The Lotus 1-2-3 Function Keys

Key	Name	Function
F1	Help	Gives you online help.
F2	Edit	Returns contents of current cell to edit line, allowing you to edit the entry.
F3	Name	Displays a list of names (files, range names, macro names, macro commands, or functions) related to the command you selected or the entry you are making.
F4	Abs	Allows you to switch the reference between relative, absolute, and mixed for a cell or range when 1-2-3 is in POINT or EDIT mode.
F5	Goto	Moves the cell pointer to a specific cell or named range in a worksheet, to a specific worksheet in the same file, or to another active file.
F6	Window	Moves the cell pointer between the windows that you have set up with one of the /Worksheet Window commands.
F7	Query	Repeats the last /Data Query command (Find, Extract, or Unique) you selected.
F8	Table	Repeats the last /Data Table command that you selected.
F9	Calc	Recalculates all formulas in all active files in READY mode. Converts a formula to its current value when a formula is on the edit line and 1-2-3 is in EDIT or VALUE mode.
F10	Graph	Displays the current graph or creates an automatic graph using the data in the vicinity of the current cell.
Alt-F1	Compose	Allows you to enter special characters not available from the keyboard by entering a compose sequence or code from the LICS (see Appendix E).
Alt-F2	Step	Allows you to turn on and off STEP mode, which is used to debug macros.
Alt-F3	Run	Allows you to select a macro name from a list and execute it (Release 2.2 only).
Alt-F4	Undo	Cancels the changes made since the last time the program was in READY mode (Release 2.2 only). You can press Undo again to restore the changes.
Alt-F5	Learn	Turns on and off LEARN mode, whereby 1-2-3 automatically records your keystrokes in a learn range defined with the /Worksheet Learn Range command (Release 2.2 only).
Alt-F6	—	No function assigned.
Alt-F7	App1	Starts the add-in program assigned to this key, if any.
Alt-F8	App2	Starts the add-in program assigned to this key, if any.
Alt-F9	App3	Starts the add-in program assigned to this key, if any.
Alt-F10	App4	Starts the add-in program assigned to this key. If none is assigned, 1-2-3 displays the Add-In menu, which enables you to install or unload or execute particular add-in programs.

Order of Precedence of Arithmetic and Logical Operators

Operator	Operation	Precedence Number	Operator	Operation	Precedence Number
^	Exponentiation	1	<	Less than	5
− or +	Negative or positive value	2	>	Greater than	5
*	Multiplication	3	<=	Less than or equal to	5
/	Division	3	>=	Greater than or equal to	5
+	Addition	4	#NOT#	Logical NOT	6
−	Subtraction	4	#AND#	Logical AND	7
=	Equal to	5	#OR#	Logical OR	7
<>	Not equal to	5	&	String concatenation	7

The Complete
Lotus 1-2-3 Release 2.2
Handbook

The Complete
Lotus® 1-2-3® Release 2.2
Handbook

♦

Greg Harvey

SYBEX®

San Francisco • Paris • Düsseldorf • London

Acquisitions Editor: Dianne King
Editor: Tanya Kucak
Technical Editor: Jon Forrest
Word Processors: Scott Campbell and Chris Mockel
Book Designer: Helen Bruno
Chapter Art and Layout: Helen Bruno
Technical Art: Jeffrey James Giese

Screen Graphics: Jeffrey James Giese
Typesetter: Winnie Kelly
Proofreader: Eddie Lin
Indexer: Julie Kawabata
Cover Designer: Thomas Ingalls + Associates
Cover Photographer: David Bishop
Screen reproductions produced by XenoFont

Library of Congress Card Number: 89-62751
ISBN 0-89588-625-1
Manufactured in the United States of America
10 9 8 7 6 5 4 3 2 1

To

Douglas Hergert

who got me started in writing computer books

and

Shane Gearing

who inspires me to keep at it

Acknowledgments

I wish to express my deepest gratitude to all the people involved in this project. First of all, I wish to thank all the talented people who worked on the book for SYBEX: Chris Mockel and Scott Campbell, word processors; Winnie Kelly, typesetter; Eddie Lin, proofreader; Helen Bruno, book designer and layout artist; Jeffrey James Giese, technical art and screen graphics; Jon Forrest, technical editor; and Julie Kawabata, indexer. In addition, a special thanks to Tanya Kucak, whose proficiency in developmental and copy editing as well as her wonderful sense of humor are ever appreciated.

At Lotus Development Corporation, I wish to thank John Shepard, who helped me immensely in the planning stages, Lisa Kosciuk and Mary Beth Rettger in Release 2.2 Beta administration, Allison Parker for Freelance Plus, Martha Isham for Magellan, and last but not least, all the folks on the Beta telephone support lines who so competently dealt with all my questions.

Finally, I wish to thank the many software vendors who supplied me with copies of their excellent software: Funk Software for Allways, Symantec Corporation for the Budget Express, Oracle Corporation for Oracle for 1-2-3, SWFTE for DataType, and Lotus Development Corporation for Lotus 1-2-3 Release 2.2, Lotus 1-2-3 Release 3.0, Magellan, and Freelance Plus.

Contents
at a Glance

Table of Contents

Part II *Generating Reports and Graphs*

Part III *Data Management and Analysis in 1-2-3*

Part IV *File Management and Organization*

Part V   *Extending the Power of 1-2-3 through Macros*

Appendices

Introduction

The Complete Lotus 1-2-3 Release 2 Handbook represents a new kind of learning aid for mastering the features of Release 2 of 1-2-3. It is a handbook both in the sense of providing you with a "handy" means for quickly learning the features of the program, and being a book you will want to keep "at hand" as you begin to transfer your understanding to your own work.

To help you find the information you need as quickly as possible, you will find that each chapter begins with a listing of all the major topics it contains, showing the page where the topic can be found. To help you make the most of the information introduced in the chapter, each chapter ends with a Summary that contains sections on troubleshooting and essential techniques.

The troubleshooting section uses the question-and-answer format that I often follow in my 1-2-3 training classes. Here, you may well find the answer to why you are encountering a particular problem as well as how to go about solving it. The essential techniques section in each Summary gives you step-by-step instructions for the most commonly used tasks covered in that chapter. Refer to this part of the chapter whenever you just want to review the steps for a particular task in 1-2-3.

To facilitate the transfer of "book" knowledge into practical 1-2-3 skills, the handbook also contains a *complete* introductory course to 1-2-3. This course covers all facets of 1-2-3, including the spreadsheet, graphics, database, and keystroke and command-language macros. It follows the organization and methodology that I have been successfully using to train business people from all backgrounds and in all lines of work for the last few years. As such, it is designed to give you practice in the most efficient ways for performing all the tasks in 1-2-3.

The special features of the handbook include:

- Each chapter contains hands-on exercises developed specifically to illustrate and explore the particular aspect of 1-2-3 that is being discussed in the chapter. These exercises give detailed instructions so that you can complete this course on your own, even if you are brand-new to 1-2-3 and without the benefit of an instructor.

- Each chapter Summary includes a Review section that lists the key terms covered in the chapter with which you should be familiar, and fill-in-the-blank questions that you can use to test your understanding. In addition, most chapters contain further exercises that you can use to deepen your understanding and further develop your skills.

- Key characteristics, features, and function keys in 1-2-3 are emphasized in the text by enclosing them in a shaded box.

Note that you should complete the exercises in chapter order, as you will find that later chapters make use of files that are created in earlier chapters. If you wish to skip around, you might want to consider ordering the sample files disk that contains all the files used in the book (see the disk offer at the end of the book for information on how to do this). That way, you will have all the files you need to complete any exercise in the handbook without having to do them in the order in which they appear. This also eliminates the need to complete an exercise that covers a part of the program with which you are already familiar just to have a file that is used somewhere later on.

Who Should Use This Handbook

This handbook is designed to meet the needs of experienced Release 2.01 users who have just upgraded to Release 2.2, as well as brand-new users with no prior 1-2-3 experience. As a new user, you will find that your exploration of 1-2-3 starts out literally from square one (that is, cell A1) and slowly and steadily builds chapter by chapter and lesson by lesson.

If you have some experience with 1-2-3 or have just upgraded to Release 2.2, you can use the book more selectively, as you would any reference. To do this, use the chapter openers to help you find specific topics of interest. Also, look for the notes in the text, which contain valuable tips on using standard features as well as information on using more advanced features of 1-2-3.

✳ *New in 2.2*   For those of you who are upgrading to Release 2.2, you will find the discussion of any features that are introduced in Release 2.2 called out with the notation *New in 2.2* in the left margin. If this notation appears directly above or to the left of the heading, you know that the entire section that follows describes and examines a feature or command found only in Release 2.2. If you are using Release 2.01, please don't mechanically skip these sections, because you can use this information to help you determine if you need to upgrade to Release 2.2.

Regardless of your background, you should be able to use this book to become familiar and comfortable with all major features of Release 2 of 1-2-3. Because of the structured nature of the handbook, you should be able to quickly come up to speed on the use of all features you need in your work. After you have attained initial mastery of the basics, you will then find the handbook to be a valuable reference in your day-to-day usage of 1-2-3.

Trainers and teachers will also find that the handbook can be used effectively as the text for formal and informal training and educational courses on 1-2-3.

Organization of the Handbook

The handbook is organized in five parts. Each part introduces a group of related chapters that present the relevant 1-2-3 commands and functions in the way most people use them. In each chapter, you will also find hands-on exercises designed to give valuable practice with these commands and features.

Part I: Mastering the 1-2-3 Spreadsheet

Part I provides an in-depth introduction to the 1-2-3 worksheet in seven chapters. This part begins by acquainting you with the electronic worksheet: what it is and how it can be used. You will learn how to move about the worksheet, add and edit data, work with cell ranges, create formulas, use built-in functions, and consolidate and link worksheets.

- **Chapter 1: The Worksheet Environment** provides a thorough introduction to the 1-2-3 worksheet display, commands, and keyboard. This is the place to start if you are new to 1-2-3.

- **Chapter 2: Techniques for Adding and Editing Data** covers moving about the worksheet, and entering and editing data of all types (labels, values, dates, and times).

- **Chapter 3: Building the Worksheet Step by Step** introduces you to the routine tasks involved in building your own worksheets. Here, you get hands-on experience with creating an income statement worksheet from start to finish. You also learn how to convert your worksheet into a template used to quickly generate new income statements.

- **Chapter 4: Cell Ranges: The Key to Managing Worksheet Data** introduces you to cell ranges and their uses in the worksheet. Here, you learn how to name ranges, protect the worksheet, and use the various /Range commands.

- **Chapter 5: Formulas and Functions: Performing Calculations** covers the creation and use of formulas in the worksheet. Here, you learn how to copy formulas, as well as how to use 1-2-3's variety of built-in @functions.

- **Chapter 6: Managing the Worksheet Environment** teaches you how to manipulate the 1-2-3 worksheet by using windows and titles, and changing column widths, as well as inserting and deleting columns and rows.

- **Chapter 7: Linking and Transferring Data between Worksheet Files** introduces you to consolidating data from multiple worksheets and extracting worksheet data into a file of its own. If you are using Release 2.2, it is here that you will learn how to create formulas that link values from other worksheets.

Part II: Generating Reports and Graphs

Part II covers the presentation aspects of 1-2-3 in three chapters. You will learn how to prepare and print worksheet reports and business graphs. In the final chapter of Part II, you will learn how to use Allways, an add-in program designed specifically to create presentation-quality reports.

- **Chapter 8: Mastering Printing** provides comprehensive coverage of all aspects of printing worksheet data. Here, you will learn how to create and format reports to your specifications.

- **Chapter 9: Representing Data Graphically** covers the creation and printing of business graphs in 1-2-3. Here, you learn how to give your worksheet data more impact by representing them pictorially.

- **Chapter 10: Using Allways to Produce Perfect Reports** teaches you all you need to know about using this add-in program to give your 1-2-3 reports a polished look. Here, you learn how to use different fonts, shading, and lines to improve the look of your reports, as well as how to integrate 1-2-3 graphs into them.

Part III: Data Management and Analysis in 1-2-3

Part III consists of two chapters that concentrate on managing and analyzing data in the worksheet. The first chapter of this part introduces you to creating 1-2-3 databases. The second chapter in this part acquaints you with formal data analysis, including what-if analysis, frequency distribution, and linear regression.

- **Chapter 11: The Database Environment** introduces you to all aspects of creating, maintaining, and querying databases in 1-2-3. This chapter includes information on sorting the data and setting up criteria for searching data, and an introduction to the built-in database functions.

◆ **Chapter 12: Data Analysis: What-If and Predictive** teaches you how to use 1-2-3's powerful data analysis tools. Here, you learn how to perform what-if analysis with data tables, calculate frequency distributions, perform matrix arithmetic, and make predictions with regression analysis.

Part IV: File Management and Organization

Part IV concerns all aspects of file housekeeping and file translation. It is divided into two chapters, the first of which covers all aspects of maintaining and managing the files you create in 1-2-3 and the second of which introduces you to ways that you can transfer data to and from 1-2-3.

◆ **Chapter 13: Organizing and Maintaining Your Files** teaches you how to organize your files into directories, protect them with passwords, change directories and list files according to type, erase unwanted files, and use the /System command to go to DOS so you can format new disks and make backup copies of your 1-2-3 files.

◆ **Chapter 14: Translating Files: Exchanging Data between 1-2-3 and Other Programs** introduces you to data exchange between 1-2-3 and other software programs. Here, you learn how to import data into the worksheet with /File Import and /Data Parse, how to export data as text files with /Print File, and how to use the Translate program to convert files directly into formats that can be used by other popular software programs.

Part V: Extending the Power of 1-2-3 through Macros

Part V provides you with a thorough introduction to all aspects of creating and using macros in two chapters. The first chapter in this part familiarizes you with keystroke macros: what they are and how they are used. The second chapter of this part acquaints you with the Lotus Command Language and its collection of advanced macro commands that further extend your ability to automate and customize the way you use 1-2-3.

◆ **Chapter 15: The Macro Environment: Automating and Customizing the Way You Work in 1-2-3** provides a step-by-step introduction to keystroke macros. Here, you learn how to plan, create, and execute a variety of commonly used utility macros. Having created these macros in a macro library, you then learn how to use them in new and existing worksheets. Release 2.2 users are provided with a thorough introduction to the creation and use of Hyperspace macros.

♦ **Chapter 16: Introduction to the Lotus Command Language** acquaints you with the advanced macro commands in the Lotus Command Language. Here, you learn how to use these commands to further automate and customize your work in 1-2-3. The macro exercises included in this chapter give you practice with branching and looping, calling subroutines, and setting up a completely menu-driven interface to automate database maintenance.

Appendices

The handbook also contains seven appendices:

♦ **Appendix A: Installation and Memory Usage** gives you detailed instructions on how to install 1-2-3. Here, you will also find information on how 1-2-3 uses your computer's memory and how you can create larger worksheets by adding expanded memory to your computer.

♦ **Appendix B: Modifying the Program Defaults** gives you information on how to permanently change 1-2-3's default settings. Specific defaults covered here include changing the help method, turning off the beep, changing the display of negative numbers, and attaching add-in programs to 1-2-3 automatically on startup.

♦ **Appendix C: Lotus 1-2-3 Menu Trees** contains menu maps that show you all the options on each 1-2-3 command menu. Refer to these maps as you learn new commands on menus with which you are unfamiliar.

♦ **Appendix D: Networking 1-2-3** acquaints you with the networked version of Release 2.2. It gives you information on how you use its reservation system to get and release control of the worksheet files shared on the network.

♦ **Appendix E: LICS (Lotus International Character Set) Table** covers the use of the Compose key (Alt-F1) to enter special symbols into your worksheet. It also contains a table that lists the codes and the compose sequences for every LICS character.

♦ **Appendix F: Answer Key to Review Questions** presents the answers to all fill-in-the-blank questions found in the Review section at the end of every chapter. Use this appendix to see how well you did after you try to answer the questions on your own.

♦ **Appendix G: Using Add-In Programs** gives you basic information on the types of add-in programs available for Release 2 of 1-2-3 and how they are used. You will also find specific information on how to use the Add-In menu to attach, invoke, and detach add-in programs once they've been installed.

The Many Faces of Release 2

This handbook is intended for users of all versions of Release 2 of Lotus 1-2-3, including Release 2.0, Release 2.01, and Release 2.2. Note that Release 2.0 was superseded by Release 2.01 shortly after its initial release. Release 2.01 represented a bug fix with no additional features, so any reference to Release 2.01 in the text covers Release 2.0 as well. Although this book is written for all Release 2 users, you will find that the handbook naturally highlights all the new features added to Release 2.2 and provides a thorough exploration and examination of each one of them.

As part of this emphasis on Release 2.2, all figures depicting the worksheet display and 1-2-3 command menus show the Release 2.2 version. Also, all menu option listings use the Release 2.2 wording (in some cases, you will find that Release 2.2 abbreviates the name of the menu option, such as *Trans* instead of *Translate* on the /Range menu).

What's New in Release 2.2

Release 2.2 incorporates many new features while retaining the familiar menu structure of the previous version. Among the most important new features are:

♦ No copy protection

♦ Minimal worksheet recalculation to speed up worksheet recalculation

♦ Undo feature, which enables you to restore your worksheet to the way it was before you made your last change

♦ File linking, which enables you to use data stored in a worksheet file on disk in a formula in the current worksheet

♦ Add-In menu located on the 1-2-3 main menu, enabling you to attach an add-in to Alt-F10 (APP4)

♦ Run key (Alt-F3), which lets you run any macro, thus allowing you to name macros with range names longer than \A through \Z

- Settings sheets, which display all the current settings for a particular operation as you select related menu options

- Search and replace feature added to /Range command

- Allways add-in included in the package to enable you to produce presentation-quality reports, incorporating 1-2-3 graphs

- LEARN mode, for creating keystroke macros, which records all your keystrokes and then writes them into the worksheet

- Enhanced STEP mode for debugging macros

- Macro Library Manager add-in, which enables you to load the macros you create into memory and then use them in any worksheet you create

- Improved graph appearance and the ability to define all graph variables in one operation

- Built-in network support with concurrency controls for sharing data files

Part I

◆

Mastering the 1-2-3 Spreadsheet

◆

1

The Worksheet Environment

In This Chapter...

Worksheet Basics

Lotus 1-2-3 combines a spreadsheet, graphics, and database management into one program. All these programs make use of the 1-2-3 *worksheet* in one way or another. The worksheet is a grid consisting of 256 columns and 8192 rows; it is on this grid that you enter the text and numbers for your spreadsheet or database. By extension, the term *worksheet* also refers to the actual data entered in the cells that make up the grid.

Only a small part of this grid is visible on your screen at any time. The part that is visible is known as the worksheet *display area*. To mark the columns of the grid, 1-2-3 shows letters in a row across the top of the worksheet display area. To mark the rows of the grid, the program shows numbers in a column down the left side of this display.

When you start 1-2-3, the program always presents you with a blank worksheet display. In this initial display, columns A through H and rows 1 through 20 are visible. You can then either begin a new worksheet application or retrieve an existing worksheet file that you have already completed and saved.

The Worksheet

> The worksheet is a table of cells with 256 columns and 8192 rows that holds your data or formulas

The Cell: Building Block of the Worksheet

The most basic worksheet unit is the *cell*, which is a block one column wide and one row deep. The cell is the repository of the text, numbers, or formulas that you enter for your spreadsheet or database. The cell also holds information on how the display of the data it contains are to be formatted. When you start 1-2-3, all cells in the worksheet are empty.

The size of the cell is not completely static. By default, a cell in a new worksheet is nine characters wide and one row deep. Although you can't change the depth of the cell, you can change its width, making it anywhere from 1 to 256 characters wide. To do this, however, you necessarily change the width of all the cells in the same column. Therefore, you are actually widening the column in the worksheet rather than widening the cell.

The Cell Address

Each cell in the worksheet has an address (or name) determined by its position in the worksheet. The *cell address* is made up of two elements:

+ The letter of the cell column

+ The number of the cell row

For example, the first cell in the worksheet display is called A1 because it is in worksheet A at the intersection of column A and row 1.

As stated earlier, the entire worksheet has 256 columns and 8192 rows. This makes a total of 2,097,152 cells. As far as cell addresses go, the number of columns available forces the doubling of letters for the column designation after column Z. Therefore, the address of the cell immediately to the right of Z1 is AA1, whereby A is added to the basic column designation of A. As you move right, the cells go from address AA1 to AZ1. Then B is added to the basic column letter, so that the cell immediately to the right of AZ1 is BA1. This system of adding the next letter in the alphabet to the string from A to Z continues until you reach the cell in the 256th column of row 1, which terminates with cell IV1.

Fortunately, the numbering of the rows of a worksheet is completely straightforward: rows start at 1 and go to 8192 as you move down the worksheet. The cell address of the first column in the fifth row of the first worksheet is, quite predictably, A5. If you move to the 500th row of this column, the cell address is A500. The very last cell in the worksheet has the address IV8192.

The Cell Address

The cell address designates the location of the cell in the worksheet

The cell address consists of two parts:
+ Letter of column (A–IV), as in A1 or AC3
+ Number of row (1–8192), as in A*1* or A*1211*

The Current Cell

Lotus 1-2-3 indicates the *current cell* in the worksheet with the *cell pointer*, which is the highlighted block that extends the entire width and depth of a single cell. You can enter or edit data only in the current cell. Any data entry or editing changes made will be placed into the current cell as soon as you press the Enter key. You must move the cell pointer to the cell you want to use before you can enter data into it or modify its contents.

Lotus 1-2-3 also keeps you informed of the cell address of the current cell by indicating it at the top of the screen. As you move the cell pointer to a new cell, the indicator in the upper left corner changes to match this location. For example, when you start a new worksheet, the cell pointer is automatically located in the first cell in the upper left corner of the worksheet display, and the cell address in the upper left corner of the screen is A1 followed by a colon, as shown in Figure 1.1. If you press the ↓ key once, the cell pointer moves down one row, and A2 becomes the current cell address.

The Types of Data That Can Be Entered in a Cell

All data entry in the 1-2-3 worksheet is done in the current cell. The program distinguishes between two basic types of entries that any cell in the worksheet can contain:

- ◆ *Label*, which consists of text-based data not subject to arithmetic calculation

- ◆ *Value*, which consists of numeric data or data returned as the result of a formula calculation

Note that even though you can't perform arithmetic calculations on labels, this doesn't mean they can't be used in formulas. As you will learn in Chapter 4, 1-2-3 contains many string functions, which allow you to perform calculations on labels. Although a string function operates on text (labels), a string function still has a value, as do all formulas entered into the worksheet.

How Labels Are Distinguished from Values

Every label entry in a cell is marked by one of the five prefix characters shown in Table 1.1. Note that none of these prefix characters are displayed with the rest of the entry in the worksheet itself. Thus, if you center the label *Year* with the caret by typing ^ *Year* in the cell, you will see only *Year* in the cell's display. Likewise, if you repeat equal signs across the entire width of a cell by typing \= you will see only equal signs in the cell's display.

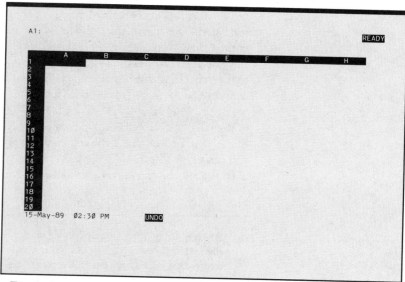

◆ **Figure 1.1:** *New worksheet with cell pointer in cell A1*

◆ **Table 1.1:** *Prefix Characters Denoting a Label*

Character	Meaning	Example
'	Left-align	'Total Due
^	Center	^ January, 1991
"	Right-align	"4th Qtr
\	Repeat following character(s) the entire cell width	\-
|	Nonprinting label	||:

Long Labels　　When you enter a label in a cell, its text is automatically left-aligned in the cell. If it contains more characters than fit in the current cell, it is referred to as a *long label*. When you enter a long label, the excess characters automatically spill over into the adjoining cells to the right, provided these cells are still empty. For example, if you enter the long label *Projected Income: 1990* as a title for the worksheet in cell A1, and cells B1 and C1 are empty, the entire title will be displayed across the cells A1 through C1. Should cell B1 be occupied, however, only the word *Projected* in the title will be visible in the worksheet. Even when this happens, the entire title that you entered in cell A1 is still safely contained in the cell; only its display in the worksheet is truncated. This means that as soon as you widen column A sufficiently, the entire title will once again be displayed in the worksheet.

Figure 1.2 illustrates the spillover of long labels into empty cells immediately to the right. Here, the description of how long labels act has been entered into cells A1 and A2 as well as A4 and A5. Because cells B1 through H2 are empty, the entire long label in A1 is displayed. Notice, however, that the display of the long label in cell A4 is truncated because cell B4 already contains the number 10. By examining the cell contents after A4: at the top of the figure, you can verify that cell A4 contains the same description as that of cell A1, even though you can see only a small part of it in the worksheet display.

Anticipating Spillover of Long Labels: The spillover effect of left-aligned long labels also takes place when a centered or right-aligned label contains too many characters for the current cell width to maintain the desired formatting. For example, if you enter a centered label that contains 12 characters in a cell that is 9 characters wide, 1-2-3 will automatically left-align the label, and the extra 3 characters will spill over to the next cell (provided that it is empty). Therefore, don't bother using the centered and right-aligned formats for labels that are longer than the current cell width.

How Values Are Identified

Values in a worksheet represent numbers or the results of calculations by formulas entered into the cell. Only some of the values in your worksheets will

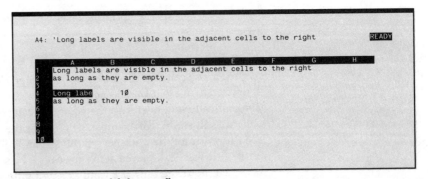

♦ **Figure 1.2:** *Long labels in a cell*

consist of actual numbers that you enter; many more will be the results of formulas that you enter in the cells of the worksheet.

Whenever you enter a value in a cell, 1-2-3 does not add any type of prefix character. Also, the program automatically right-aligns all values in the cells where they are entered. When you enter a formula to calculate a new result in a cell, the formula will begin with a number (0–9) or one of the characters denoting a value, which are shown in Table 1.2.

Values versus Labels

Values begin with a number (0–9), or −, +, @, $, (, or #

Labels begin with a letter (A–Z), label prefix (', ^ ,", | ,\), or any other character not used to denote values

Only values can be included in arithmetic formulas

Labels must be manipulated by string functions

Formulas in a Cell

A *formula* represents a mathematical expression whose calculated results are displayed in the cell that contains it. By default, 1-2-3 automatically performs the calculation called for in the formula and displays the result as soon as you enter the formula into a cell. Formulas can perform simple calculations involving addition, subtraction, multiplication, division, or raising a number to a

Table 1.2: *Prefix Characters Denoting a Value*

Character	Meaning	Example
.	Decimal	.125
+	Positive value	+600
−	Negative value	−17.5
@	Lotus 1-2-3 function	@SUM(A5..D5)
(	Group arithmetic expression	(A33−20)*G1
$	Absolute cell address	$D$2*B16
#	Logical operators	#NOT#

certain power with exponents, as well as more complex calculations involving the use of financial or statistical 1-2-3 functions.

Numbers in formulas can be entered directly (referred to as literal values) or by referencing the cell address that contains the number. In other words, entering either the formula 10/5 or 10/A1 will result in the answer of 2, provided that cell A1 already contains the value 5. As you will see when you begin to design and build worksheets in the chapters ahead, you should always keep the number of *literal values* in a formula to the minimum (that is, those entered from the keyboard such as 5, 0.67, or 3456), preferring instead to enter the value by its cell reference. That way, you can recalculate parts or all of the worksheet simply by entering new values in the cells referenced in the formulas, making it unnecessary to edit the formulas themselves.

As you would imagine, a 1-2-3 formula can contain a reference to a cell whose value, in turn, is calculated by a different formula. For example, the number 2 returned by the formula 10/A1 can be used in another formula simply by referencing the cell address that contains it. This kind of continuous referencing is quite common in spreadsheets and forms the cornerstone of good spreadsheet design.

Long Values   When you type in numbers or enter a formula whose result is a number, numbers are always right-aligned in the cell, as shown in Figure 1.3, and 1-2-3 always leaves the rightmost character in the cell containing a value

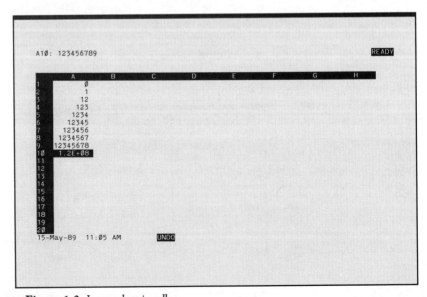

◆ **Figure 1.3:** *Long values in cells*

blank. This means that a value can hold one less character (or digit) than the total width of the cell. For instance, if the cell has the default width of nine characters, you can enter a number with eight characters (including the dollar sign, commas, and decimal point, if used).

If the number is too large for the program to display all of its digits in the current cell width, it represents a *long value*, and 1-2-3 automatically converts the number to scientific notation (which the program calls the Scientific format). Scientific notation uses a decimal number with an exponent to represent the number. Positive exponents signify the number of places the decimal point is to be moved to the right, and negative exponents indicate the number of places it is to be moved to the left. For example, if you enter 150,000,000 (that is, 150 million) in a cell, it will automatically be displayed as 1.5E+08.

If you enter a decimal number less than 1.0 that contains too many decimal places to be accommodated in the current cell width, 1-2-3 will do one of two things with its display: either you will see only zeros (0.000000), or it will be converted into scientific notation using a negative exponent (1.6E−13).

You can enter numbers directly into a cell in scientific notation. If the number is not too large to be displayed in the cell, however, 1-2-3 automatically converts it into regular notation. For example, if you enter *2.5e+2* in a cell, 1-2-3 will display it as *250*. If you enter the number *4.5e−3*, the program will display it as *0.0045*.

Note that the largest number that can be entered in a cell is 1.0E+99. The smallest number that can be entered in a cell is 1.0E−99. (Lotus always converts the *e* to uppercase but will accept and understand both.)

The Contents of the Cell

Lotus 1-2-3 differentiates between the *contents of a cell* and the *cell display*. The contents of the current cell are always shown after the cell address at the top of the 1-2-3 screen. The cell display is always shown in the cell highlighted with the cell pointer. In almost all cases, you will find a discrepancy between the contents of a cell and its display in the worksheet. In fact, only when a cell is empty, or it contains a number and no change has been made to the cell's formatting, will you find the cell contents and the cell display to be the same.

This is because the cell contents displayed after the current cell address show you how the program has calculated and/or formatted the data displayed in the current cell in the worksheet. For example, if the current cell contains a formula, the cell contents show you the formula; the cell display shows you the result. If the current cell contains a label, its contents show you the label prefix used to format the label as well as all of the characters in the label; the cell display just shows you the characters that fit in the cell width. Of course, the entire label is displayed in the worksheet, provided that the cell or cells to the right are still empty, thus allowing spillover.

Figures 1.4 and 1.5 illustrate the differences between the cell contents and cell display in the case of a left-aligned label and simple formula. In Figure 1.4, you can see that the apostrophe (the label prefix) and the word *Assets* make up the cell contents, but only the word *Assets* is shown in the cell display. In Figure 1.5, you can see that the formula *5+B1* makes up the cell contents of cell B3. However, only the result, *155*, is shown in the cell display.

Cell Contents versus
Cell Display

Cell Contents
◆ Displayed after the cell address in the upper left corner of the screen
◆ Shows you what was entered in the cell and how it is formatted

Cell Display
◆ Displayed in the current cell in the worksheet itself
◆ Shows you how the data will appear when printed

The 1-2-3 Screen Display

Now that we have examined the worksheet display area in some detail, we need to look at the rest of the screen display used by 1-2-3. Refer back to Figure 1.1 to see the worksheet display screen as it appears when you first start 1-2-3. The first three lines of the display screen, immediately above the line showing the column letters in reverse video, are called the *control panel*. The first line of the control panel contains the current cell address. If the current cell contains an entry, the program lists the cell contents after the current cell address.

The next 21 lines of the screen are taken up by the part of the current worksheet that can be seen on the screen. This area consists of two parts: the *frame*, which is the highlighted row and column indicators on the top and left sides of the screen, and the actual cells in which you enter your data. The purpose of the frame is to indicate which columns and rows are being displayed.

The last line on the screen is not part of this worksheet area: it is reserved for the display of the system date and time or file name, as well as various messages and indicators. If you are using Release 2.2, you will see the *UNDO* indicator on this line, telling you that the new Undo function is activated and ready to use.

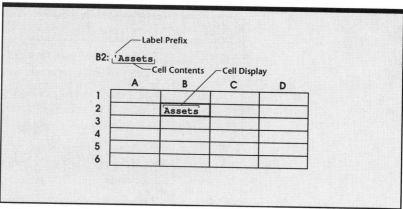

◆ **Figure 1.4:** *Cell contents and display for a label*

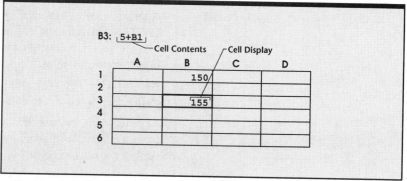

◆ **Figure 1.5:** *Cell contents and display for a formula*

The Mode Indicator

On the far right of the first line of the control panel, directly opposite of the current cell address, you find the *mode indicator*. In Figure 1.1, the mode indicator READY is displayed. As you work with the program, this indicator will change to reflect your current activity. For now, it is enough to know that 1-2-3 must be in READY mode before you can enter or edit any data in the current cell. Note also that when you type your first character of a cell entry, the mode indicator will change from READY to either LABEL or VALUE, depending upon how the program interprets your entry. When you select a 1-2-3 command from one of the program's menus, the mode changes to MENU. Refer to Table 1.3 for a complete listing of the mode indicators that can appear and their meaning.

♦ **Table 1.3:** *The 1-2-3 Mode Indicators*

Mode	Description
EDIT	Appears when you edit a cell entry with Edit (F2) or when you enter a formula incorrectly.
ERROR	Appears when an error occurs and an error message is displayed; press Esc or Enter to exit from ERROR mode and clear the error message.
FILES	Appears whenever you select a command such as /File Retrieve or /File Save where the program displays a list of file names.
FIND	Appears when you select the /Data Query Find command (either from the menu or by pressing Query, F7) and 1-2-3 locates a matching record in the database; press Enter to exit from FIND mode.
FRMT	Appears when you select /Data Parse Format-Line Edit (/DPFE) to edit a format line used to indicate where to break up long labels entered in one cell into separate cells in succeeding columns.
HELP	Appears when you select Help (F1) and 1-2-3 displays a Help screen; press Esc to exit from HELP mode.
LABEL	Appears when the first character that you type for a cell entry is a letter, label prefix, or some other keyboard symbol not used to begin 1-2-3 formulas (*see VALUE*).
MENU	Appears when you select one of 1-2-3's commands from its many menus (activated by pressing /); press Esc to back up to a higher menu level or Ctrl-Break to exit from the menus entirely.
NAMES	Appears when you select a command where 1-2-3 displays a list of the names of ranges, graphs, or attached add-in programs.
POINT	Appears when you use the cursor-movement keys to define a range or create a formula.
READY	Appears whenever 1-2-3 is ready for you to enter data or select a command; this is the default mode.

◆ **Table 1.3:** *The 1-2-3 Mode Indicators (continued)*

Mode	Description
STAT	Appears when you select either the /Worksheet Status (/WS) or /Worksheet Global Default Status (/WGDS) command and 1-2-3 displays a screen of statistics; press any key to exit from STAT mode.
VALUE	Appears when the first character that you type for a cell entry is a number, period, or some other keyboard symbol used to begin 1-2-3 formulas (−, +, @, $, #).
WAIT	Appears when 1-2-3 is processing a command or procedure and you must wait before entering data or selecting a command.

The Edit Line

When you make an entry in the current cell, the characters that you type are entered on the second line of the control panel, below the current cell address. It is only when you press the Enter key after you have finished typing the label, number, or formula that the entry is processed and the resulting label or value is actually entered into the current cell. Prior to that time, you can edit or add to the cell entry as needed. Lotus 1-2-3 also allows you to edit the contents of the current cell after it has been entered in the worksheet. When you press F2, the Edit key, the contents of the current cell are returned to the second line of the control panel, and the program goes into EDIT mode.

The 1-2-3 Command Menus

The second line of the control panel is not only used for entering and editing the contents of the current cell: it also displays the 1-2-3 command menus. To bring the command menus to this line, you press the / (slash) key. The third line of the control panel will either display the menu choices that will become available when you select the highlighted menu option on the command menu, or display a prompt that indicates what information the program needs to complete a selected command.

Figure 1.6 shows the 1-2-3 command menu as it appears when you first press the / key. Notice that the command menu on the second line of the control panel contains 11 options— Worksheet through Quit—and that only the first option, Worksheet, is highlighted. Notice, too, that the mode indicator reads

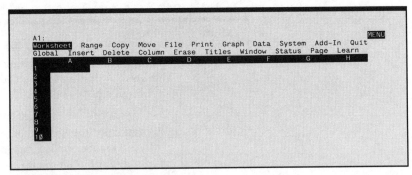

MENU and that the third line of the control panel displays the options Global through Learn (you will see the options Global through Page, if you are using Release 2.01). These represent all of the Worksheet menu options that become available if you select the Worksheet option from the command menu. In fact, should you select the Worksheet option, you will find that these menu selections replace those currently shown on the second line and that new options (those attached to the Global menu) appear on the third line.

The Hierarchy of Menus

Each option on the command menu, with few exceptions, leads to new menus containing their own options. This system is arranged in a hierarchy, where the selection of one option often leads to a new menu and, in turn, a selection from this new menu leads to still another menu, and so on down the line. As you will learn, some tasks in 1-2-3 require that you select several options in succession as you descend the menu levels.

To see how this hierarchy is organized, refer to the menu trees shown in Appendix C. The menus in 1-2-3 are traditionally named after the initial option that you select from the command menu, which is activated by pressing the / key, so the first menu is called the /Worksheet menu, the second is the /Range menu, and so on (see Figure 1.6).

✳ *New in 2.2* Settings Sheets

Several menus in Release 2.2 of 1-2-3 have *settings sheets* attached to them. In Figure 1.7, you can see the Default Settings sheet that appears when you select the /Worksheet Global Default menu. Settings sheets give you a full-screen view of all settings associated with the current menu that are presently in effect. By looking at the values displayed in the settings sheet, you can quickly determine which menu options must be used to effect the desired changes. The settings sheets in Release 2.2 include:

♦ Global Settings, activated by selecting /Worksheet Global

♦ Default Settings, activated by selecting /Worksheet Global Default or /Worksheet Status

♦ Print Settings, activated by selecting /Print Printer or /Print File

♦ Graph Settings, activated by selecting /Graph

♦ Sort Settings, activated by selecting /Data Sort

♦ Query Settings, activated by selecting /Data Query

♦ Regression Settings, activated by selecting /Data Regression

♦ Parse Settings, activated by selecting /Data Parse

If you want to see the worksheet display instead of the settings sheet, press the Window key (F6) and the settings sheet disappears (although the menu options on the control panel remain). To redisplay the settings sheet (as long as the associated menu is still displayed), press the Window key a second time.

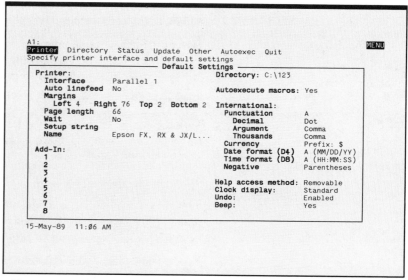

♦ **Figure 1.7:** *The Default Settings sheet*

The Status Line

The last line of the 1-2-3 display screen is called the *status line*. Here, 1-2-3 displays information about the status of your work in the current worksheet. In Figure 1.1, you can see the on-screen clock that gives the current date and time on the status line followed by the *UNDO* indicator, telling you that the Undo feature is currently active. As you build your worksheets, you will find that additional indicators appear on the right-hand side of the status line when you press special keys on the keyboard and undertake particular tasks. For example, the CAPS status indicator appears when you press the Caps Lock key, and the FILE status indicator appears when you press Ctrl-End to switch to a new worksheet file.

The Date and Time Indicator

Lotus 1-2-3 displays the current date and time at the beginning of the status line, as seen in Figure 1.1. This date and time indicator may not always be correct, because 1-2-3 displays the current date and time as they are relayed from the DOS DATE and TIME commands. If the date and/or time shown by the clock on the status line is not current, you must update it from DOS. To update the DOS date and time from within 1-2-3, take the following steps:

1. Make sure that the mode indicator in the upper right corner reads READY. If not, press Esc until it does.

2. Select the System option from the main command menu by typing /S. This takes you to DOS temporarily. If you are using 1-2-3 on a two-disk system, replace the 1-2-3 System disk with a DOS disk.

3. Type *date* and press Enter.

4. Type the current date—giving the number of the month, day, and last two digits of the year, separating each with a / or –, as in 12/16/90 or 12–16–90—and press Enter.

5. Type *time* and press Enter.

6. Type the current time by giving the number of the hour and minutes separated by a colon, as in 10:35, and press Enter. If the hour is after 12 noon (PM), add 12 hours to it; for example, enter 2:15 PM as 14:15.

7. Type *exit* and press Enter. This returns you to the 1-2-3 worksheet. If you are using 1-2-3 on a two-disk system, be sure to replace the DOS disk with your 1-2-3 System disk.

8. Check the date and time on the status line. It should now read correctly.

✱ *New in 2.2*   Note that you can change the default settings in Release 2.2 so that 1-2-3 displays the file name that you assign to the worksheet when you save it in place of the clock on the screen. To have the program replace the clock with the file name, take these steps:

1. Make sure that the mode indicator in the upper right corner reads READY. If not, press Esc until it does.

2. Select the Worksheet Global Default Other Clock options by typing /WGDOC.

3. To have the file name displayed, select the Filename option by typing F.

4. To keep the date and time indicator on the status line at all times, select the Clock option by typing C again.

5. To suppress the clock and file name display on the status line altogether, choose the None option by typing N.

In either version of Release 2, you can change the date and time indicator from the standard display of the date and time (such as 12-May-90 8:35 PM) to an international display (such as 05/12/90 20:35) by selecting the /Worksheet Global Default Other Clock International (/WGDOCI) command. As you will learn later in this chapter, you can also control the way the International date and time formats are displayed; for instance, you could have the day precede the month, as in 12/05/90.

The Status Indicators

The status indicators on the status line inform you which toggle and lock keys are currently active. The Ins (insert) key is a good example of a toggle key. By default, 1-2-3 is in insert mode, meaning that new characters typed on the edit line don't replace existing characters; instead, they displace them to the right. If you press the Ins key, the program changes to overwrite (sometimes called overstrike) mode and the OVR status indicator appears. Because Ins represents a toggle key, however, you can return to insert mode simply by pressing it again. Once you've returned to insert mode, the OVR status indicator promptly disappears.

There are three lock keys on your keyboard: Caps Lock, Num Lock, and Scroll Lock. These keys are also toggle keys, and 1-2-3 displays a different status indicator to let you know when each of them is in use.

In addition to the status indicators for toggle and lock keys, there are indicators that let you know that 1-2-3 is paused and waiting for you to take some action or press another key. For example, the END status indicator appears when you press the End key because the program is waiting for you to press one of the four arrow keys. This will cause the cell pointer to go directly to the last occupied cell in the direction of the arrow key pressed.

You will also see status indicators that inform you of a special situation that exists in the current worksheet, as does the UNDO indicator in Release 2.2. For instance, if you define a formula that contains a circular reference (that is, a formula that refers to itself either directly or indirectly), the CIRC status indicator will appear on the status line. Refer to Table 1.4 for a listing of all the status indicators that can appear on the status line and their meanings.

◆ **Table 1.4:** *The 1-2-3 Status Indicators*

Indicator	Description
CALC	Some formulas in the current worksheet need to be recalculated; press Calc (F9) to do this.
CAPS	Caps Lock is engaged and all letters that you type will be in uppercase; press Caps Lock again to disengage so you can type lowercase letters again.
CIRC	One or more formulas in the current worksheet contain circular references; use /Worksheet Status (/WS) to locate the first circular reference and then fix the formula or increase the number of iterations.
CMD	The macro you are executing is paused for data entry; enter your data, then press the Enter key.
END	You pressed the End key and 1-2-3 is waiting for you to press one of the other cursor-movement keys (End can't be used alone). Refer to Table 2.1 to see all the key combinations with End.
LEARN	You defined a learn range in the worksheet with the /Worksheet Learn Range command and turned on LEARN mode by pressing the Learn key (Alt-F5). While LEARN mode is active, 1-2-3 will enter all the keystrokes you make in the cells of the learn range until you press the Learn key a second time. (Release 2.2 only)
MEM	The amount of available memory is less than 4096 bytes, and you run the risk of getting a memory-full

♦

♦ **Table 1.4:** *The 1-2-3 Status Indicators (continued)*

Indicator	Description
	error if you continue working without first taking steps to reduce the size of the file.
NUM	Num Lock is engaged, meaning that the cursor/numeric keypad can be used to enter numbers in the worksheet; press the Num Lock key again to disengage it and enable the cursor-movement functions.
OVR	The worksheet is in overtype mode, meaning that new characters replace existing characters at the cursor; press the Ins (insert) key again to return to the default of insert mode.
RO	The current file has read-only status, meaning that you can't save any changes you make to it; this status indicator appears only when you are using Release 2.2 of 1-2-3 on a network.
SCROLL	Scroll Lock is engaged, meaning that the worksheet display as well as the pointer moves when you press a cursor-movement key; press Scroll Lock again to disengage it.
SST	The macro you are executing is being run in single-step mode; press the spacebar to have 1-2-3 execute the next step in the macro.
STEP	Single-step mode for debugging macros is enabled; select the Step option on the Record menu (Alt-F2) again to disengage single-step mode.
UNDO	The Undo feature is active, meaning that you can cancel the changes made since the program was last in READY mode by pressing Alt-F4. Press the Undo key a second time to restore your changes. (Release 2.2 only)

Keyboard Basics

The keyboard provides you with the means for communicating with 1-2-3 at all levels of program use. Because 1-2-3 was designed specifically for the IBM Personal Computer and compatibles, it makes use of the entire keyboard. Two basic keyboard designs are widely used on IBM PCs and compatibles, with several variations on both layouts.

Figure 1.8 shows you the design of the original keyboard. This keyboard has only ten function keys, arranged in two rows to the left of the alphanumeric keys, and a numeric keypad that doubles as a ten-key entry pad and a cursor-movement pad.

Figure 1.9 shows you the design of the enhanced keyboard. This keyboard has 12 function keys arranged in a single row at the top. It also separates the cursor-movement pad from the numeric pad (the numeric keypad duplicates the cursor-movement functions of the separate cursor keypad when the Num Lock key is not engaged).

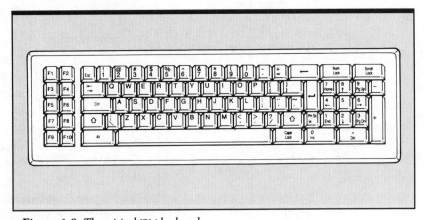

♦ **Figure 1.8:** *The original IBM keyboard*

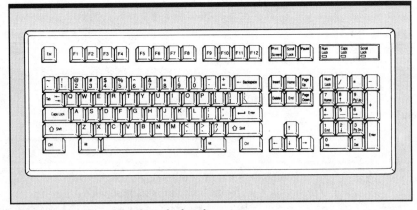

♦ **Figure 1.9:** *The enhanced IBM keyboard*

Beyond these basic differences, you will find differences in the location of many special keys not found on standard typewriters. Because these keys are used in 1-2-3, you will need to identify their position on your keyboard:

- Caps Lock

- ˜ (tilde) key

- Print Screen (PrtSc)

- Scroll Lock

Another difference between the original and enhanced keyboards is the way some keys are marked. The original keyboard did not include the name of the key along with the symbol for the Tab, Shift, and Enter keys, as does the enhanced keyboard. Note, however, that many enhanced keyboards do not mark the name of the Backspace key. In fact, on most keyboards, the only apparent difference between the ← key and Backspace is its location on the keyboard: the Backspace key is always immediately above the Enter key, and the ← key is located on the left side of the cursor keypad. (Note that the ← key on the numeric keypad is marked with a 4 above the ←.)

The Alphanumeric Keys

The alphanumeric keys on the IBM keyboard are in the traditional QWERTY arrangement, with three rows of uppercase and lowercase letters and punctuation keys and a single row of number and special-symbol keys above these. Surrounding these keys on the left and right sides are special keys that are used either in combination with one of the alphanumeric keys or alone to initiate a particular command or movement in the worksheet. On many keyboards, these keys are gray.

Using Caps Lock to Enter Uppercase Letters

To type uppercase letters in your worksheet, you need to hold down one of the Shift keys (marked with outlined arrows pointing upward) as you type. You can also engage Caps Lock by pressing the Caps Lock key once; you can then type uppercase letters without having to hold down the Shift key. The CAP status indicator lets you know that Caps Lock is on. To disengage Caps Lock, you press the Caps Lock key again, and the CAP status indicator then disappears. Note that the only function of Caps Lock is to produce uppercase letters. This means that you must still press the Shift key to enter symbols such as @ or $ from the top row.

Using the Esc Key to Cancel a Command or Clear a Value

At the beginning of the top row containing the number and symbol keys, you will find the Esc (escape) key. The Esc key is used as the cancel key in 1-2-3. When you have entered the wrong value in a cell, press the Esc key to clear it. Likewise, when you select the wrong menu option, press the Esc key to cancel your selection and return to the previous level. Although pressing the Esc key backs you out of the 1-2-3 menus a level at a time until the program returns to READY mode, you can return immediately to READY mode from any level of the menu system by pressing Ctrl-Break. Note that the exact location of the Break key varies according to the type of keyboard your computer has: on the older keyboards, it is located with the Scroll Lock key on the numeric pad; on the newer keyboards, it is sometimes located on the Pause key near the end of the top row of 12 function keys.

Using the Tab Key to Scroll Horizontally

Directly below the Esc key, you will find the Tab key (often marked with two arrows touching a vertical bar—the top one pointing left and the lower one pointing right). The lower (right-pointing) arrow indicates the direction that the Tab key will scroll the 1-2-3 worksheet display or move the cursor (when editing a cell) when Tab alone is pressed. The upper (left-pointing) arrow indicates the direction of scrolling when you press Shift-Tab (often referred to as the Backtab key).

Note that the scrolling movement performed when you press Tab is called *Big Right* and can also be done by pressing Ctrl- →. Conversely, the scrolling movement performed when you press Shift-Tab (Backtab) is called *Big Left* and can also be done by pressing Ctrl-←.

Using the Backspace and Del Keys to Delete Characters

The Backspace key is located immediately above the Enter key and is marked by a single ←. However, because it has the same marking as the ← key on the cursor/numeric keypad located to the right, be careful not to confuse them, as they have different functions.

The Backspace key is used to correct errors and make editing changes to cell entries either when they are first being entered or at a later time. When you press the Backspace key, the program deletes the character immediately to the left of the cursor. The ← key, on the other hand, is used to move the cursor one character to the left without removing or disturbing the existing characters on the edit line in any way.

If you find that you need to delete the character that the cursor is on in the edit line, press the Del (delete) key on the cursor/numeric keypad instead of the Backspace key.

You will find that you often have to use a combination of the Backspace, ←, →, and Del keys when editing existing cell entries.

The Numeric Keypad and Cursor Keypad

As a 1-2-3 user, you will really appreciate the enhanced keyboard design because it separates the cursor and numeric keypads. In the original keyboard design (still used on laptop computers), the cursor-movement keys and the ten-key number pad are joined. To toggle between numeric entry and moving the cursor, you have to press the Num Lock key. In a program like 1-2-3, the combination of these features is especially unfortunate because the constant need to use the cursor keys to move the cell pointer in the worksheet interferes with efficient use of the ten-key pad to enter columns and rows of numbers.

Using the Num Lock Key to Toggle between Cursor and Numeric Functions

If you have the enhanced keyboard, you can leave the Num Lock key engaged and just use the cursor-movement keys on the separate cursor pad to move around the worksheet.

If you don't have the enhanced keyboard, you have to use the cursor-movement keys on the numeric keypad when you want to move the cell pointer in the worksheet. To do this, make sure Num Lock is disengaged. When Num Lock is on, all the numeric functions of the keypad are active, and the NUM status indicator appears on your screen. Although this makes it easier to enter values into the current cell, it means that you can't relocate the cell pointer using the arrow keys, Home, End, PgUp, or PgDn to go to a new cell unless you first press Num Lock. Because it is tedious to continuously toggle in and out of Num Lock mode, most people who don't have the enhanced keyboard end up leaving the Num Lock function off and enter numbers in their worksheets from the top row of the keyboard.

Using the PgUp and PgDn Keys to Scroll the Worksheet Vertically

The PgUp and PgDn keys (the 9 and 3 key, respectively) on the cursor/numeric keypad are used to scroll the worksheet display up and down. If you have an enhanced IBM keyboard, you will find a second set of these keys marked Page

Up and Page Down, one above the other on the separate cursor pad next to the numeric keypad. (Remember that you can use either set if the NUM indicator is not visible at the bottom of the worksheet display.) When you press PgDn, the cell pointer moves down 20 rows, effectively bringing a new part of the worksheet into view. Conversely, when you press PgUp, the cell pointer moves up 20 rows.

Using the Home Key

When you press the Home key on the cursor/numeric keypad (on the 7 key), 1-2-3 moves the cell pointer directly to cell A1, the first cell in the worksheet, no matter which cell is current when you press it. If you combine it with the End key by pressing End and then Home, the pointer moves to the last active cell in the worksheet. This cell is at the intersection of the last occupied column and row in the worksheet.

Using the End Key

The End key on the cursor/numeric keypad is never used alone in 1-2-3: it is always used in combination with some other cursor-movement key or keys to move the cell pointer. Because the End key isn't used alone, the program displays the END status indicator when you press the End key, indicating that the program is waiting for you to press a cursor-movement key or key combination.

The Function Keys

Lotus 1-2-3 makes use of all ten IBM function keys. In addition, Release 2.01 uses the Alt key with F1 and F2, and Release 2.2 uses the Alt key with all ten function keys except F6, as shown in Table 1.5. (If you have the IBM enhanced keyboard with 12 function keys, however, neither Release 2.01 or 2.2 makes use of F11 and F12.)

Because 1-2-3 was originally designed with the IBM Personal Computer in mind, the program relies heavily on the use of these function keys. For that reason, you should make every attempt to learn the names of the function keys and their key combinations. Your 1-2-3 package includes two plastic templates indicating the function-key assignments: one for keyboards with the function keys in two columns on the left, and the other for keyboards with the function keys on the top row of the keyboard. Locate the correct template for your keyboard, and keep it on your keyboard as you learn the program.

Note that the Alt (alternate) key represents a special kind of shift key unique to the IBM Personal Computer. If you have an enhanced IBM keyboard, there

◆ **Table 1.5:** *The 1-2-3 Function Keys*

Key	Name	Function
F1	Help	Gives you online help.
F2	Edit	Returns the contents of the current cell to the edit line, allowing you to edit the entry.
F3	Name	Displays a list of names (files, range names, macro names, macro commands, or functions) related to the command you selected or the entry you are making.
F4	Abs	Allows you to switch the reference between relative, absolute, and mixed for a cell or range when 1-2-3 is in POINT or EDIT mode.
F5	Goto	Moves the cell pointer to a specific cell or named range in a worksheet, to a specific worksheet in the same file, or to another active file.
F6	Window	Moves the cell pointer between the windows that you have set up with one of the /Worksheet Window commands.
F7	Query	Repeats the last /Data Query command (Find, Extract, or Unique) that you selected.
F8	Table	Repeats the last /Data Table command that you selected.
F9	Calc	Recalculates all formulas in all active files in READY mode. Converts a formula to its current value when a formula is on the edit line and 1-2-3 is in EDIT or VALUE mode.
F10	Graph	Displays the current graph or creates an automatic graph using the data in the vicinity of the current cell.

◆ **Table 1.5:** *The 1-2-3 Function Keys (continued)*

Key	Name	Function
Alt-F1	Compose	Allows you to enter special characters not available from the keyboard by entering a compose sequence or code from the LICS (see Appendix E).
Alt-F2	Step	Allows you to turn on and off STEP mode, which is used to debug macros.
Alt-F3	Run	Allows you to select a macro from a list of range names and execute it. (Release 2.2 only)
Alt-F4	Undo	Cancels the changes made since the last time the program was in READY mode. You can press the Undo key again to restore the changes. (Release 2.2 only)
Alt-F5	Learn	Turns on and off LEARN mode, whereby 1-2-3 automatically records your keystrokes in a learn range defined with the /Worksheet Learn Range command. (Release 2.2 only)
Alt-F6	—	No function assigned.
Alt-F7	App1	Starts the add-in program assigned to this key, if any.
Alt-F8	App2	Starts the add-in program assigned to this key, if any.
Alt-F9	App3	Starts the add-in program assigned to this key, if any.
Alt-F10	App4	Starts the add-in program assigned to this key. If none is assigned, 1-2-3 displays the Add-In menu, which enables you to install, unload, or execute particular add-in programs.

are two Alt keys on the keyboard: one immediately to the left and the other immediately to the right of the spacebar. When you need to execute a Lotus function that requires you to press the Alt key as well as a function key, you do this by holding down the Alt key, pressing the appropriate function key once, and then letting up immediately on both keys.

Summary

Review

Important Terms You Should Know

cell	label
cell address	label prefix
cell display	long label
cell pointer	long value
contents of a cell	mode indicator
control panel	status indicator
current cell	status line
edit line	value
frame	worksheet
formula	worksheet display
function keys	

Test Your Knowledge

1. In a cell address, the letter represents the _____ and the number following it represents the _____.

2. A _____ can't be calculated in an arithmetic formula—only a _____ can.

3. If a label is longer than the width of the cell you enter it in and its display spills over to adjacent cells to the right, it is said to be a _____.

4. If you enter *YTD Total* in a cell, 1-2-3 will automatically add a _____ before the first character. This character represents the default label prefix and tells 1-2-3 to _____ align the label in the cell.

5. If you want to center a label in the cell at the same time you are entering it in a cell, you type the _____ label prefix as the first character.

6. The _____ mode indicator must be displayed in the worksheet display before you can enter or edit data in a worksheet.

7. To activate the 1-2-3 command menus, you press the _____ key.

8. To select a command on the menu line, you can either use one of the cursor keys to highlight it and then press Enter, or you can _____ its first letter, which combines both steps.

9. The _____ key is used to cancel a particular menu selection one level at a time; the Ctrl-_____ key, however, is used to return you to READY mode from any 1-2-3 worksheet.

10. If you press the ← key on the numeric pad and 1-2-3 enters 4 instead of moving the pointer one cell to the left, the _____ key is activated. You can verify that this is the case because the program will display the _____ status indicator on the last line of the worksheet display.

2

Techniques for Adding and Editing Data

In This Chapter...

Starting 1-2-3

I am assuming that you or someone in your office has already installed 1-2-3. If not, refer to Appendix A and install the program according to the instructions for the type of computer you have before returning here.

Starting the Program on a Hard Disk System

Many companies equip their computers (especially those on a network) with a menu from which you select and start a particular application program. If your computer displays such a menu rather than the DOS prompt when you start it, you first need to identify the number of the option that starts Release 2.

To do this, turn on the computer and look for an option named *Lotus 1-2-3 Release 2* or just *Release 2*, or possibly *Release 2.2*. After you locate it, type the option number and press the Enter key to start 1-2-3.

When looking for the Release 2 option, check to see whether there is also a Release 3 option on this menu. If there is, you must be careful not to select the Release 3 option number when you want to run Release 2, and vice versa. The easiest way to tell if you are running Release 3 instead of Release 2 (if you happen to miss the opening screen, which clearly lists the release number) is to see if the letter A appears in the upper left corner of the worksheet display (before the column A designation and above the row number). This worksheet letter appears only in Release 3; the Release 2 worksheet displays nothing to the left of column A or above row 1. Also, if you are using Release 2.2, you will notice the UNDO indicator on the status line of the blank worksheet, which is not used in Release 3 (although it too supports an Undo feature).

If your computer doesn't use such a menu and you work from the DOS prompt, you must manually enter the 1-2-3 startup command after making current the directory that contains 1-2-3 Release 2 program files. If you forget to make this directory current before you enter the 1-2-3 startup command, you'll receive the DOS message

Bad command or file name

after you type the command and press the Enter key.

To make the 1-2-3 Release 2 directory current, you must use the DOS Change Directory (CHDIR or CD) command. When installing Release 2, the program suggests C:\123 as the default name for the directory that is to contain the program files. Assuming that you accepted this as the directory name when you installed your program, type

CD\123

and press Enter at the C:> DOS prompt to make this directory current. Then you are ready to enter the 1-2-3 startup command.

Starting the Program on a Two-Disk System

If you are using a two-disk-drive system, you need to boot the computer with your DOS disk and enter the date and time. Then, once the drive light for drive A is off, you need to replace the DOS disk with a working copy of your 1-2-3 System disk. As soon as you have made this replacement and closed the door for drive A, you are ready to start 1-2-3.

The 1-2-3 Startup Commands

There are two ways to start 1-2-3: either directly by typing *123* and pressing Enter, or through the Lotus Access System by typing *LOTUS* (it doesn't matter whether you type *Lotus* in all uppercase, all lowercase, or a mix of the two) and pressing Enter.

If you use the *123* startup command, the 1-2-3 program is loaded (during which time the opening screen showing the licensing information is displayed). Once 1-2-3 is loaded, a blank worksheet appears on the screen, in which you can either begin a new spreadsheet or database application, or retrieve an existing one stored on file.

If you use the *Lotus* startup command, the program doesn't load 1-2-3. Instead, it displays the Lotus Access System menu (shown in Figure 2.1), which contains the options 1-2-3, Install, PrintGraph, Translate, and Exit. The Install option on this menu loads the installation program, which allows you to

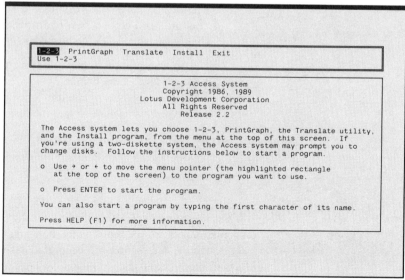

♦ **Figure 2.1:** *The Lotus Access System menu*

specify any changes in your computer hardware (such as a new monitor, printer, or plotter) so that 1-2-3 will work properly with the new equipment (for specific information on using the Install option to specify hardware, see Appendix A). You can also use the installation program to change the collating sequence that determines how data are sorted in the worksheet (for information on changing the sorting sequence, see Chapter 11). The PrintGraph option loads the graph-printing program used to print all the graphs created with the 1-2-3 program. The Translate option loads a translation program that enables you to import and export files so that you can exchange data between 1-2-3 and other application programs such as dBASE III or other spreadsheet programs (see Chapter 13).

Note that you can start either the 1-2-3 Install, PrintGraph, or Translate program directly from the DOS prompt without having to use the Lotus Access System menu. To start the Install program, type *install* and then press Enter. To start the PrintGraph program, type *pgraph* and press Enter. To start the Translate program, type *trans* and press Enter.

To start the 1-2-3 program from the Lotus Access System menu, select the 1-2-3 option either by pressing the Enter key or typing *1*. Selecting this menu option has the same affect as typing the 123 startup command from the DOS prompt. Because you won't need to use any Lotus Access System menu option besides 1-2-3 at this time, you might as well start the program directly from the DOS prompt. To do so, follow these steps:

1. **Turn on your computer; if you are using a two-disk-drive system, be sure that your DOS disk is in drive A, then enter the date and time when prompted; next, replace the DOS disk with the 1-2-3 System disk.**

2. **If you are using a hard disk system, type *cd\123* at the C> prompt and press Enter.**
   If the directory that contains the Release 2 programs on your computer isn't called *123*, be sure to type the correct directory name after cd\.

3. **At the DOS prompt (A> on a two-disk-drive system and C:\123> on a hard disk system), type *123* and press Enter.**

Moving the Cell Pointer

When the computer finishes loading the 1-2-3 program into its memory, the opening screen will be replaced by the worksheet display with a blank worksheet, and the cell pointer will be located in the first cell, A1. Before learning how to enter data in the worksheet, let's examine the most common methods for moving the cell pointer. Remember that before you enter your data in a cell, you must make that cell current by positioning the cell pointer in it. Table 2.1 outlines the techniques for moving the cell pointer using the cursor-movement keys. In addition to the methods outlined in this table, all of which use various cursor-key combinations, you can also use the function key F5 (Goto) to move to a specific cell address.

♦ **Table 2.1:** *Cell-Pointer Movement in READY or POINT Mode*

Key(s)	Name	Description
→	Right	Moves the pointer right one column.
←	Left	Moves the pointer left one column.
↑	Up	Moves the pointer up one row.
↓	Down	Moves the pointer down one row.
Ctrl-→ *or* Tab	Big Right	Moves the pointer one screen right (80 columns).
Ctrl-← *or* Shift-Tab	Big Left	Moves the pointer one screen left (80 columns).
PgDn	—	Moves the pointer down one screen (20 rows).
PgUp	—	Moves the pointer up one screen (20 rows).
Home	—	Moves the pointer to the first cell in the worksheet (A1).
End-Home	—	Moves the pointer to the last active cell in the worksheet (that is, the cell at the intersection of the last used column and row).
End-← *or* End-→ End-↑ *or* End↓	—	If the pointer is on a blank cell, moves it to the first nonblank cell in the direction of the arrow in the worksheet. If the pointer is on a nonblank cell, moves it to the last nonblank cell in the worksheet.

Practice Moving the Pointer in a Worksheet

Now is a good time to get some practice using various cell-pointer movements. Because you will be practicing in a blank worksheet, you won't yet be able to see how the commands that use the End key work with ranges of data.

1. **Move the pointer to cell D6 by pressing the ↓ key until the pointer is in row 6, and then press the → key until the pointer is in column D.**
   Note that you could just as well have moved from A1 to D6 by first pressing the → key until you were in column D and then the ↓ key until you were in row 6.

2. **Move the pointer to cell B3 using the ↑ and ← keys.**
   This time, you decide which cursor key you wish to use first. Whenever you are navigating to a cell in a new column and row a short distance away, you must move the pointer in two planes: horizontal and vertical.

3. **Press the Home key.**
   This takes the pointer immediately to cell A1 from anywhere in the worksheet.

4. **Press the Tab key once.**
   The cell address is now I1 and this cell is now in the upper left corner of the worksheet display, replacing cell A1 and displaying a new set of columns. Press Tab or Ctrl-→ to scroll the display as well as move the pointer one screen to the right.

5. **Hold down the Ctrl key and press the → key twice.**
   This makes cell Y1 the current cell. Notice the doubling of the column letter after column Z in this part of the worksheet.

6. **Hold down the Shift key and press Tab once.**
   This takes the pointer one screen left, making Q1 the current cell.

7. **Hold down the Ctrl key and press the ← key once.**
   This makes I1 the current cell again. You may find pressing Ctrl-← to be easier than pressing Shift-Tab when you want to scroll the screen to the left.

8. **Press the PgDn (Page Down) key once.**
   The PgDn key moves the pointer down 20 rows or one screen. This makes cell I21 the current cell and places it in the upper left corner of the worksheet display.

9. **Press the PgDn key twice more.**
   Cell I81 should now be the current cell.

10. **Return immediately to cell A1 by pressing Home.**
    It doesn't matter where the cell pointer is—pressing the Home key will always return it to cell A1.

Using the Goto Key (F5) to Move the Pointer

In addition to moving the pointer by using various cursor keys and key combinations, you can also move the pointer with the Goto key, F5. When you press F5, 1-2-3 responds by displaying the message *Enter address to go to:* followed by the current cell address. To move the pointer to a new cell, you simply type its address. If the cell is in the same worksheet, you don't have to include the worksheet letter; just entering the column letter and row number is sufficient. Let's try using this method of moving the pointer:

1. **Press F5, then type *H7* as the cell to go to and press Enter.**
   Notice that cell H7 is now the current cell.

2. **Press F5 again; this time, type *IV1* as the cell to go to and press Enter.**
   Column IV (the 256th) is the last column of the worksheet. That is why, with cell IV1 located in the upper left corner of the display, there are no more column letters listed to the right of IV (you just see blank highlighting along the rest of the top of the frame).

3. **Press the → key once to attempt to move the pointer one more column to the right.**
   The program responds by sounding the bell ("beeping" at you), and the pointer doesn't move. The pointer is now located at the right edge of the worksheet, and 1-2-3 will not let you move it any farther to the right.

4. **Press F5, then type *IV8192* as the cell to go to and press Enter.**
   The current cell is now IV8192. Because row 8192 is the last row of the worksheet, no more numbers are visible below it in the left part of the frame.

5. **Try moving the pointer by pressing the ↓ and the → keys.**
   Note that you can't move the pointer any farther down or to the right. This is because the pointer is now located in the last cell in the lower right corner of the worksheet.

6. Move the pointer directly to cell A1 by pressing Home.

F5: The Goto Key

> F5, the Goto key, takes the cell pointer directly to a specific cell address or to the first cell in a named range

---

Adding Data to the Worksheet

Now that you have a better idea of how to move the cell pointer so that you can position it in the cell where you want to enter data, it is time to look at the methods provided for entering and editing data in a cell. In 1-2-3, you don't enter data directly into the cell; instead, you first enter the text, numbers, or formulas in the control panel (starting on the second line). Then, once you've finished typing and have checked that the entry is correct and requires no further editing, you enter it into the cell by pressing either the Enter key or one of the four arrow keys (on the cursor or numeric keypad). Only then does the entry appear in the cell in the worksheet display. If your entry is longer than 80 characters, 1-2-3 will scroll the line of text to the left as you type.

Remember that you can enter two types of data in a cell: a label or a value. Lotus 1-2-3 lets you know which type of data you are entering by switching from READY mode to either LABEL or VALUE mode, depending upon the first character that you enter.

Entering Labels in a Cell

All labels in the worksheet *must* be prefaced by one of the label prefix characters (refer to Table 1.1). However, when your label begins with a letter, you don't *have* to type one of these prefixes before you begin entering the label because 1-2-3 will automatically insert an apostrophe (the default label prefix that left-aligns text in the cell) at the beginning of the characters you enter. This means that if you type *Qtr 1* and press Enter with the pointer in cell B1, the contents of the cell that appear after the cell address on the first line of the contol panel will be '*Qtr 1* instead of just the *Qtr 1* you typed.

If you know before you type a label that you want it centered in a cell, you can format it that way by typing ^ (the caret symbol will not be displayed in the cell) before you enter its text. Likewise, if you want the label to be right-justified in the cell, you preface it with the " symbol. However, as you will soon learn, you can also modify the alignment of a label after it has been entered in the worksheet.

Forcing a Value to Be Entered as a Label

A label entry in a cell need not consist only of text characters, such as *Current Assets*; it can also mix text and numbers, as in *4th Quarter*, or consist of numbers only, as in *1990*.

However, if your entry begins with a number or other character that Lotus considers a value—such as a period, minus sign, $, (, or #—followed by text characters, as in *4th Quarter*, Lotus won't enter it into the cell until you preface it with one of the label prefixes. The program will, instead, beep at you and place the cursor under the first text character in the entry.

If your entry consists entirely of numbers, as in *1990*, and you want it to be entered as a label rather than a value (meaning that it can't be used in arithmetic calculations), you must preface it with one of the label prefixes. You can always tell that 1-2-3 entered your number as a value because it will be automatically right-aligned in the cell. To convert a value to a label, you would then have to edit the cell's contents by adding a label prefix at the very beginning of the text. (Techniques for editing the contents of a cell are covered later in this chapter.)

Entering Numerical Values in a Cell

When entering numbers in a cell, you need enter only the significant digits of the value. Note that trailing zeros after the decimal point are not considered significant digits, but all zeros preceding the decimal point are (they are the placeholders that differentiate units from 10s, 100s, 1000s, and so on). Therefore, if you enter the decimal number 27.50 in a cell, 1-2-3 will display only 27.5, dropping the trailing zero as insignificant. Because of this, you need not bother to add such zeros to your decimal entries. Note, however, that you can have such zeros displayed by changing the formatting of numbers (a technique that you will learn in the next chapter).

If the number represents a financial figure, you may enter the dollar sign ($), although it will not be displayed in the cell. If the number includes a comma used as the thousands separator, you may *not* enter it along with the digits: doing so will cause 1-2-3 to beep at you and go into EDIT mode. This is because the comma is considered a label character that can't be used in a value. Lotus 1-2-3 adds the currency symbol, thousands separators, and a uniform number of decimal places as display formatting after you enter your numbers. As you will learn, this can be done either for a specific group of cells or for the entire worksheet.

If the number represents a percentage, you can enter it in its decimal form (divided by 100) or with all of its significant digits terminated with the percent sign (%). For example, you can enter 25% either as *.25* or *25%*. Either way, 1-2-3 will display the entry in decimal form in the cell (*0.25*).

Decimal numbers can be entered as fractions or in decimal form. For example, you can enter the number 0.75 by typing either *.75* or *3/4*. Note, however, that you can't enter mixed numbers such as *2 3/4* in their fractional form: you must enter them as decimal numbers, as in *2.75*, otherwise 1-2-3 will beep at you and go into EDIT mode (because the space between the whole number and decimal number is considered a label character).

Note that when you enter a fraction in decimal form, you don't have to enter zero before the decimal point. Lotus 1-2-3 will automatically include a leading zero in the cell display when you press the Enter key.

Entering Dates in a Cell

Dates in the worksheet are stored as special numbers, which represent the number of days that have elapsed between the turn of the century and the date in question. According to this system, 1 represents the date January 1, 1900. The largest date number that you can use is 73050, which represents December 31, 2099. Such date numbers are referred to as *date serial numbers* or just serial numbers. Lotus 1-2-3 uses date serial numbers to perform calculations involving dates.

Although the program stores the date as a serial number between 1 and 73050, you don't have to enter your dates in the worksheet in this fashion. Lotus 1-2-3 will convert your date into the correct date serial number as long as you enter it with the @DATE function. When you use this function, you type the digits of the year, month, and day separated by commas and enclosed in a closed pair of parentheses, as in

@DATE(91,3,15)

Note that when you use this (or any other) 1-2-3 function, you never type spaces between the @ symbol, the name of the function, the parentheses, and the parameters.

After you've entered the proper date serial numbers in your worksheet with the @DATE function, you format them with a data display format. Lotus 1-2-3 allows you to select between five different date formats when formatting dates that have already been entered in the worksheet. The first of these date formats is Date Format 1 (D1), which is called the Lotus standard long form. It uses the form

DD-MMM-YY

where DD represents the number of the month, MMM is the first three letters of the name of the month, and YY is the last two digits of the year. Note that the Lotus standard long form is the only date format that can't be displayed in the default column width of nine spaces. To display a cell using this date format, you must widen the column to a minimum of ten spaces using the /Worksheet Column Set-Width command.

Therefore, to enter July 14, 1989 (the bicentennial of Bastille Day), and format it with Date Format 1, you follow three steps:

1. Move the pointer to the correct cell and enter the date serial number for July 14, 1989, by typing *@DATE(89,7,14)* and then pressing Enter.

2. Select the /Range Format Date 1 command and press Enter.

3. Widen the column to ten spaces by selecting the /Worksheet Column Set-Width command, typing 10, and pressing Enter.

When you have finished the last step, you will see

14-Jul-89

displayed in the cell and

(D1) [W10] @DATE(89,7,14)

displayed as the contents of the cell. In the contents of the cell, (D1) indicates that the format used is Date 1 and [W10] indicates that the cell width is currently ten spaces.

The alternate date format you can use to format your dates is Date Format 4 (D4), which is called the Long International format (the Short International format doesn't display the year, only the month and day). Its default form is

MM/DD/YY

where MM is the number of the month, DD is the number of the day, and YY is the last two digits of the year. If you used this format on the bicentennial of Bastille Day entered with the @DATE command, it would appear as

07/14/89

in the cell display.

Note that unlike the Lotus standard long form (D1), the Long International is not invariable: you can use the International Date command on the /Worksheet Global Default Other menu (/WGDOID) to change the format according to any of the following options:

A (MM/DD/YY) B (DD/MM/YY) C (DD.MM.YY) D (YY-MM-DD)

You can also enter dates in the worksheet by using special date functions such as @NOW and @DATEVALUE. You will learn how to use these date functions in Chapter 5.

Entering Times in a Cell

As with dates, times are stored in the worksheet somewhat differently from the way you would normally enter them. In the cell, a particular time of day is represented by a decimal number between 0.000000 (for 12:00 AM) and 0.999999 (for 11:59:59 PM).

As with dates in the worksheet, you don't have to enter a time in its decimal form to have 1-2-3 interpret it as a time of day and store the correct time decimal number. Instead, you use the @TIME function where you indicate the number of the hour, minutes, and seconds (optional). For example, to enter the correct time number for 10:30 AM, you would enter

@TIME(10,30,0)

To enter the correct time number for 10:30 PM, you would enter

@TIME(22,30,0)

based on 24-hour rather than a 12-hour clock. Just as with date numbers, you will want to format time decimal numbers to one of the four formats available. You select /Range Format Date to gain access to the four time choices.

The first two time formats are based on a 12-hour clock and therefore use the AM or PM designation. The difference between Time Format 1 (T1) and Time Format 2 (T2) is that T1 allows you to enter the hour, minutes, and seconds, whereas T2 only uses hours and minutes. Both, however, separate each part of the time number with a colon, as in 10:40:15 AM (T1) or 2:30 PM (T2).

Time Format 3 (T3) is called the Long International time format, and Time Format 4 (T4) is the Short International time format. Both the T3 and T4 formats make use of a 24-hour clock, and therefore don't use the AM or PM designation. Like the T1 and T2 formats, T3 includes the seconds as well as the hours and minutes, and T4 uses only the hours and minutes.

As with the international date formats, international time formats have a default setting that you can change. By default, the T3 and T4 formats use the colon to separate each time unit, as in 13:00:25 (T3) or 20:17 (T4). If you wish, you can change this separator according to these options on the International Time menu (/WGDOIT):

A (HH:MM:SS) B (HH.MM.SS) C (HH,MM,SS) D (HHh,MMm,SSs)

You can also enter times in the worksheet by using special time functions, such as @NOW and @TIME. You will learn how to use these time functions in Chapter 5.

Editing Data in the Worksheet

You need to be familiar with several techniques for editing data in a worksheet. When we speak of editing data, we are referring to the process of making revisions, additions, or deletions to a particular cell entry on the edit lines in the control panel. You can edit a cell entry at any of these times:

+ When you're in the process of creating an entry for a blank cell and haven't yet completed it.

+ When you're in the process of creating an entry that will replace the existing entry in the cell and haven't yet completed it.

+ When the existing cell entry requires minor modifications that you wish to make to the original cell contents rather than creating a new entry to replace the original.

Techniques for Editing a Cell Entry

Table 2.2 shows you the the keys that you can use in editing and how they function in EDIT mode. As you can see from this chart, many of the keys that perform cursor movements in EDIT mode are also used to move the cell pointer in either READY or POINT mode.

+ **Table 2.2**: *Editing Keys Used in EDIT Mode*

Key(s)	Name	Description
→	Right	Moves the cursor right one character.
←	Left	Moves the cursor left one character.
↑	Up	Enters the revision and moves the pointer up one row.
↓	Down	Enters the revision and moves the pointer down one row.

◆ **Table 2.2:** *Editing Keys Used in EDIT Mode (continued)*

Key(s)	Name	Description
↵	Enter	Completes editing; the cell pointer remains in the current cell.
←	Backspace	Deletes the character to the left of the cursor.
Del	Delete	Deletes the character at the cursor.
F2	Edit	Returns the contents of the current cell to the control panel for editing; 1-2-3 goes into EDIT mode.
Esc	Escape	Erases all characters in the entry.
Ins	Insert	Toggles between insert mode and overstrike mode. In insert mode, 1-2-3 inserts new characters by moving the existing characters from the cursor position to the end of the line to the right. In overstrike mode, 1-2-3 inserts new characters by replacing existing characters at the cursor.
Home	—	Moves the cursor to the first character in the entry.
End	—	Moves the cursor to the last character in the entry.
Ctrl-→ *or* Tab	Big Right	Moves the cursor five characters to the right.
Ctrl-← *or* Shift-Tab	Big Left	Moves the cursor five characters to the left.
PgDn	—	Completes editing, then moves the pointer down one screen (20 rows).
PgUp	—	Completes editing, then moves the pointer up one screen (20 rows).

The first step in editing data before you've entered a cell is to put 1-2-3 into EDIT mode by pressing the Edit key, F2. This step is important because it allows you to move the cursor (the blinking underscore) to the left or right without entering the data in the control panel in the cell. Remember that in LABEL or VALUE mode, 1-2-3 will complete a new entry as soon as you press any arrow key; it does this to speed data entry either down a column or across a row. When you press F2 and take the program into EDIT mode, you prevent this from happening. EDIT mode enables you to use the ← and → keys to move the cursor to the place in a line that needs editing. If the entry takes up more than one line of the control panel, you can then use the ↑ and ↓ keys to move the cursor up and down the lines.

You must take an extra step when you want to edit an existing cell entry: you must first make current the cell that contains the data to be edited (that is, move the pointer onto that cell). Once this is done, you can choose between two different editing techniques:

+ Retype the entry the way it needs to be and press Enter (or one of the arrow keys). Lotus 1-2-3 will then replace the original entry with your new entry.

+ Press the Edit function key (F2) to return the cell contents to the edit line of the control panel. Then make changes to just those parts of the entry in need of revision before pressing the Enter key, whereupon 1-2-3 will replace the original entry with your edited version.

When to choose retyping over editing a cell entry depends largely on the extent of the revision required in the cell as well as on your typing skills. If the revised entry will be a great deal shorter than the original entry that it will replace, however, you will almost always find it more efficient to retype it than to edit it. For example, assume that you entered the label *2nd Quarter Sales* in the cell where you should have entered *1990*. Invariably, you would find it quicker to make this change by typing *1990* and pressing Enter rather than by pressing F2, holding down the Backspace key until the *2nd Quarter Sales* entry is deleted, then typing *1990*, and finally pressing the Enter key.

When editing, you need to keep in mind that 1-2-3 is in insert mode by default. This means that if you position the cursor at the beginning of an entry and begin typing, the program will push all existing characters to the right to make room for those you add. If you want to have the new characters replace the existing ones as you type, you need to press the Ins key to put the program in overstrike mode (shown by the OVR status indicator at the bottom of the screen).

Also, when editing an existing label, remember that the label prefix, which is not displayed in the cell, will be the very first character of the entry returned in the control panel. Be careful that you neither delete this prefix character nor insert characters in front of it. In so doing, you could inadvertently change a label into a value or make the label prefix a visible character within the cell display.

F2: The Edit Key

F2, the Edit key, puts the program in EDIT mode

If you are making a new entry in the cell, F2 enables you to edit the contents before completing the entry

If the cell already contains an entry, F2 returns the cell contents to the control panel for editing

Deleting a Cell Entry

Lotus 1-2-3 allows you either to delete part of a cell entry one character at a time or to delete the entire cell entry located on the edit lines in the control panel. As you can see from Table 2.2, two keys enable you to delete a character at a time: the Del key, which deletes the character that the cursor is located on, and the Backspace key, which deletes the character immediately to the left of the cursor.

Note that you can use the Backspace key to delete single characters without having to first switch the program from LABEL or VALUE mode into EDIT mode. This means that if you are typing a label or value and you notice that you made a typing error a few characters back, you can press the Backspace key to delete until you have wiped out all the characters up to and including the one typed incorrectly without bothering to first press the Edit key (F2).

To use the Del key to remove incorrect characters, you often have to first move the cursor to the character (or to the first character in a string of characters) that needs to be deleted. Be careful, when using the Del key to remove just the character at the cursor, that you press the key only once and don't hold it— if you do, 1-2-3 will begin pulling in and deleting characters to the right of the cursor position.

Using the Esc Key to Delete the Entire Entry

If you press the Esc key when entering or editing a cell entry in the control panel, 1-2-3 will delete the entire entry. Do it only when you decide that it would be easier to retype the entire entry than to attempt to make editing changes to it. Be aware, however, that you can't use the Undo function (see Using Undo to Restored a Deleted Entry, later in this chapter) to restore an entry to the control panel once it has been deleted with the Esc key.

In addition to erasing the entry you are editing, the Esc key can also be used to prevent you from initially making an entry in the wrong cell. Assume, for example, that you begin typing a heading one row above the one where you really want the heading to appear. After typing a few words, you notice your mistake. At that point, all you need to do is press the Esc key to clear the edit line and return to READY mode, then press ↓ to move the pointer to the correct cell and enter the heading there.

Erasing the Contents of a Cell

The Esc key, however, can't be used to erase a cell entry that you intend to leave blank: it can *only* be used to delete a cell entry from the control panel before it ever goes into the cell or to delete an existing entry that you then replace with something else. To make a cell blank once again, you *must* use the /Range Erase command.

If you want to erase only a single cell, you position the pointer on the cell, type */RE*, and then press the Enter key in response to the prompt *Enter range to erase:*. You can, of course, erase several cells at one time with this command if you need to, as you will learn in Chapter 4.

* *New in 2.2* ## Using Undo to Restore a Deleted Cell Entry

Release 2.2 of 1-2-3 includes an Undo function (Alt-F4), which can be used to restore data that has been deleted in error. When you press the Undo key (Alt-F4), 1-2-3 restores both the worksheet data and settings to the way they were the last time the program was in READY mode. After using the Undo feature, you can press the Undo key a second time to redo the deletion or return the worksheet to the state before you used the Undo feature. This means that you can use the Undo key to toggle back and forth between the worksheet as it is after a change and then back to the way it was before the change.

There is a cost for this flexibility, however: in order for 1-2-3 to restore the worksheet to its previous state, it must create a temporary backup copy of the worksheet in a special part of the RAM called the *undo buffer*. There, 1-2-3 conserves the worksheet the way it was before you began a new operation. Needless to say, this undo buffer requires memory that would otherwise be available for building your worksheet. In fact, to ensure that 1-2-3 can back up the largest worksheet you could possibly create, the program reserves about half of the conventional memory available to your computer. This significantly reduces the size of the largest worksheet you can produce when the Undo feature is active.

The Undo feature is automatically active when you first install 1-2-3, as indicated by the presence of the UNDO indicator on the status line. To turn it off, you select the /Worksheet Global Default Other Undo Disable command (/WGDOUD). To keep it turned off permanently, you must then select the /Worksheet Global Default Update command (/WGDU).

You can use the Undo feature to do more than just undelete data that have been erased in error. Indeed, this is why it is called *Undo* and not *Undelete*. If 1-2-3 is about to run out of memory during an operation when the Undo feature is on, the program will suspend the operation and display the message

You will not be able to undo this action—do you wish to proceed?

In order to have the program continue with the operation, you must type Y to select the Yes menu option. To abort the operation, you can type N to select the No option or press Ctrl-Break to return immediately to READY mode.

Alt-F4: The Undo Key

Alt-F4, the Undo key, restores the worksheet to its state the last time the program was in READY mode

Press the Undo key a second time to reinstate the deletions and/or setting changes that you undid the first time you pressed the Undo key

Undo can be turned off by selecting the /Worksheet Global Default Other Undo Disable command (/WGDOUD)

Summary

Troubleshooting

Question: When I press the Enter key to complete an entry in a cell, 1-2-3 beeps at me. What's wrong?

Answer: Check to see if the program is in EDIT mode. If so, your entry probably mixes value and label characters and starts with a number or symbol that 1-2-3 interprets as a value. Because 1-2-3 can't accept a value that contains both text and numbers, the program goes into EDIT mode and places the cursor right after the place in the entry where the mix occurs. To have such an entry accepted as a label, move the cursor to the beginning of the line and insert a label prefix (', ^, or "), then press Enter. To have the entry accepted as a value, you must remove all nonnumeric characters from the entry before you press Enter.

Question: I wanted to erase a cell entry, so I moved the pointer on a cell, pressed Edit (F2) to return the entry to the control panel, then pressed Esc and Enter to delete the entry. Although pressing Esc deleted the entry from the control panel, it didn't affect the contents of the cell when I pressed Enter. What gives?

Answer: Remember that you can only use the Esc key to clear an entry in the control panel when you then intend to replace it with some new data. The *only* way to make a cell blank once again is to use the /Range Erase command.

Question: You say that using /Range Erase is the only way to blank out a cell, yet I can do the same thing simply by pressing the spacebar and Enter. Since my technique is so much easier and quicker than having to type */RE* and press Enter, why not use it?

Answer: When you press the spacebar and press Enter, you don't make the cell blank again; you simply replace the original entry with a space. You can verify this by examining the cell's contents after performing this operation. Although you won't be able to see the space in the cell, you will see the apostrophe label-prefix that 1-2-3 enters before it. We don't replace entries with spaces in the worksheet because they can throw off the accuracy of certain formulas (especially those that use statistical functions) and queries if you are working with a database. Again, the only way to make a cell empty once you have entered data in it is to use the /Range Erase command!

Question: I deleted a cell entry with the /Range Erase command by mistake, then immediately pressed Undo (Alt-F4 and typed Y), but the deleted data didn't reappear. What am I doing wrong?

Answer: The Undo feature is probably turned off in the copy of 1-2-3 that you are using. To verify this, check the status line for the UNDO indicator. If this indicator isn't present, then the Undo feature is currently turned off. To turn it back on, type */WGDOUE* to select the /Worksheet Global Default Other Undo Enable command. If 1-2-3 goes into ERROR mode when you select this command and you receive the message *Cannot enable undo: memory required is already in use*, you will have to save your worksheet with /File Save and then clear it from memory with /Worksheet Erase Yes before retrying this command. To keep the Undo feature turned on permanently, don't forget to select the /Worksheet Global Default Update command.

Essential Techniques

To Start 1-2-3 on a Hard Disk System

1. Turn on your computer.

2. At the DOS prompt, type *CD\123R3* and press ◀─┘ to change the directory.

3. To start 1-2-3 directly, type *123* and press ◀─┘.

4. To start 1-2-3 through the Lotus Access System, type *LOTUS* and press ◀─┘. Then press Enter or type *1* to select the 1-2-3 option on the Lotus Access System menu.

To Start 1-2-3 on a Two-Disk-Drive System

1. Place your DOS disk in drive A and turn on your computer. Then enter the date and time, if necessary.

2. Replace the DOS disk with a working copy of your 1-2-3 System disk.

3. To start 1-2-3 directly, type *123* and press ◀─┘.

4. To start 1-2-3 through the Lotus Access System, type *LOTUS* and press ◀─┘. Then press Enter or type *1* to select the 1-2-3 option on the Lotus Access System menu.

To Enter a Date in a Cell of the Worksheet

1. Use the @DATE function to enter the correct date serial number in the current cell by typing @DATE(followed by the last two digits of the year, the number of the month, and the number of the day, all separated by commas, as in @DATE(90,3,4) for March 4, 1990. Type) and press Enter.

2. Format the date serial number with the /Range Format Date command by typing /RFD. Select the desired date format by entering its number from 1 through 5 and press Enter. Then press Enter again to apply the designated format to the current cell.

3. If you are using Date Format 1, the Lotus standard long form, widen the column to at least ten spaces by selecting the /Worksheet Column Set-Width command (/WCS), then enter *10* and press Enter.

To Edit an Existing Cell Entry

1. Position the pointer on the cell whose contents you want to edit.

2. Press F2 (Edit) to return the contents to the control panel.

3. Use the arrow keys to move to the place where you need to add or delete characters.

4. To add new data, begin typing as long as OVR is not on the status line. To replace existing characters, press Ins (make sure that OVR is now on the status line), then start typing.

5. Press the Del key to delete characters at the cursor, or press the Backspace key to delete characters to the left of the cursor.

6. Press the Enter key to complete editing and place your revisions in the cell.

Review

Important Terms You Should Know

date serial number
Edit key (F2)
Goto key (F5)
Long International date/time
   format

Lotus Access System
Lotus standard long form
Undo (Alt-F4)

Test Your Knowledge

1. To start 1-2-3 from the DOS prompt, you must make the _____ directory current before you enter the *123* or *LOTUS* startup command. If you start 1-2-3 on a two-disk-drive system, you must replace the DOS disk in drive A with the _____ before you enter the *123* or *LOTUS* startup command.

2. If you type *LOTUS* as the startup command, the program displays the _____ menu. To start 1-2-3 from this menu, you must select the 1-2-3 option by either pressing the _____ key or typing .

3. To move the cell pointer to the first cell in the worksheet, you press the _____ key.

4. To move the cell pointer from cell A1 to D3, you press the _____ key three times and then the _____ key twice or you press _____, type _____, and press the Enter key.

5. To move the cell pointer down one screen, you press the _____ key. To move the cell pointer up one screen, you press the _____ key.

6. To move the cell pointer right one screen, you press the _____ key or the _____ keys. To move the cell pointer left one screen, you press the _____ keys or the _____ keys.

7. The last column in the worksheet is column _____. The last row in the worksheet is row _____. This makes the last cell address _____.

8. If you enter *Net Sales* in a cell, the cell will contain _____.

9. If you enter *$1,500.00* in a cell, the cell will contain _____.

10. If you type *1990 Net Sales*, 1-2-3 will go into _____ mode when you press the Enter key.

11. To have 1-2-3 enter the number 1990 as a label, you need to enter _____ in the cell.

12. To have December 31, 1992, stored in a cell as a date serial number, you can enter _____ in the cell and then format its display, using the _____ command.

13. To clear an entry from the control panel before you enter it in the current cell, you press the _____ key.

14. To return an entry to the control panel for editing, you press _____.

15. To erase a cell entry and leave the cell blank, you must use the _____ command.

16. If you erase a cell's contents in error, press _____ to restore the data before continuing your work.

3

Building
the Worksheet
Step by Step

In This Chapter...

Beginning a New Worksheet

It's time to get some hands-on experience in building worksheets. In this chapter, you will get the opportunity to create your first 1-2-3 worksheet: a simple income statement. In so doing, you will get practice in using many of the more common 1-2-3 commands. You will also get experience with many of the basic procedures required in building almost any type of spreadsheet, such as entering data, creating formulas, using 1-2-3 built-in functions, formatting the display of the data, and saving your work in a disk file.

To begin a new worksheet, simply start 1-2-3 (refer to the beginning of Chapter 2 for instructions on how to start the program). Each time you start the program, 1-2-3 displays a new blank worksheet for you to use.

If you have already started the 1-2-3 program and have a worksheet file on your screen, you must erase the current worksheet from the computer's memory. Never clear a worksheet from memory unless you have first saved the worksheet in a disk file (or unless you intend to abandon it because you are *sure* you won't ever need to use its data again).

Data in Memory versus Data on Disk

Before discussing the actual 1-2-3 commands that can be used to erase the current worksheet from memory and then begin work on the income statement, let's quickly review the difference between data in memory and data on disk. It's not at all uncommon for people, especially when they are new to computers, to confuse computer memory with disk storage. In part, this is because both memory (specifically the RAM or random access memory) and disk space are measured in the same units: bytes, kilobytes (1000 bytes—abbreviated K), and megabytes (1000 kilobytes— abbreviated Mb).

It is important to understand the difference so that you don't lose any of your work when using 1-2-3. When you create a new worksheet, *all* the data that you enter is stored in the computer's RAM memory. Whenever you quit 1-2-3 or shut off the power to your computer, the part of the RAM that holds this data is automatically cleared. To avoid the permanent loss of worksheet data that would result should this suddenly occur, you need to save a copy of all the data in a file on disk. That way, even after the contents of a worksheet are erased from memory, you can subsequently retrieve the worksheet data from disk and restore it to memory at any time after starting 1-2-3 again.

You can run out of memory for your worksheet file and still have a great deal of storage space available. In fact, this is most often the case because the size of the average hard disk is about 40 times that of the computer's memory (a common configuration for an 80286 IBM compatible is 1Mb RAM with a 40Mb hard disk). Remember that 1-2-3 can't use the free space on your hard disk directly as it does the RAM memory of the computer. Disk space is used only as a holding area to keep a copy of the worksheet data safe so that it isn't permanently lost when you quit 1-2-3 or lose power to the computer, and you can easily retrieve worksheet data from disk when it is needed. (For more information on how 1-2-3 uses computer RAM, refer to Appendix A; for information on disk usage and 1-2-3, refer to Chapter 14.)

Erasing the Worksheet File in Memory

Before you begin entering the titles for your new income statement, you need to make sure that you are working in a new file. To create a new file when you have entered data in the worksheet display or have retrieved a file that you created earlier, you always need to use the /Worksheet Erase command. When you select this command, you have to choose between No (the default) and Yes. The prompt beneath Yes says

Erase the entire worksheet from memory

If you select the Yes option and you have made changes that haven't yet been saved, 1-2-3 will immediately erase them without giving you a second chance to retrieve them (as it does in Release 3 of Lotus 1-2-3).

If you ever erase a worksheet with this command before it's been saved and wish to retrieve it, press the Undo key (Alt-F4) before you select any other 1-2-3 command. The Undo feature will restore the entire worksheet to the worksheet display screen.

Creating an Income Statement

Now you're ready to start work on the income statement. An income statement provides a basic summary of the revenues and expenses for a business during a particular period of time (usually the fiscal year). The income statement you build will be for the period from January 1 to December 31, 1990. Figure 3.1 shows this statement as it will appear upon completion.

Setting Up the Worksheet Environment

Every new worksheet that you begin automatically partakes of the program default settings in effect. Each time you begin a new worksheet file, you need to ask yourself if any of these settings need changing (refer to Appendix B for more general information on defaults and how to change them). In this case, you will use all the worksheet default settings as they come configured when you install 1-2-3.

	A	B	C
1	INCOME STATEMENT YEAR ENDING DECEMBER 31		
2		1990	
3	Revenues	50,250	
4	Costs and expenses		
5	Product costs	12,175	
6	Marketing and sales	20,785	
7	General and administrative	17,850	
8		---------	
9	Total costs and expenses	50,810	
10			
11	Operating income (loss)	(560)	
12			
13	Other income (expenses)		
14	Interest income	4,500	
15	Interest expense	(500)	
16	Other	600	
17		---------	
18	Total other income (expenses)	4,600	
19			
20	Income (loss) before taxes	4,040	
21	Provision (benefit) for taxes	606	
22	Net earnings (loss)	3,434	
23		=======	

♦ **Figure 3.1:** *Final income statement for 1990*

Entering the Worksheet Title and Row Headings

Now let's start work on the income statement itself by adding the title for the worksheet and the headings for each row. Refer to Figure 3.1 as needed as you complete these entries:

1. **Press the Caps Lock key if the CAPS status indicator isn't already displayed at the bottom of the screen; with the pointer still in cell A1, type** INCOME STATEMENT YEAR END- ING DECEMBER 31 **and press the ↓ key.**
   Remember that if you make a mistake while typing, press the Back- space key until you delete the incorrect characters and then retype

Selecting Options from Command Menus:　　Although 1-2-3 gives you a choice in the method by which you select menu options—either move the highlight bar so that it is on the option and then press Enter, or just type the first letter of the menu option—always use the typing method as you learn 1-2-3 (even if you're not a touch typist). Not only is this method more efficient—typing the first letter of an option name combines the keystrokes required to move the highlight bar to the option and pressing Enter—but it also helps you remember the commands better because you associate the sequence of menu options required to perform a task with the sequence of letters you type. In addition, this method gives you a head start when you begin creating your own macros in 1-2-3 because you'll already be familiar with executing commands by entering the necessary menu letters, which is the way all 1-2-3 commands are actually entered in macros to record them for later playback.

the text. Notice how this long label in cell A1 spills over into columns B, C, D, and E.

2. **Press the ↓ key to move the pointer to A3, press the Caps Lock key again (the CAPS status indicator will disappear), then type *Revenues* and press the ↓ key.**
   When entering data in a worksheet, you should establish a pattern: either work down columns or across rows. For this income statement, you will find it more efficient to enter the data down each column (using the ↓ key).

3. **With the pointer in cell A4, type *Costs and expenses*, then press the ↓ key.**
   The next three row headings in cells A5 through A7 will be indented two spaces.

4. **With the pointer in cell A5, press the spacebar twice, then type *Product costs* and press the ↓ key.**
   By now, you should be getting the hang of how you enter these row headings down column A.

5. **Continue entering the titles for each of the other rows in the income statement as they are shown in Figure 3.1 (note that the headings you will be entering in cells A6, A7, A14, A15, A16, and A21 are all to be indented two spaces); when you are finished, your screen should match the one shown in Figure 3.2.**
   Remember that if you make a mistake you don't notice until after

you have completed an entry, you can edit it by moving the pointer back to the cell, and then either retype the entry or press the Edit key (F2) and make specific modifications to part of it. If you find that you have entered a label in a cell that should be blank, you must make it current and then use the /Range Erase command by typing /RE and pressing the Enter key.

6. **Press the Home key to move the pointer directly to cell A1, then use the → and ↓ keys to move the pointer to cell B2.**
   In cell B2, you need to enter *1990* as the heading for column B. Because this entry represents a title and not a value you wish to use in calculations, you need to enter it as a label.

7. **Type '1990 and then press the ↓ key.**
   Notice that 1990 is left-aligned in the cell because you entered it as a label instead of a value. You will now begin entering the cost and expense figures in column B. Remember that you can't include the comma used as the thousands separator as part of the values you enter in this column. You will add these commas later by formatting the values after you have finished entering them.

8. **Type 50250, then press the ↓ key twice.**
   Notice that the entry is automatically right-aligned in the cell, showing you that it was entered as a value.

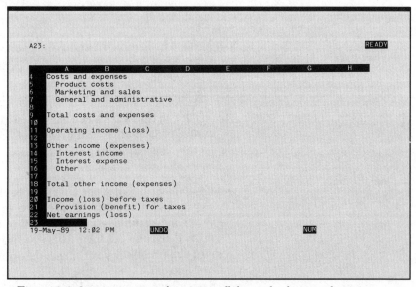

◆ **Figure 3.2:** *Income statement after entering all the row headings in column A*

9. **With the pointer in cell B5, type *12175* and press the ↓ key.**
Notice that entering this number in cell B5 has truncated the display of the row heading that you entered in A5. Instead of the full label, *Product costs*, the cell now displays only the first word, *Product*. This happens whenever you make an entry in a cell into which a long label spills. To remedy this, widen the cells in column A. Doing this now will make it easier to complete the data entry in column B.

10. **Move the pointer up and over so that it is once again located in cell A5.**
Verify that the contents of this cell is still *'Product costs*, even though only *Product* is now visible (Figure 3.3).

Using the Online Help

Now is an excellent time to explore the online help facility in 1-2-3. We will use it to look up the 1-2-3 command for changing a column width.

If you ever need help in locating a command or understanding what a particular command does, you can turn to the program's online help by pressing the Help key (F1). The help is context-sensitive, which means that the program will display help screens related to the command or function you are specifying if you press the Help key (F1) at some point during its definition.

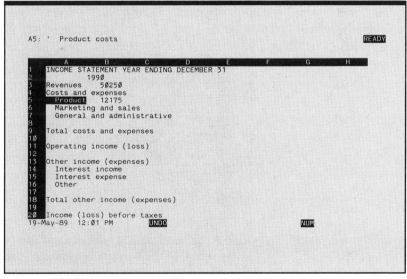

♦ **Figure 3.3:** *Income statement after truncating the display of the long label in cell A5*

If you press the Help key when the program is in READY mode, the program displays a Help Index screen that displays all the help topics in bold, or in a different color on a color monitor (Figure 3.4). To select a particular topic from this screen, you simply use the cursor keys to move the pointer until it is highlighted and then press Enter. In addition to the four arrow keys (which move the pointer one topic at a time in the direction of the arrow), you can use the Home key to move to the first topic on the screen or the End key to move to the last one. You can use the Backspace key to display the previous help screen.

The help facility helps you locate the topic you want by allowing you to approach its help topics in several ways from the index screen. For example, if you know the general category of 1- 2-3 command you need help on, but don't know on which menu it appears, select the *1-2-3 Commands* topic, which takes you to a screen where you can choose between *Worksheet commands*, *Range commands*, and so on. Selecting the correct group of commands takes you to a list of the commands on that menu for which you can get specific help.

If you need help performing a task and you don't know which command menu is used, look among the general topics listed on the Help Index screen. For example, in Figure 3.4, you can see the topic *Column Widths* listed among those in the Help Index screen. Since this is the topic we need help with, let's go ahead and use this option to find out exactly how to change the width of column A in the income statement:

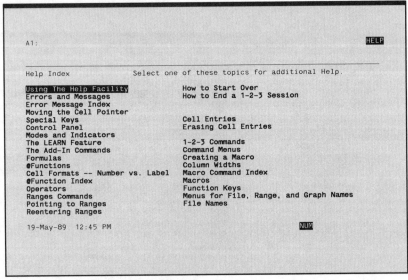

◆ **Figure 3.4:** *The 1-2-3 Help Index screen*

1. **With the pointer still on cell A5, press the Help key (F1); if you are using Release 2.01, move the pointer to *Help Index* and press Enter.**

   This takes you to the Help Index screen. Locate the Column Widths topic. Also, notice that the program is now in HELP mode (indicated by *HELP* in the upper right corner of the screen).

2. **Move the pointer to the topic *Column Widths* in the Help Index screen and press Enter.**

   You are now looking at the Column Widths help screen. Notice that the pointer is located on **/Worksheet Column** in bold on this screen (Figure 3.5). Notice that this screen tells you that the command /Worksheet Column is used to set the width of a single column.

3. **Press Enter with the pointer still on */Worksheet Column* to get more help on using this command.**

   This takes you to the first help screen for /Worksheet Column (Figure 3.6). If you are using Release 2.2, notice that the *Continued* option at the bottom of the screen is currently highlighted.

   This option lets you know that there is more information about /Worksheet Column available.

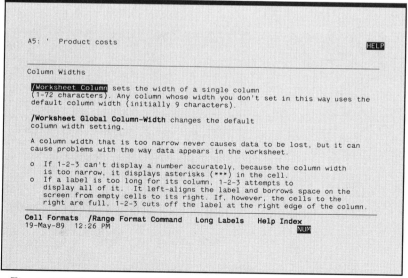

♦ **Figure 3.5:** *The Column Widths help screen*

4. **Press Enter to select the *Continued* option in Release 2.2 or the *Set-Width* option in Release 2.01 to get more help on setting new column widths.**

   This continued screen explains that you can either type a number or press the → or ← key and press Enter to set a new column width after selecting the /Worksheet Column Set-Width command. Notice the Troubleshooting option at the bottom of the screen is highlighted.

5. **Press Enter to select the *Troubleshooting* option to get special pointers on setting new column widths.**

   The troubleshooting screen for setting new columns explains that asterisks appear in a cell when the column is too narrow to display the value (either because of its size or formatting).

6. **Press Esc to exit from HELP mode and return to READY mode and the worksheet.**

Widening the First Column to Fit the Headings

As you found out from the /Worksheet Column help screen, you can set the column width either by typing a number between 1 and 240 or by using the → or ← key. Let's use the latter method so you can play with the width until you get it right, giving you visual feedback on the effect that your widening or narrowing of the column has on the worksheet display. Reserve the typing method

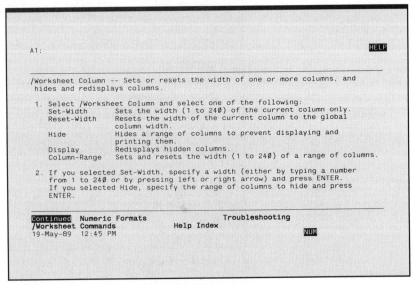

◆ **Figure 3.6:** *The first /Worksheet Column help screen*

for those situations where you know in advance how many characters will be required in a column to display all its entries.

1. **Type /WC to select the /Worksheet Column menu. Type S to select the Set-Width option.**
   You now see the prompt *Enter column width (1..240):* followed by 9, the current width of the column (the default is a width of nine characters for all cells when you start a new worksheet). Instead of typing a new number, you will change the width using the → key.

2. **Press the → key once.**
   Notice that the number after the prompt has changed from *9* to *10*.

3. **Continue to press the → key until the column-width indicator at the top of the screen reads 30.**
   Each time you press the → key, the values you entered in column B are pushed farther to the right as column A becomes wider.

4. **Press the ← key twice until the column-width indicator reads 28.**
   You can use the ← key to narrow a column whenever you have widened it too much with the → key. Notice that at a width of 28 characters, the column is just wide enough to accommodate the longest label visible in the worksheet display (that of *General and administrative* in cell A7); you'd better give yourself a few more spaces in this column.

5. **Press the → key three times until the column-width indicator reads 31, then press Enter.**
   Don't forget to press Enter when you're resetting a column width using the → or ← key (it's easy to do). Your worksheet should now resemble the one shown in Figure 3.7.

Entering a Repeating Character in a Cell

As you can see, widening column A has helped the appearance of the worksheet quite a bit. It will also make it a great deal easier to complete your data entry in column B.

1. **Move the pointer to cell B6, then enter *20785*, and press the ↓ key.**
   Now you are ready to enter the General and administrative expenses in cell B7.

2. **Type *17850*, then press the Enter key to complete this entry.**

```
A5: [W31] '  Product costs                                      READY

                       A                    B          C        D        E
1  INCOME STATEMENT YEAR ENDING DECEMBER 31
2                                         1990
3  Revenues                              50250
4  Costs and expenses
5     Product costs                      12175
6     Marketing and sales
7     General and administrative
8
9  Total costs and expenses
10
11 Operating income (loss)
12
13 Other income (expenses)
14    Interest income
15    Interest expense
16    Other
17
18 Total other income (expenses)
19
20 Income (loss) before taxes
19-May-89  12:42 PM        UNDO                            NUM
```

◆ **Figure 3.7:** *The income statement after widening column A*

The next entry you need to make in cell B8 is a row of dashes across the entire cell width. This is not done, as you might imagine, by typing a series of dashes. Instead, you will use 1-2-3's repeating label prefix, the backslash (\). Any single character or series of characters that you type after the backslash is automatically repeated across the entire width of the cell when you complete the label's entry in the cell.

You always want to use the repeating label prefix to create a line of dashes or equal signs (often used above the totals line) in the worksheet. This is because you can then change the column width and 1-2-3 will automatically increase or reduce the number of repeated characters as required to fit the new width. If you make these types of entries manually, you will have to edit them whenever you change the column width.

Also, you need to be aware that 1-2-3 won't allow you to enter a series of dashes in a cell. Normally, the program interprets an initial dash as a negative sign that precedes a value of some sort. As such, a series of negative signs is considered by the program to be an error on your part, and it brings about that all-too-common beep and the EDIT mode indicator.

To enter a repeating dash (–) in the cell:

3. **Type \– and then press the Enter key to complete the entry.**
   Notice that the dashes extend across the entire width of cell B7, although the contents of this cell is only \– as you entered it.

Creating a Formula Using a Simple @Function

For the next entry in cell B9, you need to create your first mathematical formula. This formula will total the costs and expenses for product costs, marketing and sales, and general and administrative and place this total in cell B9.

To calculate this total, your formula will use a simple 1-2-3 function called @SUM. We're going to use @SUM instead of creating an addition string (+B5+B6+B7) because @SUM is easier to build and allows you to go back later and add new expense categories by inserting rows without forcing you to redo the @SUM formula (you'll learn more about this in later chapters).

All 1-2-3 functions start with the @ symbol (this is how the program distinguishes a function from any other label) and, therefore, they are commonly referred to as *@functions* (pronounced "at functions"). As a result, entering the @ symbol as the first character automatically puts the program into VALUE mode because 1-2-3 anticipates the use of a function.

By definition, an @function is a predefined formula that returns a particular calculated result whose value is directly dependent upon the arguments (input values) made to the function. These *arguments of an @function*, which tell 1-2-3 which values to use in the calculations, differ from @function to @function. In fact, when you come across a new @function in 1-2-3, you need to learn two things about it: first, how to spell its name correctly, and second, what kind of arguments it requires.

Although some 1-2-3 functions don't require any arguments at all (they are understood by 1-2-3 to never vary), the vast majority of 1-2-3 @functions require some sort of arguments. All @function arguments are enclosed in parentheses. If the @function requires multiple arguments (as is often the case with more complex functions), they are separated by commas.

The @SUM function requires only one argument: a list of the values to be totaled. This list can be an actual listing of numbers, such as 4, 5, and 6, or—as is more commonly the case—a range of cells that contain the values. For example, to get the total of 45, 60, and 75.5 in a cell using @SUM, enter

@SUM(45,60,75.5)

in the cell.

Your formula in cell B9 will sum the values in cells B5, B6, and B7. Therefore, you need to enter this range of cells as the list argument of the @SUM function. When specifying a range of cells in 1-2-3, however, you need not list each individual cell address in the range: instead, you list only the first and last cell in the range separated by two periods (..). Entering this range as the @SUM argument tells the program to include the starting and ending cell *as well as* all cells in-between in the addition. So, your formula in cell B9 will be

@SUM(B5..B7)

@Functions

> @Functions are predefined formulas that most often require specific
> arguments to indicate which data are to be used in the calculations
>
> @Functions always begin with an @ symbol as the first character
>
> Arguments for @functions must be enclosed in parentheses: if the
> @function requires multiple arguments, they are separated by commas

Indicating a Cell Range in POINT Mode

You're now ready to enter this formula in cell B9 in your worksheet. Although
you can do this by typing *@SUM(B5..B7)* and pressing the Enter key, as you do
when entering a number or label in a cell, you will use a more reliable method
whereby you indicate the cell range for the @SUM argument by *pointing*.

Pointing, as the name implies, involves using the cursor-movement keys to
move the cell pointer to the cells in the worksheet that you want included.
When 1-2-3 is in POINT mode, the program will automatically enter the
address of the cell you are pointing to (that is, the current cell) in the formula.
As you move the pointer to new cells in the worksheet, 1-2-3 updates the cell
address in your formula.

When defining a range by pointing, you type a period (.) to anchor the range
on one of its key cells—the first or last one in a range are always good anchor
points (you will learn much more about defining and using cell ranges in the
next chapter). When you type a period to anchor a range, 1-2-3 responds by
freezing the current cell address in the formula. This is done by duplicating the
cell address separated by two periods, as in A1..A1. Once the range is anchored
on a cell, moving the pointer in any direction increases the size of the range.
As you move the pointer, 1-2-3 indicates the extent of the range just by updating the second cell address after the two periods, as in A1..A5.

Pointing out ranges when building formulas is preferable to typing them in
because the program gives you visual feedback that helps you define the range correctly. It's all too easy to type an incorrect cell address in a cell range and not notice
your mistake; as you will see now, it is much harder to make a mistake when pointing them out. Let's go ahead and define this formula by pointing:

1. **With the pointer in cell B9, type just** *@sum(* **and then stop**
   typing.
   Note that you don't have to type the name of the function in uppercase letters. Having typed *@sum(*, you are now ready to indicate the

cell range that is to be used as the argument. It's at this place exactly that you want to switch from VALUE mode to POINT mode: this is done simply by pressing one of the pointer-movement keys.

2. Press the ↑ key once.

Notice that the mode changes to POINT and that 1-2-3 enters the cell address B8 in the formula so that it now reads *@sum(B8* (Step 1 in Figure 3.8). Next, you need to move the pointer to the first cell in the range.

3. Press the ↑ key three times until the current cell is B5.

The formula now reads *@sum(B5* (Step 2 in Figure 3.8). Now that the pointer is correctly positioned on the first cell of the range, you need to anchor the range on this cell (B5).

4. Type a period (.) to anchor the cell range on B5.

The program indicates that you have anchored on a cell by changing the @SUM argument to a range so that the formula now reads *@sum(B5..B5* (Step 3 in Figure 3.8). Now that the range is anchored, you have to use the ↓ key to define its extent.

5. Press the ↓ key twice until the pointer is on cell B7.

Notice that the extent of the cell range is shown in two ways: by the highlighting of the three cells B5, B6, and B7 in the worksheet display and of the cell range B5..B7 in the @SUM function, which now reads *@sum(B5..B7* (Step 4 in Figure 3.8). Next, you need to complete the @SUM function by typing the) to close the parentheses.

6. Type).

Notice that as soon as you type), 1-2-3 moves the pointer to cell B9, the cell that actually contains the formula (Step 5 in Figure 3.8). However, the program doesn't calculate the completed @SUM function until you press the Enter key (or a pointer-movement key such as ↓).

7. Press the Enter key to have your formula calculated and entered in the cell.

You should now see the calculated total of 50810 in the cell display and the formula @SUM(B5..B7) in the cell contents (Step 6 in Figure 3.8). Notice that the calculated total of 50810 in cell B9 lacks a comma between the 0 and 8 (1-2-3 displays all calculated values in General format even when Automatic is the global format for data entry).

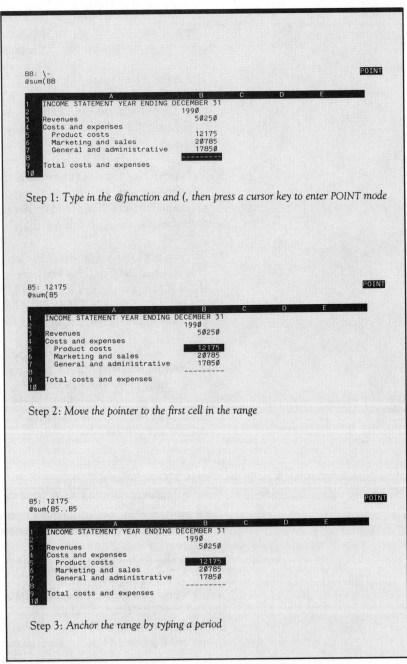

Step 1: *Type in the @function and (, then press a cursor key to enter POINT mode*

Step 2: *Move the pointer to the first cell in the range*

Step 3: *Anchor the range by typing a period*

♦ **Figure 3.8:** *Defining a cell range as the argument of an @function by pointing*

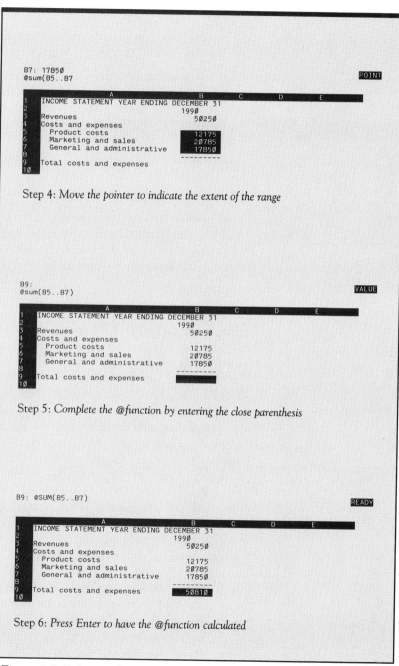

Step 4: *Move the pointer to indicate the extent of the range*

Step 5: *Complete the @function by entering the close parenthesis*

Step 6: *Press Enter to have the @function calculated*

♦ **Figure 3.8:** *Defining a cell range as the argument of an @function by pointing (continued)*

POINT Mode

> POINT mode allows you to define a cell range for a formula using the pointer-movement keys
>
> POINT mode is activated by pressing a pointer-movement key (↑, ↓, →, ←, PgUp, and so on) any place in an @function where an argument is called for after a math operator (+, −, *, /, ^, >, <, =, < >, #NOT#, #AND#, #OR#, or &) when defining a simple formula

Defining a Simple Formula in POINT Mode

The next entry you need to make in your income statement is a formula in cell B11 that calculates the operating income or loss by subtracting the total costs and expenses in cell B9 from the revenues in cell B3. This is a simple enough formula to enter either by typing or by pointing:

B3 − B9

However, there is a catch: 1-2-3 must be in VALUE mode to perform this subtraction. If you type B, 1-2-3 goes into LABEL mode. Therefore, to force the program into VALUE mode before you begin to define a formula whose initial entry is designated by a cell address (as opposed to a value such as 34 or −5), you type a plus sign (+) before you do anything else. The plus sign not only puts 1-2-3 into VALUE mode, but also doesn't modify the value of the cell in any way.

You must also enter the plus sign at the start of a formula where you mean to define the cells to be operated on by pointing (as you will do next with this formula). This is because the program won't go into POINT mode until after you have typed some sort of mathematical operator (the plus sign means addition to 1-2-3).

As with cell ranges for an @function argument, pointing is the preferred method for defining formulas (even simple ones like this) because it greatly reduces the chance of indicating the wrong cell addresses. To see how this is so, let's go ahead and define this next formula:

1. **Press the ↓ key twice to move the pointer to cell B11.**
    You always need to position the pointer in the cell where you want the calculated result to appear before you begin defining your formula (if you discover that it's not in the right cell and that you're about to replace an existing cell entry with the formula, press the Esc key to

erase it, then move the pointer). Next, you need to put 1-2-3 in VALUE mode.

2. **Type +, then press the ↑ key until the pointer in on cell B3.**
   Your formula should now read +B3. Now you're ready to enter a dash (as the operator for subtraction) before you point to cell B9, whose value is to be subtracted from that in B3.

3. **Type −.**
   Notice that as soon as you enter the subtraction operator, the program returns to VALUE mode and the pointer returns immediately to cell B11 where the formula is being entered. Next, return to POINT mode by moving the pointer to cell B9.

4. **Press the ↑ key twice until the pointer is on cell B9.**
   Notice that the formula reads +B3−B9.

5. **Press the Enter key to complete the formula in cell B11 and have it calculated.**
   As soon as you press the Enter key, 1-2-3 performs the subtraction and displays the result of −560 in cell B11.

Finishing the Income Statement

You need to enter just a few more simple formulas, numbers, and repeating labels in column B to finish your income statement. As you have some experience in doing all these types of entries, you should have no trouble with these last steps:

1. **Move the pointer down to cell B14, then type 4500 and press the ↓ key.**
   Next, you need to enter the Interest expense in cell B15. As this is an expense, you enter it as a negative number.

2. **In cell B15, type − 500 and then press the ↓ key.**
   In cell B16, you will now enter 600 for the Other category.

3. **In cell B16, type 600 and then press the ↓ key.**
   In cell B17, you need to enter another line of dashes using the repeating label prefix.

4. **In cell B17, type \− and then press the ↓ key.**
   Now, you need to enter a second @SUM function. This one will total the amounts in three cells of the Other income category.

5. **In cell B18, type** *@sum(,* **then press the ↑ key until the pointer is in cell B14; type a period (.) to anchor the range, then press the ↓ key twice until cells B14 through B16 are highlighted; finally, type) and then press the ↓ key again.**
   This formula calculates the total other income as 4600. Next, you have to create a formula that will add the operating income to the total other income. Here, it is easier to create a simple addition formula than it is to use the @SUM function.

6. **Press the ↓ key to move the pointer to cell B20; then type + to start the formula, press the ↑ key until the pointer is on cell B11; then type + again, and press the ↑ key until the pointer is on cell B18; finally, press the Enter key to complete the formula.**
   This formula calculates the income before taxes as 4040. Next, you have to enter a simple formula in cell B21 that will calculate the taxes, given the amount of income after expenses. For this amount, we will figure that we must pay 15 percent of this income figure.

7. **Press the ↓ key to move the pointer to cell B21; then type + to start the formula, press the ↑ key to highlight cell B20, type * 15 % (the * is the multiplication operator) and press the ↓ key to complete the formula.**
   This formula calculates the tax provision as 606. There is only one more formula to enter in your income statement in cell B22. This formula will calculate after-tax earnings by subtracting the amount of taxes in cell B21 from the income before taxes in cell B20.

8. **Type + to start the formula, press the ↑ key twice to highlight cell B20, and type − ; next, press the ↑ key once to highlight cell B21, and press the Enter key to complete the formula.**
   This formula calculates the net earnings as 3434. To emphasize that this is the final total in your income statement, finish the entries in this worksheet by putting a line of equal signs in cell B23.

9. **Press the ↓ key once to move the pointer to cell B23, then type \ = and press the Enter key.**
   At this point, your income statement worksheet should look like the one shown in Figure 3.9.

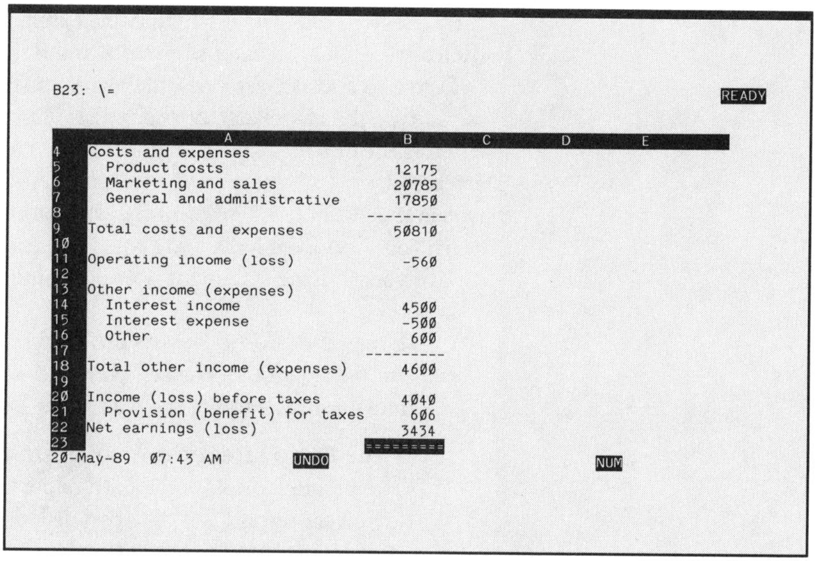

◆ **Figure 3.9:** *Income statement after completing the last entry in column B*

Saving Your Worksheet

Before you put the finishing touches on your income statement, you should save your work. As of now, all the labels, values, and formulas that you entered in the income statement exist only in RAM. Should you experience a power outage or machine failure, you would lose all this work with no way to retrieve it (the Undo feature works on data that *you* delete while the 1-2-3 program is still in memory). You would have to recreate the entire worksheet from scratch by manually redoing every step you took up to this point.

To avoid such a possibility, you will now save the worksheet on disk by using the /File Save command. That way, should you have a power failure, you can retrieve a copy of the income statement worksheet into the computer's memory from the disk file by using the /File Retrieve command.

Whenever you save a new worksheet, 1-2-3 displays a line listing of the worksheet files already saved in the current directory. For example, if the current directory is C:\123, you will see the prompt

Enter name of file to save: C:\123\ *.wk1

on the second line of the control panel. Beneath it, you will see the first part of an alphabetical listing of all Release 2 worksheets in the current directory. The *.wk1* after the path name in this prompt instructs 1-2-3 to list all files that carry the .WK1 extension, which is the extension used by Release 2.01 and 2.2 (Release 1A uses the extension .WKS and Release 3 uses .WK3).

To give your worksheet a new file name, you can simply start typing it. As soon as you type the first character, the *.wk1* disappears from the path name. When entering the new file name, remember that it can't contain more than eight characters and you can't use spaces in the name. Also, be aware that you don't have to type in the *.WK1* file extension: 1-2-3 will automatically add this to the name you assign your worksheet (unless you type in an extension of your own).

Save your income statement now by taking the following steps:

1. **Press the Home key to move the pointer to cell A1.**
   As the position of the cell pointer is saved in the file, you have to move it to the top of the worksheet before you save it.

2. **Type /FS to select the Save option from the /File menu.**
   The program displays the path name C:\123*.wk1 or A:*.wk1 (if you are using 1-2-3 on a two-disk-drive system). You are going to save your income statement under the name IS90CH3.WK1 (for the Income Statement for 1990 created in Chapter 3). However, if you are using a two-disk-drive system, you must preface this file name with a B: to prevent the program from saving the file on the 1-2-3 System disk; in this case, you must have a formatted disk in drive B and make sure that you save the file on this disk.

3. **If you are using a hard disk system and are saving the work-sheet file in the directory C:\123, type** *is90ch3* **(lowercase letters are fine) and press Enter.**
   Notice that as soon as you typed *I*, the *.wk1* disappeared but the path name C:*123*\ remained. When you finished typing the new file name, the full path name became C:*123**is90ch3*, indicating both its name and current location on the hard disk.

4. **If you are using a two-disk-drive system, press the Esc key twice until the path name A:*.wk1* disappears; then, type** *b:is90ch3* **(lowercase letters are automatically changed to uppercase) and press Enter.**
   The first time you press the Esc key, the program clears the *.wk1* from the line. The second time you press this key, it removes the path name (A:\ in this case), leaving only the prompt to enter the name of the file to save. Note that you can't enter a new drive or directory path designation until you clear the original path name by pressing Esc a second time.

◆ *New in 2.2*   *Displaying the File Name on the Status Line*

If you are using Release 2.2, you can have the program display the file name under which you save your worksheet on the status line in place of the date and time indicator. To do this, you select the /Worksheet Global Default Other Clock Filename command (/WGDOCF). After you select this command, 1-2-3 will display the date and time indicator on the status line only when the worksheet has *not* yet been saved on disk. As soon as you save the first time with the /File Save command, the name that you assign to the worksheet is displayed in the lower left corner instead of the date and time.

If you wish to make the display of the file name on the status line the new program default, you must remember to select the Update option on the /Worksheet Global Default menu before you select the Quit option to return to READY mode. With the file name displayed as the new global default, you can always tell that you haven't yet saved a new worksheet if you still see the date and time indicator at the bottom of the screen.

Figure 3.10 shows you how the file name you just gave your first worksheet appears on the status line when you activate this setting in Release 2.2. If you want to have the file names displayed on your system, take the following steps:

1. **Select the /Worksheet Global Default Other Clock Filename command by typing /*WGDOCF.**
   This returns you to the /Worksheet Global Default menu. To make

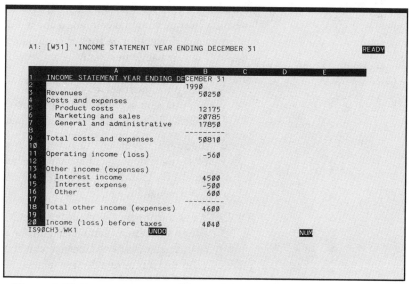

◆ **Figure 3.10:** *Income statement worksheet with file name on status line*

this a permanent change in the program, you must select the Update option. If you don't, the file name display will not be operative when you next start 1-2-3.

2. Select the Update Quit options by typing *UQ*.

This returns you to READY mode. You should now see *IS90CH3.WK1* in the lower left corner of the screen on the status line (as shown in Figure 3.10) where the date and time indicator was displayed previously. From now on, you will see the name of the worksheet file here as soon as you save or retrieve a new worksheet.

Formatting the Entries in the Worksheet

Now it is time to format the display of the values in your income statement worksheet. To do this, you will use the /Range Format command. Lotus 1-2-3 offers many choices in formatting values in a worksheet.

Although you will select a format from the /Range menu because you only need to apply it to a particular group of cells, remember that all the formats on the /Range Format menu are also available on the /Worksheet Global Format menu. The only difference is that when you select a format from the /Worksheet Global Format menu, it is automatically applied to the entire worksheet (replacing the program default of General).

Because the /Range Format command is used to format particular groups of cells, you have to specify the cell range that is to receive the format. When specifying this range, you can either type in the cell range or use pointing, as we did when defining the cell ranges for the @SUM arguments.

Let's see how the /Range Format command can help you achieve a uniform display for your values in column B of the income statement:

1. Move the pointer to cell B3.

You will next apply the formatting to the entire range of values in column B (below the 1990 column heading).

2. Type */RF* to select the Range Format command.

Note the wide range of formats that are listed on this menu (Figure 3.11). You want to select the Comma format (,) listed between Currency and General.

3. Type a comma (,) to select the Comma format.

When you select a format that allows decimal places, such as Comma or Currency (just like Comma with the addition of the dollar sign), 1-2-3 defaults to two decimal places. Notice from the prompt *Enter number of decimal places (0..15):* that your values can have up to 15 decimal places. You want only whole dollar amounts in the income statement, so set the number of decimal places to 0.

4. **Type 0 and press the Enter key.**
   The program responds by prompting you with *Enter range to format: B3..B3.* Notice that the range is anchored (you can tell this by the doubling of the cell address separated by ..). All you have to do is move the pointer to the other end of the range.

5. **Press the ↓ key to move the pointer to cell B22 (Figure 3.12), then press the Enter key.**
   Notice that now all dollar amounts in column B use the same format. Also, notice that the two negative values in cells B11 and B15 are now enclosed in parentheses—the way accountants like to see them (both the Currency and Comma formats do this automatically).

Although the income statement looks good, one more thing remains to be done to its display. Notice that the column heading 1990 in cell B2 is hard to see, as it is now aligned with the left edge of column B; it should be centered in its cell. Remember that you forced this numeric entry to be considered a label by prefacing it with the apostrophe label prefix ('), and this prefix accounts for its left-alignment in the cell.

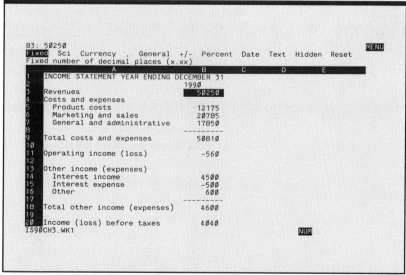

♦ **Figure 3.11:** *The /Range Format menu*

```
B22: +B2Ø-B21                                                    POINT
Enter range to format: B3..B22

                          A                    B        C        D        E
 3   Revenues                              5Ø25Ø
 4   Costs and expenses
 5       Product costs                     12175
 6       Marketing and sales              2Ø785
 7       General and administrative        1785Ø
 8                                      ----------
 9   Total costs and expenses             5Ø81Ø
1Ø
11   Operating income (loss)               -56Ø
12
13   Other income (expenses)
14       Interest income                   45ØØ
15       Interest expense                  -5ØØ
16       Other                              6ØØ
17                                      ----------
18   Total other income (expenses)         46ØØ
19
2Ø   Income (loss) before taxes            4Ø4Ø
21       Provision (benefit) for taxes      6Ø6
22   Net earnings (loss)                   3434
IS9ØCH3.WK1                                                 NUM
```

♦ **Figure 3.12:** *Indicating the range of cells to format*

You can change the alignment in one of two ways: edit the contents of the cell and change the initial apostrophe (') to a circumflex (^), or select the Center option from the /Range Label command. Since we've just begun to explore the /Range menu (and will continue to do so in the next chapter), let's give the /Range Label command a try:

1. **Move the pointer up to cell B2.**
   Always get into position before you select a /Range command, because all /Range commands automatically anchor the range on the current cell as soon as you select them.

2. **Type /RL to select the /Range Label command, then type C to select the Center option.**
   The program responds with the prompt *Enter range of labels: B2..B2.*

3. **Press the Enter key to accept this single cell range.**
   The label 1990 is now centered in the cell display: notice that the contents now reads ^1990. Because you saved the income statement before you made these formatting changes, they aren't yet saved on disk. You'd better go ahead and save it again so that there's no risk of losing even these simple changes.

4. **Press the Home key.**

   Take the pointer back to cell A1 in preparation for saving the final file. Now, when you select the /File Save command this time, 1-2-3 will suggest the file name that you originally saved it under.

5. **Type /FS, then press the Enter key to accept the suggested file name of C:\123\IS90CH3.WK1 or B:\IS90CH3.WK1 (if you are using 1-2-3 on a two-disk-drive system).**

   The program responds with a new group of options that you don't see the first time you save a file. If you are using Release 2.01, you can choose between Cancel and Replace. If you are using Release 2.2, you can choose between Cancel, Replace, and Backup. You select Cancel to abandon saving this updated version under the same file name; Replace to proceed in saving this updated version under the same file name; or Backup to keep a copy of the file as originally saved with the same file name and the extension .BAK, and then to save the updated version under the same file name and the extension .WK1.

6. **If you are using Release 2.2, type B to select the Backup option; if you are using Release 2.01, type R to select the Replace option.**

   If you selected Backup, this means that there are now two worksheet files, IS90CH3.WK1 and IS90CH3.BAK, on your disk. The most recent version (with all formatting) has the extension .WK1, and the earlier version has the extension .BAK. If you chose Replace, this means that the current version of the worksheet with all the formatting changes you made is saved under the name IS90CH3.WK1.

Creating a Template from an Existing Worksheet

The income statement is a common worksheet application—one that you are sure to need again. To simplify the creation of the income statement for the next fiscal year, you can use your income statement for 1990 to create an income statement template. A *template* is a special master worksheet that contains only the generic labels and formulas common to all worksheets of the same type. Therefore, a template doesn't contain any entries unique to a specific worksheet, and all the cells that contain numeric values and formulas in a template display zeros.

To create a worksheet from a template, you simply have to retrieve the template file, enter the values and labels that are unique to the worksheet you are building, and then save the worksheet in a new file. Because the template already contains all the necessary formulas, calculations are made automatically as you enter the data in the appropriate cells. In many ways, building a worksheet from a template is like filling out a blank form.

To create a template from your 1990 income statement is a simple procedure: simply "zero out" the cells that contain numeric values, leaving the formulas and formatting as they are. Then, you will save the modified file under a new name.

1. **Move the pointer to cell B2, then press Edit (F2).**
   This returns the label ^1990 to the control panel. Let's assume that all income statements made from the template will occur in the 90s, but not specify the last digit of the year.

2. **Press the Backspace key once to delete the trailing zero in 1990, then press the ↓ key.**
   The cell now contains 199. To later enter the proper year in an actual worksheet, all you have to do is press Edit (F2) and then type the last digit of the appropriate year.

3. **Type 0, then press the ↓ key twice.**
   All input values (such as revenues) will be zero in the template. The zeros will indicate where you must enter the values for a given year.

4. **Enter 0 in cells B5, B6, and B7.**
   Notice that as soon as you "zero out" these three cells, the total costs and expenses and the operating income both become zero. However, you will leave their formulas alone.

5. **Enter 0 in cells B14, B15, and B16.**
   As soon as you enter zero in these cells, all cells in your template display zero. Rather than have a template full of zeros, you can use the /Worksheet Global Zero Label command to either blank out the display of all zeros (Release 2.01 and 2.2) or change all zeros to a character or message of your choice (Release 2.2 only). If you are using Release 2.01, use this command to suppress the display of zeros. If you are using Release 2.2, use it to convert the zeros to question marks (?).

6. **Type /WGZ to select the /Worksheet Global Zero command; if you are using Release 2.01, type Y to select the Yes option (meaning that you do want the display of zeros suppressed globally); if you are using Release 2.2, type L to select the Label option.**

In response to the prompt *Enter label (can include label prefix):* in Release 2.2, you need to enter a question mark as the replacement string.

7. **Type *?* and press Enter.**
Notice that all zeros have been either blanked out or replaced with question marks (as shown in Figure 3.13). Now you are ready to save your template in a new file.

8. **Press the Home key to take the pointer home.**
You will change the file name from IS90CH3.WK1 to ISTMPLT.WK1.

9. **Type */FS*, then type *istmplt* and press Enter.**
This saves your changes in a file called *ISTMPLT.WK1* (if you have activated the display of the file name on the status line, you should now see *ISTMPLT.WK1* in place of *IS90CH3.WK1*). You can now use this file to create all subsequent income statements.

Building a Worksheet from a Template

Now that you have created this template, let's see just how fast and easy it is to create a new worksheet from it. To demonstrate this, you will now build an income statement for 1991. To make this exercise more realistic and introduce you to the /File Retrieve command, you will first erase the template from memory.

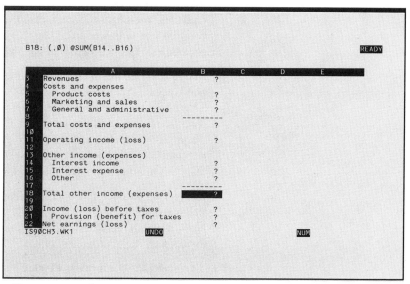

♦ **Figure 3.13:** *The income statement template with question marks for zeros*

Hiding the Display of Zeros in a Template: Many managers don't care for the appearance of a template full of zeros. If you or your boss feel this way, use the /Worksheet Global Zero command either to suppress the display of all zeros in the entire worksheet (by selecting the Yes option) or—if you are using Release 2.2—to change the display of all zeros to a label of your choice (by choosing the Label option and entering the new character or characters). If you use the Label option, 1-2-3 will automatically preface your new string with a quotation mark (") to right-align it. If you want the new string to be left-aligned, preface it with an apostrophe ('). If you want it to be centered, preface it with a circumflex (ˆ). Remember that the new label you select for displaying zeros or the global suppression of zeros aren't saved as part of the template. Therefore, when you next retrieve the template, you will see all its zeros regardless of what /Worksheet Global Zero command you use.

1. **Type /WEY to erase the template from memory.**
   You now have a blank worksheet display, the same as you see when you first start 1-2-3. Now you need to retrieve your template from disk.

2. **Type /FR.**
   When you use the /File Retrieve command, 1-2-3 shows you a line listing of the worksheet files (that is, any files with the extension .WK1). To retrieve a file, you have only to move the pointer to its name and press Enter. However, you can also type in the name of your file (you will need to do just this if you append nonstandard extensions to the file names of your worksheets).

3. **Move the pointer to the file name *ISTMPLT.WK1* and press the Enter key.**
   This retrieves your template file with the pointer in cell A1. Notice that the zeros are redisplayed automatically when you retrieve this worksheet. Neither their suppression nor their modification to question marks is saved as part of the template; therefore, zeros always reappear when you retrieve a worksheet file.

4. **Move the pointer to cell B2, press Edit (F2), then type *1*, and press the ↓ key.**
   Now, to finish up this file, you need only enter the revenues and expenses in the appropriate cells.

5. **Type *56525*, then press ↓ twice.**

6. **Type *17275*, then press ↓.**

7. **Type *22000*, then press ↓.**

8. **Type *12500*, then press the ↓ key until the pointer is in cell B14.**

9. **Type *2500*, then press ↓.**

10. **Type *– 250*, then press ↓.**

11. **In cell B16, just press the ↓ key to leave this value 0.**
    With a pretax income of 7000, you'd better change the tax rate from 15 percent to 20 percent.

12. **Move the pointer to cell B21 and press Edit (F2); then press Backspace twice to erase *15*, type *2*, and press Enter.**
    There you have it: the 1991 income statement in minutes! Now all that remains is to check your entries against those shown in Figure 3.14, and, if they are correct, save the worksheet in its own file.

13. **Press the Home key.**
    You will name this file IS91CH3.WK1.

14. **Type */FS*, then type *is91ch3* and press Enter.**
    That's all there is to it. Now is a good time to take a well-deserved break.

15. **Type */QY* to exit from 1-2-3 and return to DOS.**

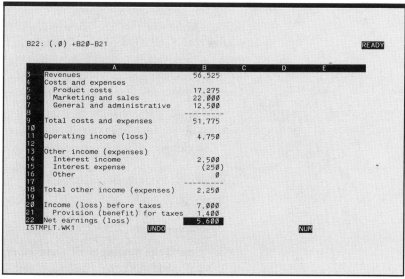

♦ **Figure 3.14:** *Income statement for 1991*

Summary

Troubleshooting

Question: How can I tell if my worksheet has been saved?

Answer: It's up to you to remember whether you have saved your worksheet with the /File Save command. If you are using Release 2.2, however, you can have the program automatically replace the date and time indicator in the lower left corner of the status line with the file name the first time you save your worksheet. To have this happen, select the /Worksheet Global Default Other Clock Filename command (/WGDOCF). To make this the new program default, be sure to select the Update option before you choose the Quit option to exit from MENU mode. After you save the worksheet initially, there is no way to tell if subsequent changes you have made to the worksheet are saved. Therefore, to avoid any loss of data, use the /File Save command often as you work, and if you're not sure that you saved your changes, err on the cautious side and save the file again.

Question: I was defining a simple formula to add the values in two cells. After starting the formula, pointing to the first cell, and typing +, I discovered the pointer returned to a cell with an existing entry and that my formula was about to replace it. What's the best thing to do to avoid replacing the entry with the new formula I'm building?

Answer: Press the Esc key to delete as much of the formula as you've defined. Make sure that you have returned to READY mode, then move the pointer to the cell where you really want the formula, and redefine it.

Essential Techniques

To Erase a Worksheet from Memory

1. Use the /Worksheet Erase command and select the Yes option if you want to clear the entire file that is active from memory, including all worksheets that you inserted in the file.

To Widen or Narrow a Column

1. Move the pointer to the column whose width you wish to change.

2. Select the Set-Width option from the /Worksheet Column menu.

3. Type in the number of characters (between 0 and 240), press the → key to widen the column a character at a time, or press the ← key to narrow the column a character at a time.

4. Press the Enter key to complete the procedure.

To Save a Worksheet the First Time

1. Select the /File Save command. Lotus 1-2-3 will display a line listing of the files saved in the current directory, using the global wildcard pattern *.wk1 (for any file with the extension .WK1).

2. To save your new worksheet file in the current directory, just start typing the file. You can enter up to eight characters with no spaces. You don't have to enter the file extension .WK1 as part of the file name, as 1-2-3 will automatically add this for you when you complete the save procedure.

3. To save the file in a new directory or on a disk in a different drive, press the Esc key twice. Then enter the complete path name before the file name. Remember that drive-letter designations must be followed by a colon (:), and each directory in the path must be separated by a backslash (\).

4. After entering the desired file name, with or without changing the path name, press the Enter key to complete the save procedure.

To Save Changes to a File Previously Saved

1. Select the /File Save command. Lotus 1-2-3 will suggest the current file name under which the worksheet was originally saved.

2. To save your changes under a new file, edit the file name or replace it, and press Enter.

3. To save your changes under the same name, press Enter to accept the file name.

4. If you are using Release 2.2, you can select the Backup option to create a backup copy of the original file when saving your changes under the same name. Select the Replace option to have the changes added to the same file. (Use the Cancel command only when you don't want to save your changes under the same name.)

Review   Important Terms You Should Know

@function	RAM
pointing	template

Test Your Knowledge

1. To clear the worksheet file on the screen to begin a new file, you select the _____ command and select the _____ option. However, you only use this command after you have saved the worksheet file on screen in a disk file using the _____ command.

2. If you delete the worksheet file in error, use the _____ feature to restore it by pressing _____.

3. To get online help about a particular feature in 1-2-3, press _____.

4. If you know what menu you should use but not which option, you should select the _____ topic from the Help Index screen.

5. If you wanted to enter a series of # symbols across the width of an entire cell, you would enter _____ in the cell.

6. To total a column of values, you should use the _____ function rather than creating a formula that adds each value individually.

7. To define a formula in cell A3 that multiplies the value in cell B3 by that in cell C3 with pointing, you first move the pointer to cell _____, type + to start the formula, then move the pointer to cell _____, type *, and finally, move the cell pointer to cell _____.

8. To right-justify labels in a range of cells after they have been entered in the worksheet, use the _____ command and select the _____ option, indicate the range of cells, and then press the Enter key.

9. To suppress the display of all zeros in a worksheet, you use the _____ command and select the _____ option. To later turn the display back on, you use the same command, only this time you select the _____ option.

Further Exercises

1. Use your ISTMPLT.WK1 file to create an income statement for 1992 using the following figures:

    | Revenues | 72,350 |
    | Product costs | 13,835 |

Marketing and sales	24,125
General and administrative	14,750
Interest income	1,500
Interest expense	−485
Other	−100

2. After you have added your data (including updating the heading for column B), save the file under the name *IS92CH3.WK1*.

4

Cell Ranges:
The Key to Managing
Worksheet Data

In This Chapter...

◆

Cell Range Basics

The cell range represents the next most complex unit in 1-2-3: above a single cell, which is its smallest unit, and below the entire worksheet, which is its largest unit. By definition, a *range* is a rectangular block of contiguous cells (*contiguous* means touching along the whole of one or more sides). In 1-2-3, a range can be as small as a single cell, as wide as an entire row, or as long as an entire column. Most ranges, however, are sized somewhere in-between so that they include parts of several columns and rows. Figure 4.1 shows you several valid cell ranges of various sizes and shapes.

Ranges, like those shown in Figure 4.1, are most often specified by their range address. The *range address* lists the address of the first and last cell in the range separated by two periods. Notice that the range address of the single cell range in Figure 4.1 is A3..A3, because the first and last cell happen to be the same. In the single-row range, C2..E2, notice that the first cell of the range is the one farthest to the left (C2) and the last cell is the one farthest to the right (E2). In the single-column range, B5..B9, note that the first cell of the range is the one at the top and the last one is the one at the bottom.

When a range forms a rectangle that includes cells in several columns and rows, as does the range D5..F8 in Figure 4.1, the first cell is the one in the upper left corner (D5) and the last cell is the one in the lower right corner (F8). Note that these corner cells are diagonally opposite one another in the range.

Look at Figure 4.2. Here you see a similar range that spans two columns and three rows: range B1..C3. Although it is most common to give the range address

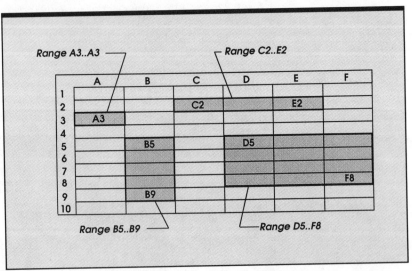

◆ **Figure 4.1:** *Sample cell ranges of various sizes and shapes*

by listing the address of the first cell and then that of the last cell, this is not the only valid way. You can, in fact, list a range address by the cell addresses of any other two corner cells that are positioned diagonally opposite each other in the range *and* in any order. So this means that 1-2-3 will accept the range address B1..C3, C3..B1, B3..C1, or C1..B3 for the range shown in Figure 4.2. Although 1-2-3 will accept any of these range addresses when designating this cell range in response to a 1-2-3 command or when entering it in a formula or function, in this book we will always give the range address by the first cell (upper left corner), then by last cell (lower right corner).

In the range address, the addresses of the first and last cells are separated by two periods, as in C2..E2 or B1..C3. When you enter a range address in response to a command or in defining a formula, however, you have to type only a single period. The program will then replace the single period that you type with two periods in the range address as soon as you complete the entry.

Entering a single period instead of two periods works when you type in the range address as well as when you define with the pointing method (called *anchoring* the range), except under one condition: that is, if you change the global default for the argument separator from a comma to a period (/WGDOIP), as you would if you wanted to follow European usage and use the comma as the decimal point. When the comma is used as the decimal point in financial figures, you must then use the period to separate the arguments in functions. When this is the case, you must enter two periods in the range address.

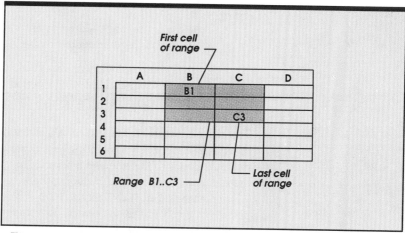

♦ **Figure 4.2:** *Range B1..C3 (or C3..B1 or B3..C1 or C1..B3)*

Referencing a Cell Not in the Current File

Release 2.2 of Lotus 1-2-3 now allows you to link worksheet files by referencing cells that aren't in the current file. If the cell is not located in the current file, you must include the *file reference* as part of the cell address. The file reference consists of the full name of the worksheet file (including the extension) enclosed in a pair of double angle brackets, as in

+ <<STORE123.WK1>>B3

which refers to the cell B3 located in the worksheet file named STORE123.WK1.

If the file that contains the cell is located in the current directory, you need only specify the file name in the pair of double angle brackets. If the file is not in the current directory, however, you must include the path as well as the full file name in the file reference, as in

+ <<C:\123\JOHN\CUSTLIST.WK1>>B3

which refers to the cell B3 in a worksheet named CUSTLIST.WK1 located in a subdirectory of the 1-2-3 directory (C:\123) called JOHN, which is not the current directory.

Specifying the Range Address by Pointing

Remember that you can specify the range address of any cell range by one of two methods:

- Type the entire range address by entering the address of the first cell, a period, and then the address of the last cell.

- Use the pointer-movement keys to highlight the range by moving the pointer to the first cell, typing a period to anchor the range, and then moving the pointer to the last cell.

The second method is referred to as *pointing* because it uses a special mode called POINT mode. Using pointing to indicate a range in building a formula or responding to a 1-2-3 command is superior to typing its range address because there is much less danger of including the wrong cells.

Remember that in POINT mode, 1-2-3 fills in the address as you move the pointer to a cell in the worksheet. To *anchor* the range on a particular cell address, you type a period (or a colon). The program indicates that a range is anchored on a particular cell by duplicating its cell address separated by two periods. For example, if you move the pointer to cell C5 after typing @SUM(

and then type a period or colon, 1-2-3 will anchor the range on this cell, which is indicated by

@SUM(C5..C5

in the control panel.

If you ever anchor a range on the wrong cell, you can *unanchor* the range by pressing the Esc key. For instance, if you discovered after anchoring the range that C5 was not the first cell of the @SUM argument range (you should have started one column over, in cell D5) and you press the Esc key, the formula in the control panel would change to

@SUM(C5

Then, by pressing the → key, you can make D5 the current cell. As soon as you do, the formula will change to *@SUM(D5* because the range is no longer anchored. To anchor the range once again, you type a period or colon a second time, which changes the formula to *@SUM(D5..D5*, indicating that it is anchored once again. At this point, you finish defining the range by moving the cell pointer to the last cell in the range and then completing the formula entry.

Table 4.1 summarizes the function of four keys: the period, colon, Backspace, and Esc. Notice that the functions of the period, colon, and Esc keys are different when the range is unanchored from when the range is already anchored.

Naming a Cell Range

In addition to specifying a range by giving its range address, you can also specify it by its *range name*. Lotus 1-2-3 allows you to give a name up to 15 characters long to any valid cell range. Once it is named, you can use the range name in place of the range address:

- ♦ In any 1-2-3 command that uses cell ranges to specify the parameters of the command

- ♦ In any 1-2-3 function that uses cell ranges to specify its arguments

- ♦ In formulas to indicate how the data in the range are to be operated on when the calculation is performed

- ♦ In macros to indicate the location of the macro commands and subroutines

- ♦ In response to the *Enter address to go to:* prompt when using the Goto key (F5) to indicate which cell to move the pointer to (1-2-3 always moves the pointer to the first cell of a named range)

♦ **Table 4.1:** *Keys Used to Specify Ranges in POINT Mode*

Key	With Anchored Range	With Unanchored Range
. (period)	Anchors the range on the current cell.	Moves the anchor cell consecutively to each corner cell of the highlighted range.
Backspace	Returns the pointer to the cell it occupied before you entered POINT mode.	Unanchors the range and returns the pointer to the cell it occupied before you entered POINT mode.
Esc	If building a formula, it clears the entry; if entering a 1-2-3 command, it returns you to the previous prompt or menu level.	Unanchors the range and returns the pointer to the cell it occupied before you entered POINT mode.

The primary benefit to using range names is that you can usually remember them more easily and enter them more quickly than you can the corresponding range addresses. Their use is made even easier in 1-2-3 because you can use the Name key (F3) to bring up a list of the range names defined in the current worksheet file. If you are using Release 2.2, to enter a particular range name from the list in a formula or in response to a command, you only have to move the pointer to it and press Enter (in Release 2.01, you must type the range name).

Defining Range Names

To assign a name to a range, you can use either the /Range Name Create command or the /Range Name Labels command. When you select the /Range Name Create command, the program prompts you to enter the range name. When creating range names, keep the following things in mind:

♦ The range name can be up to 15 characters long.

♦ The program doesn't differentiate between uppercase and lowercase letters in a range name.

F3: The Name Key and Range Names

F3, the Name key, lists all the range names defined in the current worksheet file:

* After pressing the Goto key (F5)
* After you select a 1-2-3 command that calls for a range
* After you enter a math operator when defining a formula (Release 2.2 only)
* When you are at the point in entering a function where you need to enter an argument (Release 2.2 only)

Press F3 a second time to get a full-screen listing of range names in alphabetical order

To select a range, move the pointer to its name and press Enter

* Don't use a space, comma, period, or any characters reserved by the program, including $+$, $-$, $*$, $/$, $\&$, $>$, $<$, $@$, or $\#$, in the range name. Use an underscore if you want to separate two words in a range name, such as *Product_costs*.

* Don't use any 1-2-3 @function names, key names, or macro command names as a range name, such as *@sum* or *Edit*.

* Don't use a range name that corresponds to any cell address in the worksheet, such as *B1* or *F300*.

* Don't start a range name with a number or assign a range number that is all numeric, such as *25-Feb* or *1789*.

After you select the /Range Name Create command and enter the name you wish to assign to the range, you must define the range that is being named. You can do this by typing in the range address or by pointing.

If you decide to use pointing to define the range, keep in mind that the range will already be anchored when you are prompted to enter the range (all /Range menu commands anchor the range on the cell that was current when you selected the command). If you discover that the pointer is not positioned correctly to highlight the entire range (that is, on one of the corner cells of the range), you can press the Esc key to unanchor the range, move the pointer, and then reanchor by typing a period.

If you need to assign range names to single-cell ranges and find that you can use existing labels in adjacent cells as the range names, you can use the /Range

Name Labels command instead of the /Range Name Create command. When using this command, you position the pointer on the cell that contains the label you wish to assign as the range name for an adjacent cell. When you select the /Range Name Labels command, 1-2-3 prompts you to indicate the direction of the cell you wish to name by selecting one of these options:

Right Down Left Up

Once you select the correct option, you are prompted to enter the label range. After you specify the range that contains your labels and press Enter, the program assigns whatever labels are located in the range to the cells that are immediately adjacent in the direction you selected.

If any of the cells in the label range contain values or formulas, however, these are ignored, and if any labels are more than 15 characters, only the first 15 characters are used in the resulting range names. Also, if any of the labels in the range contain spaces or any other illegal characters, these are retained in the range names, but they make it impossible to use the range names in defining formulas. The illegal characters will cause the formulas to return the special value of ERR, indicating that an error has occurred, which prevents the formula from calculating the correct answer.

Deleting Range Names

Range names take up quite a bit of memory. If you need to free up memory to be able to continue working on a worksheet, you can do so by deleting some or all of the range names in the file. To delete specific range names, you choose the /Range Name Delete command (/RND) and then type in the range name to be deleted or select it from the listing of range names in response to the *Enter name to delete:* prompt. To delete all range names in the worksheet, you select the /Range Name Reset command (/RNR). If you ever use either the /Range Name Delete or /Range Name Reset command in error, press the Undo key (Alt-F4) to restore them (Release 2.2 only).

If you use the /Range Name Delete command to delete a specific range name or the /Range Name Reset command to delete all range names in the current file, the formulas that use the range names you deleted still continue to return the correct answers. This is because 1-2-3 automatically converts a range name to the corresponding range address in any formula whenever the range is deleted from the current file.

Using the /Range Name Table Command

If, in the course of your work, you would like to refer to a list of all range names that you have defined for the current file, you can do so easily by using the

/Range Name Table command. The program will then create a two-column table that lists all the range names in alphabetical order along with their corresponding range addresses.

Note that when you use this command, 1-2-3 will prompt you for the range where the table is to be entered. Here, you only have to indicate the cell that is to contain the upper left corner of the table 1-2-3 is about to create. Be aware that the table will overwrite any existing data when it is created, however. To avoid having a range table wipe out important data (which can be recovered with Undo), you should always move the pointer to a new section of the worksheet at the beginning of a blank range sufficient to hold the range name table.

Also, be aware that the range table created with this command is static. This means that the table is not automatically updated as you continue to define new range names or delete existing ones. To have the table updated, you need to recreate it (you can recreate it on the location of the existing one).

Creating Range Names for Your Income Statement

Now it's time to get some practice in creating and using range names. Range names are so much easier to work with than range addresses that you will want to start using them in your work right away. In this next exercise, you will use the income statement for 1990 that you created in Chapter 3.

1. **Start 1-2-3, then type /FR to select the /File Retrieve command; next, move the pointer to your file *IS90CH3.WK1* and press Enter.**
   The income statement for 1990 then appears on the screen. The first range name you are going to create will be for the single cell range that contains the revenues (B3..B3). Because the label *Revenues* is already entered in an adjacent cell, you can use the /Range Name Labels command.

2. **Move the pointer to cell A3 (the cell with the label you want to use as a range name); then, type /RNL to select /Range Name Labels and type *R* to select the Right option.**
   You select the Right option because the single cell range is located to the immediate right of the label it is to take as its range name. Note that 1-2-3 is now prompting you to enter the label range and that the default label range is A3..A3.

3. **Press the Enter key to accept the default label range (don't move the pointer at all).**
   Now let's make sure that it worked.

4. Press F5 (Goto), then press F3 (Name).

You should see the range name, REVENUES, listed and highlighted.

5. Press the Enter key to move the cell pointer to the range named REVENUES.

The pointer jumps to cell B3, the cell that contains the value 50250 and is now appropriately named *Revenues*.

That was easy! And if the rest of the labels in column A didn't violate the proper naming conventions for range names (they all contain spaces and most are longer than 15 characters), you could use the /Range Name Labels Right command to assign all the row headings in column A to each adjacent cell to its right in column B in one operation.

Now you will create a formula using range names in your income statement worksheet.

6. Move the pointer to cell B5.

When you use the /Range Name Create command, move the pointer to the first cell in the range as the first step.

7. Type /RN to select the /Range Name menu, then type C to select the Create option.

The program prompts you with *Enter name:* and shows you on the line below that the range name REVENUES has already been used. Before naming a range, always check this list to see if the name you want to use is already assigned (press F3 to see a full-screen list).

8. Type *product.costs* for the range name and press Enter.

Be sure that you connect the two words in the range name with some character such as the period or the underscore (a dash or hyphen will also work). Notice that once you enter the range name, the prompt *Enter range:* appears on the right side of the screen. The default range is *B5..B5* (the program always anchors the suggested range on the current cell).

9. Press Enter to accept the default cell range.

If you had needed to, you could have used the pointer-movement keys to extend the range before pressing the Enter key, because this command allows you to define ranges of more than a single cell.

10. Press the → key to move the pointer to cell C5.

Here, you will define the formula to compare product costs to revenues. If you were defining this formula using cell addresses, it would be +*B5/B3*. However, you can make this descriptive by entering instead +*Product.costs/Revenues*.

11. **Type +, then press F3 (Name).**
    Rather than typing in the names of the ranges you wish to use in the formula, you can use the Name key to get a list of the currently defined range names and then select them by pointing.

12. **The range name PRODUCT.COSTS should already be high-lighted, so press Enter to select it.**
    The formula in the control panel now reads +*PRODUCT.COSTS*.

13. **Type / (the division operator), then press F3 (Name); move the pointer to REVENUES and press Enter to select it.**
    The complete formula should say +*PRODUCT.COSTS/REVENUES*. You are now ready to enter it in cell C5.

14. **Press Enter to complete the formula entry.**
    Your formula should return the value *0.242288*, as shown in Figure 4.3.

In addition to naming single-cell ranges, you can also name larger ranges. Assigning range names to larger ranges makes it easy to relocate the range with either /Copy or /Move (covered later in this chapter) or to print the range with the /Print command (covered in Chapter 8). Let's see how this works by naming several different ranges in the income statement.

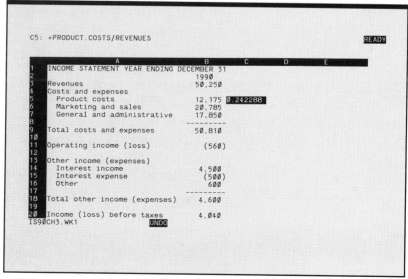

♦ **Figure 4.3:** *The ratio formula in cell C5 created with range names*

15. **Move the pointer back to B5, type /RNC, then type** *Costs* **as the range name, and press Enter.**
    The COSTS range includes cells B5 through B7.

16. **Press the ↓ key until the pointer is in cell B7 and cells B5 through B7 are highlighted, then press Enter.**
    Next, you will give the range name *Total.costs* to the single-cell range B9..B9.

17. **Move the pointer down to cell B9, type /RNC, then type** *total.costs,* **and press Enter twice.**
    Next, use the Goto key to move back up to the COSTS range.

18. **Press F5 (Goto), then press F3 (Name); the range name COSTS should be highlighted, so press Enter to select it.**
    Notice that the pointer jumps to the first cell in the named range. Finally, you will name one more cell range: this one will include all the labels, formulas, and amounts in columns A and B. You might be tempted to name this range IS1990 (for income statement in 1990) but you can't because this corresponds to a valid cell address (in column IS and row 1990). Instead, name it *INCOME.90.*

19. **Press the Home key to move the pointer to cell A1, type /RNC, type** *income.90,* **and press Enter; move the pointer down and then over to B23 (the range will read A1..B23) and press Enter.**
    Later on, you will use this range name to make it easy to print this cell range.

20. **Move the cell pointer to cell F1 by pressing the Goto key (F5), typing** *F1,* **and then pressing the Enter key.**
    The pointer is now located in cell F1, which begins a new blank panel to the right of the income statement. Here, you will type a title for your range name table.

21. **Type** *Range Names for Income Statement* **and press the ↓ key twice.**
    Now, in cell F3, you will create the range name table.

22. **Type /RNT and press Enter in response to the prompt to enter a range.**
    Notice that you can't see all the range names in the column; you have to widen column F.

23. **Type /WCS and then press the → key until you can read all the range names in column F (stop when the column is about 14 or 15 characters wide), then press Enter.**

    Your range name table should look like the one shown in Figure 4.4. Now you will give the range name table that you just created its own range name. That way, if you ever have to move it to accommodate new data in the income statement, you can do so easily.

24. **Move the pointer to cell F1, type /RNC, enter *name.table* as the range name, and then press Enter; next, move the pointer down and over until the range F1..G7 is highlighted and then press Enter.**

    One more step remains: to save the range names that you have created. If you were to quit 1-2-3 without saving the file now, you would lose the range names. When you save the file, these are also saved and will be available at any time. You will save this updated version of your file under a new file name: IS90CH4.WK3.

25. **Press the Home key to move the pointer to cell A1; type /FS, then type *is90ch4* and press Enter.**

    If you set the program so that it displays the file name instead of the date and time indicator, notice that the file name on this line has changed from IS90CH3.WK1 to IS90CH4.WK1.

You will get more practice in using named ranges in later chapters in Part I. For now, let's move on and look at the more commonly used /Range menu commands, all of which are applied to cell ranges whether they are named or not.

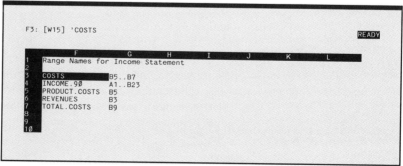

♦ **Figure 4.4:** *Range name table showing the range names defined*

Commonly Used Range Commands

The commands on the /Range menu all work with cell ranges. As such, they all automatically anchor the range on the cell that was current at the time you selected them. You can put this knowledge to work for you by remembering to move the pointer to one of the corner cells of the range to which you wish to apply the /Range command before selecting it. That way, you can just use the pointer-movement keys to enlarge the range of cells to which the command is applied as soon as you issue the proper command.

If, however, you find that you have selected a /Range command when the current cell is not on one of the corner cells of the range, you will have to press Esc or Backspace (to unanchor the range), move the pointer to one of the corner cells, type a period (to anchor the range again), and finally, use the pointer-movement keys to highlight the extent of the range.

Aligning and Formatting Data

The first two options on the /Range menu are Format and Label. These options are used to control the appearance and alignment of data in the cell display. The Format option is used most often, though not exclusively, to format the display of values in a range in the worksheet. The Label option is used exclusively to change the alignment of labels in a range of cells: you can choose between left and right alignment or centering.

In addition, the /Range menu has a Justify option that is used to control the width of the long labels in a range. This command is used much like a right margin in a word processor—to control the length of each line of text and determine where the word wrap will occur.

Using the /Range Format Command

The /Range Format command is used to override the global format (General unless changed with the /Worksheet Global Format command) and assign a new format to a specific range of cells. Table 4.2 shows you the format options that are available on this menu. Note that the Hidden format affects labels as well as values in the worksheet; all the rest affect values only. If the range you specify when using one of these formats includes cells with labels in them, the format has no effect on their display.

Any format option applied with the /Range Format menu will override the previous formatting. If you use the /Range Format Reset command on a cell range, however, it returns the formatting to the global default in effect at that time. Note that you can use this command to redisplay a cell range previously

♦ **Table 4.2:** *The /Range Format Options*

Format	Description	Cell Contents	Cell Display
+/−	Displays a graph using plus signs, minus signs, or a period. Plus signs are used to display positive numbers, minus signs are used to display negative numbers, and a period is used to display a number between −1 and 1. The number of plus or minus signs displayed is determined by the integer portion of the number entered in the cell. If the graph requires more plus or minus signs than can be displayed in the current cell width, asterisks are displayed instead.	(+) 3.5 (+) −2.7 (+) 0.67	+++ − −
, (Comma)	Uses thousands separator, up to 15 decimal places, parentheses or minus sign for negative values (depending on default set by the /WGDOIN command in Release 2.2), and leading zero for decimal values.	(,2) 4567 (,0) −23 (,1) 0.2678	4,567.00 (23) 0.3
Currency	Same as , (comma) format except that it uses the currency symbol. The currency symbol used depends on the default set by the /WGDOIC command.	(C2) 4567 (C0) −23 (C1) 0.2678	$4,567.00 ($23) $0.3
Date	Allows you to select one of five date formats (D1–D5): 1 (DD-MMM-YY); 2 (DD-MMM); 3 (MMM-YY); 4 (Long Int'l)—MM/DD/YY, default; or 5 (Short Int'l)—MM/DD, default; or Time.	(D1) 32919 (D2) 32919.5 (D3) @NOW (D4) @DATE(90,1,11) (D5) @DATE(90,1,11)	15-Feb-90 15-Feb Mar-90 01/11/90 01/11
	Time has four formats (D6–D9): 1 (HH:MM:SS AM/PM); 2 (HH:MM AM/PM); 3 (Long Int'l)—HH:MM:SS on 24-hour clock, default; and 4 (Short Int'l)—HH:MM on 24-hour clock, default.	(D6) 32919.5 (D7) @NOW (D8) @TIME(15,6,2) (D9) 0.666	12:00:00 PM 12:21 PM 15:06:02 15:59

◆ **Table 4.2:** *The /Range Format Options (continued)*

Format	Description	Cell Contents	Cell Display
	Date format can be used to display numbers between 1 (January 1, 1900) and 703050 (December 31, 2099) as dates. The program uses the integer portion of the number to determine the date and the decimal part of the number to determine the time. Numbers less than 1 or greater than 703050 display as asterisks. For negative decimal numbers, 1-2-3 calculates the time by subtracting the number from 1.		
Fixed	Displays numbers with up to 15 decimal places, a minus sign for negative numbers, and a leading zero for decimal numbers.	(F2) 156.897 (F0) −34.78 (F1) 0.2365	156.90 −35 0.2
General	Uses minus sign for negative numbers, no thousands separator, and no trailing zero for decimal values. Displays numbers in scientific format if digits left of the decimal point exceed one less than the column width. Rounds the number when the number of digits right of the decimal point exceed the column width. General is the program global default unless changed with /WGF.	(G) 156.897 (G) 0.2365 678900000000 250.11112226	156.897 0.2365 6.7890E+11 250.1111223
Hidden	Makes the cell display invisible without affecting the cell contents. Affects both labels and values in the designated range. Note that in Release 2.2, unlike Release 2.01, data formatted with the Hidden format no longer appear in the control panel when the cell is current if the cells that contain them are also protected.	(H) 'January (H) 275 (H) @SUM(B1..C10)	

♦ **Table 4.2:** *The /Range Format Options (continued)*

Format	Description	Cell Contents	Cell Display
Percent	Displays numbers as percentages with up to 15 decimal points followed by a percent sign.	(P2) 0.045 (P1) −4.2 (P0) 0.032	4.50% −420.0% 3%
Reset	Resets the range to the global default format, which is General unless changed with the /WGF command.		
Sci	Displays values in scientific notation with up to 15 decimal places in the mantissa and an exponent between −99 and +99.	(S2) 0..045 (S1) −4.2 (S0) 0.032	4.50E−02 −4.2E+00 3E−02
Text	Displays formulas as entered in the cell contents rather than their calculated values. Displays numbers in General format. If you have added notes to the formulas or numbers in the ranges, the annotations are displayed as well.	(T) +A1>25 (T) 165	+A1>25 165

made invisible with the /Range Format Hidden command (you can also make a cell range visible by assigning a /Range Format option other than Hidden to the range).

The Currency format uses the dollar sign ($) as the default *currency symbol*. To change this to a new symbol, you need to use the /Worksheet Global Default Other International Currency command. Then delete the existing symbol and replace it with a new currency symbol. Lotus 1-2-3 supports an extensive symbol set (called the Lotus International Character Set or LICS), which includes symbols such as the £ (Pound) or ¥ (Yen) that you can designate as the new currency symbol.

To create an LICS character, you press the Compose key (Alt-F1), then type the compose sequence and press Enter (all characters, code numbers, and compose sequences are listed in Appendix E). For example, to enter the Pound symbol as the new currency symbol, you would delete the dollar sign, press Alt-F1, and type *L=*. After you press Enter, 1-2-3 will prompt you to indicate whether the new symbol should precede or follow the value with these options:

Prefix Suffix

To have the new currency symbol precede the value, select the Prefix option. If it should trail the value, select the Suffix option. Note that your new default currency symbol can consist of more than one character—such as £ followed by a space.

Using /Range Label to Change Alignment

To change the alignment of a range of labels after they have been entered in the worksheet, use the /Range Label command. This command lets you choose between the following options:

Left Right Center

After selecting the appropriate option, you indicate the range of cells that contains your labels. If any of the cells in this range contain values, the /Range Label command will have no effect on them. The /Range Label command aligns labels by adding the appropriate label prefix: apostrophe (') for Left, quotation mark (") for Right, and circumflex (ˆ) for Center.

To change the global alignment for labels, use the /Worksheet Global Label-Prefix command and then choose the Left, Right, or Center option.

Using /Range Justify to Format Long Labels

The /Range Justify command enables you to format a long label by restricting the line length to the width of the cell range that you specify. You can use this command to rearrange text in a range much as you would with a word processor by resetting the document's right margin. Note, however, that besides /Range Search (added to Release 2.2) and this command, 1-2-3 lacks any other word processing capabilities and is, therefore, a poor choice for your text processing needs (for information on how to exchange text between your word processor and 1-2-3, refer to Chapter 14).

To use the /Range Justify command to format a long label, you move the pointer to the cell that contains the label, then select /Range Justify. The program then prompts you with *Enter justify range:*, whereupon you can specify the size and shape of the range into which the text of the label is to fit. If you specify a range that is too small to accommodate the label text, 1-2-3 will go into ERROR mode, beep, and display the message

Justify range is full or line too long

Press the Enter key to exit from ERROR mode and then retry the /Range Justify command, this time enlarging the justify range.

Figure 4.5 shows you a simple memorandum that requires the use of the /Range Justify command to format the text of the long label in cell A9 (this cell contains almost the maximum of 240 characters). To restrict the width of each line of text so that it will fit on an 8½-×-11-inch page, the justify range is set to A9..H12 (Figure 4.6). In Figure 4.7, you can see the result of using

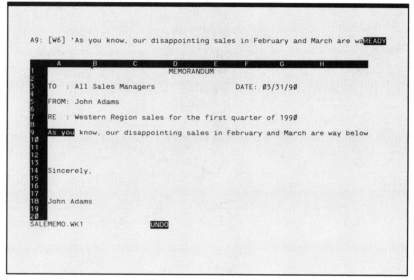

◆ **Figure 4.5:** *Memorandum with long label in cell A9*

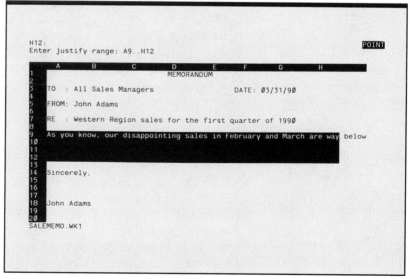

◆ **Figure 4.6:** *Setting the justify range to A9..H12*

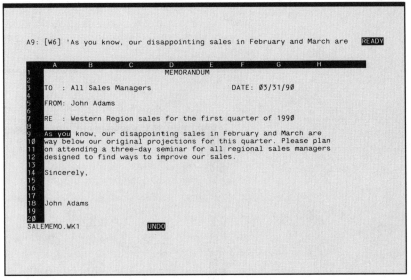

A9: [W6] 'As you know, our disappointing sales in February and March are   READY

```
        A       B       C       D       E       F       G       H
1                            MEMORANDUM
2
3   TO  : All Sales Managers                    DATE: Ø3/31/9Ø
4
5   FROM: John Adams
6
7   RE  : Western Region sales for the first quarter of 199Ø
8
9   As you know, our disappointing sales in February and March are
1Ø  way below our original projections for this quarter. Please plan
11  on attending a three-day seminar for all regional sales managers
12  designed to find ways to improve our sales.
13
14  Sincerely,
15
16
17
18  John Adams
19
2Ø
SALEMEMO.WK1                    UNDO
```

◆ **Figure 4.7:** *The memorandum after completing the /Range Justify operation*

this justify range: the text in cell A9 has now been broken up and entered into four cells, A9 through A12.

When specifying the justify range, you are usually better off defining a range that consists of multiple rows as well as multiple columns, although 1-2-3 will accept a range that uses just a single row. Figure 4.8 demonstrates what happens when you specify a justify range of A9..H9 (using only one row). As before, 1-2-3 breaks up the long label in cell A9 and puts it in four cells, A9 through A12.

Notice, however, that in Figure 4.8 the label *Sincerely,* which was originally in cell A14, has been moved down to cell A17 and the signatory *John Adams,* which was originally in cell A18, has been moved down to cell A21. This is because when defining a range with a single row, the program inserts three new rows below the last cell used in justifying the range.

The program will always insert one blank row in the worksheet for each of the rows it needs to use when justifying the long label. In the example, the range-justify operation used three rows (10–12 below the original row 9) to break the label up and restrict each line to columns A through H. Therefore, 1-2-3 inserted three new rows in the worksheet below the ones it used in justifying the label.

Specifying a single row for the justify range will protect the existing data that would fall within this range from being overwritten and thus deleted. After completing this procedure, you can delete any unnecessary blank rows that are

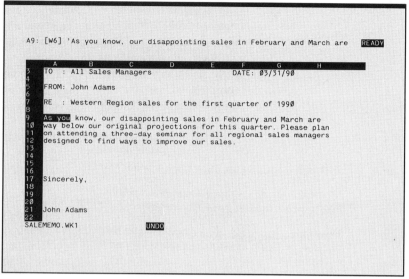

A9: [W6] 'As you know, our disappointing sales in February and March are ▐READY▌

	A	B	C	D	E	F	G	H
3	TO : All Sales Managers				DATE: 03/31/90			
4								
5	FROM: John Adams							
6								
7	RE : Western Region sales for the first quarter of 1990							
8								
9	▐As you▌ know, our disappointing sales in February and March are							
10	way below our original projections for this quarter. Please plan							
11	on attending a three-day seminar for all regional sales managers							
12	designed to find ways to improve our sales.							
13								
14								
15								
16								
17	Sincerely,							
18								
19								
20								
21	John Adams							
22								

SALEMEMO.WK1   ▐UNDO▌

+ **Figure 4.8:** *The memorandum after using the /Range Justify command with a single-row justify range*

inserted by the /Range Justify command by using the /Worksheet Delete Row command.

Erasing Ranges in the Worksheet

If you need to erase the contents of a cell range in your worksheet, use the /Range Erase command. If you ever specify a range in error, use the Undo key (Alt-F4) immediately after the /Range Erase command to restore the data. If you only need to erase a single cell, move the pointer to it and then type /RE and press Enter. Remember that replacing an existing entry with a space by pressing the spacebar is not the same as using the /Range Erase command. In the former case, the cell contains a label with a space character; in the latter, it is a blank or empty cell.

Always use the /Range Erase command instead of the /Worksheet Delete Column command to erase data in a group of columns, unless you wish to remove the *entire* column including all of its data from row 1 to 8192 for each column in the range. The same thing holds true for the use of the /Worksheet Delete Row command: use this command only when you want to remove the *entire* row including all of its data from columns A through IV; otherwise, use the /Range Erase command.

Note that when you use the /Worksheet Delete Column command, data in columns to the right of those in the deletion range move as many columns to the left as necessary to fill in the blank columns created by this deletion. As part of this process, the cell addresses in formulas that refer to the cells that moved are updated to match their new column position. The same thing happens when you issue the /Worksheet Delete Row command, except in this case, the data in the rows below those in the deletion range move up, and the row numbers are updated in formulas.

Protecting Values and Controlling Input in the Worksheet

Once you have finalized a worksheet or template, especially one that will be used by a lot of people with different levels of expertise with 1-2-3, you will often want to protect your worksheet from further changes.

To do this, you select the /Worksheet Global Protection Enable command (/WGPE) to turn on *global protection*. This prevents anyone from erasing or making any editing changes to any cells in the worksheet.

Using /Range Prot and /Range Unprot

Once you've protected the worksheet globally, you can then use the /Range Unprot command to allow changes to be made to particular cells or cell ranges. For example, in a template like the income statement template that you created, you have to make entries in just a few cells to complete a new worksheet. Therefore, after globally protecting the template file, you would use the /Range Unprot command to allow data to be entered into only these key cells (called *input cells*). Note that 1-2-3 provides a /Range Prot command that enables you to protect any cell range that you previously unprotected with the /Range Unprot command. You can always deactivate the global protection in one operation by using the /Worksheet Global Protection command again, this time selecting the Disable option.

To get a feel for how this can work, perform the following exercise using your income statement template:

1. **If necessary, type /WEY to clear worksheet file** *IS90CH4.WK1* **from memory (make sure that you saved it before you take this step); then type** */FR,* **move the pointer to** *ISTMPLT.WK1,* **and press Enter.**
Now that you have retrieved your income statement template, you next need to globally protect it.

2. **Type** /WGP **to select the** /Worksheet Global Protection com-
   mand, and then type E **to select the Enable option.**
   After turning on global protection in a worksheet with this command, nothing appears to have happened in the worksheet itself.
   However, if you look at the contents of cell A1, you will now see *PR*
   (for *protected*) at the beginning of the entry. All cells, even blank
   ones, now have this designation in the cell contents.

3. **Press F2 to edit the contents of cell A1; then press the Backspace key to delete the** 1 **of** 31 **and press Enter.**
   As soon as you press Enter, the program goes into ERROR mode,
   beeps, and displays the message *Protected cell*. The same thing would
   happen if you tried to enter a new label or value in this cell or used
   the /Range Erase command to delete its contents. All the cells in this
   worksheet are now protected from further changes.

4. **Press the Enter key to exit from ERROR mode and return to
   READY mode.**
   Next, you are going to use the /Range Unprot command to allow
   entry in the input cells.

5. **Move the pointer to cell B2 (it now contains** ^ 199), **then
   type** /RU, **press the** ↓ **key once to unprotect range B2..B3, and
   press Enter.**
   You can now make changes in these two cells, because they are
   unprotected. The program lets you know that they are unprotected in
   two ways: the entry in the cell display is either in double intensity on
   a monochrome screen or in a different color (usually green) on a color
   screen, and the cell contains a *U* (for *unprotected*). Next, you want to
   unprotect the range B5..B7 where you enter the costs and expenses for
   the income statement.

6. **Move the pointer to cell B5 and use the** /Range Unprot
   command to remove protection from the range B5..B7.
   There is one just one more cell range to unprotect: range B14..B16,
   where you enter the other income and expenses.

7. **Move the pointer to cell B14 and use the** /Range Unprot
   command to remove protection from the range B14..B16.
   That's all. You don't want to remove protection from any other cells
   because they all contain labels or formulas that shouldn't require any
   editing when building an income statement from the template.

8. **Save these changes to the worksheet by typing** /FS, **then type
   the new file name** *istmplt4* **and press Enter.**

Protecting Entries Formatted with the Hidden Format: When
you use the /Range Format Hidden command to prevent a range of cells
from being displayed in the worksheet, you are putting the data in that
range at risk unless you also protect it. Because you can't see the data, you
can easily erase them or overwrite them when moving or copying other
data. To prevent this, enable global protection (/WGPE), use the /Range
Format Hidden command to hide the display of the range, and then use the
/Range Unprot command to remove protection from the cell ranges that
aren't hidden.

Using /Range Input to Control Data Input

You can use the /Range Input command to create simple input forms in a worksheet. To do this, you specify a data-input range that contains the labels and
input cells that need to be displayed on the screen. Lotus 1-2-3 will automatically limit cell-pointer movement to those cells that you unprotect and are
therefore accessible for entry or editing. To move from unprotected cell to
unprotected cell in an input form, you can press the ↓, ↑, ←, →, Home
(first unprotected cell in the data-input range), or End key (last unprotected
cell in the data- input range). When you press the Esc or Enter key, cell-pointer
movement is no longer restricted to the data-input range defined with the
/Range Input command, and the pointer returns to the cell that was current
before you used this command.

To see how this works, you will now create a data-input range in your income
statement template:

1. **Press the Home key to move the pointer to cell A1; type /RI,
    highlight the range A1..B16 (you don't have to input data
    below this cell in the income statement), then press Enter.**
    Notice that the pointer moves to cell B2, which is the first unpro-
    tected cell in the data-input range. Let's go ahead and create an
    income statement for 1993 using this input form.

2. **Press F2, type 3 (for 1993), then press ↓.**
    The pointer is now in cell B3, where you enter the revenues
    for 1993.

3. **Type *65450*, then press ↓.**
   Now enter the costs and expenses in cells B5, B6, and B7.

4. **Type *12500*, then press ↓; type *19775*, then press ↓; type *10250* and press ↓ again.**
   Notice that the pointer jumps from cell B7 directly to cell B14 after you enter 10,250 and press the ↓ key. Finish the income statement by entering the other income and expenses for the year.

5. **Type *9975*, then press →; type *– 600*, then press →; type *– 250* and press → again.**
   Notice that when entering data in this data-input range, pressing the → key has the same effect as pressing the ↓ key (likewise, you can press the ← instead of the ↑ key). Notice that as soon as you enter the last amount of −600 for the Other category, the pointer returns to the first unprotected cell, B3 (Figure 4.9). Pointer movement remains restricted to the unprotected cells in the data-input range until you press Esc or Enter. Now try using a /Worksheet command.

6. **Type */wgd*.**
   Notice that instead of activating the 1-2-3 command menus when you type /, the program goes into LABEL mode, thus accepting /WGD as a label instead of a command. The use of the /Range Input command has disabled the command menus until you press the Esc or Enter key.

7. **Press Esc to clear */wgd* from the control panel; then press Enter to terminate the restriction of pointer movement to the data-input range.**
   The pointer immediately returns to cell A1, the cell that held the pointer before you used the /Range Input command.

8. **Check your entries against those shown in Figure 4.9; if they check, save the file under the name *IS93CH4.WK1*.**
   Remember that when you use the /File Save command to save a worksheet created from a template, you can either edit the template file name to the name you want to give the worksheet file, or type the worksheet file name from scratch—whichever you find easier to do.

```
B2: U ^1993                                                    READY

                    A                   B       C       D       E
 1   INCOME STATEMENT YEAR ENDING DECEMBER 31
 2                              1993
 3   Revenues                   65,450
 4   Costs and expenses
 5      Product costs           12,500
 6      Marketing and sales     19,775
 7      General and administrative 10,250
 8                              --------
 9   Total costs and expenses   42,525
10
11   Operating income (loss)    22,925
12
13   Other income (expenses)
14      Interest income          9,975
15      Interest expense          (600)
16      Other                     (250)
17                              --------
18   Total other income (expenses)  9,125
19
20   Income (loss) before taxes 32,050
ISTMPLT4.WK1            UNDO                         NUM
```

◆ **Figure 4.9:** *Income statement for 1993 created from the income statement template
using the /Range Input command*

Duplicating & Relocating Data in the Worksheet

Lotus 1-2-3 makes it easy to copy or move a range of data within the worksheet.
Not only can you relocate a range in the worksheet, but you can also transpose
the orientation of the data within a range so that the horizontal data are
arranged vertically and the vertical data are arranged horizontally.

As you will learn, the /Move and /Copy commands in 1-2-3 follow a similar
procedure:

1. Select the /Move or /Copy command.

2. Define the range that is to be moved or copied to a new location.
   This is in response to the prompt *Enter range to move (or copy) FROM:*
   followed by the current cell address anchored as a range.

3. After indicating the range to be moved or copied, you indicate the
   place where the range is to be moved or copied to. This is in response
   to the prompt *Enter range to move (or copy) TO:* followed by the current cell address but no longer anchored.

4. After you indicate the new location for the range (or a copy of the
   range, if you are using /Copy), 1-2-3 relocates or copies the designated range and returns the pointer to the cell it occupied at the
   beginning of this procedure.

Moving Data

The /Move command allows you to transfer a range of data to a new location within the worksheet. When you move a range, the formatting and protection status that you assigned to it in its old location is retained and transferred to the new location it occupies.

Keep in mind that 1-2-3 will overwrite and thereby destroy any existing data if you move data into the same range that they occupy. You must therefore take care that the destination range (the one you are moving to) contains no data— or at least no data that you mind losing. If you do overwrite needed data during a /Move operation, press the Undo key (Alt-F4) immediately.

Using the /Move Command

Using the /Move command is straightforward. When you select the /Move command, you are first prompted to enter the range to move FROM. You can specify this range by typing the range address or the range name or by using the pointing method. Next, you are prompted to enter the range to move TO. Here, you only have to designate the first cell of the destination range (you can do this easily, as the range is not anchored at this point). After 1-2-3 moves the data to the new range, it moves the pointer back to the cell it originally occupied when you started the move operation.

Figures 4.10 and 4.11 illustrate how this works. In this example, the range A3..F6 is being moved down several rows in the same worksheet. In Figure 4.10,

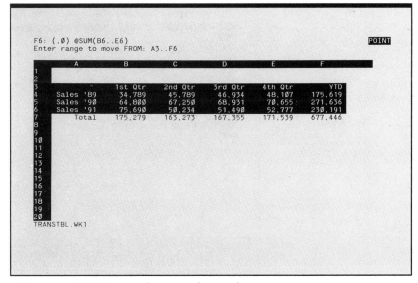

◆ **Figure 4.10:** *Designating the range to be moved*

you see the range to move FROM is defined with pointing as A3..F6. After you have completed this part of the move operation by pressing Enter, the pointer is moved down to cell A10. This cell is then designated as the range to move TO. Note that you need not define anything more than the *first* cell of the range to move TO, even though the range occupies the cell range A10..F13 as soon as the move operation is completed, as shown in Figure 4.11.

Before this move was made in this worksheet, cell B7 contained the formula @SUM(B4..B6). After the move was completed, this formula was changed to @SUM(B11..B13). The program automatically updated the cell references in this formula to reflect their new position in the worksheet.

You do have to be careful when moving data that are already referenced in formulas in the worksheet. Figure 4.12 shows you what happens to the formula in cell B7 when you move the data in cells B12 and B13 to cells B16 and B17 using the /Move command. Notice that the formula automatically expands the argument range for the @SUM function from B11..B13 to B:11..B17.

If you then enter new values anywhere within this expanded cell range, the total formula in cell B7 will be recalculated to include these values. This is what has happened in Figure 4.13, where the number 100 was entered in cell B14. Because this cell address is now included in the expanded range used by the @SUM function in cell B7, this value is now added to the total.

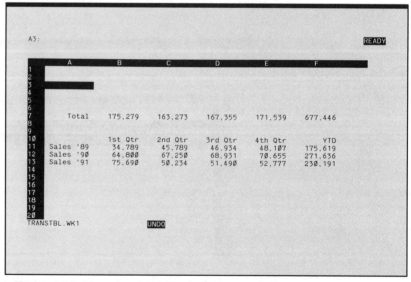

◆ **Figure 4.11:** *The range relocated by the /Move command*

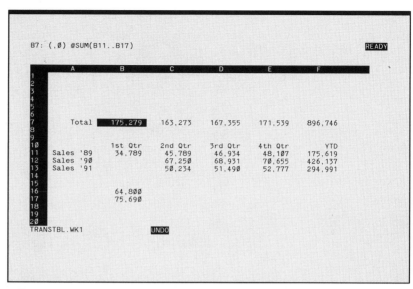

◆ **Figure 4.12:** *Expanding the range argument in a formula by moving one of the cell references*

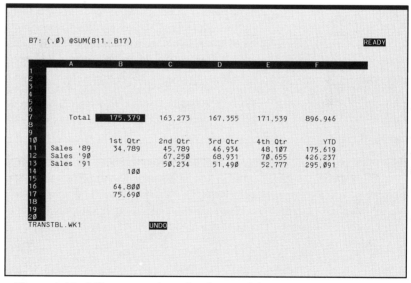

◆ **Figure 4.13:** *Adding a new value within the expanded range argument*

Figure 4.14 demonstrates another potential problem that can occur when you use the /Move command. In this figure, the /Move command was used to move the 100 entered in cell B14 to cell B17. Not only has this move replaced

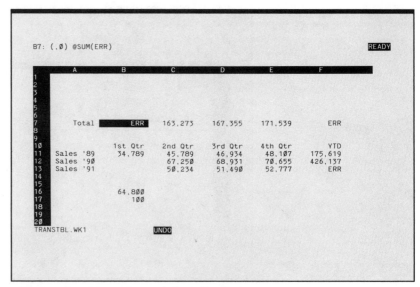

◆ **Figure 4.14:** *Moving data to the last cell in the range argument*

the original first-quarter value of 75,690 with 100 in cell B17, but it has also caused the formula in cell B7 to return the ERR value, because the argument of the @SUM function now contains the ERR value—@SUM(ERR). A function will always return ERR if you overwrite either the first or last cell in its argument range.

Copying Data

The /Copy command allows you to copy a range of data to a new location within the worksheet. When you copy a range, the formatting and protection status that you assigned to the original range is retained by the copies that are made. Be aware that the copy operation, no less than the move, will replace any existing data that are within the range chosen as the destination for the range that is being copied.

Using the /Copy Command

You can use the /Copy command to make three different kinds of copies: a *one-to-one copy*, a *one-to-many copy*, or a *many-to-many copy*. A one-to-one copy, as the name implies, copies the data in a single cell range to another cell in the worksheet. A one-to-many copy copies the data from a single cell range to multiple cells in the worksheet. A many-to-many copy copies a range consisting of many cells to another range in the worksheet.

When you select the /Copy command, you are first prompted to enter the range to copy FROM (the source range). As with the /Move command, you can specify this range by typing the range address or the range name or by using the pointing method. Next, you are prompted to enter the range to copy TO (the destination range). If you want to make only a single copy of the source range, you only have to designate the first cell of the destination range (you can do this easily, as the range is not anchored at this point). To make multiple copies of the source range, you need to designate a range of cells—each of which will hold the first cell of a copy of the source range—as the destination range.

Figure 4.15 shows the source range A3..F7 for a copy operation (one-to-one) that will copy an entire sales table from one location to another in the worksheet. Figure 4.16 shows the worksheet after the copy, which occupies the range A11..F15, has been made. To complete this copy operation, only the single cell A11 was designated in response to the prompt *Enter range to copy TO:* because when making a one-to-one copy, you only have to define the first cell of the destination range.

When you copy a range, 1-2-3 will copy any data that it contains, including labels, numbers, or formulas, from the source to the destination range. The

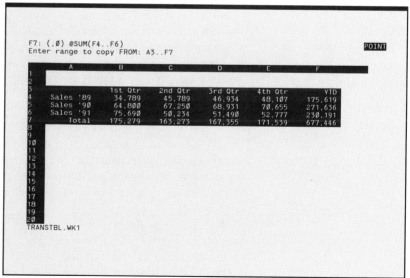

♦ **Figure 4.15:** *Defining the range to be copied*

A3:   READY

	A	B	C	D	E	F
1						
2						
3		1st Qtr	2nd Qtr	3rd Qtr	4th Qtr	YTD
4	Sales '89	34,789	45,789	46,934	48,107	175,619
5	Sales '90	64,800	67,250	68,931	70,655	271,636
6	Sales '91	75,690	50,234	51,490	52,777	230,191
7	Total	175,279	163,273	167,355	171,539	677,446
8						
9						
10						
11		1st Qtr	2nd Qtr	3rd Qtr	4th Qtr	YTD
12	Sales '89	34,789	45,789	46,934	48,107	175,619
13	Sales '90	64,800	67,250	68,931	70,655	271,636
14	Sales '91	75,690	50,234	51,490	52,777	230,191
15	Total	175,279	163,273	167,355	171,539	677,446
16						
17						
18						
19						
20						

TRANSTBL.WK1   UNDO

◆ **Figure 4.16:** *The worksheet after the one-to-one copy has been made*

program does, however, treat the copies of formulas that contain cell references differently from copies of labels and numbers. In making a copy of such formulas, the cell references are automatically adjusted, reflecting their new positions in the worksheet. Because this adjustment is not always desirable, the program provides you with the means to modify or prevent it altogether. You will learn all about how this is done in the next chapter, where we explore the use of formulas and 1-2-3 functions in depth.

Using /Range Trans to Change the Orientation of Data in a Range

The /Range Trans command (called /Range Transpose in Release 2.01) enables you to change the orientation of data when you copy it. This means that data arranged horizontally across rows of the table will be arranged vertically down columns in the copy of the range.

Figure 4.17 demonstrates how the /Range Trans command works. To produce the transposed table shown in range A10..E15 in Figure 4.17, the sales table in the range A3..F7 was defined as the FROM range for the transpose and the single cell A10 as the TO range. Note how the column and row headings are rotated along with the data in this table when the copy is made using A10 as the first cell of the range.

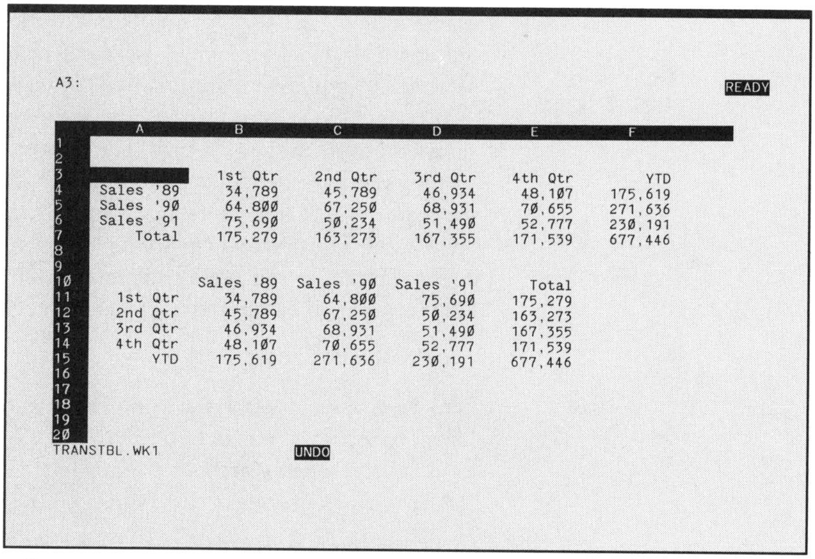

◆ **Figure 4.17**: *The original and transposed copy of the sales table*

※ *New in 2.2*

Locating Specific Data in the Worksheet

Release 2.2 includes a new search feature that enables you to quickly locate each occurrence of a particular *search string* in a cell range. The search string can be any combination of characters up to 240 characters long (the line scrolls from left to right if your search string is longer than will fit on a single line after the prompt).

The /Range Search command allows you either to locate every occurrence of your search string in the range or to replace the search string with a new string of your choosing. You can invoke the replace function on a case-by-case basis or globally.

The program allows you to select between searching formulas only, labels only, or both formulas and labels in the range. You can have 1-2-3 locate the occurrence of particular numbers in the range, as long as these values are part of a formula and you designate that formulas or both formulas and labels should be searched.

Finding a Search String in a Range

To search for a particular string, select the /Range Search command. You are then prompted with *Enter range to search:*. Unlike all the other /Range commands so far, the program doesn't display a default range because it isn't automatically anchored on the current cell. You can enter the range to be searched by typing the range address, by entering a defined range name, or by pointing. If you use pointing, you must type the period before using the pointer-movement keys to highlight the range.

After you have defined the range, 1-2-3 displays the prompt *Enter string to search for:*. You then type in your search string, up to 240 characters long, and press Enter. The find and replace functions in 1-2-3 are not case-sensitive, so it doesn't matter if you use all uppercase, all lowercase, or any combination. After entering the search string, you must select one of these options:

Formulas Labels Both

Choose Formulas to restrict the search to only the formulas in the range, Labels to restrict the search to just the labels in the range, or Both to have all formulas and labels searched.

After you choose one of these three options, the program presents two more:

Find Replace

To have 1-2-3 perform a search only, select the Find option. The program will then search the range for your search string according to the type of search you have set up. If 1-2-3 locates an occurrence of your search string, it will move the pointer to the cell that contains the string while actually highlighting the search string in the cell's contents in the control panel. The program also displays the options

Next Quit

If you want to abort the search operation at this point, select the Quit option. The program will then return to READY mode, and the pointer will remain on the cell that contains your first match. Of course, if you want to find the next occurrence instead, select the Next option.

If 1-2-3 doesn't locate a match for your search string, it goes into ERROR mode, beeps, and displays the message

String not found

If you select the Next option and there are no more matches, the same thing happens. In either situation, you must press the Esc or Enter key to exit from ERROR mode and return the program to READY mode.

The program will always remember your last search range and search string. Therefore, if you next want to perform a search on the same range using a new search string, you need only reenter or edit the search string. Conversely, when you want to perform a search on a new range using the same string, you have only to change the search range.

Replacing a Search String in a Range

When you want to use the /Range Search command to replace a string in a range, you follow the exact same procedure as the Find operation, until you are prompted to choose between the Find or Replace option. At that point, you select the Replace option and the program displays the prompt *Enter replacement string:*. Here, you can enter any combination of up to 240 characters. When entering the replacement string, pay attention to your use of uppercase and lowercase letters: 1-2-3 will enter the string in the cell exactly as you enter it.

Once you have finished entering the replacement string, the program searches for the search string in the defined range. If it doesn't find your search string, the program goes into ERROR mode and displays an error message. If 1-2-3 does locate the search string, it displays the options

Replace All Next Quit

Choose the Replace option to have 1-2-3 replace the search string with the replacement string and continue to the next occurrence in the range. To have all occurrences of the search string globally replaced without requiring your approval, select the All option. To prevent the program from replacing the current occurrence and have it search for the next one, select the Next option. And to have 1-2-3 terminate the replace operation and return to READY mode, select the Quit option.

The replace feature in 1-2-3 can be useful should you find it necessary to change a title or label throughout the worksheet or modify the use of a range name in all formulas and macros that use it. Do, however, be careful of performing global replacements: the program may replace a string that you had not intended to replace. If this happens, you can use the Undo function (Alt-F4) to return the range to its previous state, provided that you discover the problem in time (before you complete another operation that can be undone).

Summary

Troubleshooting

Question: Is it all right to give the same range more than one range name?

Answer: As long as you and the people who use the worksheet are aware that there are two range names that refer to the exact same range, 1-2-3 won't mind. In most cases, however, you won't want to use precious memory space for redundant range names.

Question: After hiding a range of data with /Range Format Hidden, I tried to protect it with the /Range Prot command. Although I thought the data were then safe, I discovered later that they had been overwritten when a co-worker moved a range in the worksheet. Why didn't /Range Prot work?

Answer: In 1-2-3, you *have* to use the /Worksheet Global Protection Enable command and then unprotect the ranges you still need to have access to with the /Range Unprot command. The only function of the /Range Prot command is to restore protection to a range that has been unprotected with /Range Unprot while the worksheet is *still* globally protected; it never works when global protection is disabled in the worksheet.

Question: I tried to make a copy of a range using pointing. When I completed the operation, however, I discovered that the range hadn't been copied and, in fact, the worksheet appeared no different! What went wrong?

Answer: You undoubtedly entered the same range in response to *both* the copy FROM and the copy TO prompts. When you do this, you are in essence making a copy of the range on top of itself and, in so doing, you don't change the appearance of the worksheet in any way.

Essential Techniques

To Name a Range

1. Move the pointer to the first cell of the range to be named.

2. Select the /Range Name Create command.

3. Type in a range name up to 15 characters long with no spaces, and press Enter.

4. Indicate the range either by typing the range address or by pointing.

To Protect a Worksheet from Further Changes

1. Select the /Worksheet Global Protection Enable command.

2. Select the /Range Unprot command to remove the protected status from any ranges in the worksheet that are now globally protected.

To Move a Range

1. Move the pointer to the first cell of the range to be moved and select the /Move command. The prompt will read *Enter range to move FROM*.

2. Indicate the source range—that is, the one that is being moved—by entering its range address or by pointing, and press Enter. The prompt will change to *Enter range to move TO*.

3. Move the pointer to the first cell in the destination range or type its address. This is the upper left corner of the range where your data is being moved to.

To Copy a Range

1. Move the pointer to the first cell of the range to be copied and select the /Copy command. The prompt will read *Enter range to copy FROM*.

2. Indicate the source range—that is, the one to be copied—by entering its range address or by pointing, and press Enter. The prompt will change to *Enter range to copy TO*.

3. If you are doing a one-to-many copy, point out the destination range or type its range address and press Enter. If you are doing a one-to-one or many-to-many copy, you only need to point out or type the address of the first cell in the destination range and press Enter.

To Search for a String in a Range (Release 2.2)

1. Select the /Range Search command.

2. Indicate the range to be searched by range address, range name, or pointing, and press Enter.

3. Specify the search string to be located in the range and press Enter.

4. Select the Formulas, Labels, or Both option.

5. Choose the Find or Replace option.

6. If you select Find, 1-2-3 will locate the first occurrence of the string and display the Next/Quit menu. When it can't find the string, the program goes into ERROR mode, and you then must press Esc or Enter.

7. If you choose Replace, 1-2-3 will locate the first occurrence of the string and display the options All, Next, Quit, and Replace. Select

All for global replace; Next to skip to next occurrence; Quit to
return to READY mode; and Replace to make the replacement and
find the next occurrence.

Review   **Important Terms You Should Know**

anchor	one-to-many copy
Compose key (Alt-F1)	one-to-one copy
currency symbol	pointing
file reference	range
global protection	range address
input cells	range name
Lotus International Character	replacement string
Set (LICS)	search string
many-to-many copy	unanchor
Name key (F3)	

Test Your Knowledge

1. To specify a range address, you indicate the _____ cell of the
   range, type a _____, and then indicate the _____ cell in the
   range.

2. To reference a cell that is not in the current file, you must be sure to
   prefix the cell address with the _____—that is, the name of the file
   enclosed in a pair of _____.

3. In pointing out a range, you type the _____ to anchor the range
   and the _____ key to unanchor it.

4. To move the pointer directly to the first cell of a named range using
   the Goto and Name keys, you first press _____, then press
   _____, move the pointer to the range name, and press Enter.

5. To name a range consisting of cells in multiple rows and columns,
   you must use the /Range Name _____ command. To name a range
   of single cells using existing labels in the row above, you use the
   /Range Name _____ command and then select the _____
   option.

6. If you wanted a range of values to display two decimal places and negative values in parentheses, you would choose the _____ format option from the /Range Format menu.

7. To prevent anyone from making further editing changes in your worksheet, you need to choose the _____ option after selecting the _____ command. To remove protection from the entire worksheet, you then select the same command, this time choosing the _____ option.

8. To exit from a data-input range set up with the /Range Input command, you must press either the _____ or the _____ key.

9. To relocate a range of data to a new place in your worksheet, you select the _____ command. If you want to make multiple copies of it, you must use the _____ command instead.

10. If you use the /Range Trans command, the data listed across each row in the original range will be listed _____ each _____ in the copy it makes.

5

Formulas and
Functions:
Performing Calculations

In This
Chapter...

Working with Formulas

Formulas are the lifeblood of the 1-2-3 worksheet. They not only perform the initial calculations in the worksheet, but also make it possible to renew or redo your computations and perform all sorts of analysis on your data, from "what-if" to goal-seeking. Without the ability to store formulas in the cells of your worksheets, you couldn't thoroughly (and almost instantly) update your work-sheet to reflect a set of new assumptions just by entering a new value in one of the *input cells* (those on which the model depends). Instead, to realize each new what-if scenario, you would have to laboriously reenter (and thereby recom-pute) each and every formula that is in any way related to your input values, just as you must when using an electronic calculator or adding machine with paper tape.

In 1-2-3, you can use three different kinds of formulas in the worksheet, each of which is designed to calculate and return a particular kind of result:

- *Numeric formulas*, which calculate numeric values and use the arithmetic operators and/or 1-2-3 mathematical, statistical, financial, date, time, or some of the special @functions

- *String formulas*, which calculate strings (characters that are treated only as labels) and use the string operator & (ampersand) and/or 1-2-3 string @functions

- *Logical formulas*, which calculate the logical value 1 (true) or the logical value 0 (false) and use the logical operators and/or some of the special @functions

Although numeric formulas are the most common, and can contain many @functions, you will also find string formulas useful if you work with data cre-ated with other programs that are imported into 1-2-3.

Logical formulas are required in setting up certain types of search criteria for performing queries in a 1-2-3 database. As such, you will learn about their use in Part III, where you will also become acquainted with a group of database @functions designed especially for use with 1-2-3 database tables.

Entering Formulas

Regardless of the type of formula you are using, the program must be in VALUE mode rather than LABEL mode when you enter it. Remember that if your formula begins with a cell reference, you must type the + (unless you need to use the nega-tive value in the cell, in which case you use −) to put 1-2-3 in VALUE mode.

When building a numeric formula, you can use any of these *arithmetic operators*:

+ (plus) for addition, as in *+D12+D13*

− (minus) for subtraction, as in *+G2−H2*

* (asterisk) for multiplication, as in *+A2*E3*

/ (slash) for division, as in *+C3/D4*

^ (circumflex) for exponentiation (raising a number to a certain power), as in *+B10^3* (the value in the cell cubed, the same as +B10*B10*B10)

The only limit on the length of the formula and the number of operators that you can use is a total of 240 characters, the maximum length for any cell entry. Note also that you can use *literal values* (numbers that you type into the formula) as well as cell references in building numeric formulas. As a rule, however, you should keep the number of literal values used in any formulas in the worksheet to a bare minimum, preferring instead to refer to the cell that contains such values. That way, you can update your worksheet much more easily.

Concatenating Strings with the String Operator

When building a string formula, you can only use one operator, & (ampersand), as in +A3&B3. This *string operator* in a string formula works much like the plus sign does in a numeric formula: it adds one string to another. However, unlike addition, which generates a new number as the sum, a string formula generates a new character string that is made up of the individual strings used in the formula. This process of joining strings, or linking them in a series, is called *concatenation*.

When building string formulas, you can concatenate two or more cells as long as they contain labels; trying to concatenate a value with a label will result in ERR. You can also concatenate a *literal string* with a cell that contains a label or even two literal strings. A literal string is some text that you type in the formula. You almost always have to enclose literal strings in quotation marks to let 1-2-3 know where the string begins and ends.

For example, if cell A3 of your worksheet contains the label *New* and you want to create a string formula in cell C3 that returns the label *New York*, you can do it by joining the literal string " *York*" to cell A3. This is accomplished by building the formula

    +A3&" York"

in cell C3. Notice in this formula that the first character after the initial quotation mark in the literal string is a space followed by the word *York*. If you didn't start the literal string with a space, the label in cell C3 would be *NewYork* instead of *New York*.

Let's assume that you've already entered the label *York* in cell A4 of the worksheet and, instead of joining a literal string to the contents of cell A3, you want to concatenate A3 and A4 in a string formula in cell C3. If you do this by entering *+A3&A4*, 1-2-3 will put the string *NewYork* in cell C3. To have the space entered between *New* and *York*, you must include it as a literal string in the formula:

> +A3&" "&A4

From this example, you begin to see that a string formula can concatenate a whole series of labels, some referred to by cell reference and others entered as literal strings. Again, the limit on the length of your string formulas and the number of strings that can be concatenated is the 240-character maximum imposed on any cell entry.

Building Logical Formulas Using the Logical Operators

Logical formulas perform a *conditional test* on a statement and indicate whether it is currently true or false. In 1-2-3, this is done by using 1 to indicate that a condition is true and 0 to indicate that it is false.

Logical formulas are built using the following *logical operators*:

> = (equal to), as in *+B3=0* or *+D2="Yes"*
>
> < (less than), as in *+D5<E10*2*
>
> <= (less than or equal to), as in *+C4<=250*
>
> > (greater than), as in *+A12>B1*
>
> >= (greater than or equal to), as in *+B7>=F1*
>
> <> (not equal to), as in *+B3<>0*
>
> #AND# (logical AND), as in *+B2>A1#AND#B2<C3*
>
> #OR# (logical OR), as in *+A12>B1#OR#B3<>0*
>
> #NOT# (logical NOT), as in *#NOT#B3=0* (same as *+B3<>0*)

Note that the last three logical operators in this list are the Boolean operators, which are often required in setting up compound conditions when setting search criteria in 1-2-3 database tables. The logical AND and OR operators are used to create compound statements in formulas. When you use the #AND# operator, *both* statements in the formula must be true in order for the condition to test true. If you use the #OR# operator, however, the condition will test true if *either* statement is true.

The Order in Which Formulas Are Evaluated

The operators used in your formulas determine the order in which operations are performed. Table 5.1 shows you the *order of precedence* given to each operator. The precedence number shown in the third column of this table indicates when the operation called for by that operator is performed: the lower the precedence number, the earlier the operation is performed. When two operators have the same precedence number, the operations are performed in strict left-to-right order.

This means that in the formula

     +A2+10−2*B2

the multiplication of 2 times the contents of cell B2 is performed first because this operation has a lower precedence number (3 as compared with 4 for addition and subtraction). After the multiplication is performed, cell A2 is then added to 10 before the product of 2 times B2 is subtracted. Because addition and subtraction have the same precedence number, addition is performed before the subtraction only because it occurs first in the formula when reading from left to right.

Overriding the Order of Precedence

You can override the order of precedence in your formulas through the use of parentheses. For example, to override the natural order of precedence in the formula +A2+10−2*B2 cited above and have the subtraction performed before the multiplication, you enter

     +A2+(10−2)*B2

in which case 8 (the result of 10−2) is multiplied by B2 and that product is then added to A2.

Just as in creating algebraic formulas, you can nest sets of parentheses within one another, up to a maximum of 32 nesting levels, when building more complex 1-2-3 formulas. With nested parentheses, operations are performed from the inmost set outward, and within a set of parentheses according to the precedence number assigned to the operator.

For example, if you nest the original set of parentheses within another pair in the sample formula, so that you have

     (A2+(10−2))*B2

♦ **Table 5.1:** *Order of Precedence in 1-2-3*

Operator	Operation	Precedence Number
^	Exponentiation	1
− *or* +	Negative or positive value	2
*	Multiplication	3
/	Division	3
+	Addition	4
−	Subtraction	4
=	Equal to	5
< >	Not equal to	5
<	Less than	5
>	Greater than	5
<=	Less than or equal to	5
>=	Greater than or equal to	5
#NOT#	Logical NOT	6
#AND#	Logical AND	7
#OR#	Logical OR	7
&	String concatenation	7

the subtraction of 2 from 10 is still performed first (it's in the inmost set). Then, however, instead of multiplying 8 times cell B2 as before, the second set of parentheses instructs 1-2-3 to add 8 to cell A2 and only then multiply this new sum by B2.

Copying Formulas

When you build any 1-2-3 formula, you can refer to the cell or range that contains the data you want calculated by its range address or range name. When building a formula, you can use three types of cell references: relative, mixed, and absolute.

Relative Addresses

When you use *relative addresses* (the default) in a formula, 1-2-3 marks the position of each cell reference in relation to the one that contains the formula (for instance, so many columns over or so many rows up from the one containing the formula). When you then make a copy of such a formula, 1-2-3 adjusts the address of each cell reference in every copy made so that the position of the formula relative to the new cell references remains the same as defined by the original formula.

Figures 5.1 and 5.2 illustrate how this works. In Figure 5.1, the simple formula +*B3*−*B4* was entered in cell B6. In reality, this formula means "subtract the cell that is two rows above the formula from the cell that is three rows above the formula." It is this information about the relative positioning of the cells to the location of the formula that is then copied in Figure 5.2, where the formula in cell B6 has been copied to the range C6..E6. Look at the contents of cell C6: when the simple subtraction formula is copied here, 1-2-3 adjusts the cell references so that it contains +C3−C4.

Note that this copied formula performs the same function as the original formula, that is, it subtracts the cell that is two rows above the formula from the cell that is three rows above the formula. If you looked at the contents of the copies in cells D6 and E6, you would see that their cell references have also been adjusted to ensure that they too perform the same type of calculation relative to their new positions in the worksheet.

Most of the time when you make copies of a formula, you make a one-to-many copy of a single formula using relative cell references, as illustrated in Figure 5.2. In some situations, however, you won't want the cell or range references to be adjusted when you copy the formula. To prevent 1-2-3 from adjusting the cell reference in a copied formula, you need to make the address absolute. An absolute address remains the same in all copies of the formula.

Absolute Addresses

To create an *absolute address*, you need to preface each part of the cell address with a dollar sign ($), as in $A$1. Lotus 1-2-3 makes it easy to create an absolute address from a relative address with the Abs key (F4). To convert a reference from relative to absolute, press the Abs key once after typing in or pointing to a cell address or when editing a formula. Note that the cursor must be on or immediately after the cell address in order for the Abs key to work.

Figure 5.3 shows you a situation that requires the use of an absolute address. In this worksheet, a constant interest rate of 8.5% (entered in cell C3) is used to calculate the potential earnings given various investments. Because the same interest rate is to be applied to each investment, the cell address for this reference must be made absolute in the original formula:

+ A7 * $C$3

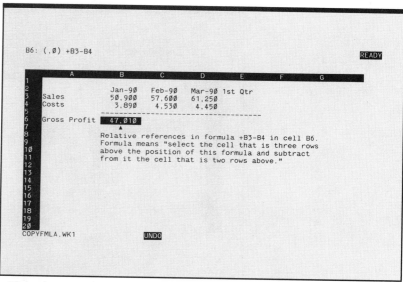

♦ **Figure 5.1:** *Simple formula in cell B6 with relative cell references*

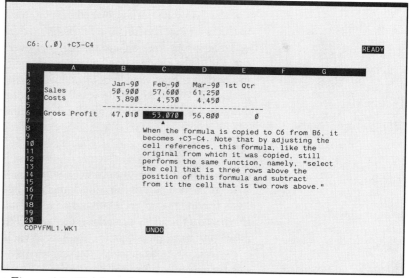

♦ **Figure 5.2:** *Worksheet after copying the formula in B6 to the range C6..E6*

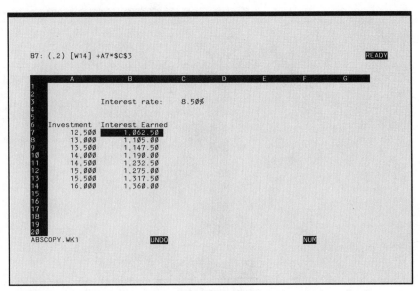

B7: (,2) [W14] +A7*$C$3   READY

	A	B	C	D	E	F	G

```
 1
 2
 3                    Interest rate:     8.50%
 4
 5
 6     Investment   Interest Earned
 7       12,500        1,062.50
 8       13,000        1,105.00
 9       13,500        1,147.50
10       14,000        1,190.00
11       14,500        1,232.50
12       15,000        1,275.00
13       15,500        1,317.50
14       16,000        1,360.00
15
16
17
18
19
20
ABSCOPY.WK1                    UNDO                        NUM
```

◆ **Figure 5.3:** *Copying a formula using an absolute address for one of its cell references*

That way, the actual cell address C3 remains constant in each copy of the formula made in the range B8..B14.

If you didn't use the absolute address for this cell reference, 1-2-3 would copy to this cell range the function of the original formula, which is to multiply the cell that is four rows up and one column over from the pointer's position by the cell in the column immediately to the left of the pointer's position. This means that the copy made in cell B8 would then contain the formula +A8*C4 instead of +A8*$C$3, giving you 0 instead of the correct answer of 1,105.00 (because C4 is blank, and a blank cell contains the value of 0).

Mixed Addresses

Between the relative and absolute addresses, there is a *mixed address*, which indicates which part of the cell address is to be made absolute (with the dollar sign), leaving the others relative. In a mixed address, 1-2-3 adjusts all the relative parts of the address in relation to the cell that contains the formula, while preserving those parts that are absolute in each copy made.

To create a mixed reference, you simply type $ before the column letter or row number as required. You can also use the Abs key (F4) to convert an address to the correct mixed address. Remember that you can convert a relative address to an absolute address by pressing F4 once. However, if you continue to press the Abs key, the program cycles the address through a series of different mixed address combinations until you return to the relative address again.

Table 5.2 illustrates this sequence and what happens if you press the Abs key successively, starting from the relative address B2. Pressing F4 always takes you through the same fixed order of changes regardless of what type of address you have when you first press the Abs key.

◆ **Table 5.2:** *Using the Abs Key to Change the Reference Type*

Press Abs key (F4) When Address Is:	Address Becomes:	Address Is Now:
B2	$B$2	Absolute
$B$2	B$2	Mixed, with row absolute and column relative
B$2	$B2	Mixed, with column absolute and row relative
$B2	B2	Relative

Reference Types for Range Names

When you use a range name in a formula, it can *only* be either relative or absolute: no mixed address combinations are possible. Further, you can't use the Abs key (F4) to convert a range name from relative to absolute; you must type the $ sign before the range name in the formula when editing it.

For example, assume that you assign the range name RATE to cell C3 in Figure 5.3 and that you wish to use this range name in building the investment earnings formula in cell B7. To make this range name absolute for copying, you first have to enter the relative formula +A7*RATE in B7. Then, you press the Edit key (F2) to return this formula to the control panel, move the cursor onto the *R* in RATE, and type $, so that the formula is

+A7*$RATE

before you copy this formula to range B8..B14 in the worksheet.

Copying Formulas and Working with Different Reference Types in the Income Statement

To get some practice in copying formulas and using absolute references, do the following exercise. In this exercise, you will add a new column of figures to your income statements to calculate the percentage of revenues represented by

F4: The Absolute Key

F4, the Absolute key, changes the type of cell address following a fixed sequence, as in A1 to $A$1, to A$1, to $A1, and then back to A1

F4 works when the cursor is somewhere on or immediately after the cell address:
♦ When building the formula after typing the address or pointing to it
♦ When editing the formula in EDIT mode (using F2)

each category in the income statement. You already have this type of percentage formula entered in cell C5 of your 1990 income statement.

1. **Retrieve the worksheet *IS90CH4.WK1* by typing /FR, highlighting its name, and pressing Enter.**
   The /File Retrieve command clears the memory of any worksheet file before it retrieves the file you select. Therefore, always be sure that the current worksheet is saved before you use this command. If you still have your IS93CH4.WK1 file on the screen, using /File Retrieve will replace it with your IS90CH4.WK1 file.

2. **Move the pointer to cell C3.**
   Here, you will enter a formula that calculates the first percentage formula. After entering this formula and formatting its display, you will copy it down the column. Because you want the amount in each category to be divided by the revenues in cell B3, you need to make this reference absolute.

3. **Type + to start the formula and move the pointer to cell B3.**
   The formula now reads +B3. Before you type the division operator (/), you need to consider whether this cell address should remain relative or be changed to absolute or some mixed form. Because you want this cell to be treated as a relative position rather than a particular cell address, you leave it relative.

4. **Type /, then move the pointer back to cell B3.**
   The formula now reads +B3/B3. The second cell address after the division operator is to remain constant in all copies made down the worksheet. To ensure that 1-2-3 will always use B3 as the divisor in each copy of the formula, you need to make this reference absolute ($B$3).

5. **Press the Abs key (F4) once so that the absolute address $B$3 is displayed after the division operator (/), then press Enter.**

   If you press the Abs key more than once by mistake and pass the absolute cell address, just keep pressing F4 until the program comes around to the address $B$3 again. The contents of your formula in cell C3 should now be *+B3/$B$3* and the answer displayed in the cell *1.* Before you copy this formula down the column, you should format it, because 1-2-3 includes all formatting in the copies made with the /Copy command.

6. **Select the /Range Format command (/RF), then choose the Percent option (P); next, type *1* for the number of decimal places and press Enter twice.**

   The percentage in C3 should be 100.0% (Figure 5.4). Note that the completed formula reads *+REVENUES/$REVENUES* instead of *+B3/$B$3* because you gave the range name REVENUES to this cell. Now you are ready to copy the formula. This will be a one-too-many formula in which you copy the formula in C3 to the range of cells C5..C22.

7. **Type /C to select the /Copy command.**

   You are prompted to enter the range to copy FROM, and the single cell range C3..C3 is listed as the default response.

8. **Press Enter to accept the default range.**

   You are next prompted to enter the range to copy TO, and the single cell C3 is listed as the default response.

9. **Move the pointer down to cell C5 and type a period (.) to anchor the range on this cell.**

   Note that this cell contains the percentage formula created with range names that you built in the last chapter. You will copy over it in this operation. The range in the control panel should now be listed as C5..C5.

10. **Use the ↓ key to highlight the range C5..C22 as the range to copy TO, then press Enter to make the copies.**

    Your worksheet should look like the one shown in Figure 5.5. Notice that you have to delete the copies that returned 0.0% because they either contain the repeating label (underscore) or divide a blank cell by the revenues in cell B3 (both labels and blanks have the value of 0 in the worksheet, so these formulas divided 0 by 50250).

11. **Move the pointer to cell C8 and delete its contents by typ-ing /RE and pressing Enter; repeat this procedure in cells C10, the cell range C12..C13, cell C17, and cell C19.**
    Your worksheet should look like the one in Figure 5.6. You are now ready to save this file under a new name.

12. **Move the pointer to cell A1 (press Home) and save the worksheet (/FS) under the file name IS90CH5.**

Controlling Recalculation in the Worksheet

When you change a number in an input cell whose value is used in a formula or make a change to the formula itself, 1-2-3 automatically recalculates that formula as well as any *dependent formulas*—that is, others that use its answer in their calculations. This is because the default recalculation mode is automatic.

 *New in 2.2*

In this mode, Release 2.2 employs a new method whereby only those cells affected by a particular change are actually recalculated (in Release 2.01 and 1A, all formulas in the worksheet are recalculated whenever any change is made). This new method greatly decreases the time it takes to recalculate a

```
C3: (P1) +REVENUES/$REVENUES                                    READY

              A                        B          C        D        E
1   INCOME STATEMENT YEAR ENDING DECEMBER 31                  .
2                                    1990
3   Revenues                         50,250   100.0%
4   Costs and expenses
5      Product costs                 12,175  0.242288
6      Marketing and sales           20,785
7      General and administrative    17,850
8                                    ---------
9   Total costs and expenses         50,810
10
11  Operating income (loss)           (560)
12
13  Other income (expenses)
14     Interest income              4,500
15     Interest expense              (500)
16     Other                          600
17                                  ---------
18  Total other income (expenses)    4,600
19
20  Income (loss) before taxes       4,040
IS90CH4.WK1                  UNDO                         NUM
```

♦ **Figure 5.4:** *Percentage formula with mixed cell reference ready for copying*

```
C3: (P1) +REVENUES/$REVENUES                                    READY

          A                        B        C        D        E
1  INCOME STATEMENT YEAR ENDING DECEMBER 31
2                                 1990
3  Revenues                      50,250    100.0%
4  Costs and expenses
5    Product costs               12,175     24.2%
6    Marketing and sales         20,785     41.4%
7    General and administrative  17,850     35.5%
8                                --------     0.0%
9  Total costs and expenses      50,810    101.1%
10                                          0.0%
11 Operating income (loss)        (560)     -1.1%
12                                          0.0%
13 Other income (expenses)                  0.0%
14   Interest income             4,500      9.0%
15   Interest expense            (500)     -1.0%
16   Other                        600       1.2%
17                                --------   0.0%
18 Total other income (expenses)  4,600     9.2%
19                                          0.0%
20 Income (loss) before taxes     4,040     8.0%
IS90CH4.WK1              UNDO                        NUM
```

♦ **Figure 5.5:** *Income statement with percentages after copying the formula*

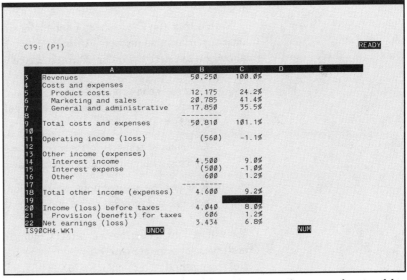

```
C19: (P1)                                                       READY

          A                        B        C        D        E
3  Revenues                      50,250    100.0%
4  Costs and expenses
5    Product costs               12,175     24.2%
6    Marketing and sales         20,785     41.4%
7    General and administrative  17,850     35.5%
8                                --------
9  Total costs and expenses      50,810    101.1%
10
11 Operating income (loss)        (560)     -1.1%
12
13 Other income (expenses)
14   Interest income             4,500      9.0%
15   Interest expense            (500)     -1.0%
16   Other                        600       1.2%
17                                --------
18 Total other income (expenses)  4,600     9.2%
19
20 Income (loss) before taxes     4,040     8.0%
21   Provision (benefit) for taxes  606     1.2%
22 Net earnings (loss)            3,434     6.8%
IS90CH4.WK1              UNDO                        NUM
```

♦ **Figure 5.6:** *Income statement with percentages after erasing the unwanted copies of the formula*

large worksheet. Even with minimal recalculation in Release 2.2, there are several @functions (covered in detail later in this chapter) that are always updated each time 1-2-3 recalculates the worksheet. These include @@, @CELL, @CELLPOINTER, @DATEVALUE, @NOW, @RAND, @STRING, @TIMEVALUE, and @VALUE, as well as any add-in @functions that you use (see Appendix G for information on using add-in @functions).

Despite these major improvements to recalculation in Release 2.2, you may want to change the mode from the default of automatic to manual. For example, you may wish to change the values for several input cells and have the worksheet(s) recalculated only after you've entered them all and had a chance to check these values. Also, you can use manual recalculation to speed up macro execution. This is because the program performs all necessary worksheet recalculations between macro steps instead of in the background, increasing the time it takes to execute the macro (see Chapter 16 for details).

To change the recalculation mode, select the /Worksheet Global Recalculation command (/WGR). This brings up the following menu:

Natural Columnwise Rowwise Automatic Manual Iteration

From this menu, select the Manual option. Thereafter, to have the worksheet recalculated, you must press the Calc key (F9). Lotus 1-2-3 informs you when a worksheet requires recalculation by displaying the CALC indicator on the status line.

Notice that the /Worksheet Global Recalculation menu includes several other options in addition to Automatic and Manual. The first three options allow you to select the order in which active worksheets are recalculated:

- *Natural* is the default. The program recalculates all formulas upon which a particular formula depends before it recalculates the value of that formula.

- *Columnwise* restricts formula recalculation to column-by-column, starting with cell A1 and moving down and across the worksheet.

- *Rowwise* restricts formula recalculation to row-by-row, starting with cell A1 and moving across and down the worksheet.

You will seldom, if ever, have to select Columnwise or Rowwise in place of Natural; these options are used only in the rare situations where you need to control the method of recalculation explicitly.

The last option, Iteration, controls the number of times the entire worksheet is recalculated (*iterations*). By default, the number of passes is set to 1. You can, however, change this to any value between 1 and 50. However, 1-2-3 uses the

---

F9: The Calc Key

F9, the Calc key, recalculates all formulas in the current worksheet file that are dependent on new values you enter

F9 works only when 1-2-3 is in manual recalculation mode (/WGRM)

The CALC indicator appears to let you know when formulas in the worksheet file need to be recalculated with the Calc key

---

Iteration value only when you set the recalculation order to columnwise or rowwise, or when a circular reference exists in one or more of the worksheet formulas.

Circular References in Formulas

A *circular reference* occurs when a cell contains a formula that refers to the cell itself. For example, if you enter the formula

  +A2 – B2

in cell B2, you create a circular reference because this formula depends upon its own answer in order to return the result. A circular reference can never be successfully resolved by the program.

When you introduce a circular reference into a formula in your worksheet, 1-2-3 immediately displays the CIRC indicator on the status line. To locate the cell that contains this reference, you can use the /Worksheet Status command: the Global Settings sheet lists the cell address of the circular reference.

Using a Converging Circular Reference to Calculate Bonuses

Although most circular references are accidental and need to be caught and fixed as soon as the CIRC indicator appears, this is not always the case. Sometimes you can use a circular reference with the Iteration control to solve worksheet problems.

To illustrate, you will now add a new expense category to your income statement for 1990: bonuses equal to 20 percent of the net earnings for the year, or +B23*0.2. This formula in itself doesn't create a circular reference. As soon as the bonus amount returned by this calculation (which depends upon the amount of net earnings in B23) is used to calculate the total of the other income in B19—which, in turn, is used to determine the net earnings in B23—a circular reference is introduced.

Fortunately, this type of circular reference can ultimately return the correct answer provided that you recalculate the dependent formulas a sufficient number of times (once is not enough). Each time the program recalculates the dependent formulas in this worksheet, the boomerang effect that a bonus amount has on the amount of net earnings gets smaller and smaller, until both figures are stabilized. That's where 1-2-3's iteration control comes in: by setting the number of iterations sufficiently high, the program will be able to resolve this circular reference without requiring any further manual recalculation.

Let's see how this works:

1. **Move the pointer to cell A16, which currently contains the label** *Other*.
   Here, you will insert a new row so that you can add the title *Bonuses* and the new formula above the Other income category. To do this, you must select the /Worksheet Insert command.

2. **Select the Row option from the Worksheet Insert menu (/WIR), and then press Enter to accept the default insert range of A16..A16.**
   This inserts a new row 16 and pushes the Other category (as well as the others below it) down one row. Not only does 1-2-3 update the references in your formulas, but it also expands the argument range for your @SUM function, moved from B18 to B19. If you examined this formula now, you would see it now contains *@SUM(B14..B17)* instead of *@SUM(B14..B16)*.

3. **Press the spacebar twice and enter** *Bonuses* **as the label in cell A16, as you move the pointer to cell B16.**
   Now you are ready to enter the formula to calculate the amount of net earnings to be set aside for bonuses. Watch the status line as you complete this formula.

4. **Type** +, **move the pointer down to B23, then type** *.2 **and press Enter.**
   As soon as you enter *+B23*0.2* in cell B16, the CIRC indicator appears on the status line (Figure 5.7). Let's use the /Worksheet Status command to see where the circular reference is located.

5. **Select the /Worksheet Status command (/WS).**
   According to the Global Settings sheet, the circular reference is located in cell B19 (Figure 5.8).

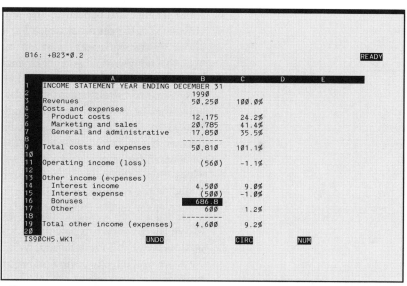

◆ **Figure 5.7:** *Creating the bonus formula that introduces a circular reference*

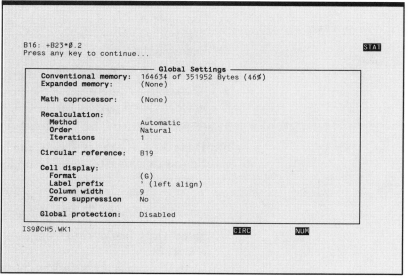

◆ **Figure 5.8:** *Locating the circular reference on the global status screen*

6. **Press any key to return to the worksheet (if you are using Release 2.01, you must press Esc or Enter).**
   Currently, the worksheet shows 686.6 as the bonus amount. However, this represents 20 percent of the current amount of net earnings before this amount has been used in recalculating the net earnings. To recalculate the dependent formulas, use the Calc key (F9). Before doing this, however, let's split the screen view so that you can see what effect recalculation has on the bonuses and net earnings. Because the income statement uses too many rows to view these two amounts in the same screen view, divide the display into two smaller windows: in the top window, you'll see the other income section including the bonuses; in the bottom window, you'll see the last section of the income statement with the net earnings.

7. **Move the pointer up to cell B13, then select the Horizontal option from the /Worksheet Window menu (/WWH).**
   Now that you have two windows, you need to adjust the view of the worksheet in each one.

8. **Press the ↓ key six times to scroll up rows 13 through 18 in the top window.**
   You can now see the other income expenses in both windows (Figure 5.9). Next, you need to move the pointer to the bottom window and adjust its view of the worksheet. This requires the use of the Window key, which moves the pointer between windows open in the same worksheet.

9. **Press the Window key (F6), then press the PgDn key.**
   This scrolls up the last part of the income statement so that it is now in view. You are ready to use the Calc key to recalculate the dependent formulas.

10. **Press the Calc key (F9) until the bonus and net earnings figures in cells B16 and B23 no longer change when you press Calc.**
    After nine iterations, the values stop changing: the bonus amount remains constant at 827.4698 and net earnings at 4137 (Figure 5.10).

11. **Select the Clear option from the /Worksheet Window menu (/WWC).**
    Next, let's format the bonus amount the same way as the other values in the worksheet.

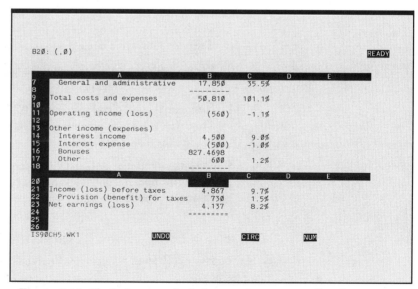

B18: (,Ø) \-   READY

	A	B	C	D	E
7	General and administrative	17,850	35.5%		
8		---------			
9	Total costs and expenses	50,810	101.1%		
10					
11	Operating income (loss)	(560)	-1.1%		
12					
13	Other income (expenses)				
14	Interest income	4,500	9.0%		
15	Interest expense	(500)	-1.0%		
16	Bonuses	686.8			
17	Other	600	1.2%		
18					

	A	B	C	D	E
13	Other income (expenses)				
14	Interest income	4,500	9.0%		
15	Interest expense	(500)	-1.0%		
16	Bonuses	686.8			
17	Other	600	1.2%		
18		---------			
19	Total other income (expenses)	4,600	9.2%		

IS9ØCH5.WK1   UNDO   CIRC   NUM

◆ **Figure 5.9:** *Creating horizontal windows to view different parts of the income statement*

B2Ø: (,Ø)   READY

	A	B	C	D	E
7	General and administrative	17,850	35.5%		
8		---------			
9	Total costs and expenses	50,810	101.1%		
10					
11	Operating income (loss)	(560)	-1.1%		
12					
13	Other income (expenses)				
14	Interest income	4,500	9.0%		
15	Interest expense	(500)	-1.0%		
16	Bonuses	827.4698			
17	Other	600	1.2%		
18		---------			

	A	B	C	D	E
20					
21	Income (loss) before taxes	4,867	9.7%		
22	Provision (benefit) for taxes	730	1.5%		
23	Net earnings (loss)	4,137	8.2%		
24		=========			
25					
26					

IS9ØCH5.WK1   UNDO   CIRC   NUM

◆ **Figure 5.10:** *The final amounts for the bonus and net earnings cells in the income statement*

12. **Move the pointer up to cell B16, select the Comma (,) option from the /Range Format menu, and set the decimal places to 0 (/RF,0) and press Enter; then press Enter again to format just the current cell.**

    Next, you need to add the percentage formula for the bonus amount in cell B16 to cell C16. To do this, you can copy the formula from the cell above it.

13. **Move the pointer to cell C16, then select the /Copy command (/C); press Esc to unanchor the range, move the pointer up to cell C15, then press Enter; finally, press Enter again to make the copy.**

    Because of the circular reference in this worksheet, you need to increase the number of iterations so that you can then change the input values in it and have the correct results calculated without having to press the Calc key nine times.

14. **Select the Iteration option from the /Worksheet Global Recalculation menu (/WGRI); then, type 9 and press Enter.**

    Let's see if this works.

15. **Move the pointer to cell B3 and change the amount of revenue to 55400.**

    The bonuses for this amount of revenues are 1,882 (Figure 5.11). See if this amount will change if you recalculate the dependent formulas.

16. **Press the Calc key (F9) a couple more times.**

    Notice that the bonus amount doesn't change.

17. **Reenter the original number, 50250, in cell B3.**

    This time, the bonus amount of 827 is returned without requiring you to press the Calc key.

18. **Save this version of the 1990 income statement under the same file name *IS90CH5.WK1* by typing /FS, then press Enter to accept the name, and type R to select the Replace option.**

Replacing Formulas with Their Current Values

As you know, 1-2-3 will recalculate the results of formulas whenever you edit or reenter new values in cells on which they are dependent. If you ever want to "freeze" an answer by converting it from a formula to its actual calculated value, you can do so by locating the pointer on its cell, pressing the Edit key, F2 (which returns the formula to the control panel), then pressing the Calc key, F9 (which converts the formula to its current value), and Enter.

```
B3: (,0) 55400                                                    READY

                         A                    B        C       D      E
3  Revenues                                55,400   100.0%
4  Costs and expenses
5      Product costs                       12,175    22.0%
6      Marketing and sales                 20,785    37.5%
7      General and administrative          17,850    32.2%
8                                          --------
9  Total costs and expenses                50,810    91.7%
10
11 Operating income (loss)                  4,590     8.3%
12
13 Other income (expenses)
14     Interest income                      4,500     8.1%
15     Interest expense                      (500)   -0.9%
16     Bonuses                              1,882     3.4%
17     Other                                  600     1.1%
18                                          --------
19 Total other income (expenses)            6,482    11.7%
20
21 Income (loss) before taxes              11,072    20.0%
22     Provision (benefit) for taxes        1,661     3.0%
IS90CH5.WK1                    UNDO              CIRC        NUM
```

♦ **Figure 5.11:** *The recalculated income statement after entering a new amount for the revenues*

If you want to convert a range of values, you should use the /Range Value command rather than this Edit-Calc method, which converts only one cell at a time. The /Range Value command works just like the /Copy command, except that all formulas in the copied range are automatically converted to their current values. To substitute values for formulas in the same range, use the /Range Value command and specify the same range address (or name) for the copy FROM and copy TO ranges.

Note that values use significantly less memory than formulas. Therefore, converting a large range of formulas to their calculated values can free up needed memory when you need to expand a particular worksheet file.

Working with Functions

The 1-2-3 @functions are built-in formulas that make it easy to perform specialized calculations. There are many different types of @functions: mathematical, statistical, date and time, financial, logical, string, database, and a miscellaneous group referred to as special. (Note that because the database @functions are used only with 1-2-3 database tables, these @functions are not covered until you learn about using database tables in Chapter 11.)

Each 1-2-3 @function has its own *syntax* (structure or pattern) that you must follow exactly. Most of the syntactical differences in @functions occur in the specific kind of arguments they require. Remember that arguments supply the @function with the information necessary for it to complete its calculations.

The @function arguments can be values, strings, or specific locations in the worksheet. These can be designated in the following ways:

+ Values can be specified by a literal number, numeric formula, or the cell address or range name of a range that contains such a number or formula.

+ Strings can be specified by literal strings (characters enclosed in a pair of quotation marks), a string formula, or the cell address or range name of a range that contains such a number or formula.

+ The location of cells or ranges in the worksheet can be specified by a cell address or a range name, or by a formula that returns such an address or range name.

Entering @Functions in the Worksheet

The first step in entering an @function in a cell is to type the @ symbol. After typing @, you type in the name of the function followed by the left parenthesis (assuming that the @function uses arguments). After entering the arguments required by the @function, be sure to remember to type the right parenthesis to complete the function before pressing the Enter key. Note that when typing in the function name, you can use uppercase or lowercase letters. Lotus 1-2-3, however, always converts the function name to all uppercase letters as soon as you complete the formula.

If you don't remember the arguments required by the @function you are using, you can get this information by pressing the Help key (F1). To get help on @functions in Release 2.2, you need to select the @Function Index topic from the Help Index screen. Then, move the pointer to the name of the @function you need help with and press Enter. Figure 5.12 shows you the online help obtained for the @SUM function by pressing the Help key, selecting the @Function Index topic from the Help Index screen, and then selecting @SUM from the second of these @function help screens.

If an @function requires more than one argument, as is the case for some of the more complex @functions, you can use either a comma or a semicolon to separate the individual arguments within the parentheses. Note, however, that if you change the default argument separator with the /Worksheet Global Default Other International Punctuation command, then only the new symbol you select will be accepted in the @functions you create from that time on.

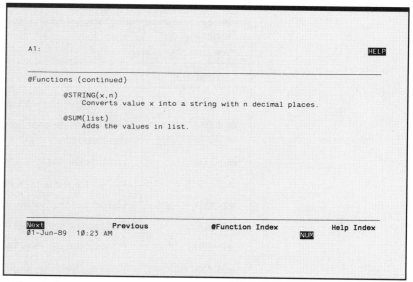

```
 A1:                                                                    HELP

 ──────────────────────────────────────────────────────────────────────────

 @Functions (continued)

        @STRING(x,n)
             Converts value x into a string with n decimal places.

        @SUM(list)
             Adds the values in list.




 ──────────────────────────────────────────────────────────────────────────

 Next               Previous              @Function Index          Help Index
 Ø1-Jun-89  1Ø:23 AM                                 NUM
```

♦ **Figure 5.12:** *Online help for the @SUM function*

The Mathematical @Functions

The first group of @functions that we will examine is the mathematical functions. Table 5.3 shows all the @functions in this group. Notice from the table that this group is composed of two subgroups: general and trigonometric @functions. Most of the arguments for the general mathematical @functions are simple values. These values can be entered as literal values, as in

   @ABS(– 49)

which will return the positive value 49, or by cell references, as in

   @ROUND(B2,3)

where cell B2 contains the literal value or a numeric formula that returns the value to be rounded, and 3 is the number of decimal places the value is to be rounded up or down.

Note the difference between the @ROUND and the @INT mathematical functions. The @ROUND function rounds the value up or down the number of decimal places, and the @INT function truncates the decimal part of the value, retaining only the integer portion. For example, if you have the value 1234.56 in cell B2 and you enter the formula

   @INT(B2)

◆ **Table 5.3:** *Mathematical @Functions*

Function & Arguments	Purpose
General	
@ABS(x)	Returns the absolute (positive) value of x.
@EXP(x)	Calculates the number e raised to the power of the value of x.
@INT(x)	Returns the integer portion of value x.
@LN(x)	Calculates the natural logarithm (base e) of value x.
@LOG(x)	Calculates the common logarithm of the value x.
@MOD(x,y)	Returns the remainder (modulus) of x divided by y.
@RAND	Returns a random number between 0 and 1.
@ROUND(x,n)	Rounds the value x to n decimal places.
@SQRT(x)	Calculates the positive square root of value x.
Trigonometric	
@ACOS(x)	Calculates the arccosine of value x (in radians).
@ASIN(x)	Calculates the arcsine of value x (in radians).
@ATAN(x)	Calculates the arctangent of value x (in radians).
@ATAN2(x,y)	Calculates the four-quadrant arctangent based on the values of coordinate x and coordinate y (in radians).
@COS(x)	Calculates the cosine of angle x (in radians).
@PI	Returns the value of the constant π.
@SIN(x)	Calculates the sine of angle x (in radians).
@TAN(x)	Calculates the tangent of angle x (in radians).

1-2-3 will return *1234* in the cell. However, if you enter the formula

@ROUND(B2,0)

the program will return *1235*. This is because the @INT function drops the decimal portion .56 and retains the 1234, whereas the @ROUND function specifying zero decimal places rounds the value up to 1235 (the decimal portion .56 is greater than .5). Figure 5.13 illustrates the effect that using @ROUND with various numbers of decimal places has on a single value.

The trigonometric @functions calculate values commonly required in trigonometry. When you use the @COS, @SIN, or @TAN function to find the cosine, sine, or tangent of an angle, you must express the angle in radians instead of degrees. If you have an angle measured in degrees, you can convert it to radians by multiplying the number of degrees by @PI/180. For example, to find the sine of a 50° angle, enter

@SIN(50*@PI/180)

Likewise, when you use any of the arc trigonometric @functions, such as @ACOS or @ASIN, 1-2-3 returns the value of the angle in radians. To convert the radians to the corresponding number of degrees, multiply the number of radians by 180/@PI:

@ACOS(0.12)*180/@PI

The Statistical @Functions

The second group of @functions that we are going to look at is the statistical functions. Table 5.4 shows you the @functions in this group. Notice that all of

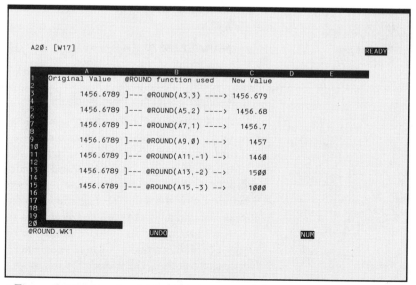

♦ **Figure 5.13:** *Using the @ROUND function to control the precision of a single value*

Rounding versus Formatting Values in the Worksheet: Remember that formatting a value with one of the /Range Format options (covered in Chapter 4) only changes the display of the value in the worksheet and not its precision in the cell. To control the precision of a calculated value, you need to use the @ROUND function. Often, you can just add the @ROUND function to the function or formula that performs the calculation. For example, if you want the square root of a value in cell C5 rounded to two decimal places, you can enter the formula

@ROUND(@SQRT(C5),2)

Notice that in this case, the entire @function @SQRT(C5) is used as the first argument of the @ROUND function.

---

these functions use the same type of argument—that is, a list of values. This *list* argument can consist of literal values, as in

@AVG(24.5,34,26)

or a list of cell addresses, as in

@AVG(A3,D4,F12)

Often, the best way to specify the *list* of values used by a statistical @function is by indicating a range of cells (entered either by its range address or range name), as in

@SUM(B2..B67)

The statistical functions will even accept multiple ranges for the list argument:

@COUNT(C5..C25;D5..D12;E5..E10)

(Note that you can use semicolons or commas to separate arguments or to separate multiple ranges in a single argument.)

If the *list* that you specify for the argument of a statistical function contains labels, these are assigned the value 0 and included in the calculation. The only exception to this is the @COUNT function, where labels aren't given the value 0 but are counted anyway because they are *nonblank* cells. Because the presence of labels in a list can skew the results of a statistical @function, you need to be sure that any ranges included in the list argument are free of labels.

Figure 5.14 illustrates what can happen when a label is included in a range. Notice that the blank cell included in the range A2..A6 that is used as the argument for the @AVG and @COUNT functions in cells A10 and A11 has no adverse effect on the results. Compare these results with those obtained when

♦ **Table 5.4:** *Statistical @Functions*

Function & Arguments	Purpose
@AVG(*list*)	Calculates the average value in the *list*.
@COUNT(*list*)	Returns the number of nonblank cells in the *list*.
@MAX(*list*)	Returns the maximum value in the *list*.
@MIN(*list*)	Returns the minimum value in the *list*.
@STD(*list*)	Calculates the population standard deviation of a *list* of values.
@SUM(*list*)	Sums the values in the *list*.
@VAR(*list*)	Calculates the population variance of a *list* of values.

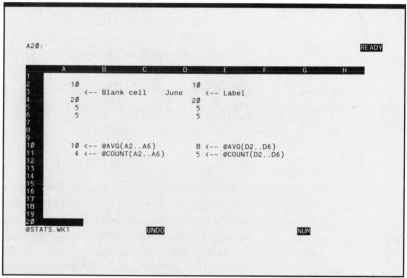

♦ **Figure 5.14:** *Statistical @functions with a blank and label in the list* arguments

the range D2..D6 is used in the @AVG and @COUNT functions in cells D10 and D11. This cell range is identical to the range A2..A6, except that it contains a label in cell D3 where cell A3 is empty. Because this label is counted in the second range, the average and count aren't correct.

Note that all the statistical functions have corresponding database functions that are used to obtain statistics about data stored in a 1-2-3 database table (see Chapter 11).

The Date and Time @Functions

As you already know, dates and times are specified by date and time numbers that make it possible to perform various arithmetic calculations with them. To facilitate date and time calculations, 1-2-3 includes a variety of date and time functions, which are listed in Table 5.5.

The @DATE function and the @TIME function provide alternate ways to convert a specific date or time into a 1-2-3 date or time number. You can enter the date number for March 4, 1990 (32936) in a cell by entering @DATE(90,3,4). Also, you could enter the command @DATEVALUE("3/4/90") or @DATEVALUE("4-mar-90") to obtain the same result.

Likewise, you can enter the correct time value for 11:05 in the morning by entering @TIME(11,5,0). Note that the @TIMEVALUE function enables you to convert labels that follow one of the time formats into actual time numbers.

After entering the correct date and time numbers in the worksheet, you then select the desired Date option from the /Range Format menu to convert the date and time numbers into an intelligible form. When you use the @NOW function, 1-2-3 returns both the date and time numbers for the current date and time. If you want to display this value as a time, format it with one of the Time formats. If you want to display this value as a date, select one of the Date formats.

The Financial @Functions

The next group of @functions is the financial functions, and the formulas they incorporate are decidedly more complex and sophisticated. As you can see in Table 5.6, the financial @functions can be subdivided into three categories: annuities, single-sum compounding, and depreciation.

The @FV, @IRR, @NPV, @PMT, @PV, and @TERM functions all analyze investments that consist of a series of cash flows (be they outflows, such as payments, or inflows, such as interest income). Such investments are known as *annuities* because all the cash flows are equal payments made at regular intervals. All the 1-2-3 financial @functions assume that the annuities are ordinary annuities, wherein the payments are made at the end of each time interval. If you are dealing with a type of investment where this is not the case, such as an annuity due, you must adjust the *term* argument accordingly.

♦ **Table 5.5**: *Date and Time @Functions*

Function & Arguments	Purpose
Date	
@DATE(*year,month,day*)	Returns the date number based on the date, as indicated by the *year*, *month*, and *day*.
@DATEVALUE(*string*)	Returns the equivalent date number for a *string* that follows one of the 1-2-3 date formats.
@DAY(*date-number*)	Returns the number for the day of the month in a *date-number*.
@MONTH(*date-number*)	Returns the number of the month in a *date-number*.
@TODAY	Returns the date number of the current date.
@YEAR(*date-number*)	Returns the value of the year in a *date-number*.
Time	
@HOUR(*time-number*)	Returns the number of hours in a *time-number*.
@MINUTE(*time-number*)	Returns the number of minutes in a *time-number*.
@SECOND(*time-number*)	Returns the number of seconds in a *time-number*.
@TIME(*hour,minutes,seconds*)	Returns the time number based on the time as indicated by the *hour*, *minutes*, and *seconds*.
@TIMEVALUE(*string*)	Returns the equivalent time number for a *string* that follows one of the 1-2-3 time formats.
Date and Time	
@NOW	Returns the number of the current date and time.

♦ **Table 5.6:** *Financial @Functions*

Function & Arguments	Purpose
Annuities	
@FV(*payments,interest,term*)	Calculates the future value of an investment based upon a series of equal *payments*, earning a periodic *interest* rate over the number of periods in the *term*.
@IRR(*guess,range*)	Calculates the internal rate of return expected from a series of cash flows listed in the *range*, using a *guess* value that represents an estimate of the rate of return.
@NPV(*interest,range*)	Calculates the net present value of a series of future cash flows listed in the *range* discounted at a fixed, periodic *interest* rate.
@PMT(*principal,interest,term*)	Calculates the amount of a periodic payment required to pay off a loan based upon the *principal*, *interest* rate, and the number of payment periods in the *term*.
@PV(*payments,interest,term*)	Calculates the present value of an investment based upon a series of equal *payments*, discounted at a periodic *interest* rate over the number of periods in the *term*.
@TERM(*payments,interest,future-value*)	Calculates the number of payment periods in the term of an investment required to accumulate a *future-value*, assuming equal *payments* and that the investment earns a periodic *interest* rate.
Single-Sum Compounding	
@CTERM(*interest,future-value,present-value*)	Calculates the number of compounding periods required for investment at *present-value* to grow to *future-value* given a fixed *interest* rate per compounding period.
@RATE(*future-value,present-value,term*)	Calculates the periodic interest rate necessary for an investment at *present-value* to grow to *future-value* over the number of compounding periods in the *term*.

♦ **Table 5.6:** *Financial @Functions (continued)*

Function & Arguments	Purpose
Depreciation	
@DDB(*cost,salvage,life,period*)	Calculates the depreciation allowance of an asset for a specified *period* using the double-declining-balance method where *cost* is the amount paid for the asset, *salvage* is the estimated value of the asset at the end of its useful life, and *life* is the number of periods required for the asset to reach salvage value.
@SLN(*cost,salvage,life*)	Calculates the depreciation allowance of an asset for a single period using the straight-line method where *cost* is the amount paid for the asset, *salvage* is the estimated value of the asset at the end of its useful life, and *life* is the number of periods required for the asset to reach salvage value.
@SYD(*cost,salvage,life,period*)	Calculates the depreciation allowance of an asset for a specified *period* using the sum-of-the-years'-digits method where *cost* is the amount paid for the asset, *salvage* is the estimated value of the asset at the end of its useful life, and *life* is the number of periods required for the asset to reach salvage value.

Many of the annuity financial @functions require both an *interest* and *term* argument. When entering these, remember that they must both be expressed in the same time units. If you enter a monthly interest rate for the *interest* argument and the number of periods in the *term* argument in years, the financial @function that you're using won't give you the correct answer.

The second group of financial @functions includes only two functions, @CTERM and @RATE. Unlike the annuities group, involving a series of cash flows, both the @CTERM and the @RATE functions involve just a single cash flow. The @CTERM function calculates the number of periods required for a single-sum investment to compound to a specific future value, assuming a constant rate of interest. The @RATE function calculates the periodic rate of interest required to compound a single-sum investment to a target future value, assuming a fixed number of periods.

The last group of financial @functions calculates depreciation allowances for assets put in use, using various standard methods: the @SLN function calculates depreciation by the straight-line method, the @SYD function calculates depreciation by the sum-of-the-years'-digits method, and the @DDB function calculates depreciation by the double-declining-balance method.

Creating a Loan Payment Table with the @PMT Function

The following exercise gives you practical experience copying a formula that uses absolute references and two types of mixed references, as well as exposing you to the use of the @PMT function. In it, you create a table that gives mortgage payments for a series of different loan amounts at various interest rates.

1. **Begin a new worksheet file by clearing any worksheet currently in memory (/WEY).**
   Use Figure 5.15 as a guide in adding the labels and data-input cells in C3, C4, and C5.

2. **Enter the worksheet title *Loan Payment Schedule* in A1, and the labels *Principal, Interest Rate,* and *Term (in years)* in cells A3, A4, and A5, respectively.**
   Next, you will enter an initial loan amount in cell C3 and format it with the Currency option.

3. **Enter *100000* in cell C3 and format it as Currency with 0 decimal places (/RFC0).**
   In the cell below, enter an initial interest rate of 6.5 percent and format this with the Percent option.

4. **Enter *6.5%* in cell C4 and format it to Percent with one decimal place (/RFP1).**
   In the last cell input cell, you will enter the initial term of 30.

5. **Enter *30* in cell C5.**
   Next, you will create the row of increasing interest rates for the loan table.

6. **Move the pointer to cell B7, type + to start the formula, then move the pointer to cell C4 (which contains the initial interest rate) and press Enter.**
   Cell B7 now contains the value *0.065*, which is *brought forward* from cell B4. Instead of directly entering the initial interest rate value in cell B7, we create this simple formula to bring its value forward to the new cell. That way, if you change the initial value in cell C4, it will automatically change in cell B7 where it was brought forward.

Notice, however, that the format was not copied when you created this formula.

7. **Format the interest rate value in cell B7 and the blank cell to its right as Percent with two decimal places by typing /RFP; press Enter to accept 2 and the → key to extend the range to B7..C7, and press Enter.**
Now you are ready to create a formula in the cell one column to the right that adds a quarter of a percentage point to the initial interest rate value that is brought forward to cell B7.

8. **Move the pointer to cell C7 and type + to start a formula; press ← to select cell B7; then type +.25% and press Enter.**
Cell C7 should now contain 6.75%. All you need to do now is copy this formula to the range D7..G7.

9. **Type /C to start the copy, then press Enter to accept C7..C7 as the range to copy FROM; move the pointer right one cell to D7, type . (period) to anchor the range, then press the → key until you have highlighted the range D7..G7 as the range to copy TO; and press Enter to make the copies.**
Good! Now, you are ready to bring the initial loan amount in cell C3 forward to cell A8.

10. **Move the pointer to cell A8, type + to start a formula, move the pointer to cell C3, and press Enter.**
Just as before, you must format the value brought forward.

11. **Format the value in cell A8 and the blank cell below to Comma (,) with 0 decimal places (/RF,0).**
Now you will set up a formula that increases the initial loan amount brought forward from the input cell C3 by $500.00.

12. **Move the pointer to cell A9, type + to start a formula, press ↑ to highlight cell A8, type +500, then press Enter.**
This time, you will copy this formula down column A to the range A9..A17.

13. **Type /C to start the copy, then press Enter to accept the range A9..A9 as the range to copy FROM; next, press the ↓ key to move the pointer to cell A10, type . (period) to anchor, and press the ↓ key until the range A10..A17 is highlighted as the range to copy TO; press Enter to make the copies.**
You're almost finished! All that remains is to create the @PMT formula that calculates the payment based on the interest rate at the top

of each column of the table for the loan amount at the beginning of
each row of the table, using the term listed in the input cell C5.
After you build this formula, you will format the results and then
copy this single formula to all the other cells in the table.

14. **Move the pointer to cell B8 and type @PMT(.**
    The @PMT function requires you first to enter the principal. In this
    formula, this is cell A8 immediately to the left. When this formula is
    copied to the other cells in the table, you need the column letter (A)
    to remain constant while varying the row number. To do this, let's
    use a mixed address, where the column is absolute and the row num-
    ber is relative.

15. **Move the pointer left to cell A8, press the Abs key (F4)**
    three times until the address reads $A8, then type ,
    (comma).
    The next argument for the @PMT function is the interest rate. This is
    found in cell B7. When copying the formula to the rest of the table,
    the column (B) must be adjusted while the row number (7) remains
    constant. To accomplish this, use a mixed address where the column
    is relative and the row is absolute. The interest rates in row 7 are
    annual interest rates. In this table, you want to calculate the monthly
    payments. Thus, be sure to convert the annual rate to
    a monthly rate by dividing it by 12.

16. **Move the pointer up to cell B7, press the Abs key (F4) twice**
    until the address reads B$7, then type /12, (comma).
    The last argument for this @function is the term. This value is not
    brought forward to the table: it is found in the input cell C5. Because
    this number is used in all copies in the table, its column and row
    reference must be absolute. Also, this term is the number of years for
    the mortgage. To calculate the monthly payment, you must express
    the term as the number of monthly periods by multiplying it by 12.

17. **Move the pointer to cell C5, press the Abs key (F4) once**
    until the address reads $C$5, then type * 12) and press
    Enter.
    You can check your answer and formula with the one in Figure 5.15.
    Next, you need to format the display before you copy this formula.

18. **Format the value in cell B8 to Comma (,) with 2 decimal places (/RF,2).**

    Now you're ready to copy this formula throughout the table.

19. **Type /C to start the copy, then press Enter to accept B8..B8 as the range to copy FROM; type . (period) to anchor (without moving the pointer), press the ↓ key until you reach cell B17, and then press the → key until you reach cell G17 to make B8..G17 the range to copy TO; finally, press Enter to make the copies.**

    Your payment schedule should now match the one shown in Figure 5.16. To see what the payments would be using a different set of interest rates or principals or even using a different term, you have only to change the values in the three input cells C3, C4, and C5. Because only these need to be changed, only they should be unprotected.

20. **Turn on global protection (/WGPE), then move the pointer to cell C3 and unprotect (/RU) the range C3..C5.**

    The last step is to save this worksheet.

21. **Save the worksheet in a file called (/FS) LOANPMT.WK1.**

    You can now experiment with the payment table by entering various new starting principals and interest rates as well as different terms.

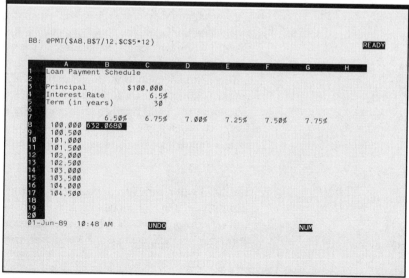

◆ **Figure 5.15:** *The completed @PMT function in cell B8*

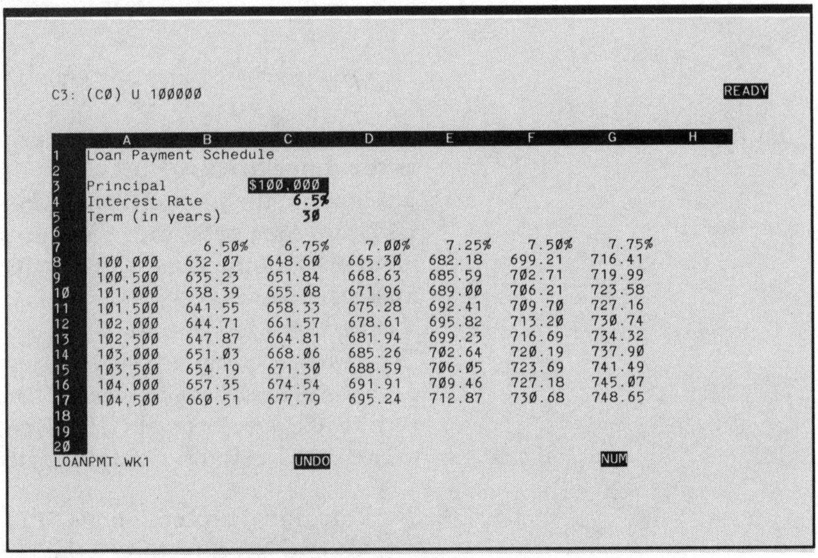

C3: (C0) U 100000 READY

	A	B	C	D	E	F	G	H
1	Loan Payment Schedule							
2								
3	Principal		$100,000					
4	Interest Rate		6.5%					
5	Term (in years)		30					
6								
7		6.50%	6.75%	7.00%	7.25%	7.50%	7.75%	
8	100,000	632.07	648.60	665.30	682.18	699.21	716.41	
9	100,500	635.23	651.84	668.63	685.59	702.71	719.99	
10	101,000	638.39	655.08	671.96	689.00	706.21	723.58	
11	101,500	641.55	658.33	675.28	692.41	709.70	727.16	
12	102,000	644.71	661.57	678.61	695.82	713.20	730.74	
13	102,500	647.87	664.81	681.94	699.23	716.69	734.32	
14	103,000	651.03	668.06	685.26	702.64	720.19	737.90	
15	103,500	654.19	671.30	688.59	706.05	723.69	741.49	
16	104,000	657.35	674.54	691.91	709.46	727.18	745.07	
17	104,500	660.51	677.79	695.24	712.87	730.68	748.65	
18								
19								
20								

LOANPMT.WK1 UNDO NUM

♦ **Figure 5.16:** *Completed loan payment schedule*

The String @Functions

The string @functions are shown in Table 5.7. A *string* is any cell entry that has been entered as a label or text enclosed in a pair of quotation marks (called a "literal string"). If a cell just contains a label prefix and no text, it is called an *empty string* and will return the value 0 when used as an argument for one of the string @functions. If you specify a value instead of a string as an argument, the @function will return ERR (except in the case of @N and @S, which evaluate whether the argument is a number or a string).

The first two @functions listed in Table 5.7 work with the Lotus International Character Set (LICS—the entire character set is in Appendix E). To determine the code number for a particular character, you use the @CODE function. For example, if you want to know the LICS code for the letter *t* (lowercase; a different code is assigned to the uppercase *T*), enter

@CODE("t")

and 1-2-3 will return *116*. If you enter a cell reference as the argument of the @CODE function and its label is longer than a single character, the program will return the LICS code for just the first character of the label. Thus, if you enter the label *tax rate* in cell B3 and then enter the formula

@CODE(B3)

1-2-3 will return *116*, the LICS code for lowercase *t*.

◆ **Table 5.7**: *String @Functions*

Function & Arguments	Purpose
@CHAR(*x*)	Returns the LICS character whose code corresponds to value *x*.
@CLEAN(*string*)	Removes certain control characters from the string. This @function is often used when importing Symphony files into 1-2-3.
@CODE(*string*)	Returns the LICS code number corresponding to the first character in the *string*.
@EXACT(*string1,string2*)	Returns the logical value 1 (true) if *string1* and *string2* match exactly; otherwise, returns the logical value 0.
@FIND(*search-string, string,start-number*)	Returns the number of the position of the *search-string* in *string* from the position indicated by the *start-number*; returns ERR if *search-string* is not found in *string*.
@LEFT(*string,n*)	Returns the first *n* characters in *string*.
@LENGTH(*string*)	Returns the number of characters in *string*.
@LOWER(*string*)	Converts all letters in *string* to lowercase.
@MID(*string,start-number,n*)	Returns *n* characters from *string* beginning at the position indicated by the *start-number*.
@N(*range*)	If the first cell in the *range* is a value, function returns that value; otherwise, returns the value 0.
@PROPER(*string*)	Converts the first letter of each word in *string* to uppercase, leaving the other letters in lowercase, thereby producing accurate capitalization.

* **Table 5.7:** *String @Functions (continued)*

Function & Arguments	Purpose
@REPEAT(*string,n*)	Reproduces the *string n* times.
@REPLACE(*original-string, start-number,n,new string*)	Replaces *n* characters in the *original-string* with characters in the *new-string*, beginning at the *start-number*.
@RIGHT(*string,n*)	Returns the last *n* characters in the *string*.
@S(*range*)	If the first cell in the *range* is a label, function returns that label; otherwise, returns a blank cell.
@TRIM(*string*)	Removes all extraneous blanks (leading, trailing, and consecutive) from the *string*.
@UPPER(*string*)	Converts all letters in the *string* to uppercase.
@VALUE(*string*)	Returns the corresponding value for a number entered as *string*; returns 0 if the *string* is a blank cell or contains an empty string, and ERR if the *string* contains nonnumeric characters.

If you need to have the program return the character for a particular LICS code, use the @CHAR function. This @function works only with values between 0 and 255 (as there are only 256 characters in the set). If you look over the character set in Appendix E, notice several characters in this set can't be displayed on the screen. If you use the code for such a character, it won't be visible in the screen display.

Several string @functions use a *start-number* argument, which represents an offset number of a character in the string counted from 0 rather than 1. For example, let's say you enter the @MID function

@MID(A3,6,5)

where cell A3 contains the string *Allan Grill*. The @function will return the string *Grill* because the *start-number* argument, 6, is counted from 0, and G is the seventh character. Note the *n* argument, which indicates how many characters to copy from the string, is counted from 1; thus, the first five characters are *G-r-i-l-l*.

Frequently, string @functions are combined to locate and return specific text from a label. For example, if you wish to copy only the first names from a range of cells that contain both the first and last names, you can do so by combining the @MID and @FIND functions. If you wanted to just copy *Allan* from cell A3, containing the full name *Allan Grill*, you would specify A3 as the *string* argument, 0 as the *start-number* argument, and then use the @FIND function to calculate the correct number of characters to return for the *n* argument of an @MID function. In doing this, you use the @FIND function to locate the first space in the string, which indicates where the first name stops, by entering @FIND(" ",A3,0). If you entered just this @FIND function, 1-2-3 would return the value 5 because the first space is in the fifth place when counting from 0 (*A-l-l-a-n-space*). So if you enter the complete formula

@MID(A3,0,@FIND(" ",A3,0))

it is the same as entering @MID(A3,0,5) and returns just *Allan* from the string *Allan Grill*.

Figure 5.17 shows you how this type of formula is put to use to copy just the first name from the cells in column A to column B. In addition, another @MID function is used to copy only the last name into column C. This formula is a bit more complex: in cell C3, it reads

@MID(A3,@FIND(" ",A3,0) + 1,@LENGTH(A3) – @FIND(" ",A3,0))

It uses the @FIND function plus one to compute the *start-number* argument for the @MID function, and then uses @LENGTH minus the @FIND function to determine the number of characters, *n*, to copy.

The Logical @Functions

The next group of 1-2-3 @functions is the logical functions, shown in Table 5.8. This is an interesting group whose primary purpose is to provide decision-making capabilities to formulas in your worksheets. As such, the most important @function in the logical group is @IF, a function that evaluates a condition and performs one set of commands if the condition is true and another set if the condition is false.

The logical functions, like all logical formulas, perform conditional tests that return the logical value *1* if the condition is true and the logical value *0* if the condition is false. For example, if cell B4 currently contains the number 25

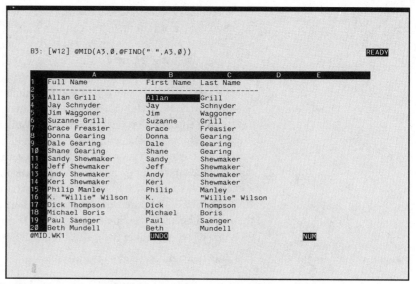

B3: [W12] @MID(A3,Ø,@FIND(" ",A3,Ø))   READY

	A	B	C	D	E
1	Full Name	First Name	Last Name		
2	---				
3	Allan Grill	Allan	Grill		
4	Jay Schnyder	Jay	Schnyder		
5	Jim Waggoner	Jim	Waggoner		
6	Suzanne Grill	Suzanne	Grill		
7	Grace Freasier	Grace	Freasier		
8	Donna Gearing	Donna	Gearing		
9	Dale Gearing	Dale	Gearing		
10	Shane Gearing	Shane	Gearing		
11	Sandy Shewmaker	Sandy	Shewmaker		
12	Jeff Shewmaker	Jeff	Shewmaker		
13	Andy Shewmaker	Andy	Shewmaker		
14	Keri Shewmaker	Keri	Shewmaker		
15	Philip Manley	Philip	Manley		
16	K. "Willie" Wilson	K.	"Willie" Wilson		
17	Dick Thompson	Dick	Thompson		
18	Michael Boris	Michael	Boris		
19	Paul Saenger	Paul	Saenger		
20	Beth Mundell	Beth	Mundell		

@MID.WK1   UNDO   NUM

◆ **Figure 5.17:** *Using the @MID function to parse full name into first and last name entries*

◆ **Table 5.8:** *Logical @Functions*

Function & Arguments	Purpose
@FALSE	Returns the logical value 0 (false).
@IF(*condition*,*x*,*y*)	If *condition* is true, returns *x*, otherwise returns *y*.
@ISAAF(*name*)	Returns the logical value 1 (true) if the *name* is a defined add-in @function, otherwise returns the logical value 0 (false). *Release 2.2 only*.
@ISAPP(*name*)	Returns the logical value 1 (true) if the *name* is an attached add-in program, otherwise returns the logical value 0 (false). *Release 2.2 only*.
@ISERR(*x*)	Returns the logical value 1 (true) if value *x* is ERR, otherwise returns the logical value 0 (false).

◆ **Table 5.8:** *Logical @Functions (continued)*

Function & Arguments	Purpose
@ISNA(*x*)	Returns the logical value 1 (true) if value *x* is NA, otherwise returns the logical value 0 (false).
@ISNUMBER(*x*)	Returns the logical value 1 (true) if *x* is a value or blank cell, otherwise returns the logical value 0 (false).
@ISSTRING(*x*)	Returns the logical value 1 (true) if *x* is a string, otherwise returns the logical value 0 (false).
@TRUE	Returns the logical value 1 (true).

and you enter the formula

> **@ISNUMBER(B4)**

in cell C4, 1-2-3 will put *1* in this cell, indicating that the condition is true (because the contents of cell B4 is indeed a number). So too, if you edit the formula in cell C4 so that instead of using the @ISNUMBER function, it now uses the @ISSTRING function, as in

> **@ISSTRING(B4)**

the contents of cell C4 will change to *0*, indicating the condition is now false (because the contents of B4 is not a string—it's a number).

The logical functions @ISERR and @ISNA perform conditional tests to see if a value is ERR or NA, respectively. Note that ERR and NA aren't labels but special values that can be entered into a cell. As you have seen, the ERR value is entered when a 1-2-3 formula is unable to perform its intended calculations. You can also enter the ERR value in a cell by using the special @ERR function. To enter the value NA (to indicate that a value is not available), you must use the special @NA function.

The @TRUE and @FALSE logical functions are the only ones that don't require an argument and don't perform a conditional test. Indeed, if you enter @TRUE in a cell, 1-2-3 displays the logical value *1* for true in the cell, and if you enter @FALSE, it displays the logical value *0* for false. These two logical functions are often used in the *condition* argument of @IF functions.

✱ *New in 2.2*   The @ISAAF and @ISAPP functions are new in Release 2.2. They are used to determine whether specific add-in @functions or add-in programs are available for use. The @ISAAF function evaluates a string and indicates whether it corresponds to a defined add-in @function. The @ISAPP function evaluates a string and indicates whether it corresponds to an attached add-in program. Both new @functions require the *name* of the add-in (@function for @ISAAF and program for @ISAPP) as the single argument. When entering the *name* argument, you can use a literal string (enclosed in quotation marks), a cell reference, or a formula that returns a string. For example, to find out if the Allways add-in program is currently attached and ready for use, you enter the @ISAPP function as

@ISAPP("Allways")

If Allways is attached, the cell containing this @function will return 1. If it hasn't been attached, it will return 0. Note that you must capitalize *Allways* in the @ISAPP argument to obtain the correct result: *@ISAPP("allways")* won't return 1 even if Allways is attached and ready for use.

Setting Up IF Conditions

The @IF function is one of the most versatile functions in 1-2-3. You can find multiple uses for this @function in any worksheet where the action should be dependent upon the outcome of a conditional test: branching one way if the outcome is true and another if the outcome is false.

For example, assume that the commission rate paid to your sales staff is based on the amount of their monthly sales: sales $25,000 and less earn 5 percent, and sales above $25,000 earn a 7 percent commission. To have 1-2-3 find the amount of the commissions, you can use the @IF function as illustrated in Figure 5.18. Here, John's commission rate in cell C3 is calculated by the formula

@IF(B3>25000,0.07,0.05)

where B3>25000 is the *condition* argument, 0.07 is the *x* argument, and 0.05 is the *y* argument. Although this @IF function just returns one rate or another in cell C3, you could also have it calculate the commissions using the appropriate rate, as in

@IF(B3>25000,0.07*B3,0.05*B3)

The @IF function is also used in the table in Figure 5.18 to return the monthly quota amount in column E and indicate in column F whether each salesperson has met the quota. The first formula for John in cell E3 is

@IF(A3="John"#OR#A3="Alice",26500,18500)

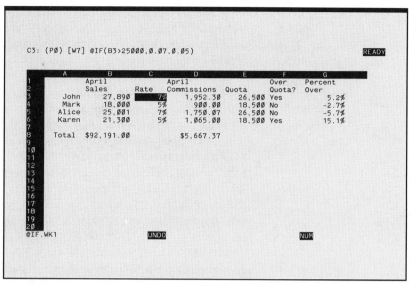

* **Figure 5.18:** *Using the @IF function to perform branching*

Here, 1-2-3 evaluates the string in cell A3 and if it matches *John* or *Alice*, it returns the rate 26,500; otherwise, it returns 18,500 (the quotas for Mark and Karen). Notice that in this *condition* argument where the logical #OR# is used, the cell reference A3 is repeated after #OR#; you must also do this when using the logical #AND# to set up compound conditions.

The formulas in column F use strings as the *x* and *y* arguments of the @IF function. The formula in cell F3 is

   @IF(B3>E3,"Yes","No")

Note that when you want the @IF function to evaluate literal strings, they must be enclosed in quotation marks.

Error Trapping with the Logical Functions

The @IF function is also especially useful in error trapping. When the ERR or NA value is entered into a cell that is referenced in a formula, that formula then returns ERR or NA. If the result calculated by that formula is used, in turn, by another formula in the worksheet, that second formula returns ERR or NA as well. This effect "ripples through" (as the 1-2-3 documentation puts it) the entire worksheet file.

Note that although the NA value is most often entered in a cell with the @NA function, the ERR value is entered by the program anytime a cell contains a formula it can't evaluate. One of the most common of these situations is when a formula calls for division by a cell and that cell contains a value of 0. Because division by 0 is an undefined operation, the program will always return ERR when this is the case.

To stop any ERR or NA value from spreading to dependent formulas, you can use the @IF function with the @ISERR and/or @ISNA function. To trap the error and prevent its spread, the @IF function returns 0 if a cell used in its calculation contains ERR or NA; only if this is not the case is the original formula calculated.

Figures 5.19 and 5.20 illustrate how this works. In Figure 5.19, an ERR value has been intentionally introduced into cell B4 with the @ERR function. Notice how this single ERR value causes ERR to ripple through other parts of the worksheet. It affects the total and average figures for the sales and commissions, the formula that calculates the sales after commissions, as well as the formulas that calculate the rate, commissions, over quota, and percentage over quota.

In Figure 5.20, the spread of the ERR values in cells B8 and D8 to cells D13 and D14, respectively, has been stopped by @IF formulas. As you can see, the formula in cell D13 is now

@IF(@ISERR(B8)#OR#@ISNA(B8),0,B8)

Because B8 contains ERR, the formula returns 0. A similar @IF function has been entered in D14 (except that it refers to cell D8, which is brought forward). Because the ERR value is stopped in cells B8 and D8, the formula in cell D16, which calculates the sales minus the commissions, no longer returns ERR.

Similarly, you could use the @IF function with @ISERR and @ISNA to stop the spread of either value to the cells with dependent formulas in row 4. Be aware that error trapping in this manner doesn't assure you of the right answers in the worksheet. Substituting zeros for the ERR or NA values in a worksheet doesn't make the numbers returned by those formulas correct; they only prevent their proliferation throughout the worksheet.

Error trapping does, however, confer definite benefits when it comes time to deal with the ERR or NA values in the worksheet. Because you have checked their spread, you can locate and fix them much more quickly. When you don't error-trap, you often spend a lot of time checking "decoy" ERR and NA values, which are themselves the result of the "real" errors or unavailable values elsewhere in the worksheet. When you successfully prohibit their spread, you know exactly where to look for ERRs and NAs that must be changed in order to have the worksheet return correct answers.

If are using Release 2.2. and the ERR or NA values were entered with the @ERR or @NA functions, you can use its new /Range Search feature to locate

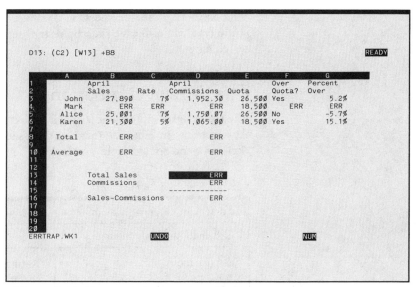

♦ **Figure 5.19:** *The spread of ERR via the ripple effect*

♦ **Figure 5.20:** *Error-trapping in the worksheet*

their position in the worksheet. To do this, enter *@ERR* or *@NA* as the search string (you can also save time by restricting the search to formulas in the search range).

The Special @Functions

The last group of @functions is known collectively as the special @functions. As you can see in Table 5.9, there are three subgroups: cell and range information, error and not available, and lookup.

♦ **Table 5.9:** *Special @Functions*

Function & Arguments	Purpose
Cell and Range Information	
@@(*location*)	Returns the contents of the cell specified by *location*.
@CELL(*attribute,location*)	Returns information about the *attribute* for the first cell in the *location*.
@CELLPOINTER(*attribute*)	Returns information about the *attribute* of the current cell.
@COLS(*range*)	Calculates the number of columns in the *range*.
@ROWS(*range*)	Calculates the number of rows in the *range*.
Error and Not Available	
@ERR	Returns the value ERR (error).
@NA	Returns the value NA (not available).
Lookup	
@CHOOSE(*offset,list*)	Returns the value whose position in *list* corresponds to *offset*.
@HLOOKUP(*x,range,row-offset*)	Returns the value whose position in the range corresponds to the column located by matching

◆ **Table 5.9:** *Special @Functions (continued)*

Function & Arguments	Purpose
	x with a value (equal to or not greater than x) in the first row of the *range* and the row specified by *row-offset*.
@INDEX(*range,column-offset, row-offset*)	Returns the value from the *range* that matches the *column-offset* and *row-offset*.
@VLOOKUP(*x,range, column-offset*)	Returns the value whose position in the range corresponds to the row located by matching x with a value (equal to or not greater than x) in the first column of the *range* and the column specified by *column-offset*.

The @functions in the first subgroup return information about a particular cell or range. These @functions are often used in macros to supply or verify information needed to successfully complete the procedure. In the case of the @@ function, the information is the actual contents of the cell; in the case of the @COLS and @ROWS functions, the information is the number of columns or rows in the worksheet, respectively. In the case of the @CELL and @CELLPOINTER functions, the information is about a particular *attribute* that is specified by name. Table 5.10 shows the attributes used in the @CELL and the @CELLPOINTER functions. Remember that when you enter literal strings as *attribute* arguments for any of these three functions, you must enclose them in quotation marks, as in @CELL(*"format"*,A5).

Using the Lookup @Functions

The last subgroup of the special @functions contains the lookup functions. Note in Table 5.9 that all four lookup @functions use an *offset* argument. Just as with the *start-number* arguments in the string @functions, the *offset* arguments are counted from 0 rather than 1. Therefore, in the @CHOOSE function

@CHOOSE(B2,"Qtr 1","Qtr 2","Qtr 3","Qtr 4")

◆ **Table 5.10:** *Attributes for the @CELL and @CELLPOINTER Functions*

Attribute	Returns
address	The absolute cell address.
col	The column, as a value from 1 to 256 with 1 for A, 2 for B, and so on.
contents	The cell contents.
filename	The name of the current file incuding the path.
format	The cell format, using these abbreviations: C0 through C15 for Currency with 0 to 15 decimal places F0 through F15 for Fixed with 0 to 15 decimal places G for General format (or label or empty cell) P0 through P15 for Percent with 0 to 15 decimal places S0 through S15 for Sci (Scientific) with 0 to 15 decimal places ,0 through ,15 for Comma with 0 to 15 decimal places + for +/− format D1 for Date 1 (Lotus standard long form), DD-MMM-YY D2 for Date 2, (Lotus standard short form), DD-MMM D3 for Date 3, MMM-YY D4 for Date 4 (Long Int'l), MM/DD/YY (default) D5 for Date 5 (Short Int'l), MM/DD (default) D6 for Time 1, HH:MM:SS AM/PM D7 for Time 2, HH:MM AM/PM D8 for Time 3 (Long Int'l), HH:MM:SS (default—24 hour) D9 for Time 4 (Short Int'l), HH:MM (default—24 hour) T for Text format H for Hidden format
prefix	The label prefix, using these symbols: ' for a left-aligned label " for a right-aligned label

◆ **Table 5.10**: *Attributes for the @CELL and @CELLPOINTER Functions (continued)*

Attribute	Returns
	^ for a centered label \ for a repeating label | for a nonprinting label no symbol (blank) for a label or empty cell
protect	The protection status, with 1 if the cell is protected and 0 if the cell is unprotected.
row	The row number, from 1 to 8192.
type	The type of data in the cell, using these abbreviations: b for an empty cell v for a cell that contains a value l for a cell that contains a label
width	The width of the cell (that is, its column).

where cells A2 and B2 contain the value 2, 1-2-3 will place *Qtr 3* in cell A2. In fact, if you want to be able to enter an *offset* value matching the number of the quarter, you have to modify the *offset* argument of the @CHOOSE function to *B2 − 1*.

The other three lookup @functions all use a range of values that are set up in tabular form like tax tables or statistical tables. The @HLOOKUP and @VLOOKUP functions work similarly: they both match the value entered as their *x* argument against values in the first row or column (called the *index* row or column) of a table range specified by the *range* argument, and then return a corresponding value from the table according to the *offset* value. In an @HLOOKUP function, 1-2-3 matches the *x* value against the first (index) row of the table, and the *offset* value is given as the number of rows down from the first row (counted as 0). In an @VLOOKUP function, the axis is inverted so that the *x* value is matched against the first (index) column of the table, and the *offset* value is given as the number of columns to the right from the first one (counted as 0).

Note that when using either @HLOOKUP or @VLOOKUP, you need to make sure the index values are arranged in ascending order. For a table using the @HLOOKUP function, this means that the values increase as you move across each column (from left to right); in a table using the @VLOOKUP function, the values increase as you move down each row. Also, in numerical tables, 1-2-3 will return the value in the offset row or column for an index value that matches *x* exactly or doesn't exceed it.

Figure 5.21 shows you an application that uses the @VLOOKUP function. Here, the @VLOOKUP formula in cell F7 uses the check amount entered in cell F5 and the percentage amount entered in cell F3 to return the appropriate amount for the tip from the tip table in range A3..C102 (the table goes from $0.00 to $99.00). This @function has returned $1.80 for the tip based on a check amount of $12.25 using a 15 percent tip. Notice that 1-2-3 returns 1.80 based on the 12.00 amount because it is the closest value that doesn't exceed 12.25. Also, notice that the @IF function determines the *column-offset* argument as 1 or 2 depending upon which value is entered into the range named PERCENT (cell F3). Remember that the 15% column of the tip table has the column offset of 1 even though it is the second column of the table, because we always start counting offsets from 0.

The @INDEX function is the last lookup @function. It differs from the @HLOOKUP and @VLOOKUP functions because you must specify both the column offset and row offset in the lookup table. If you wanted to look up the value in the second column (offset 1) of the third row (offset 2) in the worksheet of the table range A1..F15, you would enter

@INDEX(A1..F15,1,2)

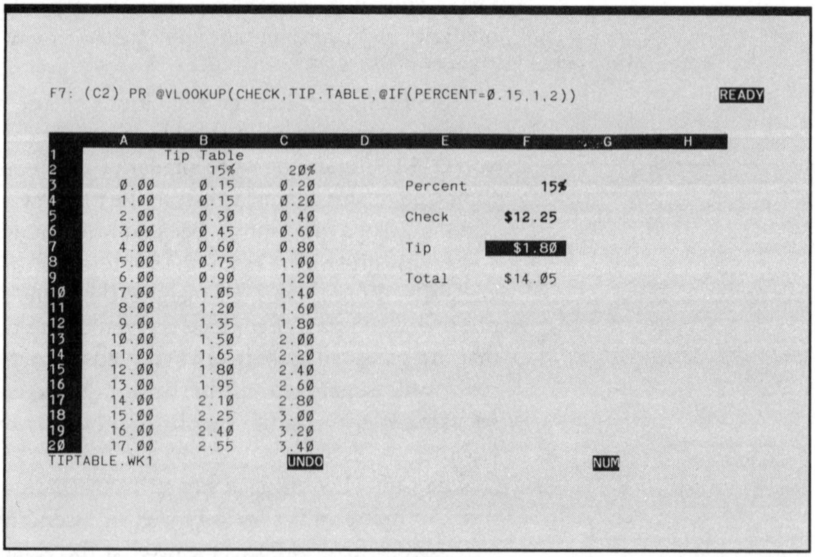

◆ **Figure 5.21:** *Using the @VLOOKUP function to figure the appropriate tip amount*

Summary

Troubleshooting

Question: I created a rather long formula and when I attempted to enter it, 1-2-3 beeped and went into EDIT mode. What's the best method for locating and fixing the error(s)?

Answer: Begin by noticing where 1-2-3 has located the cursor in the formula on the control panel: this indicates how far the program got in executing the formula. Often, although not always, the error in spelling or syntax has occurred right before the cursor position. If your formula uses an @function, make sure that the @function name is spelled correctly, that you specified enough arguments (separated by a comma or semicolon), and that you have terminated the @function with a final parenthesis. If your formula contains nested @functions, make sure that there are at least the same number of left and right parentheses.

Question: I made copies of one of my formulas and when the copies were made, I noticed that they weren't correct—some contained ERR and others zeros. How do I go about fixing this situation?

Answer: You need to check the type of cell references in the original formula: some or all may require the use of a mixed address or absolute address rather than a relative address. Analyze the problem by examining the contents of one of the copies. Ask yourself what the correct formula should be. After diagnosing the problem, edit the original formula as required, and redo the entire /Copy command.

Question: After formatting the values in my worksheet, it appears as though 1-2-3 has made some arithmetical errors! Can this be?

Answer: Most apparent errors in worksheet calculations are the result of rounding off the display with /Range Format options such as Fixed, Comma, and Currency. To prevent such errors in the display, you need to use the @ROUND function in the formulas and specify the same number of decimal places as you will use when formatting the answers.

Question: Many formulas in my worksheet are returning ERR values, although I've checked the formulas and they are correct. How can I find out what's causing the ERR values in the answers?

Answer: The first thing to look for is division by zero. Check to see if any of the formulas use division and, if so, make sure that none of the cells used as the divisor contain the value 0. If this isn't the problem, check to see if any formulas that concatenate strings (with the string operator, &) combine labels and values or labels and empty cells, as either condition will result in an ERR value. If some of the cells contain values, use the @STRING function to convert them to strings. If some cells are blank, add the @S function to each reference to prevent blanks or values in cells from causing ERR in the results.

Essential Techniques

To Create a Formula with an @Function

1. Move the pointer to the cell where the @function is to be entered.

2. Type @ followed by the @function name and the first parenthesis (.

3. Enter the argument or arguments required by the @function. If you are using cell references, you can type these or point them out. If you are using named ranges, you can type the range name or use the Name key (F3) to select it.

4. Type) to finish the @function, and then press Enter to have 1-2-3 calculate the result.

To Copy a Formula to a Range

1. Move the pointer to the cell that contains the formula you want to copy.

2. Make sure that the cell references in the formula are of the correct type (relative, mixed, or absolute) for the copy you are about to make. If not, press Edit (F2), change the address as needed, and press Enter; you can use the Abs key (F4) if you move the cursor on the address or immediately after it.

3. Type /C and press Enter in response to the prompt *Enter range to copy FROM:*.

4. Move the pointer to the first cell in the range to copy TO and type . (period) to anchor, then move the pointer to the last cell in the range and press Enter.

Review   **Important Terms You Should Know**

Abs key (F4)   literal string
absolute address   literal value
arithmetic operators   logical formula
Calc key (F9)   mixed address
circular reference   numeric formula
concatenation   order of precedence
conditional test   relative address
dependent formulas   string formula
empty string   string operator
input cell   syntax
iteration

Test Your Knowledge

1. To add two numbers in cells, use the _____, the arithmetic opera-
    tor for addition in the formula. To join two labels in cells, use the
    _____, the string operator in the formula.

2. A logical formula performs a _____ test on the statement it con-
    tains and returns the value _____ when the statement is true and
    _____ when it is false.

3. To create a logical formula that evaluates whether the value in cell
    B2 is greater than or equal to 25 *and* less than or equal to 50 (that is,
    between 25 and 50), enter the formula +B2_____25#_____#
    B2_____50.

4. Cell C5 contains the formula *(A2−(B1+B2))/B3*. If A2 contains *10*, B1
    contains *3*, B2 contains *5*, and B3 contains *2*, 1-2-3 will return
    _____ in C5.

5. You need to be concerned about the type of references (relative,
    mixed, or absolute) in a formula only when you may need to _____
    the formula.

6. To enter the cell address C10 so that the row number is relative but
    the column number is absolute, you would enter the address as
    _____ in the formula.

7. To make a range absolute in a formula that has been assigned the range name *EXPENSES*, you would enter _____ in the formula.

8. When the CALC indicator appears on the status line, you have to press the _____ key and you know that 1-2-3 is in _____ recalculation mode.

9. When the CIRC indicator appears on the status line, select the _____ command to locate the address of the circular reference.

10. If an @function requires several arguments, you can use a _____ or _____ to separate them in the formula.

Further Exercises

1. Create a new worksheet that contains the following dates in column A:
   - January 11, 1989
   - January 17, 1989
   - February 19, 1989
   - March 4, 1989
   - June 21, 1989
   - August 11, 1989

   Format these dates using the Long International date format. Then build formulas in column B that use the @NOW or @TODAY function to calculate how many days have elapsed between the current date and these dates. In column C, build formulas using the @IF function that return *Over 90* if the number of days in the cell in column B is greater than 90 and *Under 90* if the number of days is less than 90.

2. Create a new worksheet that contains the tip table and lookup capabilities illustrated in Figure 5.21. Assign the range name PERCENT to cell F3, CHECK to cell F5, and TIP.TABLE to the range A2..C102. Enter the values 0 and 1 in cells A3 and A4, and then create a formula in cell A5 that adds 1 to the cell above. Copy this formula to the range A6..A102. Enter the values .15 and .20 in cells B3 and C3. Then enter a formula in cell B4 that multiplies cell A4 by 15 percent and one in cell C4 that multiplies this cell by 20 percent. Copy these formulas to range B5..C102. Enter the @VLOOKUP function shown in Figure 5.21 in cell F7 and an @SUM formula in cell F9 that totals

cells F5 and F7. Format the values in the TIP.TABLE range using the Comma format with two decimal places. Format the PERCENT range (F3) using the Percent format with zero decimal places and format the CHECK range (F5), cell F7, and F9 using the Currency format with two decimal places. Experiment with entering different check amounts and changing the percentage. Once you know the lookup function is working correctly, format the table as shown in Figure 5.21, turn on global protection, and unprotect cells F3 and F5. Then save the file under the name *TIPTABLE.WK1*.

6

*Managing
the Worksheet
Environment*

In This Chapter...

The /Worksheet Commands

Several 1-2-3 commands affect the entire worksheet environment. You have already become familiar with some of these commands: /Worksheet Column Set-Width used to change the width of the current column, /Worksheet Erase used to clear the worksheet from memory in preparation to start a new one, /Worksheet Global Protection used to turn protection status on and off, /Worksheet Global Recalculation used to switch between manual and automatic formula recalculation and to control how the worksheet is recalculated, /Worksheet Global Zero used to suppress the zero display or to define a label to be displayed in its place (Release 2.2 only), and, finally, /Worksheet Status used to obtain information about current settings including the free memory available, current recalculation method and order, location of circular references, and so on.

In this chapter, we will take a look at some of the other commonly used /Worksheet commands. These include commands for dividing the display into windows, setting up columns and rows that remain on the screen at all times while you scroll the worksheet display, and inserting or deleting new columns and rows in the worksheet. Also, we will look at the ways you can change some of the worksheet global defaults, such as the global display format and the label prefix used by the program.

Before we begin looking at specific /Worksheet commands, it is well to remember that all commands on the /Worksheet menu affect the entire worksheet in memory in some way. Many people wonder, for instance, why the command to change the column width is located on the /Worksheet menu. This is not hard to understand if you keep in mind that widening or narrowing a column affects the entire worksheet column from row 1 through row 8192. Likewise, the commands used to insert or delete specific columns or rows in the worksheet are found on the /Worksheet menu (instead of /Range) precisely because they too work on the entire column or row of the worksheet. For a command to be located on the /Worksheet menu, it must at minimum alter or influence an entire column or row, if not all cells in the worksheet. (By contrast, /Range commands don't affect an entire row or column unless you specifically designate all cells in it as the cell range to be used.)

Managing the Worksheet Display with Windows

It's no secret that the 8-column × 20-row view of the worksheet is far from adequate in all but the most elementary applications. As you will learn in this chapter, 1-2-3 has a couple of windowing commands designed to alleviate this problem. Although neither of these commands enlarges the display, they do enable you to display separate areas in the same worksheet. This makes working with large worksheets a great deal easier.

When you select the /Worksheet Window menu, you are presented with these options:

Horizontal   Vertical   Sync   Unsync   Clear

Actually, only the first two options represent a type of window: Horizontal or Vertical. The Sync and Unsync options control whether scrolling is synchronized (the default) in the windows you create from this menu. The Clear option is used to remove any window views created from this menu and return to the normal single view.

Dividing the Worksheet Display with Horizontal or Vertical Windows

Horizontal and vertical windows simply divide the worksheet display into two windows along either the horizontal axis or the vertical axis. The sizing of a horizontal or vertical window depends upon which row or column is current when you create the windows. Remember that you have already worked a little with horizontal windows in Chapter 5, when you added the bonus formula (and circular reference) to your income statement.

You can create a horizontal or vertical window in any worksheet file to enable you to view two parts of the same sheet. Remember that you performed this kind of operation in an exercise in Chapter 5, where you created horizontal windows to display the top and bottom parts of your income statement. In this case, the top window displayed the section with the other income and expenses (including the bonus), while the bottom window displayed the last section with the net earnings.

To create a horizontal window, move the pointer to the row where you want the second window to start, and then select the Horizontal option from the /Worksheet Window menu (/WWH). If you want to divide the worksheet window into two equal windows, position the pointer in row 10 before you give the command (it doesn't matter which column the pointer's in). This will create two windows, each 80 columns × 9 rows, as in Figure 6.1. In this figure, 1-2-3 duplicates the top part of the frame, which contains the column letters.

When you create horizontal windows, all horizontal scrolling is synchronized. This means that columns always stay aligned (A over A, B over B, and so on) as you scroll right (Tab or Ctrl-→) or left (Shift-Tab or Ctrl-←). Figure 6.2 illustrates this: in this figure, the Tab key was pressed once. Notice that column letters in both the lower and upper windows are the same (column H over H, I over I, J over J, and so on).

```
A9: (G) U 13                                                    READY
        A         B         C         D         E       F        G
   1  Family    Husband's                      Wife's  Son's
   2  number    Education Job Posit. Height-in  Height " Age    Income
   3      15       H         N         70.7     69.4    10       18.8
   4     142       H         N         66.9     66.5     9.3     15.2
   5      58       H         N         68.3     62.8     7.7      9.3
   6     129       H         S         69.1     63      11       13.3
   7     115       C         N         70.9     67.5     8        13
   8       1       H         S         71       71      12.9     33
   9      13       H         N         70.7     61.4     7.3      7.5
        A         B         C         D         E       F        G
  10      87       H         N         67.1     62.5     7.6      9
  11      18       E         N         73.5     61.8     8.9      8.4
  12     104       H         S         68.8     64.9    11.7     17.6
  13      95       C         S         73       65.8    10.9     17.3
  14      50       C         S         65.7     66.2    11.2     18
  15      60       C         S         67.9     66.6    11.5     18.7
  16     124       E         N         66.9     64.4    11.1     12.5
  17      72       E         N         65.6     64.2    10.9     12.2
  18      62       E         S         71.4     67.7    15.8     29
  19     148       E         N         69.9     63.2    10.3     10.8
STATS1.WK1                    UNDO                          NUM
```

♦ **Figure 6.1:** *Worksheet with horizontal windows*

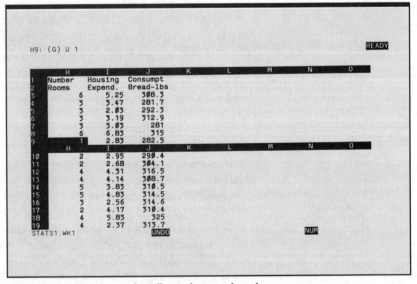

```
H9: (G) U 1                                                     READY
        H         I         J        K      L      M      N      O
   1  Number    Housing   Consumpt
   2  Rooms     Expend.   Bread-lbs
   3      6       5.25     308.3
   4      3       3.47     281.7
   5      3       2.03     292.3
   6      3       3.19     312.9
   7      3       3.03     281
   8      6       6.83     315
   9      1       2.83     282.5
        H         I         J        K      L      M      N      O
  10      2       2.95     290.4
  11      2       2.68     304.1
  12      4       4.31     316.5
  13      4       4.14     308.7
  14      5       3.83     310.5
  15      5       4.83     314.5
  16      3       2.56     314.6
  17      2       4.17     310.4
  18      4       5.83     325
  19      4       2.37     313.7
STATS1.WK1                    UNDO                          NUM
```

♦ **Figure 6.2:** *Synchronized scrolling in horizontal windows*

To scroll the current window independently of the second window, you must select the Unsync option on the /Worksheet Window menu (/WWU). Figure 6.3 shows an example of unsynchronized scrolling in horizontal windows. In this figure, the top window was scrolled left with the Ctrl-← key after selecting the Unsync option on the /Worksheet Window menu. When the scrolling is independent, the current window (the top one in this figure) scrolls independently of the bottom (resulting in column A over H, B over I, C over J, and so on).

To create a vertical window, you follow basically the same procedure, except that this time, you move the pointer to the column where you want the second window to begin before you select the Vertical option from the /Worksheet Window menu (/WWV). To create two equal vertical windows, move the pointer to column E before you use this command (assuming that all columns are still nine characters wide). Figure 6.4 shows a worksheet that has been divided roughly in two with vertical windows. Notice that in vertical windows, 1-2-3 duplicates the left part of the frame showing the row numbers.

When you create vertical windows, all vertical scrolling is synchronized. This means that rows always stay aligned (row 1 next to 1, 2 next to 2, and so on) as you scroll down (PgDn or ↓) or up (PgUp or ↑). To scroll the current window independently of the other window, you must also select the Unsync option on the /Worksheet Window menu (/WWU).

A9: (G) U 13   READY

```
        A          B          C          D          E        F         G
 1  Family     Husband's                           Wife's   Son's
 2  number     Education  Job Posit. Height-in Height "  Age     Income
 3        15          H          N       70.7     69.4      10     18.8
 4       142          H          N       66.9     66.5     9.3     15.2
 5        58          H          N       68.3     62.8     7.7      9.3
 6       129          H          S       69.1       63      11     13.3
 7       115          C          N       70.9     67.5       8       13
 8         1          H          S         71       71    12.9       33
 9        13          H          N       70.7     61.4     7.3      7.5
        H          I          J          K          L        M         O
10         2       2.95      290.4
11         2       2.68      304.1
12         4       4.31      316.5
13         4       4.14      308.7
14         5       3.83      310.5
15         5       4.83      314.5
16         3       2.56      314.6
17         2       4.17      310.4
18         4       5.83        325
19         4       2.37      313.7
STATS1.WK1                    UNDO                           NUM
```

♦ **Figure 6.3:** *Unsynchronized scrolling in horizontal windows*

D1: (G) U   READY

	A	B	C	D		E	F	G	H	
1	Family	Husband's			1	Wife's	Son's		Number	
2	number	EducationJob	Posit	Height-in	2	Height "	Age	Income	Rooms	
3	15	H	N	70.7	3	69.4	10	18.8		6
4	142	H	N	66.9	4	66.5	9.3	15.2		3
5	58	H	N	68.3	5	62.8	7.7	9.3		3
6	129	H	S	69.1	6	63	11	13.3		3
7	115	C	N	70.9	7	67.5	8	13		3
8	1	H	S	71	8	71	12.9	33		6
9	13	H	N	70.7	9	61.4	7.3	7.5		1
10	87	H	N	67.1	10	62.5	7.6	9		2
11	18	E	N	73.5	11	61.8	8.9	8.4		2
12	104	H	S	68.8	12	64.9	11.7	17.6		4
13	95	C	S	73	13	65.8	10.9	17.3		4
14	50	C	S	65.7	14	66.2	11.2	18		5
15	60	C	S	67.9	15	66.6	11.5	18.7		5
16	124	E	N	66.9	16	64.4	11.1	12.5		3
17	72	E	N	65.6	17	64.2	10.9	12.2		2
18	62	E	S	71.4	18	67.7	15.8	29		4
19	148	E	N	69.9	19	63.2	10.3	10.8		4
20	131	E	N	68.1	20	66.8	12.7	16.3		3

STATS1.WK1   UNDO

♦ **Figure 6.4:** *Worksheet with vertical windows*

To immediately clear either the horizontal or vertical windows that you have set up in the worksheet, you select the /Worksheet Window Clear command (/WWC). Note that if you save the worksheet when the display is divided into windows, these windows are saved as part of the file and will be present when you next retrieve the file.

Making a New Window Current with the Window Key

When you divide the worksheet display into horizontal or vertical windows, you use the Window key (F6) to move the pointer between them, making a new window current. With the worksheet display divided into two windows, holding down the Window key moves the pointer back and forth from one window to the other.

Once you move the pointer to a new window, you can then use the pointer-movement keys to scroll a new area of the worksheet into view or to enter or edit data in the cells visible there.

Setting Up Worksheet Titles

Even when using the windowing methods that we've just discussed, you will still often need to scroll the worksheet to bring specific data in view. To help you keep your place when scrolling through a large table of data, 1-2-3 enables

F6: The Window Key

F6, the Window key, moves the pointer to the next defined window

F6 is used to make one of the windows in the worksheet display
current to:
+ Make editing changes
+ Scroll a new section of the worksheet into view

* *New in 2.2*

F6 suppresses the display of the current setting sheet, revealing the
worksheet area beneath the menu; press the Window key a second
time to redisplay the settings sheet

you to set up *worksheet titles*, which represent specific columns and rows that
remain on the screen no matter which direction you scroll the data of the
worksheet.

In setting up worksheet titles from the /Worksheet Titles menu, 1-2-3 gives
you a choice between these options:

Both   Horizontal   Vertical   Clear

If you choose the Horizontal option, all rows above the pointer's position are
frozen on the screen. If you choose the Vertical option, all columns to the left
of the pointer's position are frozen on the screen. If you select the Both option,
all rows above and columns to the left remain on the screen. As you would
imagine, you select the Clear option when you want to remove all titles from
the current window.

Figure 6.5 shows you a worksheet where horizontal titles have been set up in
rows 1 and 2. After you set these rows up as the worksheet titles, they remain
on the screen as you scroll up new rows (notice that row 2 is followed by row 17
in this figure). These worksheet titles enable you to quickly identify the
columns of data as you scroll through the worksheet.

Once you set up titles in a worksheet, you can't move the pointer into this
area. Any attempt to move the pointer into the columns or rows they contain
will have no effect on the pointer and will cause 1-2-3 to beep. When you use
the /Worksheet Titles command after you have split the worksheet display
with one of the /Worksheet Windows commands, the titles affect only the current window. This allows you to set different title areas in each window that
you have set up.

To clear the titles that you have set up, thus giving the pointer access to this
area, you only need to select the /Worksheet Titles Clear command (/WTC).
Note, however, that if you have set up different titles in the windows you have

♦ **Figure 6.5:** *Worksheet with rows 1 and 2 designated as titles*

created, only the titles in the current window are cleared when you select this command. To clear the titles set up for the other window, you must make it current and then select the /Worksheet Titles Clear command a second time.

Using Scroll Lock with Titles: To make it easier to position a particular range on the screen in relation to the worksheet titles, use the scroll lock feature after setting up your titles with the appropriate /Worksheet Titles command. To do this, press the Scroll Lock key. The program will display the SCROLL indicator on the status line. With Scroll Lock engaged, 1-2-3 "freezes" the pointer and scrolls the data in the opposite direction of the arrow key you press. In other words, each time you press the ↓ key, 1-2-3 scrolls another row of data up, leaving the pointer stationary. Once you have positioned the data the way you want it, press the Scroll Lock key again. This frees the pointer, and the SCROLL indicator immediately disappears.

Inserting and Deleting Columns and Rows in the Worksheet

Lotus 1-2-3 makes it easy to insert or delete columns or rows in the worksheet by providing Insert and Delete options on the /Worksheet menu. When you select either /Worksheet Insert or /Worksheet Delete, 1-2-3 displays these options:

Column Row

When using either command, remember that the program will insert or delete an *entire* column or row (or range of columns or rows).

This means that you shouldn't use these commands when you just need to move or erase a range of data and there is any possibility that inserting or deleting an entire column or row (or an entire group of columns and rows) will affect other cell ranges elsewhere in the same column or row. Before you use these /Worksheet commands to insert or delete a new column, make sure that no data in unseen parts of the worksheet can be adversely affected. To do this, you can use the End key in combination with the appropriate arrow key.

For example, if you are working in a range and wish to delete the data in row 5, you can verify that it is safe to delete this row by moving the pointer to the first blank cell to the right of the range in this row and then pressing the End and → keys. Because the pointer will stop on any occupied cell in that row or the end of the worksheet (in column IV), whichever comes first, you can tell that it's safe in this direction if the pointer goes directly to column IV (you can then press End ← to move the cursor back to your data range).

Assuming that the data you wish to delete doesn't begin in column A, you will have to repeat this procedure in the first blank cell in this row to the left of the data range before going ahead with the deletion of this row. This time, you will use the ← key after the End key, and the pointer will move directly to column A instead of IV, if it's safe to proceed with the deletion. If you don't meet any occupied cells in either direction, you know that it's safe to proceed with the deletion of the row (if you are working with columns, you use End and ↑ to move directly to row 1, or the End and ↓ keys to move directly to row 8192).

Note that inserting new columns and rows can be just as hazardous to the worksheet as deleting them. This is especially true if the worksheet contains macros and you happen to insert a new row that divides the column containing a macro's commands and instructions with a blank cell; thereafter, the macro will no longer work as planned because it will shut down prematurely as soon as it reaches this new, unintentional blank cell in its midst (see Chapter 15 for more information on using macros).

If you're using Release 2.2, don't forget that you can use the Undo key (Alt-F4) to restore the deleted columns or rows (and all the data they contain) or remove newly inserted columns or rows and thus eliminate the gaps in data ranges created by their insertion. If you're using Release 2.01 or have disabled the Undo feature in Release 2.2, always make it a point to save the worksheet just before you use either the /Worksheet Delete or /Worksheet Insert command. That way, you can always retrieve the worksheet in its previous state, should you use these commands in error.

Inserting New Columns or Rows in the Worksheet

To insert a new column in a worksheet, move the pointer somewhere within the existing column where the new blank column is to be inserted (existing columns of data, including the pointer's column, will be moved one column to the right to make room for this new column), then select the /Worksheet Insert Column command (/WIC), and press Enter in response to the *Enter column insert range* prompt. If you wish to insert more than one column, anchor the range with the period key, and then use the ← or → key to extend the range as many columns to the left or right as you want new columns inserted before pressing Enter.

To insert a new row in the worksheet, you follow much the same procedure. This time, however, you move the pointer somewhere within the row where the new blank row is to be inserted (existing rows of data, including the pointer's row, will be moved down one row to accommodate the new row), then select the /Worksheet Insert Row command (/WIR), and press Enter in response to the *Enter row insert range* prompt. To insert more than one row, you need to anchor the range and then extend it with either the ↓ or ↑ key before pressing Enter.

Deleting Rows from the Worksheet

Using the /Worksheet Delete Column or /Worksheet Delete Row command to remove *entire* columns or rows from the worksheet is a similar process to that of inserting new columns and rows. Before selecting either deletion command, you need to move the pointer to the column or row that you wish deleted. If you want to delete more than one column or row, you can anchor the range and then extend it in the appropriate direction to include all columns or rows to be removed.

When you delete columns or rows from the worksheet, 1-2-3 closes the gaps that would otherwise be created by their removal by moving either the remaining columns of data to the left or the remaining rows of data up (thereby changing their cell addresses).

* *New in 2.2*   # Setting the Width for a Range of Columns

As you already know, to change the width of the current column, you select the Set-Width option on the /Worksheet Column menu. If you want to return the column to the global default column width (nine characters unless you have changed it), you choose the Reset-Width option on this menu.

To change the global default column width in the worksheet, you use the Column-Width option from the /Worksheet Global menu. Remember, however, that the value you enter here affects all columns that haven't yet been modified with the /Worksheet Column Set-Width command.

In versions of 1-2-3 prior to Release 2.2 (and Release 3.0), no command exists to change the column width for a group of columns: you could either use the /Worksheet Global Column-Width command to change the width of all columns in the worksheet, or use the /Worksheet Column Set-Width command to change the width of each column individually. Now, with the addition of the Column-Range option on the /Worksheet Column menu, you can change the width for any range of columns in the worksheet.

When you select the /Worksheet Column Column-Range command, 1-2-3 presents you with the options

Set-Width Reset-Width

To change the width of a group of columns, you choose the Set-Width option. You are then prompted to designate the range of columns whose widths are to be changed with

Enter range for column width change:

At this point, you will find that the range is anchored on the current cell. To highlight the range of columns to be changed, you only need to press the → or ← key to include the desired columns, and then press Enter. Once you have defined the range of columns, you are prompted to enter the new column width (between 1 and 240). As when setting a new width for a single column, you can indicate the new width either by typing the new width value or by pointing with the → key (to increase the width) or the ← key (to decrease the width). As soon as you press Enter, 1-2-3 will set the indicated width for all columns in the range.

If you ever want to return a group of columns to the global column width in effect, you use the Reset-Width option on the /Worksheet Column Column-Range menu (/WCCR). To return the columns to the global default, you have only to include them as part of the range specified in response to the *Enter range for column width change* prompt. As soon as you press Enter to set this range, all columns included in the range are reset to the global column width.

Modifying the Worksheet Global Settings

During your study of 1-2-3 to this point, you have become acquainted with several global settings, many of which you have learned to modify for specific areas of the worksheet with the appropriate /Range commands. For example, you know that the global default label prefix is the apostrophe, which has the effect of left-justifying a label in its cell. To override this global default, you have learned that you can either use one of the other label prefixes when entering your label or select the Center or Right option on the /Range Label menu. So too, you know that the General format is the global default for all values that you enter in the worksheet and that when you want to override this default, you select the appropriate display option from the /Range Format menu.

You may have a situation where it is more productive to change the global alignment for all labels or the global display format for all values in the worksheet rather than to constantly use the /Range Label or /Range Format command. In this case, you can change these settings for the entire worksheet by selecting the appropriate option from the /Worksheet Global menu and selecting a more appropriate setting.

Figure 6.6 shows you the /Worksheet Global options along with the Global Settings sheet. (Note that the Global Settings sheet appears only if you're using Release 2.2; if you're using Release 2.01, you need to select the /Worksheet Status command to display a full-screen version of this sheet.)

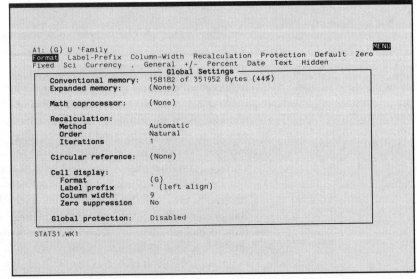

◆ **Figure 6.6:** *The /Worksheet Global menu with the Global Settings sheet*

To select a new global format for values in the worksheet, select the Format option on this /Worksheet Global menu. Doing this brings up the same selection of display formats (from General to Hidden) as when you select the /Range Format menu (except that /RF also has a Reset option). To select a new global alignment, you would choose the Label-Prefix option on the /Worksheet Global menu and then choose between the Left, Right, and Center options.

Note that in addition to selecting a new global format and label prefix on this menu, you can also select a new global column width (with the Column-Width option), modify the method of recalculation (with the Recalculation option), enable and disable global protection (with the Protection option), or change how zeros are displayed in the worksheet (with the Zero option).

The option on the /Worksheet Global menu that we've not discussed thus far is the Default option. From the /Worksheet Global Default menu, you can modify a great many of the program's default settings, including the printer used in printing your worksheets, the directory where 1-2-3 looks for your worksheets, the default setting for Long International date and time formats, and more. To get an in-depth view of what default settings you can change as well as your options in setting new defaults, refer to Appendix B.

Practice Using Windows and Titles in a Worksheet

You've already had one practical experience with creating and using windows in a worksheet. In this next exercise, you will get more practice with creating and using worksheet titles and windows to make sure that you are comfortable with these essential features.

1. **Retrieve the worksheet file *IS90CH5.WK1*.**
   This file contains the 1990 income statement complete with the bonus formula, as well as the percent formulas in column C that you entered in Chapter 5. In this exercise, you will add several columns of new figures so you can scroll the worksheet horizontally as well as vertically to view all the data it contains.

2. **Move the pointer to cell A26, then select the /Move command (/M), type *NAME.TABLE* (or select it with the Name key, F3) as the range to move FROM and press Enter, and press the Enter key to accept A26 as the range to move TO.**
   Now that you have moved the range name table below the income statement, you are ready to add some data in the columns to the right.

3. **Move the pointer to cell C3 and erase the range C3..C23.**
   You won't need to refer to the percent formulas in this exercise. In

this column, and others to the right, you will copy existing income data and then modify them slightly.

4. **Move the pointer to cell B2 and copy the range B2..B24 to cell C2; then, change the label in C2 to ^1991, change the revenues in cell C3 to 81000, and change the product costs in C5 to 22000.**

   Making these few changes differentiates the figures in column C from those in column B. Next, you will copy the newly created 1991 figures in column C to column D and modify them slightly.

5. **Move the pointer to cell C2 and copy the range C2..C24 to cell D2; then, change the label in D2 to ^1992, change the revenues in cell D3 to 83500, and change the product costs in D5 to 24700.**

   Now, you need to copy the income figures in column D to column E.

6. **Move the pointer to cell D2 and copy the range D2..D24 to cell E2; then, change the label in E2 to ^1993, change the revenues in cell E3 to 90000, and change the product costs in E5 to 28300.**

   You need to make one more copy to create some income figures for 1994 before you add some formulas that total each row of data.

7. **Move the pointer to cell E2 and copy the range E2..E24 to cell F2; then, change the label in F2 to ^1994, change the revenues in cell F3 to 99500, and change the product costs in F5 to 32600; next, select the /Worksheet Column Reset-Width command (/WCR) to return the column width to 9.**

   Next, you will add formulas in column G that total the amounts in each row.

8. **Move the pointer to G2 and enter the label *Total* in this cell; then, move the pointer to G3 and create a formula that sums the data in the range B3..F3; format the result using the Comma format with 0 decimal places; next, copy this formula to the range G5..G23; replace the zeros with repeating underscores where appropriate, and erase all other zeros in this column.**

   The income figures and totals in your worksheet should now match those shown in Figure 6.7. At this point, you should save your work in a new worksheet file before continuing this exercise.

9. **Save this worksheet under the file name** *IS5YRCH6.*
   Now you are ready to experiment with setting up windows and titles to help you keep track of the data in this worksheet.

10. **Press the Home key to move the pointer to cell A1, then move the pointer to cell B3.**
    By placing the pointer in cell B3, you can set up column A and rows 1 and 2 as the titles for this worksheet. This allows you to scroll the worksheet horizontally or vertically and still keep the column and row headings on the screen.

11. **Select the /Worksheet Titles Both command (/WTB); press the Scroll Lock key (the SCROLL indicator will appear on the status line); and press the → key twice.**
    With Scroll Lock engaged, pressing the → key scrolls the worksheet to the right without moving the pointer. Notice you can now see the first part of the income figures for the last three years (1992, 1993, and 1994) and the totals in column G (Figure 6.8).

12. **Press the ↓ key four times.**
    Pressing the ↓ key with Scroll Lock engaged causes the income data to scroll up, displaying the last part of the income statements including the net earnings figures for the last three years (1992, 1993, and 1994) and the totals in column G (Figure 6.9).

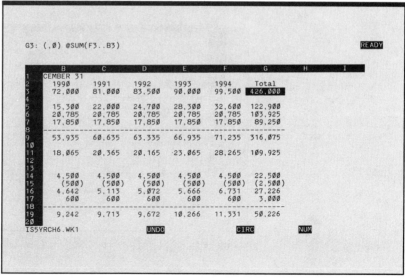

♦ **Figure 6.7:** *Income statement with income figures for 1991 through 1994*

```
D3: (,Ø) 83500                                                    READY

              A              D        E        F        G
1  INCOME STATEMENT YEAR ENDING DE
2                           1992     1993     1994    Total
3  Revenues               83,500   90,000   99,500  426,000
4  Costs and expenses
5    Product costs        24,700   28,300   32,600  122,900
6    Marketing and sales  20,785   20,785   20,785  103,925
7    General and administrative 17,850 17,850 17,850  89,250
8                         -------------------------------------
9  Total costs and expenses 63,335  66,935   71,235  316,075
10
11 Operating income (loss)  20,165   23,065   28,265  109,925
12
13 Other income (expenses)
14   Interest income        4,500    4,500    4,500   22,500
15   Interest expense        (500)    (500)    (500)  (2,500)
16   Bonuses                5,072    5,666    6,731   27,226
17   Other                    600      600      600    3,000
18                         -------------------------------------
19 Total other income (expenses) 9,672 10,266 11,331  50,226
20
IS5YRCH6.WK1        UNDO              CIRC         NUM    SCROLL
```

◆ **Figure 6.8:** *Scrolling the income worksheet horizontally*

```
D7: (,Ø) 17850                                                    READY

              A              D        E        F        G
1  INCOME STATEMENT YEAR ENDING DE
2                           1992     1993     1994    Total
7    General and administrative 17,850 17,850 17,850  89,250
8                         -------------------------------------
9  Total costs and expenses 63,335  66,935   71,235  316,075
10
11 Operating income (loss)  20,165   23,065   28,265  109,925
12
13 Other income (expenses)
14   Interest income        4,500    4,500    4,500   22,500
15   Interest expense        (500)    (500)    (500)  (2,500)
16   Bonuses                5,072    5,666    6,731   27,226
17   Other                    600      600      600    3,000
18                         -------------------------------------
19 Total other income (expenses) 9,672 10,266 11,331  50,226
20
21 Income (loss) before taxes 29,837 33,331  39,596  160,151
22   Provision (benefit) for taxes 4,476 5,000 5,939  24,023
23 Net earnings (loss)      25,362   28,332   33,657  136,128
24                         =====================================
IS5YRCH6.WK1        UNDO              CIRC         NUM    SCROLL
```

◆ **Figure 6.9:** *Scrolling the income worksheet vertically*

Creating Windows to View Different Parts of the Worksheet

Instead of worksheet titles, in the next part of this exercise, you will create windows to view different parts of the worksheet at the same time.

1. **Select the /Worksheet Titles Clear command (/WTC), press Scroll Lock, and then press the Home key.**
   You will create a horizontal window in row 15. However, you will want to see the income figures for all five years in the same screen. To do this, you will have to narrow column A before you create the horizontal windows. Otherwise, 1-2-3 will change the apparent column width for the current window *only*, leaving the width of the noncurrent window unchanged!

2. **Change the column width of column A to 27, then move the pointer to row 15 and select /Worksheet Window Horizontal (/WWH).**
   Now you will scroll up the worksheet slightly so that you can see the net earnings figures in the bottom window.

3. **Press the Window key (F6), then press the Scroll Lock key; press the ↓ key five times until you can see rows 20 through 24 in the bottom window.**
   Your worksheet display should match the one shown in Figure 6.10. Now you will change some of the figures in the first part of the worksheet. Because of the windows you have created, you will immediately see the effect of these changes on the net earnings in the bottom window.

4. **Press the Window key (F6), press the Scroll Lock key, and then move the pointer to cell C3 and enter 71500 there.**
   As soon as you change the revenues for 1991 to *71,500* in cell C3, notice that the net earnings for this year in cell C23 in the bottom window change to *15,838*.

5. **Move the pointer to cell C7 and enter 16400 for the General and administrative expenses.**
   Notice that when you change this value in cell C7, the net earnings in cell C23 in the bottom window change to *17,323*. Now that you have an idea of how horizontal windows can be used, it's time to experiment with vertical windows. In this last part of the exercise, you will move the range name table to a distant part of the worksheet, then set up vertical

```
A20: [W27]                                                              READY

            A              B       C       D       E       F
 1  INCOME STATEMENT YEAR ENDING DECEMBER 31
 2                         1990    1991    1992    1993    1994
 3  Revenues               72,000  81,000  83,500  90,000  99,500
 4  Costs and expenses
 5    Product costs        15,300  22,000  24,700  28,300  32,600
 6    Marketing and sales  20,785  20,785  20,785  20,785  20,785
 7    General and administrativ  17,850  17,850  17,850  17,850  17,850
 8                         ------- ------- ------- ------- -------
 9  Total costs and expenses  53,935  60,635  63,335  66,935  71,235
10
11  Operating income (loss)   18,065  20,365  20,165  23,065  28,265
12
13  Other income (expenses)
14    Interest income         4,500   4,500   4,500   4,500   4,500
            A              B       C       D       E       F
20
21  Income (loss) before taxes  27,307  30,078  29,837  33,331  39,596
22    Provision (benefit) for t   4,096   4,512   4,476   5,000   5,939
23  Net earnings (loss)        23,211  25,567  25,362  28,332  33,657
24  ======================================================================
IS5YRCH6.WK1                UNDO              CIRC          NUM    SCROLL
```

♦ **Figure 6.10:** *Five-year income statement with horizontal windows*

windows, and display the first part of this table in one window right next to the first part of the income statements.

6. **Select the /Worksheet Window Clear command (/WWC); then, use the Goto key (F5) to move the pointer to cell G100; select the /Move command, then either type the range name** *NAME.TABLE* **or choose it with the Name key (F3) as the range to move FROM and press Enter; finally, press Enter a second time to indicate cell G100 as the range to move TO.**
Now that you have moved this table to a distant part of the worksheet, it is time to set up the vertical windows.

7. **Move the pointer to cell D1, and select /Worksheet Window Vertical (/WWV).**
This splits the screen vertically at column D. Next, you need to make the window on the right the current one and unsynchronize scrolling.

8. **Press the Window key (F6), then select /Worksheet Window Unsync (/WWU).**
Unsynchronizing the scrolling is important. If you forget to do this, 1-2-3 will not maintain the current view of the first part of the income statements in the window on the left when you scroll the range name table into view in the window on the right.

9. **Press the Goto key (F5), then the Name key (F3), and select the range name** *NAME.TABLE* **as the range to go to.**
   You should now see the range name table in the upper left corner of the window on the right (Figure 6.11). Notice that because the scrolling is unsynchronized, the view of the income statements in the window on the left is completely undisturbed.

10. **Clear the vertical windows by selecting /Worksheet Window Clear (/WWC); move the pointer to cell A1, and then save this worksheet under the same name.**

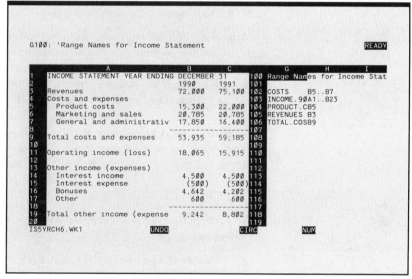

♦ **Figure 6.11:** *Five-year income statement with vertical windows*

Summary

Troubleshooting

Question: I created horizontal windows so that I could display two different parts of the worksheet at the same time, but I can't seem to figure out how to scroll the worksheet so that *both* of the desired sections are in view. What am I doing wrong?

Answer: Most of the time, you make your job much easier by selecting the Unsync option from the /Worksheet Window menu. This allows you to scroll the first section of the worksheet in the top window without affecting the view in the bottom worksheet. You can then use the Window key (F6) and scroll the second section of the worksheet into view in the bottom window. Because each window scrolls independently, you can usually achieve your desired screen view in a short time, especially if you engage Scroll Lock to help stabilize the pointer.

Question: I have to move some data in a table down to make room for some additions. I wanted to use the /Worksheet Insert Row command to insert the necessary blank rows, but I'm unable to because I found out that doing this will insert blank rows in other existing tables in the worksheet. What's the best method for creating the necessary room for adding the required data?

Answer: When you can't use the /Worksheet Insert command safely to insert the new columns or rows you need, you have to use the /Move command to cut part of the table and then paste it in a new location in the worksheet. Many times, you will have to perform more than one move operation to open up the room you need within a given table. This is because you often discover that pasting a section of the table a few columns over or rows down as planned would end up destroying part of a second existing table. To prevent this from happening, you first have to move the second data table out of harm's way before you move the section of the first table as originally planned.

Essential Techniques

To Divide the Worksheet Display into Horizontal or Vertical Windows

1. Move the pointer to the row (for horizontal windows) or column (for vertical windows) where you want to divide the screen.

2. Select the /Worksheet Window menu. Choose the Horizontal option to divide the screen horizontally at the current row, or choose the Vertical option to divide the screen vertically at the current column.

3. Use the Window key (F6) to move the pointer back and forth between windows. Choose the /Worksheet Window Unsync command (/WWU) to scroll data in the current window independently of the other window.

4. Select the /Worksheet Window Clear command (/WWC) to return to a full-screen display.

To Set Up Worksheet Titles

1. Move the pointer either to the row in the worksheet immediately below those that you wish to use as horizontal worksheet titles, or to the column immediately to the right of those that you wish to use as vertical worksheet titles.

2. Select the /Worksheet Titles command (/WT).

3. To make both the rows above and columns to the left of the pointer the worksheet columns, choose the Both option (B). To make just the rows above the pointer the worksheet columns, choose the Horizontal option (H). To make just the columns to the left of the pointer the worksheet columns, choose the Vertical option (V).

4. To clear the worksheet titles, select the /Worksheet Titles Clear command (/WTC).

Review

Important Terms You Should Know

horizontal window
Scroll Lock key
synchronized scrolling
unsynchronized scrolling

vertical window
Window key (F6)
worksheet titles

Test Your Knowledge

1. To split the worksheet display into two windows, one on top of the other and of roughly equal size, you would move the pointer to some cell in row _____ and then select the /Worksheet Window _____ command.

2. To move the pointer to a new window displayed on the screen and make that window current, you press the _____ key, which is _____ .

3. If the pointer is in cell B3 when you use the /Worksheet Titles Horizontal command, rows _____ become the worksheet titles. If you then press the ↑ key to move the pointer, 1-2-3 will respond by _____ .

4. If the pointer is in cell B3 when you use the /Worksheet Titles Vertical command, columns _____ become the worksheet titles.

5. To scroll the worksheet in the opposite direction of the arrow key you press, rather than move the pointer in the worksheet, you press the _____ key. After doing this, the _____ indicator will appear on the status line. To move the pointer freely in the worksheet once again, you have to press the _____ key again.

6. To widen a range of columns in a worksheet when using Release 2.2, you select the _____ option from the /Worksheet Column menu. Then you select the _____ option and indicate the range of columns to widen, and finally, specify the new width for the columns.

7. To insert three blank rows between rows 3 and 4 of a worksheet, you move the pointer to some cell in row _____, then select the /Worksheet Insert Row command and press the ↓ key _____ times and press Enter.

7

Linking and Transferring Data between Worksheet Files

In This Chapter...

Combining Worksheet Files in 1-2-3

Lotus 1-2-3 enables you to combine data that reside in different files by copying or consolidating data from disk files into the current file using the /File Combine command. When you use the /File Combine command, you are pulling data either from a named range or from an entire file as it is saved on disk.

Copying and Consolidating Data in Disk Files

You can use the /File Combine command to accomplish the following copy and consolidation tasks:

* Replace data in the current file with data in the disk file

* Append data in the disk file to the current file

* Add values in the disk file to values in the current file

* Subtract values in the disk file from values in the current file

The disk file containing the data you wish to replace, append to, add to, or subtract from the current file is called the *source file*. The current file that accepts the disk-based data is called the *target file*.

When you select the /File Combine command, 1-2-3 offers you three options:

Copy   Add   Subtract

Choose the Copy option when you want to copy data from the source file to the target file (which either replaces existing data or is appended to the target file, depending upon the ranges specified). As you would expect, you choose the Add option when you wish to add values in the source file to those in the target file, and the Subtract option when you wish to subtract values in the source file from those in the target file.

As soon as you select any of these three options, you receive the prompts

Entire-File   Named/Specified-Range

To copy, add, or subtract all the data in the source file to the target file, select the Entire-File option. The program then prompts you to indicate the name of the file you wish to combine: you can do this by moving the pointer to the file name on the line listing (or by pressing the Name key [F3] to get a full-screen listing) and pressing Enter, or by typing in the file name. If the file is not in the current directory, be sure to include the *path name* as part of the file name. Note that the path name refers to the drive name followed by a list of all subdirectories separated by a backslash (\), as in C:\123\DATA\SALES1.

To copy only a specific range, select the Named/Specified-Range option. When you select this option, 1-2-3 prompts you to enter a defined range name or range address with the prompt

Enter range name or address:

Here, you type in the range name or range address you want combined and press Enter. After that, you are prompted to indicate the name of the file that contains the range name or range address you just specified. You indicate the file name for the Named/Specified-Range in the same way as in the Entire-File option.

If you enter a range name that doesn't exist in the source file, 1-2-3 beeps, goes into ERROR mode, and displays the following error message:

Named range not found in worksheet file

After pressing Esc or Enter to return to READY mode, you will then have to repeat the entire /File Combine Copy command.

Copying Data with /File Combine Copy

When you use the /File Combine Copy command, 1-2-3 copies the specified data from the source file into the worksheet beginning at the current cell. Note that data copied from the source file will replace any existing data that are overlaid by the incoming data. To avoid any possibility of data loss that can occur when copying data in this way, you should always save the target file before performing a /File Combine Copy procedure. Should you happen to combine two files incorrectly, use the Undo key (Alt-F4). If you find that this doesn't work (because you performed an operation after using the /File Combine Copy command), use the /File Retrieve command to return the worksheet to the state prior to performing the consolidation.

Note that when combining files with the /File Combine Copy command, 1-2-3 doesn't transfer into the target file (that is, the current worksheet) any range names assigned to the data in the source file. Likewise, you will find that column-width settings used in the source file aren't transferred to the target file. This means that you must reassign range names and column widths for the incoming data in the current worksheet.

You can use the /File Combine Copy command whenever you need to combine worksheets saved in separate files into one file. Figure 7.1 illustrates this type of operation. In Figure 7.1, the monthly sales and commissions table for May is combined with that for April with the use of the /File Combine Copy command. This is done by placing the pointer in cell F1, then selecting the /File Combine Copy Named/Specified-Range command. The range name

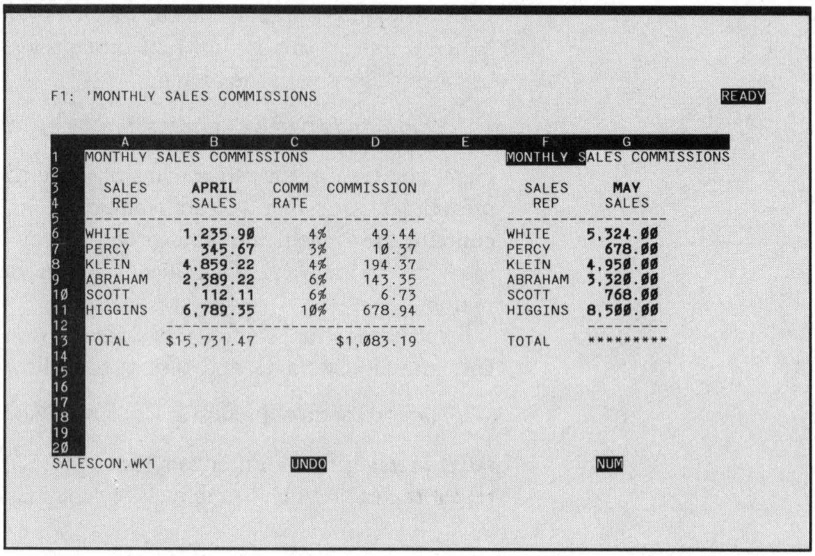

◆ **Figure 7.1:** *Combining sales and commissions tables from separate files into one worksheet*

may.sales is then entered in response to the prompt to enter the range name or address (this range name was already assigned to the sales and commissions table in the cell range A1..D13 and saved in the file SALES5.WK1). Finally, the name of the file, SALES5.WK1, that contains this range name was selected from the displayed listing of files.

Note in Figure 7.1 that column G of the target worksheet isn't wide enough to display the May sales totals in cell G13. Although the column containing this total in the source worksheet is widened sufficiently to display this total, the column-width setting isn't transferred when the data is copied into the target worksheet.

Consolidating Data with /File Combine Add or Subtract

The Add and Subtract options of the /File Combine command are used to perform calculations between numeric data in the files that are combined. In order for these calculations to be performed correctly, data in both the source and target worksheet files must be laid out in the same way. Also, make sure you locate the pointer in the first cell in the target file where you want incoming data to be added or subtracted before you perform the consolidation. Otherwise, you will not get the desired results even when the two files share a common layout that makes consolidations possible.

Just as when using /File Combine Copy, take the precaution of saving the current worksheet right before you attempt to consolidate worksheets with either the /File Combine Add or /File Combine Subtract command. That way, you can always retrieve the worksheet file in its original form, even when you can't use the Undo key (Alt-F4).

Lotus 1-2-3 will perform the addition or subtraction called for by the consolidation only when the data that occupy the same relative cell address in their respective files contain values that can be calculated. Unlike when using the /File Combine Copy command, incoming data do not replace existing data when you perform a consolidation with the /File Combine Add or Subtract command. Therefore, if the called-for calculation can't take place between the cells, the incoming data from the source file are discarded and the original data in the target are retained.

Figures 7.2 through 7.4 illustrate a simple worksheet consolidation using the /File Combine Add command. In Figure 7.2, you see the April sales and commissions report. In Figure 7.3, the May report has just been added to it by selecting the Named/Specified-Range option from the /File Combine Add menu, typing *B6.B11* (remember two periods aren't required), and then selecting the May file SALES5.WK1 from the file list. Note that except for the change to the sales figures in the range B6..B11 and the new total in cell B13, this worksheet appears the same as the one shown in Figure 7.2. For instance, cell B3 still contains *April*, even

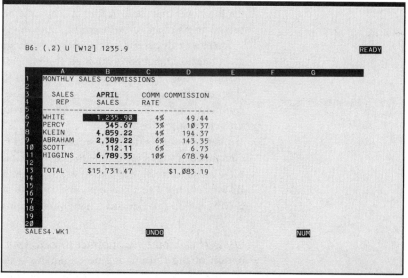

♦ **Figure 7.2:** *The April sales and commissions worksheet before the consolidation begins*

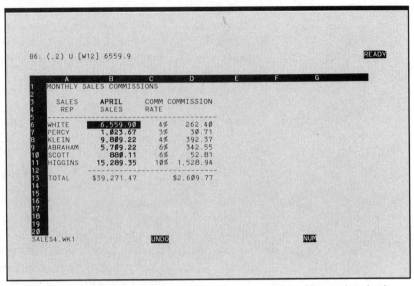

♦ **Figure 7.3:** *The April sales and commissions worksheet after adding in the sales figures from the May worksheet*

though this cell in the incoming file contains *May*. Remember that when you use /File Combine Add or Subtract, only corresponding cells in the worksheets containing values that can be added or subtracted are changed. Labels like the one in cell B3 aren't replaced by incoming data.

You can easily determine the proper range address to use because all the sales and commissions reports are built from the same template, and therefore the monthly sales figures are always entered in the range B6..B11 in every worksheet file. If you enter just the range of values that need to be calculated, 1-2-3 can perform the /File Combine Add procedure somewhat faster than if you used the Entire-File option.

Figure 7.4 shows the final worksheet after consolidating the June sales and commissions worksheet file with the /File Combine Add command (using the same range address). After this consolidation was performed, the label *April* in B3 was changed to *Quarterly*, and the file was saved under the new name SALESQ2.WK3 (for Second Quarter Sales Consolidation).

Using /File Combine Subtract to Zero Out a Worksheet   The Subtract option of the /File Combine command is used much less often than Add because you're far more likely to need the total for figures in individual worksheets than to know the difference between them. Nevertheless, besides those

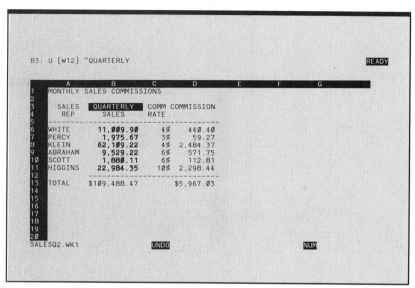

♦ **Figure 7.4:** *The Quarterly sales and commissions report after consolidating the sales figures for April, May, and June*

rare occasions when you really need to subtract two ranges in different files, another use for the Subtract option is useful.

When you want to convert a completed worksheet into a template, you can use the /File Combine Subtract command to quickly zero out the values in the new template. By using this command, you avoid having to manually replace each input value with a zero.

Figures 7.5 and 7.6 illustrate how this works. In Figure 7.5, the April sales and commissions worksheet is about to be zeroed out with the /File Combine Subtract command. In this worksheet, only the values in the range B6..B11 need to become zeros (the commissions figures are to remain in the template, as they don't vary from month to month). To complete this procedure, the Named/Specified-Range option is used, the range B6.B11 typed, and the April file SALE4.WK1 is selected. Note that by subtracting the values in the same range from the same worksheet file, you are assured of obtaining zeros as the result (unless, of course, you change the values in the current file and don't save them before you perform the subtraction), as shown in Figure 7.6.

Consolidating the Income Statements with /File Combine Add

Now it is time for you to get some experience using the /File Combine command. In the next exercise, you will first use the /File Combine Add command

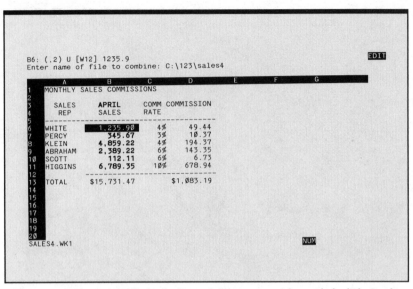

◆ **Figure 7.5:** *Converting the April sales worksheet into a template with the /File Combine Subtract command*

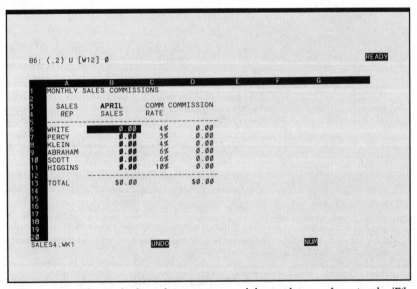

◆ **Figure 7.6:** *The April sales and commissions worksheet with zeros after using the /File Combine Subtract command*

to consolidate the various income statement worksheets that you created in earlier chapters directly from disk.

1. **Retrieve your income statement template file *ISTMPLT4.WK1*.**
    You will now use the /File Combine Add command to add the revenues and expenses in the income statement for 1990 to this new consolidation worksheet file. Here, you only need to add in the range of cells from B3..B22.

2. **Move the pointer to cell B3, where the revenues are located.**
    When using the /File Combine command, remember to locate the pointer in the first cell where you want the incoming data copied, added, or subtracted. Now you are ready to use the /File Combine Add command.

3. **Select the Named/Specified-Range option from the /File Combine Add menu (/FCAN); type *B6.B22* and press Enter; press the Name key (F3), move the pointer to the file *IS90CH5.WK1*, and press Enter.**
    The income and expense figures are copied from this worksheet into the proper cells in column B of the template file. You will now repeat this procedure until you have added in the figures for the years 1991, 1992, and 1993.

4. **Select the Named/Specified-Range option from the /File Combine Add menu (/FCAN); type *B6.B22* and press Enter; press the Name key (F3), move the pointer to the file *IS91CH3.WK1*, and press Enter.**
    When this operation is completed, the income and expenses in 1990 and 1991 should be added. Check the first few rows of values in your worksheet against those shown in Figure 7.7. (If the ones in your consolidated worksheet differ, you probably selected either the wrong /File Combine option or the wrong income statement. Clear the worksheet [/WEY], and start this exercise again.)

5. **Select the Named/Specified-Range option from the /File Combine Add menu (/FCAN); type *B6.B22* and press Enter; press the Name key (F3), move the pointer to the file *IS92CH3.WK1*, and press Enter.**
    You need to repeat this procedure once more, this time using the income statement for 1993.

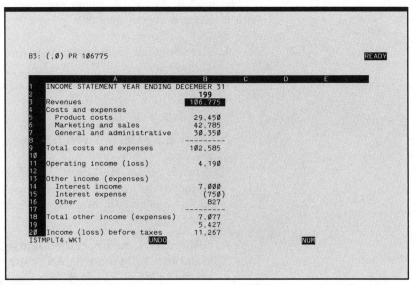

♦ **Figure 7.7:** *Consolidation worksheet after adding the income and expenses for the years 1990 and 1991*

6. **Select the Named/Specified-Range option from the /File Combine Add menu (/FCAN); type *B6.B22* and press Enter; press the Name key (F3), move the pointer to the file *IS93CH4.WK1*, and press Enter.**
   To finish the consolidated worksheet, you need to change the column heading for column B and the worksheet title, and then save the file under a new name.

7. **Move the pointer to cell B2 and erase its contents (/RE).**
   Now edit the worksheet title. Because the cell that contains this label is protected, you must remove the protection before you can make this change.

8. **Select the Disable option from the /Worksheet Global Protection menu (/WGPD).**
   With global protection turned off, you can now use the Edit key (F2) to modify the title.

9. **Move the pointer to cell A1; edit the label in this cell so that it reads *CONSOLIDATED INCOME STATEMENT FOR YEARS 1990–1993*.**
   Check your worksheet against the one in Figure 7.8. Before you save the consolidated worksheet, turn global protection on again.

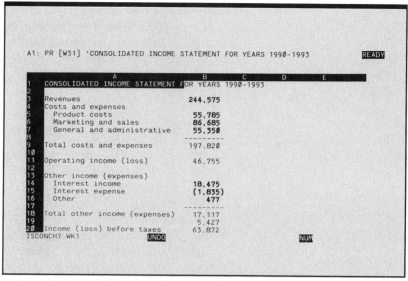

◆ **Figure 7.8:** *Consolidation worksheet after adding the income and expenses for the years 1990 through 1993*

10. **Select the Enable option from the /Worksheet Global Protection menu (/WGPE).**

    The last step is to save the consolidated worksheet under a new name.

11. **Select the /File Save command and modify the name of this worksheet to *ISCONCH7.WK1* before pressing Enter to save it.**

Combining the Income Statements with /File Combine Copy

In addition to performing a consolidation with the /File Combine Add command, you can create a composite worksheet using the /File Combine Copy command. In the next exercise, you will use the Copy option to combine your income statements stored in separate files into one worksheet.

1. **Retrieve the worksheet *IS90CH5.WK1*.**

    You will combine the other three income statements that you have created into this worksheet and then save it under a new name. But first, you will remove the Bonuses label and formula from this worksheet so that it matches the others that you are about to combine.

2. **Move the pointer to cell C16, then press End →.**
   The pointer should move directly to cell IV16, indicating that there are no other entries in this row. This means that it is safe to delete this row from the worksheet.

3. **Select the /Worksheet Delete Row command (/WDR) and press Enter to delete row 16.**
   Now you are ready to bring in the 1991 income statement. You will locate this income statement directly below the 1990 income statement.

4. **Press End ←, then move the pointer to cell A27 and select the /File Combine Copy Entire-File command (/FCCE). When prompted for the file, highlight the file name** *IS91CH3.WK1* **and press Enter.**
   The program copies in the entire 1991 income statement from cell A27 on. You can only see the worksheet title on the screen until you scroll up the 1991 income statement. In doing this, notice that this income statement lacks the percentage formulas that you created for the 1990 income statement, which compare each income statement category to the annual revenues. Before you bring in the income statement for 1992, you should add these formulas in column C.

5. **Move the pointer to cell C29, type + to begin the formula, move the pointer to cell B29, type /, then move the pointer back to cell B29, press the Abs key (F4) once, and press Enter.**
   The formula +B29/$B$29 in cell C29 should return *1* as the answer. Go ahead and format this result before you copy the formula down the column.

6. **Select the /Range Format Percent command (/RFP), then type** *1* **for the number of decimal places and press Enter twice.**
   Now, you are ready to copy this formula down column B.

7. **Type /C to start the copy and press Enter to accept the default FROM range of C29..C29; move the pointer down to cell C31, type a period to anchor the range, and press the ↓ key to extend it to cell C48, and then press Enter.**
   Before you copy the next income statement into this worksheet, you need to delete the copies of the formulas that compare the 1991 revenues to blank cells and repeating underscores.

8. **Use the /Range Erase command (/RE) to erase the contents of cells C34, C36, C38..C39, C43, and C45.**
   You will combine the 1992 income statement to the right of the 1990 income statement.

9. **Move the pointer to cell address F1 (you can use the Goto key, F5).**
   Here, you see the range name table that you created in one of the earlier lessons; before you can bring in the 1992 income statement, you need to move this table. Remember that you already named this range *NAME.TABLE* in a previous lesson.

10. **Type /M to begin the move operation; type *NAME.TABLE* or press the Name key (F3) and select this range name from the list, and press Enter; then, press the Home key and PgDn twice to move quickly to cell A41; from there, press the ↓ key until the pointer is in cell A51, and press Enter to complete the move operation.**
    You are ready to combine the third income statement, beginning at cell F1.

11. **Select the /File Combine Copy Entire-File command (/FCCE), and select the file *IS92CH3.WK1*.**
    Notice that column F isn't wide enough to display the row headings for this worksheet. You now need to widen this column.

12. **Select the /Worksheet Column Set-Width command (/WCS) and increase the column to 31 characters.**
    This income statement also lacks the percentage formulas. You will now add them in column H.

13. **Move the pointer to cell H3 and build the formula + G3/$G$3 there; format the result with the Percent format using one decimal place, then copy it to the range H5..H22, and delete all 0.00% results.**
    Now you need to bring in the 1993 income statement immediately below the 1992 income statement.

14. **Move the pointer to cell F27 and then use the /File Combine Copy Entire-File command to bring the worksheet *IS93CH4.WK1*; add the percent formulas in column H for the 1993 income statement and then delete the 0.00% results.**
    Before you save this worksheet under a new file name, you will give a range name to each income statement it now contains.

15. **Move the pointer to cell F27, select the /Range Name Create command (/RNC), and enter *INCST.93* as the range name and *F27..H49* as the range.**
    Next, assign a range name to the 1992 income statement above it.

16. **Press the PgUp key to move the pointer to cell F1; assign the range name** *INCST.92* **to the cell range** *F1..H23.*
    Now, assign range names to the 1990 and 1991 income statements.

17. **Press the Home key to move the pointer to cell A1, and assign the range** *INCT.90* **to the cell range** *A1..C23;* **then, move the pointer to cell A27 and assign the range name** *INCST.91* **to the cell range** *A27..C49.*
    Before you save your composite worksheet, you should update your range name table to include the new range names you've just added.

18. **Use the Goto key (F5) and the Name key (F3) to move the pointer to the first cell of the range name table by selecting its range name** *NAME.TABLE* **from the list; move the pointer to cell A53, then select the /Range Name Table command (/RNT) and press Enter.**
    You will save this composite worksheet under a new name so that it won't replace your IS90CH5.WK1 file.

19. **Save the worksheet under the file name** *ISC90-93.*

Extracting Data into a New File

At times, instead of combining data from individual worksheets, you may need to perform the opposite procedure, that is, to isolate a range of data or a particular schedule or table and save it in its own file. For example, if you build a worksheet file that has become too large to fit in the amount of free RAM available to 1-2-3 (indicated by the MEM indicator), you can split it into several smaller worksheet files. Then, you can continue to work with and add to the data by retrieving the appropriate worksheet file.

If your worksheet isn't too large for the RAM but becomes too large to be copied to a single 5¼-inch disk as one file, you can split the worksheet into several files that are saved on different floppy disks. Then, you use the /File Retrieve and /File Combine Copy commands to reassemble the worksheet from the individual files located on different backup disks.

When you want to extract a particular range of data from a worksheet and save it in a new file, you use the /File Xtract command. When you select this command, you must choose between these two options:

Formulas Values

If you select Formulas, 1-2-3 will copy all the formulas in the range of cells that you choose to extract. If you select Values, the program will convert any formulas in the extract range to their current values before copying all the data in this range to the new file.

When extracting formulas, be careful to copy all the data referred to in the formulas in the extract range. If you don't, you'll end up with incorrect results returned by some of the formulas in the new file, and even ERR values from those formulas that can no longer be successfully calculated.

After you choose between Formulas and Values, you are prompted to enter a new name for the file you are creating:

Enter name of file to extract to:

To save the new file in the current directory, you just start typing in a new file name, and your new name will replace the prompt *C:\123*.wk1*. To change the path name as well as the file name, press Esc twice to clear the file name and path name, and then type in the new path as part of the file name.

As soon as you finish entering the file name, 1-2-3 prompts you to designate the range of data that should be saved in the new file:

Enter extract range:

Here, you can enter the range address or a range name if one has been defined. Note that if you are extracting a named range by entering the range address but you then specify something other than the complete range, the range name will be extracted to the new file but it will no longer refer to the correct range. If the range of cells includes smaller named ranges, these range names will also be transferred to the new file.

If the file name that you entered has already been used, 1-2-3 will display the options

Cancel   Replace   Backup

just as it does when this situation arises in using the /File Save command (note, however, that the Backup option is new in Release 2.2). If you wish to abort the file extract operation, select the Cancel option. If you want to proceed and save the selected range under the same file name where it will replace the contents of the original file, select the Replace option. If you are using Release 2.2, you can save the contents of the original file in a backup file (using the extension .BAK) and save the selected range in a new file of the same name (using the extension .WK1) by choosing the Backup option.

Steps to Take in Freeing Memory: Whenever you see the MEM indicator, you need to save the worksheet file with /File Save. To free up RAM so that you can continue building your worksheet, you need to start eliminating any expendable items. If you have more than the current file in memory, start by erasing all other worksheets from RAM with the /Worksheet Delete File command. If you need to free some more memory, delete all named ranges and range name notes in the current file with the /Range Name Reset command. If you still need to free memory, you can then delete any graphs that aren't essential (you can delete all graphs with the /Graph Name Reset command). Finally, to free additional memory, you will need to split the worksheet into smaller, separate files using the /File Xtract command.

* *New in 2.2*

Linking Worksheet Files in 1-2-3

When you are building formulas in a Release 2.2 worksheet, 1-2-3 allows you to refer to the data in any other worksheet file saved on disk. When you build a formula in a worksheet that refers to data in another file, you create a *link* between the two files. When you create a linking formula in the current worksheet that refers to a cell in another file, the file in which you enter the formula (that is, the current worksheet) is called the *target file*, and the file that contains the value referred to is called the *source file*. Once these files are linked, 1-2-3 copies the value of the cell in the source file (also known as the *source cell*) to the cell in the target file (also know as the *target cell*).

Linked formulas offer you an excellent alternative to using /File Combine Copy to perform worksheet consolidations. Also, by allowing you to relate data stored in different files and update them at any time, you can effectively maintain a large spreadsheet application in several smaller worksheet files.

When creating a formula that refers to data in another file, you must follow this format:

    + < <*file reference* > >*cell reference*

Note that this format only enables you to bring forward the value of a source cell into a target cell. However, once it has been copied into the target file, you can include the target cell in any valid 1-2-3 formula.

Remember that the file reference contains the name of the file (including the extension) enclosed in double angle brackets, as in

    + <<IS90CH5.WK1>>C12

If the worksheet file is not located in the current directory, the file reference must include the path name as well as the complete file name, as in

+ <<C:\DATA\IS90CH5.WK1>>D5

The cell reference can be given by cell address or range name, if one has been assigned to the cell in the source file, as in

+ <<C:\DATA\IS90CH5.WK1>>INCOME

Note that if you enter a range name that has been assigned to a range larger than one cell, 1-2-3 copies just the first cell of this range into the target cell.

If the file to which a formula refers doesn't exist in the directory specified by the file reference (or in the current directory, if the file reference doesn't specify the directory), or if the file is later deleted from the directory, the formula will return ERR in the worksheet.

File References in Linking: If you include the path name in the file reference even when the file you are linking to is in the current directory, you will ensure the link between the two files will work even when you change the current directory. For example, if your worksheet contains the formula

+ <<DEPT_1.WK1>>C12

this formula will work only so long as the worksheet file that contains it is in the same directory as the file DEPT_1.WK1. However, if you move the file that contains this link to a different directory from DEPT_1.WK1, the formula will no longer work. It would still work, however, if you included the path name in the file reference, as in

+ <<C:\123\DATA\DEPT_1.WK1>>C12

If you don't include the path name as part of the file reference, make sure that you keep the linked worksheet files in the same directory on your hard disk. Omitting the path name from the file reference gives the added advantage of allowing you to move the linked files to a new disk and/or directory without having to edit the formulas. For example, the formula

+ <<DEPT_1.WK1>>B25

will work as long as the file that contains the formula, as well as the DEPT_1.WK1 file, are in the same directory, regardless of whether they are all in A:\, B:\DATA, C:\123\ACCTS, or another directory.

Recalculating Linked Formulas

Lotus 1-2-3 updates the target cells in the linked formulas you create only under two conditions:

- ♦ When you retrieve the target file with /File Retrieve
- ♦ When you select the /File Admin Link-Refresh command

When using Release 2.2 on a network and sharing linked files, you will want to periodically use the /File Admin Link-Refresh command (/FAL) to ensure that all links have been properly updated. You should always select /File Admin Link-Refresh before saving the worksheet.

Keeping Track of the Linked Files

Release 2.2 includes two commands to help you keep track of all files linked by formula references to the current worksheet. To obtain a full-screen listing of the files linked to the current one, use the /File List Linked (/FLL) command. To see the date and time when the file was last modified and the size of the file, you just have to move the pointer to the file in this screen. To return to the current worksheet, press Enter.

In addition to the /File List Linked command, you can also use the /File Admin Table Linked (/FATL) command. This command creates a new table in your worksheet that lists all files linked by formula reference to the current file. The table created by this command contains four columns: the first column contains the file name, the second column contains the date number when the file was last modified, the third column contains the time number when the file was last modified, and the fourth column contains the size of the file in bytes.

The linked file table created with this command, just like the range name table and the active file table, must be recreated to update its information. Also, be careful that you don't inadvertently destroy any data by specifying a table range that overlaps existing data.

Linking the Income Statement Worksheets

To get some practice in working with multiple worksheets and establishing links with formulas, perform the following exercise. In this exercise, you will create a summary worksheet that contains formulas with links to all income statement worksheet files you have created.

1. **If you still have the worksheet from the last exercise on the screen, erase it from memory using the /Worksheet Erase command.**

   You are now going to start a new summary worksheet that will bring forward the revenue figures and sum the operating costs in the income statement worksheets for the years 1990 through 1993.

2. **Refer to Figure 7.9 and enter the labels shown there; center the column headings that show the years; after entering these labels, move the pointer to column A and widen this column to 16 spaces.**

   Next, you need to create and copy two formulas required in this summary table.

3. **In cell B7, build the formula $+B4 - B5$, then copy it to the range B7..F7; in cell F4, build the formula @SUM(B4..E4) and copy it to cell F5; enter a repeating hyphen (\-) in cell B6, and copy it to the range B6..F6; finally, format the range B4..F7 using the Comma format with 0 decimal places.**

   Your worksheet should now look like the one in Figure 7.10. Now you are ready to open the income statement worksheet files for 1990 through 1993. In doing this, you will assign range names to the revenue source cell (B3) and the total expenses source cell (B9) in each of the worksheets. Before you retrieve the first worksheet, you need to save the current worksheet.

4. **Save your summary file under the file name *ISLINK*.**

   Now you need to retrieve the first worksheet, *IS90CH5.WK1*.

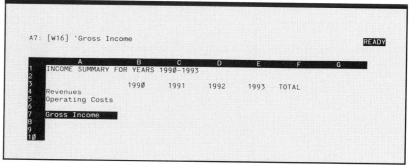

♦ **Figure 7.9:** *Entering the labels for the summary worksheet*

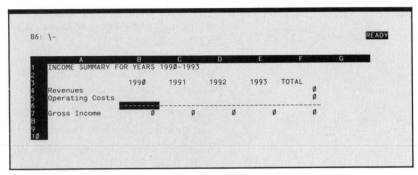

◆ **Figure 7.10:** *Building the formulas for the summary worksheet*

5. **Retrieve the file** *IS90CH5.WK1*.
   Remember that cell B3 has already been assigned the range name *REVENUES*. For this worksheet, you only have to assign a range name to cell B9.

6. **Move the pointer to cell B9, type /RNC and enter** *TOTAL.EXP* **as the range, and press Enter; then, press Enter a second time to assign this name to the cell range B9..B9; finally, save this worksheet under the same name, using the Replace option.**
   Next, you need to retrieve the income statement for 1991 and assign the range name *REVENUES* to its cell B3 and the range name *TOTAL.EXP* to its cell B9.

7. **Retrieve the worksheet** *IS91CH3.WK1*; **use the /Range Name Create command to assign the range name** *REVENUES* **to cell B3 and the range name** *TOTAL.EXP* **to cell B9; then, save the file under the same name.**
   Now you need to do the same thing for the income statement for 1992.

8. **Retrieve the worksheet** *IS92CH3.WK1*; **use the /Range Name Create command to assign the range name** *REVENUES* **to cell B3 and the range name** *TOTAL.EXP* **to cell B9; then, save the file under the same name.**
   Finally, you need to retrieve the income statement for 1993 and assign the same range names.

9. **Retrieve the worksheet** *IS93CH4.WK1*; **use the /Range Name Create command to assign the range name** *REVENUES* **to cell B3 and the range name** *TOTAL.EXP* **to cell B9; then, save the file under the same name.**

Now that you have named these source cells in each of the four income statements, you are ready to enter the linking formulas in your summary worksheet.

10. **Retrieve the worksheet** *ISLINK.WK1;* **move the pointer to cell B4, type** *+ <<is90ch5>>revenues,* **and press Enter.**
Your income summary worksheet should now resemble the one shown in Figure 7.11. The program has brought forward the value *50250* from the Revenues cell in the 1990 income statement. Notice that 1-2-3 automatically appended the extension *.WK1* to the file name you entered as the file reference for this formula: you only have to enter an extension when the source cell is in a Release 1A worksheet that uses the extension *WKS.*

11. **Move the pointer to B5, type** *+ <<is90ch5>>total.exp,* **and press Enter.**
When you complete this formula, 1-2-3 should bring forward the value *50810* from the 1990 income statement and calculate a gross loss of *−560.* Because you assigned the same range names to the Revenue and Total costs cells in each of the income statements, the only thing that differs in the rest of the formulas to be added to this table are the file references. To make it easier to finish this summary table, you can therefore copy the formulas in B4 and B5. Before you do, however, you must change the relative cell references for REVENUES and TOTAL.EXP to absolute references to prevent their being adjusted when copied.

12. **Move the pointer to cell B4 and edit the formula so that it reads** *+ <<IS90CH5.WK1>>$REVENUES,* **and press the ↓ key.**
Now you need to add the dollar sign to range name *TOTAL.EXP* in cell B5.

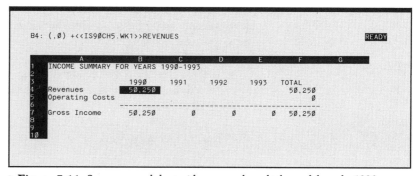

♦ **Figure 7.11:** *Summary worksheet with revenues brought forward from the 1990 income statement worksheet*

13. **Move the pointer to cell B5 and edit the formula so that it reads + <<IS90CH5.WK1>>$TOTAL.EXP, and press Enter.**
    The next step is to copy the modified formulas in B4 and B5 to the cell range C4..E5. After making these copies, you will then have to edit their file references.

14. **Copy the cell range B4..B5 to C4..E5.**
    Now you need to edit the file references in the formulas copied to C4 and C5.

15. **Move the pointer to C4 and edit the formula so that it reads + <<IS91CH3.WK1>>$REVENUES; then, edit the formula in C5 so that it reads + <<IS91CH3.WK1>>$TOTAL.EXP.**
    You need to repeat this procedure in cells D4 and D5, changing their file references so that they refer to the worksheet file IS92CH3.

16. **Edit the formula in D4 so that it reads + <<IS92CH3.WK1>>$REVENUES; then, edit the formula in D5 so that it reads + <<IS92CH3.WK1>>$TOTAL.EXP.**
    You need to repeat this procedure once more in cells E4 and E5. Here, you need to change their file references so that they refer to the worksheet file IS93CH4.

17. **Edit the formula in E4 so that it reads + <<IS93CH4.WK1>>$REVENUES; then, edit the formula in E5 so that it reads + <<IS93CH4.WK1>>$TOTAL.EXP.**
    Your summary worksheet should resemble the one shown in Figure 7.12. You are now ready to save this file.

18. **Save the file under the same name, *ISLINK.WK1*.**

Practice Working with Linked Files

Next, you will learn how to use the commands that help you keep track of the linked files you are using.

1. **Select the /File List Linked command (/FLL).**
   You should see a full-screen listing of files that includes IS90CH5.WK1, IS91CH3.WK1, IS92CH3.WK1, and IS93CH4.WK1. Now that you have viewed the linked files, let's create a table of all files linked to your income summary worksheet.

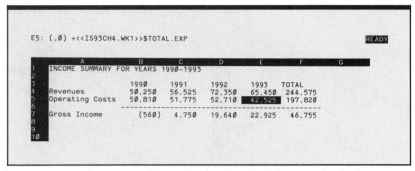

* **Figure 7.12:** *Summary worksheet after completing the linking formulas that bring forward the required income statement values*

2. **Press Enter to return to the worksheet; select the /File Admin Table Linked command (/FATL); move the pointer to cell H3 and press Enter in response to the prompt to enter the range for the table.**
   The table of linked files generated by this command contains four columns. The first column contains the name of each file, the second and third columns list the date and time serial numbers for the date and time of the most recent revision, and the last column lists the file size. Go ahead and format the table to make it easier to read.

3. **Referring to Figure 7.13, widen column H to 12 and then enter the column headings above each column; next, widen column I to 14 and then format the date numbers in this column with the D4 format (Long International); finally, widen column J to 15 and format the time numbers in this column with the T1 format (Lotus standard long form).**
   Save this table as part of the worksheet file.

4. **Press the Home key, then save the file under the same file name.**

Making Changes to Linked Values

Now let's see what happens if you change some values referenced in the linked formulas of the summary worksheet.

```
H3: [W12] 'IS90CH5.WK1                                            READY

        H            I            J             K       L       M
1                 Date of Last  Time of Last
2    File Name    Revision      Revision      Size in Bytes
3    IS90CH5.WK1    06/01/89      05:25:18 PM      3312
4    IS91CH3.WK1    06/01/89      08:08:28 AM      2381
5    IS92CH3.WK1    06/03/89      12:57:15 PM      2381
6    IS93CH4.WK1    06/02/89      05:45:28 PM      2381
7
8
9
10
```

◆ **Figure 7.13:** *Table showing the files linked to the current worksheet*

1. **Retrieve the worksheet *IS90CH5.WK1;* move the pointer to cell B5, and change the product costs for 1990 to *15300.***
   Notice that by increasing this value from *12,175,* the total costs and expenses in cell B9 have increased to *53,935.*

2. **Move the pointer to cell B3 and change the revenues to *72000.***
   Notice that by increasing this value from *50,250,* the operating income in B11 has now become *18,065.*

3. **Save the 1990 income statement under the same name; then, retrieve the summary worksheet *ISLINK.WK1.***
   Because 1-2-3 automatically refreshes the links and updates the linked formulas when you retrieve a file, the revenues for 1990 in cell B4 of the summary worksheet should now be *72,000,* the operating costs in cell B5 *53,935,* and the gross income *18,065.*

4. **Retrieve the file *IS92CH3.WK1.***
   You will modify the revenues and the marketing and sales expense in this worksheet.

5. **Move the pointer to B3 and increase the revenues to *79400;* then move the pointer to cell B6 and decrease the marketing and sales expense to *20500.***
   Notice how these changes effect your total costs and expenses in cell B9 (increased to 49,085) and your operating income in B11 (increased to 30,315).

6. **Save the 1992 income statement under the same name, then retrieve the *ISLINK.WK1* file.**

Verify that the income, operating costs, and gross income have been updated correctly in your income summary worksheet. Cell D4 should have *79,400*, D5 *49,085*, and D7 *30,315*.

Summary

Troubleshooting

Question: I used /File Combine Copy to add a data range that contains several named ranges into the current file. However, I discovered that the range names had not been transferred to the new file. Am I doing something wrong?

Answer: Lotus 1-2-3 never transfers range names when copying named data ranges from one file to another with the /File Combine Copy command; only the data themselves are transferred. You must rename the ranges in the new file. (Note that when you use the /File Xtract command, the range names are transferred.)

Question: I used the /File Xtract command to copy part of a worksheet into a new file, and although all range names were transferred from the original file, they no longer refer to the correct data in the new file. Is there any way to correct this?

Answer: This is a common problem that occurs when using /File Xtract. Because 1-2-3 copies all range names in the new file but you are copying only part of the data and they are often relocated in the new worksheet, more often than not, the range names in the new file refer to the wrong cell ranges. The only thing you can do is to delete the erroneous range names with the /Range Name Delete or /Range Name Reset command and then redefine them.

Question: I'm using Release 2.2 and was attempting to create a linked formula that would add a cell containing a total in a worksheet file in the current directory to one of the cells in the current worksheet. When I pressed the Enter key, however, instead of giving me the correct sum, 1-2-3 beeped and went into EDIT mode. What I am doing wrong?

Answer: Remember that you can *only* bring forward a value from a cell in another worksheet file; you can't use a source cell directly in any other kind of formula. This means that 1-2-3 won't accept a formula such as +<<IS90CH5>>B3+B2. If you want to add the value in cell B3 in the file

IS90CH5 to the contents of cell B2 in the current worksheet, you must first copy the value of the source cell into the current worksheet. For instance, you could do this by entering the formula $+<<IS90CH5>>B3$ in cell B1 of the current worksheet. Once this is done, 1-2-3 will allow you to add the value in the target cell B1 to that of B2 with the formula $+B1+B2$.

Essential Techniques

To Copy, Add, or Subtract Data in a Disk File to or from the Current Worksheet

1. Move the pointer to the first cell in the current worksheet where the data copied from the source file is to be located (make sure there is sufficient room, so the incoming data won't replace existing data).

2. Select the /File Combine command (/FC). To have the data copied into the current value, replacing any existing data located in the same range, select the Copy option. To add all values that overlay each other, select the Add option. To subtract all values that overlay each other, select the Subtract option.

3. Select the Entire-File option to have all data from the source file copied into the current file, or else select the Named/Specified-Range option.

4. If you selected the Named/Specified-Range option, type in the range address or range name of the data in the source file and press Enter.

5. Select the name of the source file, either by typing it in or choosing it on the line listing that appears, and press Enter.

To Save a Range of Data in Its Own File

1. Move the pointer to the first cell in the range that you want saved in its own file.

2. Select the /File Xtract command (/FX).

3. Choose the Formulas option to retain the formulas in the new worksheet file, or select the Values option to have only values copied.

4. Type in the name you wish to give the new file and press Enter. If you want to save this file in a new directory or disk, include the path in the file name.

5. Indicate the range of data to be saved, either by typing in the range address or range name or pointing it out, then press Enter to have the data saved in the new file.

Review   **Important Terms You Should Know**

link   source file
path name   target cell
source cell   target file

Test Your Knowledge

1. To copy all the data from a worksheet file on disk into the current worksheet, select the _____ option from the _____ menu.

2. To add data from a named range in a worksheet file on disk into the current worksheet, select the _____ option from the _____ menu. To enter the name of the range to combine, you can then either select it from the line list with the _____ key or type in its name.

3. To zero out all values in the current worksheet file, select the _____ option from the _____ menu. When prompted for the file name, you then enter _____.

4. To save a range of data in the current worksheet in its own file and preserve the formulas it contains, select the _____ option from the _____ menu, then enter the name for the new file followed by the range address or range name for the data to be saved.

5. When creating a link to data in another worksheet file, you must enter the _____ before the cell address or range name.

6. When creating a link that references another worksheet file not in the current directory, you must include _____ as part of the file reference used to identify the data.

7. To have the worksheet recalculated and the linked files on disk updated, select the _____ command.

8. To obtain a listing of all files linked to the current file, select the _____ command. To create a table of all files linked to the current file, select the _____ command.

Further Exercises

1. Retrieve your income summary worksheet file ISLINK.WK1, and expand the income summary table as shown in Figure 7.14: bring forward the values for the total other income from the individual income statements you have prepared into row 8 to determine the net income in row 10. In B8, enter the linking formula to bring forward the total other income value in B18 from the file IS90CH4. Change the cell reference in this formula to an absolute value and the copy this formula to the range C8..E8, then change the file references in the copied formulas so that they copy the value in the B18 source cell from the correct files (IS91CH3, IS92CH3, and IS93CH4). In cell F8, add a formula that sums the other income values in the cell range B8..E8. Format the values in the range B8..F10 using the Comma format with 0 decimal places. Save the changes to the worksheet under the same name.

2. Retrieve the worksheet file IS90CH5.WK3, and change the other interest income in cell B14 to 6000 and the other income expense in cell B15 to −150. Check the effect that these changes have on the total other income and net earnings values in this worksheet. Save these changes to the worksheet under the same name.

3. Open the ISLINK.WK1 worksheet again. Make sure that it has been properly updated.

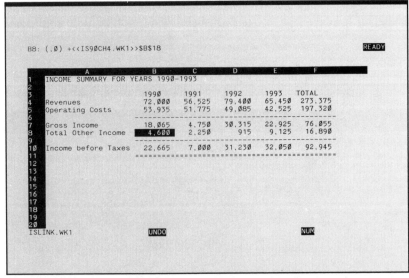

◆ **Figure 7.14:** *Adding new linked formulas to the income summary worksheet file*

Part II

♦

Generating Reports and Graphs

♦

8

Mastering
Printing

In This
Chapter...

Printing Basics

To print data in a worksheet, you use the /Print menu. When you select /Print, 1-2-3 presents you with two initial options: Printer and File. You choose the Printer option to have the program print a hard copy of the specified data, using the default text printer you installed. You choose the File option to have the program produce an ASCII text file that contains the specified data. Such text files can be imported into other programs that read ASCII files—for example, word processors such as WordPerfect or WordStar (for specific transferring information using the ASCII file format and the /Printer File command, refer to Chapter 14).

Regardless of whether you choose the Printer or File option the /Print menu, you are then presented with the same printing options. To successfully print a report from the worksheet, you need to have installed your printer as one of the text printer choices when you installed the program, have that printer selected as the current printer, and have defined the range of cells to be included in the report as the print range. The program will then print your report using its default print settings.

Setting Up Your Hardware

When you installed 1-2-3 with the Install program, you were asked to designate a text printer. In both Release 2.01 and 2.2, you can install multiple text printers. The first printer that you've installed becomes the *default printer*, that is, the one that is automatically used in printing reports every time you run the program. If you wish to print with one of the other text printers that you installed, you first need to designate it as the *current printer* before you begin printing your report. If you wish, you can not only make one of your installed printers the current printer but also the new default printer.

If you get a new printer that you wish to use in printing your worksheet reports, remember that you have to use the Install program to install this printer before you can use it in 1-2-3 (see Appendix A for more information on using new hardware with the Install program).

To make a new printer the current one, you need to select the /Worksheet Global Default Printer command (/WGDP). Figure 8.1 shows you the menu options that appear when you select this command as well as the Default Settings sheet.

If you are using Release 2.2, you can check the default printer settings on this settings sheet to see which are in effect and which require modification in making a new printer current. Notice in this figure that the Default Settings sheet shows you all settings for the default printer in the first column of the sheet arranged in the same order as the menu options in the command line above.

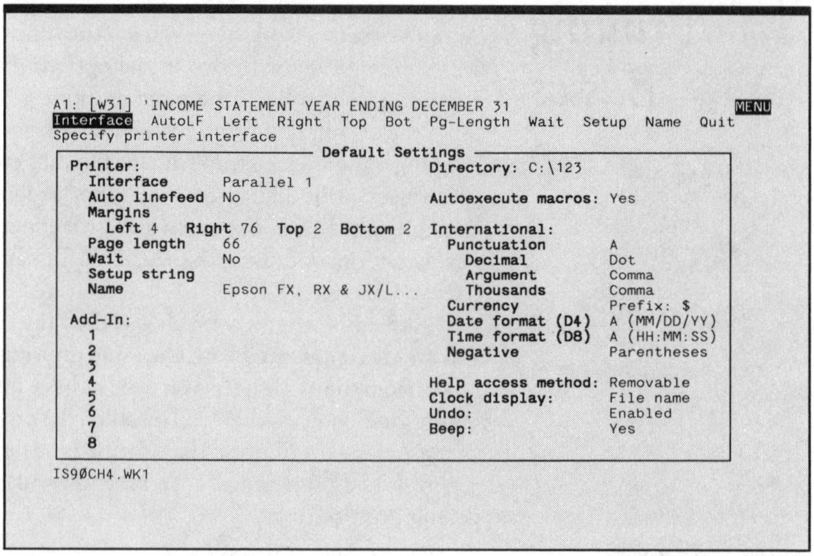

```
A1: [W31] 'INCOME STATEMENT YEAR ENDING DECEMBER 31                    MENU
Interface  AutoLF  Left  Right  Top  Bot  Pg-Length  Wait  Setup  Name  Quit
Specify printer interface
┌────────────────────────── Default Settings ──────────────────────────┐
│ Printer:                            Directory: C:\123                  │
│   Interface     Parallel 1                                            │
│   Auto linefeed No                  Autoexecute macros: Yes           │
│   Margins                                                             │
│     Left 4   Right 76  Top 2  Bottom 2  International:                │
│   Page length  66                     Punctuation     A              │
│   Wait         No                       Decimal       Dot            │
│   Setup string                          Argument      Comma          │
│   Name         Epson FX, RX & JX/L...   Thousands     Comma          │
│                                       Currency        Prefix: $      │
│ Add-In:                               Date format (D4) A (MM/DD/YY)   │
│   1                                   Time format (D8) A (HH:MM:SS)   │
│   2                                     Negative      Parentheses     │
│   3                                                                   │
│   4                                  Help access method: Removable    │
│   5                                  Clock display:    File name      │
│   6                                  Undo:             Enabled        │
│   7                                  Beep:             Yes            │
│   8                                                                   │
└───────────────────────────────────────────────────────────────────────┘
IS9ØCH4.WK1
```

◆ **Figure 8.1:** *The /Worksheet Global Default Printer menu options with the Default Setting sheet*

Notice that although this menu contains many printer options for changing the printing defaults, in selecting a new printer you are primarily interested in the Name, Interface, and AutoLF settings.

Selecting a New Printer

When making a new printer current, first select the Name option from the /WGDP menu. When you do, 1-2-3 will present you with a menu of numbers, each of which corresponds to one of the printers you have already installed with Install program. On this menu, the first option (1) always corresponds to the first text printer that you installed with the program. To make a new printer current, you must select its number from this menu (as you move the pointer to a new number option, 1-2-3 indicates the name of the printer on the line below it).

Selecting the Proper Interface

After selecting a new printer with the Name option, you may also have to change the type of printer interface with the Interface option. The printer interface designates the type of connection between your computer and printer (either parallel or serial), as well as the number of that particular kind of port. When you select the Interface option, 1-2-3 presents you with the following options, numbered 1 through 8:

1. Parallel 1, which is the first parallel port attached to your computer (also known as LPT1)

2. Serial 1, which is the first serial port attached to your computer (also known as COM1)

3. Parallel 2, which is the second parallel port attached to your computer (also known as LPT2)

4. Serial 2, which is the second serial port attached to your computer (also known as COM2)

5. DOS Device LPT1

6. DOS Device LPT2

7. DOS Device LPT3

8. DOS Device LPT4

The last four options, 5 through 8, describe logical output devices used by some networks to describe the printer interface. Unless you are using 1-2-3 on a network, you won't use any of these options.

If your printer uses a serial interface and you choose either option 2 or 4, you must then select the option that corresponds to the correct baud rate (that is, the rate at which data are transmitted to the printer). The baud rate options are numbered from 1 through 9 and correspond to the following rates:

1. 110 baud	6. 2400 baud
2. 150 baud	7. 4000 baud
3. 300 baud	8. 9600 baud
4. 600 baud	9. 19200 baud
5. 1200 baud	

Option 1 is the default. To select a new baud rate, merely type the number of the option that corresponds to the correct rate setting. (To obtain the correct baud rate for your printer, you need to refer to your printer documentation.)

When printing with a serial port, other settings need to be specified, including the data bits, stop bits, parity, and XON/XOFF settings. When you use a serial text printer with 1-2-3, make sure that the data bits are set to 8, the stop bits are set to 1 (unless the baud rate is 110, in which case set the stop bits to 2), parity is none, and XON/XOFF is enabled. Note that none of these settings can be changed from within 1-2-3 itself: they must be the current settings by the time you start printing your reports with the program.

Changing the Auto-Linefeed Setting

The AutoLF option (for automatic linefeed) tells 1-2-3 whether to transmit a carriage return and linefeed or just a carriage return to the printer after each line in the report. When you select a new printer, you sometimes have to change the AutoLF setting as well as the type of interface. The default setting for this option is No, meaning the program only sends a carriage return at the end of each line.

This default setting is fine as long as your printer interprets a carriage return as meaning "move the printhead to the left edge of the paper *and* advance the page by one line," as most do. Some printers, however, only move the printhead to the left edge of the page when they receive a carriage return. Such printers require a separate linefeed signal to advance the page by one line. With such printers, you need to change the AutoLF setting from No to Yes to avoid having 1-2-3 overprint each line of the report.

Making the Current Printer the Default Printer

After you select a new printer with the Name option, and change its Interface and AutoLF options if necessary, it becomes the current printer. All reports that you print in 1-2-3 are sent to this printer during the rest of your work session. If, however, you want to make this printer the default printer that is used whenever you print reports in subsequent work sessions, you need to select the Update option from the /Worksheet Global Default menu before you quit the program. Otherwise, 1-2-3 will once again use the printer that you first installed as the default printer, the next time you start 1-2-3.

Printing a Basic Report

As soon as you have selected your printer, you are ready to print. When you select the /Print Printer (or /Print File) command, the main printing menu with the following options appears:

Range Line Page Options Clear Align Go Quit

If you are using Release 2.2, you will also see a Print Settings sheet below this menu like the one shown in Figure 8.2. As you define the settings required for your report, this Print Settings sheet is updated to reflect your selections.

```
A1: [W31] 'INCOME STATEMENT YEAR ENDING DECEMBER 31          MENU
Range  Line  Page  Options  Clear  Align  Go  Quit
Specify a range to print
                              ┌── Print Settings ──
  Destination:  Printer

  Range:

  Header:
  Footer:

  Margins:
    Left 4      Right 76    Top 2    Bottom 2

  Borders:
    Columns
    Rows

  Setup string:

  Page length:  66

  Format:        As-Displayed (Formatted)

IS90CH4.WK1
```

♦ **Figure 8.2:** *The main printing menu with the Print Settings sheet*

Selecting the Print Range

In order to print data from your spreadsheet the first time, you must choose the Range option and indicate the range of cells to be printed. This range can consist of all cells used in the worksheet or just some of them. Note that the program remembers this print range and stores it as part of the worksheet when you next save it with the /File Save command.

The print range is defined just like any other in 1-2-3: either by typing in the range address, typing the range name or selecting it with the Name key (F3), or pointing it out. If you want to print all worksheet data in your report, the easiest way to designate this range is to select the /Print Printer Range command (/PPR), press the Home key to move the pointer to cell A1, type a period to anchor the range, then press the End and Home keys to move the pointer to the last active cell in the worksheet. When you use the End and Home keys to make the last active cell in the worksheet the last cell of the print range, 1-2-3 will automatically expand the print range to include the last active cell as you add data to the worksheet, thereby changing its address.

When defining the print range, be sure to include all the data you want printed. If there are long labels in the range whose final characters spill over into a new column, you must be certain that you include this new column as part of the print range. If you don't, you will find these labels are truncated in the printed report: only the text and numbers displayed within the highlighted print range are included in the printed report.

Starting the Printing

The program assumes that you are printing your report on 8½-×-11-inch continuous-feed paper. As long as this is the case, you can print your report by selecting the Align and Go commands (AG) on the main printing menu as soon as you have finished defining the print range with the Range option. Always select the Align option (though nothing obvious will appear to happen when you select it) before the Go option when you begin printing a report, because this tells 1-2-3 that the current position of the printhead is the top of form (of course, you should manually make sure that the printhead is at the top of the page before printing).

If you need to stop the printer, press the Ctrl–Num Lock key combination. This acts as a printer pause. The WAIT indicator continues to flash, and the printer waits until you press any key. If you wish to abort the printing of the report before it is finished, press the Ctrl-Break key, and then press the Esc or Enter key when you receive the *Printer Error* message and the program goes into ERROR mode.

Advancing the Paper in the Printer

Lotus 1-2-3 stops printing the report as soon as it reaches the last row in the print range. On the last page of the report, this occurs before the printhead has reached the bottom of the page. To advance the printhead to the top of form at the beginning of the next page, you should use the Page option on the main /Print menu.

If you are using a laser printer, such as the HP LaserJet Series II, 1-2-3 won't even eject the last page until you select the Page option. If you are printing with a printer that uses continuous-feed paper, such as an Epson FX dot-matrix printer, you can select the Page option a second time to issue a form feed to the printer, thereby advancing the paper another complete page. This enables you to remove the report from the printer without disturbing the paper in the tractor feed. If you don't want to advance the paper an entire page, you can use the Line option to advance it a line at a time.

Make a habit of using the Page or Line option on the /Print Printer (or File) menu to advance the paper instead of advancing it manually or taking the printer offline and advancing it with the printer's form-feed or linefeed controls. This is because when you advance the page using any method besides the Page or Line option, 1-2-3 loses track of the printhead's position on the page.

Suppose, for example, that 1-2-3 has just finished printing the last page of your report and the printhead is positioned in the middle of the page. In your eagerness to read the report over, you go over to the printer and manually advance the page until the printhead is located at the top of the next full page after you remove the report. Then, after reading over the report, you notice a couple of mistakes. After fixing these errors, you give the command to print the same report. If you don't select the Align option before the Go option, 1-2-3 will still act as if the printhead is positioned in the middle of the page. This means that after printing several lines of the first page of the report, the program will insert a page break in the middle of the page (because it assumes the printhead is now at the end of the page). And once the first page of the report is paged incorrectly, all subsequent pages will also be printed inaccurately.

The only way to avoid such problems when printing is either to always select the Align option before the Go option when you print or to use the Line and Page options to advance the paper. Actually, a combination of both techniques will ensure that you don't have unpleasant surprises waiting for you at the printer.

Printing Multiple Ranges in a Single Report

The only time you don't want to use the Page option to advance to the next top of form when the printing stops, or use the Align option before Go when starting the printing, is when you want to print more than one range continuously as part of a single report. In that case, as soon as the printer finishes printing the first range, you select the Range command and define the second range as the print range without first selecting the Page option to advance the paper to the next top of form. Then, to start printing the newly defined print range at the printhead's current position on the page, you select the Go option without first selecting the Align option (because the printhead hasn't been moved to the top of form). Only when you have printed the last range you wish to include in the report in this manner will you use the Page option to advance the printhead to the next top of form.

Formatting Your Reports

The default format settings used by 1-2-3 (shown in the Print Settings sheet shown in Figure 8.2) are perfectly adequate when you simply need a quick printout of a particular range of data in your worksheet. The program does, however, offer several format options that give you a good deal of control over the appearance of a printed report and enable you to enhance their readability. In formatting your report, you can set new margins, add a header and footer, change the page length, print certain columns and rows as borders on each page, and insert setup strings that send codes to your printer producing such enhancements as bold, italics, compressed, or expanded type.

In addition to the format controls offered by these options on the /Print Options menu, you will also learn how you can add manual page breaks to your report and add special print enhancements to sections of the body of the report by inserting setup strings in the worksheet itself.

Modifying the Margin Settings

The default margin settings are a left margin 4 spaces from the left edge of the page, a right margin 76 spaces from the left edge of the page, a top margin two lines from the top of the page, and a bottom margin two lines from the bottom of the page. To change any of these margin settings for your report, you must select Margins from the /Print Printer Options menu (/PPOM). When you select this command, 1-2-3 presents you with these options:

Left Right Top Bottom None

The left- and right-margin settings are reckoned as the number of spaces or characters from the left edge of the page.

With the default left margin of 4, 1-2-3 begins printing each line at the fifth space from the left edge of the paper. To increase or decrease the left margin in a report, select Margins Left from the Options menu and enter the number of spaces between 0 and 240.

Because the right-margin setting is also reckoned from the left edge of the page, it overlaps the left-margin setting in effect. When using the default left and right margins of 4 and 76, this means that the maximum line length in the report is 72 spaces (76−4) or about 7¼ inches long. With 76 as the right margin, the longest line in the report will end about half an inch from the right edge of the page.

To change the right margin for your report, select Margins Right from the Options menu and enter the number of characters from the left edge between 0 and 240. Note that the right-margin setting must exceed the left-margin setting, otherwise 1-2-3 won't be able to print your report. Also, you need to make the difference between the left- and right-margin settings equal to or greater than the widest column in your print range. This is because 1-2-3 won't print just a partial column on a page: if the program can't accommodate a column within the margin settings on a particular page, it prints the entire column on the next page of the report. To print the longest line possible on the page, be sure to set the left margin to 0 and then set the right margin to the maximum setting that can be used by your printer given the width of paper and size of type you are using.

When setting the right margin, you must make sure that it is compatible with the width of the paper as well as the size of type you are using. The standard type size used by 1-2-3 in printing is pica, which gives you 10 characters per inch. At this size, you can fit a maximum line length of about 80 characters when using an 8½-inch-wide sheet of paper. If you use 14-inch-wide paper and print in pica type, you can have a maximum line length of about 132 characters.

Most printers can produce compressed type, which gives you about 17 characters per inch (you will learn how to use compressed type later in this chapter). When you use compressed type, you can increase the maximum line length to about 132 characters on an 8½-inch-wide sheet of paper. If you are using 14-inch-wide paper and compressed type, the maximum line length increases to about 240 characters.

If you specify a right-margin setting for your report that is longer than the maximum number of characters that can be printed on one line, 1-2-3 will wrap the extra characters to the next line on the page, making your report difficult to read. Also, if you change to compressed type, be sure to remember to increase the right-margin setting before you send the report to the printer. Otherwise, although each page of the report will be printed in smaller type, you will find that 1-2-3 hasn't included any more information on the page than it did when you printed the report using pica type.

✷ *New in 2.2*   In addition to the Left, Right, Top, and Bottom options, Release 2.2 includes an option called None on the /Print Printer Options Margins menu. This option allows you to set all four margins in one operation to maximize the line length for reports printed on a 14-inch-wide page in compressed type. Therefore, when you select the None option, 1-2-3 automatically sets the left, top, and bottom margins to 0 and the right margin to 240.

If you aren't using 14-inch-wide paper and compressed type for your report and you use the None option, remember to select the Margins Right option and decrease the right-margin setting accordingly before you send your report to the printer, to prevent long lines from wrapping to new lines in the report.

Defining Headers and Footers

Lotus 1-2-3 allows you to define a one-line header and/or footer for your report, using the Header and Footer options on the /Print Printer Options menu. A *header* is a heading that is printed on the third line down from the top of each page in the report, assuming that you are using the default top margin of 2 lines. A *footer* is a heading that is printed on the third line up from the bottom of each page in the report, assuming that you are using the default bottom margin of 2 lines.

The program always separates the header or footer line from the body of the report by two blank lines. In the case of the header, 1-2-3 puts two blank lines below the line that contains the header before the first line of the report on the page. In the case of the footer, the program places two blank lines after the last line of the report on the page before the line that contains the footer. Note that 1-2-3 reserves these three lines at the top and bottom of the page whether or not you define a header and footer for your report. Also, these three lines are in addition to the top- and bottom-margin settings you use for the report (2 lines at the top and 2 at the bottom, by default).

To create a footer for your report, you select the /Print Printer Options Header command (/PPOH) and then type in the line of text for this heading exactly as you want it to appear in the printout, terminated by the Enter key. The process for defining a footer is identical, except that you select Footer rather than Header from the /Print Printer Options menu. If you are using Release 2.2, you will be able to see the first 55 characters of the header and footer you define for the report in the Print Settings sheet.

Aligning Text in the Header or Footer

When you enter the text for your header and footer, it is automatically aligned with the left margin of the report. When you add the header or footer text, 1-2-3 also enables you to center or right-align it.

To effect the alignment of part or all of the header or footer text, you enter the vertical bar (|) character, which works as an alignment code. (This character is located on the same key as the backslash, \, and is shifted.) To center all text of a header or footer between the left and right margins of the report, you enter the vertical bar (|) before typing in the text. To align all text with the right margin of the report, you enter two vertical bars (||) with no spaces between them before typing the text to be right-aligned.

If you have three elements in your one-line header or footer, and you want to spread them across the page so that the first is left-justified, the second is centered, and the third is right-justified, you would enter the first text, a vertical bar, the second text, another vertical bar, and then the third text.

Adding the Date and Page Number to the Header or Footer

To have the current date (as supplied to DOS and shown in the on-screen clock) entered in a header or footer, you enter the @ symbol. To have the program automatically number the pages of the report, you use the # symbol. In the report, it will substitute the number of the page wherever this symbol occurs, beginning with the number 1. The program cannot begin numbering your pages from a different number.

For example, if you wanted the title of the report to appear left-justified in a header with the current date right-justified, you would enter the text of the header as:

> **Personnel Report | | @**

If you then wanted the page numbers to appear centered at the bottom of the report with the word *Page* preceding each number, you would enter the text of the footer as:

> **| Page #**

If you had three elements to be entered in the header and wanted them spaced across this line, you would modify the header as follows:

> **Personnel Report | Revision 2 | @**

In this header, the title *Personnel Report* would be printed flush left, *Revision 2* would be centered, and the date would be printed flush right. Assuming that the current date were July 20, 1991, it would appear in the header as 20-Jul-91. To change the appearance of the date, you can change the global date format using the /Worksheet Global Format Date command before printing the report.

Changing the Page Length of the Report

The default page length used by 1-2-3 in printing reports is 66 lines, which represents the total number of lines on an 11-inch page when using single spacing (where there are 6 lines per vertical inch). The total number of lines that 1-2-3 will print on any page is equal to the page length minus the three lines at the top reserved for the header, the three lines at the bottom reserved for the footer, and the number of lines in the top and bottom margins.

If you print your report using all the program printing defaults, 1-2-3 will print a maximum of 56 lines of data on the page. This represents the page length of 66 lines, minus 2 lines for the top, 3 lines for the header, 2 lines for the bottom margin, and 3 lines for the footer ($66-2-3-2-3=56$).

When you change the line spacing used in the report or the size of the form you are printing your report on, remember to indicate the new page length by selecting the Pg-Length option on the /Print Printer Options menu and entering the total number of lines (between 1 and 100) that can be printed on that form. For example, if you enter the printer code to print 8 lines per inch instead of the standard 6 lines per inch, you need to select the Pg-Length option and set the page length to 88 before printing your report. Note that if you are using Release 2.2, the current page-length number is displayed in the Print Settings sheet near the bottom. Also, although 1 is theoretically the smallest page-length number accepted by 1-2-3, practically speaking, your page length can't be any smaller than the number of lines in the top and bottom margins plus at least 7 (6 for the lines allotted to the header and footer and 1 to print just a single line of data).

If you don't set the proper page length for the type of line spacing and the size of the form you are using, the page breaks will occur at the wrong places in the report (in fact, they may even start to "creep" down each succeeding page). Nowhere is the problem of creeping page breaks more obvious than when printing a report with a laser printer such as the HP LaserJet Series II using the default page length of 66 lines. Although this is the correct page length for most printers when using 11-inch paper, it is too many lines for this LaserJet. This is because this type of printer won't allow you to set zero margins at top and bottom (and left or right, for that matter): the smallest margin you can set on any side is 1/4 inch. This means that you have about 4 1/2 fewer lines available when printing a single-spaced report on an 8 1/2-×-11-inch page.

As a result, you should not use a page length of more than 60 lines when printing a single-spaced report (this gives you about 50 text lines per page, if you maintain the 2 lines each for top and bottom margins). If you use the default page length of 66 lines, you will find that the printed report is paged incorrectly: in counting 66 lines before a page break, the 5 blank lines for the bottom margin and the footer of page 1 are placed at the top of page 2, right above the 5 blank lines for the top margin and header for page 2. This creates 10 blank lines at the top of page 2 before the program even begins counting the next 66 lines that constitute the second page. As a result, the blank space for the bottom margin and footer from the previous page, mixed with the space for top margin and header of the current page, continues to "creep" down each subsequent page of the report.

Adding Borders to the Report

The Borders option on the /Print Printer Options menu allows you to specify headings in particular rows or columns of the spreadsheet as borders for the report, meaning that they will be printed on each page of the report. When you select the Borders option on this menu, you are presented with two options:

Columns Rows

If you want both a column of labels and some rows of headings to be included on each page, use the Borders command twice: first the Columns option, and then the Rows option.

When you want to specify a row containing column headings that should appear in the top line of the body of the report on every page, you use the Rows option. You will be prompted to enter the range for the border rows. To do so, move the pointer to one of the cells in the row that contains these headings and press the Enter key. If you want to designate more than one row for the borders, you move the pointer to the first row, type a period to anchor the cell range, and use the appropriate pointer-movement key to highlight the rows you want included (you do not have to indicate the number of columns as part of this range, as this number is determined by the right-margin setting for the report).

When you want to specify a column containing row headings to appear on the left side of each page of the report, you use the Columns option. You indicate the column or columns to be used as borders in the same way as you do when specifying rows for the borders.

When defining border columns and/or rows, be sure not to include these columns and rows as part of the print range. The labels and data in these border areas will automatically be printed in the report. If you include them in the print range, they will be printed twice on the first page of the report.

Figures 8.3 and 8.4 illustrate how borders can help in a multiple-page report. In this example, rows 1 and 2 in the worksheet are defined as border rows in the report. These rows contain the column headings that explain what type of data each column contains. Notice in Figure 8.4 that these column headings are reprinted at the top of the second page of the report. Always define borders in a report rather than copying headings in the worksheet itself. That way, you don't have to spend a lot time moving headings around the worksheet as you increase the number of rows in the print range. Also, remember not to include the border rows and/or columns as part of the print range, or 1-2-3 will print the borders twice on the first page of the report.

Printing the Column Letters and Row Numbers in the Report

You will sometimes want to include the worksheet column letters and row numbers for the data printed in your report. Unfortunately, neither Release 2.01 nor 2.2 of 1-2-3 includes a printing option that automatically prints the accompanying worksheet column and/or row borders as part of the report (this feature has been added to Release 3). You can, however, use the Borders Columns and Rows options to add them when you need a printout that contains these letters and numbers.

To do this, you must insert a new row at the top of the print range with the /Worksheet Insert Row command and enter the column letters as they are displayed in the spreadsheet border above. Note that you can use the /Range Label Center command to center the row of cells that contain these column letters.

```
Family Statistics Populations 1 & 2

                                           Wife's   Son's            No. of
Family  Husband's Job                                               
number  Education Posit.  Height-in  Height "   Age      Income    Rooms
   15      H        N       70.7      69.4       10       18.8        6
  142      H        N       66.9      66.5       9.3      15.2        3
   58      H        N       68.3      62.8       7.7       9.3        3
  129      H        S       69.1      63         11       13.3        3
  115      C        N       70.9      67.5        8       13          3
    1      H        S       71        71         12.9     33          6
   13      H        N       70.7      61.4       7.3       7.5        1
   87      H        N       67.1      62.5       7.6       9          2
   18      E        N       73.5      61.8       8.9       8.4        2
  104      H        S       68.8      64.9       11.7     17.6        4
   95      C        S       73        65.8       10.9     17.3        4
   50      C        S       65.7      66.2       11.2     18          5
   60      C        S       67.9      66.6       11.5     18.7        5
  124      E        N       66.9      64.4       11.1     12.5        3
   72      E        N       65.6      64.2       10.9     12.2        2
   62      E        S       71.4      67.7       15.8     29          4
  148      E        N       69.9      63.2       10.3     10.8        4
  131      E        N       68.1      66.8       12.7     16.3        3
   64      C        S       66.7      68.5       12.6     25          4
   80      H        N       66.7      64.4       8.3      11.9        2
  112      H        N       71.1      65.6       8.9      13.8        4
  107      E        S       68.9      63         14.7     17          4
   12      H        N       63        62.1       7.5       8.2        2
   29      H        N       69        73         10.3     22.3        5
   26      H        S       68.5      66.8       12.3     21.6        5
   27      E        N       66.6      62.3       9.5       9.2        3
   82      H        S       65        62.1       10.8     11.3        2
   83      H        N       69.9      65.2       8.7      13.3        3
   38      C        N       68.5      63         7.1       5          2
   40      E        N       68.1      62.8       10.1     10          3
  128      H        N       69.5      67.2       9.5      16.3        3
    2      E        N       67        59         7.4       5          2
   36      E        N       69.2      61         8.3       7.6        2
  145      E        N       68.2      69         13.8     19.5        3
   76      H        N       67.7      68.6       9.9      18.1        5
   45      H        N       65.5      60.2       7.1       5          2
    2      E        N       67        59         7.4       5          2
   95      C        S       73        65.8       10.9     17.3        4
   52      H        S       71.3      65.6       12       19.3        2
   55      E        N       71.9      63.7       10.6     11.4        2
   54      E        N       64.5      60.2       7.7       6.3        3
   33      E        N       67.2      60.6        8        7.2        1
  117      H        S       66.5      64.4       11.5     16.4        4
  122      E        N       68.4      64.9       11.4     13.3        3
   49      E        N       67.4      62.5       9.8       9.6        3
   48      C        S       70.1      67.4       12       21          5
   13      H        N       70.7      61.4       7.3       7.5        1
  134      H        N       72.3      65.7        9       14.1        4
  108      C        S       69.3      67.7       11.8     19.7        4
  148      E        N       69.9      63.2       10.3     10.8        4
  121      H        S       71.7      63.6       11.3     14.7        4
   82      H        S       65        62.1       10.8     11.3        2
   50      C        S       65.7      66.2       11.2     18          5
  120      H        N       68.3      66.8       9.3      15.5        3


03-Jun-89                                                          Page 1
```

• **Figure 8.3:** *First page of report using border rows (58% actual size)*

```
Family Statistics Populations 1 & 2

Family  Husband's Job              Wife's    Son's          No. of
number  Education Posit. Height-in Height "  Age     Income Rooms
   133  E         N         66.1      66.3    12.4     15.5      3
    31  E         N         72.5      69.8    14.1     21.5      5
    61  E         S         71.6      63.7    14.9     18.3      5
   124  E         N         66.9      64.4    11.1     12.5      3
    23  E         S         71.7      65.7    15.3     22.3      5
   116  H         N         72        65.9     9       14.3      4
    24  H         N         69.5      63       7.8      9.7      3
   123  C         S         66.1      64.2     9.9     14.7      4
   106  H         N         68.6      64.9     8.6     12.7      3
    66  E         N         63        66.1    12.3     15.2      2
TOTAL                     4397.80  4144.30  663.30   915.10 212.00
AVG                         68.72     64.75   10.36    14.30   3.31
```

• **Figure 8.4:** *Second page of report using border rows (58% actual size)*

Using the Period to Change Print Range: Remember that pressing the period key (.) once a cell range has been highlighted has the effect of changing the anchor cell. If you type a period four times, 1-2-3 will change the anchor cell to each of the four corners of the highlighted range in succession (moving clockwise). You can put this feature to good use when you have to alter the size of the print range slightly, as you often do after defining border rows and columns for the report. For instance, suppose that currently the print range is defined as B3..H115 and you have just defined rows 3 and 4 as border rows for your report. To have the first page of the report printed correctly, you need to redefine the print range to B5..H115 so that it doesn't include the border rows 3 and 4. The easiest way to do this is to select the Range option on the /Print Printer menu, type the period twice until the anchor cell is B3, then press the ↓ key twice to reduce the print range by two rows so that it is now H115..B5, and press Enter. Note that this technique for changing the anchor cell to make it possible to change the size of a range with the pointer-movement keys is not limited to this application (it is often quite useful in macros).

To add the row numbers, you insert a new column at the beginning of the print range with the /Worksheet Insert Column command. To add the row numbers, move the pointer down one row and then enter each row number as a left-aligned label by prefacing it with the apostrophe ('). After entering all row numbers, you can narrow the column with the /Worksheet Column Set-Width command.

Select the Columns option from the /Print Printer Options Borders command (/PPOBC) and designate the new column containing the row numbers as the border column for the report. Next, select the Rows option from the same menu and designate the row containing the worksheet letters as the border row for the report. Before sending the report to the printer, be sure that the print range does not include the column and row assigned as borders for the report.

Figure 8.5 illustrates how this arrangement would appear on the screen, and Figure 8.6 shows the final printed report with the column letters and row numbers that were added to the worksheet and designated as the row and column borders for the report.

Defining Setup Strings for the Report

Most printers can produce various print attributes, such as a bold or italic type style or a compressed or expanded type size. To print a 1-2-3 report with such

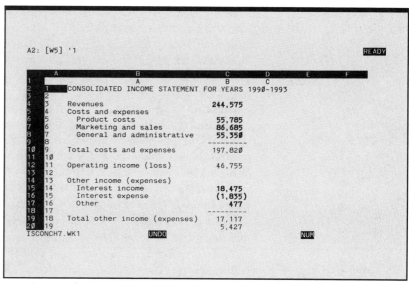

A2: [W5] '1   READY

	A	B	C	D	E	F
1	CONSOLIDATED INCOME STATEMENT FOR YEARS 1990-1993					
2						
3	Revenues	244,575				
4	Costs and expenses					
5	Product costs	55,785				
6	Marketing and sales	86,685				
7	General and administrative	55,350				
8		---------				
9	Total costs and expenses	197,820				
10						
11	Operating income (loss)	46,755				
12						
13	Other income (expenses)					
14	Interest income	18,475				
15	Interest expense	(1,835)				
16	Other	477				
17		---------				
18	Total other income (expenses)	17,117				
19		5,427				

ISCONCH7.WK1   UNDO   NUM

♦ **Figure 8.5:** *Adding worksheet letters and row numbers to be used as the border row and column in the printed report*

	A	B	C
1	CONSOLIDATED INCOME STATEMENT FOR YEARS 1990-1993		
2			
3	Revenues	244,575	
4	Costs and expenses		
5	Product costs	55,785	
6	Marketing and sales	86,685	
7	General and administrative	55,350	
8		---------	
9	Total costs and expenses	197,820	
10			
11	Operating income (loss)	46,755	
12			
13	Other income (expenses)		
14	Interest income	18,475	
15	Interest expense	(1,835)	
16	Other	477	
17		---------	
18	Total other income (expenses)	17,117	
19		5,427	
20	Income (loss) before taxes	63,872	
21	Provision (benefit) for taxes	9,581	
22	Net earnings (loss)	54,292	
23		=========	

♦ **Figure 8.6:** *Printed report with worksheet letters and row numbers (00% actual size)*

attributes, you must enter special code sequences, called *setup strings*, that are sent to your printer at print time.

To enter a setup string, you select the Setup option on the /Print Printer Options menu, type in the setup string, and press Enter. The setup string that you enter affects the printing of the entire report (that is, the print range as well as the header and footer and any border columns or rows).

The setup string required to perform a particular action (such as printing in compressed type) differs according to the type of printer you have. Table 8.1 shows you several frequently used setup strings for the more commonly used printers. Notice that each setup string in this table begins with a backslash. When you use setup strings from this table, be careful to type the codes exactly as they are shown. You must follow the capitalization exactly, and not type an *l* where the code requires a *1* and vice versa.

If your printer is not listed in this table, you will have to refer to the documentation that came with your printer to find the appropriate code numbers. In looking up printer codes, you may find that your manual refers to these codes as escape codes or escape sequences. This is because many printer codes are preceded by the escape character (code 027). For example, to print 8 lines per inch in a report with an Epson FX, RX, or MX or IBM Graphics printer, you enter the setup string

   \0270

which is the equivalent of *Esc 0* because 027 is the ASCII decimal code that sends the Escape code to the printer. Note that you can also enter this same code as

   \027\048

because 048 is the ASCII decimal code equivalent of 0. Note, however, that when you convert each part of the printer code into its ASCII decimal code, you must separate each three-digit code in the setup string with a backslash of its own.

Lotus 1-2-3 allows you to create a setup string that controls more than one printer function; in fact, you can create a compound setup string up to 39 characters long. To combine attributes, you simply enter their particular setup strings in succession, separating each string with a backslash. For instance, if you use an Epson printer and want to print the report in compressed print with 8 lines per inch, enter the following setup string:

   \015\0270

where \015 is the setup string to produce compressed print on such a printer and \0270 is the setup string to print 8 lines per inch.

Deleting the Setup String and Clearing the Printer

The program remembers the setup string that you enter with the /Print Printer Options Setup command. If you save the worksheet after defining a setup string, it will be saved as part of the file. To delete a setup string, you need to select the /Print Printer Options Setup command, press the Esc key, and then press Enter.

If, however, you have just printed a report using the current setup string and then delete it, you may find that the printer retains the previous settings put into effect by the setup string. To clear the effect of the previous setup string from the printer, you must either turn the printer off and on again or reset the printer by entering the code that initializes the printer as the setup string. If you use the initialize printer code as the setup string, 1-2-3 will reset the printer to all of its default print settings before it sends your report. Note that with some printers, you can also reset the printer by selecting the All or Format option from the /Print Printer Clear menu (/PPCA or /PPCF).

Embedding Setup Strings in the Worksheet

As noted earlier, the setup string that you enter when using the /Print Printer Options Setup command affects the entire report. This is fine when you want the entire report printed with a particular enhancement, such as compressed print or using 8 lines per inch. When you don't want to use the attribute throughout the report—as when specifying bold or italic type to emphasize particular parts of the report, such as the title or subtotals and totals—you must embed the setup code in the worksheet itself.

To do this, you enter the setup code prefaced by two vertical bars (||) in a blank cell in its own row in the leftmost column of the print range. When you enter the setup code in this cell, only the second vertical bar will be displayed in the cell along with the digits and backslashes of the code itself. Note that the print attribute controlled by the embedded setup code is applied to all rows of data below it in the print range until either the program encounters an embedded setup code that counteracts the attribute or the program reaches the end of the print range.

Many print setup strings are naturally paired—those that turn on and off boldfacing, underlining, italics, and compressed and expanded type. This means that if you only want a row or two of a report printed with a particular

◆ **Table 8.1:** *Commonly Used Setup Strings*

	Compressed	Expanded	3 Lines per Inch (Double Spacing)	6 Lines per Inch (Single Spacing)	8 Lines per Inch
C. Itoh 8510A	\027Q	\014	\027T48	\027A	\027B
Epson FX, MX, or RX	\015	\027W1	\027\065\024	\0272	\0270
Epson LQ1500	\027x0\015	\027W1	\027\065\024	\0272	\0270
HP LaserJet	\027&k2S	—	\027&l3D	\027&l6D	\027&l8D
HP ThinkJet	\027&k2S	\027&k1S	—	\027&l6D	\027&l8D
IBM 5182 Color Printer	\015	\027\087\001	—	\027\050	\027\048
IBM Color Jetprinter	\015	\027\087\001	\027\087\001	\027\050	\027\048
IBM Graphics	\015	\027\087\001	—	\027\050	\027\048
IBM Proprinter	\015	\027\087\001\014	\027\051\0272	\027\050	\027\048
IBM Quietwriter, Models 1 & 2	—	\027\087\049	\027\065\024\027\050	\027\050	\027\048
Okidata Microline	\029	\030\031	\027\037\057\048	\027\054	\027\056
Okidata Pacemark	\027\066	\027\054\027\067	\027\037\057\048	\027\052	\027\053
Star Micronics Gemini	\015	\027\087\001	\027\065\024	\050	\0270\048
TI 850, 850XL, 855, 856	\027P	\014	\027\065\024	\0272	\0270
Toshiba P351, P1350, P1351, 321SL, 351SX, 321LC, 351C	\027*0\027[	\027!	\027L16	\027L08	\027L06

◆ **Table 8.1:** *Commonly Used Setup Strings (continued)*

	Bold On	Bold Off	Underline On	Underline Off	Reset
C. Itoh 8510A	\027!	\027\034	\027X	—	—
Epson FX, MX, or RX	\027E	\027F	\027-1	\027-0	\027@
Epson LQ1500	\027E	\027F	\027\045\001	\027\045\000	\027@
HP LaserJet	\027(s3B	\027(s0B	\027&dD	\027&d@	\027E
HP ThinkJet	\027(s1B	\027(s0B	\027-1\027&dD	\027&d@	\027E
IBM 5182 Color Printer	\027\069	\027\070	\027\045\001	\027\045\009	\027E
IBM Color Jetprinter	\027\071	\027\070	\027\045\001	\027\045\000	—
IBM Graphics	\027\069	\027\070	\027\045\001	\027\045\000	—
IBM Proprinter	\027\069	\027\070	\027\045\001	\027\045\000	\024
IBM Quietwriter, Models 1 & 2	—	—	\027\045\001	\027\045\000	—
Okidata Microline	\027\084	\027\073	\027\067	\027\068	\027\024
Okidata Pacemark	\027\066\027\067	\027\090\027\054	\027\085	\027\086	—
Star Micronics Gemini	\027\069	\027\070	\027-1	\027\045\000	\027\064
TI 850, 850XL, 855, 856	\027G	\027H	—	—	—
Toshiba P351, Pl350, Pl351, 321SL, 351SX, 321LC, 351C	\027K2	\027\077\027M	—	—	—

enhancement, you must embed the setup string that turns on the enhancement in the row right above those to receive the attribute, and embed the setup string that turns off the enhancement in the row immediately below these rows.

Note that embedded setup strings can only be applied to entire rows of the print range. You can't use them when you want the attribute to be applied to only a partial row, such as a single cell that contains a subtotal or total. To apply print enhancements to cell ranges that don't include entire rows of the print range, you need to use a print utility such as Allways. If you are using Release 2.2, Allways is included as part of your 1-2-3 package. If you are still using Release 2.01, you can purchase Allways as a separate utility. Note, however, that Allways requires a hard disk: if you are not using 1-2-3 on a hard-disk system, you can't use this add-in program no matter what release of the program you are using. See Chapter 10 for specific information on how to use Allways to produce high-quality, professional-looking reports.

Clearing the Print Settings

The program remembers all print settings that you define for your report. When you save the worksheet, the print settings in effect are saved as part of the file. In defining new reports, you can clear some or all of these print settings by selecting the /Print Printer Clear command. When you select this command, you are presented with four options:

All   Range   Borders   Format

If you select the All option, all print settings are immediately returned to their default settings. This includes not only the margins, page length, border columns and rows, headers, and footers, but also the print range itself.

If you simply want to clear the print range and leave all other print settings in effect, choose the Range option. Many times, you will find this option the most efficient way to define a new print range with pointing. This is because you don't have to spend time unanchoring the pointer from a previously defined print range (as you would if you didn't first cancel the current print range).

If you only need to cancel the border columns and rows that you have defined for a report, you can do this in one operation by selecting the Borders option on the /Print Printer Clear menu. You use the Format option on this menu when you want to return to the default settings for the margins, page length, and setup string (if you haven't defined a default setup string, this option clears the setup string).

Controlling the Page Formatting of the Report

When the print range you define is too large to be printed on a single page, 1-2-3 will automatically break the report into separate pages. How much data can be printed on each page depends upon the margin settings and page length in effect for the report. These settings, in turn, are dependent upon the type size, number of lines per inch, and the orientation selected for the report (some printers can print in landscape mode, where the printing is rotated 90 degrees counterclockwise on the page so that it runs across the long side of the paper).

In paging a report, 1-2-3 uses a consistent system, regardless of the amount of data that it can fit on each page. In this system, the program always prints as many complete columns and rows from the upper left part of the print range as possible on the first page. Then, assuming that there are more rows to be printed than fit on the first page, the program prints the same columns as on the first page, this time using the next set of rows in the print range. When 1-2-3 has finished printing all columns and rows in the upper left part of the print range, it will begin printing the next group of columns to the right in the print range. After that, it will use the same group of columns, this time printing the next set of rows in the print range. The program will continue in this manner, moving down each section before moving to the right, until the entire print range has been printed.

When paging a report, you must remember that 1-2-3 never prints just part of a column on one page and the rest of it on another page. If the program can't fit the entire column on the page, given the current left- and right-margin settings, it will shift the entire column over to a different page in the report (the next page, if all columns fit on the current page).

To estimate how many full columns can be accommodated on each page, you need to subtract the left-margin setting from the right-margin setting to determine the maximum line length in characters. If the columns have a uniform width, you can then just divide the maximum line length by the width of each column. For example, if you use the default margin settings of 4 for the left margin and 76 for the right margin, the line length is 72 characters. If all columns in the print range still use the default width of 9 characters, each page of the report can contain 8 columns (72/9=8).

If the widths of the columns in the print range aren't uniform, you have to add their widths and compare them against the maximum line length. For instance, assume that the margins remain 4 and 76 but that columns A through C are widened to 10 characters ($3 \times 10 = 30$), column D and E to 12 characters ($2 \times 12 = 24$), and column F to 17 characters, and that columns A through K are included in the print range. In such a case, the first page of the printed report will contain only the first six columns (A through F) because together they total 71 characters (30+24+17=71) and 72 characters per line is the maximum.

Using Compressed Print in a Report

One of the most common ways to get more information on each page of the report and, therefore, cut down on the amount of pages and the splitting up of information across multiple pages, is to print the report in compressed print. When you use compressed print, you can fit about 17 characters per inch (some printers, such as the HP LaserJet, give you only 16.6 characters per inch in compressed mode) as opposed to the regular 10 characters per inch.

As we've already discussed, to turn on compressed print, you must enter the correct setup string used by your printer. In addition to adding the appropriate setup string, don't forget to change the right-margin setting. If you do forget, 1-2-3 will not increase the number of columns on each page, even though they will be printed in smaller print and will take up only the first part of the page. If your paper is 8½ inches wide, you can increase the right margin to something like 128. If your paper is 14 inches wide, you can increase it to about 236 characters.

To further maximize the amount of data that can be printed on each page, you should also set the left, top, and bottom margins to 0. If you do, you can then further increase the right-margin setting by 4 (to 132 for 8½-inch paper or 240 for 14-inch paper). Remember that you can use the None option on the /Print Printer Options Margins menu (/PPOMN)to immediately set the left, top, and bottom margins to 0 and the right margin to 240, if you are using Release 2.2 and are printing on 14-inch-wide paper.

Inserting Manual Page Breaks

Many times, you will find that 1-2-3 has inserted a page break in an inappropriate place in the printed report. To decide where a page should break in the report, you can insert a *manual page break* with the /Worksheet Page command (/WP). Before you use this command, move the pointer to the first column of the print range in the row directly beneath the last row of the data you want to remain on a page. As soon as you type /WP, 1-2-3 inserts a new row in the worksheet containing two colons in the cell containing the pointer (: :). This is the symbol for a manual page break.

Any rows of data in the print range below the row containing this symbol will begin printing on a new page of the report. If you have a table of data that you want to make sure is printed on its own page of the report, you would enter manual page breaks both in the row above the first row of the table and in the row after its last row.

After printing the report, remove the page breaks inserted with the /Worksheet Page command by positioning the cell pointer in one of the cells in the row containing the page-break symbol, and then selecting the /Worksheet Delete Row command (/WDR).

Hiding Columns in the Print Range

Some reports that you create do not require all columns of data that are actually entered in the worksheet itself. Rather than having to resort to the time-consuming task of moving and rearranging columns to create a print range that consists of just those you want printed, 1-2-3 offers a much simpler method by enabling you to temporarily hide the columns that you don't want printed. Then, after you have printed the report, you can display the hidden columns in the worksheet once again.

To hide a particular column, you move the pointer to any row within that column, select the Hide option from /Worksheet Column menu (/WCH), and press Enter in response to the *Specify column to hide:* prompt. All data in the entire column (from row 1 through 8192) then disappear from view. Note that the only way you can tell that a column has been hidden is by referring to the column letters on the top frame. When you hide a column, 1-2-3 doesn't adjust the column letters at the top of the frame. Therefore, you know that a column has been hidden if a particular column letter is missing. For example, after hiding columns D and E from the worksheet, you would see

> A B C F G H I J

along the top frame of the leftmost part of the worksheet.

Note that you can hide a range of columns with the /Worksheet Column Hide command (/WCH). To do this, be sure to position the pointer either in the first or last column of the range before issuing the command. Then, enter the range address or type a period to anchor the range and use the → or ← keys to highlight the columns to be included (there is no need to include more than a single row in the range address or in pointing, as this command affects all rows in the selected columns).

To display the columns that you have hidden once again, you need to use the /Worksheet Column Display command (/WCD). When you use this command, 1-2-3 redisplays the hidden columns and presents you with the prompt *Specify hidden columns to redisplay*. At this point, you will notice the column letters of the redisplayed columns are followed by asterisks. For example, if you had hidden columns D and E and then selected the /Worksheet Column Display command, you would see

> A B C D* E* F G H

in the worksheet frame at the top.

To have 1-2-3 once again display these columns shown with asterisks, you must move the pointer to either column D or E, type a period to anchor the range, and then use the appropriate pointer-movement key to highlight the second column in the range (or type in a range address that includes columns D and E) before pressing Enter. Note that if you simply select the /Worksheet Column Display command and then press Enter without first specifying the column or column range to redisplay, the hidden columns will once again disappear from view when the program returns to READY mode.

Pausing the Printing between Pages

In printing a report, 1-2-3 automatically assumes you are using continuous-feed paper. As soon as the program finishes printing one page, it begins printing the next page without pausing. If you are using manual-feed paper, where the printer must pause between pages until you have had a chance to feed a new sheet to the printer, you must change the global printer default to Wait Yes before sending your report to the printer. To do this, you select the /Worksheet Global Default Printer Wait command (/WGDPW), then choose the Yes option.

With the Wait option turned on, 1-2-3 will print a single page of the report, then beep and pause the printer until you press a key. During this pause, you can insert a new sheet of paper. After you press any key, the program will print the next page and then pause. This process continues until the last page of the report is printed.

Be sure to turn the Wait option off as soon as you switch back to continuous-feed paper. You do this by choosing the No option after selecting the /Worksheet Global Default Printer Wait command.

Printing Unformatted Reports

Most of the time, you will want to use the many printing options to format your worksheet data into a formal report. On some occasions, however, you just want the data printed and aren't terribly concerned about the formatting. For such times, you can print an unformatted report in which 1-2-3 ignores the top and bottom margins, the page-length setting, and any header or footer that has been defined. In this type of report, the specified print range is printed continuously without any page breaks, leaving no gaps between the last line of data at the bottom of one page and the first line of data at the top of the next page of the report. Although the top and bottom margins are ignored in an unformatted report, the left- and right-margin settings remain in effect. Also, if the report contains too many columns to fit onto one page, 1-2-3 will divide them onto separate pages, using the same system that it does for formatted reports.

To create an unformatted report, you select the /Print Printer Options Other command (/PPOO). This brings up the following menu options:

As-Displayed Cell-Formulas Formatted Unformatted

From this menu, you select the Unformatted option. Note that if you are using Release 2.2, 1-2-3 will update Format on the Print Settings sheet so that it reads *As-Displayed (Unformatted)* after you select this option. After you print the report, you can once again put your print formatting settings back into effect by selecting the /Print Printer Options Other Formatted command (/PPOOF).

The first time you print your worksheet data, you may find it useful to produce a draft printout of the report by selecting the Unformatted option, turning on compressed print, changing the line spacing to 8 lines per inch, setting the left margin to 0, and making the right margin as large as you can for the paper size you are using. You can then use this draft version of the report to decide how the final version of the report should be formatted. Figure 8.7 shows you a report printed using such "draft" settings.

Printing the Formulas in the Worksheet

Besides allowing you to switch between formatted and unformatted reports, the /Print Printer Options Other menu contains two options, As-Displayed (the default) and Cell-Formulas, that enable you to switch between printing the cells as they appear in the worksheet display (the normal way they are printed) and printing their contents as they appear in the control panel, including formatting codes and formulas.

To obtain a listing of the contents of each cell in the currently defined print range, you select the Cell-Formulas option. When you send the report to the printer, 1-2-3 prints the contents of each cell on its own line in the report. The contents printed in the report matches exactly the way they appear in the control panel. Note, however, that blank cells in the print range aren't included in this listing (unless you have assigned a display format to them).

Figure 8.8 shows you the first page of a report printed using the Cell-Formulas option. Notice that the biggest drawback of such a report is that it does not follow the column and row layout of the worksheet itself. Instead, the contents of each cell are printed consecutively in a very long listing. This makes it a little more difficult to locate a particular cell in the printed report and compare it with the cell in the worksheet itself.

Family number	Husband's Education	Job Posit.	Height-in	Wife's Height "	Son's Age	Income	No. of Rooms	Housing Expend.	Consumpt Bread-lbs
15	H	N	70.7	69.4	10	18.8	6	5.25	308.3
142	H	N	66.9	66.5	9.3	15.2	3	3.47	281.7
58	H	N	68.3	62.8	7.7	9.3	3	2.03	292.3
129	H	S	69.1	63	11	13.3	3	3.19	312.9
115	C	N	70.9	67.5	8	13	3	3.03	281
1	H	S	71	71	12.9	33	6	6.83	315
13	H	N	70.7	61.4	7.3	7.5	1	2.83	282.5
87	H	N	67.1	62.5	7.6	9	2	2.95	290.4
18	E	N	73.5	61.8	8.9	8.4	2	2.68	304.1
104	H	S	68.8	64.9	11.7	17.6	4	4.31	316.5
95	C	S	73	65.8	10.9	17.3	4	4.14	308.7
50	C	S	65.7	66.2	11.2	18	5	3.83	310.5
60	C	S	67.9	66.6	11.5	18.7	5	4.83	314.5
124	E	N	66.9	64.4	11.1	12.5	3	2.56	314.6
72	E	N	65.6	64.2	10.9	12.2	2	4.17	310.4
62	E	S	71.4	67.7	15.8	29	4	5.83	325
148	E	N	69.9	63.2	10.3	10.8	4	2.37	313.7
131	E	N	68.1	66.8	12.7	16.3	3	4.1	325
64	C	S	66.7	68.5	12.6	25	4	5.17	292.5
80	H	N	66.7	64.4	8.3	11.9	2	3.75	289
112	H	N	71.1	65.6	8.9	13.8	4	2.87	296.2
107	E	S	68.9	63	14.7	17	4	3.97	322.5
12	H	N	63	62.1	7.5	8.2	2	2.59	287.5
29	H	N	69	73	10.3	22.3	5	5.61	288.3
26	H	S	68.5	66.8	12.3	21.6	5	5.28	299.3
27	E	N	66.6	62.3	9.5	9.2	3	1.9	307.5
82	H	S	65	62.1	10.8	11.3	2	3.15	307
83	H	N	69.9	65.2	8.7	13.3	3	3.14	294.6
38	C	N	68.5	63	7.1	5	2	1.37	295
40	E	N	68.1	62.8	10.1	10	3	2.18	305
128	H	N	69.5	67.2	9.5	16.3	3	4.3	291
2	E	N	67	59	7.4	5	2	1.12	302.5
36	E	N	69.2	61	8.3	7.6	2	2.04	289.6
145	E	N	68.2	69	13.8	19.5	3	4.5	302.5
76	H	N	67.7	68.6	9.9	18.1	5	4.17	301.7
45	H	N	65.5	60.2	7.1	5	2	1.62	291.7
2	E	N	67	59	7.4	5	2	1.12	302.5
95	C	S	73	65.8	10.9	17.3	4	4.14	308.7
52	H	S	71.3	65.6	12	19.3	2	4.83	292.1
55	H	N	71.9	63.7	10.6	11.4	2	3.25	303
54	E	N	64.5	60.2	7.7	6.3	3	1.1	307.5
33	H	N	67.2	60.6	8	7.2	1	2.5	295.9
117	H	S	66.5	64.4	11.5	16.4	4	3.66	313.5
122	E	N	68.4	64.9	11.4	13.3	3	3.08	317.9
49	E	N	67.4	62.5	9.8	9.6	3	2.08	309.1
48	C	N	70.1	67.4	12	21	5	5.06	295
13	H	N	70.7	61.4	7.3	7.5	1	2.83	282.5
134	H	N	72.3	65.7	9	14.1	4	3.22	297.9
108	C	S	69.3	67.7	11.8	19.7	6	5.5	290.7
148	E	N	69.9	63.2	10.3	10.8	4	2.37	313.7
121	H	S	71.7	63.6	11.3	14.7	4	3.53	316.2
82	H	S	65	62.1	10.8	11.3	2	3.15	307
50	C	S	65.7	66.2	11.2	18	5	3.83	310.5
120	H	N	68.3	66.8	9.3	15.5	3	3.7	285
133	E	N	66.1	66.3	12.4	15.5	3	3.64	321
31	E	N	72.5	69.8	14.1	21.5	5	5.17	311.7
61	E	S	71.6	63.7	14.9	18.3	5	4.39	327.5
124	E	N	66.9	64.4	11.1	12.5	3	2.56	314.6
23	E	S	71.7	65.7	15.3	22.3	5	5.5	327.5
116	H	N	77	65.9	9	14.3	4	3.34	298.7
24	H	N	69.5	63	7.8	9.7	3	2.13	293.2
123	C	S	66.1	64.2	9.9	14.7	4	3.59	309
106	H	N	68.6	64.9	8.6	12.7	3	2.72	292.1
66	E	N	63	66.1	12.3	15.2	2	4.5	319.5
TOTAL			4397.80	4144.30	663.30	915.10	212.00	223.62	19434.00 .
AVG			68.72	64.75	10.36	14.30	3.31	3.49	303.66

◆ **Figure 8.7:** *Unformatted report using compressed print (58% actual size)*

```
A1: [W31] ||\027E
A2: [W31] 'INCOME STATEMENT YEAR ENDING DECEMBER 31
F2: [W31] 'INCOME STATEMENT YEAR ENDING DECEMBER 31
B4: ^1990
G4: ^1992
A5: [W31] ||\027F
A6: [W31] 'Revenues
B6: (,0) 72000
C6: (P1) [W7] +REVENUES/$REVENUES
F6: [W31] 'Revenues
G6: (,0) 79400
H6: (P1) [W7] +G6/$G$6
A7: [W31] 'Costs and expenses
F7: [W31] 'Costs and expenses
A8: [W31] '  Product costs
B8: (,0) 15300
C8: (P1) [W7] +PRODUCT.COSTS/$REVENUES
F8: [W31] '  Product costs
G8: (,0) 13835
H8: (P1) [W7] +G8/$G$6
A9: [W31] '  Marketing and sales
B9: (,0) 20785
C9: (P1) [W7] +B9/$REVENUES
F9: [W31] '  Marketing and sales
G9: (,0) 20500
H9: (P1) [W7] +G9/$G$6
A10: [W31] '  General and administrative
B10: (,0) 17850
C10: (P1) [W7] +B10/$REVENUES
F10: [W31] '  General and administrative
G10: (,0) 14750
H10: (P1) [W7] +G10/$G$6
B11: (,0) \-
G11: (,0) \-
A12: [W31] 'Total costs and expenses
B12: (,0) @SUM(COSTS)
C12: (P1) [W7] +TOTAL.COSTS/$REVENUES
F12: [W31] 'Total costs and expenses
G12: (,0) @SUM(G8..G10)
H12: (P1) [W7] +G12/$G$6
A14: [W31] 'Operating income (loss)
B14: (,0) +REVENUES-TOTAL.COSTS
C14: (P1) [W7] +B14/$REVENUES
F14: [W31] 'Operating income (loss)
G14: (,0) +G6-G12
H14: (P1) [W7] +G14/$G$6
A16: [W31] 'Other income (expenses)
F16: [W31] 'Other income (expenses)
A17: [W31] '  Interest income
B17: (,0) 4500
C17: (P1) [W7] +B17/$REVENUES
F17: [W31] '  Interest income
G17: (,0) 1500
H17: (P1) [W7] +G17/$G$6
A18: [W31] '  Interest expense
B18: (,0) -500
C18: (P1) [W7] +B18/$REVENUES
F18: [W31] '  Interest expense
G18: (,0) -485
H18: (P1) [W7] +G18/$G$6
A19: [W31] '  Other
B19: (,0) 600
C19: (P1) [W7] +B19/$REVENUES
F19: [W31] '  Other
G19: (,0) -100
```

♦ **Figure 8.8:** *First page of report listing the contents of the cells in the print range (58% actual size)*

Changing the Printing Defaults

If, in the course of your work with 1-2-3, you find that you are routinely changing any of the printing defaults before printing your reports, you should consider changing the printing defaults permanently.

To change a printing default, you need to use the /Worksheet Global Default Printer menu (/WGDP). From this menu, you can change the default left, right, top, or bottom margin, as well as the page length. To change any defaults, select the appropriate option, type in the new value, and press Enter, then choose the Quit option. This returns you to the /Worksheet Global Default menu. From here, be sure to select the Update option before you select this menu's Quit option to return to READY mode. Doing this ensures that new defaults are saved on disk in the 1-2-3 configuration file, making them the new permanent defaults.

Defining a Default Setup String

If you find that you are regularly using a particular setup string in the reports you are producing, you can make that setup string the default. To do this, you need to choose the Setup option from the /Worksheet Global Default Printer menu. Then, type in the new default setup string, press Enter, and select the Quit option. Just as when changing other printing default settings, be sure that you select the Update option on the /Worksheet Global Default menu before you select Quit a second time to return to READY mode.

Printing Your Worksheets

Now it's time to get some practice in printing reports with 1-2-3. In your first printout, you will use all of the program's printing defaults. Then, you will begin to experiment with changing the defaults and enhancing your reports. Before you start the printing exercises, be sure that your printer is turned on and that it has plenty of paper. If your printer requires you to manually feed each sheet of paper, select the Yes option from the /Worksheet Global Default Printer Wait menu (/WGDPW) before doing this exercise.

1. **Retrieve the worksheet file *IS90CH5.WK1*.**
   This worksheet already contains the range name *INCOME.90*, which includes all the information you want to print.

2. **Select the /Print Printer Range (/PPR) command, then press the Name key (F3) and select the range name *INCOME.90* before you press Enter.**
   If you are using Release 2.2, you will notice that the program now lists *A1..B24 (INCOME.90)* after Range in the Print Settings sheet. You are ready to print.

3. **Select the Align Go Page options (AGP).**
   Remember that the Align option informs 1-2-3 that the printhead is at the top of form, the Go option starts the printing, and the Page option advances the printhead to the next top of form (the income statement uses only about half of the page). Next, try printing the income statement so that it is more centered on the page.

4. **Select Options Margins Left (OML), type 22, and press Enter; then, select Quit to return to the main printing menu and select Align Go Page (QAGP) to print the income statement with this new left margin.**
   In this second printout, the income statement should be centered between the left and right margins on the page. When you have a small print range that fits comfortably on a single page, you can use the left- and top-margin settings to position the range as you want. Next, you will add a header for the report.

5. **Select Options Header (OH), then type *Preliminary Report* || @, and press Enter.**
   If you are using Release 2.2, you can check the text of your header in the settings sheet as it will now appear after Header. The header you just created will print the text *Preliminary Report* aligned with the left margin of the report, and the @ symbol will print the current date aligned with the right margin (because you separated the two parts of the header with *two* vertical bars). Remember, however, that you changed the left margin from 4 to 22. This will indent the first part of the header too much.

6. **Select Margins Left (ML), then type 8, and press Enter.**
   Now, the first part of the header will be indented about 1/2 inch from the left edge of the page. This means, however, that the income statement will also no longer be centered when printed. To center the body of the report without affecting the alignment of the header text, you have to move the print range to the right by inserting a blank column.

7. **Select Quit twice to return to READY mode; move the cell pointer to cell A1, select the /Worksheet Insert Column command (/WIC), and press Enter to accept the default range of *A1..A1*.**
   Inserting a column nine characters wide isn't quite enough to center the income statement on the page, so you'd better widen this column.

8. **Select the /Worksheet Column Set-Width command (/WCS), and increase the column width to 14 characters.**
Note that inserting a blank column before the print range doesn't have any effect on the positioning of the range unless that column is included *as part of* the print range.

9. **Select the /Print Printer Range command (/PPR).**
The program highlights the range B1..C24, and you now need to extend it to include the newly inserted column A. This is a perfect opportunity to use the period key to change the anchor cell in the range, greatly simplifying this procedure.

10. **Press the period key twice so that B1 becomes the anchor cell (you can tell that this is the anchor cell by the presence of the blinking underscore in the middle of this cell) and the range reads C24..B1; then press the ← key once to include column A (the range changes to C24..A1), and press Enter.**
Try printing your report now.

11. **Select Align Go Page (AGP).**
Your report should be similar to the one shown in Figure 8.9. Next, try adding a footer that prints the page number centered at the bottom of the report.

12. **Select Options Footer (OF), type | *Page #*, and press Enter.**
If you're using Release 2.2, you should see the text of your footer in the Print Settings sheet. The page number will be centered between the left and right margins because you only entered a single vertical bar. Try printing the report with the new footer.

13. **Select Quit Align Go Page (QAGP).**
Check two things in this new printout: that the page number is printed on the first page of the report and that it is centered between the margins. If the footer is printed on the second page, either the printhead is not positioned high enough at the top of the page or the page-length setting is too large. Experiment first with the position of the printhead by manually advancing the next sheet of paper down slightly, then print this report again to see if this takes care of the problem. If this doesn't work (or if you're using a printer—such as a laser printer—where you have no physical control over where the printing starts at the top of the page), try reducing the page-length setting (it's located on the Options menu). Before ending this exercise, let's try printing the income statement once more, this time including the column of percentages immediately to the right of the income and expense column in the worksheet.

14. **Select the Range option (R), press the → key once to include column D so that the print range becomes** *A1..D24,* **and press Enter.**

    Before you begin printing, you need to decrease the size of column A if you want the body of the report to remain centered.

15. **Choose the Quit option (Q), then select the /Worksheet Column Set-Width command (/WCS) and decrease the column width to 9 characters.**

    Now try printing this version of the report.

16. **Select /Print Printer and then choose the Align Go Page options (/PPAGP).**

    Your report should match the one shown in Figure 8.10 (except that the date in your report header should be current).

17. **Save the file under the same name.**

    When you save the file, 1-2-3 saves all the report print settings as part of it.

```
Preliminary Report                                         02-Jun-89


                  INCOME STATEMENT YEAR ENDING DECEMBER 31
                                                  1990
                  Revenues                       72,000
                  Costs and expenses
                     Product costs               15,300
                     Marketing and sales         20,785
                     General and administrative  17,850
                                                 --------
                  Total costs and expenses       53,935

                  Operating income (loss)        18,065

                  Other income (expenses)
                     Interest income              4,500
                     Interest expense             (500)
                     Bonuses                      4,642
                     Other                          600
                                                 --------
                  Total other income (expenses)   9,242

                  Income (loss) before taxes     27,307
                     Provision (benefit) for taxes 4,096
                  Net earnings (loss)            23,211
                                                 =========
```

♦ **Figure 8.9:** *The 1990 income statement report with left- and right-aligned header and body centered between margins (58% actual size)*

```
Preliminary Report                                          02-Jun-89


              INCOME STATEMENT YEAR ENDING DECEMBER 31
                                  1990
              Revenues                    72,000      100.0%
              Costs and expenses
                Product costs             15,300       21.3%
                Marketing and sales       20,785       28.9%
                General and administrative 17,850      24.8%
                                          --------
              Total costs and expenses    53,935       74.9%

              Operating income (loss)     18,065       25.1%

              Other income (expenses)
                Interest income            4,500        6.3%
                Interest expense            (500)      -0.7%
                Bonuses                    4,642        6.4%
                Other                        600        0.8%
                                          --------
              Total other income (expenses) 9,242      12.8%

              Income (loss) before taxes  27,307       37.9%
                Provision (benefit) for taxes 4,096     5.7%
              Net earnings (loss)         23,211       32.2%
                                          ========


                            Page 1
```

◆ **Figure 8.10:** *The 1990 income statement report with percentages (58% actual size)*

♦

Printing Multiple-Page Reports

Now that you have gained some experience with printing single-page reports, you are ready to work with larger print ranges that require multiple pages to be printed. For this exercise, you will use the composite worksheet that you created in the last chapter using the /File Combine Copy command.

1. **Retrieve the worksheet file *ISC90-93.WK1*.**
   Remember that this file consists of four income statements and the range name table. Begin by printing all of this information to see how 1-2-3 pages this report.

2. **Select the /Print Printer Range command (/PPR), type a period, press End Home, and press Enter.**
   Pressing End Home highlights the range A1..H63 by moving the pointer to the last active cell in the worksheet. This range extends as far down as row 63 because of the range name table (not visible on your screen). Now that you've defined this as the print range, go ahead and print it.

3. **Select the Align Go Page options (AGP) to print this range.**
   To print this range requires three pages. Notice how 1-2-3 pages the report: the 1990 and 1991 income statements along with the first few lines of the range name table are printed on the first page, the rest of the range name table is printed on the second page, and the 1992 and 1993 income statements on the third page. Except for splitting the range name table across two pages, this arrangement is fine. Use the /Worksheet Page command to ensure that the entire range name table is printed on the second page.

4. **Select the Quit option (Q), then move the pointer to A51 and select /Worksheet Page (/WP).**
   Note that as soon as you type /WP, 1-2-3 inserts a new row in the worksheet and places two colons (: :) in cell A51. When you use the /Worksheet Page command to insert a manual page break, remember that you must position the pointer in the leftmost column of the print range (column A in this example), right on the row that you want to appear at the top of a new page (row 51 in this example). Now print the report again to see the effect of using /Worksheet Page.

5. **Select /Print Printer Align Go Page (/PPAGP) to print the report a second time.**
   This time, the range name table should be printed completely on page 2 of the report. Now try printing the entire print range on one page by turning on compressed mode and increasing the right-margin setting.

6. **Refer to Table 8.1 or your own printer documentation to determine the ASCII printer code that your printer uses to turn on compressed print; then, select Options Setup (OS) and enter the appropriate setup string (for example, if you have an Epson printer, type \015 and press Enter).**
Remember that to increase the amount of information that can be printed on the single page, you must increase the right-margin setting as well as enter the setup string to print with compressed type.

7. **Select Margins Right, type *132*, and press Enter.**
Now you are ready to print the report in compressed print.

8. **Select the Quit option (Q), then choose Align Go Page (AGP).**
Figure 8.11 shows you the first page of this report (the range name table is still printed by itself on the second page). As you see, in compressed mode, 1-2-3 can accommodate all four income statements on the first page of the report. If you add the setup code for your printer to change from 6 lines per inch to 8 lines per inch, you can also print the range name table on the first page.

9. **Select the Quit option (Q) to return to the worksheet; move the pointer up to row 51, then select /Worksheet Delete Row (/WDR), and press Enter to remove the manual page break.**
Now you need to add the print codes for printing 8 lines per inch to the setup string.

10. **Select /Print Printer Options Setup (/PPOS), add the appropriate codes from Table 8.1 or your printer documentation (be sure to separate each part with a backslash) to the existing setup string, and press Enter.**
When you increase the number of lines per inch, you need to increase the page length accordingly to accommodate more lines per page.

11. **Select the Pg-Length option (P), type 88, and press Enter.**
Now you are ready to print the report a second time, using this new setup string and page length.

12. **Select the Quit option (Q), then choose Align Go Page (AGP).**
Figure 8.12 shows you the report printed with this setup string. For many printers, this is the smallest type size and line spacing they can produce.

```
INCOME STATEMENT YEAR ENDING DECEMBER 31        INCOME STATEMENT YEAR ENDING DECEMBER 31
                        1990                                            1992
Revenues                72,000    100.0%        Revenues                79,400    100.0%
Costs and expenses                              Costs and expenses
  Product costs         15,300     21.3%          Product costs         13,835     17.4%
  Marketing and sales   20,785     28.9%          Marketing and sales   20,500     25.8%
  General and administrative      17,850  24.8%   General and administrative      14,750  18.6%
                        ----------                                      ----------
Total costs and expenses 53,935    74.9%        Total costs and expenses 49,085    61.8%

Operating income (loss) 18,065     25.1%        Operating income (loss) 30,315     38.2%

Other income (expenses)                         Other income (expenses)
  Interest income        4,500      6.3%          Interest income        1,500      1.9%
  Interest expense        (500)    -0.7%          Interest expense        (485)    -0.6%
  Other                    600      0.8%          Other                   (100)    -0.1%
                        ----------                                      ----------
Total other income (expenses)  4,600  6.4%      Total other income (expenses)   915  1.2%

Income (loss) before taxes  22,665  31.5%       Income (loss) before taxes  31,230  39.3%
  Provision (benefit) for taxes  3,400  4.7%      Provision (benefit) for taxes  4,685  5.9%
Net earnings (loss)     19,265     26.8%        Net earnings (loss)     26,546     33.4%
                        =========                                      =========



INCOME STATEMENT YEAR ENDING DECEMBER 31        INCOME STATEMENT YEAR ENDING DECEMBER 31
                        1991                                            1993
Revenues                56,525    100.0%        Revenues                65,450    100.0%
Costs and expenses                              Costs and expenses
  Product costs         17,275     30.6%          Product costs         12,500     19.1%
  Marketing and sales   22,000     38.9%          Marketing and sales   19,775     30.2%
  General and administrative      12,500  22.1%   General and administrative      10,250  15.7%
                        ----------                                      ----------
Total costs and expenses 51,775    91.6%        Total costs and expenses 42,525    65.0%

Operating income (loss)  4,750      8.4%        Operating income (loss) 22,925     35.0%

Other income (expenses)                         Other income (expenses)
  Interest income        2,500      4.4%          Interest income        9,975     15.2%
  Interest expense        (250)    -0.4%          Interest expense        (600)    -0.9%
  Other                      0      0.0%          Other                   (250)    -0.4%
                        ----------                                      ----------
Total other income (expenses)  2,250  4.0%      Total other income (expenses)  9,125  13.9%

Income (loss) before taxes   7,000  12.4%       Income (loss) before taxes  32,050  49.0%
  Provision (benefit) for taxes  1,400  2.5%      Provision (benefit) for taxes  4,808  7.3%
Net earnings (loss)      5,600      9.9%        Net earnings (loss)     27,243     41.6%
                        =========                                      =========
```

◆ **Figure 8.11:** *First page of the four-year income statement report printed in compressed print (58% actual size)*

```
INCOME STATEMENT YEAR ENDING DECEMBER 31      INCOME STATEMENT YEAR ENDING DECEMBER 31
                     1990                                          1992
Revenues                72,000  100.0%        Revenues                79,400  100.0%
Costs and expenses                            Costs and expenses
   Product costs        15,300   21.3%           Product costs        13,835   17.4%
   Marketing and sales  20,785   28.9%           Marketing and sales  20,500   25.8%
   General and administrative 17,850  24.8%      General and administrative 14,750  18.6%
                        --------                                      --------
Total costs and expenses 53,935  74.9%        Total costs and expenses 49,085  61.8%

Operating income (loss) 18,065   25.1%        Operating income (loss) 30,315   38.2%

Other income (expenses)                       Other income (expenses)
   Interest income       4,500    6.3%           Interest income       1,500    1.9%
   Interest expense       (500)  -0.7%           Interest expense       (485)  -0.6%
   Other                   600    0.8%           Other                  (100)  -0.1%
                        --------                                      --------
Total other income (expenses) 4,600  6.4%     Total other income (expenses) 915   1.2%

Income (loss) before taxes 22,665 31.5%       Income (loss) before taxes 31,230 39.3%
   Provision (benefit) for taxes 3,400 4.7%      Provision (benefit) for taxes 4,685 5.9%
Net earnings (loss)     19,265   26.8%        Net earnings (loss)     26,546   33.4%
                        ========                                      ========


INCOME STATEMENT YEAR ENDING DECEMBER 31      INCOME STATEMENT YEAR ENDING DECEMBER 31
                     1991                                          1993
Revenues                56,525  100.0%        Revenues                65,450  100.0%
Costs and expenses                            Costs and expenses
   Product costs        17,275   30.6%           Product costs        12,500   19.1%
   Marketing and sales  22,000   38.9%           Marketing and sales  19,775   30.2%
   General and administrative 12,500  22.1%      General and administrative 10,250  15.7%
                        --------                                      --------
Total costs and expenses 51,775  91.6%        Total costs and expenses 42,525  65.0%

Operating income (loss)  4,750    8.4%        Operating income (loss) 22,925   35.0%

Other income (expenses)                       Other income (expenses)
   Interest income       2,500    4.4%           Interest income       9,975   15.2%
   Interest expense       (250)  -0.4%           Interest expense       (600)  -0.9%
   Other                     0    0.0%           Other                  (250)  -0.4%
                        --------                                      --------
Total other income (expenses) 2,250  4.0%     Total other income (expenses) 9,125  13.9%

Income (loss) before taxes  7,000 12.4%       Income (loss) before taxes 32,050 49.0%
   Provision (benefit) for taxes 1,400 2.5%      Provision (benefit) for taxes 4,808 7.3%
Net earnings (loss)      5,600    9.9%        Net earnings (loss)     27,243   41.6%
                        ========                                      ========

Range Names for Income Statement

COSTS                   B5..B7
INCOME.90               A1..B23
INCST.90                A1..C23
INCST.91                A27..C49
INCST.92                F1..H23
INCST.93                F27..H49
NAME.TABLE              A51..B57
PRODUCT.COSTS           B5
REVENUES                B3
TOTAL.COSTS             B9
TOTAL.EXP               B9
```

◆ **Figure 8.12:** *Four-year income statement report printed in compressed print with 8 lines per inch (58% actual size)*

Enhancing the Composite Income Statement Report

For the last printing exercise, you will get some more practice in defining headers and footers. In addition, you will enhance the basic report by embedding setup strings to print some income statement titles in bold and hiding some columns. When you are finished, you should be able to print the essentials from all four income statements on a single page without having to use compressed print.

Currently, the print settings in effect include compressed printing on, a line spacing of 8 lines per inch, a page length of 88 lines, and a right-margin setting of 132. You can verify this by referring to the Print Settings sheet shown in Figure 8.13. For this next report, you will want to clear the setup string to return the type size to pica (10 characters per inch) and the line spacing to 6 lines per inch, reset the page length to the default of 66 lines, and return the right-margin setting to 76. In 1-2-3, rather than changing each of these values separately, you can accomplish the same thing by simply selecting the Format option on the /Print Printer Clear menu.

1. **Select Clear Format (CF).**

   This clears the setup string and returns the page length to the default of 66 and the right margin to 76. In this report, you won't bother to print the range name table that occurs at the bottom of the print range. To eliminate it from the report, you need to modify the print range.

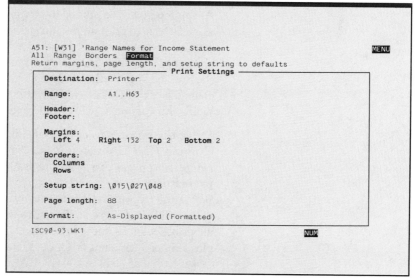

```
A51: [W31] 'Range Names for Income Statement                          MENU
All   Range   Borders   Format
Return margins, page length, and setup string to defaults
                              ┌──────── Print Settings ────────
    Destination:   Printer

    Range:         A1..H63

    Header:
    Footer:

    Margins:
      Left 4      Right 132   Top 2    Bottom 2

    Borders:
      Columns
      Rows

    Setup string:  \015\027\048

    Page length:   88

    Format:        As-Displayed (Formatted)

ISC90-93.WK1                                                          NUM
```

♦ **Figure 8.13:** *Print Settings sheet showing the current print settings*

2. **Select the Range option (R), then press the ↑ key until the range *A1..H49* is highlighted, and press Enter.**
Next, you need to increase the left margin and bottom margin slightly and define a header and footer.

3. **Select Options Margins Left (OML), type 8, and press Enter; then, select Margins Bottom (MB), type 4, and press Enter again.**
The entire text of the report header will be right-aligned. To do this, you must remember to type two vertical bars (without any space between them) before entering the text.

4. **Select Header (H), type || *Income Statements 1990–1993*, and press Enter.**
The text of the footer will be split so that the current date is aligned with the left margin and the page number is aligned with the right margin. To do this, you must enter the two vertical bars between these two elements.

5. **Select Footer (F), type @ || *Page #*, and press Enter.**
If you are using Release 2.2, you should look over your header and footer in the Print Settings sheet to make sure that you entered the codes correctly. Next, you need to return to the worksheet to make some changes in the print range itself.

6. **Select the Quit option twice (QQ) to return to READY mode.**
As this report will be printed in pica type instead of compressed, you won't be able to print all the income statement data for the four years on one page unless you either restrict the print range or hide some of the columns. In this report, you really don't need to repeat the row headings for the 1992 and 1993 income statements in column F of the worksheet. Try getting all the data on one page by hiding this column as well as column E to its left.

7. **Move the pointer to column F, and select the /Worksheet Column Hide command (/WCH); type a period to anchor the range, and press the ← key to include column E before you press Enter.**
Before you try printing this report, try to determine whether the print range will fit on one page. To do this, you need to add the widths of all visible columns in the print range: Column A at a width of 31, plus 5 times 9 (columns B, C, D, G, and H are all still 9 characters), makes a total of 76 ($9 \times 5 = 45 + 31 = 76$). Although this would

just make it if your left margin were 0, it will be 8 too many with the new left margin of 8 (meaning that column H will be printed on its own page).

8. **Move the pointer to column C and decrease its width from 9 to 7; then, move the pointer to column D and make it 3 characters wide; finally, move the pointer to column H and reduce it from 9 to 7 as well.**

    Narrowing these three columns by these few characters should make it possible to print the entire print range on a single page. Before you try printing the report, however, make one more enhancement: print the worksheet title and year column headings in bold type. To do this, you must embed the setup strings in the worksheet that turn bold on and off.

9. **Press the Home key to move the pointer to cell A1; then, select the /Worksheet Insert Row command (/WIR), and press Enter to insert a new row above the worksheet title.**

    Now you are ready to embed the setup string that turns on bold type (this attribute is referred to as *doublestrike* in some printer manuals).

10. **With the pointer in A1, enter || (two vertical bars) followed by the setup string used by your printer to turn on bold (refer to Table 8.1 or your own printer manual) in this cell; for example, if you have an Epson FX printer, to do this you would type || \027E, and press Enter.**

    Displayed in cell A1, you should now see one of the vertical bars you entered followed by the setup string to turn bold on. You only want the title in cell B1 and the year column headings in B3 and G3 bold, so you will need to turn bold off in row 4 of the report. First, separate the worksheet title from the year column headings by inserting a new row in the worksheet.

11. **Move the pointer to row 3 (the column doesn't matter), select the /Worksheet Insert Row command (/WIR), and press Enter to accept the default range.**

    Now you are ready to turn bold off in the report. To do this, you will need to insert a row below what is now row 5 and embed the setup string to turn bold off in the new cell A5.

12. **Move the pointer to row 5, insert a single row, and then enter || (two vertical bars) followed by the setup string to turn bold**

off in this cell; for instance, if you have an Epson FX printer, to do this you would type || \027F, and press Enter.

Check your screen against the one shown in Figure 8.14. Of course, the actual setup strings displayed in your cell A1 and A5 may differ, but otherwise your screen should match the one in this figure. Now you need to turn bold on and off for the 1991 and 1993 column headings in row 31 of the worksheet. You don't, however, need to print *INCOME STATEMENT YEAR ENDING DECEMBER 31* in row 30 because this title will already appear at the top of the page in bold.

13. **Move the pointer to cell A30, select /Range Format Hidden (/RFH), and press Enter to hide the display of this title.**
    You need not insert a new row in the worksheet in which to embed the code to turn bold on again; instead, you can use the empty cell in A29 above the now hidden title in cell A30.

14. **Move the pointer to cell A30, and copy the embedded setup string entered in cell A1 to this cell; then, move the pointer to A32, insert a new row in the worksheet, and copy the embedded setup string entered in cell A5 into the empty cell in A32.**

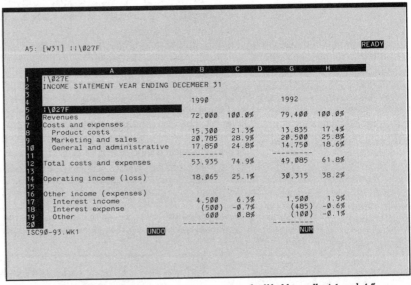

◆ **Figure 8.14:** *Embedded setup strings to turn on and off bold in cells A1 and A5*

You are finished making modifications in the worksheet. Only one more thing remains to be done before printing the report: you need to increase the print range slightly to include row 1 with the embedded setup string to turn on bold. When you inserted this new row for the setup string, you pushed down the print range.

15. **Select /Print Printer Range (/PPR), press the period key twice, then press the ↑ key once to include row 1 as part of the print range, and press Enter.**
    Now you are ready to print this report.

16. **Select Align Go Page (AGP).**
    Your report should pretty much match the one shown in Figure 8.15 (the current date in the footer will, of course, be different). You should save these report settings as part of the worksheet. To retain the compressed print settings from the previous exercise, you will also rename the worksheet.

17. **Quit the print menu and then save the worksheet under the file name *ISCONRPT*.**

Summary

Troubleshooting

Question: When I selected the Align Go options on the /Print Printer menu, the program beeped, went into ERROR mode, and displayed the error message *Printer error*. What is the cause of this?

Answer: You will get this error from 1-2-3 whenever the current printer either isn't turned on or isn't cabled properly. If you are using Release 2.2, check the Default Settings sheet by selecting /Worksheet Global Default (/WGD) to make sure that the correct printer and interface are selected. If not, use the Name and, if necessary, the Interface options on the /Worksheet Global Default Printer menu (/WGDP) to make these settings correct. If this is not the problem or the problem persists, make sure the printer is turned on and that all cable connections between your computer and printer are secure.

Question: When printing a second copy of my report, I discovered that the page numbers in the footer don't begin from 1 as they're supposed to but continue from the last page number in the first copy. What caused this to happen?

```
                                              Income Statements 1990-1993


INCOME STATEMENT YEAR ENDING DECEMBER 31

                              1990                1992
Revenues                      72,000   100.0%    79,400   100.0%
Costs and expenses
   Product costs              15,300    21.3%    13,835    17.4%
   Marketing and sales        20,785    28.9%    20,500    25.8%
   General and administrative 17,850    24.8%    14,750    18.6%
                             ---------           ---------
Total costs and expenses      53,935    74.9%    49,085    61.8%

Operating income (loss)       18,065    25.1%    30,315    38.2%

Other income (expenses)
   Interest income             4,500     6.3%     1,500     1.9%
   Interest expense             (500)   -0.7%      (485)   -0.6%
   Other                         600     0.8%      (100)   -0.1%
                             ---------           ---------
Total other income (expenses)  4,600     6.4%       915     1.2%

Income (loss) before taxes    22,665    31.5%    31,230    39.3%
   Provision (benefit) for taxes 3,400   4.7%     4,685     5.9%
Net earnings (loss)           19,265    26.8%    26,546    33.4%
                             =========           =========


                              1991                1993
Revenues                      56,525   100.0%    65,450   100.0%
Costs and expenses
   Product costs              17,275    30.6%    12,500    19.1%
   Marketing and sales        22,000    38.9%    19,775    30.2%
   General and administrative 12,500    22.1%    10,250    15.7%
                             ---------           ---------
Total costs and expenses      51,775    91.6%    42,525    65.0%

Operating income (loss)        4,750     8.4%    22,925    35.0%

Other income (expenses)
   Interest income             2,500     4.4%     9,975    15.2%
   Interest expense             (250)   -0.4%      (600)   -0.9%
   Other                           0     0.0%      (250)   -0.4%
                             ---------           ---------
Total other income (expenses)  2,250     4.0%     9,125    13.9%

Income (loss) before taxes     7,000    12.4%    32,050    49.0%
   Provision (benefit) for taxes 1,400   2.5%     4,808     7.3%
Net earnings (loss)            5,600     9.9%    27,243    41.6%
                             =========           =========




03-Jun-89                                                  Page 1
```

◆ **Figure 8:15:** *Final report using embedded setup strings to bold titles (58% actual size)*

Answer: You didn't select the Align option before the Go option when you printed the second copy of the report. Without the Align signal, the program doesn't know that you are starting a new report and, therefore, doesn't begin renumbering the pages from 1.

Question: I know that I can prevent 1-2-3 from printing particular columns in the print range by using the /Worksheet Column Hide command. Is there a comparable command that will allow me to prevent the printing of particular rows in the print range?

Answer: Although there is no specific 1-2-3 command like the /Worksheet Column Hide command for hiding particular rows, you can accomplish this by using the same technique you use to embed setup strings within the print range. By prefacing the contents of the first cell in the row (that is, the leftmost cell in the print range) with a single vertical bar (|), 1-2-3 will ignore the entire row when printing the report. For example, if the first cell of a particular row in the print range contains the label '*Expenses* and you wish to prohibit the printing of this row in the report, edit the cell so that its contents are | '*Expenses* (in the cell display, you will then see '*Expenses*). When 1-2-3 prints the report after you make this editing change, all data in the row that contains the | '*Expenses* label will be missing from the report. Also, 1-2-3 will not place a blank line in the report for this report, but will ignore it totally as though it didn't exist in the print range.

Question: I'm using an HP LaserJet Series II to print my 1-2-3 reports. Sometimes the printer, for no apparent reason, ejects a page of the report before it has finished printing. What is going on here?

Answer: This problem occurs when you embed setup strings in the print range to turn on and off attributes such as bold, underlining, or italics, and the like, and you begin such setup strings with the reset code \027E. This reset code for the LaserJet printers not only clears all prior codes but also sends the code to eject the page from the printer. Therefore, eliminate this reset code from your embedded setup strings and you should eliminate the random page ejections.

Essential Techniques

To Print a Report Using the Default Print Settings

1. Select the /Print Printer Range option. Move the pointer to the first cell to be printed, type a period to anchor the range, and then move the pointer to the last cell to be included and press Enter.

2. Select the Align Go options on the /Print Printer menu.

3. Select the Page option on the the /Print Printer menu to advance the printhead to the next top of form and complete the last page. Select this option a second time to issue a form feed to the printer to advance the last page so that you can remove it from the printer.

To Change the Print Settings for Your Report

1. To modify the margin settings for your report, select Options Margins from the /Print Printer menu, then choose the appropriate margin option (Left, Right, Top, or Bottom), and enter the new setting.

2. To turn on compressed print, change the line spacing, or add a particular attribute (such as doublestrike) to the entire report, select Setup from the Options menu, then type the setup string required by your printer.

3. To change the page length, select Pg-Length on the Options menu and enter the total number of lines that can be printed on the page. This number depends upon the length of the paper you are using as well as the line spacing in effect.

4. To define a header and/or footer for the report, select Header or Footer on the Options menu and type in one line of text to appear on every page of the report. To enter the current date in the header or footer, type the @ symbol. To enter the page number, type the # symbol. Use vertical bars to change the alignment of parts of the header or footer. Precede the text with one vertical bar (|) to center it. Precede the text with two vertical bars (||) to right-justify it.

5. To define borders for your report, select Borders from the Options menu. Then select the Columns option and designate a range of columns, to have the group of columns printed at the left edge of each page of the report. Select the Rows option and designate a range of rows, to have the group of rows printed at the top of each page of the report. Be sure that the columns and rows designated as borders for the report aren't included in the print range.

6. To have 1-2-3 ignore the headers, footers, and top and bottom margins when printing the report, select Other Unformatted from the Options menu. Return to the Options Other menu and select the Formatted option when you wish to have the header and footer printed in the report and the top- and bottom-margin settings used once again.

7. To have 1-2-3 print the contents of each cell in the print range (rather than its display, as is usual), select Other Cell-Formulas from the Options menu. Return to the Options Other menu and select the As-Displayed option when you wish to have the report printed normally.

Review

Important Terms You Should Know

borders	parallel port
current printer	print range
default printer	serial port
footer	setup string
header	

Test Your Knowledge

1. To select a new printer to use, you choose the _____ option on the _____ menu, then select the number of the printer from this new menu.

2. If the printer that you select uses a different port, you must also choose the _____ option and select the number of the correct port.

3. To print a report using the printing default settings, all you need to do is define the _____ and then begin printing. To do this, you select the _____ option on the _____ menu. To begin the printing, you select the _____ and _____ options.

4. When 1-2-3 has finished printing your report, you must remember to select the _____ option to advance the printhead to the next top of form (or eject the last page, if you are using a laser printer).

5. To change one of the margin settings for your report, you select _____ and then select either the Left, Right, Top, or Bottom option. If you're using Release 2.2 and want to optimize the amount of data that can be printed on a page, you can select the new _____ option on this menu to set the left, top, and bottom margins to 0 and the right margin to 240.

6. To create a header that prints the current date aligned with the right margin, you select the _____ option from the /Print Printer Options menu and then enter _____.

7. To create a footer that prints the page number centered between the left and right margins, you select the _____ option from the /Print Printer Options menu and then enter _____.

8. To print a report in compressed print, you must select the _____ option from the /Print Printer Options menu and then enter _____. After doing this, you must increase the _____ setting from 76 to _____ as well (assume that you are using 8½-×-11-inch paper).

9. To print a report using 8 lines per inch as the line spacing, you must select the _____ option from the /Print Printer Options menu and then enter _____. After doing this, you must increase the _____ setting from 66 to _____ as well (assume that you are using 8½-×-11-inch paper).

10. To insert a manual page break in a report, you must move the pointer to _____ and then select the _____ command.

11. To have 1-2-3 pause after printing each page of the report to allow you to manually feed a new page to your printer, you must select the _____ option on the _____ menu.

12. To obtain a printout of the contents of each cell in the print range, you must select the _____ option on the _____ menu.

Further Exercises

1. Retrieve the worksheet *IS90CH5.WK1*. Delete the blank column A you inserted in the earlier printing exercise, and then save this file under the same name.

2. Retrieve the worksheet *ISLINK.WK1*. Define the print range for this worksheet as A1..F11. Change the left-margin setting to 8, and define

```
                        Consolidated Income Report Dated: 04-Jun-89

INCOME SUMMARY FOR YEARS 1990-1993

                    1990     1991     1992     1993    TOTAL
Revenues          72,000   56,525   79,400   65,450  273,375
Operating Costs   53,935   51,775   49,085   42,525  197,320
                  -----------------------------------------------
Gross Income      18,065    4,750   30,315   22,925   76,055
Total Other Income 9,242    2,250      915    9,125   21,532
                  -----------------------------------------------
Net Income        27,307    7,000   31,230   32,050   97,587
                  ===============================================




INCOME STATEMENT YEAR ENDING DECEMBER 31
                                1990
Revenues                       72,000    100.0%
Costs and expenses
    Product costs              15,300     21.3%
    Marketing and sales        20,785     28.9%
    General and administrative 17,850     24.8%
                               ---------
Total costs and expenses       53,935     74.9%

Operating income (loss)        18,065     25.1%

Other income (expenses)
    Interest income             4,500      6.3%
    Interest expense            (500)     -0.7%
    Bonuses                     4,642      6.4%
    Other                         600      0.8%
                               ---------
Total other income (expenses)   9,242     12.8%

Income (loss) before taxes     27,307     37.9%
    Provision (benefit) for taxes 4,096    5.7%
Net earnings (loss)            23,211     32.2%
                               =========




                            Page 1
```

◆ **Figure 8.16:** *First page of report printed with print ranges in different files (58% actual size)*

a right-aligned header that says *Consolidated Income Report Dated:* followed by the current date, as shown in Figure 8.16. Define a centered footer that prints the current page number. Then select the Align Go options. When 1-2-3 finishes printing the income summary, select the Line option seven times to advance the printhead a line at a time. Then exit from the /Print menu and save this worksheet under the same name.

3. Retrieve the worksheet *IS90CH5.WK1* again. Define the print range as A1..C24 and then select the Go option to start printing (don't select the Align option this time). After 1-2-3 prints the 1990 income statement below the income summary, use the Line option until 1-2-3 prints the footer on this page (your report should resemble the one shown in Figure 8.16). Exit from the /Print menu, and save this file under the same name.

9

Representing Data Graphically

In This Chapter...

Lotus 1-2-3 Graphics Capabilities

Lotus 1-2-3 makes it easy to enhance your spreadsheet data with professional-looking business graphics. The program allows you to represent your worksheet data in a variety of standard business graph formats: line graph, bar graph, XY graph (or scatter chart), stacked-bar graph, or pie chart. Creating graphs in Lotus 1-2-3 is a straightforward process of choosing one of these graph types and defining the various data ranges in the worksheet that are to be represented pictorially.

All the graphs you create in a worksheet file are saved with that file. Lotus 1-2-3 allows you to generate as many different graphs as you want. To print them, however, you must save the graphs in separate files in a special format, then exit from 1-2-3 and use the PrintGraph program.

Viewing Your Graphs on the Screen

To view a graph on the screen, you can use the /Graph View command when you are still using the /Graph menu, or press the Graph key (F10) when you are back in the worksheet and the program is in READY mode. When you select either method, 1-2-3 replaces the worksheet display with the current graph. To return to the worksheet display after viewing a graph, you can press any key. Lotus 1-2-3 always considers the graph that you most recently viewed as the *current graph*.

F10: The Graph Key

F10, the Graph key, displays full-screen view of the current graph provided that:
 * Your computer is equipped with some type of graphics adapter
 * You have created a graph in the current worksheet file

Press any key to return to the worksheet display

F10 can be used only when the program is in READY mode

Graphics Displays

To view the graphs you create, your computer must be equipped with some type of graphics adapter. If your computer doesn't support graphics, 1-2-3 will simply beep at you when you select the /Graph View command or press the Graph key (F10). (You can, however, still generate graphs and print them, although you won't be able to preview them prior to printing.)

If you have a monochrome monitor, you need a monochrome graphics card, such as the Hercules Graphics Card, to view your graphs on the screen. If you have a color monitor, you need to have some type of graphics card to view your graphs. Release 2.2 supports the use of CGA, EGA, or VGA color graphics. With a color system, you can choose between viewing your graphs in color or black and white (the default). To switch from black and white to color, you select the /Graph Options Color command. To then switch back to black and white, you need to select the /Graph Options B&W command.

Components of 1-2-3 Graphs

A graph is essentially a pictorial representation of data values that often enables you to evaluate their significance more quickly. Most types of graphs make use of a grid system that plots the change of one variable in relation to one or more other variables on an xy coordinate system.

The basic reference lines of this xy coordinate system are referred to as the *axes* of the graph. The horizontal reference line is called the *x-axis* of the graph. Often, it represents the changes over time. For example, the units of time can be weeks, months, or years. The vertical reference line is called the *y-axis* of the graph. It usually represents changes in the values of the data variables. The program automatically creates the scale for the y-axis and adds the values at regular intervals based on the lowest and highest values in the data ranges.

This xy coordinate system is used by every 1-2-3 graph type except for the pie chart. Lotus 1-2-3 scales the x- and y-axes of a graph automatically according to the type of graph chosen, the number of values in each data variable, and the number of data variables graphed.

The values to be graphed are assigned by their cell range or ranges in the worksheet itself. Each group of values in a single cell range represents one *data variable*. You can define up to six separate data variables (A–F) for all graph types except the pie chart. Lotus 1-2-3 graphs are dynamically linked to the values in these cell ranges. If you change these values, the graph using them will automatically be modified to illustrate these changes the next time the graph is drawn.

Generating Graphs

Graphs are defined and named from the /Graph Menu (/G). This menu is a "sticky" menu (like the /Print menu) that allows you to define each graph component without returning you to READY mode each time. As such, it includes a Quit option that you can use to return directly to READY mode and the spreadsheet.

If you are using Release 2.2, the program displays the Graph Settings sheet shown in Figure 9.1 when you activate the /Graph menu. You can refer to this sheet as you define your graph to see exactly which settings are in effect.

The /Graph menu has many levels. To orient yourself to the graph commands, refer to the /Graph menu tree shown in Figure 9.2.

Selecting the Type of Graph

As shown on the menu map, the first level of menu options on the /Graph menu begins with the Type option. This is used to choose the type of graph you wish to use. When you select the /Graph Type command, 1-2-3 presents the following menu options:

Line Bar XY Stacked-Bar Pie

By default, 1-2-3 will produce a line graph from the data ranges you define as data variables if you do not choose one of the other four types with the Type menu option. You can, however, always change the type of graph after defining the data variables. This allows you to view the graph in several different formats to determine the most appropriate type before naming and saving the graph as part of the worksheet.

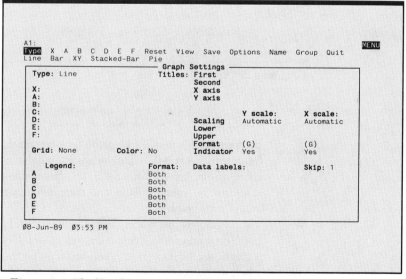

♦ **Figure 9.1:** *The /Graph main menu with the Graph Settings sheet (Release 2.2 only)*

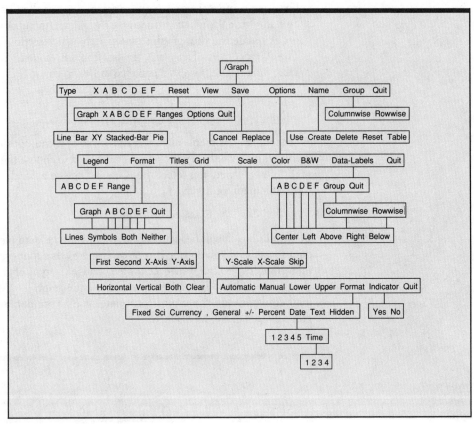

◆ **Figure 9.2:** *The /Graph menu tree*

Assigning Data Variables

Each data range used in the graph is assigned a data variable represented by a letter between A and F. This means you can have up to six different data variables in a single graph. You define the data variables to be used in the graph by selecting the variable letter and then defining the range that contains the values to be graphed.

If the ranges you use in defining the A through F data variables for your graph contain labels instead of values, 1-2-3 will ignore them when generating a graph. If all data variables contain only labels, 1-2-3 won't draw anything when you select the /Graph View command or use the Graph key (F10).

The X option on the /Graph menu specifies the data range for the x-axis of the graph. This option defines the labels that appear at the bottom of the graph below the tick marks of the x-axis for the line, bar, and stacked-bar graphs.

When you create a pie chart, the labels in the X data range are used to identify each segment of the pie. When you create an XY graph, the range defined as the X range contains the values to be used in generating the x-axis rather than a range of labels that identify the tick marks on the x-axis (the y-axis values are assigned to the A data variable).

Clearing Data Variables and Graph Options

The program remembers all X and A–F data ranges that you assign with the /Graph X and A–F commands. This enables you to reuse them in any new graph you are building. However, if you are beginning a new graph that doesn't share the data variables assigned in the previous graph, you can use the /Graph Reset (/GR) command to clear one or all of the data variables. When you select this command, 1-2-3 presents you with the following options:

Graph X A B C D E F Ranges Options Quit

Note that if you are using Release 2.01, the /Graph Reset menu includes the Graph, X, A–F, and Quit options only; Ranges and Options are newly added to Release 2.2.

To clear all graph settings, including all ranges assigned to data variables and graph options, choose the Graph option. To clear a specific data variable, choose its letter. If you are using Release 2.2, you can select Ranges when you want to clear all data variable ranges (X and A–F) and Options when you want to clear all settings selected from the /Graph Options menu.

Using the /Graph Group Command to Assign All Data Variables at One Time

✳ *New in 2.2*

Release 2.2 has added a new Group option to the /Graph menu that enables you to specify all data variables (X and A–F) in one operation. When you use the /Graph Group command, you specify the cell range that contains the data to be graphed either by typing the range address, selecting or typing the range name, or defining the range with pointing.

After you specify the range, the program presents you with the options

Columnwise Rowwise

You select the Columnwise option if you want 1-2-3 to assign each data variable (X and A–F) using the values in each column of the range. Otherwise, you select the Rowwise option to have the program assign each data variable using the values in each row of the range.

When you use the /Graph Group command, 1-2-3 assigns the values in the first column or row to the X data range, the next column to the right or the next row down to the A data range, and so on, until either all columns and rows are assigned to data variables or data variable F has been assigned (any data in the eighth column or row of the range is disregarded).

Figures 9.3, 9.4, and 9.5 illustrate how the /Graph Group command can be used to quickly generate a line graph with multiple data variables. In Figure 9.3, the cell range A5..D10 is being designated as the group range with the /Graph Group command. After designating this as the group range, the Columnwise option is selected to let 1-2-3 know that each column in the group range represents a different data variable.

Figure 9.4 shows you the Graph Settings sheet that appears immediately after designating A1..D10 as the group range and selecting the Columnwise option. Notice that 1-2-3 has automatically designated A5..A10 as the X range, B5..B10 as the A data variable range, C5..C10 as the B data variable range, and D5..D10 as the C data variable range.

Figure 9.5 shows you the resulting line graph that is drawn when you select the View option from the /Graph menu. Notice that the labels assigned to the X range (A5..A10) appear along the x-axis of this graph. The values in the three ranges assigned to data variables A, B, and C are used to draw the three lines, representing the three months of the first quarter.

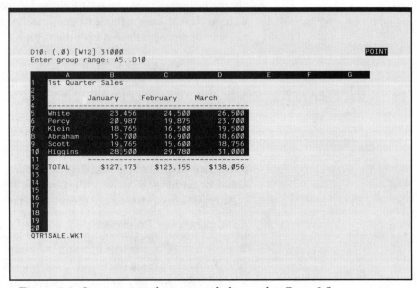

◆ **Figure 9.3:** *Group range used to generate the line graph in Figure 9.5*

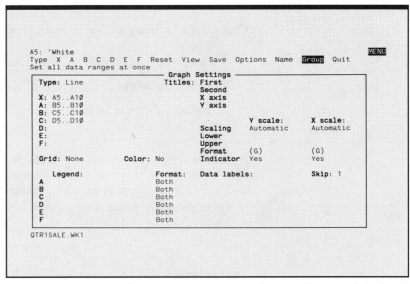

◆ **Figure 9.4:** *The Graph Settings sheet showing the data variable ranges defined with /Graph Group*

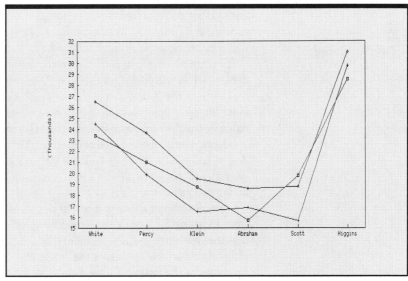

◆ **Figure 9.5:** *Line graph generated with group graph range shown in Figure 9.3*

Creating Graphs

Creating graphs from your worksheet data is essentially a three-step process:

1. Select the type of graph you wish to create.

2. Define the data ranges to be graphed as the appropriate data variables.

3. Enhance the basic graph by selecting options from the /Graph Options menu.

To help in choosing which type of graph to create, the following sections describe the characteristics of each 1-2-3 graph type. In this section, you will also find information on which data variables are required by the particular type of graph and how they are represented.

Line Graphs

The line graph is the default graph type in 1-2-3 and is a good choice for showing the changes in values over a certain period of time. This type of graph displays various data points connected by lines, which help illustrate trends or projections during a particular period. If the line graph includes multiple data variables, each data variable is represented by its own line, which uses a different symbol to represent its data points. Data variable A is represented by squares, B by pluses, C by diamonds, D by triangles pointing upward, E by Xs, and F by triangles pointing downward.

To create a line graph, you only need to assign the appropriate data ranges to data variables with the /Graph X and A–F commands. The cell range that you designate as the X data range for the graph becomes the x-axis labels, with a label for each tick mark on the horizontal axis (which corresponds to each value in the A–F data variable ranges). The program automatically scales the y-axis and selects the tick marks based on the high and low values in the ranges designated as data variables A–F. As with any graph that uses the xy coordinate system, you can override the automatic scale for the y-axis and set the lower and upper values manually.

Figure 9.6 shows a line graph that describes pictorially the VCR sales in all store locations for a company over a five-year period (1990–1994). This graph uses the row range in the worksheet that contains the total annual sales as the single data variable A. It uses the single-row range that contains the column headings for the years 1990 through 1994 for the X data range.

Figure 9.7 shows a line graph that uses multiple data variables, A through D, each representing the amount of annual sales for each item sold. In this graph,

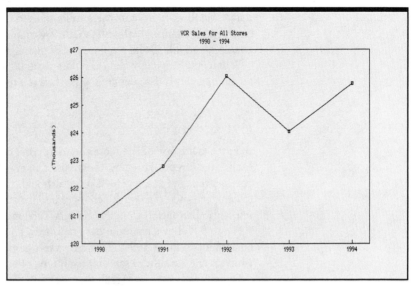

♦ **Figure 9.6:** *Line graph with a single data variable*

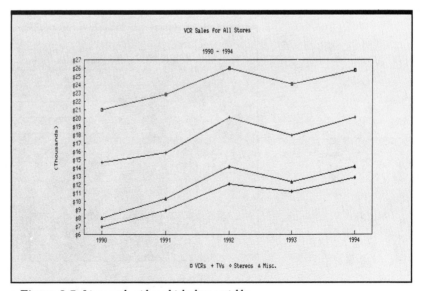

♦ **Figure 9.7:** *Line graph with multiple data variables*

data variable A represents the annual sales in dollars of VCRs, data variable B represents the annual sales of TVs, data variable C the annual sales of stereos, and data variable D the annual sales of miscellaneous equipment.

When graphing more than one data variable, it is customary to add a legend to the line graph that explains what data are represented by each symbol.

Bar Graphs

Bar graphs are one of the most common types of business graphs. In this type, each value is represented by its own bar. Bar graphs are frequently used to compare related data at a specified time, although they can also be effectively used to compare and contrast the changes in data over time. To create a bar graph, select the Bar option from the /Graph Type menu (/GTB).

Figure 9.8 shows a simple bar graph that compares the total sales for each equipment item in 1990. This bar graph graphs just one data variable (A), which is the amount of sales for each type of equipment.

Figure 9.9 shows a bar graph that uses four data variables. When you create a bar graph with multiple data variables, each one is assigned its own color or hatch pattern by the program (you can't, however, override the selections made by 1-2-3). Notice in the bar graph in Figure 9.9 that a *legend* has been

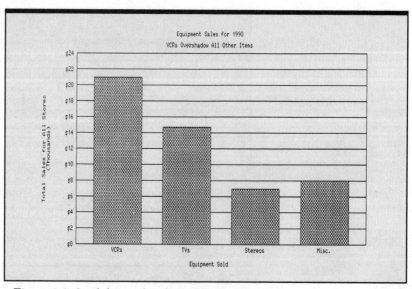

♦ **Figure 9.8:** *Simple bar graph with one data variable*

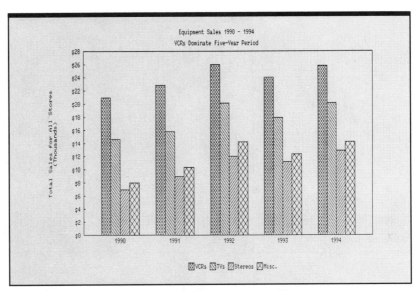

Equipment Sales 1990 - 1994
VCRs Dominate Five-Year Period

◆ **Figure 9.9:** *Clustered-bar graph using multiple data variables*

created to correlate the type of data represented by each data variable (A through D) with the fill type (hatch pattern in this figure) used in the bars. Also, notice how the bars representing each data variable are clustered at each x-axis label (the year, in this example). For this reason, bar graphs with multiple data variables are also known as *clustered-bar graphs*.

XY Graphs

The next type of graph that we are going to examine is the XY graph. This type of graph is sometimes referred to as a *scatter chart*. It differs significantly from the other types we've looked at because it correlates two sets of *numerical* values (or data variables): one set plotted against the y-axis and the other set plotted against the x-axis.

To create an XY graph, you select the XY option from the /Graph Type menu (/GTX), assign the values to be plotted on the x-axis as the X data variable, and then assign the values to be plotted on the y-axis as the A data variable.

Figure 9.10 shows an XY graph generated by 1-2-3 from two sets of data. The worksheet range containing the number-of-rooms data was assigned to the X data range, and the range containing the monthly expenditures was assigned to the A data variable.

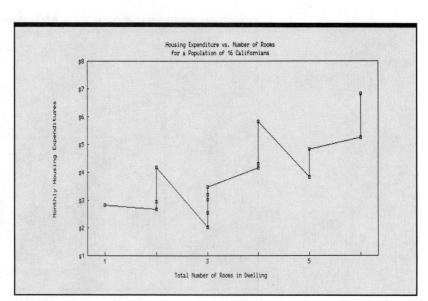

◆ **Figure 9.10:** XY *graph showing the correlation between monthly housing expenditure and the number of rooms*

Stacked-Bar Graphs

Stacked-bar graphs display multiple data variables in a single bar, where each value is stacked on top of the others. To differentiate each data variable represented in a single bar, 1-2-3 assigns a unique color or hatch pattern to each value. Stacked-bar graphs display the cumulative total in each stacked bar and tend to emphasize the individual groups of data (in each bar) and their relationship to each other.

Figure 9.11 shows a stacked-bar graph that was created from the same data as the clustered-bar graph shown in Figure 9.9. In fact, the only step required to convert that clustered-bar graph into the stacked-bar graph in this figure was to select the Stacked-Bar option from the /Graph Type menu (/GTS).

Pie Charts

Pie charts represent a special type of graph that does not use the xy coordinate system. Instead, they show how each value in a single data variable relates proportionally to the whole. Visually, a circle (the pie) represents the sum of all values, and each segment, or pie slice, is scaled according to the percentage it represents.

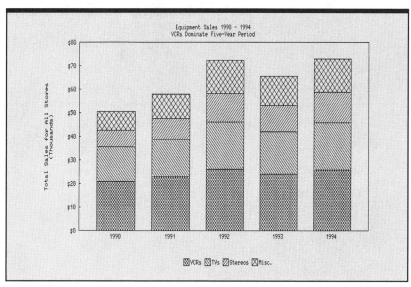

+ **Figure 9.11**: *Stacked-bar graph showing the relationship of equipment sales to the annual sales*

To create a pie chart, you select the Pie option from the /Graph Type menu (/GTP), and define the cell range in the spreadsheet that contains the values for the A data variable. To label the segments of the pie chart, you designate the range in the worksheet that contains the appropriate labels as the x-axis range. Lotus 1-2-3 automatically calculates and displays the percentage that each segment (or value in the data variable range) represents.

Figure 9.12 shows you a typical pie chart, showing the equipment sales by category in 1990.

Assigning Fill Types and Exploding Sections of a Pie

When creating a pie chart, 1-2-3 draws each segment of the pie without assigning any fill type to it. You can, however, select a hatch pattern for the individual segments as well as emphasize specific segments by exploding them. When you *explode* a segment of a pie chart, the program separates it somewhat from the rest of the pie.

To use these enhancements, you enter code numbers in a new cell range in the worksheet and then assign this range as a B data variable for the pie chart you are creating. Each code number from 1 through 7 represents a different hatch pattern. Note that if you enter 0 or any lower number, or 8 or any higher number, 1-2-3 won't use any hatch pattern.

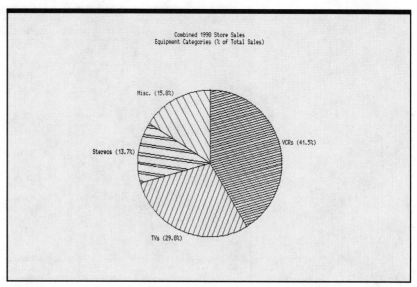

♦ **Figure 9.12:** *Pie chart showing sales by equipment category for 1990*

If you have a color monitor and have selected Color from the /Graph Options menu, 1-2-3 will color the hatch patterns it assigns to individual segments of the pie chart. The colors assigned to the hatch patterns by each of these code numbers vary with the type of monitor and the color or graphics card you are using, and you will want to experiment with them to see what colors they produce on your monitor. The hatch patterns, however, are standard across different types of monitors, and Figure 9.13 shows the hatch pattern associated with each code number.

To explode a segment of a pie graph, you add 100 to the code number representing the hatch pattern that you want to assign to it. For example, to assign pattern 5 to the first segment of your pie chart and explode it at the same time, you would enter the value *105* in the first cell of the worksheet range assigned as the B data variable for the graph. You can explode as many segments of your pie graph as you want. To explode a segment and leave it blank, you merely enter the number 100 in the appropriate cell of the cell range defined as data variable B.

Figure 9.14 shows a pie chart where codes have been used to assign hatch patterns to each segment of the pie as well as to explode the last segment. To accomplish this, a range of values that controls the hatch pattern assigned to each pie segment is entered in the worksheet and defined as the B data variable in this graph. The last segment (representing Higgins' sales) is exploded in

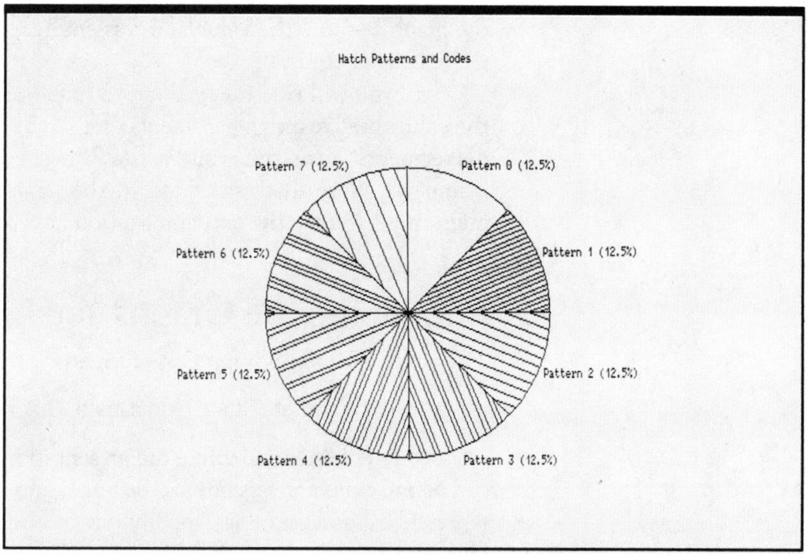

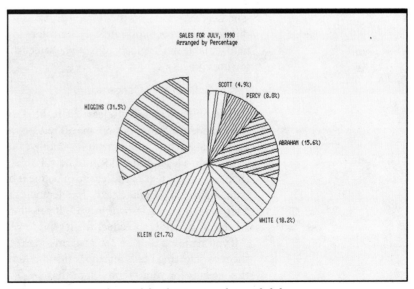

Hatch Patterns and Codes

Pattern 7 (12.5%) Pattern 0 (12.5%)
Pattern 6 (12.5%) Pattern 1 (12.5%)
Pattern 5 (12.5%) Pattern 2 (12.5%)
Pattern 4 (12.5%) Pattern 3 (12.5%)

◆ **Figure 9.13:** *Hatch patterns that can be assigned to segments of a pie chart by code number*

SALES FOR JULY, 1990
Arranged by Percentage

SCOTT (4.9%)
PERCY (8.0%)
HIGGINS (31.5%)
ABRAHAM (15.6%)
WHITE (18.2%)
KLEIN (21.7%)

◆ **Figure 9.14:** *Pie chart with hatch patterns and an exploded segment*

the graph because the value *106* was entered as the first value of the B data range instead of just 6.

Often, you will find it expedient to hide the display of ranges that contain the values used to assign particular colors and/or hatch patterns and to explode pie segments. To do this, you use the /Range Format Hidden command (/RFH) command. Note that once hidden, the ranges can easily be erased, so you might want to take the extra precaution of protecting the worksheet globally.

Enhancing the Graphs You Create

The choices on the /Graph Options menu

Legend Format Titles Grid Scale Color B&W Data-Labels Quit

are used to enhance and refine the presentation of your graphs. From here you can define titles and legends for the graph, alter the way the data variables are represented, add grid lines, modify one or both graph scales (in an XY graph, both the x- and y-axis are numeric), switch between a black-and-white and color display, and identify the contents of each data variable.

Using Legends to Label the Data Variables Represented

The Legend option on the /Graph Options menu (/GOL) is used to label the different symbols, crosshatching, or colors assigned by the program to each data variable in the graph. When you select this option, you are given the following choices:

A B C D E F Range

Note that if you're using Release 2.01, the /Graph Options Legend menu does not include the Range option: in this release, you have to define the legend for each data variable in the graph separately.

To assign a legend to a specific data variable, you select its letter option. You then type in the text of the legend or define it by referencing a cell that already contains the appropriate text. To reference such a cell, you precede the cell address with a backslash, as in \A1. If you change or erase the contents of the label in this cell, it will affect the legend to which it is assigned.

If you are using Release 2.2, you can assign legends from a range in the worksheet by selecting the Range option and entering the cell range that contains the legends for your graph. Note that 1-2-3 will assign the contents of the cells that you specify as the legend range to data variables in the graph in order, so that the contents of the first cell becomes the legend for data variable A, the second becomes the legend for data variable B, and so on, for as many cells as there are in the range and for as many data variables defined for the graph.

Legends are always displayed at the bottom of the graph below the x-axis line. The number of characters that 1-2-3 displays in the legend depends upon the resolution of your display monitor as well as the number of legends. Legends that would extend beyond the border of the graph will either be truncated or not be displayed at all. In a few cases, you may find that legends displayed properly on the screen are truncated when printed due to the resolution of your printer. To take care of this, you will have to return to 1-2-3 and modify the graph's legends by reducing the number of characters they use.

Changing the Display of Line and XY Graphs

When you create a line or XY graph, the symbols assigned to each data point representing each value of the data variable are automatically connected to one another by lines. To change this formatting, you can use the Format option on the /Graph Options menu (/GOF). When you do, you are presented with options that allow you to choose between a specific data variable (A–F) or Graph. Choosing A–F formats the line defined by the specified data range. Choosing the Graph option formats all lines in the graph.

Once you choose the letter of the data variable or Graph (for all data variables), you are presented with these options:

Lines Symbols Both Neither

To display only lines in the graph, select the Lines option. To display just the symbols, choose the Symbols option. If you wish to suppress the display of a data variable entirely, choose the Neither option. The Both option is used to reset the graph to the default of displaying both the symbols and lines connecting them.

Figure 9.15 shows you the same XY graph shown in Figure 9.10 after changing the format from both lines and symbols to symbols only.

Adding Titles to a Graph

You can assign several titles to any graph you create, using the Titles option on the /Graph Options menu (/GOT). The title choices include:

First Second X-Axis Y-Axis

The First and Second titles are general headings that are automatically centered and placed at the top of the graph. The X-Axis title is centered on the line beneath the x-axis labels and above the legend (if used). The Y-Axis title is rotated 90 degrees counterclockwise so that it is read up the left side of the graph (see Figure 9.15 for an example).

Just as when assigning legends, you can enter these graph titles either by typing in the text or by referencing a cell in the worksheet that already contains the

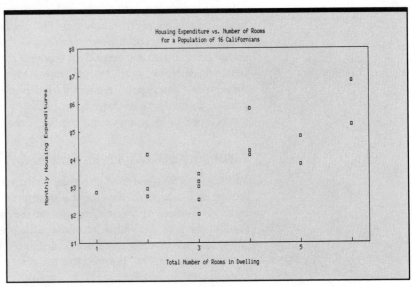

◆ **Figure 9.15:** XY *graph formatted with symbols only*

appropriate title. If you reference a cell address, preface it with the backslash, as in \A5. When using this system, be careful not to erase or move the contents of such a cell, or else the title that uses it will be missing from the graph.

Adding Grid Lines to a Graph

The /Graph Options Grid command (/GOG) is used to add either horizontal, vertical, or both types of grid lines to a graph. When you select this command, you are presented with these options:

Horizontal Vertical Both Clear

When you select the Horizontal option, 1-2-3 will draw lines across the graph from the tick marks on the y-axis. To have vertical grid marks drawn from the tick marks on the x-axis, you select the Vertical option on the /Graph Options Grid menu. If you want the grid drawn both horizontally and vertically, you select the Both option. To suppress the use of any grid lines in your graph, you select the Clear option.

Adding grid lines can sometimes make a graph easier to read by making it clear when individual values in the graph exceed or fall below the values called out by the tick marks. However, they can also clutter a graph and possibly obscure the symbols used by Lotus 1-2-3 to represent the data points, especially if you are creating a line or XY graph.

When the program draws grid lines in a graph drawn in Release 2.01, they go right through the graph symbols used. When used with a bar or stacked-bar graph, the grid lines detract from the graph's presentation, as they intersect the bars and appear in the foreground. In Release 2.2, grid lines added to bar and stacked-bar graphs never intersect the bars and, therefore, always appear as the background against which the graph is drawn. You will find, however, that grid lines sometimes intersect the data labels that you have assigned in either release of 1-2-3.

Modifying the Graph Scales

Lotus 1-2-3 allows you to make several different types of modifications to the x- and y-scales of your graph, not the least of which is to manually set their upper and lower limits. To make modifications to either graph scale, you select the /Graph Options Scale command (/GOS) and then choose the appropriate scale from this menu:

Y-Scale X-Scale Skip

After you choose Y-Scale or X-Scale (the Skip option is discussed separately in the next section), a new menu appears:

Automatic Manual Lower Upper Format Indicator Quit

Manually Adjusting the X- and Y-Scales   When 1-2-3 scales the y-axis, it chooses the upper and lower limits for the scale based on the highest and lowest values of the data assigned to the various data variables. It then subdivides this range into equal increments and displays a tick mark with its appropriate value labeled on the y-axis line. When it scales the x-axis, it takes the number of values in each data variable and spaces them equally along the x-axis reference line. Each value represented is given its own *tick mark* on this horizontal line.

Although 1-2-3 handles this scaling of the x- and y-axis automatically, it does allow you to set the upper and lower limits for either axis manually. You may want to adjust the scaling when you are creating several graphs that are to be compared with one another. It is always easier to compare graphs when they use the same scale. If you leave it to automatic scaling, they will probably all have slightly different y-scales due to the differences in high and low values in the spreadsheet data used to create each graph.

To set the selected scale manually, you must select the Manual option as well as *both* the Lower and Upper options (you can do this in any order). When you select the Lower or Upper option, you type in the new value for these limits and press Enter. Make sure the values you use are sufficient to display all the data included in the defined data variables.

Should you enter new lower and upper limits for the scale but fail to select Manual, the new values will be ignored in the graph. To return to automatic scaling for the selected graph scale, return to this menu and select the Automatic option.

Formatting the Values on the X- or Y-Scale   To format the values that appear next to the tick marks on the x-axis or y-axis, you choose the Format option. This leads you to a menu of formatting options similar to the one that appears when you select the /Worksheet Global Format or /Range Format command.

Most often, you will use this command to format the values on the y-axis to give the reader an idea of what type of units are represented on this graph axis. For instance, you could use the Currency format option to let the reader know that these graph units are measured in dollars (if the Currency default symbol is still the dollar sign and not set to some other symbol, such as £). When using the scaling format options, you must also designate the number of decimal places to be displayed, just as when choosing a format from the /Range Format menu.

This Format command can also be applied to the x-axis scale, although this is seldom done except when you are creating an XY graph and its x-axis represents numeric values that would benefit from formatting.

Suppressing the Scale Indicator   When 1-2-3 sets the y-axis scale for the graph you are building, it often uses an *order of magnitude* other than 0 for the numbers that appear. When this is the case, the program adds a scale indicator such as Thousands to let you know what units are expressed.

The Indicator option allows you to remove this scale indicator. When you select this option, 1-2-3 allows you to choose between Yes and No options. To suppress the display of the scale indicator entirely, you select the No option. To later redisplay it, you need to return to this menu and select the Yes option.

Using the Skip Option to Display Fewer X-Axis Labels   The Skip option, which appears with the Y-scale and X-scale options when you choose the /Graph Options Scale command, is used to determine which values assigned to the X data range are displayed at each tick mark along the bottom of the graph. You use this option when these labels overlap in the graph display.

The Skip option allows you to specify a "skip factor," telling the program how many values to skip in the range assigned as the X data variable. For instance, if you designate a Skip value of 3, every third label or value in this cell range would be displayed below its tick mark on the x-axis. Lotus 1-2-3 would display all tick marks, but only tag every third one. Using the appropriate "skip factor" therefore eliminates the overlapping that can occur when all values or labels are displayed.

Figure 9.16 shows you a bar graph that uses a skip factor of 2 to have 1-2-3 display the name of every other month along the x-axis of the graph. This avoids the crowding that otherwise occurs when 1-2-3 tries to display the names of all 12 months along the x-axis.

Switching between Color and Black-and-White Displays

Even if you have a color graphics card and a color monitor, 1-2-3 automatically displays your graphs in black and white as though you only had a monochrome system. To view your graph in color, you must select the Color option from the /Graph Options menu (/GOC). Note, however, that 1-2-3 always chooses its own colors for each variable in the graph and that you have no way to override them and select colors of your own.

You can always return to a black-and-white display by then choosing /Graph Options B&W. Note, however, that if you name a graph when viewing it in color, it will continue to be displayed in color whenever you view it even after you have reactivated black-and-white display of your graphs with the /Graph Options B&W command. To have it converted to black and white and saved that way, you will need to name it again with the /Graph Name Create command (see Naming Graphs, later in this chapter).

If you display your graphs on a color monitor but print them on a black-and-white printer, you will need to convert your bar and stacked-bar graphs from

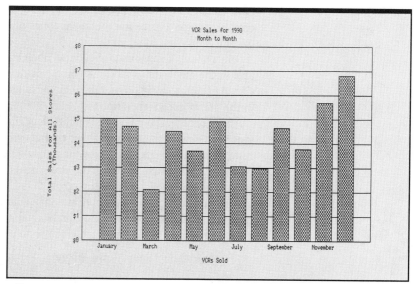

♦ **Figure 9.16:** *Bar graph using a skip factor of 2 to avoid crowding x-axis labels*

color to black and white to have them printed correctly with the PrintGraph utility. To do this, be sure to select the B&W option from the /Graph Options menu after you make the bar or stacked-bar graph current, but before you save it with the /Graph Save command (see Saving Graphs, later in this chapter, for more information).

Taking this step ensures that the PrintGraph program will use different hatching patterns to differentiate the data variables represented in the graph when printing the graph on a black-and-white printer. Otherwise, all data variables in the graph will be printed in solid black and will, therefore, be indistinguishable from each other.

If you display your graphs on a monochrome monitor but print them on a color printer, you don't need to select the Color option on the /Graph Options menu before saving your graphs because you select the colors to be used in printing the graphs in the PrintGraph program instead of in 1-2-3.

Using Data Labels to Annotate Your Graph

The Data-Labels option on the /Graph Options menu (/GOD) allows you to place the actual data values that have been graphed, or the labels contained in a range of cells in the worksheet, near the data variable within the graph. When you use this command, 1-2-3 displays these options:

A B C D E F Group Quit

Note that if you are using Release 2.01, this menu does not include the Group option: you have to define the range containing the data labels for each data variable in the graph separately.

Select the A–F options to assign the labels in a data range to each data variable in the graph individually. If you are using Release 2.2, you can select the Group option to assign the range that contains the labels for *all* data variables in the graph in one operation.

After selecting an option between A–F or the Group option, you must then specify the range in the worksheet that contains your data labels. If you are using the Group option, you must also choose between Columnwise and Rowwise, indicating whether the data labels are to be applied down each column or across each row of the range.

After indicating the range containing the labels, you must specify the position of the data labels relative to the data variable to which they apply. There are five position options from which to choose:

Center Left Above Right Below

If your graph is a bar or stacked-bar type, 1-2-3 will automatically locate the data labels above all bars representing positive values and beneath all bars representing negative values when you choose the Above option. If you choose the Below option, the data labels will still appear centered, although they will be lower so that they appear embedded in the bar (making them very hard to see). Note that selecting the Center, Left, or Right options has no effect on the positioning of your data labels with these types of graphs.

You cannot assign data labels to a pie chart (assigning a cell range for the X data range is the equivalent of data labels for this kind of graph).

The full complement of positioning options can, however, be used with line or XY graphs. With these graphs, however, you may need to locate data labels for different data variables in different positions to avoid overlapping and keep the graph legible, depending upon the number of data variables graphed. If necessary, you can label some values and not others for a particular data variable by leaving some of the cells blank in the range that you assign as the data-label range.

Annotating a Line or XY Graph: You can use data labels with the Neither option on the /Graph Options Format menu to add notes to your graph. To do this, you must define a new data variable for your graph, whose values are used only to determine the position of the note in the graph. After adding this data range and assigning it to a new data variable, you need to enter the text of the note you wish displayed in the graph as a label in the worksheet and then assign this cell as the data label for the new data variable you just added. Then, you need to select the /Graph Options Format command, choose the letter of the new data variable, and select Neither to suppress the display of symbols and lines in the graph. Figure 9.17 illustrates this technique: in this line graph, the range B10..E10 was designated as the new B data variable. The first cell of this range, B10, contains the value 92,000 and the rest of the range is left blank (you must include as many cells in this range as there are in the ranges that are actually graphed, although they all don't have to contain values). The value of 92,000 determines the vertical position of the note in the graph. The text of this note is entered in cell B12 in the worksheet, and this cell is designated as the data label for this new B data variable. The Left position option is used to format the note so that it fits within the graph frame. The selection of the Neither option on the /Graph Options Format menu suppresses the display of the symbols and lines for the B data variable, leaving only the data label annotation visible.

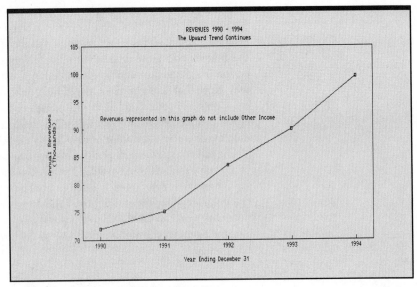

♦ **Figure 9.17:** *Line graph with annotation*

Deleting Data Labels   Data labels are not easy to remove from a graph; 1-2-3 provides no express menu options that will remove them. But when you use the /Graph Reset command to clear the range used for a particular data variable, 1-2-3 automatically clears the data labels assigned to it as well. You may not want to use this method to delete data labels when you still wish to retain the data variable. If you do use /GR, you will have to take the time to redefine the range for the data variable.

The other alternative for removing data labels from the graph is to redefine the data label range, this time referencing a blank range in the worksheet. Although, strictly speaking, this doesn't delete the data labels from the graph, it does suppress their display in the graph.

Naming Graphs

When creating multiple graphs for a worksheet file, you need to assign names to them so that you can retain the settings. In 1-2-3, only one graph can be current at any one time. Although the program remembers all settings that you assign a graph (including the type, data ranges, and all options), if you don't name the graph before you go on to create a new graph that uses different settings, the original graph settings will be lost.

To prevent this, you should use the /Graph Name Create command (/GNC). When you select this command, 1-2-3 prompts you to enter the graph name. You can then type in a name up to 15 characters long (with no spaces). When using this command, 1-2-3 shows you a line listing of the currently assigned graph names. If you reassign a graph name, you will lose the original graph.

After naming your graphs, you still need to save the worksheet file with the /File Save command to have them saved as part of the file. If you fail to save the file before you clear the worksheet display or use /File Retrieve to replace the current file(s) in memory, you will lose all your graphs even if you have taken the trouble to name them. These named graphs must be saved on disk in the worksheet file, if you want to be able to view and/or print them the next time you use the worksheet.

If you update some of the graph settings after naming the graph, these settings won't be saved under the graph name unless you make the graph current by selecting the /Graph Name Create command. Then choose the graph from the line listing by moving the pointer to it and pressing Enter. Remember that you still need to select the /File Save command to save the updated graph settings on disk.

Making a New Graph Current

You can make one of the named graphs that are saved as part of the worksheet current by choosing the /Graph Name Use command (/GNU) and selecting the appropriate graph name from the line listing (press the Name key, F3, to get a full-screen listing of all named graphs). As soon as you complete this command sequence, 1-2-3 immediately draws the graph (press any key to return to the worksheet and the /Graph menu).

Deleting Named Graphs

To delete named graphs from the file, you use the /Graph Name Delete command (/GND) and then select the appropriate graph name from the line listing (press the Name key, F3, to get a full-screen listing of all named graphs), or type in the graph name and press Enter. As soon as you complete this command sequence, 1-2-3 immediately deletes the graph.

To delete all graphs in a file in one command, select the /Graph Name Reset command (/GNR). This immediately clears all graph names from the current worksheet file. If you ever find that you have used the /Graph Name Delete or /Graph Name Reset command in error when using Release 2.2, immediately exit from MENU mode, and press the Undo key (Alt-F4) to restore the graph name or names that were deleted.

✳ New in 2.2   *Creating a Graph Name Table*

To help you keep track of the named graphs in the worksheet, Release 2.2 allows you to create a graph name table with the /Graph Name Table command (/GNT). When you select this command, 1-2-3 prompts you to indicate the placement of the table with

Enter range for name table:

Move the pointer to the cell where you want the upper left corner of the table to be and press Enter. As with other tables generated by the program (such as range name tables), you need to make sure that the pointer is located at the beginning of a blank area sufficiently large to accommodate the table without overlapping any existing data. Otherwise, 1-2-3 will replace the existing data with part of the graph table.

If you wish to view the graph name table without having to quit the /Graph menu, you need to press the Window key (F6) to suppress the display of the Graph Settings sheet to display the area of the worksheet containing the table that lies beneath it. To redisplay the Graph Settings sheet, you just press the Window key a second time.

The graph name table created with this command has three columns and as many rows as there are named graphs plus one blank row. The first column of the table lists the name of the graph, the second the type of graph, and the third the first line of the graph's title. Figure 9.18 shows you a graph name table

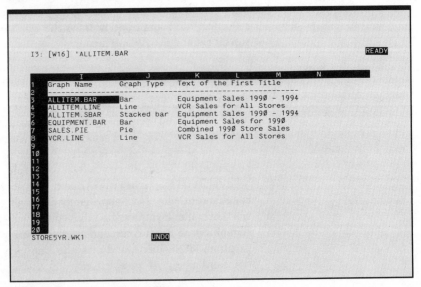

◆ **Figure 9.18:** *A graph name table*

generated with this command. In this figure, the column headings and underscores were added after the table was generated with the pointer in cell I3. In addition, the widths of column I and J were adjusted to display the entire name and type for each graph.

Printing Your Graphs

The graphs that you create and display on the screen in 1-2-3 can't be printed from within the program. To obtain hard copies of each 1-2-3 graph, you must exit from the program and start the PrintGraph program. Before you do, however, you must use the /Graph Save command to save each graph in its own file in a format (called a PIC file) that PrintGraph can use. Not only must your graphs be saved in separate files in the PIC format, but you must have installed a printer that can print graphics (not all printers can) to successfully print the graphs you create in 1-2-3.

Saving Graphs as PIC Files to Be Used by PrintGraph

The graphs that you create are saved under the names assigned to them with the /Graph Name Create command as soon as you save the worksheet file with the /File Save command. The Save option on the /Graph menu is therefore used only to save your graphs in separate files in the PIC format that can be used by the PrintGraph program.

When you use /Graph Save, 1-2-3 automatically saves the current graph in the PIC file format and appends the extension .PIC to the file name you give it. If your worksheet contains many named graphs and you wish to print each of them, you must first select the /Graph Name Use command to make each graph current, and then select the /Graph Save command to save it in its own PIC file.

Starting the PrintGraph Program

You can start the PrintGraph program from the Lotus Access System menu by selecting the PrintGraph option, or directly from the DOS prompt by typing *PGRAPH* and pressing the Enter key. When starting PrintGraph from DOS on a hard disk system, remember that the directory containing the PrintGraph files (usually the same one that contains 1-2-3) must be current.

When starting the PrintGraph program on a two-disk-drive system, you have to replace the 1-2-3 System disk with a copy of the PrintGraph disk. If you enter the program startup command from the DOS prompt or select the Print-Graph option on the Lotus Access System before swapping disks, you will be prompted to replace the System disk with the PrintGraph disk.

The first time the PrintGraph program is loaded into memory, you will see the screen shown in Figure 9.19. This screen contains the PrintGraph main menu and initial settings sheet. Notice that unlike 1-2-3, the PrintGraph program main menu is always displayed on the screen. When using this menu, you don't have to type / (slash) before typing the initial character of the option you wish to use.

Selecting the Hardware Settings

The first time you use PrintGraph, you need to check the hardware settings in the last column of the settings sheet to make sure that they are correct. Most of the time, you will have to modify the graphs and/or fonts directory listed under Hardware Settings even if all the other settings are correct (especially if you are using PrintGraph on a hard disk). In addition to changing any incorrect settings, you will have to select the printer that you will be using to print your graphs.

To make changes to the hardware settings, you need to select the Settings option (S) on the PrintGraph main menu. This brings up the following menu:

Image Hardware Action Save Reset Quit

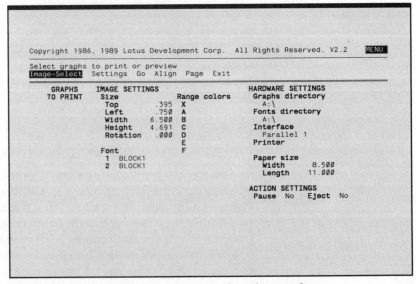

◆ **Figure 9.19**: *The PrintGraph main menu and initial settings sheet*

Select the Hardware option (H) from this menu, and you will see these options:

Graphs-Directory Fonts-Directory Interface Printer Size-Paper Quit

Indicating the Directory That Contains the Graphs to Print

If the directory listed after *Graphs directory* on the PrintGraph settings sheet
isn't the one that contains the graphs that you wish to print, you need to select
Settings Hardware Graphs-Directory (SHG) and type in the correct drive and
directory path. As soon as you begin typing a new path, the current directory
listing disappears from the prompt line.

If you are using 1-2-3 on a two-disk-drive system, you will most likely need to
make B: the graphs directory, as this is where you keep the data disk containing
your worksheet and PIC files (while drive A contains the PrintGraph disk). If
you are using 1-2-3 on a hard disk system, the directory containing your graphs
depends upon where you saved your graph files when you used the /Graph Save
command: this could either be a data disk in drive A or a directory on your
hard drive.

Indicating the Directory That Contains the PrintGraph Fonts

The PrintGraph program allows you to choose among 11 different fonts for
printing the titles and other text in your graphs. These fonts are supplied as
part of the 1-2-3 program on the PrintGraph disk and in files that are given the
extension .FNT. Before the PrintGraph program can print your graphs, it must
know the location of these FNT files.

If you are using 1-2-3 on a two-disk-drive system, the directory that contains
these files is the same one that contains the PrintGraph disk (the default of
A:\). If you are using 1-2-3 on a hard disk, these files are most likely in the same
directory as the 1-2-3 programs. If you don't know for sure where these files
were copied on your hard disk, try changing the Fonts directory to C:\123
(assuming that this is the name of the directory that contains the 1-2-3 files).

To change the Fonts directory, select Settings Hardware Fonts-Directory
(SHF) and then type in the name of the drive and directory that contains the
FNT files before pressing the Enter key.

Selecting the Printer to Use

The first time you use the PrintGraph program, you must select the printer you
wish to use. To do this, you choose Settings Hardware Printer (SHP). When
you do, a list of the printers you installed as your graphics printers
when you installed 1-2-3 will appear on the screen.

Figure 9.20 shows this screen when the Epson FX dot-matrix and HP LaserJet Series II laser printer have been installed as the graphics printers. In this figure, notice that although only two different types of printers were installed, four options are listed on this screen. This is because you can choose not only which printer to use, but also the resolution or density at which it will print.

Selecting the Printer Interface

The default printer interface on the PrintGraph settings sheet is Parallel 1 (the first parallel port). If the printer you have selected is connected to a different port, you must remember to select Settings Hardware Interface (SHI). When you select the Interface option, the program presents you with the following eight options:

1. Parallel 1, which is the first parallel port attached to your computer (also known as LPT1)

2. Serial 1, which is the first serial port attached to your computer (also known as COM1)

3. Parallel 2, which is the second parallel port attached to your computer (also known as LPT2)

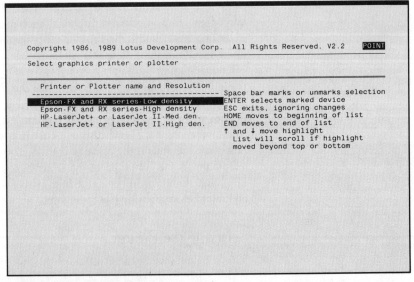

◆ **Figure 9.20:** *Selecting the printer to use*

4. Serial 2, which is the second serial port attached to your computer (also known as COM2)

5. DOS Device LPT1

6. DOS Device LPT2

7. DOS Device LPT3

8. DOS Device LPT4

Options 5 through 8 describe logical output devices used by some networks to describe the printer interface. Unless you are using PrintGraph on a network, you won't use any of these options.

Select the option number corresponding to your correct interface from the Interface menu. If your printer uses a serial interface and you chose either option 2 or 4, you must then select the option that corresponds to the correct baud rate (that is, the rate at which data is transmitted to the printer). The baud rate options are numbered from 1 through 9:

1. 110 baud

2. 150 baud

3. 300 baud

4. 600 baud

5. 1200 baud

6. 2400 baud

7. 4000 baud

8. 9600 baud

9. 19200 baud

Option 1 is the default. To select a new baud rate, merely type the number of the option that corresponds to the correct rate setting. (To obtain the correct baud rate for your printer, refer to your printer documentation.)

When printing with a serial port, you need to specify other settings, including the data bits, stop bits, parity, and XON/XOFF settings. When using a serial text printer with 1-2-3, make sure that the data bits are set to 8, the stop bits are set to 1 (unless the baud rate is 110, in which case set the stop bits to 2), parity is none, and XON/XOFF is enabled. None of these settings can be changed from within PrintGraph itself: they must be the current settings by the time you start printing your reports with the program.

Changing the Paper Size

PrintGraph assumes that you will be printing your graphs on 8½-×-11-inch paper. If you are using another size of paper in your printer or plotter, you need to select Settings Hardware Size-Paper (SHS). The program will then display these choices:

Length Width Quit

To change the length, you select the Length option (L) and type in the new page length in inches. For example, if the page you were using was 8¼ inches long, you would enter 8.25 as the new length.

To change the width, you select the Width option (W) and enter the new width in inches. When you have finished setting the new page dimensions, select the Quit option (Q) to return to the Hardware menu.

Controlling the Action of the Printer between Printing Graphs

After you're done making all necessary changes to the Hardware settings, check them over in the PrintGraph settings sheet. If they are correct, select the Quit option (Q) on the Hardware menu to return to the Settings menu. On this menu, you can use the Action option (A) to control two action settings: Pause, which pauses the printer before printing each graph, and Eject, which advances the page after printing each graph.

If your printer requires single sheets of paper that you must feed manually, you will want to select the Pause option (P) on the Action menu and change the default of No to Yes (Y). When the printing is paused, the program will beep continuously at you until you press the spacebar to resume the printing of your graphs. During this time, you can feed a new sheet of paper to your printer.

The Eject option on the Action menu controls whether the printer advances to the top of the next page after printing each graph. Be default, PrintGraph prints two graphs on each 8½-×-11-inch page. If you want the program to automatically advance to the next top of form after printing just one graph, you need to choose the Eject option (E) and then change the default setting from No to Yes (Y). When the Eject and Pause settings are both turned on, PrintGraph will print one graph, then eject the sheet, and pause the printing until you press the spacebar.

Selecting the Image Settings for Your Graphs

Several options allow you to control the appearance of your graph by specifying its size, orientation, the top and left margins on the page, and the fonts and colors to be used. When you choose Settings Image, these options appear:

Size Font Range-Colors Quit

The changes that you make on this menu are reflected under the heading IMAGE SETTINGS in the central part of the PrintGraph settings sheet.

By referring to Figure 9.19, you can see the default graph size is 4.691 × 6.5 inches, the rotation is 0, the top margin is 0.395, the left margin is 0.75, both fonts are BLOCK1, and the color for all six data ranges is black by default.

Setting the Size and Orientation of the Graph

The default graph size and top and left margins enable PrintGraph to print two graphs on a single 8½-×-11-inch page in portrait mode (Figure 9.21). You can change the size and orientation of the graphs you are printing by selecting the Size option (S) on the Image menu. When you select Settings Image Size (SIS), you are presented with these options:

Full Half Manual Quit

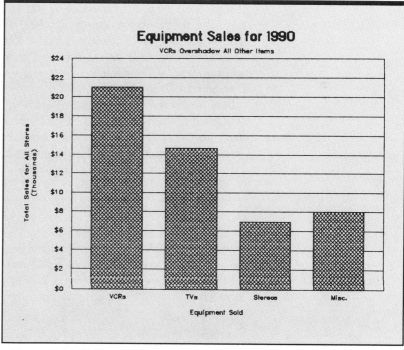

♦ **Figure 9.21:** *Half-size graph printed in portrait mode (0-degree rotation)*

The default size and orientation are represented by the Half option on this menu.

To have PrintGraph print a single graph on an 8½-×-11-inch page in landscape mode (rotated 90 degrees counterclockwise), you choose the Full option (Figure 9.22). When you do, the size changes to 6.852 × 9.445, the top margin to 0.25, the left margin to 0.5, and the rotation to 90 (degrees).

To print your graphs in a size other than half or full, you must select the Manual option (M) on the Size menu. Here, you can specify the left and top margins, the width and height of the graph, and the rotation (if any). When you select Settings Image Size Manual (SISM), you are presented with these options:

Top Left Width Height Rotation Quit

When sizing your graph manually, you must be sure that the width, height, and margin settings that you specify can be accommodated on the size of paper that you are using. When you choose the Top, Left, Width, or Height option on this menu, you are prompted to enter the new dimension to be used in inches. Each change you make will be immediately reflected in the PrintGraph settings sheet.

The Rotation option on this menu allows you to specify the orientation of the graph on the page by selecting a rotation between 0 and 360. This value represents the number of degrees that the graph is to be rotated counterclockwise on the page. Note that values such as 45 (degrees) will cause the graph to be oriented diagonally on the page and, as a result, it will appear distorted when printed, as PrintGraph doesn't deal very well with orientations other than portrait (0) and landscape (90).

In setting new dimensions for the width and height of the graph, you must also guard against a different kind of distortion that can happen when you don't maintain the correct ratio between the width and the height of the graph. The correct width-to-height ratio when the rotation is 0 degrees is 1.385 to 1. This means that if you set the width of the graph to 3.75 inches, ideally, you should set the length to about 2.7 inches when it is printed in portrait mode. When the graph is rotated 90 degrees, the correct width-to-height ratio becomes 1 to 1.385. As a result, if you set the width to 4.25 inches, you should set the length of the graph to about 5.89 inches when it is printed in landscape mode. Although the width and height dimensions that you choose for your graph don't have to maintain this width-to-height ratio exactly to avoid distortion, be aware that the more they vary from this "ideal" ratio, the more distortion will be apparent in the printed graph.

Selecting the Fonts to Be Used

PrintGraph enables you to choose the fonts to be used in printing the text portions of your graphs. Samples of these text fonts are shown in Figure 9.23.

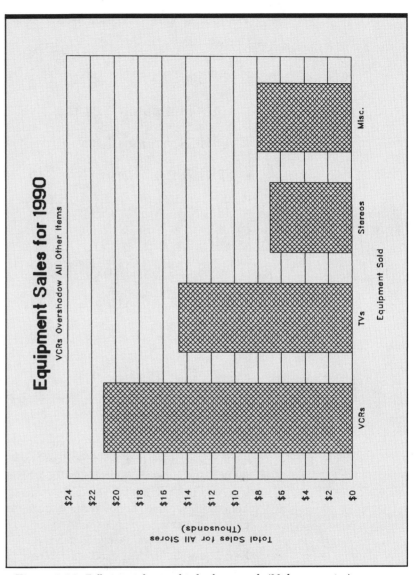

♦ **Figure 9.22:** *Full-size graph printed in landscape mode (90-degree rotation)*

You can specify up to two different fonts for a single graph. The first font (Font 1) is used to print the first title of the graph. The second font (Font 2) is used to print all other titles and labels in the graph, including the second line, x-axis, and y-axis titles and the text in the x-axis range, y-scale, legends, and data labels defined for the graph.

This is a sample of the BLOCK1 Font

This is a sample of the BLOCK2 Font

This is a sample of the BOLD Font

This is a sample of the FORUM Font

This is a sample of the ITALIC1 Font

This is a sample of the ITALIC2 Font

This is a sample of the LOTUS Font

This is a sample of the ROMAN1 Font

This is a sample of the ROMAN2 Font

This is a sample of the SCRIPT1 Font

This is a sample of the SCRIPT2 Font

♦ **Figure 9.23:** *Samples of the PrintGraph fonts*

The default font for Font 1 and Font 2 is BLOCK1. If you wish to use a different font for the first title, select Settings Image Font 1 (SIF1). This brings up the list of font choices shown in Figure 9.24. Note that the current font choice is indicated by the # symbol before the name of the font. To select a new font from this list, move the pointer to it, press the spacebar to mark it, and then press the Enter key.

Note that when you change Font 1, this selection is automatically applied to Font 2 as well. To then choose a different font for Font 2, you must select the Font 2 options on the Image menu and select a new font from the list.

You will notice on the Font screen that the fonts BLOCK, ITALIC, ROMAN, and SCRIPT are paired. In these cases, the 1 and 2 refer to the darkness or heaviness of the printed font, so that ROMAN2 produces a heavier type than ROMAN1. They both, however, produce the same type style.

You will find that some of the more cursive fonts—LOTUS, ITALIC, and SCRIPT—produce suitable results when printed with a plotter or a laser printer.

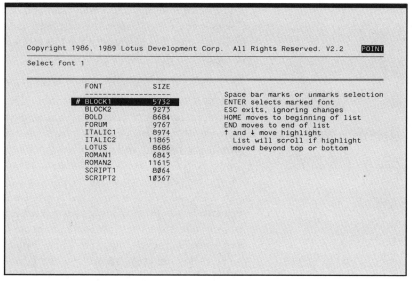

Copyright 1986, 1989 Lotus Development Corp. All Rights Reserved. V2.2   POINT
Select font 1

```
        FONT          SIZE
       ------------------------
    #  BLOCK1          5732          Space bar marks or unmarks selection
       BLOCK2          9273          ENTER selects marked font
       BOLD            8684          ESC exits, ignoring changes
       FORUM           9767          HOME moves to beginning of list
       ITALIC1         8974          END moves to end of list
       ITALIC2        11865          ↑ and ↓ move highlight
       LOTUS           8686            List will scroll if highlight
       ROMAN1          6843            moved beyond top or bottom
       ROMAN2         11615
       SCRIPT1         8064
       SCRIPT2        10367
```

◆ **Figure 9.24:** *Selecting a new Font 1 for the graph*

If you are using a dot-matrix or inkjet printer, you should avoid these fonts and stick with the BLOCK or BOLD fonts. You may also find the ROMAN font acceptable as long as you specify the heavier version, ROMAN2.

Selecting the Colors to Be Used

If you have a color printer or plotter, you can use the Range-Colors option on the Image menu to select colors for each data range in the graph. Before you can assign the colors to be used in printing with this option, you must already have selected the color printer or plotter as the device to use (with the Settings Hardware Printer command).

When you select Settings Image Range-Colors, you are presented with these options:

X A B C D E F Quit

When selecting the color for the X option, you are not only assigning the color for the labels along the x-axis in the graph, but also the graph frame and all its titles. Only the legend, data labels, and the data range itself aren't affected by this color choice. In fact, it is only when you select a new color for each data variable A–F that you select the legend and data label associated with that data variable.

The color options that appear after you select X or A–F from the Range-Colors menu depend upon the particular color printer or plotter that is currently selected. For example, if the IBM PC Color Printer is the current printer, you will have the following color options:

Black Cyan Magenta Yellow Orange Green Violet Brown

Be careful when selecting options from color menus, as they sometimes contain color names that begin with the same letter—as is the case with Black and Brown in this menu. Here, you can't just type *B* to select the color Brown because the program will choose the first match, Black. You have to move the pointer to the menu option and press Enter to select Brown.

If you are printing a pie chart with a color printer, the colors that you select with the X and A–F options on the Range-Colors menu are applied to different segments of the pie according to the numbers you assigned to them as the B data variable (remember that these values are entered in the worksheet and are used to specify the hatch pattern when displaying the pie chart on the screen).

The following table shows you the correspondence between the value assigned in the B range of the pie chart and the Range-Colors option:

Value in B Range	Range-Colors Option
1 or 101	X
2 or 102	A
3 or 103	B
4 or 104	C
5 or 105	D
6 or 106	E
7 or 107	F

According to this system, if you assign the color yellow to variable A on the Range-Colors menu, the segment of the pie chart assigned the value 2 or 102 (which explodes it) from the B range will be printed in yellow.

After choosing the colors for each data variable in the graph, you need to select the Quit option (Q) to return to the Image menu.

Selecting the Graphs to Be Printed

To choose the graphs you want to print with the settings you have specified, you use the Image-Select option (I) on the PrintGraph main menu. When you select this option, the program presents you with a listing of all files with the extension .PIC that are located in the current graphs directory. If there are no PIC files in this directory, PrintGraph will display a message indicating that this is the case.

To select a graph to be printed, you move the pointer to its name and press the spacebar to mark it. PrintGraph will then place the # symbol before its name. The program will allow you to mark as many graphs as you wish, in effect creating a *print queue*, which determines the number of graphs that will be printed and the order in which they will be processed when you select the Go option.

To unmark a graph that you select in error, you need to move the pointer to it and press the spacebar a second time: this removes the # symbol from its file name. You can display the graph on the screen by moving the pointer to it and pressing the Graph key (F10). Note that this on-screen display doesn't show the graph exactly as it will be printed (it resembles the graph display in 1-2-3 more than the printed version); this feature is intended, instead, to enable you to take a quick look at the graph when you need to see it again to determine if you want to print it.

After you have marked all the graphs you want printed, press Enter to return to the PrintGraph main menu. There you will see the names of the graphs in the order that you have marked them on the left side of the PrintGraph settings sheet.

Printing the Selected Graphs

After specifying the print settings and selecting the graphs to be printed, you are ready to begin the printing. To do this, you select the Align and Go (AG) options from the PrintGraph main menu, just as you do when printing a worksheet report in 1-2-3. Remember that the Align option tells the printer that the printhead is at the top of form, and the Go option actually starts the printing.

After you select the Go option, the PrintGraph program will load the font files it needs from the fonts directory and then load the PIC file containing the first graph to be printed from the graphs directory.

Note that it takes much longer to print graphs than it does worksheet reports, so you need to plan your printing session around natural breaks in your work day when you don't have to access the computer or do more work in 1-2-3 (the lunch hour is often an ideal time to print graphs).

If you need to stop the printing of your graphs for any reason, press Ctrl-Break (just as you do when printing worksheet reports). When you do, Print-Graph will beep and display the message

    CTRL-BREAK
    Press ESC or ENTER
      to continue.

After you press Esc or Enter, the program will return to MENU mode (the printing stops as soon as the print buffer is empty). Note that after aborting the printing with Ctrl-Break, you will have to manually reset the top of form before starting the printing again with the Align and Go options.

When PrintGraph finishes printing all graphs in the print queue, you'll need to select the Page option on the main menu to advance the printhead to the next top of form or to eject the last page, if you are using a laser printer.

When you are finished using PrintGraph, select the Exit option followed by the Yes option (EY). If you started PrintGraph from the Lotus Access System menu, you will be returned to this menu; otherwise, you will be returned to the DOS prompt.

Saving PrintGraph Settings

All the print settings that you select, including the image and hardware settings, are used in printing the marked graphs when you select the Go option on the main menu. These print settings remain in effect during current PrintGraph session until you change them with the appropriate menu options.

If you want these print settings to be in effect for future PrintGraph sessions, you must select the Settings Save options before you use the Exit option to quit the program. When you select this option, the current print settings are saved in the configuration file (PGRAPH.CNF) that is read at the start of each PrintGraph session. If, after changing some of the settings in a PrintGraph session, you decide that you want to return to the most recently saved settings (that is, those in the PGRAPH.CNF file), you simply select the Settings Reset options.

Creating Your Own Graphs

Now it's time for you to get some practice in creating your own graphs. In the following exercises, you will graph data from the composite income statement worksheet that you created in Chapter 6, which tracks the income for the five-year period 1990–1994. You will get an opportunity to generate graphs of different types and complexities.

Creating a Line Graph

Your first graph will be a simple line graph, comparing the annual sales for each year.

1. **Retrieve the file named IS5YRCH6.WK1.**
   This file is a composite worksheet that contains income and expense figures for five years, 1990 through 1994. The first graph will use the

year headings in B2..F2 as the X range and the annual sales in B3..F3 as the A data range. If you are using Release 2.2, you can define both these ranges in one operation using the Group option. If you are using Release 2.01, you must define these ranges separately.

2. **If you are using Release 2.2, select the /Graph Group command (/GG), move the pointer to cell B2, type a period to anchor, move the pointer to cell F3, and press Enter, then select the Rowwise option (R); if you are using Release 2.01, type X, then move the pointer to B2, anchor the range, move to F2, and press Enter, then type A, and specify B3..F3 as the A data range in the same manner.**

   If you are using Release 2.2, you should see that the X data range is now B2..F2 and that the A data range is B3..F3. Regardless of the version you're using, you should now preview your graph.

3. **Type *V* to select the View option.**

   Your graph should resemble the one shown in Figure 9.25. Note the y-scale for this line graph corresponds with the first value for 1990. As a result, this value is touching the lower part of the graph "box" or frame. You will change this shortly by manually scaling the graph. But now, experiment with different graph types to see what impact the type of graph has on the data.

4. **Press any key to return to the /Graph menu; if you have a color monitor, select Options Color Quit (OCQ) to view your graph in color; regardless of monitor type, you should then select the Type Bar View options (TBV) to change the line graph to bar graph and display it on the screen.**

   The program now represents the data as a bar graph (in color, if you have a color monitor). Notice that although you can tell that income increases steadily over the five-year period, this bar graph doesn't emphasize that point as much as the line graph did. Next, change the graph type to Pie to see how the data look in a pie chart.

5. **Press any key to return to the /Graph menu, then select the Type Pie View Options (TPV).**

   Notice how slowly 1-2-3 draws the pie chart: it takes a longer time to draw curves than it does straight lines. Note that the X labels that appeared along the x-axis of the line and bar graphs are used to label the segments of the pie. Also, note that this graph type adds some new information not present in either of the two previous formats: what percent the annual sales for each year represent of total sales during the five-year period. Now change the graph type back to Line.

6. **Press any key to return to the /Graph menu, then select the Type Line options (TL).**
   Next, you will add some titles to this line graph. Start with the first title.

7. **Select Options Titles First (OTF), then type** *REVENUES 1990–1994*, **and press Enter; then select Titles Second (TS), type** *The Upward Trend Continues,* **and press Enter; next, select Titles X-Axis (TX), type** *Year Ending December 31,* **and press Enter; finally, select Titles Y-Axis (TY), type** *Annual Revenues,* **and press Enter.**
   You've now added all four titles to your line graph. Before you display the graph again, you should use the Scale option on this menu to manually set the upper and lower limits of the y-scale of the graph. To avoid having the symbol representing the 72,000 revenues in 1990 touch the bottom of the frame, you will change the lower limit of the y-scale to 70,000. You will then set the upper limit of this scale to 105,000 (the largest value in the A data range is 99,500).

8. **Select the Scale Y-Scale Lower options (SYL), then type** *70000,* **and press Enter; select the Upper option (U), type** *105000,* **and press Enter; then select the Manual option (M) to change the scaling from automatic to manual and, finally, select the Quit option (Q) to return to the Options menu.**
   If you're using Release 2.2, you will be able to see your new lower and upper limits for the y-scale as well as verify that scaling is manual by looking at the Graph Settings sheet. Before you preview the graph, try making one more enhancement: add grid lines to the line graph.

9. **Select the Grid Both options (GB), and then select the Quit option to return to the /Graph main menu; once there, select the View option to display your graph on the screen.**
   Your graph should now resemble the one shown in Figure 9.26.

Naming and Saving Your Graph

Before you go on and create another graph, you should take the time to both name your line graph and save its settings as part of the worksheet. Remember that if you don't name the graph and then go on to create another graph, the original graph settings will be lost.

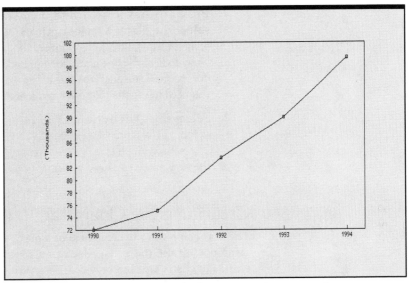

♦ **Figure 9.25:** *Line graph showing annual income for a five-year period*

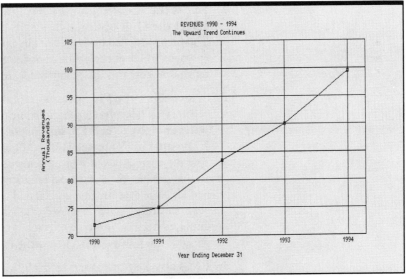

♦ **Figure 9.26:** *Line graph after adding titles, modifying the y-scale, and adding grid lines*

1. **Press any key to return to the /Graph main menu, then select the Name Create options (NC), type *INCOMELN* as the graph name, and press Enter.**
   Now, to save the line graph settings under the graph name *INCOMELN* (for Income Line graph) as part of the worksheet file under this name, you need to use the /File Save command.

2. **Select the Quit option (Q) to return to READY mode; next, select /File Save (/FS), type *IS5YRCH9*, and press Enter.**
   The named graph is now saved as part of this worksheet file under the new name you have given it.

Creating a Pie Chart

The next graph you will create will be a pie chart. Remember that this type of graph doesn't use the xy coordinate system shared by all other 1-2-3 graph types. Pie charts also use only one data variable (A), as they compare each value in the data range as a percentage of the total value in the range. For your pie chart, you will graph the product costs for each year in the five-year period, comparing the percentage each year represents of the total five-year expenses.

1. **Select the A option on the /Graph Reset menu (/GRA), then select the Quit option (Q).**
   This clears the A data range used in the previous line graph. Next, you need to select the pie chart as the type of graph and assign the range that contains the product costs to data variable A.

2. **Select the Type Pie options (TP), then type A, move the pointer to B5, type a period to anchor the range, move the pointer right to cell F5, and press Enter; next, select the View option (V) to see the pie chart on the screen.**
   Your pie chart is now displayed, showing the relationship between annual product costs and total product costs for the entire five-year period. Note that the first and second titles and X range from the previous line graph are retained (the x-axis and y-axis titles aren't displayed because this type of graph doesn't use the xy coordinate system). You now need to change the titles for this graph.

3. **Press any key to return to the /Graph menu; select Options Titles First (OTF), change just the *REVENUES* portion of this title to *PRODUCT COSTS*, so that this title reads *PRODUCT COSTS 1990–1994*, and press Enter; select Titles Second (TS), press Esc to clear the title, and press Enter; select Titles**

X-Axis (TX) and Titles Y-Axis (TY), and remove these titles in the same manner.

If you are using Release 2.2, you can see in the Graph Settings sheet that your pie chart still retains the grid and the manual scaling settings from the previous line graph. You can't tell that these settings are still in effect when the graph is displayed on the screen because pie charts don't use the xy coordinate system; nevertheless, you should clear them, as they play no part in this graph.

4. **Select Grid Clear (GC), then Scale Y-Scale Automatic (SYA), then Quit Quit (QQ) to return to the /Graph main menu.**

To enhance your pie chart, you will now experiment with adding the codes to assign hatch patterns and explode specific segments of the graph. Remember that this is done by adding numbers in the worksheet and then assigning them to the graph as the B data range. You will add these values in the cell range B4..F5 (you can only assign five different patterns, as your pie chart only has five segments). In entering the code numbers in this range, you will explode the fourth segment as well as assign a new hatch pattern to it and all the other pie segments.

5. **Select the Quit option (Q) to return to READY mode, then move the pointer to cell B4 and enter 6 there; enter 4 in cell C4, 2 in cell D4, 107 in cell E4, and 1 in F4; next, select /Graph B (GB), type a period to anchor the range, move the pointer up to cell B4 to highlight the range F4..B4, and press Enter; finally, select the View option (V) to see how your pie chart looks.**

Your pie chart should now look like the one shown in Figure 9.27. Notice how the fourth segment is exploded. If you wish, you can experiment with using different hatch pattern codes and/or exploding different segments by changing the values in the range B4..F4. Each time you change a value in this range, press the Graph key (F10) to have the pie chart redrawn to reflect the change. Next, you need to hide the values in the B data range.

6. **Press any key to return to the /Graph main menu, then select the Quit option (Q) to return to READY mode; select the /Range Format Hidden (/RFH) command, press End ←, then the → key, and press Enter.**

Formatting the values with the Hidden format ensures that they won't be printed as part of any worksheet reports that use this range. Now you are ready to name the graph and then save the worksheet file again (saving the graph as part of it).

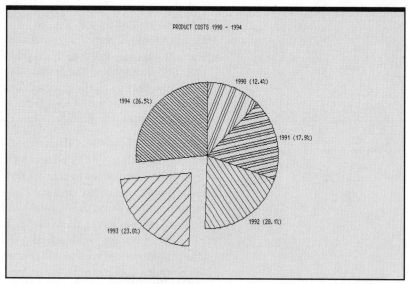

◆ **Figure 9.27:** *Pie chart after assigning B data range whose values control which segments are exploded and which hatch patterns are used*

7. **Select the /Graph Name Create command (/GNC), type**
   ***PRDCSTP* (for Product Cost Pie chart), and press Enter; then**
   select the Quit option (Q) and the /File Save command (/FS),
   press Enter, and choose the Replace option (R) to save the
   changes under the same name.

Graphs with Multiple Data Variables

Thus far, you have only graphed one data variable. In this next exercise, you will create a bar and a stacked-bar graph that compare three data variables: product costs, marketing and sales, and general and administrative. In creating this graph, you will get a chance to work with some new enhancements, including legends and data labels. You will begin by changing the graph type and clearing the A and B data ranges.

1. **Select the /Graph Type Bar command (/GTB), then select**
   Reset A B Quit (RABQ).
   Because the current X data range can be used for this graph, you only needed to clear the A and B ranges. Now you are ready to define the A, B, and C data variables for this bar graph. The first data range containing the product costs is B5..F5, the second containing the

◆

marketing and sales cost is B6..F6, and the third containing the general and administrative expenses is B7..F7.

2. **Select option A, move the pointer to cell B5, type a period to anchor, move the pointer to cell F5, and press Enter; then select B and define the range B6..F6 as the second data range in the same manner; next, select option C and define B7..F7 as the third data range; finally, select View to display the bar graph on the screen.**
   At this point, your graph should resemble the one shown in Figure 9.28. Notice that the first title retained from your pie chart needs to be changed.

3. **Press any key to return to the /Graph menu; select Options Titles First (OTF), then change just the *REVENUES* portion of the title to *COSTS AND EXPENSES* so that the entire title reads *COSTS AND EXPENSES 1990–1994*, and press Enter.**
   Next, you will select horizontal grid lines.

4. **Select Grid Horizontal (GH).**
   When your graph contains more than one data variable, as is the case in the bar graph, you need to add a legend that indicates which data are represented by which bar in the graph. The legend will appear at the bottom of the graph and will match each hatch pattern or color of each bar to a label indicating what type of data are represented. You can either type in the labels for the legend or refer to existing labels in the worksheet. You will use this latter method by indicating the cells that contain the row headings for each data range.

5. **Select Legend A (LA), type \A5, then press Enter; select Legend B (LB), type \A6, and press Enter again; select Legend C (LC), type \A7, and press Enter a third time.**
   When entering the cell references for the legends, be sure that you type a \ (backslash) and not a / (forward slash). If you don't use the \, 1-2-3 will not use the contents of the cell address as the legend label but the cell reference itself. Before you view your graph, make one more enhancement to it: format the y-scale to currency so that it is obvious that its values represent money.

6. **Select Scale Y-Scale Format Currency (SYFC), then type 0 for the number of decimal places and press Enter; next, select the Quit option twice (QQ), and then choose the View option (V) to see how your bar graph looks.**
   Your bar graph should resemble the one shown in Figure 9.29. Be sure that your legend at the bottom of the graph contains the correct

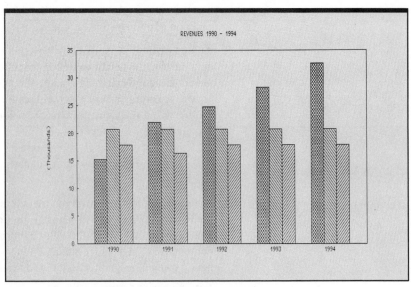

◆ **Figure 9.28:** *Bar graph using three data variables*

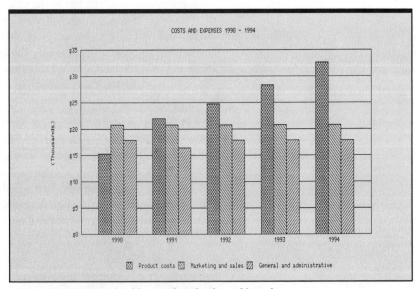

◆ **Figure 9.29:** *Completed bar graph with titles and legends*

labels. Now you are ready to name and save its settings as part of the worksheet.

7. **Press any key to return to the /Graph main menu; select Name Create, type** COSTBAR, **and press Enter; select Quit (Q), and then save the worksheet under the same name with the /File Save command, using the Replace option.**
You should now see how this bar graph with three data variables looks as a stacked-bar graph.

8. **Select the /Graph Type Stacked-Bar option (/GTS), then select the View option (V) to display the graph on the screen.**
Notice that as a stacked-bar graph, the total costs and expenses for each year are emphasized, although you still get a good idea of what portion of the total each category is responsible for. To stress the total expenses even further, you will add data labels that display the total costs for each year. These data labels will appear above each bar.

9. **Press any key to return to the /Graph menu, then select Options Data-Labels C (ODC); move the pointer to cell B9, type a period to anchor, then move the pointer to cell F9 to highlight the range B9..F9, and press Enter; finally, select the Above option (A) and then the Quit option (Q).**
You may wonder why you assigned the range B9..F9 as the data labels for variable C. This was done because the third data variable (C) is represented in the stacked-bar graph by the segment at the top of each bar. To have the totals in the range B9..F9 appear centered above each bar in the graph, you had to assign them as the data labels for this topmost stack and then select the Above position option to have them drawn above this stack (and, therefore, the entire bar). If you are using Release 2.2, notice in the Graph Settings sheet that it now lists the range B9..F9 as the data labels for variable C; the [A] before the range indicates that you selected the *Above* position option.

10. **Select the Quit option (Q), then select the View option (V) to see the data labels in the stacked-bar graph.**
Note that the horizontal grid lines make it difficult to read the data label over the fourth bar; you should remove these grid lines to make it easier to read these values. While you're doing this, you can also make some modifications to the first line title and add a second line, x-axis, and y-axis title as well.

11. **Press any key to return to the /Graph main menu, and select Options Grid Clear (OGC); next, select Titles First (TF), backspace over the text *1990–1994* to delete it, then press the Home key to move the cursor to the beginning of the line, type *TOTAL* and press the spacebar so the revised title reads *TOTAL COSTS AND EXPENSES*, and press Enter; then select Titles Second (TS), type *1990–1994*, and press Enter; select Titles X-Axis (TX), type *Year Ending December 31*, and press Enter; finally, select Titles Y-Axis (TY), type *Annual Expenses in Thousands*, and press Enter.**

    Because your Y-Axis title includes the word *Thousands*, you no longer need the scale indicator. Go ahead and remove it.

12. **Select Scale Y-Scale Indicator No (SYIN), then select the Quit option twice (QQ), and choose the View option (V) to see your completed stacked-bar graph.**

    Your graph should now resemble the one shown in Figure 9.30. You are ready to name this graph and save its definition as part of the worksheet.

13. **Press any key to return to the /Graph menu; select Name Create, type *TOTEXPSB* (for Total Expenses Stacked-Bar), and press Enter; then select the /File Save command (/FS), press Enter, and select the Replace option (R).**

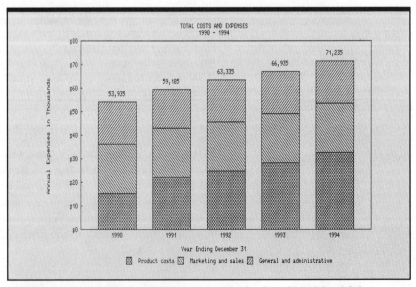

◆ **Figure 9.30:** *Completed stacked-bar graph with titles, legends, and data labels*

Printing Your Graphs

Before you can print the graphs you have created, you need to save them with the /Graph Save command. When you use this command, you create separate files in the PIC format that can be used by the PrintGraph program. After saving each of the four graphs that you have named and saved as part of the worksheet in PIC files, you must exit from 1-2-3 and start the PrintGraph program.

The following printing exercise assumes that you have already installed your printer as one of the graphics printers with the Install program and that this printer is turned on. You will begin the exercise by saving the current graph in its own PIC file. The current graph is the stacked-bar graph that you completed.

1. **Select the /Graph Save command (/GS), type** *TOTEXPSB*, **and press Enter.**

   This saves the stacked-bar graph comparing the total costs and expenses during the five-year period in its own file that can be printed (note that the graph name and file name are purposely the same). To save the other three graphs in their own PIC files, you must make each one current and then save it with /Graph Save. To make a new graph current, you have to use the Name Use options.

2. **Select Name Use (NU), move the pointer to** *PRDCSTP*, **and press Enter.**

   As soon as you press Enter, 1-2-3 automatically draws the graph on the screen. Now that your pie chart is the current graph, you will use /Graph Save to save it in a PIC file, using the same name as the graph name.

3. **Press any key to return to the /Graph menu; select Save (S), type** *PRDCSTP*, **and press Enter.**

   Notice that it takes a much longer time for 1-2-3 to save the pie chart than it did the stacked-bar graph before it. Now you need to make your line graph current and save it with /Graph Save.

4. **Select Name Use (NU), move the pointer to** *INCOMELN*, **and press Enter; then select Save (S), type** *INCOMELN*, **and press Enter.**

   All that remains is to make the bar graph that compares the costs for each year current and save it as a PIC file.

5. **Select Name Use (NU) and press Enter to select** *COSTBAR*; **then select Save (S), type** *COSTBAR*, **and press Enter.**

   Now that all four graphs are saved in their own PIC files, you are ready to exit from 1-2-3 and start PrintGraph.

6. Select the Quit option (Q) to return to READY mode, then select /QY to exit from 1-2-3; if this returns you to the Lotus Access System menu, select the PrintGraph option (G); otherwise, if you're at the DOS prompt, type *PGRAPH* and press Enter.
   In PrintGraph, you must first make sure that the graphs directory and fonts directory are correct and choose your printer.

7. Select Settings Hardware Graphs-Directory (SHG), type in the drive and directory that contain your graphs, and press Enter (if the directory is already correct, just press Enter); next, select Fonts-Directory (F), type in the drive and directory that contain your font files (most often the same ones that contain your 1-2-3 files), and press Enter (if the directory is already correct, just press Enter); finally, select Printer (P), move the pointer to the name of the printer (you can select the low- or medium-resolution version for this exercise), press the spacebar to mark it, and press Enter.
   Check your selections in the last column of the PrintGraph settings sheet.

8. If the printer you selected isn't connected to the first parallel port of your computer, select the Interface option (I) and choose the number that corresponds to the interface (if you choose a serial port—2 or 4—you need to select the number that corresponds to the correct baud rate) before you select the Quit option (Q); if you don't need to change the port, just select the Quit option (Q).
   Before you select the graphs to be printed, you will change the fonts to be used. For Font 1 (the one used to print the first line title), you will use BOLD. For Font 2 (the one used to print all other text in the graph), you will use BLOCK2 (a slightly heavier version of BLOCK1). Remember that when you change Font 1 to BOLD, PrintGraph will automatically change *both* Font 1 and 2 to BOLD.

9. Select the Image Font 1 options (IF1), then move the pointer to BOLD, press the spacebar, and press Enter; next, select Font 2 (F2), move the pointer to BLOCK2, press the spacebar, and press Enter; finally, select the Quit option twice (QQ) to return to the PrintGraph main menu.
   Now you are ready to select the graphs to print. You will select all four graphs. Remember that, by default, PrintGraph will print your graphs half-size, with two per page.

10. **Choose Image-Select (I); the names of the four PIC files you created should be displayed on the screen; move the pointer to PRDCSTP and press the spacebar to mark it; move the pointer to INCOMELN and press the spacebar to mark it; move the pointer to COSTBAR and press the spacebar to mark it; move the pointer to TOTEXPSB and press the space-bar to mark it; and press Enter.**

You should see the names of these four files listed on the left side of the PrintGraph settings sheet in the order you marked them. Now you are ready to print these graphs; because it will take a little while, you will probably want to take a break after taking the next step.

11. **If your printer takes continuous-feed paper, start the printing by selecting Align Go (AG). If your printer requires hand-fed paper, select Settings Action Pause Yes Quit Quit (SAPYQQ) before selecting Align and Go, then press the spacebar when prompted after feeding the first sheet of paper to your printer.**

When the printing stops, you are ready to advance the page to the next top of form and exit from PrintGraph.

12. **Select Page (P) and then select Exit Yes (EY) to quit Print-Graph and return to either the Lotus Access System or the DOS prompt.**

Summary

Troubleshooting

Question: When I try to view my graph with the View option in the /Graph menu or the Graph key (F10) in the worksheet, 1-2-3 either beeps at me or just displays a blank screen. What am I doing wrong?

Answer: Several factors could account for this:

• Your computer doesn't have a graphics adapter that can display graphs.

• You selected the wrong type of display when installing 1-2-3.

• You selected the /Graph Options Scale Manual command and haven't set new limits with the Lower and Upper options.

♦ You chose the XY graph type but haven't defined both an X and A data range.

Question: I tried to create a graph with the Group option in Release 2.2, but 1-2-3 graphed the wrong data.

Answer: Remember that to successfully define all data ranges for your graph in one operation with the new /Graph Group command, the X and A–F data ranges must follow each other in successive columns or rows in a single range in the worksheet. If the data to be assigned to the X and A–F data variables aren't arranged in this way, you shouldn't use the Group option to define them but should, instead, define each data range separately. If this isn't the problem, then you probably chose the wrong option after assigning the group range; try this command again, defining the same group range but this time selecting the opposite orientation option (Columnwise if you chose Rowwise before, or Rowwise if you chose Columnwise previously).

Question: I saved my graph in 1-2-3 with /Graph Save, then quit the program and printed the graph with PrintGraph. When I returned to 1-2-3, however, I could no longer display the graph on the screen. What am I doing wrong?

Answer: You forgot to name the graph and then save the worksheet before you quit 1-2-3 to use PrintGraph. Remember that /Graph Save creates a separate PIC file for the graph that is used in printing. To name the graph and save its definition as part of the worksheet so that you can review it and make changes to it, you must use /Graph Name Create and assign it a name (up to 15 characters long), and then use /File Save to save this name and the graph definition associated with it as part of the worksheet.

Essential Techniques

To Create Graphs

1. Select the type of graph that you wish to create with the /Graph Type command.

2. Define the data ranges for the data variables used in the graph. Select the X option to define the values or labels to appear along the x-axis. Select the A–F options to define the data variables required by the type of graph you are building.

3. Preview the graph with the View option when using the /Graph menu or the Graph key (F10) when in the worksheet. Press any key to return to the /Graph menu or worksheet.

4. Add all desired enhancements—including titles, legends, grid lines, modification to the graph scales, and data labels—using the /Graph Options command.

5. To retain the settings, select the /Graph Name Create command to assign a name up to 15 characters long to the graph.

6. To save the graph name and definition as part of the worksheet, select the /File Save command.

7. To save a copy of the graph in the PIC file format so that it can be printed with the PrintGraph program, select the /Graph Save command and assign a file name up to 8 characters long to the graph (1-2-3 will automatically add the extension .PIC to the file name you assign).

To Print Graphs

1. Exit from 1-2-3 and start the PrintGraph program by selecting the PrintGraph option on the Lotus Access System, or by typing *PGRAPH* and pressing Enter at the DOS prompt.

2. Make sure that the drive and directory listed for the Graphs directory and Fonts directory and the printer type and interface listed on the PrintGraph settings sheet are correct. If not, select Settings Hardware and use the appropriate options on this menu to make them correct.

3. Select the size, fonts, and colors (if you are using a color printer) for your graph by selecting the Settings Image options and using the appropriate options on this menu.

4. Select the graphs to be printed by choosing the Image-Select option on the PrintGraph main menu. Mark each graph to be printed by moving the pointer to it and pressing the spacebar, then press Enter.

5. Make sure that the Action settings on the PrintGraph settings sheet are correct for your printer and that your printer is turned on. Select the Align Go options to begin printing all marked graphs in the order they appear on the PrintGraph settings sheet.

Review   Important Terms You Should Know

data variable	scale indicator
Graph key (F10)	tick mark
grid	x-axis
hatch pattern	x-scale
PIC file	y-axis
print queue	y-scale

Test Your Knowledge

1. To assign all data variables to a graph using the values in the columns of a table of data in one operation in Release 2.2, you choose the _____ command, define the data range, and select the _____ option.

2. To create a line graph that displays only the symbols used to represent each data variable, select the _____ command and then choose the _____ options.

3. To convert a line graph to a bar graph, select the _____ command and then choose the _____ option.

4. When creating an XY graph, you assign the data range for the x-axis to the _____ data variable and the data range for the y-axis to the _____ data variable.

5. To assign your own hatch patterns to the segments in your pie chart, you enter a range of values representing the _____ in the worksheet and assign this range as the _____ data variable.

6. To assign a range of labels in the worksheet as the legends for your graph, you select the _____ command and then select the _____ option, enter the range name or range address, and press Enter.

7. To set 1500 as the lower limit and 9500 as the upper limit of the y-scale of your graph, you select the _____ command, choose the Y-Scale option, then select the _____ option and enter *1500*,

choose the _____ option and enter 9500, and finally, choose the _____ option from the menu.

8. To format the values on the y-scale so that they display the percent sign and no decimal places, you select the _____ command, choose the Y-Scale option, then select the _____ option and enter _____ before pressing Enter.

9. To assign data labels to data variable A in your line graph so that the values are displayed centered over each symbol representing a data point, you select the _____ command, then choose the A option, define the range that contains the values, and finally, select the _____ options.

10. To name the current graph, select the _____ command. To make a named graph current, choose the _____ command.

11. To save a graph name and graph definition as part of the worksheet, select the _____ command.

12. To save the current graph as a PIC file, you select the _____ command.

13. To print your graphs, you must _____ 1-2-3 and start the _____ program.

14. To print your graphs full-size rotated 90 degrees counterclockwise on the page, you need to select the _____ options from the Print-Graph main menu.

15. To abort the printing of your graphs in PrintGraph, you press the _____ keys and then press the _____ key.

Further Exercises

1. Create a line graph that compares the revenues and operating costs for the four-year period 1990–1993 in your worksheet ISLINK.WK1, using Figure 9.31 as a guide. Assign the column headings with the years 1990 through 1993 as the X data range. Assign the revenues for 1990 through 1993 as the A data range and the operating costs for

these years to the B data range. Format the y-scale with the Currency format, using zero decimal places. Create legends for each of the two data variables by using the contents of cells A4 and A5, add the first and second titles, and add the grid lines as shown in Figure 9.31. Name the graph *REVOPRLN* and then save it in its own PIC file under the same name.

2. Save the worksheet under the same name, exit from 1-2-3, and start PrintGraph. Print your new REVOPRLN.PIC file full-size, using BLOCK2 for Font 1 and ROMAN2 for Font 2.

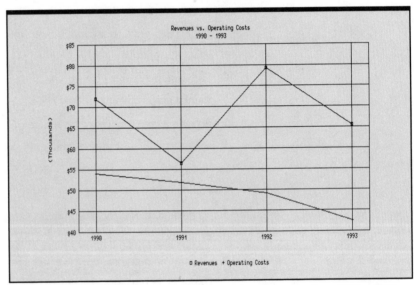

♦ **Figure 9.31:** *Line graph comparing revenues and operating costs from 1990 to 1993*

10

Using Allways
to Produce Perfect
Reports

In This Chapter...

Getting Acquainted with Allways

Allways is a spreadsheet publishing utility that enables you to enhance the printing of all the worksheets you produce in 1-2-3. This program was created by Funk Software, Inc., the same company that developed Sideways, a printing utility that makes it possible to print 1-2-3 reports in landscape mode. Allways is an example of a Lotus 1-2-3 add-in program. This means that it is loaded into memory from within 1-2-3, using a special Add-In menu.

Allways is included as part of the Release 2.2 package. If you are still using Release 2.01 and don't plan to upgrade to Release 2.2, you can still use Allways; however, you must purchase the program separately. You can only use Allways on a computer with a hard disk, so it is of no use to you if you are using 1-2-3 on a two-disk-drive system, regardless of which 1-2-3 release you have. Allways does, however, work with a wide variety of printers, including the many models of dot-matrix and laser printers supported by 1-2-3.

The advantages to using Allways to print your worksheet reports instead of the /Print Printer commands in 1-2-3 include:

+ WYSIWYG (what-you-see-is-what-you-get) display of the formatting added to the report in Allways (provided that your computer has graphics capabilities).

+ The ability to use any font supported by your printer or any of the three *soft fonts* supplied by Allways, and to combine up to eight different fonts in a single report.

+ The ability to add bold, underline, or double underline to any cell or cell range in the print range.

+ The ability to draw boxes or horizontal or vertical rules in the report or to outline or enclose cells in the print range in boxes.

+ The ability to shade areas of the report using light, dark, or solid black shading.

+ The ability to print graphs on the same page as worksheet data in the report.

Taken together, these features offer you sophisticated controls over the look and presentation of your worksheet reports. As you will see shortly, Allways is easy to learn and use because it uses the same type of menu system that you are familiar with in 1-2-3.

Installing Allways

Allways isn't automatically installed as part of the Lotus 1-2-3 installation procedure. To install the program, you need to locate Disk 1 (the Setup Disk) in the set of Allways disks and then take these steps:

1. **Insert Disk 1 into drive A of your computer.**
   Next, you need to make drive A current.

2. **Type A: and press Enter.**
   The DOS prompt should now read *A*>.

3. **Type *AWSETUP* and press Enter to start the installation procedure.**
   The opening screen for the Allways installation program will appear.

4. **Press Enter to continue with the installation of Allways.**
   You will now see the main menu of the Allways installation program on your screen (Figure 10.1). Note that the *First Time Installation* option is highlighted.

5. **Press Enter to begin the first time installation procedure.**
   During this procedure, you will be asked to name the drive and directory containing 1-2-3, the type of display your computer has, and the

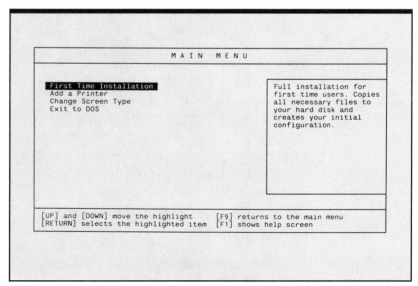

♦ **Figure 10.1:** *Main menu of the Allways installation program*

type of printer(s) you will be using to print your Allways reports. First, you need to indicate the drive and directory that contains 1-2-3 on the hard disk.

6. **Press Enter to accept the default drive and directory of C:\123, or type in the letter of the drive and the name of the directory containing 1-2-3 if the program is located some-where else, and then press Enter.**
After you indicate the location of 1-2-3, the Allways installation program automatically displays the type of screen that it detects.

7. **Press Enter to accept the screen type listed, or move the pointer to the No option and press Enter; then select the appropriate screen type from the list (see Figure 10.2) and press Enter (if your computer isn't equipped with a color or Hercules monochrome graphics adapter, you must select the No graphic adapter option on this screen).**
After indicating the type of screen, the program copies some files from Disk 1 and then asks you to indicate the type of printer you have from the list of printers (Figure 10.3). Just as with 1-2-3, you can install more than one printer for use with Allways. The first printer that you select will become the default printer in Allways, so if you

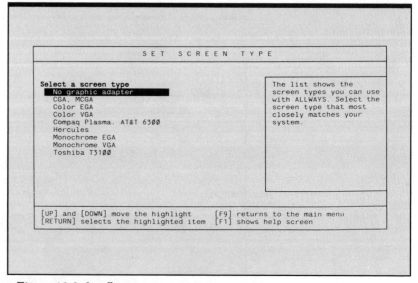

◆ **Figure 10.2:** *Installing a new screen type*

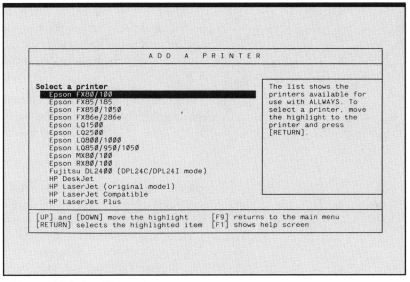

```
                    A D D   A   P R I N T E R

 Select a printer                          ┌─────────────────────┐
   Epson FX80/100                           │The list shows the   │
   Epson FX85/185                           │printers available for│
   Epson FX850/1050              ,          │use with ALLWAYS. To │
   Epson FX86e/286e                         │select a printer, move│
   Epson LQ1500                             │the highlight to the │
   Epson LQ2500                             │printer and press    │
   Epson LQ800/1000                         │[RETURN].            │
   Epson LQ850/950/1050                     │                     │
   Epson MX80/100                           │                     │
   Epson RX80/100                           │                     │
   Fujitsu DL2400 (DPL24C/DPL24I mode)      │                     │
   HP DeskJet                               │                     │
   HP LaserJet (original model)             │                     │
   HP LaserJet Compatible                   │                     │
   HP LaserJet Plus                         └─────────────────────┘

 [UP] and [DOWN] move the highlight      [F9] returns to the main menu
 [RETURN] selects the highlighted item   [F1] shows help screen
```

♦ **Figure 10.3:** *Installing a printer*

have more than one printer connected to your computer, begin by installing the one that you will be using most often.

8. **Move the pointer to the name of the printer you wish to install as the default printer in Allways, and press Enter.**
   At this point, Allways will prompt you to place the disk that contains the driver for the printer you've selected in the disk drive.

9. **Replace Disk 1 in drive A with the disk whose number is indicated on your screen, and press Enter.**
   After copying the driver from the disk, the installation program will ask you if you would like to choose another printer.

10. **If you want to install another printer, move the pointer to the Yes option and press Enter (you may then be prompted to replace the disk currently in drive A with another one that contains the driver for the printer you just selected); when you are finished installing printers, press Enter to select the No option.**
    After you choose No, the installation program will copy more files from each of the Allways disks, prompting you each time it needs you to replace the disk in drive A with a new one. When this process is completed, the install program will return you to the main menu.

11. **On the main menu, move the pointer to the *Exit to DOS*
    option and press Enter, then move the pointer to the Yes
    option and press Enter to return to the DOS prompt.**
    This terminates the installation procedure and returns you to the
    A > prompt.

12. **Type C: and press Enter to change to drive C, then remove
    the last Allways disk from drive A.**

Loading Allways into Memory

After you have installed Allways on your hard disk, you need to start 1-2-3 (just
as you normally do) before you can load Allways into the computer's memory.
To load add-in programs such as Allways, you choose the Attach option on the
Add-In menu, then select the key that will be used to start the program. In
Release 2.2, you can assign add-in programs to keys Alt-F7, Alt-F8, Alt-F9, and
Alt-F10. In Release 2.01, you can assign them to keys Alt-F7, Alt-F8, and
Alt-F9 only. Note that although the menus and documentation list the Alt
key, you can use the Shift key instead. For example, if you assign Allways to
Alt-F7, you can start it by pressing Alt-F7 *or* Shift-F7.

If you are using Release 2.2, you can bring up the 1-2-3 Add-In menu by
either typing /A or pressing Alt-F10 (provided that you haven't already
assigned an add-in program to this key). If you are using Release 2.01, however,
you can only use Alt-F10 to activate this menu (this is why you can't assign
Alt-F10 as the startup key for an add-in program in this version).

The steps you use to load and start Allways are as follows:

1. **Select the /Add-In menu (/A) if you are using Release 2.2, or
   press Alt-F10 if you are using Release 2.01, to bring up the
   Add-In menu.**
   To load Allways, you need to select the Attach option from the Add-In
   menu that appears.

2. **Select Attach (A) and select *ALLWAYS.ADN* on the menu line;
   you should be able to do this simply by pressing Enter, as
   this file name should already be highlighted.**
   Next, you need to indicate which key is to be used to start Allways.
   The Release 2.2 menu choices are No-Key, 7 (for Alt-F7), 8 (for
   Alt-F8), 9 (for Alt-F9), and 10 (for Alt-F10). The Release 2.01 menu
   choices are No-Key, 7, 8, and 9.

3. **Type 7 to assign Alt-F7 as the startup key for Allways.**
   You will see the Allways startup screen as this program is loaded into memory, and then you will be returned to the 1-2-3 Add-In menu.

4. **To start Allways, select the Invoke option (I) from Add-In menu, then select *ALLWAYS* from the menu line; you should be able to do this simply by pressing Enter, as it should already be highlighted.**
   You can always start an attached add-in program by using the Invoke option on the Add-In menu (this is how you have to start add-in programs to which no key has been assigned). Because you assigned Alt-F7 as the Allways startup key, you can also use this to start the program. To see how this works, exit from Allways and then restart using Alt-F7.

5. **Press Esc to return to 1-2-3.**
   You can always press Esc to exit from Allways and return to 1-2-3. Now try starting Allways with Alt-F7.

6. **Press Alt-F7 to start Allways.**
   From now on, until you quit the program or unload the program from memory (using the Detach option on the Add-In menu), you can exit from Allways and return to 1-2-3 by pressing the Esc key, and then restart Allways simply by pressing Alt-F7.

The Allways Display

Figure 10.4 shows the Allways display as it would appear on your monitor with a 1-2-3 worksheet. The arrangement of this display is intentionally similar to that of 1-2-3. The top part of this screen is called the *control panel*, just as it is in 1-2-3. In Figure 10.4, you will see that the first line of this control panel differs slightly from 1-2-3: in the upper left corner, the program displays information on the format of the current cell, including the font, text color, and use of any other attribute such as bold, underline, shading, or lines instead of the contents of the current cell. Notice, however, that Allways displays its MODE indicator in the upper right corner on the first line of the control panel, just as in 1-2-3. In Figure 10.4, you see that the format for the current cell is *FONT(1) Triumvirate 10 pt* (the default font assigned to every cell in the worksheet) and the mode is *ALLWAYS*.

On the second line of the control panel, Allways displays the contents of the current cell. When you activate the Allways menu system, this information is temporarily replaced by the menu options.

```
FONT(1) Triumvirate 10 pt                                           ALLWAYS
A1: 'INCOME STATEMENT YEAR ENDING DECEMBER 31

                  A            B       C       D       E       F       G
1    INCOME STATEMENT ENDING DECEMBER 31
2                             1990    1991    1992    1993    1994    Total
3    Revenues               72,000  75,100  83,500  90,000  99,500  420,100
4    Costs and expenses
5      Product costs        15,300  22,000  24,700  28,300  32,600  122,900
6      Marketing and sales  20,785  20,785  20,785  20,785  20,785  103,925
7      General and administrative 17,850 16,400 17,850 17,850 17,850  87,800
8                          --------  ------  ------  ------  ------  -------
9    Total costs and expenses 53,935 59,185 63,335 66,935 71,235  314,625
10
11   Operating income (loss) 18,065 15,915 20,165 23,065 28,265  105,475
12
13   Other income (expenses)
14     Interest income       4,500   4,500   4,500   4,500   4,500   22,500
15     Interest expense       (500)   (500)   (500)   (900)   (500)  (2,500)
16     Bonuses               4,642   4,202   5,072   5,666   6,731   26,314
17     Other                   600     600     600     600     600    3,000
18                          --------  ------  ------  ------  ------  -------
19   Total other income (expenses) 9,242 8,802 9,672 10,266 11,331 49,314
20
21   Income (loss) before taxes 27,307 24,717 29,837 33,331 39,596 154,789
22     Provision (benefit) for taxes 4,096 3,708 4,476 5,000 5,939 23,218
06/08/89   09:32                                         CIRC
```

◆ **Figure 10.4:** *The Allways display*

Below the control panel, you see the worksheet display. Note that the
Allways display shows more columns and rows of the worksheet than the 1-2-3
display (this is because the program displays the worksheet in graphics mode
rather than text mode).

You can move the pointer around the Allways worksheet display using the
same pointer-movement keys and commands as you do in 1-2-3. When you
need to specify a range in the Allways worksheet display, you can use the same
methods as in 1-2-3, including pointing, typing the range address or range
name, or selecting the range name from a menu using the Name key (F3).

There is, however, one thing you can't do in the Allways worksheet display:
you can *never* edit the contents of the cells in any way. If you discover that you
need to make a change to the contents of the worksheet while in Allways,
you must exit from the program (by pressing Esc or selecting /Quit on the
Allways main menu) and then make this change in 1-2-3 itself.

Beneath the worksheet display, you see the Allways status line (on line 25 of
the screen). No significant difference exists between the status line in 1-2-3
and the status line in Allways. They both display any status indicator (you can
see the CIRC indicator in Figure 10.4) that appears in the 1-2-3 worksheet.
There is, however, one minor difference between the two: if you are using
Release 2.2 and have the file name on the status line replace the date and time
indicator in the lower left corner, the Allways status line will show the date
and time indicator even when 1-2-3 displays the file name.

The Allways Menu System

As you would expect, the Allways menu system is arranged similarly to 1-2-3's and operates in the same way. To bring up the main menu for Allways, you press the / (slash) key, just as you do in 1-2-3. To select options from this menu, you can either type the initial character of the option name or use the arrow keys to move the pointer to it and press the Enter key.

The only difference between the Allways menu system and the 1-2-3 menu system is that Allways contains pull-down menus—that is, menus whose options are numbered and are arranged vertically—which are totally absent from 1-2-3. Figure 10.5 shows you a pull-down menu that is used to select a new color for printing.

The difference between an Allways pull-down menu and a standard horizontal menu is more than cosmetic: to select an option from a pull-down menu, you *must* type the number of the option *and* press the Enter key. If you try to select an option by typing the initial character of the option name, as you do with normal 1-2-3 and Allways menus, the program will beep at you. Also, typing the number just highlights the option in the menu; you must press Enter to actually select it. For example, to select blue as the print color from the pull-down menu shown in Figure 10.5, you must type *4* and press Enter; typing *B* for *Blue* will have no effect.

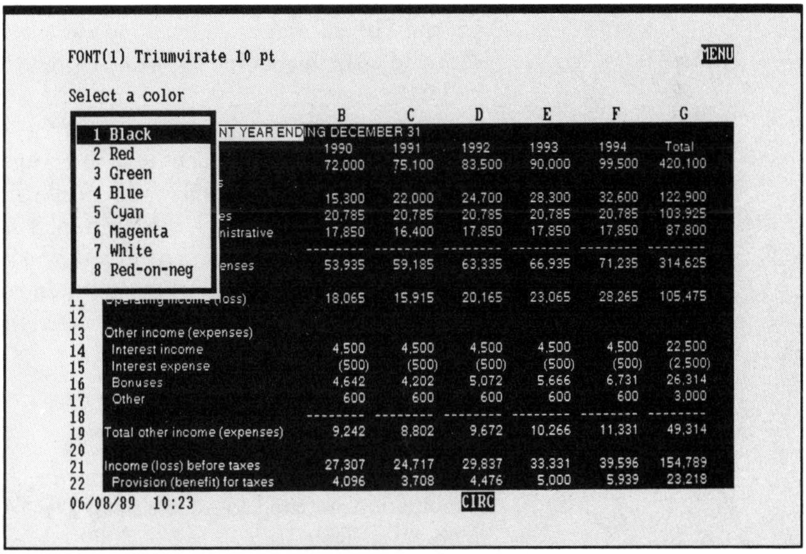

◆ **Figure 10.5:** *The Allways /Format Color pull-down menu*

The Allways Main Menu

When you activate the Allways main menu with the / (slash) key, the following options are displayed:

Worksheet Format Graph Layout Print Display Special Quit

As in 1-2-3, the selection of most of these options leads to new menus. If you select a menu option in error, you can return to the previous menu by pressing the Esc key. Also, you can press Ctrl-Break to immediately return to ALLWAYS mode (the equivalent to READY mode in 1-2-3) from anywhere in the Allways menu system.

The Allways Function Keys

Allways uses several function keys in the same way as 1-2-3. For example, you can press F3 to bring up a list of range names or files in Allways, just as you do in 1-2-3. In addition, the program assigns a few unique functions not shared in 1-2-3 to some of the keys. For instance, you can press F6 to switch between graphics and text mode in Allways, whereas you use this key to make a new window active in 1-2-3 (worksheet windows defined in 1-2-3 aren't displayed in Allways).

Table 10.1 lists the function keys in Allways. As you can see, Allways uses far fewer function keys than 1-2-3. Of those that Allways does use, the keys F1, F3, F5, and F10 are used much the same way as they are in 1-2-3. Note, however, that the assignments for F4, Shift-F4, and F6 in Allways are not shared by 1-2-3.

In Allways, you can change the size of the worksheet display provided that the program is in graphics mode (and that your computer can display graphics). To enlarge the size of the display, you can use Shift-F4, and to reduce it, you can use F4 (you can also select a specific display size by selecting the appropriate option on the /Display Zoom menu). Provided that your computer has some type of graphics adapter, you can toggle in and out of graphics mode by pressing F6 (you can also do this by choosing between the Graphics and Text options on the /Display Mode menu).

The Allways Accelerator Keys

In addition to the function-key assignments, Allways includes special Alt-key combinations referred to as *accelerator keys*. All accelerator-key assignments are listed in Table 10.2.

♦ **Table 10.1:** *The Allways Function Keys*

Key	Name	Usage
F1	Help	Gives you online, context-sensitive help. Allways help is organized much like 1-2-3's.
F3	Name	Displays a list of range names or file names, depending upon the command. When presenting a list of range names, Allways displays the options in a pull-down menu.
F4	Reduce	Reduces the size of the Allways display. This key reduces the display by cycling through the same sizes as offered by the Tiny, Small, Normal, Large, and Huge options on the /Display Zoom menu.
Shift-F4	Enlarge	Enlarges the size of the Allways display. This key enlarges the display by cycling through the same sizes as offered by the Tiny, Small, Normal, Large, and Huge options on the /Display Zoom menu.
F5	Goto	Moves the pointer to a specific cell address (can be used with range names specified by the Name key, as in 1-2-3).
F6	Display	Switches the Allways display between graphics and text modes.
F10	Graph	Turns the display of a 1-2-3 graph brought into an Allways report on and off. When the display is on, the graph is actually displayed in Allways. When the display is off, the graph is represented by a shaded box that indicates its position on the page.

Accelerator keys save you keystrokes when you use some of the more common Allways commands. Note that each of the commands listed in Table 10.2 has Allways menu equivalents. Nevertheless, if you use Allways a great deal, you will find that using the accelerator-key alternatives can speed up your work considerably.

◆ **Table 10.2:** *The Allways Accelerator Keys*

Key	Usage
Alt-1	Selects Font 1
Alt-2	Selects Font 2
Alt-3	Selects Font 3
Alt-4	Selects Font 4
Alt-5	Selects Font 5
Alt-6	Selects Font 6
Alt-7	Selects Font 7
Alt-8	Selects Font 8
Alt-B	Toggles bold on or off
Alt-G	Toggles grid lines on or off
Alt-L	Selects lines: outline, all, or none
Alt-S	Selects shades: light, dark, solid, or none
Alt-U	Selects underline: single, double, or none

Some accelerator keys (Alt-B and Alt-G) toggle on and off a particular attribute or effect. For example, if the pointer is located in a cell that contains a normal label, pressing Alt-B the first time will make the label bold, and pressing Alt-B a second time will return it to normal.

Other accelerator keys (Alt-L, Alt-S, and Alt-U) cycle you through different formats. For instance, if the pointer is located in a cell that contains a normal label, pressing Alt-U the first time will add a single underline to the label, pressing it a second time will add a double underline to the label, and pressing it a third time will remove the double underlining and return it to normal. This means, therefore, that if you want to use the Alt-U accelerator key to remove single underlining from a cell, you must move the pointer to it and press Alt-U twice (you can do this by holding the Alt key and then pressing U two times): the first time, Allways changes the single underlining to double, and the second time, the program removes the double underlining from the current cell.

Specifying Ranges in Allways

When adding an attribute to a single cell, you merely move the pointer to it and press the appropriate key combination. When adding an attribute to a range of cells, however, you must have already selected the range *before* you press the key combination. To select a range before pressing an accelerator key, you *must* select it by pointing, that is, by moving the pointer to the first cell of the range, typing the period key to anchor the range, and then moving the pointer to the last cell of the range. Just as in 1-2-3, Allways highlights all the cells that you select when pointing.

You will find that you can point out the range that you want a command applied to before you choose *any* Allways command that accepts a range. This is unlike 1-2-3, where you must always select the desired command and wait to be prompted before you specify the range of cells to which it is to be applied.

Like 1-2-3, however, Allways will prompt you to enter a range after you select a command if you have not already specified a range. You may want to follow the more conventional order because it allows you to specify the range by range address, range name, or pointing (when you specify the range before selecting the command, you are restricted to the use of pointing).

Displaying the Worksheet in Allways

As a spreadsheet publishing program, Allways displays your report on the screen more or less as it will appear when printed, provided that your computer is equipped with a graphics adapter and the program is in graphics mode. Because of this WYSIWYG capability, the discrepancies between the report as it appears on the screen in Allways and as it appears on the screen in 1-2-3 will become progressively greater as you format your report in the program.

Note that if your computer doesn't have graphics capabilities, you can still use Allways, although the program will always remain in text mode and you won't know how your report is going to look until you actually print it. If you plan to use Allways regularly to produce your 1-2-3 reports, I highly recommend that you add graphics capabilities to your system to avoid wasting a lot of time and effort trying to design your reports without seeing how they will appear printed.

If your computer does have graphics capabilities, Allways offers several commands that enable you to control the screen display. These are a part of the Allways /Display menu, which is illustrated in Figure 10.6. Notice that the first option on the /Display menu is Mode, whose suboptions are Graphics and Text. You use these options to toggle between graphics mode, which shows you the area of the worksheet currently on the screen almost exactly as it will appear when printed (including the different fonts, text sizes, and attributes used) and text mode, which is how the area of worksheet currently on the screen appears in 1-2-3. Remember that you can use the Display key (F6) to toggle between graphics and text mode in Allways instead of /Display Mode Graphics (/DMG) and /Display Mode Text (/DMT).

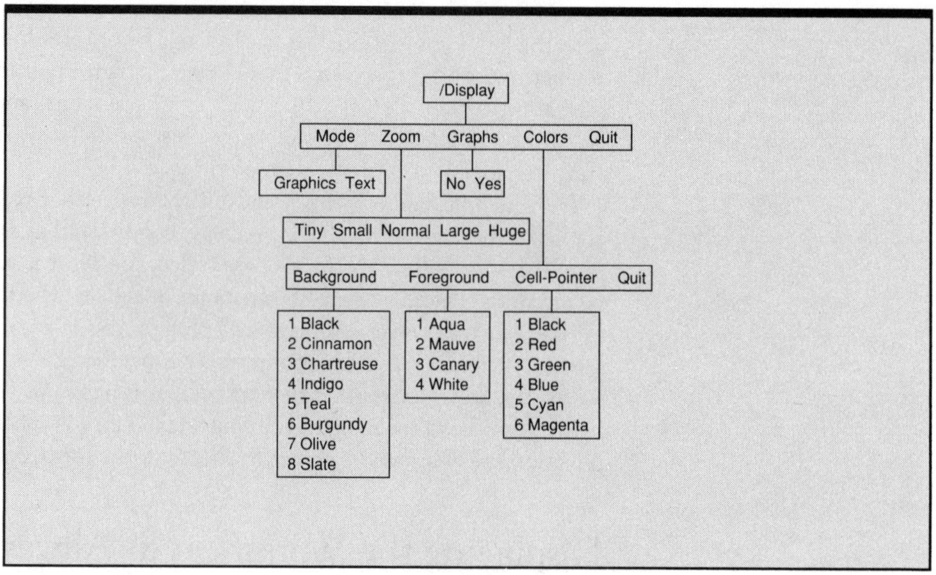

♦ **Figure 10.6:** *The Allways /Display menu tree*

The second option on the /Display menu is Zoom. It contains five size options that enable you to enlarge or reduce the size of the worksheet display. Figure 10.7 shows you how the worksheet display looks in Allways when you select Tiny, the smallest /Display Zoom option, and Figure 10.8 shows you how it appears when you select Huge, the largest /Display Zoom option. As you can imagine just by looking at the extreme sizes illustrated in these figures, you can use these Zoom menu options effectively either to zoom out to get an over-view of how larger sections of the report look, or to zoom in to see more details in smaller sections of the report.

When you select a size option from the /Display Zoom menu, Allways won't redraw the screen until you select Quit from the /Display menu to return to ALLWAYS mode, so you have to type /DZHQ to have the screen enlarged to huge size. To avoid using so many keystrokes to reduce or enlarge the screen display, you can use the Enlarge key (Shift-F4) or Reduce key (F4). If the screen is normal size and you want to enlarge it to huge size without using the /Display Zoom menu, press the Enlarge key (Shift-F4) twice: once to increase the size to large and a second time to increase it to huge. If you then want to reduce the screen display back to normal, press the Reduce key (F4) twice. To further reduce the screen display from normal, continue to press the Reduce key: once to reduce to small and a second time to reduce to tiny.

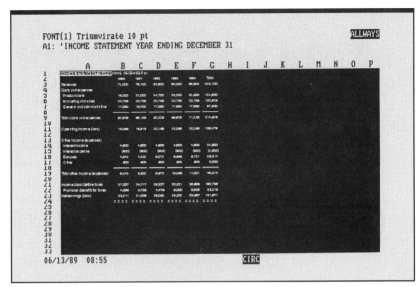

♦ **Figure** 10.7: *The Allways display after selecting /Display Zoom Tiny*

♦ **Figure** 10.8: *The Allways display after selecting /Display Zoom Huge*

The Graphs option on the /Display menu is used when you have added 1-2-3 graphs to the worksheet so that they will be printed as part of the Allways report (you will learn how to do this later in this chapter). When you add a 1-2-3 graph to a worksheet in Allways, the program doesn't display any details of the graph. Instead, it draws a crosshatched box in the worksheet that indicates only its size and position on the page.

If you want to preview the graph, you need to choose the Yes option from the /Display Graphs menu (/DGY). To return to crosshatched boxes, you use the /Display Graphs No command. Normally, you will want to display the crosshatched boxes instead of the graphs themselves in the worksheet, because their display slows the response time of the program quite a bit. You can then turn on their display when you need to preview the graphs when relocating or resizing them, or right before printing the report. Allways makes this easy to do because it includes the Display key (F10), which duplicates the functions of /Display Graphs Yes and No. The Display key is another toggle key in Allways: the first time you press it, the graphs replace the crosshatched boxes in the worksheet; the second time you press it, the crosshatched boxes replace the graphs.

If you have a color monitor, you can use the Colors option on the /Display menu to change the colors of the background, foreground, and cell pointer (which sets the color for the pointer as well as all highlighting of ranges in the worksheet) in the Allways display. Note that none of the color selections made on the /Display menu affect the colors used in printing if you are using a color printer (this is done with the /Format Color command). You can see the various color options available for each part of the screen display in Figure 10.6. As in 1-2-3, the colors vary according to the type of graphics adapter and monitor, and you will have to experiment to see how colors such as Teal and Mauve actually appear on your display.

Creating Reports in Allways

As you would expect, Allways is rich in formatting and layout features designed to give you maximum flexibility in creating presentation-quality reports. Figure 10.9 shows you all the options on the /Format menu. You can use this menu to change the font or add attributes to your report.

After changing the fonts and adding various print attributes such as underlining, bold, boxes, or shading from the /Format menu in Allways, you will sometimes also need to adjust the column width and/or row height. This is done from within Allways, using the options on its /Worksheet menu, shown in Figure 10.10. Here, you can also create manual page breaks for your report.

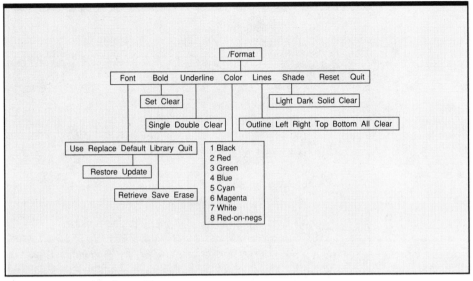

◆ **Figure 10.9:** *The Allways /Format menu tree*

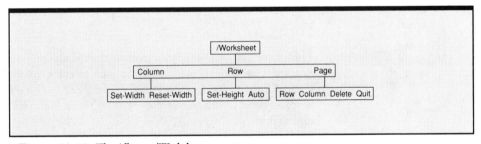

◆ **Figure 10.10:** *The Allways /Worksheet menu tree*

To change the page length or margins, or create a header, footer, or borders, you use the Allways /Layout menu, shown in Figure 10.11. In addition, from this menu, you can increase or decrease the heaviness of the printing or have column and row grid lines printed in the report. From this menu, you can also save your layout settings and reuse them in other worksheets you print with Allways.

We will begin looking at the many ways you can enhance a 1-2-3 report in Allways with the /Format menu before examining the uses of the options on the /Worksheet and /Layout menus.

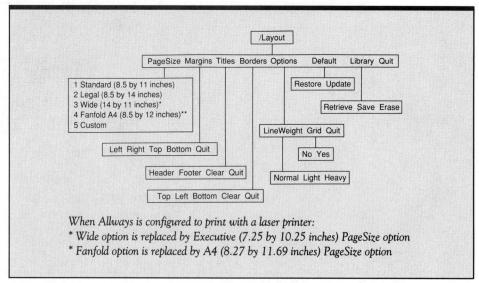

When Allways is configured to print with a laser printer:
* Wide option is replaced by Executive (7.25 by 10.25 inches) PageSize option
* Fanfold option is replaced by A4 (8.27 by 11.69 inches) PageSize option

♦ **Figure 10.11:** *The Allways /Layout menu tree*

Fonts in Allways

The first option on the /Format menu is Font. This option enables you to select new fonts for your report. You can use up to eight different fonts in a worksheet. Allways considers a *font* to be a typeface of a particular size. The program provides you with three typefaces: Times, Triumvirate, and Courier in a range of sizes from 5 to 24 points. If you are using a laser printer, such as the LaserJet Series II, you can use the other typefaces that are available for your printer as well.

Type sizes are measured in one of two ways: points or pitch. A *point* is a vertical measurement, with each point equal to approximately 1/72 inch. Common point sizes are 10, 12, 14, and 20 (10 point type is the default in Allways). The fonts supplied by Allways (Courier, Triumvirate, and Times) and laser-printer fonts are measured in points. *Pitch* is a horizontal measurement that measures the number of characters in an inch of type. Common pitch sizes are 10, 12, and 17 (often called compressed type). Most fonts for dot-matrix printers (other than the Allways fonts) are measured by pitch.

The Default Font Set

When you start Allways, the program offers a default *font set*. This set contains eight fonts that you can use right away in the report by choosing the /Format

Font option, moving the highlight to its name and size, and pressing Enter. Figure 10.12 lists the fonts in the default font set. As you can see from this figure, this set contains four choices for Triumvirate and four choices for Times. Note that the italic versions of 10 point Triumvirate and 10 point Times are considered to be different fonts in Allways.

To use one of these fonts in the worksheet, you choose /Format Font (/FF), move the pointer to the description of the font that you wish to use in the pull-down menu that appears, and select it by choosing the Use option (U) or pressing Enter. Allways will then prompt you to indicate the range to which the font is to be applied. As in 1-2-3, the range will be anchored on the current cell. At that point, you can press Esc to unanchor the range, use the pointer-movement keys to increase the size of the range, type in the range address or range name, or press the Name key (F3) and select the range name.

Remember that you can also use the accelerator keys, Alt-1 through Alt-8, to select specific fonts in the worksheet. When you press Alt-1, Allways applies whatever font is currently the first one in the font set to whatever range is highlighted (if no range is highlighted, the program applies it to the current cell).

Figure 10.13 shows a part of a worksheet where new fonts have been specified. For the title in cell A1, 14 point Triumvirate is selected. For the year and total headings in the row below, 14 point Times is used, and for the rest of the cells in the worksheet, 10 point Times is assigned.

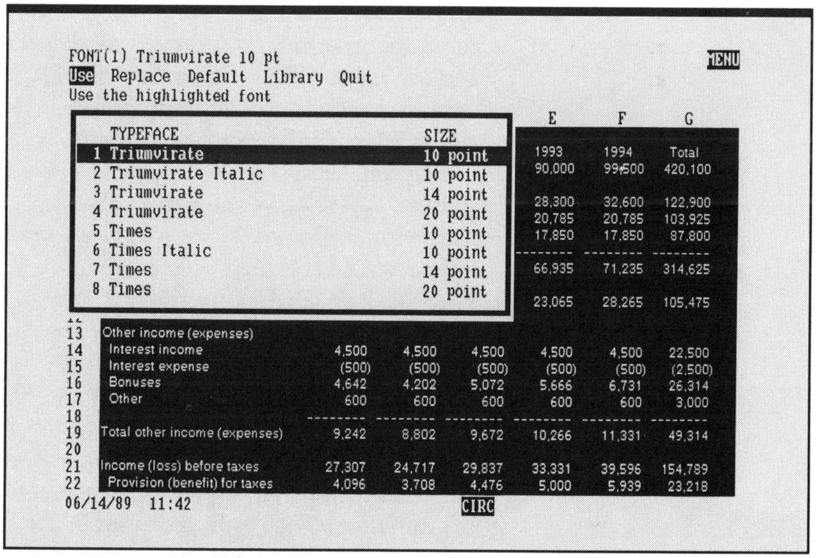

♦ **Figure 10.12:** *The Allways default font set*

```
FONT(3) Triumvirate 14 pt                                    ALLWAYS
A1: 'INCOME STATEMENT YEAR ENDING DECEMBER 31
```

	A	B	C	D	E	F	G
1	INCOME STATEMENT YEAR ENDING DECEMBER 31						
2		1990	1991	1992	1993	1994	Total
3	Revenues	72,000	75,100	83,500	90,000	99,500	420,100
4	Costs and expenses						
5	Product costs	15,300	22,000	24,700	28,300	32,600	122,900
6	Marketing and sales	20,785	20,785	20,785	20,785	20,785	103,925
7	General and administrative	17,850	16,400	17,850	17,850	17,850	87,800
8							
9	Total costs and expenses	53,935	59,185	63,335	66,935	71,235	314,625
10							
11	Operating income (loss)	18,065	15,915	20,165	23,065	28,265	105,475
12							
13	Other income (expenses)						
14	Interest income	4,500	4,500	4,500	4,500	4,500	22,500
15	Interest expense	(500)	(500)	(500)	(500)	(500)	(2,500)
16	Bonuses	4,642	4,202	5,072	5,666	6,731	26,314
17	Other	600	600	600	600	600	3,000
18							
19	Total other income (expenses)	9,242	8,802	9,672	10,266	11,331	49,314

```
06/14/89   17:11                              CIRC
```

♦ **Figure 10:13:** *Worksheet using different fonts in the default font set*

Adding New Fonts to the Font Set

To add a new font to the font set, you use the Replace option on the /Format Font menu. This brings up a new pull-down menu that displays the font choices for the current printer. Note that the printer that is current in 1-2-3 when you start Allways is also the current printer in this add-in program. If you have installed a second printer for 1-2-3, you can use it in Allways as well. However, you must first make it current by selecting the /Print Configuration Printer command.

Figure 10.14 shows you part of the font selections that appear when you select /Format Font Replace in Allways with the Epson FX80/100 selected as the current printer. As this is a dot-matrix printer with limited font capabilities, this list includes only three printer fonts: Pica, Pica Italic, and Proportional, in addition to the fonts supplied by Allways (which are considered to be *soft* fonts, as opposed to *printer* fonts).

To select a new font to use, you choose /Format Font Replace (/FFR). Make sure that the pointer is on a font you no longer wish to use in the report. Then move the pointer to the name of the font you wish to add, and press Enter. Allways will display a new pull-down menu containing size choices. In the case of printer fonts such as Pica (shown in the Figure 10.14), these size numbers will represent different pitches. In the case of soft fonts such as Courier, these size numbers will represent points. You then move the pointer to the size you wish to add and press Enter.

```
FONT(1) Triumvirate 10 pt                                    MENU

Select typeface

      TYPEFACE                    SIZE           E       F       G
    1 Triumvirate                 10 point      1993    1994    Total
    2 Triumvirate Italic          10 point     90,000  99,500  420,100
    3 Triumvirate                 14 point
    4 Triumvirate                 20 point     28,300  32,600  122,900
    5 Times                       10 point     20,785  20,785  103,925
    6 Times Italic                10 point     17,850  17,850   87,800
    7 Times                       14 point     66,935  71,235  314,625
    8 Times                       20 point
                                               23,065  28,265  105,475
 13  Other income (expenses)        TYPEFACE              KIND
 14    Interest income           1 Pica                   printer    500
 15    Interest expense          2 Pica Italic            printer    500)
 16    Bonuses                   3 Proportional           printer    314
 17    Other                     4 Courier                soft       000
 18                              5 Courier Italic         soft
 19  Total other income (expe    6 Times                  soft       314
 20
 21  Income (loss) before taxe                                       789
 22  Provision (benefit) for taxes    4,096   3,708   4,476  5,000  5,939  23,218
06/14/89  11:44                                CIRC
```

♦ **Figure 10.14:** *Choosing a new font to add to the default font set*

Restoring or Updating the Default Font Set

If you find that you have replaced a font in error or wish to restore the default font set for any other reason, you can do so by selecting the Restore option on the /Format Font Default menu (/FFDR). Doing this will immediately reestablish the font choices as they are saved in the default font set.

If, on the other hand, you find that you would prefer the replacements you have made to the original default font set to be permanent and become the new default font set for Allways, you can accomplish this simply by selecting the Update option on the /Format Font Default menu (/FFDU).

Saving and Reusing Modified Font Sets

Allways enables you to save the changes you make to the current font set in its own file. To save your modifications, you select the Save option from the /Format Font Library menu (/FFLS), then enter a file name (using the same rules as you apply when naming worksheets), and press Enter. Allways automatically appends the extension .AFS (Allways Font Set) to the file name you enter.

To use an AFS file that you have created, you select the Retrieve option on the /Format Font Library menu (/FFLR). This brings up a full-screen listing of all AFS files in the current directory. To retrieve a file so that you can use its fonts, you simply move the pointer to the file you wish to make active and press Enter.

Use the Erase option on the /Format Font Library menu to delete a font set that you no longer need or want (/FFLE). As when retrieving an AFS file, you then have to indicate the file name, either by typing it or pointing it out. Note that erasing font sets differs from erasing worksheet files in 1-2-3, because Allways won't ask you to confirm your deletion: as soon as you indicate the name and press Enter, the file is erased. Furthermore, if you're using Release 2.2, you can't use the Undo feature to retrieve this file. As a result, be very careful when using this option to clear out old AFS files.

Enhancing the Report with Attributes on the /Format Menu

Fonts are not the only enhancements that you can add to your Allways reports using the /Format menu. You can also add boldfacing, underlining, color, outlining, or shading to a single cell or multiple cell range (Figure 10.9).

Figure 10.15 shows you how some of these attributes appear on the screen in Allways. In this figure, the shading is applied to the title in cell A1 by selecting the Shade Light option. The column headings in the row below it are outlined with the Lines Outline option, and the revenue figures in the row below this are individually outlined with the Lines All option. The row headings in column A are boldfaced with the Bold Set option. The single underlining separating the rows containing the general and administrative costs and the total

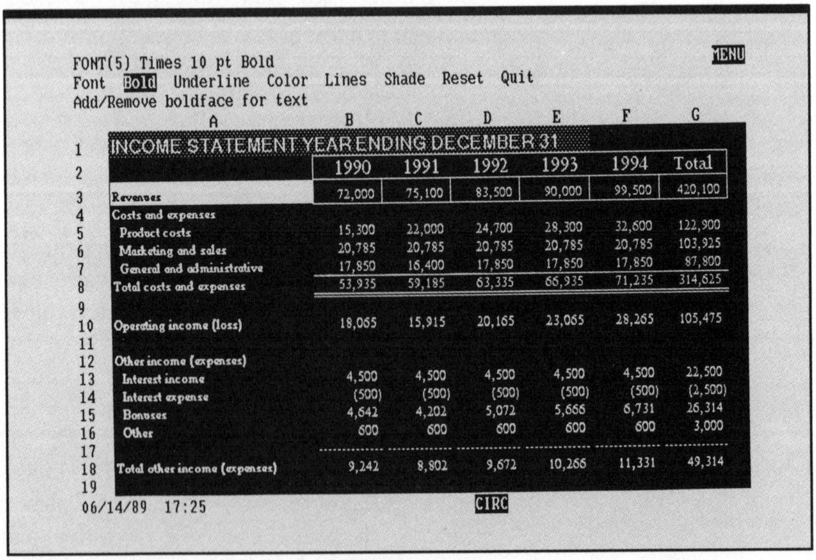

◆ **Figure 10.15:** *A typical worksheet displaying a variety of Allways attributes*

costs and expenses is created by selecting the Lines Bottom option, and the double underlining below the total costs and expenses rows is created by selecting the Underline Double option.

Boldfacing Ranges in the Worksheet

To add boldfacing to the worksheet, you select the /Format Bold Set command (/FBS) and indicate the range to be emboldened. If you wish to remove the bold attribute, you can do so by selecting /Format Bold Clear (/FBC) and indicating the range. Instead of these menu commands, you can use the accelerator key Alt-B to toggle bold on and off. Remember that to add or remove bold from more than the current cell, you must have already highlighted the range before you press Alt-B.

Underlining Ranges in the Worksheet

Allways offers you two underlining choices. To underline a range of cells with single underlining, you use /Format Underline Single (/FUS). To underline a range with double underlining, you use /Format Underline Double. As with all other attributes on the /Format menu (except Color), you use the Clear option on the /Format Underline menu to remove either type of underlining from a particular cell or range in the worksheet.

Allways provides an accelerator key, Alt-U, that can be used to select single underlining, double underlining, or no underlining at all. This accelerator key cycles through these choices, affecting the highlighted range or, if no range is selected, the current cell.

Note that when you use single underlining, the program places underscores only under the characters that have been entered in each cell of the selected range. When you use double underlining, however, Allways places double underscores across the entire width of each cell of the selected range, whether the cells are empty or not.

Assigning Colors to Ranges in the Worksheet

If you have a color printer, you can assign colors to different cells and cell ranges in the worksheet by selecting /Format Color and then choosing the number (between 1 and 8) of the color you wish to use (Figure 10.9 lists the color choices). Note that unlike assigning colors with the PrintGraph program, the color choices on this menu never vary in Allways: you always select 1 to use Black, 2 to use Red, and so on. This doesn't mean, however, that your printer can necessarily produce all of the colors on this menu. Note also that option 8, Red-on-negs, instructs Allways to print all negative numbers in the report in red.

Drawing Lines and Outlining Ranges in the Worksheet

The Lines option on the /Format menu offers you several options for drawing rules or outlining ranges in the worksheet:

Outline Left Right Top Bottom All Clear

You select the Outline option to have lines drawn around the perimeter of a particular range. Select the Left option if you want the line drawn only along the left edge of the range; the Right option to have it drawn only along the right edge of the range; the Top option to have it drawn only along the top edge of the range; or the Bottom option to have it drawn only along the bottom edge of the range. You select the All option only when the range consists of more than one cell and you wish to have lines drawn along all edges of every cell in the range. As usual, select the Clear option when you want to remove any type of lines that you added to the worksheet.

Although Allways includes an accelerator key, Alt-L, you can use it only to select the Outline, All, or Clear option on the /Format Lines menu. If you want to use the Left, Right, Top, or Bottom option, you must do so from this menu.

Note that when you add lines to a cell, the contents in the control panel indicates their type by using abbreviations for the direction. For instance, if you place the pointer in a cell that has been outlined with the All option, you will see

LINES:LRTB

after the name of the font. In this designation, *L* stands for left, *R* for right, *T* for top, and *B* for bottom.

Shading Ranges in the Worksheet

You can apply three types of shading to areas of the worksheet: light, dark, and solid black. The light and dark shading can be applied to cells that contain text or numbers to draw attention to them in your report. The solid black shading can be used to create thick horizontal or vertical lines in the report. Don't ever apply this type of shading to cells that contain labels or values that you want displayed in the printed report. Unlike light or dark shading, solid shading makes it impossible to read any text to which you apply it.

To shade an area of the worksheet, select the /Format Shade command and then choose between:

Light Dark Solid Clear

After choosing the option, you indicate the range to be affected, as when applying any other format in Allways. Remember that the Allways accelerator key, Alt-S, can also be used to select light, dark, solid, or no shading for the selected range or current cell.

Changing Column Widths and Row Heights in the Report

As you change the fonts and add attributes to your reports in Allways, you will find occasions when you need to adjust the column widths or row heights to accommodate your modifications. This is an especially common situation after you have selected a new font for part of the report, especially those in much larger or smaller type sizes. Such adjustments are made with the Set-Width option on the Allways /Worksheet Column and /Worksheet Row menus, shown in Figure 10.10.

Unlike 1-2-3, where you can only increase or decrease the width of worksheet columns, Allways allows you to increase or decrease the height of worksheet rows as well. By increasing or decreasing the height of rows in the worksheet, you can introduce more or less vertical space between lines of the report. Understand, however, that changes made to the size of the worksheet columns and rows in Allways have no effect on their counterparts in the 1-2-3 worksheet. This means that if you narrow column A from 27 to 23 characters using Allways' /Worksheet Column Set-Width command, it will continue to be 27 characters when you return to 1-2-3. Also, realize that increasing the height of the row in Allways never has any effect on its height in 1-2-3. This means that if you increase the height of a row from 12 to 18 points using Allways' /Worksheet Row Set-Height command, it will continue to be 12 points high when you return to 1-2-3.

The Set-Width and Reset-Width options on the /Worksheet Column menu and the Set-Height option on the /Worksheet Row menu in Allways work much like corresponding options on the /Worksheet Column menu in 1-2-3. This means that you can change the width of the current column either by typing in the number of characters (between 1 and 240) or by pressing the ← or → key until the column is the width you desire, and then pressing Enter. When setting a new height for the current row, you can either enter the number of points (between 0 and 255) or press the ↑ or ↓ key until the row is the height you want it.

Selecting the Reset-Width option on the /Worksheet Column menu immediately resets the current column to the width it has in 1-2-3. The counterpart of the Reset-Width option on the /Worksheet Row menu is the Auto option. When you select this option, Allways resets the height so that it can accommodate the largest size of type it contains.

Note that you can change the width of multiple columns or the heights of multiple rows simply by highlighting the range of columns or rows before selecting either the Set-Width option from /Worksheet Column or the Set-Height option from /Worksheet Row.

Special Formatting Commands

Allways contains some special formatting commands that make it easy to format worksheets of the same type or to copy formats to areas of the same worksheet. These commands are located on the /Special menu, shown in Figure 10.16.

Copying and Moving Formats to Ranges in the Worksheet

The /Special Copy and /Special Move commands on this menu allow you to copy or move the format of a cell or cell range to a new range in the same worksheet. Note that although these commands use the same prompts as their 1-2-3 counterparts, /Copy and /Move, they copy or move *only* the format of the source range to the target range (they never affect the data of the worksheet itself). This means that you can use these commands to copy or move the font, boldfacing, underlining, lines, colors, and shades of the source range to the target range and nothing more. The /Special Copy command makes it easy to format tables of the same type in the worksheet by adding the fonts and attributes to the first table and then copying them to all other similar tables.

Copying Formats from Other Worksheets

Not only can you copy formats from one range to another within the same worksheet, but you can also copy formats from one worksheet to another with

◆ **Figure 10.16:** *The Allways /Special menu tree*

the /Special Import command. With this command, you can add the fonts and attributes saved in one worksheet to the worksheet you are currently working on (Allways saves all report settings in a separate file using the same name as the worksheet but with the .ALL extension, when you save the worksheet with /File Save).

To use /Special Import, your worksheet needs to use the same layout as the one whose format you wish to copy. When you select the name of the ALL file whose formats should be imported, Allways removes any formats that you've already assigned to the worksheet and replaces them with those in the ALL file.

Justifying Text in an Allways Report

In addition to the /Special commands for moving or copying formats (either within or between worksheets), this menu contains a Justify option, which is used like the Justify option on the 1-2-3 /Range menu, to format long labels in a cell or cell range. The Allways /Special Justify command is used to wrap text in accordance with the fonts and attributes you've selected for the range in Allways. Because Allways allows you to vary the type size (unlike 1-2-3), you will often find that the ranges you have formatted with /Range Justify in the worksheet require the use of /Special Justify in Allways after you select a new font for the range.

You use the /Special Justify command just like you do /Range Justify. Select the command, indicate the range within which you want the text justified, and press Enter to reformat the long labels in the range. If this justify range is not large enough to accommodate the reformatted text, the program will beep, go into ERROR mode, and display the message

Justify range too small—text would be truncated

At this point, you have to press Esc or Enter to return to ALLWAYS mode and then redo the command, this time increasing the size of the justify range.

Page Layout in Allways

Page formatting for Allways' reports is mostly accomplished with the options on the /Layout menu (Figure 10.11). As with 1-2-3, Allways supplies default layout settings, all of which you can modify. Figure 10.17 shows you these settings as they appear in the Allways layout settings sheet that appears when you choose /Layout.

In an Allways report, unlike a 1-2-3 report, you can set all four margins, and these margins are measured in inches from the edge of the sheet of paper. This means that a right margin of 1 is one inch from the right edge of the paper,

```
FONT(1) Triumvirate 10 pt                                              MENU
PageSize Margins Titles Borders Options Default Library Quit
Set page width and length


   Page Size: Standard (8.5 by 11 inches)

   Margins (in inches)        Borders            Options
       Left:  1.00              Top:                 Line weight: Normal
      Right:  1.00             Left:                 Show grid: No
        Top:  1.00           Bottom:
     Bottom:  1.00

   Titles
     Header:
     Footer:



17  Other                    600      600      600      600      600    3,000
18                        -------  -------  -------  -------  -------  -------
19  Total other income (expense:  9,242    8,802    9,672   10,266   11,331   49,314
20
21  Income (loss) before taxes  27,307   24,717   29,837   33,331   39,596  154,789
22  Provision (benefit) for taxes  4,096    3,708    4,476    5,000    5,939   23,218
06/15/89  11:59                              CIRC
```

◆ **Figure 10.17:** *The Allways /Layout menu with settings sheet showing the defaults*

whereas a bottom margin of 2 is two inches up from the bottom edge of the paper.

If you are using Allways on a laser printer, you can change the orientation of the printing from the default of portrait mode to landscape mode (using the /Print Configuration Orientation command). When you change to landscape mode, the print area on the page is rotated 90 degrees clockwise. Note that the margins rotate along with the print area, so the top margin in landscape mode is the one normally considered the right margin in portrait mode, and so on with the other three margins around the borders of the page, as shown in Figure 10.18.

Selecting a New Page Size

If you plan on using a different paper size in printing your Allways report, you need to select the PageSize option on the /Layout menu and then choose the number of the page size you are using. The size options that appear when you select the Page-Size option depend upon the type of printer you are using. For example, if the HP LaserJet Series II is the current printer, the size options will be:

1. Standard (8.5 by 11 inches)

2. Legal (8.5 by 14 inches)

3. Executive (7.25 by 10.5 inches)

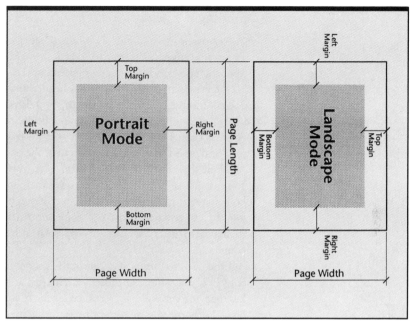

♦ **Figure** 10.18: *Portrait and landscape mode in Allways*

4. A4 (8.27 by 11.69 inches)

5. Custom

If, however, you make the Epson FX80/100 the current printer, option 3 on this menu will be Wide (14 by 11 inches) instead of Executive (7.25 by 10.5 inches).

If you are using a paper size that doesn't correspond to the first four size options, you need to choose Custom (press 5 and Enter). When you do, you will be prompted to enter the page width followed by the page length in inches (with up to two decimal places). The new page size you select for your report will be reflected at the top of the layout settings sheet.

Setting New Margins

To set new margins for your report, you select /Format Margins followed by the appropriate margin option (Left, Right, Top, or Bottom). As stated earlier, margins are measured in inches from the outer edges of the page. As you change the margins with the appropriate options on the /Layout Margins menu, your new values will be displayed under *Margins* on the layout settings sheet.

Adding a Header or Footer to Your Report

In Allways, you can define a one-line header and footer just as you do in 1-2-3. The main difference is that in Allways you select the Header or Footer option from the /Layout Titles menu (instead of the /Print Printer Options menu in 1-2-3). Also, if you don't define a header and footer for your report, Allways doesn't reserve three lines at the top and three lines at the bottom of the page (as 1-2-3 does, whether or not you define either one in the report). Instead, Allways begins printing the report at the top of the page at the top-margin setting, and ends the text at the bottom of the page at the bottom-margin setting.

When you create your header or footer, you can enter up to 240 characters. You can also use the @ symbol to have the current date printed and the # symbol to have the page number included. Note, however, that Allways has a command that enables you to change the initial page number in the report (remember that 1-2-3 always starts with 1) by using the /Print Settings First command.

If you need to format sections of the header or footer, you can use the vertical bar (|) to center or right-justify them, just as you do in 1-2-3 reports. Remember that one vertical bar (|) precedes the text to be centered, and two vertical bars (| |) precede the text to be right-justified. You can, however, left-justify, center, and right-justify different sections of the same header or footer by placing the bars before each section of text, as in the following example:

@ | CONFIDENTIAL | Page #

which would produce the following alignment:

03-Jul-90   CONFIDENTIAL Page 1

assuming that the current date is July 3, 1990, and this is the first page of the report.

Adding Borders to Your Report

Allways allows you to print title rows and/or columns on each page of a multiple-page report, just as you can in 1-2-3. To add borders to the report, you select the /Layout Borders command, which brings up the options

Top Left Bottom Clear Quit

Although you specify the border range in Allways just as you do for a 1-2-3 report, Allways gives you an extra option (Bottom). You use it in the rare cases where you want to designate a range of rows to be printed at the bottom of each page of the report.

On the /LB menu, the Allways Top option corresponds to the Rows option on the /Print Printer Options Borders menu in 1-2-3. You use this option to select a range of rows that are to be printed at the top of each page.

The Left option corresponds to the Columns option on the /Print Printer Options Borders menu in 1-2-3. You choose this option when you want to designate a range of columns to be printed on the left side of each page of the report.

Remember that just as in 1-2-3, any columns or rows defined as report borders are *not* to be included in the print range. This is to prevent the border columns and/or rows from being printed twice on the first page of the report.

Setting the Line Weight and Adding Grid Lines to the Report

The /Layout Options menu allows you to change the weight of all lines that you have added to the worksheet with the /Format Lines menu options or the Alt-L accelerator key, or to add grid lines. *Grid lines* are dotted lines that separate each column and row in the worksheet, thus outlining every cell. Note that when you turn on grid lines, Allways doesn't print the worksheet column letters and row numbers (this must still be done by adding them to the worksheet in 1-2-3); it only prints grid lines that help you line up the information across rows and down columns.

When you select LineWeight on the /Layout Options menu, Allways displays three choices: Normal, Light, and Heavy. Note that when you select one of these options, the new line weight affects *all* lines drawn with /Format Lines or Alt-L; there is no way to control the weight of individual lines in the report.

To add grid lines to your report, you select the /Layout Options Grid command and then select the Yes option. To turn them off again, use /Layout Options Grid and choose No. Remember that Allways also includes an accelerator key, Alt-G, that can be used to toggle grid lines on and off in the worksheet.

Saving and Reusing Your Page Layout Settings

Allways enables you to save your layout settings in separate files that can be reused in much the same way as you save and reuse font sets in AFS files with /Format Font Library commands.

To save the changes you've made to page layout settings in a separate file, you choose the /Layout Library Save command, and enter a new file name. Allways will append the extension .ALS (Allways Layout Settings) to your file name.

To retrieve an ALS file and activate its layout settings, you use /Layout Library Retrieve. Allways then displays a full-screen listing of all ALS files in the current directory. To retrieve a file from this list, move the pointer to it or type the file name, and press Enter. As soon as you complete this procedure, Allways makes current all settings saved in the file that you have retrieved.

To delete a page layout that was previously saved in an ALS file, you select the Erase option on the /Layout Library menu, then select the file name that contains the page layout settings you want to delete.

If you wish to institute new page layout defaults for Allways, you can do so by selecting the Update option on the /Layout Default menu. The program will then make whatever page layout settings are in effect the new program defaults. Should you select this option in error or wish to return to the settings saved as the previous defaults, select the Restore option from this menu.

Adding Manual Page Breaks to Your Report

The amount of data that will be printed on each page is determined by the size of the page and the margin settings in effect. Allways shows how much worksheet data will fit on each page by outlining its borders with dashed lines as soon as you define the print range with the Allways /Print Range Set command. The placement of the vertical dashed lines indicates how many columns will be printed on each page, whereas the placement of the horizontal dashed lines indicates how many rows will be printed on each page. Just as in 1-2-3, Allways will not print partial columns: if it cannot fit the entire column on a page, it moves the entire column to a subsequent page in the report.

Allways uses the same system as 1-2-3 to break the print range into pages and print these pages. If the print range exceeds the width of the page as well as the length, it first prints the page in the upper left portion of the print range, then the one below it, and so on until it prints the last row in the range. Then, the program moves to the top of the print range and prints the pages to the right of the first set, proceeding in this way until all data in the print range are printed.

Allways enables you to add your own page breaks, so you can prevent data that should stay together from being separated across pages by awkward column or row page breaks created by the program.

To add manual page breaks in Allways, you select the /Worksheet Page command and then choose the Row or Column option. If you wish to have certain rows at the bottom of one page printed on the following page, you select the Row option, move the pointer to the row that is to be the first row printed on the next page, and press Enter. Allways will then draw a horizontal dashed line (representing the manual page) that extends the entire width of the worksheet.

If you wish to have certain columns near the right edge of the page printed on the next page to the right (not necessarily the next page printed), you select the Column option, move the pointer to the column that is to be the first column on this page, and press Enter. Allways will then draw a vertical dashed line representing this manual page break that extends the entire length of the worksheet.

To remove a manual page break, you first choose the Delete option on the Allways /Worksheet Page menu (/WPD). Then, to delete a column page break, move the pointer somewhere in the column that is immediately to the right of the vertical dashed line that represents the manual page break (that is, the first column of the new page) and press Enter. To delete a row page break, select /WPD, move the pointer somewhere in the row immediately below the manual page break you wish to remove (that is, the first row of the new page), and press Enter.

Incorporating Graphs into Your Reports with Allways

One of the greatest strengths of Allways as a publishing utility is its ability to incorporate 1-2-3 graphs in the report you create. In allowing you not only to import graphs but also to size them and position them as you wish in relation to the worksheet data, Allways overcomes a major weakness in 1-2-3's report capabilities. With Allways, you can bring in up to 20 graphs in a single worksheet, positioning them as you see fit.

The 1-2-3 graphs that you bring into Allways must already be saved as PIC files (with the /Graph Save command in 1-2-3). Note that if you make changes to a graph in 1-2-3 that you've already placed in the worksheet with Allways, the changes will be reflected in Allways only after you use /Graph Save in 1-2-3 to save the changes in the PIC file.

To attach PIC files to the current worksheet, you use the Allways /Graph menu. The options on this menu are shown in Figure 10.19.

Adding Graphs to the Worksheet

To add a graph to the current worksheet, you select the /Graph Add command (/GA). Allways will then display a line listing of all PIC files in the current directory (this line listing also takes up the entire screen). You select the graph file you wish to add by either moving the pointer to its name or typing in the file name (including path, if the file isn't located in the same directory), and press Enter. The program will then prompt you to enter the range for the graph (you will notice that the range is automatically anchored on the current cell). In response, you can point out the range to contain the graph or type in the range address and press Enter. If you are indicating the range by pointing and find that the range isn't anchored on the correct cell, press Esc (as you would in 1-2-3) to unanchor the range, then move the pointer to the correct cell, and type a period to anchor the range on this new cell.

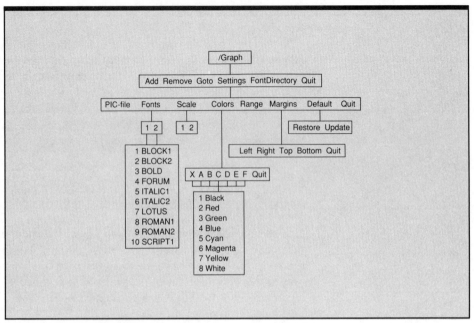

◆ **Figure 10.19:** *The Allways /Graph menu tree*

The graph range that you indicate determines not only the position of the graph in the worksheet but also its size. Be careful not to make the range too narrow or too short for the graph. If you do, Allways will still bring the graph into the worksheet, but you won't be able to read it either on the screen or in the printed report. To rectify such a situation, you need to choose the /Graph Settings Range command (/GSR) and modify the size of the graph range accordingly.

Viewing the Graphs on the Screen   When Allways attaches the graph to the range you have defined, it doesn't show the graph but rather a cross-hatched box, indicating its size and position in the worksheet. To have the program display the graph itself in this range, you need to turn on the graph display by selecting /Display Graphs Yes Quit (/DGYQ) or pressing the Graph key (F10) when the program is in ALLWAYS mode.

Once you have previewed the graph to see if it's the one you want and to see if the range that contains it is large enough, you will want to turn the graph display off again by selecting /Display Graphs No Quit (/DGNQ) or pressing the Graph key (F10) again. Keeping the graph display turned off avoids the considerable slowdown in the program's response time that occurs when Allways has to redraw the graphs in detail on the screen each time you select a command or move the pointer in the worksheet.

Locating the Directory Containing the 1-2-3 Graph Fonts   In order to display and print graphs, Allways uses the 1-2-3 graph fonts that you assigned to the graph when using the PrintGraph program. If you turn on the graph display and Allways can't find these 1-2-3 graph font files (the FNT files usually stored in the same directory as 1-2-3), the program will beep, go into ERROR mode, and display an error message explaining that it can't read the graph font that you selected as Font 1 for the graph. When you press Esc to get out of ERROR mode, the program will draw the graph but won't include any of its titles or labels.

To then have the titles and labels added to the graph, you have to select the /Graph FontDirectory command (/GF) and enter the name of the directory that contains the 1-2-3 font files. As soon as you press Enter (assuming that you've entered the correct directory), Allways will redraw the graph (or graphs) on the screen, this time including all titles and labels.

Finding a Particular Graph in the Worksheet   The Allways /Graph menu includes a Goto option to make it easy to locate a particular graph in the worksheet. When you select /Graph Goto (/GG), Allways displays a pull-down menu showing the file names of all the graphs you've added to the current worksheet. To move the pointer directly to the first cell of the range that contains a particular graph, you just type its number or use the ↑ or ↓ key to move the pointer to its name in the list, and then press Enter.

Deleting a Graph from the Worksheet   If you no longer need a graph that you've added to a worksheet or have added one in error, you can use the /Graph Remove command (/GR) to delete it. When you select this command, just as when you select /Graph Goto, Allways displays a pull-down menu showing the file names of all graphs added to the current worksheet. To remove a graph, type its number or use the ↑ or ↓ key to move the pointer to it before you press Enter. As soon as you press Enter, Allways removes the graph. Note that if you are using Release 2.2, you can't undo this deletion with the Undo key: you'll have to redo the /Graph Add procedure to restore the graph you just removed to its former place in the worksheet.

Modifying the /Graph Settings

Each graph that you add to your worksheet has its own settings sheet. The graph settings displayed on this sheet include the path name of the PIC file; the worksheet range that contains the graph; the left, right, top, and bottom margins from the outer edges of the graph range; the fonts assigned to Font 1 and Font 2; the scale factor assigned to each of these fonts; and the colors assigned to each graph range.

To display the settings sheet and change any of these settings, you need to select the /Graph Settings command (/GS). If the pointer is located on a graph in the worksheet, Allways will then bring up the Settings menu and display its settings sheet for that graph. If the pointer isn't located on any of the graphs in the worksheet, you first have to select the graph from a pull-down menu showing the file names before the program will display the /Graph Settings menu options along with its settings sheet. Figure 10.20 shows you the /Graph Settings menu options and the settings sheet for a graph named VCRLNE.PIC.

Replacing the Graph   The PIC-file option on the /Graph Settings menu is used to replace the current graph with another graph. This allows you to change graphs without having to use /Graph Remove and then /Graph Add. When you enter a new PIC file after selecting this option, Allways replaces the graph with the selected file using the graph range currently defined on the settings sheet.

Modifying the Graph Fonts and Scaling Them   Allways allows you to change the fonts used in printing the graphs if the ones that were selected in PrintGraph aren't appropriate. To change the font, select the Fonts option on the /Graph Settings menu. If you want to modify Font 1, select option 1. If you want to modify Font 2, select option 2. Whenever you select either option, you are presented with a pull-down menu displaying 10 of the 11 fonts available in

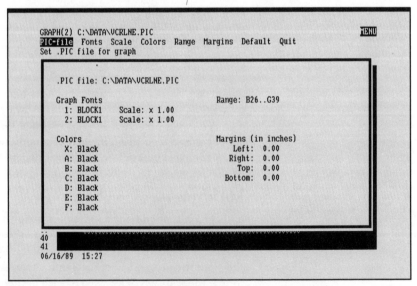

◆ **Figure 10.20:** *The Allways /Graph Settings menu with settings sheet*

PrintGraph (to select the Script2 font, you must scroll the selections). To select a new font, move the pointer to its name or type its number (be aware that typing 1 will probably select 11 and then 12 before it chooses 1) and press Enter. Unlike in 1-2-3, when you select a new font for Font 1 in Allways, the choice for Font 2 remains unchanged.

In addition to selecting the font to be used in printing your graphs, Allways enables you to adjust the size of the text in graphs by applying a scaling factor to Font 1 and/or Font 2. To change the size of the font, you select the Scale option on the /Graph Settings menu followed by 1 to adjust Font 1, or 2 to adjust Font 2. Then, you enter a number between 0.5 and 3 representing a scale factor. The default scale factor of 1 produces the text at the same size as PrintGraph, and a scale factor of 2 would produce text twice as large.

When applying a scale factor to Font 1 or Font 2, you need to display the graph before printing the report to make sure that none of the text overlaps. This often happens when the graph contains many titles and labels (first and second titles as well as data labels and legends) and you increase the size of the text. By displaying the graphs when using the Scale option, you can experiment with the scale factor until you achieve the best text size for the graph.

Selecting Colors for Printing the Graph   If you are printing your Allways reports with a color printer, you can use the /Graph Settings Colors option to assign colors to each data range in the graph. You assign colors to each range after selecting /GSC by choosing the appropriate range letter (X or A–F). Unlike 1-2-3, however, where the color choices differ according to the type of printer you are using, the color choices are unvarying in Allways (refer to Figure 10.19 for the color options). Remember that the color you choose for the X range is the color used to print the majority of the graph, including the frame, graph elements, first and second titles, and x-range labels.

Modifying the Graph Range   The Range option on the /Graph Settings menu is used to change the size and/or location of the graph range. When you select /Graph Settings Range (/GSR), Allways displays the current graph range on the screen. To change the size of the range without moving it, you can then use the cursor-movement keys to increase or decrease the highlighting (you can also press the period key to change the anchor cell, just as you can in 1-2-3). To move the range, press Esc to unanchor the range, then move the pointer to the first cell of its new location, type a period to anchor, move the pointer to the last cell, and press Enter.

Setting Margins in the Graph Range   When you select the graph range for your graph, Allways sizes the graph so that it uses the entire range. If you

wish, you can add left, right, top, and bottom margins that specify the amount
of space between the graph and the outer borders of the graph range. The
graph margins are set in inches, just like the report margins. To set graph margins, choose the appropriate margin (Left, Right, Top, or Bottom) from the
/Graph Settings Margins menu, then enter the number of inches (you can
enter up to two decimal places), and press Enter. The /Graph Settings menu is
a "sticky" menu, so you can enter new values for as many of the margins as you
wish before selecting the Quit option to return to the /Graph Settings menu.

Restoring or Updating the Default Settings   The Default option on the
/Graph Settings menu allows you to restore the default settings to the current
settings sheet or to save its modified settings as the new graph default settings.

To restore the default graph settings, you choose the Restore option from
/Graph Settings Default menu (/GSDR). To save the current graph settings as
the new default, select the Update option from this menu instead (/GSDU).

Printing with Allways

Printing with Allways is similar to printing in 1-2-3 using the /Print Printer
menu. Figure 10.21 shows you the options on the Allways /Print menu. As is
true in 1-2-3, you can't print a report in Allways until after you have defined
the print range. In this program, you use the /Print Range Set command (/PRS)
to do this. When you are prompted to enter the print range, you can indicate it
by pointing, typing the range address or range name, or selecting the range
name from a pull-down menu after pressing the Name key (F3). As in 1-2-3,
you can press the period key to move the anchor cell, which makes it easier to
increase or decrease the range on a particular side by using the pointer-
movement keys.

After you set the print range for the report, the program indicates the page
breaks on the screen by drawing a dashed line around the boundaries of each
page. If, in examining the page breaks, you find that a graph is going to be split
across pages, you will need to resize or relocate the graph before you print the
report. If you see that a table of data is going to split across pages, you can try
using a smaller font for the table or inserting a manual page break to have it
printed on a subsequent page.

When you are ready to print, you can send the report either to the printer, by
selecting the Go option on the /Print menu (there is no Align option in
Allways), or to a disk file by selecting the File option. Allways keeps you
informed of its progress by displaying the number of the row that is currently
being printed. As in 1-2-3, you press Ctrl-Break to stop the printing at any time
before the program reaches the end of the print range.

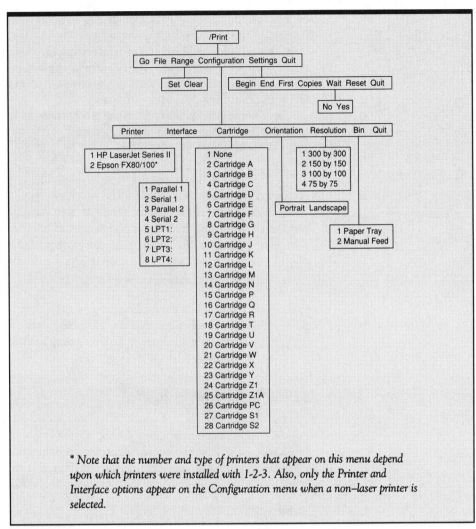

* *Note that the number and type of printers that appear on this menu depend upon which printers were installed with 1-2-3. Also, only the Printer and Interface options appear on the Configuration menu when a non-laser printer is selected.*

♦ **Figure 10.21:** *The Allways /Print menu tree*

Printing to Disk in Allways

The /Print File command in Allways, which is used to create a disk file containing the report, does not work exactly the same way as the /Print File command in 1-2-3 (see Chapter 13). In 1-2-3, you use /Print File to create a text file version of the print range saved in ASCII format. This type of file doesn't include specific printer codes for producing attributes such as bold and under-lining.

In Allways, you use /Print File to create a disk file version of the print range that contains *all* codes required by your printer to produce all the special attrib-utes used in the print range (including graphics, if this range includes graphs and your printer has graphics capabilities).

When you select /Print File, Allways prompts you to enter the name of the file in which this information is to be saved. If you don't add an extension to this file name, Allways will automatically append the extension .ENC (for Encoded file) to it.

The encoded file that is created by Allways should be printed from the DOS prompt after you exit from Allways and 1-2-3, using the DOS COPY command with the /B switch. When you use the DOS COPY command, you must specify the name of the file as well as the interface to which the file is to be sent. For example, to print the file named SUMMARY.PRN with the printer that is con-nected to the first parallel port, LPT1, you would enter the command

COPY   SUMMARY.PRN/B   LPT1:

and press Enter at the DOS prompt. Note that the /B switch entered after the name of the file causes no end-of-file codes to be sent to the printer. If you don't include this switch, some printer codes may be misinterpreted as end-of-file codes, causing the printing to stop prematurely.

Selecting the Printer to Use

You can use any printer that you've installed for use in 1-2-3 in printing your Allways report. Choose the /Print Configuration Printer command (/PCP), and select its number from the pull-down menu that appears. The number and type of printer options that are displayed when you select this command depend upon how many and what type of printers you installed in 1-2-3. Remember that if you select a printer that uses an interface different from the previously selected printer, you must choose the appropriate port option on the /Print Configuration Interface menu (/PCI) before trying to print your Allways report.

Laser Printer Configuration Options   When you select a laser printer such as the HP LaserJet Series II with the /Print Printer menu, Allways adds four new options—Cartridge, Orientation, Resolution, and Bin—to the /Print Configuration menu (shown in Figure 10.21). When you select a laser printer such as the LaserWriter Plus, Allways adds only the Orientation, Resolution, and Bin options, because this laser printer doesn't use cartridges.

Figure 10.21 shows you the 28 cartridge options that appear on the /Print Configuration Cartridge menu when you select the HP LaserJet as the printer to use. To use the fonts on a particular cartridge, you must have that cartridge inserted in one of the printer's slots and select its number from this menu.

To change the orientation of the print area from the default of portrait to landscape for a laser printer, you select the Landscape option from the /Print Configuration Orientation menu (/PCOL). Remember that in landscape mode, Allways rotates the print area 90 degrees clockwise. As part of this rotation, the margins are shifted so that the top margin remains the one above the print area (see Figure 10.18).

The Resolution option on the /Print Configuration menu allows you to change the printing resolution, which is measured in dots per inch. The default is 300 by 300, the best resolution that the laser printer is capable of. You may find, however, that if your printer has only 512K memory (standard for the HP LaserJets), Allways cannot print a complex page when it uses many formatting attributes and includes 1-2-3 graphs. If Allways gives you an *Out of memory* error message when you are printing a report, you can try printing it again after decreasing the resolution (also try disabling the Undo feature if you're using Release 2.2). For example, you might try printing it after selecting the 100 by 100 Resolution option, as this requires quite a bit less printer memory than the 300 by 300 option.

The Bin option on the /Print Configuration menu offers only two options: Paper Tray (the default) or Manual Feed. If you are using a paper size that you must feed to the laser printer manually because you don't have the proper paper tray, be sure to remember to select the Manual Feed option from this menu before printing the Allways report.

Modifying the Print Settings

The Allways /Print Settings menu options enable you to print just single pages or a selected range of pages in the report, set a page number other than 1 for the first page of the report, indicate the number of copies to be printed, and have the printer pause after printing each page of the report. Figure 10.22 shows you the options on the /Print Settings menu and the settings sheet that appears when you select it.

To reprint just selected pages of the report, you choose the Begin option and enter the starting page number (between 0 and 9999), then choose the End option and enter the ending page number (between 0 and 9999). If you have changed the number of the first page with the First option, you need to enter starting and ending page numbers that reflect this change. For example, if you

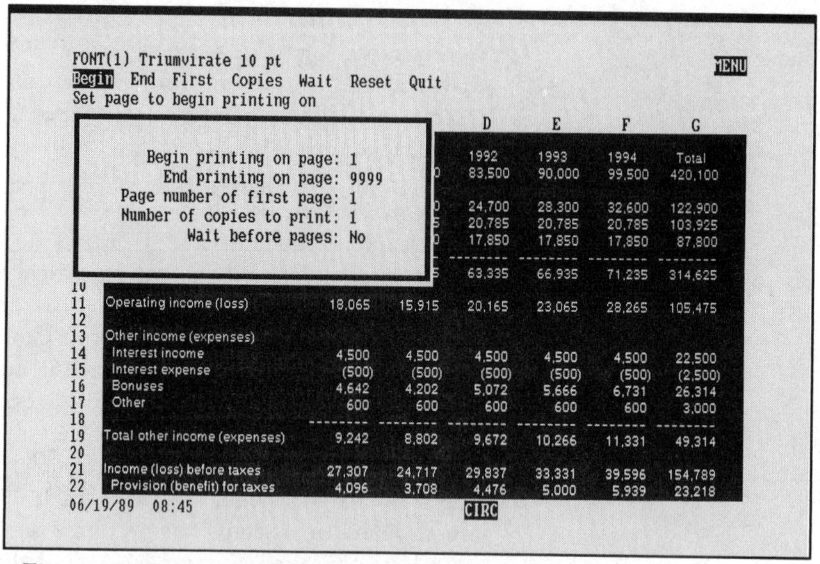

◆ **Figure 10.22:** *The Allways /Print Settings menu with settings sheet*

need to reprint the second and third pages of the report but have set the first page number to 4, you would enter 5 as the starting page with Begin and 6 as the ending page number with End, because 5 is the new page number of the *second* page of the report and 6 is the page number of the *third* page.

The First option on the /Print Settings menu allows you to specify a page number other than the default of 1 when you have used the # symbol in a header or footer. To have the page numbering begin with a new number, you select the First option and enter a number between 0 and 9999.

Allways also includes a setting for printing multiple copies of the report. Unlike 1-2-3, where you have to repeat the /Print Printer Align Go command to print subsequent copies of the same print range, Allways enables you to do this by selecting the Copies option on the /Print Settings menu and then specifying the number of copies to be printed (between 1 and 9999).

The Wait option on the Allways /Print Settings menu is used just like the Wait option on the 1-2-3 /Worksheet Global Default Printer menu: to pause the printer after printing each page of the report. To turn this feature on, you select the Yes option on the /Print Settings Wait menu. To restore continuous printing at any time, you then choose the /Print Settings Wait No command.

To reset all the print settings to their default values, you can choose the Reset option on the /Print Settings menu rather than selecting each option on this menu and reentering the default value.

Creating Your Own Reports in Allways

Now you are ready to perform the following printing exercise with Allways. This exercise is designed to show you how easy it is to create great-looking reports with this add-in program. It assumes that you have already installed Allways and attached it to add-in key Alt-F7 (see the instructions for installing and loading the program at the beginning of this chapter, if you still need to do this).

1. **Retrieve the worksheet file** *IS5YRCH9.WK1*.
   In this report, you will outline and underline the title in A1 to make it stand out. To underline it with a heavy black line, you need to insert a blank row in the worksheet, to which you will assign solid shading. Also, you'll use Allways' double underlining for the totals in rows 8, 18, and 24 instead of the repeating hyphens and equal signs added in 1-2-3. This means that you will need to delete or hide them in worksheet.

2. **Move the pointer somewhere in row 2 and insert a blank row here; then delete row 9 and row 19, which contain the repeating hyphens, and hide the repeating equal signs in the range B23..G23 with the Hidden format.**
   Now that you have made these modifications in the worksheet, you are ready to start Allways and begin formatting the report.

3. **Start Allways by pressing Alt-F7, and press the Home key to move the pointer to cell A1.**
   You will begin formatting the report by adding the lines to it. Start by outlining range A1..G1, which holds the title.

4. **Select /Format Lines Outline (/FLO), then move the pointer down to cell A2 and over to G2 so that the range A1..G2 is highlighted, and press Enter.**
   Allways has outlined the specified range. Next, you will outline each cell in the summary income statement by using the All option on the /Format Lines menu.

5. **Move the pointer to cell A3, select /Format Lines All (/FLA), and move the pointer over to cell G3 and then down to G23 to highlight the range A3..G23, and press Enter.**
   Each cell in the range you selected should now be outlined. Now you should select a larger font for the title.

6. **Press Home to move the pointer to A1; select /Format Font (/FF), then type 7 and press Enter to select Times 14 point; press Enter again to select the default range of A1..A1.**

Note that although the title is now quite a bit larger, it is not centered across the top of the report. Centering is the one area that Allways is weak in: to center this title, you must return to 1-2-3 and insert spaces preceding the text to push the title to the right. You won't know what effect this has on the centering of the title, however, until you return to Allways.

7. **Press Esc to return to 1-2-3, then press the Edit key (F2); next, press Home and the → key to position the cursor after the apostrophe but before the first word in the title; then press the spacebar 17 times (only 15 times if you are using a laser printer such as the HP LaserJet) and press Enter; return to Allways by pressing Alt-F7.**

   The title should appear pretty well centered in the outlined range. Now see how it would look if you change the font to an italic style. To do this, you will have to replace one of the fonts in the default font set. In this case, you can replace Times 20 point with Times Italic 14 point, and then apply it to cell A1.

8. **Select /Format Font (/FF), then press the ↓ key to highlight 8 *Times* and select the Replace option (R); press the ↓ key to highlight *Times Italic*, press Enter, then press the ↑ key to highlight *14.00* and press Enter; finally, select the Use option (U) and press Enter to apply the new font to the title in A1.**

   See how this font looks in bold.

9. **Press Alt-B to boldface the title in cell A1.**

   Next, you will add the underline in row 2 by adding solid shading to the range A2..G2 and then decreasing the height of this row.

10. **Select /Format Shade Solid (/FSS), then move the pointer to G2 and press Enter.**

    The line as it stands now is much too thick; use the /Worksheet Row Set-Height command to make it thinner.

11. **Select /Worksheet Row Set-Height (/WRS), press the ↑ key until the row is only 4 points high, and then press Enter.**

    With the title set in 14 point, you need to add more vertical space in row 1.

12. **Move the pointer to A1, select /Worksheet Row Set-Height (/WRS), press the ↓ key until the row is 21 points high, and then press Enter.**

Now you are ready to format the column headings in row 3. You will use a larger font for these headings and make them bold.

13. **Move the pointer to cell B3, which contains 1990, then type a period to anchor the range and move the pointer to G3; press Alt-B to boldface this range, then select /Format Font, type 3, and press Enter to select Triumvirate 14 point.**
Notice that you save some keystrokes by selecting the range before you select the font from the Allways menus. Next, you need to increase the height of this row.

14. **Select /Worksheet Row Set-Height; press the ↓ key until the row is 20 points high, then press Enter.**
For the body of the report in the range B4..G22, you will use the Times font in 10 point size; for the row headings in the range A4..A22, you will use the Times font in 12 point size. Begin by assigning Times 10 point to the body of the report.

15. **Move the pointer to cell B4, type a period to anchor, then move the pointer to G22; select /Format Font (/FF), type 5, then press Enter.**
To use the Times font in 12 point size, you must replace one of the fonts in the default font set: in this case, you will replace the Times Italic font (6).

16. **Move the pointer to cell A4, type a period to anchor, then move the pointer to A22; select /Format Font (/FF), type 6, then select the Replace option (R). Next, press the ↑ key once to highlight *Times*, press Enter, then press the ↓ key once to highlight *12.00*, and press Enter again; finally, select the Use option (U), and press the Home key to move the pointer to cell A1.**
Your report should now look like the one shown in Figure 10.23. You're almost ready to print this report, but before you do, you should add some light shading to the rows and column that contain totals to make them stand out. When you do, you will also boldface the numbers so that they contrast better against the gray background.

17. **Move the pointer to G3, type a period to anchor, and move the pointer down to G22; then press Alt-S to add light shading to the range and Alt-B to boldface it.**
Notice how quickly you assign attributes by using the accelerator keys on a range that is already selected. Next, you will apply these same affects to the ranges A9..F9, A18..F18, and A22..F22. After adding

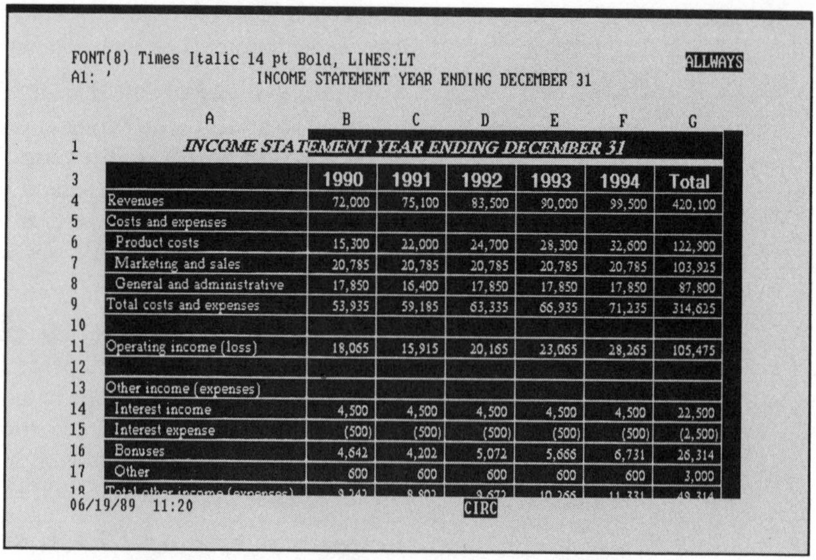

◆ **Figure 10:23:** *Income statement report after changing the fonts*

the shading and boldfacing to these ranges, you can also add double underlining to each row of totals. Start by adding these attributes to the totals in row 9.

18. **Move the pointer to cell A9, type a period to anchor it, then move the pointer to F9; press Alt-B, then press Alt-S; move the pointer to cell G9, type a period to anchor it, move the pointer to A9, and press Alt-U twice to add double under-lining across the whole row of the report; select the /Worksheet Row Set-Height command and increase the height to 17 points.**

The first time you press Alt-U, Allways adds single underlining to the values in each cell. The second time you press it, however, the pro-gram adds double underlining across all cells in the range. You need to follow this same procedure in rows 18 and 22 of the report.

19. **Apply bold and light shading to the cell range A18..F18, then apply double underlining to the range G18..A18; next, repeat this procedure of assigning bold and light shading in the cell range A22..F22.**

Instead of double underlining for the net earnings figures in row 22, you will add a thick underline in row 23 by using solid shading and then narrowing the height of the row.

20. **Move the pointer to cell A23, select the range A23..G23, press Alt-S three times to select solid shading, then make the height of this row 4 points.**
    With the highlighting extended across the entire range, you can't see the solid shading you've assigned, so press the → key to reduce the pointer to a single cell.

Previewing, Saving, and Printing Your Report

The report is ready to be printed. To do this, you must define the print range. Then, before sending the report to the printer, you will use the Reduce key to preview it. You will also learn how to save the report so that it can be reused.

1. **Select /Print Configuration and check that the printer and interface listed in the settings sheet are correct; if they are correct, select the Quit option (Q) to return to ALLWAYS mode; if they aren't correct, select the Printer and/or Interface option and choose the proper printer and port before selecting the Quit option.**
    Next, you are ready to define the print range for the report.

2. **Press the Home key to move the pointer to cell A1, select /Print Range Set (/PRS), then move the pointer to cell G23 and press Enter; select the Quit option (Q) to return to ALLWAYS mode.**
    If you're using a LaserJet with only 512K memory, you may get an *Out of memory* error message when you try to define the print range (press Esc to clear the error message and then Enter to finish defining the print range). In such a case, you must exit from Allways and select the /Worksheet Global Default Other Undo Disable Quit command (/WGDOUDQ) to free up sufficient memory before you try to print this report. Once you've set the print range, notice that two vertical dashed lines appear on your screen: one between columns F and G and the second along the right edge of column G. This means that column G won't be printed on the first page with the rest of the columns. Before you take care of this problem, you should use the Reduce key to make sure that all rows in the print range will fit on one page.

3. **Press the Reduce key (F4) until you can see all 23 rows on the screen (you will have to reduce the display to Tiny to view the entire print range).**

The dashed line between rows 23 and 24 in the display tells you that all the rows in the print range will fit on the same page. Now try narrowing the widths of the columns in the print range to fit them on one page.

4. **Press the Enlarge key (Shift-F4) twice to return to the normal-size view; then move the pointer to a cell in column B, type a period to anchor, and press the → key to include columns C through G; select /Worksheet Column Set-Width, press the ← key once, and press Enter to reduce the width of these six columns to 8 characters each.**

   If you are using a laser printer such as the HP LaserJet Series II, as soon as you press Enter to narrow the columns, you will notice that the second vertical dashed line has disappeared. If you are using a dot-matrix printer such as an Epson FX80 or FX100, you will still see the two vertical dashed lines. To take care of this paging problem for this type of printer, you must decrease the width of column A slightly (if you are using a LaserJet, leave the column set at 27).

5. **Move the pointer to a cell somewhere in column A and narrow the column from 27 to 26 characters.**

   That should take care of this paging problem for both types of printers, but it will introduce a new one: in narrowing the columns sufficiently to print the entire worksheet on one page, the title is no longer centered on the page. To prevent it from being printed too far to the right, you must remove some of the spaces.

6. **Press Esc to return to 1-2-3; move the pointer to cell A1 and press Edit (F2), followed by the Home and → keys; then press the Del key four times to remove this many spaces from the title; return to Allways by pressing Alt-F7.**

   Make sure that the printer is on and loaded with paper. If you have manually fed the paper, you need to select the Yes option on the /Print Settings Wait menu before you start the printing.

7. **Select /Print Go to print the report.**

   Figure 10.24 shows the report as it appears when printed with an HP LaserJet. Now you are ready to save the Allways report.

8. **Press Esc to return to 1-2-3 and save the file under the same name with the /File Save command.**

   Allways provides no save command of its own, but it will save your report when you save the worksheet in 1-2-3 with the /File Save command. In this case, the program saves the report under the file name *IS5YRCH9.ALL*.

INCOME STATEMENT YEAR ENDING DECEMBER 31						
	1990	**1991**	**1992**	**1993**	**1994**	**Total**
Revenues	72,000	75,100	83,500	90,000	99,500	420,100
Costs and expenses						
Product costs	15,300	22,000	24,700	28,300	32,600	122,900
Marketing and sales	20,785	20,785	20,785	20,785	20,785	103,925
General and administrative	17,850	16,400	17,850	17,850	17,850	87,800
Total costs and expenses	53,935	59,185	63,335	66,935	71,235	314,625
Operating income (loss)	18,065	15,915	20,165	23,065	28,265	105,475
Other income (expenses)						
Interest income	4,500	4,500	4,500	4,500	4,500	22,500
Interest expense	(500)	(500)	(500)	(500)	(500)	(2,500)
Bonuses	4,642	4,202	5,072	5,666	6,731	26,314
Other	600	600	600	600	600	3,000
Total other income (expenses)	9,242	8,802	9,672	10,266	11,331	49,314
Income (loss) before taxes	27,307	24,717	29,837	33,331	39,596	154,789
Provision (benefit) for taxes	4,096	3,708	4,476	5,000	5,939	23,218
Net earnings (loss)	23,211	21,009	25,362	28,332	33,657	131,571

♦ **Figure 10.24:** *The Allways income statement report printed on a LaserJet printer*

Adding a Graph to Your Allways Report

In this exercise, you will add the stacked-bar graph *TOTEXPSB.PIC*, which you created in the preceding chapter, at the bottom of this report. Remember that to add a graph to a worksheet, you must save the graph in a PIC file with the /Graph Save command in 1-2-3 and then attach that file to the report in Allways.

Begin this exercise by verifying that the graph you wish to add to your report is indeed in the current directory.

1. **While you are still in 1-2-3, select /File List Graph (/FLG) and look for the** PIC **file** *TOTEXPSB.PIC* **in the full-screen listing, then press Enter to return to the worksheet.**

    If you didn't see this graph file listed, you probably need to copy the file from another data disk or another directory (refer to Chapter 13 for information on copying files).

2. **Start Allways by pressing Alt-F7, then press the Goto key (F5), type A24, and press Enter.**
   Now you are ready to add the stacked-bar graph.

3. **Select /Graph Add (/GA), press the End key to move the pointer to the end of the file name listing, press the ← key until *TOTEXPSB.PIC* is highlighted, and press Enter; move the pointer first right to cell G24 and then down to G40 to highlight the range A24..G40 as the graph range before pressing Enter.**
   You will see a crosshatched box representing the graph in the cell range A24..G40. You should preview the graph to make sure you've chosen the right one.

4. **Select the Quit option (Q) to return to ALLWAYS mode, then press the Graph key (F10) to view the graph.**
   If you get an error message telling you that Allways can't find the BLOCK1 font, you know that the font directory isn't correct. To change this, press Esc, then select /Graph FontDirectory and enter the letter of the drive and name of the directory that contains the FNT files (usually the same one that contains 1-2-3 and PrintGraph). When you get the graph drawn correctly, notice how close the Y-Axis and First titles and legend labels are to the left, top, and bottom boundaries of this range. To add some space, you will set margins for the left, top, and bottom of the graph. Doing this will allow you to draw an outline around the graph range, joining it to the rest of the report. But first, before you do this, you should lengthen the graph by adding more rows to the graph range.

5. **Press the Graph key (F10) again; then select /Graph Settings Range (/GSR), press the ↓ key until the range A24..G43 is highlighted, and press Enter.**
   Now make the left, top, and bottom margins of the graph about 1/8 inch each.

6. **Select Margins Left (ML), type *.12*, and press Enter; then select Margins Top (MT), type *.12* again, and press Enter; and finally, select Margins Bottom (MB), type *.12* a third time, and press Enter.**
   Now you are ready to outline the graph range and see how it looks.

7. **Select the Quit option twice (QQ) to return to ALLWAYS mode; then select /Format Lines Outline (/FLO), move the**

pointer to cell G43 so that the range A24..G43 is highlighted,
and press Enter.

Now is a good time to preview the graph once again.

8. **Press the Graph key (F10) to view the graph on the screen.**
   Your screen should look like the one shown in Figure 10.25. Before
   you print the report again, you should change the fonts used in the
   graph so that they harmonize better with the fonts used here and add
   a solid underline in row 44 to mark the end of the page.

9. **Press the Graph key (F10), move the pointer to A44, type a
   period to anchor the range, move the pointer to cell G44,
   and press Alt-S three times to select solid shading; then,
   reduce the height of row 44 to 4 points.**
   To change the fonts, you must return to the /Graph Settings menu.

10. **Select /Graph Settings (/GS) and press Enter to select TOTEX-
    PSB.PIC; next, select Fonts 1 (F1), type 7, and press Enter to
    choose Lotus for Font 1; then, select Fonts 2 (F2), type 9,
    and press Enter to choose Roman2 for Font 2.**
    View the graph now to see how these font changes look.

11. **Select the Quit option (Q), then press the Graph key (F10).**
    Notice that Lotus is an italic font like the one you chose for the
    report title at the top of the page. Now you are ready to print the
    final report. To do this, remember that you must expand the print
    range to include the graph you've added.

12. **Press the Graph key (F10), select /Print Range Set (/PRS) and
    press the ↓ key until the range is extended to row 44
    (A4..G44), then press Enter and select the Go option (G) to
    begin printing.**
    Note that if you are using Release 2.2 with only 640K RAM, you must
    not try printing this expanded report, which includes the stacked-bar
    graph, before you have disabled the Undo feature. If you do, you will
    surely get an *Out of memory* error as soon as the printer reaches the
    first line of the graph in row 24. After printing the report, you need
    to save it. Figure 10.26 shows you the printed report produced on an
    HP LaserJet.

13. **Press Esc to return to 1-2-3, then save the worksheet under
    the same name with the /File Save command (/FS), using the
    Replace option (R).**

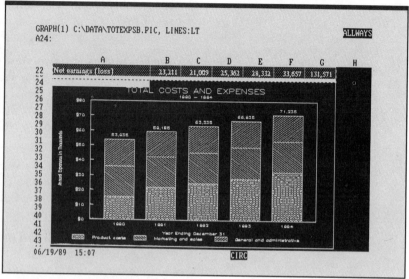

◆ **Figure 10.25:** *Stacked-bar graph added to the income statement report*

Summary

Troubleshooting

Question: When I selected the Go option on /Print menu in Allways after creating a report, nothing printed. What can be the trouble?

Answer: There are several possibilities, but the most likely—assuming that you haven't forgotten to define the print range, the printer is turned on, and the printer cable is secure—is that the wrong printer or, at least, the wrong type of interface is selected. To check this, select the /Print Configuration command (/PC) and examine the printer and interface listed in the settings sheet. If the printer needs to be changed, select the Printer option (P) and choose the number of the correct one shown in the pull-down menu. If the printer port is not correct, select the Interface option (I) and select the number of the port used by the printer. After making these changes, try printing the report again.

Question: When printing my report, Allways suddenly went into ERROR mode, displaying the *Out of memory* error message. What steps can I take to get my report printed?

INCOME STATEMENT YEAR ENDING DECEMBER 31						
	1990	1991	1992	1993	1994	Total
Revenues	72,000	75,100	83,500	90,000	99,500	420,100
Costs and expenses						
Product costs	15,300	22,000	24,700	28,300	32,600	122,900
Marketing and sales	20,785	20,785	20,785	20,785	20,785	103,925
General and administrative	17,850	16,400	17,850	17,850	17,850	87,800
Total costs and expenses	53,935	59,185	63,335	66,935	71,235	314,625
Operating income (loss)	18,065	15,915	20,165	23,065	28,265	105,475
Other income (expenses)						
Interest income	4,500	4,500	4,500	4,500	4,500	22,500
Interest expense	(500)	(500)	(500)	(500)	(500)	(2,500)
Bonuses	4,642	4,202	5,072	5,666	6,731	26,314
Other	600	600	600	600	600	3,000
Total other income (expenses	9,242	8,802	9,672	10,266	11,331	49,314
Income (loss) before taxes	27,307	24,717	29,837	33,331	39,596	154,789
Provision (benefit) for taxes	4,096	3,708	4,476	5,000	5,939	23,218
Net earnings (loss)	23,211	21,009	25,362	28,332	33,657	131,571

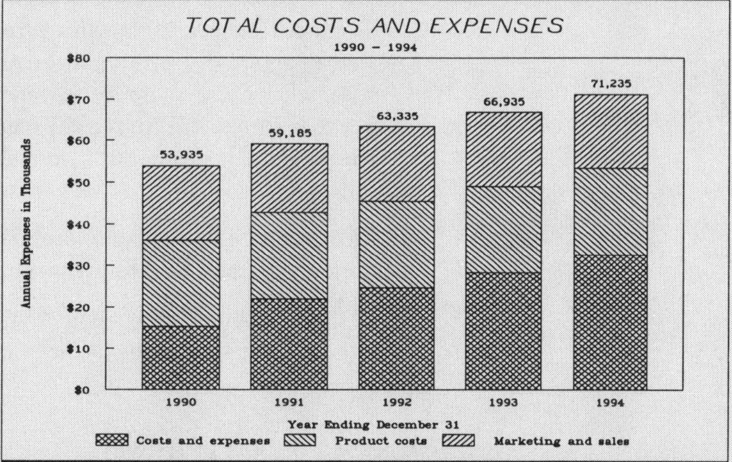

- **Figure 10.26:** *Allways income statement report with graph printed on a LaserJet printer*

Answer: If you are using Release 2.2, you should immediately clear the error by pressing Esc, and then exit from Allways and return to 1-2-3 by pressing Esc again. Check the status line in 1-2-3. If you see the UNDO status indicator, select the /Worksheet Global Default Other Undo Disable command (/WGDOUD). Next, quit the /Worksheet Global Default menu, restart Allways, and try printing your report again. If you are using a laser printer to print the report, you can also try selecting a lower resolution if you still get an *Out of memory* error. To do this, select the /Print Configuration Resolution command (/PCR), then choose a resolution such as 75 by 75 or 100 by 100 from the pull-down menu. If, after reducing the resolution, you still get an *Out of memory* error, you will have to reduce the size of the print range. Try especially to reduce the range to the point that it contains fewer graphs or no graphs at all.

Essential Techniques

To Attach and Start Allways

1. Start 1-2-3 as you normally would.

2. Type /A if you're using Release 2.2, or press Alt-F10 if you're using Release 2.01, to select the Add-In menu. Select the Attach option (A) from this menu, then highlight the file *ALLWAYS.ADN*, and press Enter. Select the key with which to start this add-in program (7, 8, 9, or 10 in Release 2.2, and 7, 8, or 9 in Release 2.01).

3. To start Allways without exiting from the Add-In menu, select the Invoke option (I), then highlight *ALLWAYS*, and press Enter. Otherwise, select the Quit option (Q) and then press Alt plus the function key that corresponds to the key number you choose when attaching the program. For example, if you selected 7, you press Alt-F7 to start Allways.

4. To exit from Allways and return to 1-2-3, press Esc or select the Quit option (/Q) from the Allways menu.

5. To detach Allways and free up RAM, select the Add-In menu (/A or Alt-F10), then select the Detach option (D), highlight *ALLWAYS*, and press Enter.

To Create a Report in Allways

1. Retrieve the worksheet in 1-2-3 for which you wish to develop the Allways report.

2. Start Allways (see technique above).

3. Select the fonts you wish to use in the report, and assign them to the various ranges in the worksheet using the /Format Font menu options.

4. Select the attributes—bold, underlining, shading, and outlining—that you wish to add to the report using the options on the /Format menu (or the accelerator keys Alt-B, Alt-U, Alt-S, and Alt-L).

5. Change the width of the columns and height of the rows to suit the fonts and attributes that you have selected with /Worksheet Column Set-Width and /Worksheet Column Set-Height.

6. Add a header and/or footer, define border columns or rows, make any changes to the page size, margins, or line weight, or add grid lines using the options on the /Layout menu.

7. Make sure that the printer is correct by selecting the /Print Configuration menu (/PC). Select the range to be printed using the /Print Range Set command (/PRS), then send the report to the printer using the Go option (G).

8. Save the Allways report by exiting from the program (press Esc or select the Quit option on the Allways menu) and then using the /File Save command in 1-2-3.

To Add a Graph to Your Report

1. Select the /Graph Add command (/GA), select the PIC file from the line listing by moving the pointer to it, and press Enter. Indicate the range to hold the graph either by typing in the range address or range name, or by pointing it out.

2. Select the Quit option (Q) on the /Graph menu to return to ALLWAYS mode, then press the Graph key (F10) to view the graph.

3. To delete a graph from the worksheet, select the /Graph Remove command (/GR), then select the graph file name from the pull-down menu by typing its number or moving the pointer to it and pressing Enter.

4. To replace a graph, use the /Graph Goto command (/GG) and then select the graph file name from the pull-down menu to make current the graph you wish replaced. Next, select /Graph Settings PIC-File (/GSP), select the file name of the graph to replace the current graph from the line list, and press Enter.

5. To change the size or location of a graph, use the /Graph Goto command (/GG) and then select the graph file name from the pull-down menu to make the graph current. Next, select /Graph Settings Range (/GSR). To resize the graph, move the pointer to change the extent of the highlighting and press Enter. To move the graph, press Esc to unanchor the range, move the pointer to the beginning of the new range, type a period to anchor, move the pointer to the end of the new graph range, and press Enter.

6. Assign new fonts to Font 1 and Font 2, increase or decrease the size of the fonts, print different parts of the graph in different colors, or add margins in the graph range, by using the appropriate options on the /Graph Settings menu.

Review   Important Terms You Should Know

accelerator key	printer font
font set	pull-down menu
pitch	soft font
point	WYSIWYG

Test Your Knowledge

1. To be able to use Allways, your computer system must be equipped with _____.

2. In loading Allways in Release 2.2, you can assign the key combination _____, _____, _____, or _____ to it.

3. If you need to remove Allways from RAM in order to load another add-in program or increase the size of your worksheet, you need to select the _____ option on the Add-In menu.

4. To add bold to the current cell in Allways, you can select _____ on the Allways menu or press the accelerator key _____.

5. To double-underline a range of cells using the Allways accelerator key, Alt-U, first you need to _____ using the _____ method, then press Alt-U _____ times.

6. To draw a heavy black line that is three characters wide between columns in an Allways report, you need to highlight the range of cells in that column using the pointing method, then press the accelerator key _____ three times. Then, you need to select the _____ command and reduce the width to three characters.

7. To create a header in the report that prints the current date aligned with the right margin, you select the Header option from the _____ menu and then enter _____.

8. To print the range B3..B10 in an Allways report in Triumvirate Italic 10 point, you must select the _____ option on the /Format menu, then type _____ and press Enter to select this font, and finally, highlight the range B3..B10 and press Enter.

9. To print the title in cell A2 in Courier 20 point bold (by replacing Times 14 point), you need to move the pointer to cell A2, select the _____ option on the /Format menu, then type _____ to select Times 14 point, choose the _____ option, type _____ to select Courier, move the pointer to _____ in the pull-down menu, and press Enter. Finally, to apply this font to cell A2, you select the _____ option on the /Format Font menu.

10. To save the changes you've made to the default font set under the name *BUDGFNT*, you select the _____ option from the _____ menu, then type _____ and press Enter. When you wish to use this font set again, you select the _____ from the same menu and select the font file from the line list. Allways automatically appends the extension _____ to *BUDGFNT* so that it will appear as _____ on this menu.

11. To add the 1-2-3 graph COSTBAR.PIC to your report in cell range A25..G32, you select the _____ option on the /Graph menu, then highlight the graph file name on the line list, press Enter, and indicate the _____ by typing in the range address or pointing it out.

12. To print a report for the first time, you must first indicate the print range by selecting the _____ option on the /Print Range menu. To start printing the range, you choose the _____ option. To save the print range in a file (print to disk), you select the _____ option and enter a file name for it. If you don't add an extension of your own, Allways will automatically append _____ to it.

13. Allways indicates the boundaries of page breaks by drawing _____ lines on the screen. To prevent a graph from being split between the bottom of page 1 and the top of page 2 of a report, you would move the pointer to the _____ that is to apppear first on the following page and then select the _____ option on the /Worksheet Page menu.

14. To preview a report to make sure that it is paged properly, you can reduce the worksheet display from the normal size to the smallest size by selecting the _____ option on the _____ menu or by pressing the Reduce key (_____) _____ times.

Further Exercises

1. Retrieve the worksheet *IS5YRCH6.WK1*. Delete rows 8, 18, and 24 from the worksheet.

2. Start Allways and then create the report shown in Figure 10.27. Outline the range A1..G21. Add the lines between columns B, C, D, E, and F. Add the lines above and below rows 3, 10, 17, and just above 21. Assign the font Triumvirate 14 point bold to the title in cell A1, and center it in the outlined area. Increase the height of this row to 20 points. Assign the font Times 10 point bold to the column headings in row 2, then increase the height of the row to 14 points. Add light shading to the outlined area at the top of the report as shown in Figure 10.27. Assign the font Times Italic 12 point to cells A3, A10, A17, and A21. Boldface the ranges B3..G3, B10..G10, B17..G17, and B21..G21. Increase the height of rows 3, 10, 17, and 21 to 17 points. Add light shading to the last row of this report as shown in Figure 10.27.

INCOME STATEMENT YEAR ENDING DECEMBER 31						
	1990	1991	1992	1993	1994	Total
Revenues	72,000	75,100	83,500	90,000	99,500	420,100
Costs and expenses						
Product costs	15,300	22,000	24,700	28,300	32,600	122,900
Marketing and sales	20,785	20,785	20,785	20,785	20,785	103,925
General and administrative	17,850	16,400	17,850	17,850	17,850	87,800
Total costs and expenses	53,935	59,185	63,335	66,935	71,235	314,625
Operating income (loss)	18,065	15,915	20,165	23,065	28,265	105,475
Other income (expenses)						
Interest income	4,500	4,500	4,500	4,500	4,500	22,500
Interest expense	(500)	(500)	(500)	(500)	(500)	(2,500)
Bonuses	4,642	4,202	5,072	5,666	6,731	26,314
Other	600	600	600	600	600	3,000
Total other income (expenses)	9,242	8,802	9,672	10,266	11,331	49,314
Income (loss) before taxes	27,307	24,717	29,837	33,331	39,596	154,789
Provision (benefit) for taxes	4,096	3,708	4,476	5,000	5,939	23,218
Net earnings (loss)	23,211	21,009	25,362	28,332	33,657	131,571

◆ **Figure 10.27:** *Revised Allways income statement report*

3. Define the print range as A1..G21. Narrow the columns as required to print the entire range on one page, and then print two copies of this report. Exit from Allways, and save the worksheet under a new file name, *IS5YCH10*.

Part III

♦

Data Management and Analysis in 1-2-3

♦

11

The Database Environment

In This
Chapter...

Definition of a Database

A 1-2-3 *database* is a table of related worksheet data organized in columns and rows. Each column of the table is called a *field* and represents a particular category of information in the database. For example, consider the product database shown in Figure 11.1. This database contains four fields: product number in column A, item description in column B, price in column C, and quantity in column D. Notice that the data in each of these fields consists of the same type of information.

A 1-2-3 database field can be one of two types: character or numeric. If a field is the character type, all of its entries must be labels (that is, preceded by some type of label prefix). If a field is the numeric type, all of its entries must be values (in the form of numbers or formulas).

Each row of the table is called a *record* and represents a collection of information about each item in the database. For instance, in the product database in Figure 11.1, each row gives you complete information about each piece of furniture carried by the store.

In a 1-2-3 database, the first row must contain the *field names*, that is, labels that describe what type of information each field (column) contains. The field names that you assign must be unique within the database. In Figure 11.1, the field names are PRODUCT#, DESCRIPTION, PRICE, and QUANTITY in row 2 of the worksheet.

The row below the one that contains the field names for your database must contain the first record; you must not insert a blank line or one that contains repeating dashes to separate the field names from the first record. If you enter the field names for your database in row 2, as they are in Figure 11.1, then row 3, by necessity, will contain the first record.

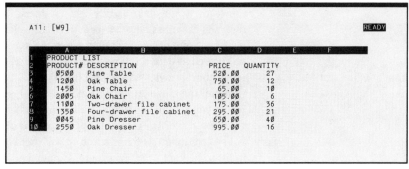

♦ **Figure 11.1:** *Product database*

Because the database uses the columns of the 1-2-3 worksheet as fields, you are constrained to a maximum of 256 fields in any database. And because the database uses the rows of the worksheet as records and must reserve the first row for the field names, you are limited to a maximum of 8,191 records (one less than the total of 8,192 rows).

Designing a 1-2-3 Database

In designing a 1-2-3 database, you must first decide which information you need to track and maintain. This process requires looking carefully at the overall purpose of the database and then deciding what constitutes a complete record within it.

After deciding these aspects, you must then determine the best way to split up the information into separate fields in each record. For instance, in a client or personnel database you have a choice of how to keep the names of each person. You could keep each full name in its own field, or split each part of the name into two or more separate fields. Doing the former may make it more difficult to rearrange the data and use it in other applications, such as mailing labels or form letters; doing the latter will require using more columns of the worksheet.

After deciding which items require their own fields, you need to decide what type of field (character or numeric) each should be. In making this decision, you can use the following rule of thumb: make all fields character unless they contain date or time numbers or contain values that you might need to use in calculations. For example, you would make a zip code field a character field and enter all of its numbers as labels because its data are *never* used in calculations. You would make a price field a numeric field, however, and enter all of its numbers as values because its data could well be used in calculations (such as quantity times price to obtain the extended price). Also, note that dates should be entered as date serial numbers with the @DATE function and times as time serial numbers with the @TIME function.

In making these types of decisions, it helps to try to think of every type of report you will have to produce from the database. Often, particular requirements of the reports determine what items must be kept in individual columns.

The last design step is to come up with field names that best describe the data items to be kept in each column. Remember, each field name must be unique and can only be entered in a single cell of the first row of the database.

Creating the Database

Once you have decided the fields to use and their field names, you must decide where to locate the database in the worksheet. To maximize the number of records that the database can contain, you should always enter the field names in the first few rows of the worksheet. Then, to allow for expansion of the database, you should not enter any other data below the last record in the database, leaving all the columns used as fields free for the database (all the way down to the last row of the worksheet). To minimize the amount of memory used by the database, you will probably want to make column A or one close to it the first field of the database.

If you need to add another database to the worksheet, place it in the columns to the right of the database, making sure that you leave at least one blank column between the last field of the first database and the first field of the second database that you add to its right.

After deciding which columns to use and which row to begin with, you need to enter the field names in the first row. After that, vary the width of each column according to the longest entry you anticipate it will hold (you may end up having to change the column width several times based upon the data you enter there).

Entering Records in the Database

When entering records in the database, don't skip any rows: always append each new record to the bottom of the database by adding to the row immediately below the last one used. That way, the database remains a single range that is easier to maintain and manipulate.

Entering data in the fields of the database is no different from entering data into any 1-2-3 worksheet cell. The same distinction exists between entries made as labels and values as in spreadsheet applications. In fact, you may find that the biggest problem in doing data entry in a 1-2-3 database is remembering when you need to preface an entry with the apostrophe label prefix to ensure that it is entered as a label in a field that you have decided should be a character field.

This is not so much a problem with entries such as *123 Elm Street* in an address field, because 1-2-3 won't accept such a mix of numbers and letters *unless* you add a label prefix, but it can be a problem when entering numbers such as 99234 in a zip code field. In this case, 1-2-3 will accept such an entry without complaint, and you may not notice that it is entered as a value while the rest of the entries in the field are entered as labels until you begin obtaining unexpected results when you sort the database or search it for data meeting your criteria.

Suffice it to say that it is very important to maintain complete consistency with regard to the type of entry you make in each database field. If the field is a character field, make sure all its entries are labels. If the field is a numeric type, make sure that all its entries are values.

After entering new records in the database, you can format fields containing labels with the /Range Label Format command, changing them from their left-justified default setting to either centered or right-justified. Conversely, you can also format fields containing values to any of the numerical or date formats available from the /Range Format command.

Using /Data Fill to Number Records in a Database

Unlike some stand-alone database management software, 1-2-3 does not automatically assign a record number to each record as it is added to the database. Without such record numbers, you may find it difficult, if not impossible, to rearrange the records in their original order once you sort the database with /Data Sort, should such a step become necessary. By adding a field for record numbers, you can easily restore the original order simply by sorting on the record number field. Note that you can always keep the record numbers from being printed in a final database report by using the /Worksheet Column Hide command to temporarily remove the record number field from the print range.

When you first create the database, you can easily add such record numbers to your database by first entering all the records, then inserting a new column in the worksheet to create a new field and using the /Data Fill command to assign a consecutive number to each record. Most often, you won't want to add these record numbers until after the database has been sorted to the most favored arrangement, such as last name, first name alphabetical order with the /Data Sort command (see next section).

When you use the /Data Fill command to automatically enter a sequence of numbers in the worksheet, you must indicate four things: the fill range (that is, the range of cells that is to contain the sequence of numbers), the start value (0 is the default), the step value (1 is the default), and the stop value (8191 by default). When you finish entering these four items, 1-2-3 enters a sequence of numbers in the fill range beginning with the start number, incrementing each number in the following cell of the range by the step number until either the range is filled or the stop value is reached. Note that in the event that 1-2-3 reaches the stop value before filling the entire fill range, the program erases the remaining cells in the range.

Figure 11.2 demonstrates the use of /Data Fill to assign numbers to each record entered in the product database. The first step in this process was to insert a new column in the worksheet at the beginning of the database (in column A) for the new record number field, and then to enter its name *REC#* in cell A2. Next, the pointer was moved down to cell A3, then /Data Fill was selected. The cell range A3..A10 was made the fill range, 1 was used as the start and step values, and 8191 was accepted as the stop value. Finally, column A was narrowed from 9 to 5 characters with the /Worksheet Column Set-Width command.

The use of the /Data Fill command is not limited to numbering records in 1-2-3 databases. In fact, it can be used in any worksheet that requires the entry of a series of numbers, so long as the numbers increase or decrease by a constant amount throughout the entire series. Remember, however, that if you use a negative value as the stop value, the start value *must* be larger than the stop value (since you are diminishing the start value by the step value either until you reach the lesser stop value or fill the entire range). Also, keep in mind that you don't have to enter a number when defining the start, step, or stop values to be used in /Data Fill: the program will accept a formula that calculates a value as well as a cell reference, range address, or range name containing a value or a formula that returns a value.

Sorting the Database

Once the database has been set up and all the initial data have been entered, you will often want to sort its records in a new preferred order. As you continue to add new records to the database, you will need to re-sort the database to maintain the preferred order. You may also find times when you need to sort

♦ **Figure 11.2:** *Using /Data Fill to create record numbers for the product database*

the database in a different order to meet a special need. For example, although you might normally keep your client database sorted by last name and first name, you would sort it by zip code prior to using it to generate mailing labels.

Rearranging the order of the records in a 1-2-3 database is a fast and effortless process. To sort your data, you use the /Data Sort command. When you select this command, 1-2-3 displays the following options:

Data-Range Primary-Key Secondary-Key Reset Go Quit

If you are using Release 2.2, the program will also display a Sort Settings sheet beneath these options, which keeps track of the data range and sorting keys that you set up (Figure 11.3). Note that the /Data Sort menu, like the /Graph menu, is a sticky menu that allows you to select more than one option without returning to READY mode. Also, it contains a Reset option that is used to clear all sort settings in one operation.

Defining the Data Range

The first option, Data-Range, is used to indicate which data are to be rearranged during sorting. You indicate this range after selecting /Data Sort Data-Range (/DSD) as you do any range in 1-2-3 (by entering the range address or range name or pointing).

When sorting the records of a database, you must be careful that you don't include the row of field names at the top of the database as part of the /Data Sort data range. Therefore, be sure that the data range you define includes only the rows that hold records, but that it includes all the records. Also be sure that you include *all* the fields in the database. Otherwise, the fields that aren't included in the range won't be rearranged along with those that are included when you sort the database, thereby mixing fields from the different records and corrupting the entire database.

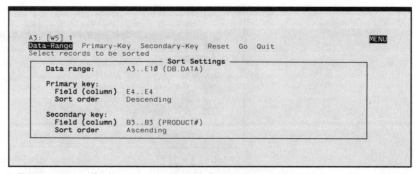

♦ **Figure 11.3:** *The /Data Sort menu with the Sort Settings sheet*

Defining the Sorting Keys

The /Data Sort command allows you to sort the records of the database on up to two different keys. A *sorting key* is the field of the database whose values determine the new order in which the records are arranged during sorting. The first key is defined by using the Primary-Key option, and the second with the Secondary-Key option. When defining either key, you only have to indicate the column that contains the field (the row is unimportant and can even be outside the confines of the data range).

Either sorting key can be specified in either *ascending order* or *descending order*. In ascending order, 1-2-3 arranges numbers in standard numerical order (lowest to highest) and letters in standard alphabetical order (from A to Z, ignoring capitalization). In descending order, 1-2-3 arranges numbers in reverse numerical order (highest to lowest) and letters in reverse alphabetical order (Z to A, ignoring capitalization).

When you select ascending order using a character field as the key that contains both numbers and letters entered as *labels*, 1-2-3 arranges the numbers (from lowest to highest) before the letters (from A to Z). When you select descending order using such a key, 1-2-3 reverses this order, arranging the numbers (from highest to lowest) after the letters (from Z to A). Note that you can change this default sorting sequence, called Numbers First, by changing the collating sequence in the Install program (a technique discussed later in this chapter).

After you select either the Primary-Key or Secondary-Key option and indicate the column containing the field to be used as that key, the program will display the prompt

Sort order (A or D): D

To accept the default of descending (D), you just press Enter. To change the sort order to ascending, type A and press Enter. Note that 1-2-3 remembers the sort order that you select for each key and will make that the new default until you change it again or end the work session.

You only need to define a secondary key when the primary key that you define allows for duplicates that need to be arranged in an order different from the way they were originally entered. The most common example of this is when sorting the database alphabetically by the last name field. Those people with the same last names will be listed together in the order their records were entered. If you need to refine this sort, you would select the column containing the first name field as the secondary key and perform the sort on both last and first name fields in ascending order. In this way, all records for people with the same last name would be arranged alphabetically by their first name, regardless of the order in which the records were originally entered.

Performing the Sorting Operation

After defining the data range, primary key, and secondary key (if required), you select the Go option to have 1-2-3 perform the sorting operation. Remember to always save a copy of the worksheet in its original order before performing the sorting arrangement. This allows you to retrieve a copy of it in its previous order should you specify the wrong data range or keys to be used. If you are using Release 2.2, however, you can use the Undo key (Alt-F4) to restore the database to its original order.

Although sorting is normally associated with arranging records in a database, it can also be used to rearrange any data in a spreadsheet. Just be sure when using it to sort data that the data range you specify does not include any column headings, or these will be sorted into the resulting arrangement. Also, be sure the data range does include any row headings that are supposed to remain part of the row whose data may be rearranged.

Sorting on More Than Two Keys

Even the new release of 1-2-3, Release 2.2, doesn't allow you to sort on more than two keys (although Release 3.0 does). When you need to sort the data on more than two keys, you must perform a couple of sort operations with the /Data Sort command to arrive at the final desired order.

For instance, to sort the personnel database shown in Figure 11.4 so that it is in the order shown in Figure 11.6 (that is, arranged alphabetically first by department, then by position, and finally by last name) requires two sorting operations using different keys. (The reason for sorting on a third key is to arrange the people in the Sales department, because they all have the same position title of Account Executive.)

The first time the database is sorted, it is done by defining the POSITION field (column E) as the Primary-Key and the LAST.NAME field (column C) as the Secondary-Key (both in ascending order). After the database is sorted, you use the /Data Fill command in the REC# field in column G to renumber the records now ordered alphabetically by position and then last name (Figure 11.5). Then use the /Data Sort command a second time, this time defining the DEPT field (column D) as the Primary-Key and the REC# field (in column G) as the Secondary-Key (again, both in ascending order).

The result of this second sorting operation is shown in Figure 11.6. There, you can see that the account executives in the Sales department are listed in alphabetical last name order. This is the result of using the renumbered record

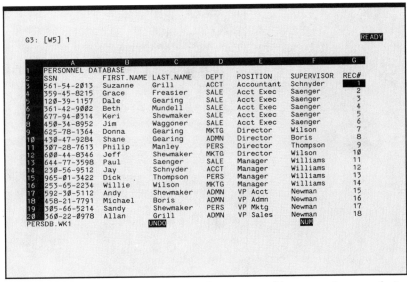

```
A1: [W13] 'PERSONNEL DATABASE                                    READY

            A            B          C          D         E           F        G
1   PERSONNEL DATABASE
2   SSN          FIRST.NAME LAST.NAME  DEPT     POSITION   SUPERVISOR  REC#
3   360-22-0978  Allan      Grill      ADMN     VP Sales   Newman       1
4   230-56-9512  Jay        Schnyder   ACCT     Manager    Williams     2
5   450-34-8952  Jim        Waggoner   SALE     Acct Exec  Saenger      3
6   561-54-2013  Suzanne    Grill      ACCT     Accountant Schnyder     4
7   359-45-8215  Grace      Freasier   SALE     Acct Exec  Saenger      5
8   625-78-1364  Donna      Gearing    MKTG     Director   Wilson       6
9   120-39-1157  Dale       Gearing    SALE     Acct Exec  Saenger      7
10  430-47-9284  Shane      Gearing    ADMN     Director   Boris        8
11  305-66-5214  Sandy      Shewmaker  PERS     VP Mktg    Newman       9
12  600-44-8346  Jeff       Shewmaker  MKTG     Director   Wilson      10
13  592-30-5112  Andy       Shewmaker  ADMN     VP Acct    Newman      11
14  677-94-0314  Keri       Shewmaker  SALE     Acct Exec  Saenger     12
15  307-28-7613  Philip     Manley     PERS     Director   Thompson    13
16  253-65-2234  Willie     Wilson     MKTG     Manager    Williams    14
17  965-01-3422  Dick       Thompson   PERS     Manager    Williams    15
18  458-21-7791  Michael    Boris      ADMN     VP Admn    Newman      16
19  644-77-3598  Paul       Saenger    SALE     Manager    Williams    17
20  361-42-9002  Beth       Mundell    SALE     Acct Exec  Saenger     18
PERSDB.WK1                   UNDO                            NUM
```

♦ **Figure 11.4:** *The order of the personnel database before sorting*

```
G3: [W5] 1                                                      READY

            A            B          C          D         E           F        G
1   PERSONNEL DATABASE
2   SSN          FIRST.NAME LAST.NAME  DEPT     POSITION   SUPERVISOR  REC#
3   561-54-2013  Suzanne    Grill      ACCT     Accountant Schnyder     1
4   359-45-8215  Grace      Freasier   SALE     Acct Exec  Saenger      2
5   120-39-1157  Dale       Gearing    SALE     Acct Exec  Saenger      3
6   361-42-9002  Beth       Mundell    SALE     Acct Exec  Saenger      4
7   677-94-0314  Keri       Shewmaker  SALE     Acct Exec  Saenger      5
8   450-34-8952  Jim        Waggoner   SALE     Acct Exec  Saenger      6
9   625-78-1364  Donna      Gearing    MKTG     Director   Wilson       7
10  430-47-9284  Shane      Gearing    ADMN     Director   Boris        8
11  307-28-7613  Philip     Manley     PERS     Director   Thompson     9
12  600-44-8346  Jeff       Shewmaker  MKTG     Director   Wilson      10
13  644-77-3598  Paul       Saenger    SALE     Manager    Williams    11
14  230-56-9512  Jay        Schnyder   ACCT     Manager    Williams    12
15  965-01-3422  Dick       Thompson   PERS     Manager    Williams    13
16  253-65-2234  Willie     Wilson     MKTG     Manager    Williams    14
17  592-30-5112  Andy       Shewmaker  ADMN     VP Acct    Newman      15
18  458-21-7791  Michael    Boris      ADMN     VP Admn    Newman      16
19  305-66-5214  Sandy      Shewmaker  PERS     VP Mktg    Newman      17
20  360-22-0978  Allan      Grill      ADMN     VP Sales   Newman      18
PERSDB.WK1                   UNDO                            NUM
```

♦ **Figure 11.5:** *Personnel database sorted by position and last name after renumbering records*

numbers in the REC# field as the secondary key to maintain the arrangement created by the first sort operation when sorting the database by department.

In this procedure, note that the first sort is performed using the second and third keys, POSITION and LAST.NAME, respectively. Then, once these are arranged, the second sort is performed using the first key, DEPT, and REC# renumbered (which retains the arrangment of the first sort). Whenever you have to sort a 1-2-3 database on three keys, you always use the second and third keys in the first sorting operation and then use the first key and one that retains the arrangement of the first sort in the second sorting operation.

Modifying the Collating Sequence

The default sorting sequence (called the *collating sequence* by the program) used by 1-2-3 is called Numbers First (numbers precede letters entered as *labels* when sorting on a key in ascending order). You can change the default collating sequence in the Install program.

To do this, you must start the Install program either by selecting the Install option (I) on the Lotus Access System menu or by typing *INSTALL* and pressing Enter at the DOS prompt. Once the Install program is loaded into memory, you

```
A1: [W13] 'PERSONNEL DATABASE                                        READY

        A            B          C          D         E           F         G
1  PERSONNEL DATABASE
2  SSN           FIRST.NAME LAST.NAME  DEPT      POSITION    SUPERVISOR  REC#
3  561-54-2013   Suzanne    Grill      ACCT      Accountant  Schnyder      1
4  230-56-9512   Jay        Schnyder   ACCT      Manager     Williams     12
5  430-47-9284   Shane      Gearing    ADMN      Director    Boris         8
6  592-30-5112   Andy       Shewmaker  ADMN      VP Acct     Newman       15
7  458-21-7791   Michael    Boris      ADMN      VP Admn     Newman       16
8  360-22-0978   Allan      Grill      ADMN      VP Sales    Newman       18
9  625-78-1364   Donna      Gearing    MKTG      Director    Wilson        7
10 600-44-8346   Jeff       Shewmaker  MKTG      Director    Wilson       10
11 253-65-2234   Willie     Wilson     MKTG      Manager     Williams     14
12 307-28-7613   Philip     Manley     PERS      Director    Thompson      9
13 965-01-3422   Dick       Thompson   PERS      Manager     Williams     13
14 305-66-5214   Sandy      Shewmaker  PERS      VP Mktg     Newman       17
15 359-45-8215   Grace      Freasier   SALE      Acct Exec   Saenger       2
16 120-39-1157   Dale       Gearing    SALE      Acct Exec   Saenger       3
17 361-42-9002   Beth       Mundell    SALE      Acct Exec   Saenger       4
18 677-94-0314   Keri       Shewmaker  SALE      Acct Exec   Saenger       5
19 450-34-8952   Jim        Waggoner   SALE      Acct Exec   Saenger       6
20 644-77-3598   Paul       Saenger    SALE      Manager     Williams     11
PERSDB.WK1                       UNDO                         NUM
```

◆ **Figure 11.6:** *Personnel database sorted the second time by department and record number*

select Advanced Options on the main menu by moving the pointer to it and pressing Enter. On the Advanced Options menu, you need to select the Modify Current Driver Set option by moving the pointer to it and pressing Enter.

This brings up the screen that shows you the current driver types used by 1-2-3. Here, you need to move the pointer down to the Collating driver type and press Enter. This leads you to the Collating Sequence menu shown in Figure 11.7. To choose a new collating sequence, move the highlight to it and press Enter.

After that, press F9 to return to the main menu, and then select the Exit Install Program option. Press Enter to select the Yes option to save your changes, and then press Enter a second time to save the collating sequence in the default driver set (123.SET unless you changed it when installing 1-2-3). If you are ready to exit from the Install program, press Enter a third time, then move the pointer to the Yes option and press Enter a final time. This will take you back either to DOS or to the Lotus Access System.

Table 11.1 shows you the three available collating sequences and their effect on sorting when you select *ascending* order when defining the key. If you select descending order when defining a key, this reverses the order shown in this table.

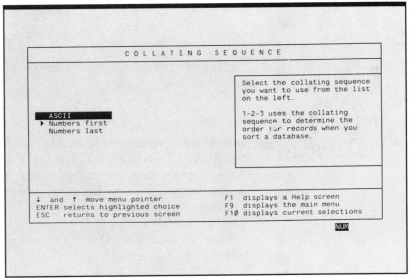

♦ **Figure 11.7:** *The Collating Sequence menu in the Install program*

◆ **Table 11.1:** *The Collating Sequences in 1-2-3*

Collating Sequence	Sequence Followed (Using Ascending Order)
Numbers First	1. Blank cells 2. Labels beginning with numbers in numerical order 3. Labels beginning with letters in alphabetical order (ignoring capitalization) 4. Labels beginning with other characters 5. Values in numerical order
Numbers Last	1. Blank cells 2. Labels beginning with letters in alphabetical order (ignoring capitalization) 3. Labels beginning with numbers in numerical order 4. Labels beginning with other characters 5. Values in numerical order
ASCII	1. Blank cells 2. Labels arranged by ASCII value in numerical order 3. Values arranged by ASCII value in numerical order

Querying the Database

Lotus 1-2-3 offers several commands that enable you to quickly search the database to locate specific information that you can then edit, delete, or copy to a new range in the worksheet. The process of searching the database and then performing such operations on the data that are located there is called querying the database (from the Latin verb *quaerere*, meaning to seek to obtain). Therefore, it should come as no surprise that 1-2-3 commands used to perform these operations are all located on the /Data Query menu.

When you select /Data Query (/DQ), you are presented with the following options:

Input Criteria Output Find Extract Unique Delete Reset Quit

If you are using Release 2.2, the program will also display a Query Settings sheet beneath the /Data Query menu, as shown in Figure 11.8. Also, if you are

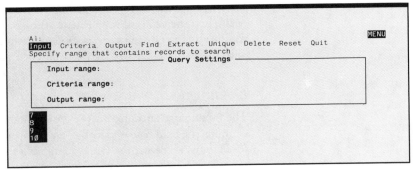

◆ **Figure 11.8:** *The /Data Query menu and Query Settings sheet*

still using Release 2.01, you will notice that the program uses the singular form, *Criterion*, instead of the plural form, *Criteria*, used in Release 2.2. There is no difference in the way these options are used in the two versions: you type C to select this option from either menu.

Preparing to Query the Database

The Input, Criteria, and Output options on the /Data Query menu are used to define the ranges in the worksheet that are needed to query the database with the Find, Extract, Unique, and Delete options that follow them. The input range defines the data that you want to query, the criteria range defines the conditions under which the database is queried, and the output range defines the range where the records that match the search criteria are copied. You must define the input and criteria ranges in order to perform any of the four query operations on the database; you only need to define the output range when you want to copy records from the database using the Extract or Unique options on the /Data Query menu.

Lotus 1-2-3 remembers all three ranges once you have defined them. When you save the worksheet containing the database, 1-2-3 saves the input, criteria, and output ranges that you have defined as part of the file. You can use the /Data Query Reset command (/DQR) to delete all three ranges at one time. If you do this in error and are using Release 2.2, you can restore them by immediately selecting the Quit option (Q) to exit from the /Data Query menu and then selecting Undo (Alt-F4).

To redefine any of these ranges, select the appropriate option from the /Data Query menu, and 1-2-3 will highlight the currently defined range on the screen. To redefine the range by pointing, press Esc to unanchor the range, move the pointer to the first cell of the new range, type a period to anchor again, and then indicate the extent of the new range. Otherwise, you define the new range by typing in its range address or range name (or choosing it with the Name key, F3).

Defining the Input Range

The input range encompasses the entire database, including the first row that contains the field names as well as all its records. After selecting /Data Query Input, you can define the range containing the database as you do any other range in 1-2-3—by entering the range address or range name or pointing it out. If you choose to use the pointing method and the database contains no blank records or blank cells in the last field, you can type a period to anchor the range, then press End → to highlight through the last field and End ↓ to highlight through the last record.

Whatever method you choose, be sure that you include all the records in the database. If you include only part of the records, the results you obtain from your searches may very well be incorrect.

Defining the Criteria Range

The criteria range indicates which records to search for in the input range. The first row contains the names of the fields you are searching, and the subsequent rows contain the criteria to be used in the search. The criteria range can contain up to 32 field names from the database specified in the input range. To define the criteria range, you select /Data Query Criteria (/DQC) and indicate the range of cells that hold the field names and search criteria to be used in the next query operation.

The field names that appear in the first row of the criteria range must exactly match those in the input range. For this reason, you should use the 1-2-3 /Copy command to copy the field names from the first row of the input range (database) to the area in the worksheet where you are placing the criteria range. Always locate the criteria in a part of the worksheet that gives you sufficient room so that your search criteria won't overlap either the input or output range (if used).

Defining the Output Range

The output range is required *only* when you want to perform the /Data Query Extract or /Data Query Unique operation, both of which copy records matching your search criteria from the input range (database) to a new part of the worksheet. (These commands differ from one another only in that Unique doesn't copy duplicate records from the input range, whereas Extract does.)

Like the criteria range, the first row of the output range must contain the names of the fields you wish extracted from the database entered exactly as they are in the database. Note that the fields you enter in the output range don't have to appear in the same order as they do in the input range or be the same as the ones used in the criteria range. However, if you want the complete set of matching records copied into the output range exactly as they are entered in the input range (database), you should use the /Copy command to copy the row containing the field names to the area of the worksheet you wish to use for the output range.

In defining the output range with the /Data Query Output (/DQO) command, you have two choices: you can either specify a single-row output range consisting of only the row that contains the field names—in which case 1-2-3 will use as many rows beneath as it needs to copy the records matching your search criteria—*or* you can specify a multiple-row output range consisting of the row containing the field names along with a number of blank rows beneath—in which case 1-2-3 will use only those blank rows included in the output range in copying the matching records.

When you define a single-row output range, you must take care that there are sufficient blank rows beneath the row of field names to accommodate all matching records, because 1-2-3 will copy over any existing data when you perform your /Data Query Extract or /Data Query Unique operation. Remember that you may often not know how many records will match your search criteria *before* you execute the extract operation. Afterward, when you discover that 1-2-3 has replaced existing data with the copied records, you will not be able to recover the existing data unless you are using Release 2.2 with Undo enabled or you've saved the worksheet before performing the query (both safeguards are highly recommended).

To be sure that 1-2-3 can't overwrite any data, you can locate the output range to the right of the input range (database) beneath the criteria range without using any of the rows below all the way to the end of the worksheet (this type of arrangement where you work in "panels" is the one that you will follow in the database management exercises later in this chapter). That way, you can specify a single-row output range without having to worry that your extract queries can harm the database, criteria range, or any other worksheet data.

In situations where such an arrangement isn't possible (you may lack the RAM needed to use new panels of the worksheet) and there is a danger that an extract query might overwrite data, you can prevent this by specifying a multiple-row output range containing as many blank rows as you have available beneath the field names. Be aware, however, that if there are more records to be copied than will fit into the output range that you have defined, 1-2-3 will beep, go into ERROR mode, and display the following error message:

Too many records for Output range

In such a case, the program will fill the output range with as many records as it can accommodate as soon as you press Esc or Enter to recover from the error. However, you will then have to increase the size of the output range and perform your query operation a second time to obtain the correct results.

Setting Up Search Criteria

You enter the search criteria in the blank cells beneath the appropriate field names in the criteria range. You can enter labels or values precisely as they are entered in the database when you want 1-2-3 to match the criteria exactly. You can use wildcard characters in the labels or values when you're not completely sure how they are entered in the database. In addition, you can also enter logical formulas as search criteria when you want the program to match a range of values.

Searching for Exact Matches in the Database

To have 1-2-3 search for exact matches in the input range (database), you need to enter the label or value beneath the correct field name in the criteria range. Remember that if the entries in the field to be searched are entered as labels, you must enter the criterion as a label beneath the field name (this means entering one of the label prefixes before numeric entries). Similarly, if the entries are input as values, you must enter the criterion as a value.

When entering a criterion label, you don't have to worry about matching its capitalization to the entries in the database unless you've changed the 1-2-3 collating sequence to ASCII in the Install program (the default is Numbers First, which ignores capitalization). Unless this change has been made, this means that you can enter *adams*, ADAMS, or *Adams* as the search criterion beneath LAST.NAME to locate the records in the database where *Adams* is entered as the last name.

Using Wildcards in Search Criteria

If you don't know exactly how the label that you wish to use as the search criterion is entered in the database, you can use the asterisk (*) or question mark (?) wildcard characters (just as they are used in DOS). The question mark entered in the criterion label matches any single character in the same position in the label. For example, if you enter *d?n* under the field name FIRST.NAME in the criteria range, *Dan* and *Don* in this field will both match.

The asterisk entered in the criterion label matches all characters to the end of the label. For instance, if you enter *d** under FIRST.NAME in the criteria range, *Dan*, *Don*, *Dean*, *Doris*, and *Dorothy* will all match. In fact, any name of any length, as long as it starts with *D* (including *D* alone), is a match to *d**.

Locating the Exceptions

In addition to these two wildcard characters, you can precede a criterion label with a tilde (˜) when you want 1-2-3 to search for all labels *except* that one. For example, if you enter ˜ *IL* under the field STATE in the criteria range, all records where the state code is anything besides *IL* are matches. You can use the tilde in search criteria effectively when performing extraction queries on the database where you want to work with all records except for those of a particular kind (such as records from all cities except New York and Los Angeles).

Creating AND and OR Search Conditions

When setting up your criteria range, you can create compound criteria involving AND or OR conditions just by the way you position the labels and/or values that you enter in the criteria range. To create an AND condition where 1-2-3 considers a record to match only when all criteria are met, you enter the labels or values that make up the various criteria in the *same* row of the criteria range. To create an OR condition where 1-2-3 considers a record to match when either of its criteria are met, you enter the labels or values in *different* rows of the criteria range.

Figure 11.9 illustrates an AND condition entered in row 3 of the criteria range (H2..M3). In this figure, two criteria—*Shewmaker* under the field name LAST.NAME and *Acct Exec* under the field name POSITION—must be true in a record for 1-2-3 to consider it a match, because they are both entered in the same row of the criteria range.

Figure 11.10 illustrates an OR condition using the same two criteria. In this figure, the first criterion label, *Shewmaker*, is entered in row 3 and the other one, *Acct Exec*, is entered in row 4, and the criteria range is enlarged from H2..M3 to H2..M4. Here, only one of the two criteria need be true for 1-2-3 to consider it a match, because they are entered in different rows of the criteria range; the program will match records that contain just *Shewmaker* in the last-name field, or *Acct Exec* in the position field, or even those that contain both *Shewmaker* and *Acct Exec*.

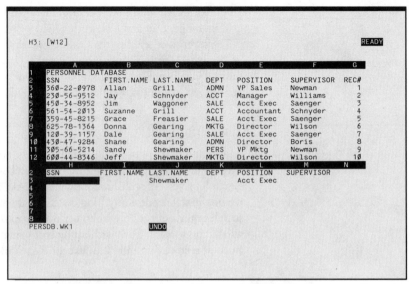

♦ **Figure 11.9:** *AND condition set up in the same row of the criteria range*

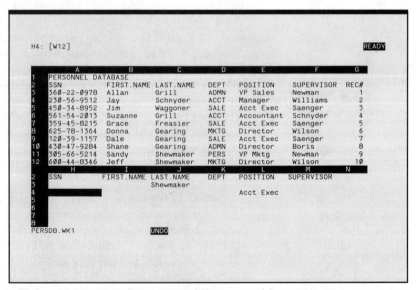

♦ **Figure 11.10:** *OR condition set up in different rows of the criteria range*

Figure 11.11 illustrates another common OR condition. Here, the OR criteria are entered in a single column under the appropriate field name (in this case, the department field). When a query operation is undertaken using these criteria, 1-2-3 will match any record where the department is administration (ADMN), accounting (ACCT), or sales (SALE). Note, however, that for the OR condition to succeed, the criteria range must include all three rows beneath the one containing the field name (in this example, the criteria range would be enlarged to H2..M5 to include all three departments).

When setting up compound criteria in this way, you must make sure that the criteria range includes all of the labels and values that you want to use. So too, when you want to exclude certain criteria, you need to remember to restrict the criteria range so that it no longer includes the unwanted labels or values.

By the way, it is not enough to just erase such labels or values from the rows of the criteria range with /Range Erase when you no longer want to use them; you must also restrict the criteria range so that it no longer includes these new blank rows. If you don't, their presence will badly skew the query operation you perform because a blank in the criteria range matches any entry in the corresponding field of the input range (database)!

You can always verify the extent of the criteria range and change it if necessary by selecting the /Data Query Criteria command (/DQC).

♦ Figure 11.11: OR *condition with three criteria in a single field*

Using Logical Formulas as Search Criteria

Lotus 1-2-3 also allows you to enter logical formulas when you need to search the database for records within a range of values, such as all records where the amount of sale is between $500.00 and $2,500.00, or if the date of the sale is between January 11, 1990, and February 15, 1990. Remember that logical formulas perform a *conditional test* on the cell they refer to and indicate whether the condition is currently true or false in that cell by returning the value 1 for true or the value 0 for false. As with all formulas in 1-2-3, logical formulas are limited to a maximum of 240 characters.

When 1-2-3 performs a query operation using the logical formula in the criteria range, the program performs its conditional test on all entries in the field that is being evaluated and considers every record where the formula returns 1 (true) to be a match. To have every record in the database evaluated by the logical formula, you always enter the cell address or range name that corresponds to the column that holds the field to be evaluated and the row that holds the first record of the database, making this the *test cell* whose result (0 or 1) is displayed in the cell containing the logical formula.

Therefore, if you want to set up a criterion formula to search the product database for all quantities greater than 10, and the QUANTITY field is in column E and the first record of the database is row 3, you would enter the formula

    +E3>10

in the criteria range under the field name QUANTITY (as shown in Figure 11.12). Notice that this formula returns the answer 1 in cell K3. This indicates that this condition is true in cell E3 (indeed, the quantity is 36 in this first record).

When you enter a logical formula in the criteria range, 1-2-3 always returns either the value 1 or 0 in the cell, as shown in Figure 11.12, based on whether the statement is true or false when evaluating the contents of the test cell in the formula. However, when you perform the query operation, 1-2-3 evaluates the same conditional test on all the remaining entries of the same field included in the input range.

Because you are not primarily interested in the answer returned by criterion formulas, you may want to format the cells that contain them with the /Range Format Text command (/RFT). When you use the Text option, 1-2-3 displays the formula entered into the cell instead of the answer, so that instead of 1, you would see +E3>10 in cell K3 in Figure 11.12. Note, however, that many criterion formulas are quite long, requiring you to widen their columns quite a bit to see the formulas in the worksheet display.

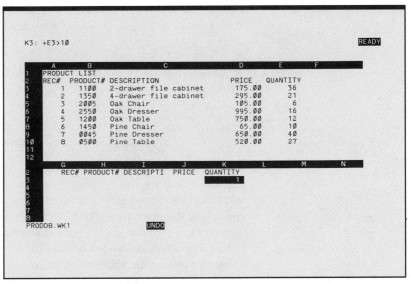

♦ **Figure 11.12:** *Criterion formula to locate records where the quantity is greater than 10*

When you create criterion formulas, you can use any logical operators. Remember that these include the following:

= (equal to), as in +B3=0 or +D2="*Yes*"

< (less than), as in +D5<E10*2

<= (less than or equal to), as in +C4<=250

> (greater than), as in +A12>B1

>= (greater than or equal to), as in +B7>=F1

<> (not equal to), as in +B3<>0

#AND# (logical AND), as in +B2>A1#AND#B2<C3

#OR# (logical OR), as in +A12>B1#OR#B3<>0

#NOT# (logical NOT), as in #NOT#B3=0 (same as +B3<>0)

Also, when building criterion formulas, you must use relative cell addresses (or range names) when referring to test cells within the input range (database) and absolute cell references when referring to cells outside of this range. For example, if you are setting up a criterion formula to search the product database for all records where the value entered in the QUANTITY field of the database in column E is unequal to a single value entered in cell Z90 (well out-side of the input range), you would enter the logical formula

   + E3 < > $Z$90

in the criteria range. You make the cell address outside the input range absolute to indicate that the same value is to be used each time the formula is evaluated throughout the database.

AND and OR Conditions in Criterion Formulas

You can use the #AND# and #OR# Boolean operators to create compound con-ditions. When you set up compound conditions in logical formulas using #AND# or #OR#, you aren't concerned with their position in the criteria range (just make sure they are within the criteria range as defined). Such formulas don't require the same kind of horizontal and vertical stacking as AND and OR conditions using exact match criteria do.

When creating a compound condition in a logical formula that restricts matching values to a particular range, you must remember to repeat the cell reference in both parts of the formula. For instance, consider a condition to locate all records where the date of sale is between January 11, 1990, and Feb-ruary 15, 1990 (inclusive). Assume that the first record is in row 2 and the DATE.OF.SALE field is in column D. You would then enter the following crite-rion formula somewhere in the criteria range:

   + D2 > = @DATE(90,1,11)#AND#D2 < = @DATE(90,2,15)

Notice that although each part of the condition refers to the same test cell (D2, which contains the first date of sale entry), this cell reference must be repeated after the #AND# operator. Also, notice that you must use the @DATE function to return the appropriate date numbers (assuming that this field contains date numbers and not labels).

When creating compound logical formulas, you can refer to different fields in the database in each part of the formula. For instance, if you wanted to locate all records where the date of sale is after March 31, 1990, and the amount of sale is greater than or equal to $5,000.00 (assume that this field is in column C), you could enter the formula:

   + D2 > @DATE(90,3,31)#AND#C2 > = 5000

Note that you can enter this formula under the field name DATE.OF.SALE or AMOUNT.OF.SALE in the criteria range. In fact, because the formula contains the necessary cell references indicating which fields and records in the input range (database) are to be evaluated, you can place this criterion formula under *any* valid field name in the criteria range. The same is true for all criterion formulas: they can be placed under any field name in the criteria range (nevertheless, it is wise to place them under related field names so you don't become confused as to their function).

Note that if the criterion formula refers to a field whose entries are all labels, you must remember to enclose the criteria in a pair of quotation marks. For example, assume that you wish to locate all Joneses in the database who make a salary in excess of $30,000 a year. If the test cell for the LAST.NAME field is B2, you would enter the following criterion formula

   +B2 = "Jones"#AND#C2>30000

Note in this example that the 30000 is not enclosed in quotation marks. This is because the SALARY field in column C is a numeric field. If, however, your criterion formula were evaluating a character field, whose entries are all labels, you would enclose the number in quotation marks. For instance, to locate all Joneses in the database who live in the zip code 94511 or greater (entered as labels in column J), you would enter the criterion formula

   +B2 = "Jones"#AND#J2> = "94511"

Using /Range Name Labels Down to Assign the Field Names as the Range Names for the First Entries: If you use the /Range Names Labels Down command (/RNLD) to assign the row of field names in the first row of your database to the entries in each field in the first record below, then you can use their range names when building criterion formulas. This makes such formulas easier to create as well as to interpret. Instead of having to look up the appropriate cell address to build a logical formula in the criteria range, you can simply type a plus (+) to start the formula, then press the Name key (F3) to bring up the list of range names, select the appropriate range name (which is the same as the name of the field to be evaluated) from the list, and type in the rest of the formula. When you enter the formula in the criteria range, you will see the range name rather than the cell address. For instance, if you did this with the criterion formula shown in Figure 11.12, you would see +QUANTITY>10 in the contents of the cell, which is far more descriptive of its function than +E3>10. If you then formatted the criterion cell with the Text option on the /Range Format menu (/RFT), you would also see the logical formula with the range name in the cell display.

Performing Query Operations on the Database

You can perform several different types of query operations once you have defined the necessary ranges and set up your search criteria. These include:

- ◆ /Data Query Find, which is used to individually locate all records in the database that match the search criteria.

- ◆ /Data Query Delete, which is used to remove all records from the database that match the search criteria.

- ◆ /Data Query Extract, which is used to copy all records from the database that match the search criteria to the output range.

- ◆ /Data Query Unique, which is used to copy all unique records from the database that match the search criteria to the output range.

The first time you perform any of these operations, you must select the appropriate option from the /Data Query menu. However, if you then have to repeat the same operation (usually with new search criteria or to a new output range), you can do so from READY mode by pressing the Query key (F7). Note, however, that this doesn't work in the case of the /Data Query Delete operation: you must always select this command from the 1-2-3 menus.

The Query key is unlike any other function key in 1-2-3 because its function is defined by the last query operation you selected from the /Data Query menu. If the last query operation you selected was /Data Query Find, then the Query key performs a find operation. If the last operation you selected was /Data Query Extract or /Data Query Unique, then the Query key performs the appropriate extract operation. This enables you to modify the search criteria in the criteria range without having to constantly return to the /Data Query menu to perform the same operation. Note that when you first create a 1-2-3 database, the Query key has no function at all: if you press this key before you have selected a query operation from /Data Query menu, the program will merely beep at you.

Using /Data Query Find

The /Data Query Find command (/DQF) locates records in the database matching your criteria. It is used primarily when you need to edit particular records. When you use this command, 1-2-3 highlights the first matching record in the input range that matches the current criteria. If there are no matching records, 1-2-3 beeps at you.

F7: The Query Key

F7, the Query key, has no function until you select a /Data Query option

F7 performs either /Data Query Find, /Data Query Extract, or /Data Query Unique, depending upon which operation was the one last selected on the /Data Query menu

When the you select the /Data Query Find command and the first matching record is found in the input range, the program goes into FIND mode. While in FIND mode, you can move around the input range by using any of the pointer-movement keys indicated in Table 11.2. If you need to edit the contents of a field in a matching record, you can move the cursor to the field with the → or ← key and then press the Edit key (F2) to edit its contents. Once you have made your modifications to the field entry, you press the Enter key (press Esc to abandon your changes).

◆ **Table 11.2:** *Cursor- and Pointer-Movement Keys Used in FIND Mode*

Key	Usage
↑	Moves the pointer to the previous record that matches the current criteria; if no such record is located in this direction, 1-2-3 beeps.
↓	Moves the pointer to the next record that matches the current criteria; if no such record is located in this direction, 1-2-3 beeps.
←	Moves the cursor left one field in the highlighted record.*
→	Moves the cursor right one field in the highlighted record.*
End	Moves the pointer to the last record in the input range.
Home	Moves the pointer to the first record in the input range.

* Press the Edit key (F2) to edit the contents of the current field in the highlighted record.

To exit from FIND mode, you can press Esc or Enter. You are then returned to the /Data Query menu or READY mode (if you used the Query key {F7} to initiate the operation).

Using /Data Query Delete

The /Data Query Delete command (/DQD) removes all records from the database matching the current criteria. In addition, the command automatically shrinks the input range so that there are no blank rows left in the database due to the deletions. When you select the Delete option from the /Data Query menu, 1-2-3 prompts you to continue with the deletion operation by displaying these options:

Cancel Delete

To abandon the operation and avoid deleting all matching records, select the Cancel option (C). To complete the deletion of all matching records, select the Delete option (D).

You should always save the worksheet just prior to using the /Data Query Delete command. That way, you can always retrieve the previous version of the database should you delete records in error. If you are using Release 2.2, you can use the Undo key (Alt-F4) to restore all records deleted with this command.

Using /Data Query Extract

The /Data Query Extract command (/DQE) is used to copy records matching the current criteria from the input range to the output range. Remember that unlike when using /Data Query Find or /Data Query Delete—which require just input and criteria ranges—/Data Query Extract requires an output range as well.

When you select /Data Query Extract, 1-2-3 copies the fields from the matching records in the order they are arranged in the output range. Note that if you perform a second extract operation using the same output range, 1-2-3 will erase all the data in this range beneath the field names. Therefore, if you wish to preserve the results of an extraction, you must either move the matching records to a new area of the worksheet, copy them to a new worksheet using /File Xtract, or redefine the output range to a new area of the worksheet that doesn't overlap any of the matching records.

Using /Data Query Unique

The /Data Query Unique command (/DQU) works just like /Data Query Extract, except that it doesn't copy duplicate records matching the current criteria to the output range. Note, however, that 1-2-3 uses the fields in the *output* range to match duplicates. This means that even if two records are not identical in the input range, they may still not both be copied to the output range if the fields contained in that range are the same in each.

Figure 11.13 illustrates such a situation. In this example, the output range contains just one of the fields (LAST.NAME) in the database. The single criterion for the extract is that the department be Marketing, shown by *MKTG* under the DEPT field name in the criteria range J1..P2. When the /Data Query Unique command is selected, 1-2-3 copies just three last names—Gearing, Shewmaker, and Wilson—to the output range. Notice, however, that there are actually two Shewmakers in the database that meet this criterion: both Sandy *and* Jeff Shewmaker are in the Marketing department (look at D10 and D11 in the figure).

If the Extract option had been chosen instead of Unique, the name *Shewmaker* would be copied twice to the output range under LAST.NAME in column J: once for Sandy and once for Jeff. When Unique is used, however, 1-2-3 uses just the LAST.NAME field (in the output range) to determine duplicates and therefore copies the name *Shewmaker* only once.

You can use the /Data Query Unique command not only to eliminate identical records from the database that are entered in error, but also to determine how many unique entries are in a particular field of the database. For example,

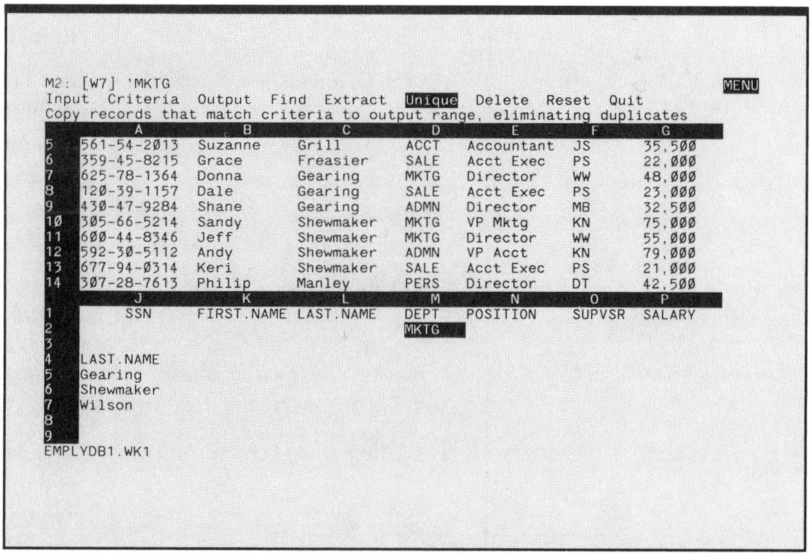

♦ **Figure 11.13:** *Eliminating duplicates with the /Data Query Unique command*

assume that you are working with a client database and want to know how many states are represented in the database. To do this, you would restrict the output range to the STATE field and select /Data Query Unique. That way, 1-2-3 will copy only unique state codes to the output range, allowing you to see how many different states are represented in the input range (without giving you any indication as to how many times each is entered in the database).

The Database @Functions

Lotus 1-2-3 includes statistical @functions that are used only with databases. The database @functions (shown in Table 11.3) parallel the statistical @functions in 1-2-3. They are formed by adding a *D* to the names of these @functions, so that @SUM becomes @DSUM, and @AVG becomes @DAVG.

♦ **Table 11.3:** *The Database @Functions*

Function Name & Arguments	Usage
@DAVG(*input,field,criteria*)	Calculates the average or mean of the values in the field of the *input* range (database) given by the *field* argument, according to the *criteria* entered in the criteria range.
@DCOUNT(*input,field,criteria*)	Calculates the number of the nonblank cells in the field of the *input* range (database) given by the *field* argument, according to the *criteria* entered in the criteria range.
@DMAX(*input,field,criteria*)	Calculates the highest values in the field of the *input* range (database) given by the *field* argument, according to the *criteria* entered in the criteria range.
@DMIN(*input,field,criteria*)	Calculates the lowest values in the field of the *input* range (database) given by the *field* argument, according to the *criteria* entered in the criteria range.

♦ **Table 11.3:** *The Database @Functions (continued)*

Function Name & Arguments	Usage
@DSTD(*input*,*field*,*criteria*)	Calculates the standard deviation of the values in the field of the *input* range (database) given by the *field* argument, according to the *criteria* entered in the criteria range.
@DSUM(*input*,*field*,*criteria*)	Calculates the sum of the values in the field of the *input* range (database) given by the *field* argument, according to the *criteria* entered in the criteria range.
@DVAR(*input*,*field*,*criteria*)	Calculates the variance of the values in the field of the *input* range (database) given by the *field* argument, according to the *criteria* entered in the criteria range.

As you can see in Table 11.3, all database @functions share the same three arguments: input, field, and criteria. The *input argument* is the range that contains the database including the field names. It corresponds to the input range used by /Data Query operations.

The *field argument* is the offset number of the field that the particular @function uses in calculating. It represents the field's position in the input range, so that the first field of the input range has an offset number of 0, the second field has an offset of 1, and so on.

The *criteria argument* is a range that indicates under which conditions the @function is to operate. Like the criteria range for /Data Query commands, this range must include at least one field name from the database, with the criteria you want 1-2-3 to use placed in the cell underneath it.

You will find times when the criteria range for your database @function will be the same as the criteria range used in the /Data Query commands. Note, however, that you can't use a database @function in a criteria range defined for performing various /Data Query operations. If you do, 1-2-3 will beep, go into ERROR mode, and display the following error message when you select your query operation:

Criterion range contains database statistical function(s)

Creating and Querying Your Own Database

In the following exercises, you will get a chance to create a database that you will then use to practice setting up criteria and performing various query operations. The database is shown in Figure 11.14. It is a personnel database that maintains information about the department, position, supervisor, salary, and start date for each employee. As you can see in Figure 11.14, the database also includes the social security number for each employee as the first field.

Begin this exercise by starting 1-2-3 and clearing the worksheet display.

1. **Enter the field names in row 1 of the new worksheet as they are shown in Figure 11.14; center *SSN* in cell A1, and right-align *SALARY* in G1 and *START.DATE* in H1.**

    Next, you will enter the social security numbers in column A. Remember that this is a character field, meaning that all of its entries must be entered as labels—that is, prefaced with the apostrophe label prefix.

2. **Enter the social security numbers in the SSN field following Figure 11.14: remember to begin each entry with an apostrophe (') to enter these numbers as labels.**

    Next, enter the labels in the next five fields of the database.

3. **Enter the data as shown in Figure 11.14 for the FIRST.NAME, LAST.NAME, DEPT, POSITION, and SUPRVSR fields.**

    The SALARY field in column G is a numeric field. This means that you must enter only the numbers shown in Figure 11.14 (not the commas). Then, you must use the Comma (,) format on the /Range Format menu to alter their display to match the ones shown in Figure 11.14.

4. **Enter the values for the SALARY field as they are in Figure 11.14; then, format these values with the Comma (,) format with 0 decimal places.**

    The START.DATE field is the last one in the personnel database. This field is also a numeric field, but unlike the SALARY field, you can't just enter the values directly: you must use the @DATE function and

	A	B	C	D	E	F	G	H
1	SSN	FIRST.NAME	LAST.NAME	DEPT	POSITION	SUPRVSR	SALARY	START.DATE
2	360–22–0978	Allan	Grill	ADMN	VP Sales	KN	85,000	16–Jul–72
3	230–56–9512	Jay	Schnyder	ACCT	Manager	RW	56,000	11–Sep–83
4	450–34–8952	Jim	Waggoner	SALE	Acct Exec	PS	25,000	05–Feb–88
5	561–54–2013	Suzanne	Grill	ACCT	Accountant	JS	35,500	03–Oct–80
6	359–45–8215	Grace	Freasier	SALE	Acct Exec	PS	22,000	17–Aug–82
7	625–78–1364	Donna	Gearing	MKTG	Director	WW	48,000	01–Jul–85
8	120–39–1157	Dale	Gearing	SALE	Acct Exec	PS	23,000	27–Dec–89
9	430–47–9284	Shane	Gearing	ADMN	Director	MB	32,500	25–Oct–72
10	305–66–5214	Sandy	Shewmaker	MKTG	VP Mktg	KN	75,000	15–Jul–80
11	600–44–8346	Jeff	Shewmaker	MKTG	Director	WW	55,000	31–Mar–81
12	592–30–5112	Andy	Shewmaker	ADMN	VP Acct	KN	79,000	01–Apr–82
13	677–94–0314	Keri	Shewmaker	SALE	Acct Exec	PS	21,000	12–Jan–83
14	307–28–7613	Philip	Manley	PERS	Director	DT	42,500	27–Dec–80
15	253–65–2234	Willie	Wilson	MKTG	Manager	RW	64,500	06–Mar–88
16	965–01–3422	Dick	Thompson	PERS	Manager	RW	65,000	19–Jun–86
17	458–21–7791	Michael	Boris	ADMN	VP Admn	KN	78,500	21–Sep–70
18	644–77–3598	Paul	Saenger	SALE	Manager	RW	56,000	02–Apr–63
19	361–42–9002	Beth	Mundell	SALE	Acct Exec	PS	26,800	07–Nov–73

♦ **Figure 11.14:** *Sample personnel database*

then format the results with the /Range Format Date 1 command. Remember that the arguments for the @DATE function are year, month, and day, so you would enter 16-Jul-72 as @DATE(72,7,16).

5. **Enter the date numbers for the dates shown in the START.DATE field in Figure 11.14; then, format these values with the Date 1 option on the /Range Format menu.**
Now you are ready to save the database.

6. **Press Home to move the cursor to the first cell, then save the worksheet under the file name *PERSNLDB*.**

Defining the Input, Criteria, and Output Ranges for the Database

Because you will get an opportunity to practice using all of 1-2-3's query operations, you will need to define not only the input and criteria ranges but the output range as well. To make it easier to define the input range not only for the /Data Query commands but also in the database @functions, you will assign a range name to the database. You will locate the criteria and output range in the columns to the right of the database. You will then use a horizontal window to display parts of the three query ranges on the same screen.

1. **With the pointer in cell A1, select /Range Name Create (/RNC), then type *db* as the range name and press Enter; to indicate the range, press End → followed by End ↓ and press Enter.**
When defining the extent of the database for any 1-2-3 command, you will find that using the End key with the ↓ and → keys saves you time. The range *DB* includes the field names and all the records. Now you are ready to copy the field names in range A1..H1 to J1 to create the criteria range. Remember that the field names in the criteria range must match those in the input range exactly.

2. **Move the pointer to cell A1, then use the /Copy command to copy the range A1..H1 to J1.**
Before you copy some of the field names for the output range beneath the criteria range, you should split the worksheet display with the horizontal window and then scroll the field names for the criteria range into view.

3. **Move the pointer to row 4, then select /Worksheet Window Horizontal (/WWH), press the Window key (F6), and select /Worksheet Window Unsync (/WWU); press Scroll Lock, then press Tab and the → key twice to move the pointer to column J; next, press the ↑ key until row 1 is in view in the lower window.**

   The field names for the output range must be located well enough below those for the criteria range that you can enter multiple criteria in the same column (for OR conditions). You will alter the order of the fields in the output range as well as omit the SSN field.

4. **Press Scroll Lock again, then move the pointer to cell K1 and copy the field names FIRST.NAME in K1 and LAST.NAME in L1 to cells J5 and K5, respectively; next, enter or copy POSITION in cell L5, SALARY in M5, DEPT in cell N5, and SUPRVSR in cell O5; when you have finished, widen the columns J, K, and L to 11 characters all at once with the /Worksheet Column Column-Range Set-Width command (/WCCS) if you are using Release 2.2, or individually with /Worksheet Column Set-Width (/WCS) if you are using Release 2.01.**

   Your screen should resemble the one shown in Figure 11.15. Next, assign a range name to the range that you will define as the output range.

5. **With the pointer in J5, select /Range Name Create (/RNC), type output as the range name, and press Enter; then press End → to highlight J5..O5, and press Enter again.**

   Now you are ready to define the input, criteria, and output ranges.

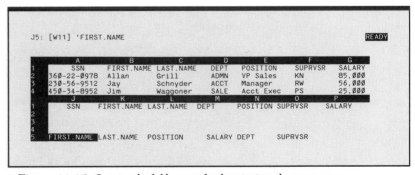

♦ **Figure 11.15:** *Copying the field names for the criteria and output ranges*

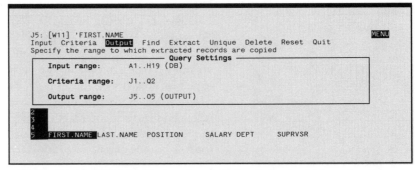

```
J5: [W11] 'FIRST.NAME                                                   MENU
Input  Criteria  Output  Find  Extract  Unique  Delete  Reset  Quit
Specify the range to which extracted records are copied
─────────────────────────── Query Settings ───────────────────────────
    Input range:        A1..H19 (DB)

    Criteria range:     J1..Q2

    Output range:       J5..O5 (OUTPUT)

2
3
4
5  FIRST.NAME LAST.NAME  POSITION      SALARY DEPT      SUPRVSR
```

◆ **Figure 11.16:** *The Query Settings sheet displaying the input, criteria, and output ranges*

6. **Select /Data Query Input (/DQI), press the Name key (F3), move the pointer to *DB*, and press Enter; next, select Criteria (C), move the pointer to J1, type a period to anchor the range, press End →, then press the ↓ key to highlight J1..Q2, and press Enter; select Output (O), press the Name key (F3), move the pointer to *OUTPUT*, and press Enter.**
   If you are using Release 2.2, you should now check the three ranges in your Query Settings sheet against those shown in Figure 11.16.

Practice Setting Up Criteria and Performing Query Operations

Now that you have defined the three ranges, you are ready to practice entering different types of criteria in the criteria range and performing different types of query operations. Before you do, however, you should save your changes to the worksheet.

1. **Select the Quit option (Q) to exit from the /Data Query menu; then, save the worksheet under the same name with the /File Save command.**
   For your first query operation, you will locate the records for all employees in the Sales department.

2. **Move the pointer to cell M2 under DEPT, then enter *SALE* in this cell; select /Data Query Find (/DQF).**
   The first part of the personnel database fills the lower window, and Jim Waggoner's record is highlighted as the first match. See how many others there are.

3. **Press the ↓ key until the last matching record (which happens to be the last record in the database) is highlighted; then, press the ↑ key twice to return to the previously selected records before pressing the Home key to jump directly to the first record in the input; finally, press Esc to exit from FIND mode.**

When you press the ↑ and ↓ keys in FIND mode, 1-2-3 jumps to matching records above and below in the database. When you press the Home and End keys in FIND mode, the program jumps to the first and last record, whether they match the criteria or not. Try another find query, using slightly different criteria.

4. **Select Quit (Q) to return to READY mode; move the pointer to cell N2 under *POSITION* and enter ˜ *Acct Exec* in this cell.**

Remember the tilde is used to find the exception. This means you are looking for records where the position is something other than Acct Exec (account executive). Because this criterion label is entered in the same row as *SALE* in cell M5, you have created an AND condition. This query will locate records where the department is Sales and the position is *not* account executive.

5. **Press the Query key (F7) to perform the /Data Query Find operation using these new criteria.**

The highlight jumps to Paul Saenger's record.

6. **Press the ↑ key, then press the ↓ key.**

Each time you do, 1-2-3 beeps, indicating there are no more matching records.

7. **Press Esc to exit from FIND mode.**

Now you will get some practice in editing records. You are going to increase the salaries for the vice presidents in the company. To do this, you will have to change the criterion label under *POSITION* and erase the one under *DEPT*.

8. **Enter *VP** in cell N2, then move the pointer to M2 and erase the label with /Range Erase.**

The asterisk after VP will match any succeeding characters (VP Sales, VP Mktg, and so on). Remember that you must use /Range Erase to remove criteria from this range—never press the spacebar to replace the current entry with a space, because this will skew the results of your query.

9. **Press the Query key (F7); when Allan Grill's record is high-lighted, press the → key until the cursor is under 85,000; then press Edit (F2) and the Backspace key until you erase the number 80000; type 90000 and press Enter.**
   When you need to edit a field entry, you must use this method.

10. **Press the ↓ key; change Sandy Shewmaker's salary from 75,000 to 85,000 by pressing Edit, then deleting the current number and replacing it with 85000 before pressing Enter.**
    Notice that you didn't have to move the cursor to make this update.

11. **Press the ↓ key and increase Andy Shewmaker's salary to 83,000; press the ↓ key again and increase Michael Boris' salary to 82500; then press Esc.**

Performing Extract Operations

Although /Data Query Find is useful when you need to edit records in the database, you may find more use for /Data Query Extract, which enables you to copy subsets of the database to a new part of the worksheet. Once records are copied into the output range, you can copy them into their own file (with /File Xtract), where you can sort the data and graph it, as well as print reports (prepared with 1-2-3 or Allways).

To see how /Data Query Extract works, you will start by copying all records where the supervisor's initials are RW.

1. **Erase the label in cell N2, and enter RW in cell O2; then select /Data Query Extract (/DQE).**
   There are four employees who report to RW (shown in Figure 11.17). You had to initiate this new query operation from the /Data Query menu because the Query key was programmed to perform a /Data Query Find. However, you can now use it in future queries because it is now reprogrammed to perform /Data Query Extract.

2. **Replace RW in O2 with JS, then press the Query key (F7).**
   Only one employee, Suzanne Grill, reports to JS. Next, try creating an OR condition. Remember that this involves stacking the criteria in the same field, and it also requires modifying the criteria range.

3. **Enter PS in cell O2, WW in cell O3, and MB in cell O4; then select /Data Query Criteria (/DQC), press the ↓ key twice to include the labels in cells O3 and O4 in the criteria range, and select Extract (E).**

Notice that the new matching records have replaced the one copied by the previous extract operation. Also, notice that 1-2-3 has copied the records where the supervisor's initials are PS or WW or MB. If, however, you had forgotten to increase the criteria range to include rows 3 and 4, the program would have used the initials PS only. Next, you will create a compound AND and OR condition by adding the criterion label *Director* to the POSITION field.

4. **Select Quit (Q), then enter *Director* in cell N2 and copy it to N3..N4; press the Query key (F7) to perform the extract operation.**
   Notice that fewer records meet this condition. This is in large part because none of PS's people hold the position of director (they are all account executives).

Practice Creating and Using Criterion Formulas

In this next exercise, you will switch from entering criteria that must match exactly (such as PS under SUPRVSR) or closely (with the use of wildcard characters such as * or ?) to criteria that fall within a range. Remember that to set up this type of criteria, you must create logical formulas in the criteria range. To

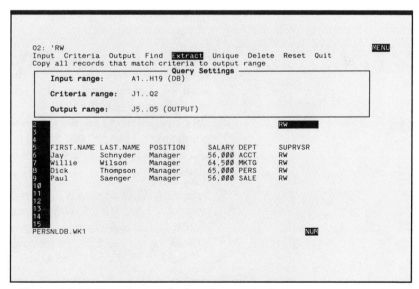

♦ **Figure 11.17:** *Extracting records where the supervisor is RW*

help you create them, you will assign range names to the data in the first record using the field names above them.

1. **Press the Window key (F6), move the pointer to A1, select /Range Name Labels Down (/RNLD), press End →, and then press Enter.**
   This assigns each field name to the first entry directly below it. When building your criterion formulas, you can now refer to these cells by range name (that is, field name).

2. **Press the Window key (F6) again; then erase all the criterion labels in the range N2..O4.**
   Your first criterion formula will find the records where the salaries are greater than $55,000.

3. **Move the pointer to P2, type +, press the Name key (F3), press the → key until the pointer is on SALARY, then press Enter; now type >50000 (the entire formula will read + SALARY>50000), and press Enter.**
   Cell P2 should now display a result of 1, because the contents of test cell G2 is 90,000 (which is greater than 50,000). Before you perform the extract operation to locate all records that meet this condition, you *must* remember to decrease the size of the criteria range (it currently includes two blank rows). If you don't modify the range before you perform the extract, you will get unexpected results.

4. **Select /Data Query Criteria (/DQC), and press the ↑ key twice to shrink the criteria range so that it just includes the row with the formula and the row with the field names; then select Extract (E).**
   Look carefully at the salaries in the output range, verifying that they are all greater than $50,000. Next, you will modify the criterion formula to extract only those records where the salaries are greater than $50,000 and less than or equal to $65,000.

5. **Select the Quit option (Q), then press the Edit key (F2) and type #AND#SALARY< = 65000, and press Enter.**
   Notice that P2 now contains 0, because this compound condition is false for the test cell G2. The formula in this cell should now read +SALARY>50000#AND#SALARY<=65000.

6. **Press the Query key (F7) to perform this extract operation.**
   Verify that all salaries in the SALARY field in the output range are

greater than $50,000 and less than or equal to $65,000 (notice that Dick Thompson's salary is $65,000 exactly). Now try creating a different criterion formula to find the records where the start date is on or after January 1, 1980, and on or before December 31, 1986.

7. **Erase the formula in cell P2, then move the pointer to cell Q2; type +, press the Name key (F3), select the range name START.DATE, and press Enter; then enter > = @DATE(80,1,1)# AND#, select START.DATE again with the Name key, and type < = @DATE(86,12,31), and press Enter.**
   You can check your criterion formula against the one shown in cell Q2 in Figure 11.18.

8. **Press the Query key (F7) to perform the extract operation.**
   Notice that although 1-2-3 copies many records into the output range, you can't tell if they meet your criteria because you haven't included the START.DATE field in the output range. Add this field now.

9. **Copy the contents of cell Q1 to cell P5, then select /Data Query Output and press the → key to include cell P5; select Extract (E), and then Quit (Q); finally, widen column P to 10 characters.**
   This time, with the dates included in the output range, you should be able to verify that all the dates are within the range specified by the criterion formula in Q2 (see Figure 11.18). Next, you will create a criterion formula that refers to a cell outside the input range. This formula will locate all records where the years of service are greater than 18. It will calculate this using the dates in the START.DATE field.

10. **Erase the criterion formula in cell Q2, then move the pointer to cell L2 under the FIRST.NAME field name.**
    Although this formula doesn't logically belong under the FIRST.NAME field, remember that it doesn't matter which field name is used as long as it is a valid field name. The logical formula that you are going to enter in this cell uses the @NOW function to return the current date, then subtracts it from the date in the START.DATE field, and divides this number by 365.25 to derive the years the employee has been with the company (it also uses the @ROUND function to round this result to the nearest whole number). Then, the calculated number of years is compared to the number that you will enter in cell J3.

11. **Type @ROUND((@NOW – START.DATE)/365.25,0)>, move the pointer to cell J3, and press the Abs key (F4) to change the cell reference to $J$3; then press Enter.**

This formula should return the value of 1, because cell J3 is still blank (so that any number of years calculated by the formula has got to be greater than the value of this cell). Remember that you had to make the reference to cell J3 absolute because this cell is outside of the input range.

12. **Move the pointer to cell J3, enter 7 in this cell, and press the Query key (F7).**

When you press the Query key to perform the extract operation, 1-2-3 copies the records for the employees who have worked for the company 7 years or longer. See how many employees have 10 or more years of service.

13. **Enter 10 in J3, then press the Query key (F7).**

As you can see, there are fewer employees with 10 years of service. See how many employees have 20 or more years of service.

14. **Enter 20 in J3, then press the Query key (F7).**

There is only one employee, Paul Saenger, who has been with the company that long.

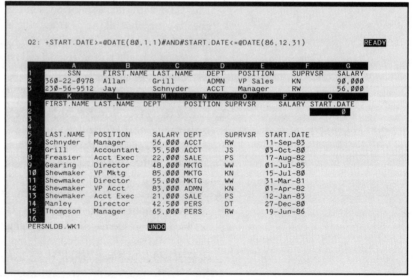

◆ **Figure 11.18:** *Criterion formula to find all records where the start date is on or after January 1, 1980, and on or before December 31, 1986*

Using Database @Functions

Now it's time to get some practice using the database @functions. You can use these @functions to find out many interesting statistics about the personnel database. For example, you can use them to compute the average salary for the employees working in the accounting department, calculate the number of employees who make an annual salary over $75,000, or find the lowest-paying position in the database.

In using the database @functions, you will specify the range name *DB* as the input argument (same as the input range). The field argument depends upon which field you want to query (there are eight fields in the database, so the off-set numbers run from 0 to 7). The criteria argument will also depend upon which field determines the criteria used by the @function.

Let's see how this works by first calculating the average salary of the employees who work in the accounting department. To obtain this statistic, you will use the @DAVG function, which you will enter in cell K3. The field argument is 6: the @function is operating on the values in the SALARY field, and as the seventh field in the database, 6 is its offset number. You will enter the criteria ACCT in cell M2 under the DEPT field name in cell M1 so that the criteria argument is M1..M2.

1. **Move the pointer to cell M2 and enter the criterion label ACCT there.**
   This establishes the criterion on which the average will be calculated when the @DAVG function is entered in cell K3.

2. **Move the pointer to cell K3, then type @DAVG(DB,6,M1.M2) and press Enter.**
   This @function calculates the average salary in the department as $45,750. Note that you didn't have to erase the criterion in cell L3 because the @DAVG function uses a different range as its criteria argument.

3. **Move the pointer to cell K3 and format the value using the Comma (,) format with 0 decimal places; then move the pointer to cell M2 and enter ADMN as the new criterion label.**
   The @DAVG function recalculates the average salary ($72,000) for the new criteria as soon as you press Enter. Next, you will enter a new formula that will calculate the number of records where the salary is above $75,000. The number is calculated by using the @DCOUNT function, which returns the number of nonblank cells in the chosen field that meet your criteria.

4. **Move the pointer to cell P2, enter** + *SALARY* > *75000* **in this cell, then move the pointer to cell L3 and enter** @*DCOUNT(DB,6,P1.P2).*

According to this @function, three records meet this condition. For your last practice database @function, find out which is the lowest-paying position in the database. To do this, you will use the @DMIN function, which returns the minimum number in the chosen field that meets your criteria (in this case, you will leave the criterion cell blank, as you simply want to know which salary is the lowest without regard to any other conditions). After this @function returns the lowest salary, you can then perform a find operation using the cell that contains this result as the criterion value for this operation.

5. **Move the pointer to cell P2 under the field name** SALARY, **then enter** @*DMIN(DB,6,J1.J2).*

You used the range J1..J2 as the criteria argument because it contains no criterion entries or formula but does include a valid field name (SSN). You should now see *21000* in cell P2. Next, you will convert this formula into its calculated value (remember that you can't have database @functions in the criteria range), and then use it to perform the /Data Query Extract command to copy the record where the salary is $21,000. Then, you can use the copied record to find out which position draws this salary.

6. **Press Edit (F2), Calc (F9), and Enter; next, select /Data Query Criteria (/DQC), then press Esc, move the pointer to cell P1, type a period (.) to anchor, press the ↓ key to extend the range to P2, and press Enter; finally, select Extract (E) followed by Quit (Q).**

You can see from the POSITION field in Keri Shewmaker's record that the account executive position is the lowest-paying at this time.

Sorting Your Database

Sorting in 1-2-3 is both easy and fast. You will now abandon your query exercises in favor of those that involve sorting the data in the personnel database using various keys. In this exercise, you won't need to use the horizontal window that you created for querying the database, as you will want to have as many records in the database as possible on the screen.

As a prerequisite for sorting the records in the database, you will add a new record-number field. That way, you can easily return the database to its original order simply by sorting the records in ascending order, using this new field as the primary key.

1. **Select /Worksheet Window Clear (/WWC) to remove the horizontal window.**
   Now you will add the record-number field in column A.

2. **Move the pointer to a cell in column A and select /Worksheet Insert Column (/WIC), then press Enter.**
   Next, you need to add the field name *REC#* and narrow the column width.

3. **With the pointer in cell A1, type *REC#*, then press ↓; narrow the column width to 4 characters.**
   You will now use /Data Fill to enter the record numbers in this new field.

4. **With the pointer in cell A2, select /Data Fill (/DF), highlight the range A2..A19 as the fill range, then press Enter, type *1* as the start number, and press Enter three times more.**
   Now you need to save the worksheet so that the record numbers are saved on disk before you begin rearranging the order of the records themselves with the /Data Sort command.

5. **Use the /File Save command to save the worksheet containing the personnel database on disk under the same file name (PERSNLDB.WK1).**
   To sort the database, you must define the data range (all the data to be sorted) and at least the primary key (by specifying the column holding the field on which to sort). In this case, you will sort all the records (not including the top row of field names) in the database alphabetically by last name.

6. **Select /Data Sort Data-Range (/DSD), move the pointer to cell A2, type a period (.) to anchor the range, then press End → followed by End ↓, and press Enter.**
   This defines the range A2..I19 as the data range for sorting. Now you are ready to define the primary key, which is the last-name field in column D, and select ascending as the order by replacing *D* with *A*.

7. **Select Primary-Key (P), then move the pointer to column D and press Enter; then type *A* for Sort order and press Enter; finally, select the Go option (G) to perform the sort.**
   Notice how fast 1-2-3 sorts these records when you press Go. Your screen at this point should resemble the one in Figure 11.19. Note

that the Gearings and the Shewmakers are in alphabetical order only by last name. They still don't follow alphabetical order in the first-name field. Rectify this by making the first-name field the secondary key and then sorting the database again.

8. **Select /Data Sort Secondary-Key (/DSS), then move the pointer to column C, press Enter, type A, and press Enter again; next, select Go (G) to sort the database a second time, using both keys.**
   Your screen should now look like the one in Figure 11.20. By adding this second key, you were able to sort the records alphabetically by both first and last name. Next, you will sort the database first by department, then by position.

9. **Select /Data Sort Primary-Key (/DSP), move the pointer to column E, and press Enter twice; then select Secondary-Key (S), move the pointer to column F, and press Enter twice; select Go (G) to sort the database.**
   Try another sort, this time sorting the records first by department and then by salary. The department names will be in ascending order (A–Z) and the salaries in descending order (highest to lowest).

10. **Select /Data Sort Secondary-Key (/DSS), move the pointer to column H, press Enter, type D, press Enter, and then select Go (G) to perform the sort.**
    You will have to scroll the screen to the right until you can see the SALARY field heading to verify that the records are now sorted the way you want them. Try one more sort, this time restoring the original order to the database by sorting numerically on the record-number field.

11. **Select /Data Sort Primary-Key (/DSP), move the pointer to column A, press Enter twice, then select Go (G) to perform the sort.**
    Scroll the screen to the left until you can see the REC# field heading. You can see that records are once again returned to the order in which you entered them. Note that the secondary key of the salary field in column H is not used (although it is still defined) because all the entries in the record-number field are unique—you need only define one key when the entries in that key contain no duplicates.

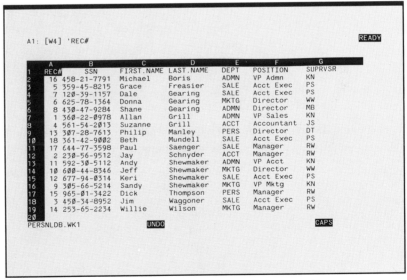

◆ **Figure 11.19:** *Personnel database sorted alphabetically by last name*

```
A1: [W4] 'REC#                                                          READY

        A         B           C          D         E         F          G
  1   REC#      SSN        FIRST.NAME  LAST.NAME  DEPT   POSITION    SUPRVSR
  2     16  458-21-7791   Michael     Boris      ADMN   VP Admn     KN
  3      5  359-45-8215   Grace       Freasier   SALE   Acct Exec   PS
  4      7  120-39-1157   Dale        Gearing    SALE   Acct Exec   PS
  5      6  625-78-1364   Donna       Gearing    MKTG   Director    WW
  6      8  430-47-9284   Shane       Gearing    ADMN   Director    MB
  7      1  360-22-0978   Allan       Grill      ADMN   VP Sales    KN
  8      4  561-54-2013   Suzanne     Grill      ACCT   Accountant  JS
  9     13  307-28-7613   Philip      Manley     PERS   Director    DT
 10     18  361-42-9002   Beth        Mundell    SALE   Acct Exec   PS
 11     17  644-77-3598   Paul        Saenger    SALE   Manager     RW
 12      2  230-56-9512   Jay         Schnyder   ACCT   Manager     RW
 13     11  592-30-5112   Andy        Shewmaker  ADMN   VP Acct     KN
 14     10  600-44-8346   Jeff        Shewmaker  MKTG   Director    WW
 15     12  677-94-0314   Keri        Shewmaker  SALE   Acct Exec   PS
 16      9  305-66-5214   Sandy       Shewmaker  MKTG   VP Mktg     KN
 17     15  965-01-3422   Dick        Thompson   PERS   Manager     RW
 18      3  450-34-8952   Jim         Waggoner   SALE   Acct Exec   PS
 19     14  253-65-2234   Willie      Wilson     MKTG   Manager     RW
 20
PERSNLDB.WK1                          UNDO                              CAPS
```

◆ **Figure 11.20:** *Personnel database sorted alphabetically by first and last name*

Summary

Troubleshooting

Question: When I try to perform a /Data Query Extract on my database, 1-2-3 merely beeps at me. What could be the problem?

Answer: The beep indicates that one or more of the /Data Query ranges—input, criteria, or output—aren't properly defined. Check each of these three ranges by selecting first /Data Query Input (/DQI), then Criteria (C), and finally Output (O). This process is easier if you are using Release 2.2, because you can check these ranges in the Query Settings sheet. After you have verified each range and made all necessary corrections, select the Extract option (E) to try your query again.

Question: I built a criterion formula to search for all part numbers greater than 2000. But when I performed my /Data Query Extract, 1-2-3 didn't locate a single matching record, and I know there are at least 50 or more in the database. What's the matter with the program?

Answer: The problem you are having could come from one of two sources: either the part numbers in the database are entered as labels and therefore the number 2000 must be enclosed in quotation marks, as in "2000", in the criterion formula, or you used the less than or equal to symbol (<=) instead of greater than or equal to (>=) in the formula.

Essential Techniques

To Create a 1-2-3 Database

1. Decide which data items you want in the database and how they are to be arranged.

2. Enter field names for each item of data to be entered in the database. Don't skip any columns when entering these field names.

3. Enter the first record in the row immediately below the one containing the field names. Don't skip any rows when entering records in the database.

4. Always enter the same type of data in each field: if the field tracks cities, don't enter states in it. Also, make all entries in a particular field of the same type. If the field contains labels, make all of its entries labels (even if this requires the use of a label prefix), and if the field contains values, make all of its entries values.

To Sort a Database

1. Save the worksheet containing the database.

2. Select /Data Sort Data-Range (/DSD), and define as the sort range all records in the database. Be sure, however, that you don't include the row containing the field names as part of this range.

3. Select the Primary-Key option (P), and indicate the column that contains the field on which the database is to be sorted. After moving the pointer to its column (the row doesn't matter; the row can even be outside of the data range), press Enter. Type A to have the records sorted in ascending order, or press Enter to have the records sorted in descending order (the default).

4. If the primary key contains duplicate entries and you wish to further refine the final arrangement of the records, select the Secondary-Key option (S). Indicate the column that contains the secondary key, then choose between ascending and descending order.

5. Select the Go (G) option to sort the database. Then select the Quit option to return to READY mode.

To Query a Database

1. Copy the names of the fields you wish to use as the search criteria in your queries to a new part of the database. If you retype their names rather than copy them with /Copy, you must make sure that they exactly match the way the field names appear in the database. Enter the criterion labels or values beneath the appropriate field names (arranged vertically for OR conditions and arranged horizontally for AND conditions), or enter a criterion formula using the appropriate logical operators and test cells.

2. If you are planning to extract records from the database with either /Data Query Extract or /Data Query Unique, you need to copy the names of the fields you wish copied to a new part of the worksheet. These field names will be used in the output range. Note that their order in the output range doesn't have to match that of the input range (database). Also, you don't have to include every field in the input range in the output range.

3. Select /Data Query Input (/DQI), and define the entire database (including the row of field names and all records) as the input range.

4. Select the Criteria option (C), and define the range that contains the copied field names and criteria placed beneath them as the criteria range.

5. Select the Output option (O), if you plan to select either Extract or Unique, and define the range that contains the copied field names to be used in the output range. Restrict the output range to just the field names, and include no blank rows beneath if you want to allow 1-2-3 to use as many rows as necessary to copy matching records below the field names. Include blank rows as well as the field names to allow copying of matching records to only those blank rows (thus preventing 1-2-3 from overwriting any existing data in the rows below when performing the extraction).

6. Select the appropriate query option—Find (F), Extract (E), Unique (U), or Delete (D)—then select the Quit option (Q) to return to READY mode.

Review   Important Terms You Should Know

ascending order	input range
ASCII sorting sequence	output range
criteria range	primary key
database	Query key (F7)
descending order	record
field	secondary key
field names	

Test Your Knowledge

1. A _____ is a table of related worksheet data organized in columns and rows. Each column of the table is a _____ and each row is a _____.

2. When designing a 1-2-3 database, you must enter the _____ in its very first row and begin adding the _____ in the rows right below without skipping any in-between.

3. When entering data in the fields of the database, you must make sure that they are all of the same _____.

4. To sort a database, you must define the _____, which includes all the data to be sorted, and at least one _____, which indicates which field to use in reordering the database.

5. In sorting, you can choose between _____ order and _____ order. If you wanted to alphabetize your database using the last-name field as the primary key, you would select the _____ order.

6. You only select a secondary key when the field that you have selected as the primary key contains _____.

7. If there are blank entries in the field used as the primary sort key, their records will be placed at the _____ of the database.

8. If there are numbers entered as values in the field used as the primary sort key, their records will be placed at the _____ of the database.

9. To locate a record that needs editing, you would select the _____ option on the /Data Query menu.

10. To copy records that need to be included in a special report to a new area of the worksheet, you would select the _____ option on the /Data Query menu.

11. When you use the /Data Query Find or the /Data Query Delete command, you must have defined both a _____ range and a _____ range. When you use the /Data Query Extract or the /Data Query Unique command, you must have defined a _____ range as well.

12. When defining either a criteria or output range, the field names that you use must _____ those in the input range.

13. To make the size of the output range directly dependent on the number of records that match your search criteria, you include only the _____ when defining the size of this range.

14. Your database contains a STATE field, and you wish to locate all records where the state is either Georgia or Florida. You've copied the field name STATE to cell N1 to set up the criteria range. To enter

your search criteria, you enter GA in cell _____ and *FL* in cell _____ and define the criteria range as _____.

15. You now wish to locate all the records except for those in California. To do this (using the same database as in Question 15), you replace GA with _____ and then redefine the criteria range as _____.

16. Your database contains an amount of sale field, and you wish to find all records where the sale was greater than or equal to $500.00 and less than or equal to $1,000.00. You've copied the field name AMT.SALE to cell P1 to set your criteria range. The first entry for the field AMT.SALE is in cell E3. To set up the search criteria for this query, you enter the logical formula _____ in cell _____ and define _____ as the criteria range.

17. If the last query operation you performed in 1-2-3 was /Data Query Extract, you can use the _____ key by pressing _____ to perform your next extraction when you are in READY mode.

18. When you use /Data Query Unique, 1-2-3 uses the field names in the _____ range to determine which records are duplicates.

Further Exercises

1. Retrieve the worksheet *PERSNLDB.WK1.* Then sort the personnel database by starting date (START.DATE) in descending order.

2. Next, sort the database first by department in ascending order, then by position in ascending order, and finally, by last name in ascending order. Remember that to sort a 1-2-3 database using three keys, you must perform two sorts (review the section on sorting on more than two keys if you need help).

3. Sort the database so that it is restored to its original order.

4. Perform an extract operation on the personnel database to locate all records where the start date is prior to January 1, 1985.

5. Perform an extract operation on the personnel database to locate all records where the supervisor's initials are either RW or KN *and* the salary is greater than $65,000 and less than or equal to $85,000.

6. Perform an extract operation on the personnel database to locate all records where the supervisor's initials are either RW or KN *or* the salary is greater than $65,000 and less than or equal to $85,000.

12

Data Analysis:
What-If
and Predictive

In This Chapter...

What-If Analysis in 1-2-3

Undoubtedly one of the most important uses for the 1-2-3 worksheet is *what-if* analysis, whereby you revise certain basic assumptions in your worksheet model to see what effect these have on the remaining calculated values. One of the most widespread and basic examples of *what-if* analysis in the worksheet is the projected income statement. Here, you make your best guess about the future revenues over the next few months, four quarters, or whatever the case may be, to determine what net income you could then expect.

To accomplish this, many projected income statements build a growth factor into the formulas that increase the revenues by specific percentages over the period covered. In working with projected income statements, you must often revise the assumed growth factor many times to realize the hoped-for net income. It is also common to modify the growth assumptions so as to create both best-case and worst-case scenarios, to show what net income may be expected under the best and worst conditions.

Under normal circumstances, to test new assumptions in the formulas of your worksheet, you must alter one of the input values and then recalculate the worksheet. The problem is that the original input value must then be restored or the new results must be saved in a new worksheet file if you wish to keep a record of the original results. Also, when using this method, you must keep changing the input value and recalculating the formula to subject it to further analysis using other possible values.

Using Data Tables to Perform What-If Analysis

To subject a worksheet to what-if analysis without having to continually change the input values in the formula or formulas in question, you can use the 1-2-3 /Data Table commands to create a data table. The program supports two types of data tables: a *one-variable* (or one-input) table created with /Data Table 1, or a *two-variable* (two-input) table created with /Data Table 2.

By creating data tables with the /Data Table commands, you can keep a record of the effect of testing multiple input values without disturbing the original result or having to continually update the input value and recalculate the formula. Such tables are saved as part of the same worksheet, making it unnecessary to create multiple copies of the spreadsheet. Also, the /Data Table commands arrange the results in a concise table whose results can be easily graphed.

Because the results in the table are returned as actual values, they are not recalculated when new values are entered or changed elsewhere in the worksheet. If you wish to perform further what-if analysis in the same data table, you can use the Table key (F8) to update the results in the data table after you enter new input values.

Because the data tables created with the /Data Table commands are static and can only be recalculated by using the Table key, their presence in the worksheet does not slow down the recalculation of the spreadsheet as you continue to build or refine it. Also, being stored as values, they use up less memory than would be required if you copied a basic formula and used slightly different input values in each copy.

F8: The Table Key

F8, the Table key, has no function until you select a /Data Table command

F8 performs either the /Data Table 1 or /Data Table 2 command, depending upon which operation was last selected, and recalculates the table using the new input values you enter

Creating Data Tables

To use /Data Table to automate what-if analysis, you must have a formula (sometimes called the *master formula*) that contains a variable, plus a list of *input values* that you want 1-2-3 to substitute for the variable in the formula. As mentioned earlier, 1-2-3 supports two types of data tables. You use the /Data Table 1 command to create the first type of table, when you are using a master formula that contains only one variable for which a list of input values is to be substituted. You use /Data Table 2 to create the second type of table, when you are using a master formula that contains two variables for which different ranges of input values are to be substituted.

Using the /Data Table 1 Command

You use the /Data Table 1 command to create a table that shows the effect of changing one variable in one or more master formulas. When you select the /Data Table 1 command (/DT1), you are prompted to enter the table range. This range must include the master formulas arranged in succeeding columns and the input values arranged in succeeding rows.

Figure 12.1 shows you this type of layout. Notice in this diagram that the cell in the upper left corner of this range, which forms the intersection of the row with the two master formulas and the column containing the input values, is the first cell of the table range and is left blank. In this example, the first master formula (A1*B1) is brought forward from cell C1 to cell C3, which, in turn, is used in the second master formula in D3. Note that if this table used only one master formula, it would be entered in cell C3 and the table range would then be B3..C9 instead.

After you enter the table range, you are prompted to indicate the location of input cell 1. The input cell 1 is the cell where 1-2-3 places the values it substitutes for the variable in the master formula(s) when it performs the calculations. This cell must be unprotected in order to allow this to happen. In Figure 12.1, the input cell is A1. After you indicate A1 as the location of input cell 1, 1-2-3 creates data table 1.

In creating this data table, 1-2-3 will substitute each of the input values from the range B4..B9 into the input cell in A1. It will then perform the first calculation—multiplying the substituted value in A1 by 15 in cell B1 (as called for in the first master formula, +C1)—and place this answer in the same row in column C, multiply the product by 7 (as called for in the second master formula, +C3*7), and place that answer in column D.

Note that as soon as the program finishes generating the data table, 1-2-3 always returns the original value to the cell designated as the input cell (in the example in Figure 12.1, this value is 10).

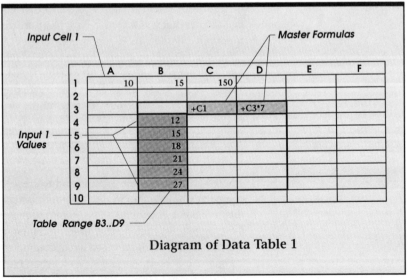

* **Figure 12.1:** *Diagram of a data table 1*

Using the /Data Table 2 Command

You use the /Data Table 2 command to create a table that shows the effect of changing two variables in a single master formula. As with /Data Table 1, when you select the /Data Table 2 command (/DT2), you are first prompted to enter the table range. This range must include the master formula in the first cell of the range, with the input values for the first variable arranged in succeeding rows underneath it, and the input values for the second variable arranged in succeeding columns to its right in the same row.

Figure 12.2 illustrates this type of layout. Notice in this diagram that the cell in the upper left corner of this range, which contains the master formula, forms the intersection of the row containing input values for the second variable and the column containing input values for the first variable.

After you enter the table range, you are prompted to indicate the location of input cell 1 and then the location of input cell 2. Input cell 1 is the cell where 1-2-3 places the values it substitutes for the first variable in the master formula, and input cell 2 is the cell where the program places the values it substitutes for the second variable. Both cells must be unprotected in order to allow this to happen. In Figure 12.2, input cell 1 is A1 and input cell 2 is B1. After you indicate these cells, 1-2-3 creates data table 2.

In creating this data table, 1-2-3 substitutes each of the input 1 values from the range B4..B9 into the input cell 1 in A1 and each of the input 2 values

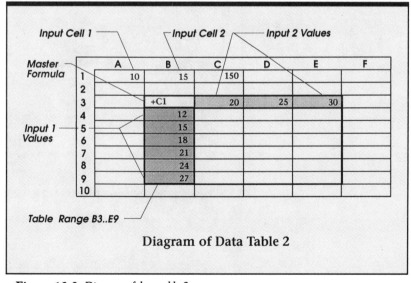

Diagram of Data Table 2

♦ **Figure 12.2:** *Diagram of data table 2*

from the range C3..E3 into input cell 2 in B1. The program then performs the first calculation of multiplying the substituted value in A1 by the substituted value in B1 (as called for by the master formula, +C1) and places this answer in the cell at the intersection of the input cell 1 row and the input cell 2 column values used in the calculation.

Note that as soon as the program finishes generating data table 2, 1-2-3 always returns the original values to the cells designated as input cell 1 and input cell 2 (in the example in Figure 12.2, these values are 10 and 15, respectively).

Analyzing a Database with Data Tables

In addition to making it easy to perform extensive what-if analysis on a spreadsheet, the 1-2-3 /Data Table commands can be used when working with databases to perform statistical analysis, summarizing the data contained within them. This is done by setting up master formulas that contain specific database statistical @functions, such as @DSUM, @DAVG, @DCOUNT, @DMAX, and @DMIN. (Table 11.3 summarizes these functions.)

Using a one-variable data table allows you to generate different summary statistics with these database @functions. Using a two-variable data table allows you to generate cross-tabulated statistics from the database using a single database function, but based on two different values in two fields. In both cases, the

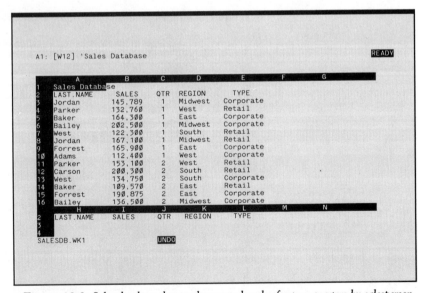

♦ **Figure 12.3:** *Sales database that tracks quarterly sales for two quarters by salesperson, region, and type*

list of input variables is used as successive criteria in the master formula that contains the appropriate database @function.

Using Database @Functions in One-Variable Data Tables

Figure 12.3 shows a sales database that tracks the quarterly sales figures for eight account executives. It not only records the amount of sales made by each, but also the quarter in which they were made, the region where the sales were made, and the type of sale, either directly to a corporate customer or to a retail outlet.

The database (range A2..E16) was given the range name DB, and this range name was then used to designate the input range with the /Data Query Input command. This figure also shows the criteria range, H2..L3, in a lower window. This range is given the range name CRIT and was used to define the database criteria range with the /Data Query Criteria command.

Figure 12.4 shows two different one-variable data tables that were generated with the /Data Table 1 command to create summary statistics charting the totals, averages, and number of sales made by each salesperson and in each region.

```
P1: [W11] 'LAST.NAME                                              READY

        P            Q                  R                  S
1  LAST.NAME  @DSUM(DB,1,CRIT) @DAVG(DB,1,CRIT) @DCOUNT(DB,1,CRIT)
2  Adams            112,400          112,400                  1
3  Bailey           339,000          169,500                  2
4  Baker            273,870          136,935                  2
5  Carson           200,300          200,300                  1
6  Forrest          356,775          178,388                  2
7  Jordan           312,889          156,445                  2
8  Parker           285,860          142,930                  2
9  West             257,050          128,525                  2
10
11 REGION     @DSUM(DB,1,CRIT) @DAVG(DB,1,CRIT) @DCOUNT(DB,1,CRIT)
12 East             630,645          157,661                  4
13 Midwest          651,889          162,972                  4
14 South            457,350          152,450                  3
15 West             398,260          132,753                  3
16
        H          I         J        K        L        M        N
2  LAST.NAME     SALES     QTR    REGION    TYPE
3
4
SALESDB.WK1                    UNDO
```

* **Figure 12.4:** *One-variable data tables that summarize the totals, averages, and number of sales by salesperson and region*

The three master formulas in both data tables return sales figures according to the various input variables in column P used as the criteria arguments of the database @functions. These @functions return sales figures because the master formulas use *1* as the field (or offset) argument, which refers to the second field in the sales database containing the quarterly sales.

In the first data table, the input variables include all salespeople entered into the database. The input cell for this data table was given as cell H3. In the second data table, the variables include the four regions serviced by these salespeople, and the input cell was given as cell K3.

Three master formulas containing the @DSUM, @DAVG, and @DCOUNT functions were used in generating the statistics in both data tables. When the /Data Table 1 command was used to generate the first data table, the table range was entered as P1..S9, and the input cell as H3. This corresponds to the input cell beneath the LAST.NAME field name in the criteria range (named CRIT). The program then generated the results shown in the first table by substituting each of the last names in the list of input values (the cell range P2..P9) in this criterion cell. This meant that the first total in cell Q2 was calculated using last name equal to Adams as the criteria argument. Next, 1-2-3 substituted Bailey as the criteria argument and calculated his total, and so on, using all names in this list. The same process was used to return the averages and the number of sales made by each.

The only difference between the first data table and the second shown in Figure 12.4 is that the list of input values has been changed. This, in turn, changes the criteria argument used to calculate the sales totals, averages, and counts. In the second data table (in the cell range P11..S15), the four sales regions were used as the criteria arguments. When indicating the input cell for this data table, the cell K3 (the one right below the field name REGION) was used.

Using Database @Functions in Two-Variable Data Tables

Beyond this type of one-way analysis, the /Data Table commands can also be used to perform two-way statistical analysis. By creating a master formula that includes a database @function and setting up a two-variable data table with the /Data Table 2 command, you can also generate cross-tabulated statistics from your 1-2-3 databases.

You can see how this type of analysis is done using the same sample sales database. Here, you use a two-variable data table to correlate the total sales made by each salesperson with the type of sale. Further, you can create a data table that correlates the total amount of each type of sale (either Corporate or Retail) with the regions in which they were made.

Figure 12.5 shows the two data tables that generated these statistics. Notice that just as when using two-variable data tables with spreadsheets, the ranges of input values are arranged below and to the right of the single master formula. However, in these examples, these input values represent the criteria by which each result is totaled with the @DSUM function.

In the first data table (U1..W9), the last names of the salespeople in the range U2..U9 are used as the input 1 values and the types of sales in the range U1..W1 are used as the input 2 values. The cell range named CRIT (which contains all field names copied from the database with a single empty cell below each) is again used as the criteria argument in the master @DSUM formula. When indicating input cell 1, cell H3 (below the field name LAST.NAME) is used. When indicating input cell 2, cell L3 (below the field name TYPE) is given.

When 1-2-3 generated this two-variable data table, it substituted each pair of values into the criteria range used by the @DSUM formula. In other words, the first total in cell V2 was generated using the criteria LAST.NAME equal to Adams and TYPE equal to Corporate, then the second total in V3 used the criteria LAST.NAME equal to Bailey and TYPE equal to Corporate, and so on until totals were calculated using every pair of input values as criteria.

To generate the second data table, the input 1 values were changed to the range U12..U15, the range containing each of the four sales regions. Then when issuing the /Data Table 2 command, the cell range U11..W15 is designated as the table range, cell K3 is used as input cell 1, and cell L3 is used as input cell 2.

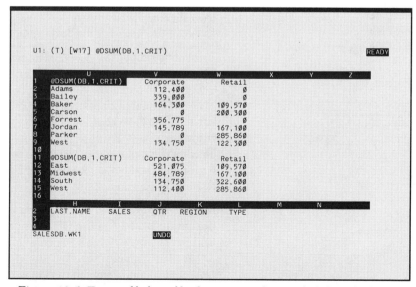

◆ **Figure 12.5:** *Two-variable data tables that summarize by type of sale for each salesperson and region*

Creating Your Data Tables

Creating data tables to perform what-if analysis is easy. To see how easy it can be, you should perform the following exercises on creating data tables.

Creating a One-Variable Data Table

In the first exercise, you will create a one-variable data table with /Data Table 1 that calculates how much money a nursery can expect to make on a daily, weekly, or monthly basis, when it gets $15.00 (wholesale) for each dozen roses sold but the number of dozens sold varies.

1. **Enter the labels *Price/dozen*, *Dozens/day*, and *Daily income* in cells A1, A2, and A3, respectively; then widen column A to 12 characters.**
   In cell B1, you will now enter the price per dozen of $15.00. In cell B2, you will enter 8 as the initial number of dozens expected to be sold, and in cell B3, you will enter the formula +B1*B2.

2. **Move the pointer to cell B1, enter *15*, and format the cell to Currency (C) with 2 decimal places; next, enter *8* in cell B2; finally, enter the formula *+B1*B2* in cell B3 and format the result, using the same format as in cell B1.**
   Next, you will bring forward the formula in cell B3 that calculates the expected daily earnings from rose sales, then add the formulas to calculate the weekly and monthly amounts.

3. **Enter the labels *Daily*, *Weekly*, and *Monthly* in cells C5, D5, and E5, respectively; then enter the formula *+B3* in cell C6, the formula *+C6*7* in cell D6, and the formula *+D6*4* in cell E6; format the range C6..E6 with the Text format (/RFT) so that you can see the formulas displayed in their cells.**
   To enter the range of input values to be substituted in the three master formulas you just entered in cells C6, D6, and E6, you can use the /Data Fill command.

4. **Move the pointer to cell B7, and select /Data Fill (/DF); then designate *B7..B17* as the fill range and *8* as the start value, and press Enter twice to accept 1 as the step value and 8191 as the stop value.**
   Now that you have entered the input values in column B, you are ready to use the /Data Table 1 command to generate the data table.

5. **Move the pointer to cell B6, select /Data Table 1 (/DT1), and designate the range *B6..E17* as the table range and cell *B2* as input cell 1; format the results using the Comma (,) format with 2 decimal places; widen columns D and E to 11 characters.**
    Your worksheet should match the one shown in Figure 12.6. Now see how easy it is to recalculate the data table with the Table key (F8) after entering new input values.

6. **Select /Data Fill (/DF), press Enter to accept the same range, type *19* as the start number, and press Enter twice more to accept the step and stop defaults; then press the Table key (F8) to recalculate the data table using these new input values.**
    As soon as you press the Table key, 1-2-3 recalculates the entire table using the new assumptions. Your new potential earnings should match those shown in Figure 12.7. Save this worksheet before going on to create a two-variable data table with the /Data Table 2 command.

7. **Save the worksheet under the file name *DT1CH12.WK1*.**

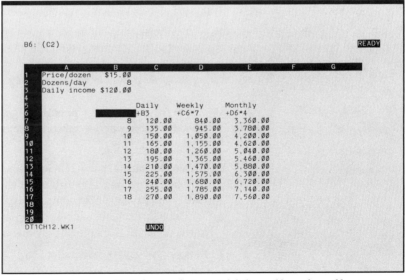

♦ **Figure 12.6:** *Data table 1 showing the potential daily, weekly, and monthly earnings from flower sales*

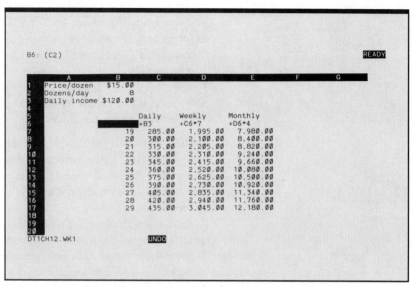

♦ **Figure 12.7:** *Data table 1 after changing the input values and recalculating the table with the Table key*

Creating a Two-Variable Data Table

In this next exercise, you will create a two-variable data table that will calculate the potential daily earnings not only when the number of dozens of roses varies but also when the price per dozen varies. You will create this data table from the one-variable data table that you just saved.

1. **Erase the entries in the cell range C5..E6.**
   This data table will use only one formula, which calculates the daily sales total in B3.

2. **Move the pointer to cell B6, then enter the formula +B3 in this cell; format the result with the Text format (/RFT) so that you can see this formula displayed in B6.**
   For these first calculations, you will want to return the input 1 values in the range B7..B17 to their previous values.

3. **Select /Data Fill (/DF), press Enter to accept the fill range B7..B17, type 8 as the start value, and press Enter twice more to accept the step and stop default values.**
   Now you must enter the input 2 values, to vary the price per dozen, in row 6 after the column (B) that holds the master formula.

4. **Select /Data Fill (/DF) again, press Esc to unanchor the fill range, move the pointer to cell C6, type a period (.) to anchor the range, move the pointer to cell G6, and press Enter; type *15* as the start value and press Enter twice more to accept the next two defaults; format the range C6..G6 as Currency (C) with 2 decimal places.**
   Now you are ready to generate the two-variable data table with the /Data Table 2 command.

5. **Select /Data Table 2 (/DT2), then press the → key twice to extend the table range to include column G (B6..G17), and press Enter; press Enter to accept cell B2 as input cell 1, then press the ↑ key to move the pointer to cell B1 and press Enter to make this cell input cell 2 and generate the table; finally, format the range C7..G17 as Comma (,) format with 2 decimal places.**
   Your data table should match the one shown in Figure 12.8. Next, let's change some of the assumptions in this data table (both input 1 and input 2 values) and then recalculate the table with the Table key.

6. **Use /Data Fill to change the price per dozen in row 6 so that it ranges from $10.00 to $14.00 across the range C6..G6;**

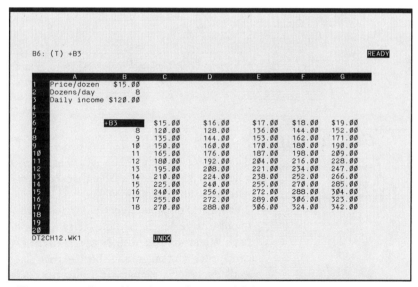

♦ **Figure 12.8:** *Data table 2 showing the potential daily income from rose sales when the number of dozens and price per dozen vary*

**next, change the number of dozens sold in column B so that
it ranges from 5 to 15 down the range B7..B17; recalculate
the two-variable data table by pressing the Table key (F8).**
Your new data table should match the one shown in Figure 12.9.
Now save this table in its own worksheet file.

7. **Save the worksheet under the file name *DT2CH12.WK1*.**

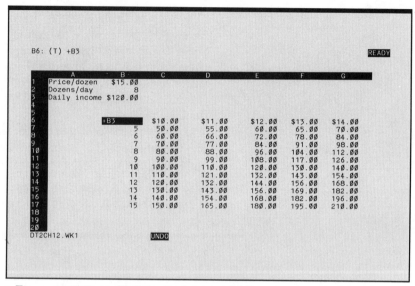

◆ **Figure 12.9:** *Data table 2 showing the potential daily income from rose sales after
modifying the number of dozens and price per dozen*

Calculating Frequency Distribution

Lotus 1-2-3 provides an easy way to determine the category to which worksheet
data belong with the /Data Distribution command. This command enables
you to quickly generate a table that shows you how often values in a range fall
within specified numeric ranges.

Frequency distribution of this kind has many practical uses, chief of which is
to tally the values that fall into certain intervals in order to graph the distribution. When working with large sets of data, this provides a practical way for
condensing and organizing them so that you can present them in one of the
available graphic formats. It is also especially useful when analyzing market
potential or market share for the company's products or services by categoriz-
ing and analyzing data obtained from research records or surveys.

Figure 12.10 illustrates how the /Data Distribution command works and how it can be used to analyze data. This figure shows the results of a survey that asked each of the respondents to indicate, among other things, the annual income and whether the company rented, leased, or owned the building in which they were quartered. This information was then entered in a worksheet. Once all the responses are recorded in the worksheet, the /Data Distribution command is used to determine how many of the companies responding to the survey fall into various income brackets. Seven different income brackets are established: up to $500,000, $500,001–$1,000,000, $1,000,001–$1,500,000, $1,500,001–$2,000,000, $2,000,001–$2,500,000, $2,500,001–$3,000,000, and over $3,000,000.

After the brackets are established, they are entered into the worksheet as shown in Figure 12.10 in the range E4..E9. Notice that only six intervals are actually entered in this range, and each is established by entering its upward limit. There is no need to enter an interval for the last bracket, those with incomes greater than $3,000,000. The /Data Distribution command automatically calculates the number of values that exceed the last interval (this is why the value 4 is in cell F10 in this figure).

When using the /Data Distribution command, you are required to indicate two ranges: the range that contains all the values for which the frequency

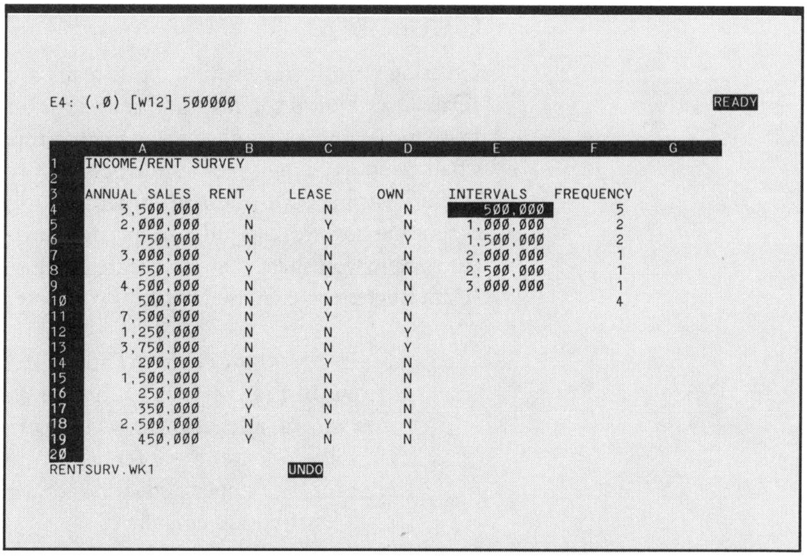

◆ **Figure 12.10:** *Using /Data Distribution to determine the number of companies in the survey that fall into each income bracket*

distribution is to be calculated (called the *values range*), and the range that contains the numeric intervals by which they are tallied (called the *bin range*).

In Figure 12.10, the values range is A4..A19, and the bin range is E4..E9. Regardless of where the pointer is located in the worksheet when the /Data Distribution command is used, the frequency values it returns are always entered in the column immediately to the right of the bin range, in the same row as its first cell. In this example, the frequency values returned by the /Data Distribution command are placed in the range F4..F10.

Because the program always locates the results of the /Data Distribution command right next to the bin range in this manner, you must always be sure that these cells are empty before using it. Any existing entries located in these cells would be overwritten by the calculated frequency values.

When setting up the bin range in a worksheet, you may often find it convenient to use the /Data Fill command, as long as the intervals are equal. It cannot, however, be used to generate bin ranges that do not have equal intervals. For instance, if the intervals for the bin range were set as 1000, 2500, 7500, and 9000, the /Data Fill command could not be used. In such circumstances, you must enter the bin range values manually.

Practice Using the /Data Distribution Command

Creating a frequency distribution is really a quick and easy process using the /Data Distribution command. In the next exercise, you will get to observe this firsthand as you set up a worksheet containing a list of salaries and ages for a small sample of employees at a hypothetical company. You will then use the /Data Distribution command to perform a frequency distribution that will determine how workers fall into specific income and age categories. Note that the sample worksheet that you create for this exercise will also be used in the /Data Regression exercise later in this chapter.

1. **Begin a new worksheet, and enter the labels and values shown in Figure 12.11; change the width of column A to 12 characters, and column C to 5 characters.**
   You will now enter the intervals for the salaries to be used as the bin range for the frequency distribution, which you will perform with the /Data Distribution command.

2. **Enter INTERVALS in cell D1 and widen the column to 10; move the pointer to D2 and use the /Data Fill command to fill the range D2..D5 with a series of numbers starting with**

30000, and increasing by 10000 each step, to enter intervals
from 30000 to 60000 in this range; then format this range of
values with Comma (,) and 0 decimal places.

Now you are ready to perform the frequency distribution indicating
how many salaries fall into each interval.

3. **Enter the label** FREQUENCY **in cell E1 and widen the
    column to 10; then select /Data Distribution (/DD), and
    indicate the range B2..B10 as the values range and D2..D5 as
    the bin range.**

    Your worksheet should now match the one shown in Figure 12.12.
    Remember that the first frequency value in cell E2 means that there
    are two salaries in the sample between 0 and $30,000, and the last
    frequency value in cell E6 means that there are three salaries above
    $60,000. Next, you will perform a frequency distribution for the ages
    in the sample.

4. **Copy the labels** INTERVALS **and** FREQUENCY **in cells D1 and
    E1 to cells F1 and G1; then widen columns F and G to 10.**

    Now you are ready to enter the interval numbers for the ages in the
    cell range F2..F5. This range will start at 25 and increase by 5s to 40.
    You can enter these values manually or with the /Data Fill command.

5. **Enter the values 25, 30, 35, and 40 in the cells F2, F3, F4,
    and F5, respectively.**

    Because the /Data Distribution command doesn't have a Reset
    option, you will have to unanchor the values range and bin range
    when performing the next frequency distribution.

6. **Select /Data Distribution (/DD), then press Esc to unanchor
    the values range, move the pointer to C2, type a period to
    anchor again, move the pointer down to C10, and press
    Enter; next, press Esc to unanchor the bin range, move
    the pointer to F2, type a period to anchor again, move the
    pointer down to F5, and press Enter.**

    Your worksheet should match the one shown in Figure 12.13. Now
    you are ready to save this worksheet.

7. **Move the pointer to cell A1, and save the worksheet under
    the file name** FREQCH12.WK1; **then clear the worksheet
    display.**

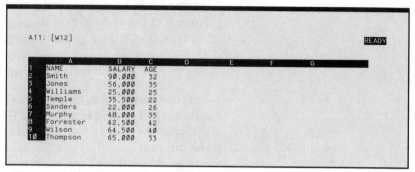

♦ **Figure 12.11:** *Salary worksheet with sample salaries and ages*

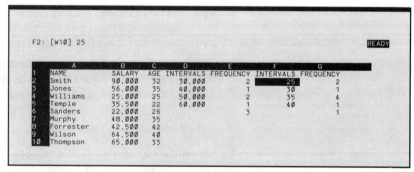

♦ **Figure 12.12:** *Salary worksheet after performing frequency distribution of sample salaries*

♦ **Figure 12.13:** *Salary worksheet after performing frequency distribution of sample ages*

Matrix Mathematics

Lotus 1-2-3 provides you with two powerful /Data Matrix commands, Multiply and Invert, which you can use to solve problems that call for matrix algebra. A *matrix* is nothing more than a rectangular array whose values are laid out in rows and columns, but matrix algebra is a tedious process when its calculations must be performed by hand. Matrix multiplication, which is often applied to problems involving probabilities, represents a specialized method for multiplying the contents of one matrix by another.

Matrix inversion is most often applied to solving simultaneous equations. It has fewer direct business uses, though it can be effectively applied to some business problems, such as those involving the allocation of resources. It involves finding the reciprocal or inverse values for those in a matrix, providing a method analogous to division (division in matrix algebra is not defined).

Multiplying Matrices

The /Data Matrix Multiply command enables you to multiply the columns of one matrix by the rows of a second matrix to produce a third matrix that contains the results of the multiplication. Note, however, that you can multiply two matrices only when the number of columns in the first matrix is equal to the number of rows in the second matrix.

When you select /Data Matrix Multiply (/DMM), the program prompts you to enter the first range to multiply. After you indicate the range that contains the first matrix (just as you would any other in 1-2-3), you are then prompted to enter the second range to multiply. After defining the range that holds the second matrix, you are prompted to enter the output range.

When defining the output range, you have to indicate only the first cell of the range that is to hold the product of these two matrices. Make sure, however, when indicating the location of the output range, that there are sufficient blank cells to hold the product of this multiplication. Otherwise, 1-2-3 will replace existing data in the output range with the newly calculated values.

When deciding if there are sufficient blank cells to hold the product, keep in mind that the /Data Matrix Multiply command creates an output range that contains as many rows as there are in the first range and as many columns as there are in the second range. Therefore, if the first range uses five rows and the second range uses three columns, you know that the output range will take up a range three columns wide and five rows long.

Inverting a Matrix

The /Data Matrix Invert command is used to create an inverse of a matrix. Only square matrices can be inverted, but not all such matrices have inverses.

If you should use the /Data Matrix Invert command on a matrix that has no inverse, the program will beep, go into ERROR mode, and display the error message

Cannot invert matrix

If you try to invert a matrix that isn't square (that is, one where the number of columns is *not* equal to the number of rows), 1-2-3 will display the error message

Not a square matrix

when the program goes into ERROR mode.

When you select the /Data Matrix Invert command (/DMI), 1-2-3 prompts you to enter the range to invert. After you define this range, the program prompts you to enter an output range. When defining the location of the output range, you only have to specify the first cell of this range. The output range will be the same size as the original matrix, so be sure that your worksheet has a sufficient number of blank cells to accept the values calculated during the inversion without having to overwrite existing data.

Practice Using the /Data Matrix Commands

One of the best business applications for the /Data Matrix Multiply command is to calculate the expected outcome for a particular business venture. In this next exercise, you will use matrix multiplication to determine the maximum daily profits for a florist who sells roses at $25.00 a dozen that cost $5.00 a dozen.

As the florist, you must choose between ordering 12, 13, or 14 dozen a day. To figure out which is most economical, you must determine the profit you can expect from ordering each quantity. As part of computing probable daily profits, you must take into consideration how likely it is that you will sell all the flowers you order (roses being perishable, all unsold dozens are worthless and must be replaced with new stock). For this problem, assume that you have a 55 percent chance of selling 12 dozen, a 33 percent chance of selling 13 dozen, and a 12 percent chance of selling 14 dozen roses.

To determine how many dozens to order daily to maximize daily profit, you have to construct a simple profit table and then multiply this by the probability factor associated with each quantity using the /Data Matrix Multiply command.

1. **Begin a new worksheet by entering the label *Estimated sales* in cell A2 and *Probability* in cell A3, and widen column to 15; then enter *12* in cell C2, *13* in cell D2, and *14* in cell E2;**

next, enter *55%* in cell C3, *33%* in cell D3, and *12%* in cell E3; then format the range C3..E3 to Percent (P) with 0 decimal places.

This establishes the probability matrix that will be multiplied by the values in the profit that you will now set up.

2. **Enter the label *Number of dozens ordered* in cell C6 and *Possible sales/day* in cell A7; then, enter the values *12, 13,* and *14* in the cell ranges C7..E7 and B8..B10, and move the pointer to cell C8.**

In cell C8, you will enter the formula to determine the daily profit for each amount. This formula is simply total revenue minus total cost. The total revenue is determined by multiplying the number of dozens that can be sold by 25 (each dozen is sold for $25.00). Total cost is determined by multiplying the number of dozens that can be sold by 5 (each dozen costs you $5.00).

3. **Enter the formula *($B8*25) – (C$7*5)* in cell C8; then format the result with the Comma (,) format with 2 decimal places and copy this formula to the range C8..E10.**

There are some problems with the resulting profit table. For one thing, the maximum possible profit when you order 12 dozen is 240.00 (at which point you are sold out), so the profits of 265.00 and 290.00 in cells C9 and C10 aren't feasible. The same illogic occurs in the next column at cell D10, where a profit of 285.00 from selling 14 dozen isn't conceivable when you have ordered only 13 dozen. You must correct these values before you multiply the matrices.

4. **Enter *240* in cells C9 and C10; then enter *260* in cell D10.**

Now the possible sales per day are correct in the profit table according to the number of dozens ordered. Next, enter the labels for the table that you will create with the /Data Matrix Multiply command.

5. **Copy the range of labels in C6..E7 to cell C13; then enter the label *Expected profit* in cell A15.**

You are now ready to multiply the probability matrix (C3..E3) by the profit matrix (C8..E10).

6. **Select /Data Matrix Multiply (/DMM), then indicate C3..E3 as the first range to multiply, C8..E10 as the second range to multiply, and C15 as the output range; format the results in C15..E15 with Currency (C) and 2 decimal places.**

Your worksheet should now match the one shown in Figure 12.14. From the results of this multiplication, you can see that you will

```
C15: (C2) 240                                                    READY

         A         B         C         D         E         F         G
1
2  Estimated sales              12        13        14
3  Probability                 55%       33%       12%
4
5
6                   Number of dozens ordered
7  Possible sales/day           12        13        14
8              12     240.00    235.00    230.00
9              13     240.00    260.00    255.00
10             14     240.00    260.00    280.00
11
12
13                  Number of dozens ordered
14                            12        13        14
15 Expected profit        $240.00   $246.25   $244.25
16
17
18
19
20
   DMMCH12.WK1                    UNDO
```

* **Figure 12.14:** *Determining probable daily profits from rose sales with /Data Matrix Multiply*

maximize your daily profits by ordering 13 dozen roses even if you only have a 33 percent chance of selling them all.

7. **Save this worksheet under the file name** *DMMCH12.WK1*, **then clear the screen.**

Solving Resource Allocation Problems with /Data Matrix Invert

To illustrate one of the business applications for inverting matrices, you will use this technique to solve a simple resource allocation problem. Figure 12.15 shows an example in which a filling station owner must determine the number of mechanics and service station attendants he must hire to staff a new full-service gas station.

During a typical eight-hour shift, the owner estimates that a mechanic should spend 3/4 of the time repairing automobiles and 1/4 of the time pumping gas, while an attendant will spend all of the time pumping gas and attending to the motorists' needs. The owner estimates that on the average it requires 1/10 of a man-hour to service each automobile that comes in for gas. Further, he reckons that the new station will need to sell gas to 320 autos a day and have at least 24 man-hours of the mechanics' time available for repair work.

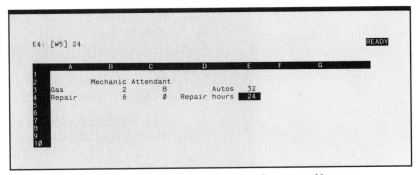

♦ Figure 12.15: *Setting up the filling station resource allocation problem*

To figure out how many attendants and mechanics to hire, a square matrix is set up in the cell range B3..C4 containing the time allotted to mechanics and attendants for pumping gas and doing repairs. A second matrix, containing the time for pumping gas and doing repairs, is set up in the cell range E3..E4. Because 320 autos are anticipated and it is estimated that it requires 1/10 of a man-hour to service each, the first value in the matrix is entered as 320/10, or 32 man-hours. The second value is 24 man-hours required to do repairs during a single day's business.

After setting up this table in the worksheet, you will use the /Data Matrix Invert command to invert the first matrix (B3..C4) into the output range B7..C8. You will then use the /Data Matrix Multiply command to multiply this output matrix by the man-hour matrix to determine the number of mechanics and attendants to hire in its output range E7..E8.

1. **Referring to Figure 12.15, enter the labels and values shown there; format the labels in the range D3..D4 so that they are right-aligned in their cells, and widen column D to 15; then narrow column E to 5.**
   Now you are ready to invert the first matrix, B3..C4.

2. **Select /Data Matrix Invert (/DMI) and indicate the range B3..C4 as the range to invert, then indicate B7 as the output range.**
   To find out how many mechanics and attendants are needed, you must multiply the inverted matrix in B7..C8 by the matrix E3..E4.

3. **Enter *Mechanics* in cell D7 and *Attendants* in D8, and then right-align them in their cells; next, select /Data Matrix Multiply (/DMM), and indicate B7..C8 as the first range to**

multiply, E3..E4 as the second range to multiply, and cell E7 as the output range.

When you press Enter after indicating the first cell of the output range in E7, you should see 4 as the number of mechanics and 3 as the number of attendants needed (Figure 12.16). Now save this worksheet and clear the screen.

4. **Save this worksheet under the file name *DMICH12.WK1*, then clear the worksheet display.**

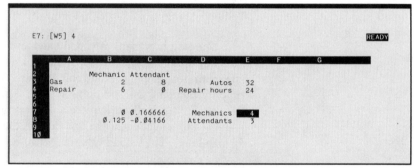

◆ **Figure 12.16:** *Filling station resource allocation problem solved with the /Data Matrix commands*

Performing Linear Regression Analysis

The /Data Regression command is used to obtain statistics that indicate the strength of the relationship between two or more sets of data in a worksheet. If a strong relationship, or high correlation, is shown to exist between them, then these statistics can be used to predict future trends and returns. These commands can be applied to a wide range of financial problems of any type where you have sample data and wish to examine how one sample might be related to another. It is also particularly useful in marketing activities where research or survey data must be correlated.

Specifically, the /Data Regression command provides you with the means to perform simple or multiple *linear regression analysis*. Simple linear regression involves correlating sample data for the dependent variable with those for a single independent variable. Multiple linear regression involves correlating sample data for the dependent variable with those for up to 75 independent variables (only 16 independent variables can be used if you are still using Release 2.01).

To perform regression analysis, you must have at least two paired sets of data—one representing the dependent variable and another representing the independent variable. The *dependent variable* contains the predicted values and is designated as the y variable. The *independent variable* contains the known values and is designated as the x variable. If the data in these variables are shown to be strongly related to each other, then a change in the x variable will predict the amount of change in the y variable.

The relationship between variables can be shown graphically by plotting them in a scatter diagram (just like a 1-2-3 XY graph). A straight line (thus the name *linear regression*) describing the best fit between the observed data in the sample containing the actual values of the dependent and independent variables can be drawn in such a diagram. This is called the estimated regression line, and it can be expressed mathematically by the equation

$$y = a + bx$$

where *a* is the y-intercept—or the point on the y (vertical) axis where the regression line intersects when the value on the x (horizontal) axis is zero—and *b* describes the slope of the line. This *b* value, referred to as the coefficient of x, tells you how much the line rises or falls on the y-axis for an increase of one unit along the x-axis.

Whenever you use the /Data Regression command, 1-2-3 creates a Regression Output table in the worksheet that contains a standard set of regression statistics. These include:

- *Constant*, which is the value of the y-intercept of the estimated regression line.

- *Std Err of Y Est*, which is the average of the differences between the estimated values on the regression line and observed values of the dependent variable.

- *R Squared*, which is the coefficient of determination. This statistic gives you an idea of the strength of the relationship between the variables. Note that if 1-2-3 displays a value less than zero, you selected Zero as the Intercept option when it was not appropriate to do so.

- *No. of Observations*, which is the number of values in the sample data.

- *Degrees of Freedom*, which is the number of observations minus the number of independent variables minus 1. If you use a zero intercept, the degrees of freedom equal the number of observations minus the number of independent variables.

* *X Coefficient(s)*, which is the slope of the estimated regression line (or lines, if multiple regression analysis involving several independent variables has been performed).

* *Std Err of Coef.*, which is the average difference between the x coefficient of the estimated regression line and those of the independent variable.

Figure 12.17 shows you the Regression Output table in the range A10..D18 created with the /Data Regression command using the sample data shown in range A2..A7 (Y range) and B2..B7 (X range) of the worksheet.

When you select /Data Regression (/DR), 1-2-3 presents you with the following menu of options:

X-Range Y-Range Output-Range Intercept Reset Go Quit

If you are using Release 2.2, the program also displays the Regression Settings sheet beneath the menu (Figure 12.18).

From the /Data Regression menu, you will have to specify three cell ranges: X-Range, which contains the data representing the independent variable or variables (you can specify up to 75 independent variables in Release 2.2 or 16 in Release 2.01 when performing multiple linear regression); Y-Range, which

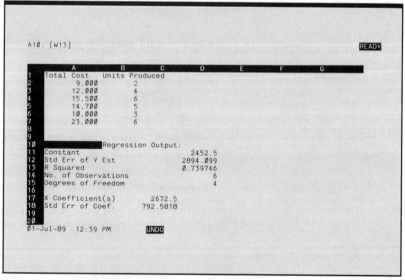

◆ **Figure 12.17:** *Typical Regression Output table created with the /Data Regression command using one independent variable*

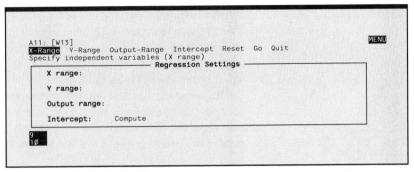

◆ **Figure 12.18:** *The /Data Regression menu with the Regression Settings sheet*

contains the data representing the dependent variable; and Output-Range, where the program places the table containing all the regression statistics.

This output range must be located in an area of the worksheet that contains a sufficiently large area of blank cells to accommodate the Regression Output table without destroying existing data. Such a table requires nine rows of the spreadsheet and two more columns than the number of columns used to indicate the y- and x-ranges (Figure 12.17). When indicating the location of the output range, you need only indicate the cell address or point to the location of the first cell in it.

When entering your sample data in the worksheet, organize the dependent variable in one column of the worksheet. When using more than one independent variable, you must arrange the values in a contiguous cell range with each adjacent column containing the values for each succeeding independent variable. The number of rows in each range must be the same, since regression analysis requires the use of paired data variables.

The /Data Regression menu is a sticky menu, like the /Print menu, where you can define various parameters before using the Go option to have the program perform the regression analysis. However, unlike when using the /Print menu, you don't have to select the Quit option on the /Data Regression menu to return to READY mode. Instead, you are automatically returned to READY mode as soon as the calculations are complete and 1-2-3 has created the Regression Output table in the worksheet.

To use the /Data Regression command, select the X-Range option on the /Data Regression menu (/DRX), then indicate the cell range containing the independent variable values. You may indicate this cell range by typing in the cell addresses or range name or by pointing to it. Next, select the Y-Range option (Y) to indicate the cell range containing the dependent variables in a similar manner. Then select the Output option (O) and indicate the location of the first cell of the range that is to hold the Regression Output table.

After defining these ranges, you can also select the Intercept option to change the default from Compute, where 1-2-3 calculates the constant or the y-intercept point, to Zero, where the program uses 0 as the constant (this affects all other regression statistics—most importantly, the x coefficient, which determines the slope of the regression line).

After selecting all these options, you choose the Go option (G) to have the program perform the necessary calculations and copy them into the area of the worksheet designated as the output range. The program remembers the options defined from the /Data Regression menu during a work session, and these will be saved in the worksheet file when you next use the /File Save command. If you wish to perform regression analysis using new data variables in the worksheet, you can select the Reset option (R) to clear all previously used variables and settings. This makes it a lot easier to define new x- and y- or output ranges if you are doing this by pointing.

Making Predictions Using the Regression Statistics

Of all the statistics returned by the /Data Regression command, the most important are the Constant and the X Coefficient(s) which you can use to predict future values and trends if the statistics show a strong relationship between your dependent and independent variables.

The equation for predicting the value of y for a given value of x using statistics in the Regression Output table is

$$y = Constant + (X \, Coefficient * x)$$

This means that once you have determined the Constant and the X Coefficient with the /Data Regression command, you can then use these values in this formula to predict what other values for x outside your sample will be given different values for y.

Practice Performing Regression Analysis

In this exercise, you will perform regression analysis on the salary and age data for which you generated the frequency distributions. In this case, the age data represent the independent variable (x) and the salaries represent the dependent variable (y). After generating the Regression Output table with the /Data Regression command, you will then use this data to predict the salary that one might expect to receive at different ages.

1. **Retrieve the worksheet *FREQCH12.WK1* that you created when practicing the use of the /Data Distribution command.**
   You will place the Regression Output table below the worksheet and frequency distribution data.

2. **Select the X-Range option on the /Data Regression menu (/DRX) and indicate the range C2..C10; next, select the Y-Range option (Y) and indicate the range B2..B10; select the Output-Range option (O) and indicate cell A11 as the range; then select the Go option (G).**
   Your Regression Output table in the range A11..D19 should match the one shown in Figure 12.19. Now you will use the Constant and X Coefficient in this table to set up a formula that will predict your salary in this company based on your age.

3. **Enter the labels *AGE* in cell F12 and *SALARY* in cell F13; enter *50* in cell G12, and the formula *+D12+(C18*G12)* in cell G13; then format this cell with the Comma (,) format using 0 decimal places.**
   Figure 12.20 shows you this formula and its result. Based upon this limited sample, you should expect to be making more than $76,000 a year at age 50. Now see what salary is predicted by this formula at age 40.

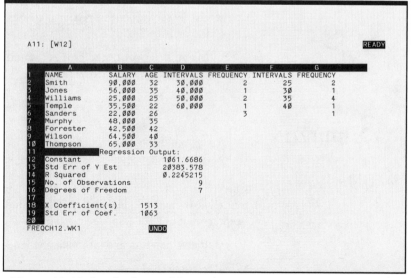

♦ **Figure 12.19:** *Sample salary worksheet with Regression Output table correlating salary with age*

```
G13: (,Ø) [W1Ø] +D12+(C18*G12)                                    READY

         A          B        C      D         E         F         G
 1  NAME           SALARY   AGE  INTERVALS FREQUENCY INTERVALS FREQUENCY
 2  Smith          90,ØØØ   32   3Ø,ØØØ        2        25         2
 3  Jones          56,ØØØ   35   4Ø,ØØØ        1        3Ø         1
 4  Williams       25,ØØØ   25   5Ø,ØØØ        2        35         4
 5  Temple         35,5ØØ   22   6Ø,ØØØ        1        4Ø         1
 6  Sanders        22,ØØØ   26                 3
 7  Murphy         48,ØØØ   35
 8  Forrester      42,5ØØ   42
 9  Wilson         64,5ØØ   4Ø
1Ø  Thompson       65,ØØØ   33
11              Regression Output:
12  Constant                   1Ø61.6686            AGE          5Ø
13  Std Err of Y Est          2Ø383.578            SALARY      76,742
14  R Squared                     Ø.2245215
15  No. of Observations               9
16  Degrees of Freedom                7
17
18  X Coefficient(s)    1513
19  Std Err of Coef.    1Ø63
2Ø
FREQCH12.WK1                        UNDO
```

◆ **Figure 12.20:** *Using the regression statistics to predict salary based on age*

4. **Move the pointer to G12 and enter 40 in this cell.**
   According to this formula, a person 40 years of age should expect to
   be making at least $60,000 a year at this company. Finish this exer-
   cise by saving your regression statistics in this worksheet under a new
   file name.

5. **Move the pointer to cell A1, then save the worksheet under
   the file name *REGRCH12.WK1*.**

Summary

Troubleshooting   **Question:**   I've tried to use the /Data Matrix Multiplication command to
multiply two matrices, but as soon as I finish defining the second range, 1-2-3
beeps, goes into ERROR mode, and displays the error message

   Matrices incompatible for multiplication

What's causing this?

Answer: You receive this error message whenever you try to multiply two matrices whose sizes aren't compatible. Remember that you can only successfully multiply

matrices when the number of *columns* in the first matrix is equal to the number of *rows* in the second matrix.

Question: I've tried to invert a square matrix with the /Data Matrix Invert command, but as soon as I finish defining the output range, 1-2-3 beeps, goes into ERROR mode, and displays the error message

Cannot invert matrix

What is the reason for this?

Answer: When 1-2-3 inverts a matrix, it finds the reciprocal or inverses of the values in the matrix. However, not all matrices have inverses that can be expressed. When this is the case and you use the /Data Matrix Invert command, 1-2-3 indicates this by going into ERROR mode and displaying this error message.

Essential Techniques

To Set Up a One-Variable Data Table

1. Enter the master formulas in a single row of the worksheet.

2. Enter the input values in a single column to the left of the column containing the first master formula, starting in the row beneath the one holding the master formulas.

3. Select the /Data Table 1 command and enter the range containing the input values and master formulas.

4. Indicate the location of input cell 1. This cell must be located outside of the table range.

To Set Up a Two-Variable Data Table

1. Enter the master formula in a cell of the worksheet.

2. Enter the input 1 values in a single column beneath the master formula.

3. Enter the input 2 values in a single row to the right of the master formula.

4. Select the /Data Table 2 command, and enter the range containing the master formula and both sets of input values.

5. Indicate the location of input cell 1. This cell must be located outside of the table range.

6. Indicate the location of input cell 2. This cell must also be located outside of the table range.

To Perform Regression Analysis

1. Enter your values for the dependent variable in the worksheet.

2. Enter your values for the independent variable(s) in the worksheet. Remember that you can have up to 75 independent variables (16 if you are using Release 2.01), but these must be arranged as part of a contiguous range with the values for each variable in adjacent columns.

3. Select the X-Range option on the /Data Regression menu (/DRX), and indicate the range containing the independent variable(s).

4. Select the Y-Range option (Y), and indicate the range containing the dependent variable.

5. Select the Output-Range option (O), and indicate the cell in the upper left corner of the range to hold the Regression Output table (make sure that 1-2-3 will not overwrite any existing data by creating this table in this part of the worksheet).

6. Select the Intercept Zero options to force 1-2-3 to use 0 as the y-axis intercept (the default is Compute, whereby the program calculates this intercept automatically).

7. Select the Go option (G) to have 1-2-3 compute the regression statistics and create the Regression Output table in the worksheet.

Review   Important Terms You Should Know

constant or y-intercept	master formula
dependent variable (y)	matrix
frequency distribution	one-variable table
independent variable (x)	Table key (F8)
input cell	two-variable table
input values	x coefficient or slope
linear regression analysis	

Test Your Knowledge

1. To perform what-if analysis with a single variable in a group of formulas, you would use the _____ command to set up a _____ .

2. To perform what-if analysis with two variables in a single formula, you would use the _____ command to set up a _____ .

3. To have 1-2-3 recalculate the values in a data table after entering new input values, you press the _____ key, which corresponds to function key _____.

4. To perform frequency distribution on a range of sample values, you must enter a range of numbers that represents the upper limits of the various _____ (called the _____ range by the 1-2-3 /Data Distribution command).

5. To multiply two matrices with the /Data Matrix Multiply command, the number of _____ in the first matrix must be equal to the number of _____ in the second matrix.

6. The size of the output range created when multiplying two matrices with the /Data Matrix Multiply command is equal to the number of _____ in the first range and the number of _____ in the second range.

7. To invert a matrix with the /Data Matrix Invert command, the matrix must be _____.

8. Linear regression analysis performed with the /Data Regression command correlates data in the _____ or _____ variable (the one containing predicted values) with data in the _____ or _____ variable (the one containing the known values).

9. When you perform regression analysis with the /Data Regression command, the output range contains _____ rows and _____ more columns than the number of columns used to indicate the y- and x-ranges.

10. To predict new values with the regression statistics obtained from the Regression Output table, you use the _____ and _____ statistics.

Further Exercises

1. Referring to Figure 12.21, create the sales forecast worksheet in the range A1..G8. In this model, the sales in February and March are calculated by increasing the previous month's salary by the growth

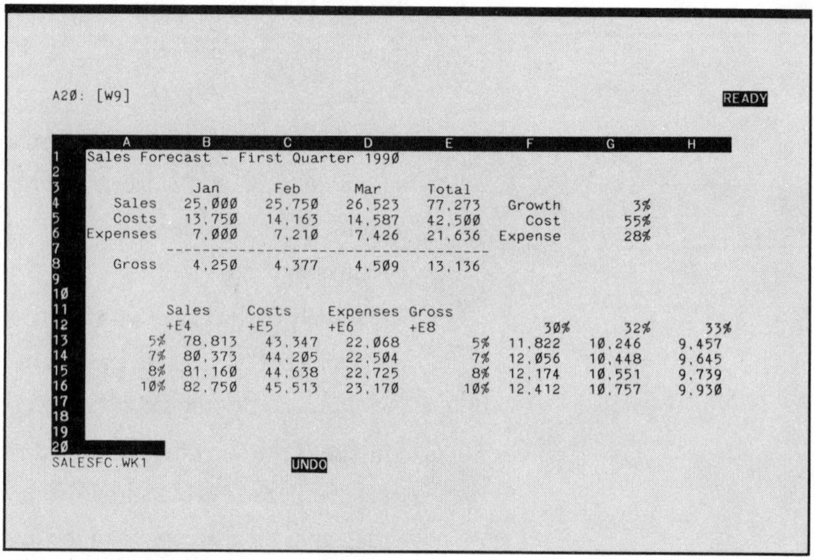

◆ **Figure 12.21:** *Sales forecast worksheet with data tables*

percentage entered in cell G4 so that the formula in cell C4 is
+B4*(1+$G$4). The costs for all three months in row 5 are calculated
by multiplying the sales for the month by the cost factor in cell G5.
The expenses for all three months in row 6 are calculated by multiplying the sales by the expense factor in cell G6. The gross income
figures in row 8 are calculated by subtracting the costs and expenses
for the month from the sales, so that the formula in cell B8 is
+B4−@SUM(B5..B6).

2. After you finish creating the forecast spreadsheet, create the one-
variable data table in the range A12..D16. Start by entering the labels
in cells B11, C11, and D11. Then bring forward the formulas that
calculate the total sales, total costs, and total expenses in cells B12,
C12, and D12 (format these cells with the Text format). Enter the
percentages shown in column A in the range A13..A16, then compute
the data table with the /Data Table 1 command (designate cell G4 as
the input cell 1).

3. After you finish creating the one-variable data table, create the two-
variable data table in the range E12..H16. Start by entering the label
Gross in cell E11. Then, bring forward the formula that calculates
total gross income in cell E12 (format this cell with the Text format).
Copy the percentages from the range A13..A16 to E13..E16, and enter

the expense percentages 30%, 32%, and 33% in the range F12..H12. Select the /Data Table Reset command, then compute this data table with the /Data Table 2 command (designate cell G4 as input cell 1 and G6 as input cell 2).

4. Save this worksheet under the file name *SALESFC.WK1*.

Part IV

♦

File
Management and
Organization

♦

13

Organizing and Maintaining Your Files

In This Chapter...

Organizing Your Worksheet Files in Directories

If you are using 1-2-3 on a two-disk-drive system, the worksheet files that you create with the program are normally saved on a data disk in the B drive of your computer. If your B drive is a standard 5¼-inch double-density drive, your data disk can hold about 360K of data. If your B drive is a 5¼-inch high-density drive, your data disk can hold about 1.2Mb (megabytes) of data (almost four times the storage capacity of a 5¼-inch double-density disk). For a 3½-inch double-density drive, your data disk can hold about 720K of data; a 3½-inch high-density drive can hold about 1.44Mb of data (about twice the storage capacity of a 3½-inch double-density disk).

If you are using 1-2-3 on a hard disk system, you can store your 1-2-3 worksheet files either on a data disk in drive A (which can be either a 5¼-inch double-density, 5¼-inch high-density, 3½-inch double-density, or 3½-inch high-density drive) or in your own directory on the hard disk.

Keeping related 1-2-3 worksheet files together in the same directory on your hard disk makes it much easier to locate them when you need them again. Although directories are most often used to partition the hard disk into smaller, more manageable units, you can also create and use directories on removable disks. This is especially true when using high-density disks that hold as much as 1.2Mb to 1.44Mb of data.

Creating Directories

File directories can only be created in DOS. To create a directory you must use the change directory command, which you can enter either as *MD* or *MKDIR*. When entering the name of the directory, you must obey the same naming conventions as you do when naming worksheet files; this means that directory names can't be longer than eight characters long and can't include spaces, although they can include a three-character extension after the file name preceded by a period.

Directories are structured as a hierarchy, with the *root directory* at the top. The name of the root directory at the top of the hierarchy depends upon the name of the drive. For example, the root directory on the first hard disk in your computer is called C:\, and the root directory on a floppy disk in drive A is called A:\.

Directory levels are indicated by the backslash (\) in the path name. For example, if you use the make directory command to create a directory named *DATA* when C:\ is the current directory, as in

    C:\>MD DATA

the directory will be located one level beneath the root directory and its path name will be C:*DATA*.

On this second level, directly beneath the root directory, you most often install application programs such as 1-2-3 or dBASE IV. You can, of course, also create directories at lower levels than this. For example, if C:\123 is the current directory and you enter the make directory command to create a directory called *DATA*, as in

C:\123>MD   DATA

this DATA directory will be located on the third level, two levels beneath the root directory, and its path name will be *C:\123\DATA*.

In organizing your hard disk and creating the directories that you wish to use with 1-2-3, you may locate your data directories either directly beneath the root directory (as in C:\DATA) or immediately beneath the 1-2-3 directory (as in C:\123\DATA); the program supports both arrangements.

Figure 13.1 shows a diagram that uses the first arrangement, whereby each person who uses the computer has his or her own directory, located directly below the root directory on the same level as the programs (1-2-3, Word-Perfect, and dBASE IV). Under this system, users keep all the files they create in their own directory, regardless of what program is used to create them. For example, under this system, Andrea's directory in Figure 13.1, C:\ANDREA, contains all her files whether created with WordPerfect, 1-2-3, or dBASE IV.

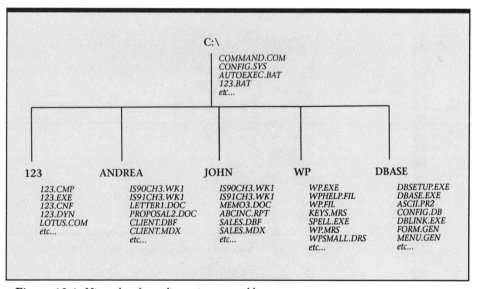

♦ **Figure 13.1:** *Hierarchy of user directories arranged by user*

Figure 13.2 illustrates the second arrangement, whereby files of a similar type or that perform the same function are maintained in their own directories, located directly below the one containing the program with which they were created. Under this system, all related or similar files are kept together in the same directory regardless of who created them. For instance, in Figure 13.2 all the budget worksheets prepared with 1-2-3 are located in C:\123\BUDGETS.

Whether you organize your own hard disk more along the lines of the arrangement shown in Figure 13.1 or the one shown in Figure 13.2 depends upon how many different people share the computer and use its various application programs, as well as upon the type of files you generate in your work.

Changing Directories in DOS

To make a new directory current once you have created it with the make directory (MD) command in DOS, you use the change directory command, which

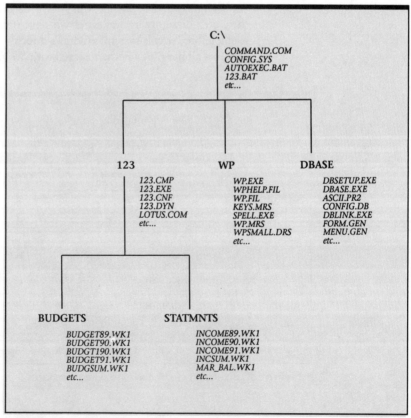

◆ **Figure 13.2:** *Hierarchy of user directories arranged by function*

you can enter as either *CD* or *CHDIR*. You can use the change directory command to go to one of the directories on the next level down in the hierarchy simply by typing *CD*, pressing the spacebar, typing the name of the directory, and pressing Enter. For example, if C:\123 is the current directory and you wish to make the DATA directory below it current, you can simply enter

CD   DATA

and press Enter at the DOS prompt. If, however, the C:\123 directory is current and you wish to make the C:\WP directory (on the same level) current, you must enter *CD\WP*. The backslash between *CD* and *WP* tells DOS to go back up to the root level (C:\) and then back down to the WP directory.

The directory one level up on the same path is called the *parent directory* in DOS. Note that you can always move to the parent directory using the CD command by simply typing *CD*.. (the double period after *CD* denotes the parent).

Deleting Directories

To remove a directory from your disk, you must use the remove directory command in DOS, which you can enter as either *RD* or *RMDIR*. DOS won't let you delete a directory until all the files it contains have been erased, so you will have to use the ERASE or DELETE command to remove all files before you try to use RD. Note that after emptying the directory of all files, you must first use the CD.. command to make the parent directory current before you can successfully use the RD command to remove the directory (DOS never allows you to delete the directory that you are in).

Changing the Default Directory in 1-2-3

When you start 1-2-3, the program makes the directory that is listed as the default directory current. When you first install the program, this default directory is the same as the one that contains the 1-2-3 program files—that is, A:\ on a two-disk-drive system and C:\123 on a hard disk system.

On a two-disk-drive system, you will want to change the default directory from A:\ to B:\, where you keep your data disk (drive A usually contains the 1-2-3 System disk). On a hard disk system, although you may leave C:\123 as the default directory, you will find your data files much easier to manage if you change the default directory to one of the worksheet data directories that you have created so that worksheets aren't saved in the same directory as the program files.

To change the default directory, select the /Worksheet Global Default Directory command (/WGDD) and then enter the path name of the directory that you wish to make the new default. Lotus 1-2-3 allows you to edit the path name of the default directory as soon as you access this command. If you wish to retype the path name, you must first press the Esc key to clear the current path. For instance, if you are changing the default directory on a two-disk-drive system from A:\ to B:\ and wish to retype the path name, you would type /WGDD, then press Esc to clear A:\ from the edit line before typing B:\ in response to the *Enter default directory:* prompt, and press Enter.

If you enter the name of a directory or its path incorrectly when assigning a new default, then 1-2-3 will beep, go into ERROR mode, and display the error message

Directory does not exist

After you change the default directory, be sure to select the Update option on the /Worksheet Global Default menu (/WGDU) to have your new directory saved as part of the permanent program defaults. That way, the next time you start 1-2-3, the program will automatically make the new default directory current.

Changing the Current Directory

To change the current directory without making it the new default directory, you use the /File Directory command. As the current directory, 1-2-3 automatically lists all the worksheet files it contains when you select a file command such as /File Save or /File Retrieve (you can, however, override the current directory simply by typing the complete drive and directory path as part of the file name). Note that the directory you select with the /File Directory command remains current only during your work session in 1-2-3; it reverts back to the default directory when you next start the program.

When you select the /File Directory command to change the current directory, you must retype the entire directory path, because 1-2-3 won't let you edit the existing one (this is just the opposite of the way the /Worksheet Global Default Directory command works). To do this, just begin typing the whole path name (including the drive letter, colon, and all the directories separated by backslashes). Once you've begun typing the path name, you can edit the characters you've entered. As soon as you finish entering the path, press Enter, and you will be returned to READY mode in the worksheet. The next time you select a file command such as /File Save or /File Retrieve, you will notice that 1-2-3 now lists only the worksheet files in the new current directory.

Assigning File Names When Saving Your Worksheets

As you know, all worksheets created in 1-2-3 must be saved in disk files with the /File Save command if you want to retain permanent copies of them.

When you use this command the first time, the program prompts you to enter a file name.

When assigning a file name to a worksheet, you must obey all DOS file-naming conventions. Basically, this means that you are limited to an eight-character file name that cannot include the following:

- ◆ Spaces (replace all spaces with hyphens or underscores)

- ◆ Periods, except to denote the beginning of a three-character file name extension

- ◆ These reserved characters: * + = [ ] : ; " ? / \ < >

Any lowercase letters used in a file name are automatically converted to upper-case in directory listings.

If you don't enter a file extension, 1-2-3 will automatically append its own extension to the file name you enter. This extension varies according to the version of the program you are using: Release 1A worksheets are given the extension .WKS; Release 2.01 and 2.2 are given the extension .WK1; and Release 3.0 worksheets are given the extension .WK3.

When you name a worksheet, 1-2-3 does allow you to add your own file name extensions. To do this, you must enter the complete file name including a period and the extension you wish to use. Because the /File Retrieve command only lists worksheets that follow the .WK? extension, you will have to enter the complete file name each time you wish to retrieve files with other extensions. You can, however, use the /File List Other command to obtain a directory listing that includes these files.

After you have saved a worksheet once, 1-2-3 suggests the file name you originally gave it when you next select the /File Save command to save the updates made to the worksheet. If you want to save your changes under the same file name, you accept the file name by pressing Enter. The program then supplies three further choices: Cancel, Backup, and Replace (Release 2.01 displays only Cancel and Replace; the Backup option is new in Release 2.2). Choose the Replace option to have your updates to the worksheet saved under the same file name. Choose the Backup option to have the current disk version of the worksheet saved under the same file name with the .BAK extension and the updated version in memory saved under the same file name with the .WK1 extension (that way, you can still retrieve the unedited version by retrieving the .BAK copy). The Cancel option (the default) is supplied in case you access the command by mistake and want to return to the spreadsheet without saving it.

To save the updated worksheet under a new file name, you can either retype the file name (the current file name disappears as soon as you type the first character of the new file name) or press the spacebar and then edit only those characters in the file name that require changing. To remove the current file name from the edit line before you start typing, you can press the Esc key twice. To remove the drive letter and directory path from the edit line, you need to press Esc a third time. This allows you to save the file on a new disk or in a new directory.

Using Passwords to Protect Worksheet Files

When saving your worksheet, you can also add a password, which you must enter each time you retrieve the worksheet. This means that if you don't know the password assigned to a file, you will not be able to successfully retrieve it. Although this type of protection limits access to only those entrusted with the password, it can also prevent you from using your own worksheets if you forget the password.

To assign a password to a file, you press the spacebar, type *p*, and press the Enter key after entering the file name. The program will then prompt you to enter the password. The password that you enter can be up to 15 characters long and is case-sensitive (this means you must remember whether you entered the letters in a password in uppercase or lowercase). As you enter the password, the characters that you type aren't echoed on the screen (this makes it impossible for anyone else who can see your screen to read the password as you enter it).

After you press Enter, you receive a second prompt to verify the password just entered. Here, you must type the password a second time, exactly as you originally entered it (as before, the characters that you enter aren't displayed on the screen as you type them). If the two passwords do not match in every detail, 1-2-3 will abort the save operation altogether, and you will have to start over by issuing the /File Save command again. If they do match, the program will save the file with your password.

Retrieving a Password-Protected File

When you select the /File Retrieve command and choose a password-protected file, you are immediately prompted to enter the password. Failure to enter the password exactly as it was assigned to the file will result in 1-2-3's aborting the /File Retrieve operation and returning you to READY mode.

Remember that if you can't reproduce the password, you won't be able to regain access to the worksheet (meaning not only that you can't revise it, but also that you can't print it). Also, when you copy a worksheet file that has been password-protected, its password is copied as well. This means that you must either remove the password protection from the file before giving a copy to a co-worker, or you must inform him or her of the password assigned to the file.

Removing Password Protection from a File

Each time you save a password-protected file, you see the message [PASSWORD PROTECTED] following its file name. If you press Enter and select the Replace or Backup option, all updates to the worksheet are saved under the same file name along with the same password.

If, however, you no longer wish to have the file password-protected, select /File Save and then press either the Esc or Backspace key to delete the [PASSWORD PROTECTED] message, and press Enter. When you then select the Replace or Backup option, the file is saved under the same name, but without password protection. To remove the password and save the file under a new name, press the Esc key twice—the first time to delete the password-protected message, and the second time to remove the current file name. Then type in the new file name without entering a new password.

File Maintenance Operations

You can accomplish almost all routine file maintenance operations—such as formatting new data disks, making backup copies of files, erasing unwanted files, creating new directories and moving files into them, and listing files in a directory—while running 1-2-3. You can perform a couple of these tasks—listing files and erasing files in the current directory—from the /File menu within 1-2-3 itself. You must perform the others within DOS using the appropriate operating-system command. However, by using 1-2-3's /System command, you can temporarily go to DOS, where you can perform all the required maintenance tasks and then return directly to 1-2-3 (even when working on a worksheet). This eliminates the need to save your worksheet before quitting 1-2-3, and then restart the program after performing the maintenance tasks in DOS.

Before examining the /System command, let's look at the file maintenance tasks that you can perform from the /File menu within 1-2-3.

Obtaining a Listing of Files

To obtain a directory listing of all files of a certain type, such as worksheet files (using the .WKS, .WK1, or .WK3 extension) or graph files (using the .PIC extension), you use the /File List command. When you select /File List, you are presented with options that enable you to select the type of files you wish to see:

Worksheet Print Graph Other Linked

(Note that the Linked option is new in Release 2.2: Release 2.01 doesn't support linked formulas in worksheets.) When you choose one of these options,

1-2-3 displays a full-screen listing of all files of that type in alphabetical order by file name. This screen also lists the date and time of the last update, as well as the size in bytes of the first file on this screen. To see these same statistics for another file on this screen, just use the cursor-movement keys to move the pointer to it. If there are no files of the type you selected in the current directory, the program displays the prompt

Enter extension of the files to list:

followed by the path name of the current directory, such as C:\123\. At this point, you are free to enter a DOS search pattern or press Esc twice to return the /File menu.

When you select one of the first four options on this menu, the program segregates the directory listing by file type, using the appropriate DOS search pattern. For example, to produce a listing of all worksheet files when you select the Worksheet option on the /File List menu, the program uses the pattern *.WK?. The asterisk (*) before the period matches any file name. Note that the file extension includes the question mark (?) after *WK* so that it will match *WKS*, used by Release 1A; *WK1*, used by Release 2.01 and 2.2; or *WK3*, used by Release 3.0.

When you select the Print option on the /File List menu, the program gives you a listing of all ASCII files created with the /Print File command (see Chapter 14), which carry the extension .PRN (for Print file), by using the pattern *.PRN. Similarly, you obtain a listing of all graph files in the current directory by using the /File List Graph command. In this case, the program employs the search pattern *.PIC (the extension given to all graphs saved with the /Graph Save command).

Because you can replace the automatic worksheet extension .*WK1* with your own file name extensions when saving worksheets, 1-2-3 provides the Other option on the /File List menu to enable you to obtain a directory listing of them. With the Other option, the program uses the global search pattern *.*. This means that all files regardless of file name or extension in the current directory or on the data disk are to be listed.

✳ *New in 2.2*   You use the Linked option on the /File List menu to obtain a directory listing of all files in the current directory that are linked to the current worksheet. Because linking is new in Release 2.2, this option is new to this menu. For more information on linking worksheets and using this command, refer to Chapter 7.

✳ *New in 2.2*   *Creating a Table Listing the Files in the Current Directory*

Release 2.2 includes a Table option on its new /File Admin menu that you can use to create a table in the worksheet listing all files of a particular type in the directory of your choice. When you select the /File Admin Table command (/FAT), you are presented with the same five options as are found on the /File List menu:

Worksheet Print Graph Other Linked

When you select any of the first four options, the program first displays the prompt *Enter directory:* followed by the path name of the current directory. The directory referred to here is the one containing the files to be listed in the worksheet table. To use the current directory, press Enter. To use any another directory, edit the path name before pressing Enter.

After you indicate the directory to use, you are prompted to enter the table range. As when creating a range name table with the /Range Name Table command, you only have to indicate the address of the first cell of the table (that is, the one in the upper left corner) when responding to this prompt. As with all other 1-2-3 table commands, such as /Range Name Table and /Graph Name Table, the program overwrites any existing data in the range it uses when creating any of these file tables, so you must be sure that the location you select leaves sufficient room for the table.

All file tables created with the /File Admin Table command use four columns of the worksheet: the first column contains the file names arranged alphabetically; the second column has the date numbers of the dates the files were last revised; the third column has the time numbers of the times the files were last revised; and the fourth column has the size of the files in bytes. The number of rows required by the file table depends, of course, upon the number of files and types of files in the selected directory. If you select the Other option (which includes all files in the directory) for a large directory, your file table may require hundreds of rows in the worksheet.

When you select the Worksheet option, 1-2-3 uses the search pattern *.WK?, so this file table will include all worksheet files regardless of whether they were created in Release 1A, Release 2.01 or 2.2, or Release 3.0. When you select the Print option, the program uses the search pattern *.PRN, so this file table will include only those files in the directory that have the extension .PRN. When you select the Graph option, 1-2-3 uses the pattern *.PIC to create a table with all graph files. And when you select the Other option, the program uses the pattern *.* to include all files in the directory.

Figure 13.3 shows you the file table created with the Other option, listing all files in the C:\PRACTICE directory (you can see only the first part of this listing in the figure). Note that I added the headings in the first three rows of this table and formatted the date and time serial numbers after the file table was created by 1-2-3.

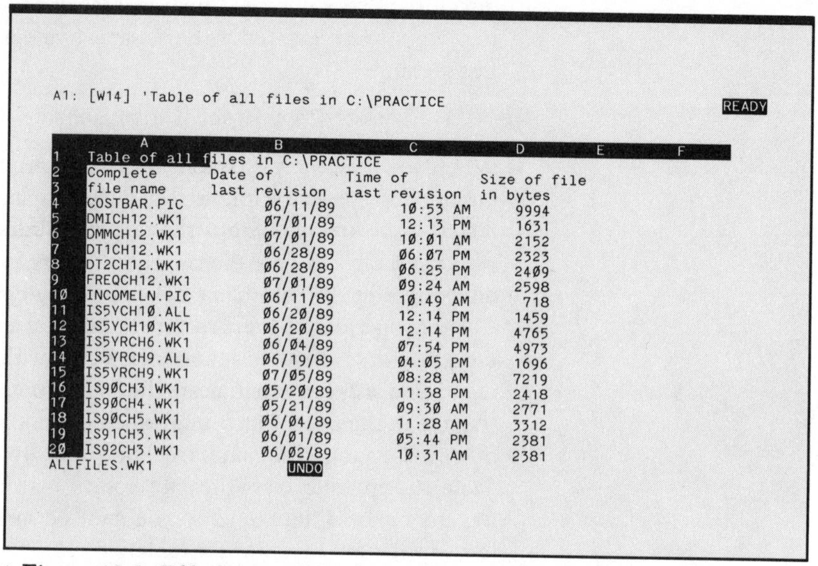

A1: [W14] 'Table of all files in C:\PRACTICE READY

	A	B	C	D
1	Table of all files in C:\PRACTICE			
2	Complete	Date of	Time of	Size of file
3	file name	last revision	last revision	in bytes
4	COSTBAR.PIC	06/11/89	10:53 AM	9994
5	DMICH12.WK1	07/01/89	12:13 PM	1631
6	DMMCH12.WK1	07/01/89	10:01 AM	2152
7	DT1CH12.WK1	06/28/89	06:07 PM	2323
8	DT2CH12.WK1	06/28/89	06:25 PM	2409
9	FREQCH12.WK1	07/01/89	09:24 AM	2598
10	INCOMELN.PIC	06/11/89	10:49 AM	718
11	IS5YCH10.ALL	06/20/89	12:14 PM	1459
12	IS5YCH10.WK1	06/20/89	12:14 PM	4765
13	IS5YRCH6.WK1	06/04/89	07:54 PM	4973
14	IS5YRCH9.ALL	06/19/89	04:05 PM	1696
15	IS5YRCH9.WK1	07/05/89	08:28 AM	7219
16	IS90CH3.WK1	05/20/89	11:38 PM	2418
17	IS90CH4.WK1	05/21/89	09:30 AM	2771
18	IS90CH5.WK1	06/04/89	11:28 AM	3312
19	IS91CH3.WK1	06/01/89	05:44 PM	2381
20	IS92CH3.WK1	06/02/89	10:31 AM	2381

ALLFILES.WK1 UNDO

◆ **Figure 13.3:** *Table showing all files in the* C:\PRACTICE *directory*

The Linked option on the /File Admin Table menu creates a special table that lists all worksheets in the specified directory that are linked by formula references to the worksheet in memory. This is the only /File Admin Table option that requires you to have an actual worksheet in memory at the time you use it; all the others can be used to create their file tables in a blank worksheet.

You have already had some experience with the /File Admin Table Linked command. Remember that in Chapter 7, you created this type of file table in your ISLINK worksheet, which listed all the files linked to it by formula reference (for an illustration of this type of file table, see Figure 7.13).

Deleting Files

To delete an unwanted file from the current directory or data disk, you use the /File Erase command. When you select /File Erase (/FE), 1-2-3 presents you with the options

Worksheet Print Graph Other

Select the option that matches the type of file you wish to delete, or select the Other option (O) to obtain a listing of all files in the current directory.

After you choose the file type, the program displays a single-line listing of all files, just as it does when you use /File Retrieve (to obtain a full-screen listing, press the Name key, F3). After you select the file to delete by moving the pointer to it and pressing Enter, 1-2-3 displays the options

No Yes

Select No by pressing Enter or typing *N* if you wish to abort the erasing of the file. Otherwise, type *Y* to select the Yes option and carry out its deletion. Remember, however, that once you select the Yes option, the file is gone and cannot be retrieved again with 1-2-3. The Undo feature in Release 2.2 is powerless to restore a file that has been erased with the /File Erase command. The only way to retrieve a file erased in error is with the use of a stand-alone DOS utility program such as PC Tools Deluxe or The Norton Utilities.

Because this method of deletion allows you to erase only a single file at a time, it is much more efficient to use the DELETE or ERASE command in DOS with appropriate wildcard characters when you need to delete a particular group of 1-2-3 files or all data files in the directory.

Using the /System Command to Go to DOS

The /System command on the 1-2-3 main menu enables you to go temporarily to DOS, where you can use such commands as FORMAT, DIR, COPY, DELETE, ERASE, CHKDSK, MD, CD, and RD to perform routine file maintenance. When you select the /System command, the program starts a new version of the command processor so that you aren't actually returned to the DOS processor from which you started 1-2-3 (this second version is known as a *DOS shell*). During the time you are in the DOS shell, the 1-2-3 program and whatever worksheet you had in memory at the time you selected /System remain in RAM.

In addition to being able to use a wide variety of DOS commands to perform file maintenance tasks, you can also start other programs from the DOS shell, provided that your computer has enough memory to store the 1-2-3 program and any worksheet you were working on, as well as the new program. If there isn't enough memory, you will receive the error message

Program too big to fit in memory

when you enter the startup command for the new program. Note that because Release 2.2 requires more memory than Release 2.01, you may find it difficult to start any other application program while running 1-2-3.

Although it's safe to use most DOS commands (including all those listed at the beginning of this section) from the DOS shell, you *cannot* use any DOS commands or start any other utility applications that stay resident in RAM after you start them (such programs are called *TSRs*, for Terminate and Stay Resident). This includes programs such as Sidekick, as well as the DOS commands PRN, GRAPHICS, and MODE. If you do start a TSR from the DOS shell, 1-2-3 will probably "freeze up" or crash when you return to the program.

As soon as you select /System from the 1-2-3 menu, you are presented with the DOS prompt and are located in the directory where you started 1-2-3. If you are using the program on a two-disk-drive system, you will have to replace your 1-2-3 System disk with a DOS disk unless you have copied COMMAND.COM on the 1-2-3 System disk. To return to 1-2-3 and any worksheet at any time from the DOS prompt, you type the word EXIT and press the Enter key. Never turn off the computer after using the /System command if you have a worksheet in RAM that has either never been saved or contains edits that have not yet been saved.

Everyone who uses 1-2-3 should be made familiar with the workings of the /System command (especially those users whose DOS skills are minimal and would never intentionally use this command). This is because it is so easy to select this command accidentally by transposing the F and S when entering the command /FS to save a file with /File Save.

New users may become unsettled when they suddenly see the DOS prompt instead of having a file saved. If they do not understand the meaning of the EXIT message and panic in some manner, the worksheet in RAM could be lost. The most common panic reaction is to try to restart 1-2-3 at the DOS prompt by entering the 123 or LOTUS startup command. Of course, should a second copy of 1-2-3 be started in the DOS shell, it won't contain the worksheet that the user was trying to save at the time the /System command placed him or her in DOS.

Note that if you are using Release 2.2, 640K is not sufficient memory to enable you to load a second copy of the program into RAM. When you try, you will receive the error message

1-2-3 cannot start because there is not enough memory available.
(Press any key to exit)

It is, however, possible to start a second copy of Release 2.01 in the DOS shell if your computer has 640K and the worksheet in memory isn't too large.

Formatting Data Disks from the DOS Shell

Before you can save data on a new disk, you must prepare it with the DOS FORMAT command. You can do this from the DOS shell by using the /System command. This is especially helpful if you find yourself in a situation where you need a data disk in order to save the worksheet you have created and have no prepared data disks available.

As soon as you are at the DOS prompt, you can change to the DOS directory containing the FORMAT.COM file and then use the FORMAT command to prepare a new data disk. When you are finished formatting disks, you can then return to 1-2-3 by typing EXIT and pressing Enter, whereupon you can save your worksheet on the newly formatted disk by selecting /File Save.

Making Backup Copies of Your Data Files

You can also use the /System command to make backup copies of your data files while running 1-2-3 in the background. When doing this, you can use the DIR command to obtain a listing of all files or a specific group of files. You can also use the MD (MKDIR) command to create a new directory to hold the backup files, and then use the COPY command to copy them to it. More commonly, you will use the COPY command to copy your data files located on drive C or B to a backup disk in drive A.

Practice Organizing and Maintaining Your 1-2-3 Files

The exercises for this chapter will give you practice in the organizing and housekeeping of your 1-2-3 files. As part of the organizing, you will learn how to create a directory for your 1-2-3 files and copy them into it. As part of the housekeeping chores, you will learn how to make backup copies of these files as well as delete those that are no longer needed.

If you have completed all the exercises up to this point in the book (the supplementary exercises at the end of most of the chapters as well as those in the text), you now have a total of 31 files (five of which are graph files and two of which are Allways files, the rest being worksheet files). If you are working on a two-disk-drive system, I assume that these files are all on one data disk in drive B (in the root directory B:\). If you are working on a hard disk system, I assume that these files are all in the same directory as your 1-2-3 program files (C:\123). If you are inexperienced with the DOS commands used in these exercises, I urge you to proceed slowly, checking that you have typed each command correctly before you press the Enter key.

1. **Clear the worksheet display, if necessary, with the /Worksheet Erase command.**
   Before you can do anything with the 1-2-3 files that you've created, you must be in the directory that contains them.

2. **Select /File Directory (/FD); if the directory listed is indeed the one containing your practice files, press Enter; if not, type the name of the directory that contains them (such as B:\ or C:\123).**
   Next, verify that all your practice worksheet files are located in this directory by using the /File List Worksheet command.

3. **Select /File List Worksheet (/FLW).**
   Your screen should be similar to the one shown in Figure 13.4. If you have created all the practice worksheets, yours will contain the same

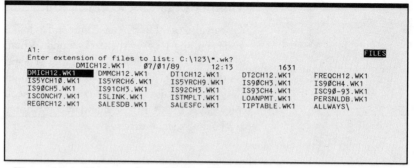

◆ **Figure 13.4:** *Obtaining a listing of all worksheet files in the current directory*

files. If you have a hard disk and have installed Allways, yours will
also display the ALLWAYS\ directory at the end of the listing (1-2-3
always displays the subdirectories of the current directory at the end
of the file listing). Next, obtain a listing of all the graph files in the
current directory.

4. **Press Enter to return to the worksheet; then select /File List
   Graph (/FLG).**
   If you did all the graph exercises in Chapter 9, you will see five PIC files
   listed on this screen. Now see what other files are in this directory.

5. **Press Enter to leave this screen; then select /File List Other
   (/FLO).**
   If your current directory is C:\123, you will see a listing similar to the
   one shown in Figure 13.5. If your current directory is B:\123, you
   will see a mix of your WK1 and PIC files on the screen. If you did the
   exercises with the Allways add-in program in Chapter 10, perform
   the next step to restrict the listing to just the Allways files in the
   current directory.

6. **Press Esc, then type *.ALL and press Enter.**
   When you press Esc, 1-2-3 takes you out of the directory listing
   screen and clears the search pattern (while leaving the path). In this
   case, you replaced the search pattern *.* used to list all files with
   *.ALL to restrict the listing to just those files with the .ALL extension.
   You should see two such files on your screen (*IS5YCH10.ALL* and
   IS5YRCH9.ALL) before the directory name *ALLWAYS*.

7. **Press Enter to return to READY mode in the worksheet.**

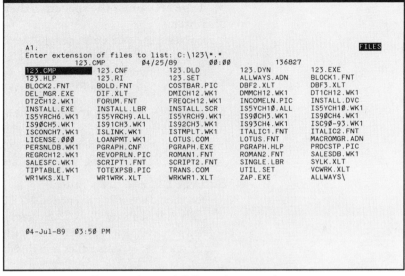

```
A1.
Enter extension of files to list: C:\123\*.*                                    FILES
          123.CMP        04/25/89      00:00          136827
123.CMP        123.CNF        123.DLD        123.DYN        123.EXE
123.HLP        123.RI         123.SET        ALLWAYS.ADN    BLOCK1.FNT
BLOCK2.FNT     BOLD.FNT       COSTBAR.PIC    DBF2.XLT       DBF3.XLT
DEL_MGR.EXE    DIF.XLT        DMICH12.WK1    DMMCH12.WK1    DT1CH12.WK1
DT2CH12.WK1    FORUM.FNT      FREQCH12.WK1   INCOMELN.PIC   INSTALL.DVC
INSTALL.EXE    INSTALL.LBR    INSTALL.SCR    IS5YCH10.ALL   IS5YCH10.WK1
IS5YRCH6.WK1   IS5YRCH9.ALL   IS5YRCH9.WK1   IS90CH3.WK1    IS90CH4.WK1
IS90CH5.WK1    IS91CH3.WK1    IS92CH3.WK1    IS93CH4.WK1    ISC90-93.WK1
ISCONCH7.WK1   ISLINK.WK1     ISTMPLT.WK1    ITALIC1.FNT    ITALIC2.FNT
LICENSE.000    LOANPMT.WK1    LOTUS.COM      LOTUS.FNT      MACROMGR.ADN
PERSNLDB.WK1   PGRAPH.CNF     PGRAPH.EXE     PGRAPH.HLP     PRDCSTP.PIC
REGRCH12.WK1   REVOPRLN.PIC   ROMAN1.FNT     ROMAN2.FNT     SALESDB.WK1
SALESFC.WK1    SCRIPT1.FNT    SCRIPT2.FNT    SINGLE.LBR     SYLK.XLT
TIPTABLE.WK1   TOTEXPSB.PIC   TRANS.COM      UTIL.SET       VCWRK.XLT
WR1WKS.XLT     WR1WRK.XLT     WRKWR1.XLT     ZAP.EXE        ALLWAYS\


04-Jul-89   03:50 PM
```

♦ **Figure 13.5:** *Obtaining a listing of all files in the current directory*

Creating a Directory for Your Practice Files

In this exercise, you will use the /System command to go to DOS. Once in the DOS shell, you will create a new directory to contain your practice files. After creating this directory, you will copy your practice files to it.

1. **Select the /System command; if you are using a two-disk-drive system, replace the 1-2-3 System disk with a copy of your DOS disk if you get an error message indicating that DOS can't locate the file called COMMAND.COM.**
   You should see the DOS prompt, A:\> on a two-disk-drive system or C:\123> on a hard disk system. Notice the message *(Type EXIT and press ENTER to return to 1-2-3)* at the top of the screen above the information listing the version of DOS you are using. Before you create a new directory with the make directory command, you need to change to the root directory of the correct drive.

2. **Type B: and press Enter if you are using a two-disk-drive system; type CD\ and press Enter if you are using a hard disk system.**
   You should now see the DOS prompt B:\> on a two-disk-drive system or C:\> on a hard disk system. You will now create a directory called PRACTICE, one level below the root directory.

3. **Type *MD*, press the spacebar, then type *PRACTICE*, and press Enter.**

   If you get the DOS error message *Unable to create directory*, this means that your disk already has a PRACTICE directory. In such a case, try the MD command again, this time entering the directory name as *PRACTIC* (without the *E*). Next, make your new directory current.

4. **Type *CD*, press the spacebar, then type *PRACTICE*, and press Enter.**

   The DOS prompt should now be B:\PRACTICE> or C:\PRACTICE>. Obtain a directory listing of your new directory.

5. **Type *DIR* and press Enter.**

   You should see only two entries, .<DIR> and ..<DIR>. The .<DIR> entry represents the PRACTICE directory itself, and the ..<DIR> entry represents its parent directory (B:\ or C:\). Now let's copy all the practice worksheet files into this directory.

6. **If you are using a two-disk-drive system, type COPY B:*.*WK1* and press Enter; if you are using a hard disk, type COPY C:\\123*.*WK1* and press Enter; in either case, be sure to enter a space between the command COPY and the drive letter designation.**

   When you press Enter, DOS begins copying all the worksheet files in the specified directory (B:\ or C:\123) to the current directory. When it is finished, you should see the message *24 File(s) copied* at the bottom of the list. Next, copy the graph files you created to this new directory.

7. **Press F3, then press the Backspace key until you have erased only the characters *WK1*; then type *PIC* and press Enter.**

   This time, DOS copies five files to the new directory. If you created the Allways reports in Chapter 10, you now need to copy them to this directory as well.

8. **Press F3 again, then press the Backspace key until you have erased only the characters *PIC*; then type *ALL* and press Enter.**

   This time, the program copies the two Allways files into the PRACTICE directory. Now it's time to obtain a complete listing of all files in the current directory. If you created all 31 files, there are too many to display in one screenful when using a standard directory listing. To see all the files in one screen, use the /W (Wide) switch with the DIR command.

9. **Type** *DIR/W* **and press Enter.**
   Your directory listing should be similar to the one shown in Figure 13.6 (although the drive letter may be different). Now, you are ready to return to 1-2-3 (remember that it's still running in the background).

10. **Type** *EXIT* **and press Enter.**
    You should now be returned to the worksheet display. Did you notice that the message instructing you to type EXIT to return to 1-2-3 has long since scrolled off the screen? Unfortunately, the program displays this message only once when you first exit to the DOS shell; when it's no longer visible on the screen, it's up to you to remember that 1-2-3 is still running in the background.

Erasing Unwanted Files

Now that you have copied your practice files to the new directory and checked that they are all there, you can safely proceed with the next exercise, where you will get practice in erasing files both with the /File Erase command in 1-2-3 and the DEL (DELETE) command in DOS. Under no circumstances should you do this exercise if you haven't copied all your practice files to the PRACTICE directory *and* verified that they are all there.

1. **Select /File Directory (/FD) and verify that your PRACTICE directory is** *not* **the current directory; instead, the directory listed should be the one from which you copied your practice files into the PRACTICE directory; if this is the case, press Enter; if not, type the name of this directory, then press Enter.**
   Now that you have ascertained that the correct directory is current, you are ready to delete some files with the /File Erase command.

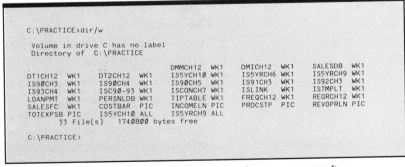

```
C:\PRACTICE>dir/w

   Volume in drive C has no label
   Directory of  C:\PRACTICE

               .         ..            DMMCH12  WK1    DMICH12  WK1    SALESDB  WK1
   DT1CH12  WK1    DT2CH12  WK1    IS5YCH10 WK1    IS5YRCH6 WK1    IS5YRCH9 WK1
   IS90CH3  WK1    IS90CH4  WK1    IS90CH5  WK1    IS91CH3  WK1    IS92CH3  WK1
   IS93CH4  WK1    ISC90-93 WK1    ISCONCH7 WK1    ISLINK   WK1    ISTMPLT  WK1
   LOANPMT  WK1    PERSNLDB WK1    TIPTABLE WK1    FREQCH12 WK1    REGRCH12 WK1
   SALESFC  WK1    COSTBAR  PIC    INCOMELN PIC    PRDCSTP  PIC    REVOPRLN PIC
   TOTEXPSB PIC    IS5YCH10 ALL    IS5YRCH9 ALL
            33 File(s)   1740800 bytes free

C:\PRACTICE>
```

♦ **Figure 13.6:** *Directory listing of all files copied to the new PRACTICE directory*

2. **Select /File Erase Worksheet (/FEW); make sure that the file DMICH12.WK1 is highlighted, then press Enter to select it and type Y to confirm the erasure of this file.**
   Check to see that this file has, indeed, been deleted.

3. **Select /File List Worksheet (/FLW) and check that the file DMICH12.WK1 is no longer listed in this directory (press the Name key, F3, if necessary); after verifying that this file is gone, press Enter to return to READY mode.**
   Next, erase one of your graph files with the /File Erase Graph command.

4. **Select /File Erase Graph (/FEG), move the pointer to the file INCOMELN.PIC, and press Enter; then type Y to select the Yes option.**
   Verify that this file is gone with the /File List Graph command.

5. **Select /File List Graph (/FLG); when you have verified that INCOMELN.PIC is no longer among those graph files listed, press Enter to return to READY mode.**
   Unfortunately, 1-2-3's /File Erase commands allow you to delete only one file at a time. To delete the remaining worksheet and graph files in this directory using these commands will take far too long. Instead, you can speed things up considerably by selecting the /System command to go to DOS, and then using the DOS DELETE or ERASE command with appropriate wildcard characters to erase multiple files in one operation.

6. **Select /System (/S); if you are using a two-disk-drive system, type B: and press Enter to make B:\ the current directory; if you are using a hard disk system, C:\123 will be the current directory (as long as this is the directory from which you copied your practice files, you don't need to make any changes).**
   To delete several files of a certain type with the DELETE command, you will use the DOS * wildcard character with the 1-2-3 file extension.

7. **Type DIR *.WK1 and press Enter to obtain a listing of all worksheet files in the current directory; as long as you don't see any in this list that are *not* practice worksheets that you created, type DEL *.WK1, and press Enter.**
   Verify that all worksheet files have been removed from this directory.

8. **Type** *DIR* ∗*.WK1* **and press Enter.**
   You should receive the message *File not found*. Next, delete the graph files.

9. **Type** *DIR* ∗*.PIC* **and press Enter to obtain a listing of all graph files in the current directory; as long as you don't see any in this list that are** *not* **practice graph files that you cre-ated, type** *DEL* ∗*.PIC*, **and press Enter.**
   If you created the Allways files as part of the exercises in Chapter 10, you also need to erase them from this directory.

10. **Type** *DIR* ∗*.ALL* **and press Enter to obtain a listing of all graph files in the current directory; as long as you don't see any in this list besides the two practice Allways files that you created, type** *DEL* ∗*.ALL*, **and press Enter.**
    Now you are ready to return to 1-2-3.

11. **Type** *EXIT* **and press Enter.**
    Make your practice directory the current one.

12. **Select /File Directory (/FD); if you are using a two-disk-drive system, type** *B:\PRACTICE* **as the directory name and press Enter; if you are using a hard disk system, type** *C:\PRACTICE* **and press Enter.**
    Examine all the files in this directory.

13. **Select /File List Other (/FLO) to obtain a listing of all files in this directory.**
    You should see not only all your practice worksheet files listed here, but also all the graph and Allways files that you created.

14. **Press Enter to return to READY mode in the worksheet display.**

Making Backup Copies of Your Files

This last exercise is designed to give you practice in making backup copies of your practice files. Regardless of whether you keep your data files in a directory on the hard disk or on a data disk kept in drive A or B, you need to make an additional backup copy of each file. That way, you are protected in the event that your hard disk goes down or your computer cannot read your data disk.

To perform this next exercise, you need a new (blank) disk. If you don't have a new disk, be sure that the one you choose doesn't contain any data that you still need, because you will be formatting this disk in the exercise—a procedure that destroys *all* the data on the disk.

1. **Select the /System command (/S); if you are using a two-disk-drive system, replace the 1-2-3 System disk with a copy of your DOS disk.**

   Now you need to get your new blank disk. If you don't have a new disk, don't substitute one that contains data you still need, or you will lose your data.

2. **Place your new blank data disk in drive B (if you are using a two-disk-drive system) or drive A (if you are using a hard disk system) and close the drive door.**

   Note that if you are using a double-density disk in a high-density drive (either 5¼-inch or 3½), you will not want to format the disk to the 1.2Mb or 1.44Mb high-density capacity. Instead, you will need to add switches to the command to instruct DOS to format the disk to double-density capacity only. If you are using a 3½-inch disk, you add the switches /T:80/N:9 to your basic format command to format the disk to 720K capacity, and if you are using a 5¼-inch disk, you add the switches /T:40/N:9 to format your disk to 360K capacity.

3. **If you are using a two-disk-drive system, type FORMAT B:/V at the A:\> DOS prompt, and press Enter; if you are using a hard disk system, type FORMAT A:/V at the C:\123> prompt, and press Enter; note that if you need to add the other switches for double-density to either FORMAT command, you type them after the /V with no spaces between the slashes (/).**

   You should now see the message *Insert new diskette for drive A: (or B:) and strike ENTER when ready* on your screen. If have a hard disk system and you see the error message *Bad command or file name*, you must change the directory to the DOS directory that contains the FORMAT.COM file before you can format the disk. To do this, type CD\DOS and press Enter; then repeat step 3.

4. **Press the Enter key to begin the formatting.**

   When the format is complete, you will be asked to enter a volume label for the disk (this is the result of using the /V switch in the FOR-MAT command).

5. **Type PRACTICEBAK as the volume label and press Enter; then type N and press Enter in response to the prompt to format another disk.**

   Now you are ready to use the DOS COPY command to copy all files in your PRACTICE directory to your newly formatted data disk. But before you do that, you will make the PRACTICE directory current and get a directory listing of its files.

6. **If you are using a two-disk-drive system, replace the DOS disk in drive A with your original data disk (the one that contains your PRACTICE directory), then type** *CD\PRAC-TICE* **and press Enter; if you are using a hard disk system, type** *CD\PRACTICE* **and press Enter.**
   Next, obtain a listing of all files in this directory.

7. **Type** *DIR/W* **and press Enter.**
   At the bottom of the listing, you should see the message *33 File(s)* (the current and parent directory add 2 to your 31 data files). Now copy all your data files using the global pattern *.* with the DOS COPY command.

8. **If you are using a two-disk-drive system, type** *COPY *.* B:* **and press Enter; if you are using a hard disk system, type** *COPY *.* A:* **and press Enter.**
   Make sure that your practice backup disk contains all your files.

9. **If you are using a two-disk-drive system, type** *DIR B:/W* **and press Enter; if you are using a hard disk system, type** *DIR A:/W* **and press Enter.**
   The file listing of the PRACTICE.BAK volume should match that of the previous directory listing.

10. **Remove your backup disk from its drive. If you are using a two-disk-drive computer, put your original data disk back in drive B and your 1-2-3 System disk back in drive A.**
    Next, you need to label your backup disk and return to 1-2-3.

11. **Identify your backup disk by filling out an adhesive label (you can call it** *Practice Files: Backup*)—**use** *only* **a felt-tip pen if you have already placed the label on the disk—then type** *EXIT* **to return to 1-2-3.**

Summary

♦

Troubleshooting

Question: I protected one of my worksheet files with the password DTD (don't tell dad). The next time I tried to retrieve it, however, 1-2-3 wouldn't accept this password as valid and I couldn't open my file. As I'm sure this is the password I assigned to this worksheet, what can the problem be?

Answer: As long as you're sure you assigned the three letters *DTD* as the password for this file, you have probably forgotten the correct combination of uppercase and lowercase letters you originally used. Remember that letters in passwords are case-sensitive; this means the three letters *DTD* can yield eight different passwords depending upon which combination of uppercase and lowercase letters are used: dtd, dtD, dTD, DTD, DtD, Dtd, dTd, DTd. To retrieve your file, you will have to try each one of these possible combinations until you hit on the one you actually used. If you use passwords a lot, you should decide upon a consistent scheme for entering uppercase and lowercase letters (all caps, all lowercase, capitalize the first letter only, and so on), and stick with it to avoid wasting time trying to figure out which case you used.

Question: In our office, several people share the same computer, and all of them will be using 1-2-3. To provide for this, we purchased a system with a very large hard disk that will be partitioned into a C, D, E, and F drive. We have installed 1-2-3 on the C drive in the directory C:\123. Will we run into any trouble with 1-2-3 if we don't keep all our worksheet files in directories on the same drive (C) as the program?

Answer: No, you can keep your worksheet files on other drives on the hard disk, just as you can keep your files on a floppy disk in drive A or B and still run the program on the C drive. Just remember that you will have to specify not only the directory path but also the drive letter when you use the /File Directory command to make current the directory you want to work in.

Question: I have trouble remembering which worksheet a file contains just by looking at the the cryptic DOS file names I'm forced to use, with the result that I often waste a great deal of valuable time retrieving various likely looking candidates before finding the worksheet I need to revise. Is there anything I can do to alleviate this situation?

Answer: If you are running 1-2-3 on a hard disk, you might consider using Magellan, a stand-alone utility designed to aid in the location of files on a hard disk, which is also from Lotus Development Corporation. With Magellan, you can not only obtain a file listing of all 1-2-3 worksheets in a particular directory, but also view the contents of each one in rapid succession. This is accomplished by dividing the screen into two windows: the window on the left contains an alphabetical listing of all worksheet files that you can scroll through, and the window on the right displays the first part of the worksheet that contains the pointer. When you locate the worksheet you want to use, you can both start 1-2-3 and have it retrieve this file from within Magellan.

Essential Techniques

To Password-Protect a Worksheet File

1. Select /File Save, enter the file name, press the spacebar, and type *p*.

2. You will then be prompted to enter a password. Type in a password up to 15 characters and press the Enter key. If you use letters in the password, remember that passwords are case-sensitive. Note that you will be typing blind, as the program suppresses the display of the password on the screen as you type it.

3. You will next be prompted to verify your password. Retype the password exactly as you originally entered it and press the Enter key. Again, you will be typing blind when you reenter the password for verification.

4. As long as the passwords match exactly, 1-2-3 will save your worksheet (you will receive the Cancel, Replace, and Backup options, if you are saving the file under the same name). Thereafter, to retrieve the worksheet file, you must enter the password correctly after selecting the file. Failure to do so will cause 1-2-3 to abort the /File Retrieve procedure.

To Remove a Password from a Worksheet File

1. If the worksheet is not already on the screen, select /File Retrieve, select the worksheet file, type in the password, and press Enter.

2. Select /File Save, then press the Esc or Backspace key to delete the message [PASSWORD PROTECTED] after the file name.

3. Press Enter and then select the Replace or Backup option to save the file under the same name without the password.

4. Press the spacebar to edit the existing file name, or begin typing the file name to save the worksheet under a new name without the password.

Review

Important Terms You Should Know

backup copy
current directory
default directory

DOS shell
root directory

Test Your Knowledge

1. To create a directory to hold your 1-2-3 files, you must use the DOS _____ command.

2. To make a directory current in DOS, you use the _____ command. To make it current in 1-2-3, you use the _____ command.

3. To be able to delete a directory from the hard disk, you must first remove all its _____. Then, you need to move up a level by entering _____ at the DOS prompt and then use the _____ DOS command to remove the directory.

4. To change the default directory, you must select the _____ option on the _____ menu and type in the directory path. Then, you must select the _____ option to make sure that this change is saved before choosing Quit to return to READY mode.

5. To assign the password *NEPO* (*open* spelled backwards) to the current worksheet when saving it for the first time under the file name *SALARY1.WK1*, you select /File Save, type the file name *SALARY1*, press the _____, type _____, and then enter _____. Next, you must type _____ again and press Enter.

6. To remove the password protection from your *SALARY1.WK1* file but save it under the same name, you must select /File Save, press the _____ key to remove _____, then press Enter, and select the _____ option.

7. To obtain a listing of all PIC files in the current directory in 1-2-3, you select the _____ option on the _____ menu.

8. If you are using Release 2.2, you can create a table of all PIC files in the current directory starting in cell A100 by selecting the _____ option on the _____ menu. Then, to indicate which directory to use, you press _____, and to indicate the table range, you type _____ and press Enter.

9. To go to DOS temporarily, you select _____ from the 1-2-3 main menu. To return to 1-2-3, you type _____ and press Enter.

10. To delete a single worksheet file, you can select the _____ option on the _____ menu in 1-2-3. To delete a group of files, however, you must use the _____ command to go to DOS and then use its _____ or _____ command with appropriate wildcard characters.

14

Translating Files: Exchanging Data between 1-2-3 and Other Programs

In This Chapter...

Exchanging Data

If you use other application programs besides 1-2-3, or work in an office where several different applications are supported, chances are good that you will find times when you need to exchange data between 1-2-3 and the other program you are using. As you are probably aware if you have experience with even a few IBM PC applications, each program saves the files that it creates in a slightly different file format, requiring some translation to take place before the exchange can occur.

Lotus 1-2-3 offers two basic methods for exchanging data: translating the file into the ASCII file format and then importing or exporting the ASCII data, or translating the file directly into the program's native format. The ASCII (American Standard Code for Information Interchange) file format provides a standardized code for representing all letters, punctuation symbols, numbers, and many printer control codes used by the computer. In 1-2-3, you can convert worksheet files to the ASCII format by using the /Print File command and import a file in the ASCII format with the /File Import command. To translate a 1-2-3 worksheet into another file format or translate another file into a WK1 format, you use the Translate program.

Saving Other Program Files in ASCII Format

To create an ASCII or *text file* version of your data file so that you can use 1-2-3's /File Import command to bring it into a worksheet, you need to find out how your program goes about creating such files. Often, programs provide a special save or export command, sometimes separate from the program itself, that is used to create ASCII files. Some programs create ASCII files with a print-to-disk command (this is the method that 1-2-3 uses to create ASCII files with its /Print File command). When the program prints the file to disk rather than to your printer, it is automatically saved in ASCII code.

When a file is saved in the ASCII format, special formatting characters, such as those that boldface and underline text, are not saved. The text, numbers, and punctuation used in the document are often saved as separate lines, each terminated with a carriage return and linefeed character. Also, if you translate a document or report that contains headers, footers, or footnotes, these are not transferred to the new ASCII file.

Note that some word processing programs, such as WordPerfect, always refer to ASCII files as *text files*. If your word processor has a facility for creating text files, you use this whenever you need to transfer data from a word processed document into a 1-2-3 worksheet. The name refers to the fact that you can display the contents of an ASCII file on the screen as readable text, using the DOS TYPE command.

If your word processor is WordPerfect, to save your document in ASCII format, first press the Text In/Out key (Ctrl-F5), select the DOS Text option (1 or T), and then select Save (1 or S). If your word processor is WordStar, you create your new file as an ASCII file by opening your document in Non-Document mode (choose N from the main menu instead of D to edit the document). When you've finished creating it, you save it with ^KD as you normally do.

Some programs have translate utilities or export commands that create *delimited files*. A delimited ASCII file is one in which all text is enclosed in quotation marks, and all individual text items and numeric data are separated by either commas, spaces, colons, or semicolons. Note that numeric data in the file don't have to be enclosed in quotation marks (that is, delimited), as is the case with text.

Saving 1-2-3 Worksheets in the ASCII Format

To save a worksheet file in the ASCII file format to use in another program that can import or directly use text files, you use the /Print File command. When you select /Print File, you are prompted to enter a name for the text file. The file name that you enter here must obey the DOS file naming conventions, and 1-2-3 will automatically append the extension .PRN to it unless you enter an extension of your own. If you wish, you can save the text file version under the same name as the worksheet, because the two versions are automatically differentiated by extension (.WK1 for the worksheet and .PRN for the text file).

Specifying Your Print Settings

After you enter the file name for your new text file, you are presented with the same menu as when you select /Print Printer. All options on this menu work just as they do when you create a worksheet report to send to the printer.

After you enter the file name, you need to select the Range option to define the range of worksheet data you wish included in the new text file. After specifying the print range but before selecting the Go option to create the file, you should make sure that the right-margin setting is sufficient to include all columns in the print range. Select Margins Right from the Options menu and enter the number of characters in the longest row of the print range to do this. Also, you will most often want to set the left margin to zero by selecting Margins Left from the Options menu and entering 0. If you do not, each line of data will be indented in the text by the number of spaces set by the left-margin setting.

Before using the Go option to save the new text file, you should also select the Other Unformatted option from the Options menu. When you create a text file with the Unformatted option in effect, 1-2-3 suppresses any headers, footers, or page breaks that you may have previously specified when defining a worksheet report, as well as top and bottom margins in effect. If you don't select this option, the resulting text file will contain extra lines at the top and bottom of each "page" in the text file, as well as in the text of any header or footer you defined.

After defining the print range, changing the left- and right-margin settings, and selecting the Unformatted option, you are ready to select the Go option from the main /Print File menu. When you do, 1-2-3 will save the data in the print range as a text file under the name you specified in the current directory.

Remember that you can get a file listing of all text files created with the /Print File command in the current directory by selecting the Print option on the /File List menu.

Using Your Text File in Another Program

After creating a PRN text file in 1-2-3, you can retrieve this file with any program that can read ASCII files. Some word processors, such as WordStar, will retrieve ASCII files without requiring any prior conversion. Other word processors, such as WordPerfect and Microsoft Word, require you to convert the file before it can be loaded into the word processor. This means that you will have to use its utility program or import text command before you can edit it.

You may find that once you have retrieved the text file, you need to edit it, especially when the data are to be arranged in a tabular format. Many times, it helps to set up an appropriate ruler line right before the place in the document where you intend to bring in the 1-2-3 data stored in the PRN file. This is especially important if the line length of the data in the 1-2-3 file exceeds that of the right margin currently used in the document. You will almost always find it necessary to insert tabs (decimal tabs, most often) to format the data into columns as you want them to appear in the final printed report.

Note that once you have finished editing the text file, you should save it in the program's native file format.

Practice Saving a Worksheet as an ASCII File

This next exercise will give you practice in using the /Print File command to save one of your worksheets in the ASCII file format. If you have access to a word processor, you should try retrieving the resulting text file into it after you've completed this exercise to get a feel for how easy it is to bring 1-2-3 data into your word processing documents.

1. **Select /File Directory (/FD) to make sure that** *B:\PRACTICE* **(for a two-disk-drive system) or** *C:\PRACTICE* **(for a hard disk system) is the current directory; if it is, press Enter; if it is not, enter the directory name and press Enter.**
   You will now retrieve your *IS5YCH10.WK1* worksheet, then you will save the summary income table in its own text file.

2. **Retrieve the file** *IS5YCH10.WK1*; **then make sure you can see all the characters in the headings in Column A and, if not, widen the column to 31.**
   Now you are ready to select the /Print File command and name the new text file you are about to create.

3. **Select /Print File (/PF), type** *INCSUM* **as the file name, and press Enter.**
   Next, you need to define the print range.

4. **Select Range (R), anchor the range on cell A1, then move the pointer to cell G21, and press Enter.**
   Now set the left and right margins for the new file. With column A set at a width of 31 characters plus 6 columns of 9 characters (6 × 9 = 54), you will need a right margin of 85 (31 + 54 = 85) after you set the left margin to 0.

5. **Select Options Margins Left (OML), type O, and press Enter; then select Margins Right (MR), type 85, and press Enter.**
   Before you select the Go option on the main /Print File menu to create the text file, you need to select the Unformatted option on the Other menu.

6. **Select Other Unformatted (OU); then select Quit (Q) to return to the main /Print File menu, select Go (G) to create the text file, and select Quit (Q) again to return to READY mode.**
   Verify that your text is saved in your PRACTICE directory.

7. **Select /File List Print (/FLP); you should see** *INCSUM.PRN* **listed on this screen; press Enter to return to the worksheet.**
   Remember that 1-2-3 always appends the extension .PRN to all text files you create with /Print File unless you add an extension of your own. Before you leave this exercise, go to DOS and use the TYPE command to examine the contents of this text file.

8. **Select /System (/S), type** *CD\PRACTICE*, **and press Enter; then type** *TYPE INCSUM.PRN* **and press Enter.**

Notice the lines of this file are too wide to be displayed on the screen without wrapping part of the text; this is what caused the apparent double-spacing in this report (see Figure 14.1). To take such a file into a word processing document, you would have to modify the margin settings to accommodate such a long line length before retrieving this file into your document, or the same kind of wrapping would happen there.

9. Type *EXIT* to return to 1-2-3.

Importing ASCII Files into 1-2-3

You use the /File Import command to take files created in other programs and saved in ASCII format into the 1-2-3 worksheet. The /File Import command works much like the /File Combine command, in that it reads in data from the pointer's position, making it easy to add such data to an existing worksheet or database. Be careful when using the /File Import command; just as when using the /File Combine Copy command, it will also overwrite any existing data that are located in the range used in the import operation.

When you select /File Import, you are presented with these options:

Text Numbers

```
.625
Operating income (loss)          18,065   15,915   20,165   23,065   28,265   105
,475
Other income (expenses)
  Interest income                 4,500    4,500    4,500    4,500    4,500    22
,500
  Interest expense                (500)    (500)    (500)    (500)    (500)   (2
,500)
  Bonuses                         4,642    4,202    5,072    5,666    6,731    26
,314
  Other                            600      600      600      600      600     3
,000
Total other income (expenses)    9,242    8,802    9,672   10,266   11,331    49
,314

Income (loss) before taxes      27,307   24,717   29,837   33,331   39,596   154
,789
  Provision (benefit) for taxes   4,096    3,708    4,476    5,000    5,939    23
,218
Net earnings (loss)             23,211   21,009   25,362   28,332   33,657   131
,571

C:\PRACTICE>
```

◆ **Figure 14.1:** *Last part of the PRN file displayed on the screen with the TYPE command*

The Text option imports each line in the ASCII file as a long label in a single cell, with each line of the file placed on its own row in the worksheet. Note that each line of a nondelimited file must be terminated by a carriage return or linefeed, and cannot exceed 240 characters. This option is used only when the ASCII file is not a delimited file.

The Numbers option on the /File Import menu imports numeric data and quoted text into separate columns of the worksheet, with each line of data placed on its own row in the worksheet. Always choose the Numbers option when you are importing an ASCII delimited file into the worksheet.

After choosing between Text and Numbers, you are prompted to select the text file to be imported. The program automatically displays a line listing (which you can change to a full-screen listing by pressing the Name key, F3) of all the PRN files in the current directory. To select the file to be brought into the worksheet, you can either type in its name or move the pointer to it in the list and press Enter. As soon as you press Enter, 1-2-3 copies all data in the PRN file into the worksheet starting from the current cell (the one with the pointer), using as many rows as there are lines in the text file. If you choose the Numbers option, the program will also use as many columns as there are delimited items in each line of the file. As is customary in 1-2-3, the program will overwrite existing data with the data from the incoming PRN file, so be careful that the pointer is positioned in an area of the worksheet where data can't be destroyed.

Figures 14.2 and 14.3 illustrate the use of the /File Import Text command to bring a nondelimited ASCII file into the worksheet. Figure 14.2 shows you how this text file appears when displayed on the screen with the DOS TYPE command. This particular file was created in WordPerfect. The columns in this table were created by entering tabs between each item in the line. When this document is converted to an ASCII file, these tabs are automatically converted to an equivalent number of spaces between each item.

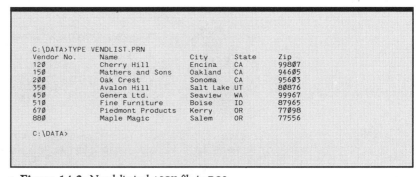

```
C:\DATA>TYPE VENDLIST.PRN
Vendor No.    Name                City        State    Zip
120           Cherry Hill         Encina      CA       99807
150           Mathers and Sons    Oakland     CA       94605
200           Oak Crest           Sonoma      CA       95603
350           Avalon Hill         Salt Lake   UT       80876
450           Genera Ltd.         Seaview     WA       99967
510           Fine Furniture      Boise       ID       87965
670           Piedmont Products   Kerry       OR       77098
880           Maple Magic         Salem       OR       77556

C:\DATA>
```

◆ **Figure 14.2:** *Nondelimited ASCII file in DOS*

Figure 14.3 shows you how the file appears in 1-2-3 after being imported with the /File Import Text command. Look at the contents of cell A1 in this figure: notice that all five column headings are actually entered in this cell, although they appear to be in different columns in the worksheet display (this is due entirely to the spillover effect of long labels when the column to the right is empty, as is the case in column B). Not only are the column headings in the first row entered as a long label in cell A1, but all the data in this table are entered as long labels in their respective rows of the worksheet. This means that the only cells in this worksheet that contain data are in the range A1..A9: all the other cells in it are still blank.

Having all the data in this worksheet entered as long labels can cause some problems. For one thing, unless each data item is entered in its own column, you can't use this table as a 1-2-3 database and perform /Data Query operations on it (remember that this requires each item of information to be entered in its own field—that is, column). For another thing, you can't perform any calculations on the numbers contained in this table because they are entered as part of the labels in a single cell and not as values in their own cells.

Lotus 1-2-3 includes a /Data Parse command that is designed for just this situation. With it, you can convert a column of long labels into a range of labels and values, all entered in their own cells (you will learn how to use this command in the next section).

Figures 14.4 and 14.5 illustrate the use of the /File Import Numbers command to bring a delimited ASCII file into the 1-2-3 worksheet. In Figure 14.4, you see the text file as it appears when displayed on the screen with the DOS TYPE command. Compare the appearance of these data with those shown in Figure 14.3. Notice that in a delimited file, all text items are enclosed in quotation marks and all items are separated from one another with commas.

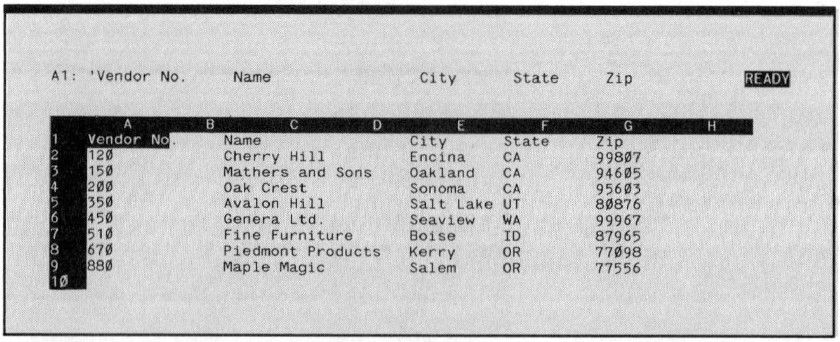

A1: 'Vendor No.   Name   City   State   Zip   READY

	A	B	C	D	E	F	G	H
1	Vendor No.		Name		City	State	Zip	
2	120		Cherry Hill		Encina	CA	99807	
3	150		Mathers and Sons		Oakland	CA	94605	
4	200		Oak Crest		Sonoma	CA	95603	
5	350		Avalon Hill		Salt Lake	UT	80876	
6	450		Genera Ltd.		Seaview	WA	99967	
7	510		Fine Furniture		Boise	ID	87965	
8	670		Piedmont Products		Kerry	OR	77098	
9	880		Maple Magic		Salem	OR	77556	
10								

♦ **Figure 14.3:** *Nondelimited ASCII file brought into 1-2-3 with /File Import Text*

```
C:\DATA>TYPE VENDELIM.PRN
"Vendor No.","Name","City","State","Zip"
120,"Cherry Hill","Encina","CA","99807"
150,"Mathers and Sons","Oakland","CA","94605"
200,"Oak Crest","Sonoma","CA","95603"
350,"Avalon Hill","Salt Lake","UT","80876"
450,"Genera Ltd.","Seaview","WA","99967"
510,"Fine Furniture","Boise","ID","87965"
670,"Piedmont Products","Kerry","OR","77098"
880,"Maple Magic","Salem","OR","77556"

C:\DATA>
```

♦ **Figure 14.4:** *Delimited ASCII file in DOS*

In this ASCII delimited file, only the first item, the vendor number, is numeric (and not enclosed in quotation marks). All the remaining data items are entered as text, including the zip code numbers at the end of each line of data. Because these numbers are enclosed in quotation marks, they will be imported into the worksheet as labels instead of values.

Figure 14.5 shows you how the data in this delimited file appear once imported into the worksheet with the /File Import Numbers command. Notice that the contents of cell A1 in this figure is just *'Vendor No.* Because the delimited file contains all the necessary information on where each data item occurs as well as its type, 1-2-3 can automatically parse the data into separate columns when you use the Numbers option to import the PRN file. In this figure, columns B and C have been widened so that you can see that all data items have been completely and correctly imported.

Parsing Imported Data

As mentioned earlier, to convert a column of long labels into a range of labels and values entered into separate cells, you use the /Data Parse command. When you access the /Data Parse command, the following menu options are displayed:

Format-Line Input-Column Output-Range Reset Go Quit

If you are using Release 2.2, you also see the Parse Settings sheet below the menu that shows you the range currently specified for Input-Column and Output-Range (Figure 14.6).

To use /Data Parse to break up a column of long labels into individual cell entries, you follow this basic four-step process:

1. Use the Format-Line Create options on the /Data Parse menu to set up format lines that contain codes to indicate where the long label is

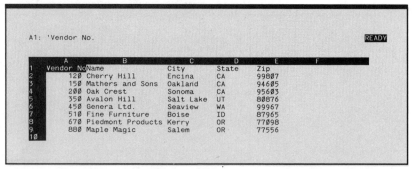

◆ **Figure 14.5:** *Delimited ASCII file brought into 1-2-3 with /File Import Numbers*

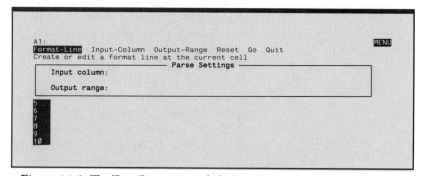

◆ **Figure 14.6:** *The /Data Parse menu with the Parse Settings sheet*

to be split into separate entries and what type of entry (label, value, date, or time) each of these represents.

2. Use the Format-Line Edit options on the /Data Parse menu to fine-tune the format lines (this step is required only when 1-2-3 misinterprets the type entry in a label or when you need to modify the length of entries or the spacing between them).

3. Select the Input-Column option to define the range that contains the long labels to be parsed, and select the Output-Range option to define the range where the parsed data is to be located.

4. Select the Go option to perform the parsing operation.

Creating Format Lines

The Format-Line option is used to create or edit format lines that determine how the long labels are parsed. To create a format line, you position the pointer in the first cell of the range that contains the long labels, and then select /Data Parse Format-Line Create (/DPFC). The program then enters a format line in the worksheet as a long label. In doing this, 1-2-3 inserts a new row in the worksheet and precedes the format line with the | (vertical bar) label prefix. If you're using Release 2.2, remember that you can use the Window key (F6) to temporarily remove the display of the Parse Settings sheet if it obscures the display of the format line in the worksheet. To display the Parse Settings sheet again, press the Window key a second time.

The format line contains the codes that indicate where 1-2-3 will break the label into individual cell entries and what type of data it will assign to these entries. Each new section of a format line is called a *data block*. A format line can contain the following code letters and symbols, which define the various types of data blocks:

Code	Meaning
D	Date block
L	Label block
S	Skip block, to indicate characters in the data block that you don't want 1-2-3 to include when the labels are parsed
T	Time block
V	Value block
>	Characters in a data block
*	Blank space in a data block, which can become part of the data block if a label contains extra characters

You can create as many different format lines as are required to format all long labels in the imported text file correctly. Each format line controls all labels below it. Therefore, when adding a new format line, you select the Quit option (Q) on the /Data Parse menu to return to READY mode, then position the pointer on the cell containing the label that requires the new format line and select /Data Parse Format-Line Create (/DPFC) again.

You most often need to create a new format line when the type or width of the entries in labels below the format line doesn't match its data blocks. This is often the case with tables that contain a row of column headings above the columns of data. When parsing the table, you need to create one format line to correctly parse the column headings in the first long label and at least one more format line to correctly parse the data in the long labels in each column below.

Figure 14.7 shows you a nondelimited text file after it has been imported into 1-2-3 with the /File Import Text command. To break the long labels imported

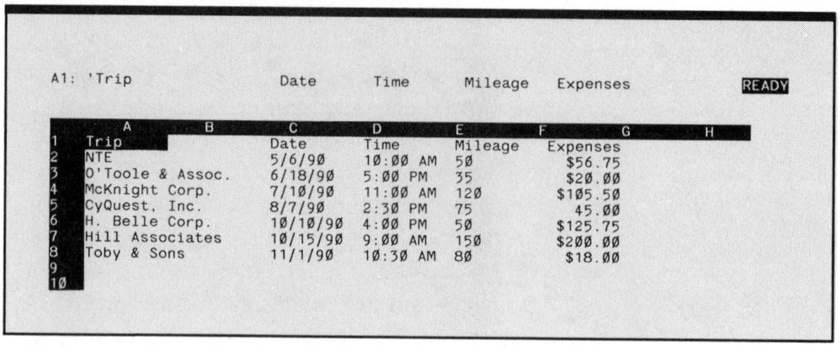

A1: 'Trip   Date   Time   Mileage   Expenses   READY

	A	B	C	D	E	F	G	H
1	Trip		Date	Time	Mileage	Expenses		
2	NTE		5/6/90	10:00 AM	50	$56.75		
3	O'Toole & Assoc.		6/18/90	5:00 PM	35	$20.00		
4	McKnight Corp.		7/10/90	11:00 AM	120	$105.50		
5	CyQuest, Inc.		8/7/90	2:30 PM	75	45.00		
6	H. Belle Corp.		10/10/90	4:00 PM	50	$125.75		
7	Hill Associates		10/15/90	9:00 AM	150	$200.00		
8	Toby & Sons		11/1/90	10:30 AM	80	$18.00		
9								
10								

• **Figure 14.7:** *A nondelimited text file imported in 1-2-3 with /File Import Text*

into the cell range A1..A8 by the /File Import Text command into individual cell entries, you must use the /Data Parse command. Figure 14.8 shows you the format line created for this file when the pointer is positioned in cell A1 and you select the /Data Parse Format-Line Create command. Notice that 1-2-3 has divided this format line into five label blocks using the column headings in the row below.

Although this format line will correctly parse the column headings in the first label in cell A2, its data blocks will not work when applied to the entries in the remaining long labels because these labels contain dates, times, and values in addition to labels. To have these data parsed correctly, you must locate the pointer in cell A3 and select the /Data Parse Format-Line Create command a second time.

Figure 14.9 shows you the second format line that 1-2-3 creates when you do this. You can see that 1-2-3 has divided this format line into six data blocks, including a date block, a time block, two value blocks, and two label blocks.

Editing Format Lines

When you select the /Data Parse Format-Line Create command to create a format line, 1-2-3 uses the entries in the first unparsed long label below where the format line will be inserted to decide what type each data block is to be and how wide to make it. Sometimes you will have to edit the format line because either the width of the data blocks, the type of the data blocks, or the number of data blocks it contains are incorrect.

An incorrect format line can be the result of an entry in the long label to which 1-2-3 could assign more than one data type. When the program encounters an ambiguous entry, it uses the following order of precedence: value, date, time, and label. For example, if the label contains *10/92*—which could represent the date October 1992, the fraction 10/92nds, or even the label 10 per

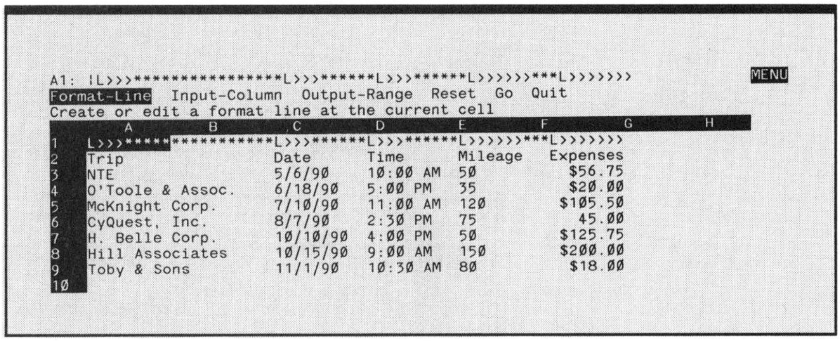

◆ **Figure 14.8:** *Text file after adding a format line*

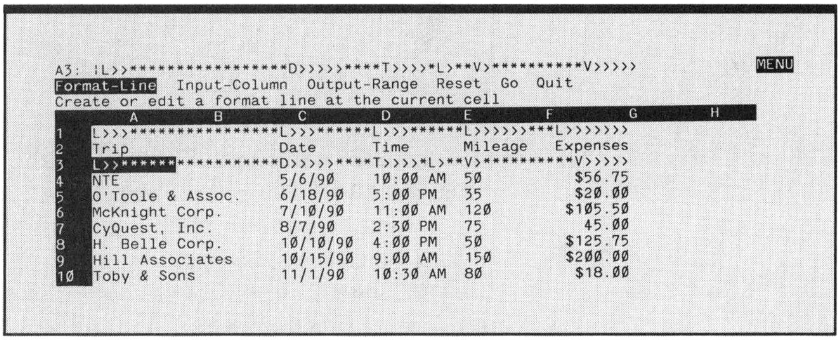

◆ **Figure 14.9:** *Text file after adding a second format line*

92—using this order of precedence, 1-2-3 will interpret it as a value data block (10/92nds or 10 divided by 92). An incorrect format line can also be the result of a single entry made up of two words that are separated by a space, causing 1-2-3 to create two data blocks where you want just one.

Figure 14.9 illustrates this particular situation. Notice that the space between *10:00* and AM in the long label in cell A4 caused 1-2-3 to interpret these entries as two data blocks: the first as a time block and the second as a label block. Because the AM and PM designations are part of the time, you must edit this second format.

To edit a format line, you need to position the pointer on the cell containing the format line and then select the /Data Parse Format-Line Edit command (/DPFE). If you are using Release 2.2, 1-2-3 will place the format line you are editing in the box containing the Parse Settings sheet (beneath the *Input column:* heading), as shown in Figure 14.10. Note in this figure that the program goes into FRMT mode when you edit a format line. It remains in this mode until you either press Ctrl-Break (to abort your edits) and return to READY mode, or press Enter to return to MENU mode.

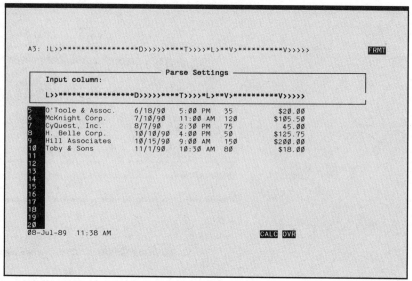

◆ **Figure 14.10:** *Editing a format line in Release 2.2*

When you edit a format line, the program is in overtype mode, indicated by the OVR status indicator at the bottom of the screen (you change to insert mode by pressing the Ins key). You will also see the CALC indicator immediately to its left in Figure 14.10. (This remains on the screen until you press the Enter key to have the format line updated.)

Once the program is in FRMT mode, you can move the cursor to the code letter above the incorrectly identified data block and type the > symbol or the code letter of the correct type of data block over it. When you edit a format line, some of the editing keys work slightly differently from the way they do when you are editing a cell entry. Table 14.1 shows the special key functions that you can use in FRMT mode.

Once you have finished making modifications to this format line, you press Enter to have them updated and to return to the /Data Parse menu. If you wish to leave the format line without having your changes recorded, press Ctrl-Break to return to READY mode. Do not press the Esc key: doing so will erase the entire format line, leaving a blank cell, when the program returns to READY mode. If this happens, you cannot recreate the format line with the /Data Parse Format-Line Create command without first deleting the blank row in the worksheet (with /Worksheet Delete Row).

When you edit a format line, you can change the type of entry by typing a new letter code over the one entered by the program. For instance, if you want an item identified as a value with a V in the format line to be entered as a label,

♦ **Table 14.1:** *Special Functions of the Editing Keys in* FRMT *Mode*

Key	Function
↑	Scrolls the unparsed labels below the format line up one row at a time
↓	Scrolls the unparsed labels below the format line down one row at a time
Ctrl-Break	Abandons all edits made to the format line and returns you to READY mode
Esc	Erases the format line but does not delete its row in the worksheet
Home	Returns the cursor to its original position on the format line and displays the unparsed labels that were visible before you started scrolling
PgDn	Scrolls the unparsed labels beneath the format line down one screen at a time
PgUp	Scrolls the unparsed labels beneath the format line up one screen at a time

you would move the cursor to it and type an L in its place. You must be careful when manually editing the codes, because you cannot make an item that begins with a letter or punctuation symbol into a value. If there are spaces or letters in entries designated as a value, date, or time block type, 1-2-3 will parse these entries as labels.

You can also use the letter S as a code to have the program ignore the data below it in the same column. Data blocks below an S will not appear in the cells when the data is parsed. You can use this code whenever you have an entry in the imported data that you do not want to keep in the worksheet.

Also, 1-2-3 can only translate entries into date and time serial numbers if they match one of its date or time formats. If the dates have been entered in the form 10/31/92, you can convert them into date serial numbers by using the D format letter code. However, if they were entered in the form 10–31–92, they would not be successfully translated into date serial numbers (they would be parsed as labels even if you used the D code).

Figure 14.11 shows the second format line after the time data block has been edited so that it includes the AM or PM designations that follow the hour. You do this by selecting the /Data Parse Format-Line Edit command (/DPFE), then move the cursor to the *L after the T>>>> in the format line, and type >>

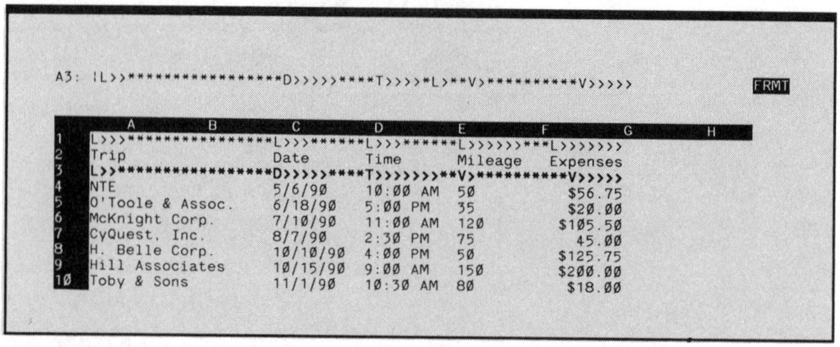

• **Figure 14.11:** *The second format line after editing to extend the time block*

over these two characters, thus including the AM or PM designation in the time data block.

Parsing the Data

Once you have created and edited all format lines required to correctly parse your data, you select the Input-Column option on the /Data Parse menu (/DPI) to identify the range of cells in the column that contains both the format lines and the data to be parsed. You can indicate this range by typing the cell addresses or by pointing. If you use pointing, you will find that the range is not yet anchored, allowing you to move the pointer to the cell containing the first format line. Once you have positioned it in this cell, type a period and use the ↓ key or the End ↓ combination to mark all entries and subsequent format lines in that column. Then press Enter to mark the range and return to the /Data Parse menu.

After that, you need to indicate the location of the output range. To do this, select the Output-Range option (O) from the /Data Parse menu (/DPO). When defining this range, you need to indicate only the first cell of this range. When designating the output range, make sure there are no existing data in the same area of the worksheet that could be destroyed when the long labels are parsed into separate cells. Remember that the output range will require as many rows as there are in the input column and as many columns as there are data blocks in format lines.

After defining the output range, you select the Go option (G) to have the long labels in the input column parsed in the output range. Once the data have been copied into separate cells in the output range, you can erase the original labels and format lines in the input column using the /Range Erase command.

If you wish, you can then move the newly parsed data to another place in the worksheet with the /Move command. Also, you will want to format any date and time serial numbers created during the parsing operation with one of the date and time formats available on the /Range Format menu. You may also want to format other values using one of the other formats available on the /Range Format menu.

If you find that your data are not correctly parsed and you wish to use the same output range when you redo the command, first erase the existing data. Because the /Data Parse command does not work like the /Data Query Extract command by erasing the output range before writing in new data, there is a chance that some of the old data may still exist in the cell range even after you have made changes to the format lines and reissued the command.

The /Data Parse command contains a Reset option, which will clear both the current input and output ranges. Use it if you need to parse labels in a new part of the worksheet during the work session. This makes it easier when you define the new input and output ranges, especially if you do this by the pointing method.

Figure 14.12 shows the data after parsing. To perform this operation, you define the range A1..A10 as the input column and cell A12 as the output range. Notice, in the parsed data table, that 1-2-3 has converted the dates and times in the input column into their equivalent date and time serial numbers in columns B and C of the output range. Also, notice that the expenses in column E in the output range are converted to values using the global General format. Figure 14.13 shows you the same output after formatting the values and widening the columns.

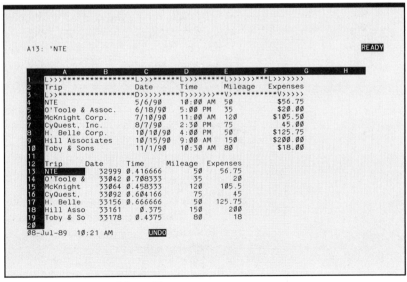

♦ **Figure 14.12:** *Parsed data table*

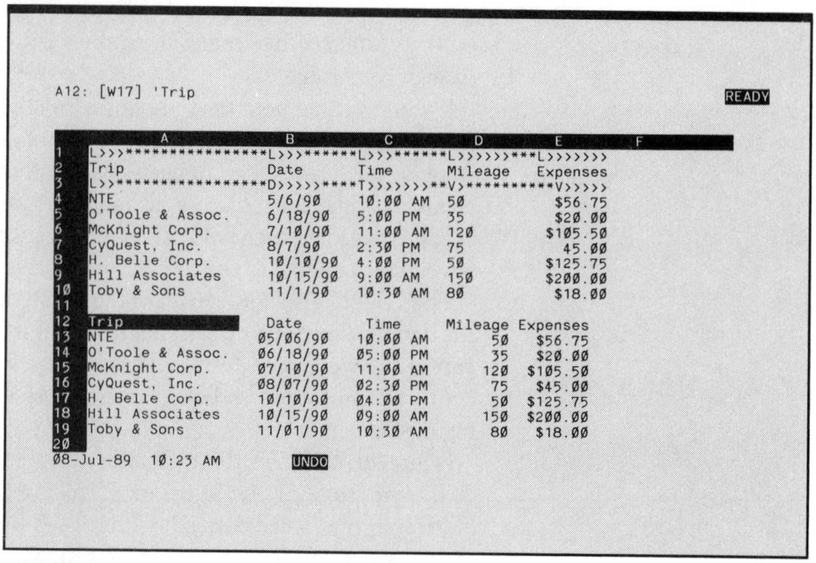

◆ **Figure 14.13:** *Parsed data table after formatting*

Practice Importing and Parsing a Text File

The next exercise gives you some practice in importing an ASCII data file into 1-2-3 and parsing its data. As part of this practice, you will import the text file *INCSUM.PRN*, which you created in the preceding exercise. As this file is a nondelimited text file, you will have to use the Text option on the /File Import menu when you bring its data into the worksheet. Once in the worksheet, you will use the /Data Parse command to convert the range of long labels it contains into separate entries.

1. **Clear the worksheet display of the *IS5YCH10.WK1* file if it is still on your screen.**
   Now you will import your *INCSUM.PRN* file into a blank worksheet. Because this is a nondelimited ASCII file, you must use the Text option on the /File Import menu.

2. **Select /File Import Text (/FIT), then select *INCSUM.PRN* by moving the pointer to it (if necessary) and pressing Enter.**
   Verify that 1-2-3 has imported each line in this text file as a long label in column A.

3. **With the pointer in cell A1, press the ↓ key and examine the contents of cells A2, A3, and A4.**

Each "row" of data that you examined was really a long label, beginning with the apostrophe label prefix and spilling over to column I in
the worksheet. Now, you need to create your first format line for
parsing this data.

4. **Move the pointer back to cell A1, then select /Data Parse
   Format-Line Create (/DPFC); if you're using Release 2.2,
   press the Window key (F6) to hide the display of the Parse
   Settings sheet.**
   Your screen should now be similar to the one shown in Figure 14.14.
   Notice 1-2-3 has divided the worksheet title into six different data
   blocks. You must edit this format line so that the program uses only
   one label block.

5. **Select Format-Line Edit (FE), move the cursor past the first *L*
   in the format line, and then replace all remaining format
   code letters with >; once you have extended the label block
   the full length of the worksheet title, press Enter.**
   You now need to create a second format line for the long label in
   row 3 that contains the column headings.

6. **Select Quit (Q), move the pointer to cell A3, and select
   /Data Parse Format-Line Create (/DPFC); if you're using
   Release 2.2, press the Window key (F6) to hide the display
   of the Parse Settings sheet.**
   Your screen should be similar to the one shown in Figure 14.15.
   Notice that 1-2-3 has interpreted the year column headings as values
   instead of labels by making them value data blocks. You must edit
   this format line, changing the value data blocks to label data blocks.
   You must also add a new label block at the beginning of this format
   line to prevent 1-2-3 from parsing the column headings starting in
   column A rather than column B.

7. **Select Format-Line Edit (FE), type *L* over the first * at the
   beginning of the format line, then move the cursor to each
   V in the line and type *L*; once you have replaced the last V,
   press Enter.**
   You need to add at least one more format line before parsing the data.
   This format line will control the division of the row headings and
   income and expense values.

8. **Select Quit (Q), move the pointer to cell A5, and select
   /Data Parse Format-Line Create (/DPFC); if you're using**

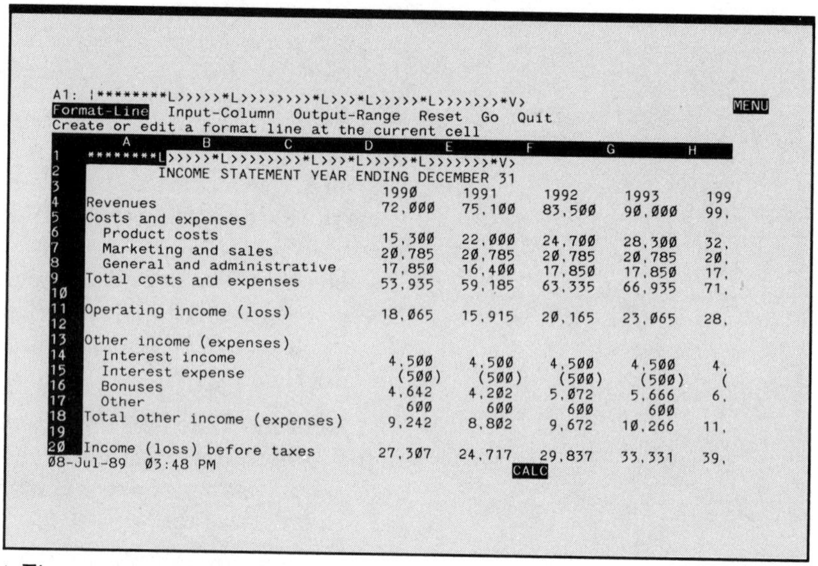

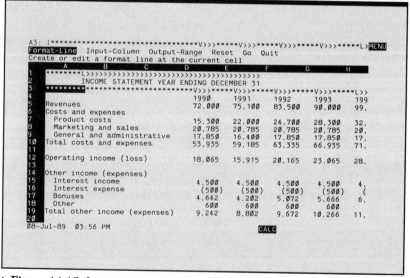

◆ **Figure 14.14:** *Income summary text file after adding the first format line*

◆ **Figure 14.15:** *Income summary text file after adding the second format line*

Release 2.2, press the Window key (F6) to hide the display
of the Parse Settings sheet.

Your screen should now be similar to the one shown in Figure 14.16.
This format line needs no editing, as 1-2-3 was able to interpret the
data block type and width correctly for all the remaining long labels.
You are now ready to perform the parse operation. Begin this operation by defining the input column.

9. **Select Input-Column (I), move the pointer to cell A1, type a
period to anchor the range, move the pointer to cell A24,
and press Enter.**

   Now all you need to do is to define the output range and select the
   Go option. You will locate the output range below the input column.

10. **Select Output-Range (O), move the pointer to cell A27, and
select the Go option (G) to have 1-2-3 parse the data.**

    Now check that 1-2-3 parsed the data correctly.

11. **Select Quit (Q) to return to READY mode, then press the
Goto key (F5), type *A27*, and press Enter.**

    Your screen should now match the one shown in Figure 14.17. All
    that remains is to format the parsed data and widen some of the
    columns.

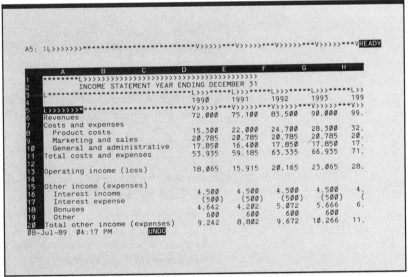

♦ **Figure 14.16:** *Income summary text file after adding the third format line*

```
A27: 'INCOME STATEMENT YEAR ENDING DECEMBER 31                          READY

      A         B        C        D        E        F        G        H
27 INCOME STATEMENT YEAR ENDING DECEMBER 31
28            1990     1991     1992     1993     1994     Total
29 Revenues    72000    75100    83500    90000    99500   420100
30 Costs and expenses
31    Product  15300    22000    24700    28300    32600   122900
32    Marketi  20785    20785    20785    20785    20785   103925
33    General  17850    16400    17850    17850    17850    87800
34 Total cos   53935    59185    63335    66935    71235   314625
35 Operating   18065    15915    20165    23065    28265   105475
36 Other inc(expenses)
37    Interes   4500     4500     4500     4500     4500    22500
38    Interes   -500     -500     -500     -500     -500    -2500
39    Bonuses   4642     4202     5072     5666     6731    26314
40    Other      600      600      600      600      600     3000
41 Total oth    9242     8802     9672    10266    11331    49314
42 Income (1   27307    24717    29837    33331    39596   154789
43    Provisi   4096     3708     4476     5000     5939    23218
44 Net earni   23211    21009    25362    28332    33657   131571
45
46
08-Jul-89   04:13 PM        UNDO
```

• **Figure 14.17:** *Parsed income summary*

12. **Widen column A to 31 characters.**

    Notice that *(expenses)* in row 36 has been parsed into cell B36 instead of remaining part of the heading in A36.

13. **Delete *(expenses)* in cell B36, then press the Edit key (F2), press the spacebar, type *(expenses)*, and press Enter.**

    Next, center the column headings in row 28.

14. **Change the alignment of the labels in the range B28..G28 from left-aligned to centered with the /Range Label command.**

    Now format the values in this summary with the Comma (,) format.

15. **Format the range B29..G44 with the Comma (,) format with 0 decimal places.**

    Your worksheet should look like the one in Figure 14.18.

16. **Move the pointer to cell A1, then save the worksheet under the name *PARSEC14.WK1*.**

```
A27: [W31] 'INCOME STATEMENT YEAR ENDING DECEMBER 31          READY

            A                        B       C       D       E
27 INCOME STATEMENT YEAR ENDING DECEMBER 31
28                            1990    1991    1992    1993
29 Revenues                   72,000  75,100  83,500  90,000
30 Costs and expenses
31    Product costs           15,300  22,000  24,700  28,300
32    Marketing and sales     20,785  20,785  20,785  20,785
33    General and administrative  17,850  16,400  17,850  17,850
34 Total costs and expenses   53,935  59,185  63,335  66,935
35 Operating income (loss)    18,065  15,915  20,165  23,065
36 Other income (expenses)
37    Interest income          4,500   4,500   4,500   4,500
38    Interest expense         (500)   (500)   (500)   (500)
39    Bonuses                  4,642   4,202   5,072   5,666
40    Other                      600     600     600     600
41 Total other income (expenses)  9,242   8,802   9,672  10,266
42 Income (loss) before taxes  27,307  24,717  29,837  33,331
43    Provision (benefit) for taxes   4,096   3,708   4,476   5,000
44 Net earnings (loss)         23,211  21,009  25,362  28,332
45
46
08-Jul-89   04:35 PM          UNDO
```

• **Figure 14.18:** *Parsed income summary after formatting*

The 1-2-3 Translate Program

The Translate program enables you to exchange data between several different programs and 1-2-3 (including different versions). You can also use it to convert file formats that do not even involve 1-2-3 worksheets. Thus, you can not only convert a dBASE III file to a Release 2 worksheet file, but you can also convert a dBASE III file to a Symphony file with Translate.

Direct conversion to a program's native file format provides a much more efficient method of exchanging data between 1-2-3 and other programs than the method of creating and exchanging ASCII files that we've already examined. Whenever possible, use Translate rather than /Print File or /File Import in 1-2-3 to export and import data files.

When using Translate, you must specify both the *source file*, which is the file format of the program that was used to create the file, and the *target file*, which is the file format of the program that uses the converted file. Table 14.2 lists the translations that are possible with the Translate program.

When It Is Unnecessary to Use Translate

In some cases, translations that can be performed in Translate are not necessary. You can often use the /File Retrieve command to load a file created from another version of 1-2-3 or another Lotus program such as Symphony. For

◆ **Table 14.2:** *Translations Possible with the Translate Program*

Source File Format (FROM)	Target File Format (TO)
1-2-3 1A	1-2-3 2, 2.01, *or* 2.2 1-2-3 3 dBASE II dBASE III DIF Symphony 1.0 Symphony 1.1, 1.2, *or* 2.0
1-2-3 2, 2.01, *or* 2.2	1-2-3 1A 1-2-3 3 dBASE II dBASE III DIF Symphony 1.0 Symphony 1.1, 1.2, *or* 2.0
dBASE II, dBASE III, DIF, Multiplan (SYLK), *or* VisiCalc	1-2-3 1A 1-2-3 2, 2.01, *or* 2.2 Symphony 1.0 Symphony 1.1, 1.2, *or* 2.0
Symphony 1.0	1-2-3 1A 1-2-3 2, 2.01, *or* 2.2 1-2-3 3 dBASE II dBASE III DIF Symphony 1.1, 1.2, *or* 2.0
Symphony 1.1, 1.2, *or* 2.0	1-2-3 1A 1-2-3 2, 2.01, *or* 2.2 1-2-3 3 dBASE II dBASE III DIF Symphony 1.0

example, although you can translate a Release 2.01 or 2.2 file to Release 3.0 with this program, this is unnecessary because Release 3.0 can retrieve all .WK1 files without conversion. Similarly, you can use /File Retrieve in Release 2.01

or 2.2 of 1-2-3 to directly load a Symphony Release 2.1 WR1 file. Note, however, that because the Symphony file extensions .WRS and .WR1 don't match the extension search pattern of .WK?, you must enter the complete file name when using /File Retrieve.

When you use /File Retrieve in Release 2.01 or 2.2 to load a worksheet file created with another version of 1-2-3 or Symphony and you save your work with /File Save, 1-2-3 will use the same file name but append the .WK1 extension. After you select the Replace option, the updated worksheet will be saved in the Release 2 file format. You may then find that this worksheet file is no longer directly retrievable with the 1-2-3 or Symphony version used to create it.

Exchanging Data between Release 2 and Release 3 of 1-2-3

Release 3.0 worksheets use the file extension .WK3. Although such worksheet files will be among those listed when you use /File Retrieve, their format is not compatible with Release 2.01 or 2.2 and, therefore, they are not directly retrievable.

Release 3.0 worksheet files can, however, be saved in a format that can be directly used by Release 2.01 or 2.2 simply by naming the file with the .WK1 file extension when you save the worksheet in Release 3.0. This method can only be used, however, when the Release 3.0 file does not include features that aren't supported in Release 2, such as multiple worksheets. If the Release 3.0 file does include such unsupported features, you must use the Release 3.0 Translate program to convert the file before it can be used in any version of Release 2.

As stated earlier, the WK1 file format used by both Release 2.01 and 2.2 is completely compatible with Release 3.0 and requires no conversion to be retrieved by Release 3.0.

Starting the Translate Program

You can start Translate from the Lotus Access System menu by choosing the Translate option (T), or directly from DOS by typing the command *TRANS* and pressing Enter. Note that you can use the /System command to exit to DOS and start Translate safely from the DOS shell; just remember to type *EXIT* when you have finished your conversions and you wish to return to 1-2-3.

If you are using 1-2-3 on a two-disk-drive system, you must replace the 1-2-3 System disk with the Utility disk before you enter the Translate startup command or when prompted to do so. If you are running 1-2-3 on a hard disk system, the directory that contains the Translate program files (usually the same one that contains the 1-2-3 program files) must be current when you give the startup command.

When you start the Translate program, you are presented with the list of options shown in Figure 14.19. Here, you indicate the source file format by first using the ↓ or ↑ cursor key to move the pointer to the appropriate program option and then pressing Enter.

After you select the format to translate from, you are presented with a new list of target file formats (from which you indicate the type of file you want the source file translated into). The kind and number of programs that are displayed vary depending upon the format of the source file. To see what target file formats are available for each source file type, refer to Table 14.2.

After you select the target file format by moving the pointer to the appropriate program and pressing Enter, the Translate program will display a screen of information outlining guidelines for a successful translation. If there is more than one screen of information, you will see the message *Press [Return] for next page* displayed at the bottom of the screen. Be sure to read all information screens before proceeding if you are unfamiliar with the requirements for successfully performing the type of translation you have called for.

After you've read the information, press the Esc key to continue. If you wish to abort the translation operation, press Ctrl-Break and you will be returned

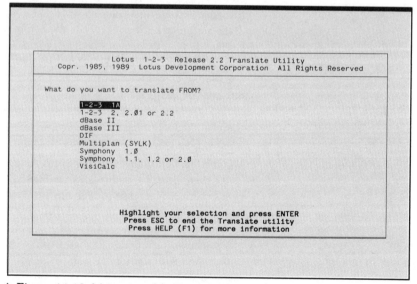

♦ **Figure 14.19:** *Main menu of the Translate program*

immediately to the first menu screen. From there, you can exit from the Translate program by pressing the Esc key and typing Y if you need to make changes to your file before performing the planned translation.

If you wish to continue with the translation, you must choose the source file to be translated. The Translate program will display a partial listing of all files in the current directory that carry the extension associated with the source file type. If there are no files of this type in the current directory, you will receive a message indicating that no files were found that match the source specification.

At this point, if the current directory is A:\ or B:\, you can replace the data disk if your file is located on a different floppy disk and press Enter to have the program search it for files matching the source specification. If your file is located on the hard disk but the current directory is not correct, you can press the Esc key to clear the message and edit the file name. You can use the Backspace key to delete characters, and then retype them. If you wish to clear the entire file name, you press the Esc key again and type in the full path name. Then press Enter to have the program search this new directory for matching files.

Once Translate displays a listing of the source files in the current directory, move the pointer to the one you want translated and press Enter. Translate will then display the full file name of both the source and target files. They will be the same, except for their extensions. You will then be prompted to edit the file specification. If you wish to change the target file name as well, you can do so. Press the Esc key if you want to make changes to the file name (press Esc a second time to clear the entire file name and then retype it, including its path name). Once you have finished editing the target file name or the specification type by editing only the extension (or if you don't want to make any changes), press Enter.

You will then be prompted to confirm the translation with three options: Yes, No, and Quit. Choose the Yes option to have the program perform the translation. Choose the No option to return to the file selection menu to select another file for translating. Choose the Quit option if you wish to abort the translation and return to the Translate main menu. From there, you can either choose another type of translation or press the Esc key and type Y to exit from the Translate program.

After the translation has been completed, you will be automatically returned to the Translate main menu screen, where you can press the Esc key and type Y to return to the Lotus Access System or DOS, where you can perform another translation.

The Translate program will not allow you to convert any password-protected file into any another file format. Therefore, you must first remove the password protection from the WK1 file (by retrieving and saving it again without a password) before you can use it as the source file in a translation.

Translating Release 2 Worksheets to Release 1A

If your office uses both Release 1A and 2 of 1-2-3, you may find many occasions when you will need to use the Translate program to convert Release 2 worksheets to Release 1A so that fellow workers who use Release 1A can have access to the data you have generated. Remember that although Translate includes an option to translate Release 1A worksheets to Release 2, it is never required: you use /File Retrieve to load any Release 1A worksheet file.

Because of the substantial changes to Releases 2.01 and 2.2, you must be aware of problems and discrepancies that can arise before attempting the translation:

- ◆ Releases 2.01 and 2.2 handle computer memory much differently than Release 1A. As a result, a worksheet that can be loaded in its original WK1 format may cause a memory-full error when you try to load the file after it has been translated to the WKS format. If this occurs, you must try to reduce the overall area of the WK1 worksheet or delete extraneous data (perhaps graphs and range names) and try the translation a second time. You can also break the worksheet into several files as a last resort.

- ◆ The size of the Release 2.01 or 2.2 worksheet is much larger than that of Release 1A. If your WK1 spreadsheet contains data in rows past 2048, they will not be translated into the corresponding WKS file. If the formulas that are successfully translated contain references to the missing data in these rows, their results will not be trustworthy and may contain ERR values.

- ◆ Many Release 2.01 and 2.2 @functions and macro keynames and keywords have no counterparts in Release 1A. Any @function that is not recognized will be translated as a label entry in the new file. Trying to use macros that contain Release 2.01 or 2.2 keynames or keywords will cause a macro error to occur.

- ◆ Release 1A does not support the use of the LICS codes. If you have entered any special characters in the WK1 file you are translating to WKS, they will be represented by fallback characters (these are illustrated on the last two help screens that are displayed when you set up a Release 2 to Release 1A translation).

Translating dBASE Files to 1-2-3

Because of the widespread use of dBASE II, dBASE III PLUS, and dBASE IV as corporate database management systems, the Translate program provides for direct translation of dBASE data to and from 1-2-3 worksheet files. Note that if you are translating a dBASE IV database file, you need to select dBASE III as the source file format.

When translating data from a dBASE database file into a 1-2-3 worksheet, you need to keep a few things in mind:

♦ Records in the dBASE file after record 8191 will not be translated.

♦ If you are translating a dBASE III PLUS or dBASE IV file, any Memo fields used in the database will not be translated (these are stored in a separate text file with the extension .DBT).

♦ Records that are deleted in the database file (marked for deletion but not yet packed) will not be translated into the 1-2-3 worksheet.

Whenever you wish to translate a dBASE III PLUS database into a Release 2 worksheet, always use the 1-2-3 Translate program rather than copying the database from dBASE, because Translate will make a more faithful translation than the dBASE COPY TO command with the WKS parameter.

To translate 1-2-3 worksheets into dBASE files, you must make sure that your database is organized correctly to ensure a successful translation. All data you want included in the dBASE file must be organized as a 1-2-3 database. If you are translating the entire worksheet, then the first row of the file must consist only of the field names, with succeeding rows consisting of data records. Before translating the file, delete any criterion or output ranges. You can, however, save the database under a range name and specify that it, rather than the entire worksheet, be translated. In that case, any other ranges or data outside the database proper can remain in the file.

When preparing your 1-2-3 database for translation to dBASE, keep the following things in mind:

♦ dBASE field names cannot be longer than 10 characters and must not contain spaces. If you have spaces in the 1-2-3 field names, replace them with underscores.

♦ dBASE field names must begin with a letter, and the colon is the only embedded punctuation character that can be used. If you have any field names that begin with other characters or have used other embedded punctuation characters, edit their names before attempting the translation.

• All data in the cells of the worksheet must be displayed in order for the complete field entries to be translated (any characters not displayed will be truncated). Make sure all columns are wide enough to display all the characters in every field entry before translating the worksheet.

• If you are translating the worksheet into a dBASE II file, you can translate only the first 32 database fields into the dBASE file. If you are translating a Release 2 worksheet into a dBASE III PLUS file, you can translate only the first 128 fields.

• The field type in the resulting dBASE file is determined by the type of entries in the first record of the 1-2-3 database. Labels are converted into Character fields, values into Numeric fields, and serial date numbers into Date fields (in dBASE III PLUS). If you have any blank fields (cells) in the first record, make sure they are formatted so that their type can be correctly interpreted during translation (better yet, put in a "dummy" value or label that can later be deleted in dBASE).

Summary

Troubleshooting

Question: When I converted one of my worksheet files to another file format with the Translate program, I received all sorts of error messages. What's causing this?

Answer: When translating files, 1-2-3 often generates error messages. Some of these are spurious and cause no real problems, whereas others do indicate genuine problems with the translation. One leading cause of such translation problems is selecting, as the source file, a worksheet file that has been saved with /File Xtract instead of /File Save. To successfully translate a worksheet that was created with /File Xtract, you first need to retrieve the worksheet with /File Retrieve and then save it with /File Save before you start the Translate program.

Question: Many translations of my 1-2-3 worksheet files created with the Translate program lack the formatting and precision of the original files. Is there any way to preserve these parts of the worksheet?

The only way to ensure the preservation of all formatting, punctuation marks, trailing zeros, and the like is to convert the 1-2-3 worksheet into an ASCII or text file with the /Print File command rather than convert it directly into another program's file format using the Translate program.

Essential Techniques

To Save a 1-2-3 Worksheet as an ASCII File

1. Retrieve the worksheet, then select the /Print File command (/PF).

2. Enter a new file name for the ASCII file and press Enter (if you don't enter an extension, 1-2-3 will add .PRN to the file name).

3. Select the Range option (R) and define the print range, which is all the data you want copied to the new file in ASCII code.

4. Set the left margin (OML) to 0, and set the right margin (MR) wide enough to accommodate the line length.

5. Select the Unformatted option from the Other menu (OU).

6. Select the Quit option (Q), then select Go (G) to create the file.

To Import an ASCII File into the Worksheet

1. Move the pointer to the first cell of the range in the worksheet that is to contain the imported ASCII data, and select /File Import (/FI).

2. Select the Text option (T) if the ASCII file is not delimited. Otherwise, select the Numbers option (N).

3. Select the ASCII file to be imported from the line list (to obtain a full-screen listing, press the Name key, F3) by moving the pointer to it and pressing Enter.

To Parse ASCII Data

1. Move the pointer to the first label in the column of long labels to be parsed.

2. Select the /Data Parse Format-Line Create command (/DPFC).

3. If necessary, edit the format line by selecting the Format-Line Edit options (FE). When you've finished modifying the codes, width, or number of the data blocks in the format line, press Enter.

4. Select the Quit option (Q) to return to READY mode, then repeat steps 2 and 3 until you have created all the format lines required by the data items in the column of long labels to correctly parse it.

5. Select the /Data Parse Input-Column command (/DPI) and define the range of cells that contain the long labels to be parsed. Then select the Output-Range option (O) and indicate the location of the first cell of the range to hold the parsed data.

6. Select the Go option (G) to parse the data.

Review   Important Terms You Should Know

ASCII file	format line
data block	parse
delimited file	text file

Test Your Knowledge

1. If you have typed a table of figures in your word processor and want to import it into 1-2-3, you would save the document in the _____ file format and then use the _____ option on the _____ menu to bring it into the worksheet.

2. If your database program creates delimited files and you want to import one of your database files into 1-2-3, you would use the _____ option on the _____ menu to bring it into the worksheet.

3. If a file is saved in the ASCII file format, you can use the DOS command _____ to display its data on the screen.

4. In a delimited ASCII file, each item of data is separated by a _____ and each text item is enclosed in _____.

5. To convert a column of long labels into individual cell entries, you use the _____ command.

6. If you want 1-2-3 to ignore the last two digits of a number in the long labels you wish to parse, you select the _____ command and type _____ in the format line above the digits you don't want.

7. To use a Release 2 worksheet in Release 3, you must select the _____ command.

8. To use a Release 2 worksheet in Release 1A, you must use the
   _____ program.

9. To bring a dBASE III database file into 1-2-3, you should use the
   _____.

10. When you wish to convert an entire 1-2-3 database into a dBASE III
    database, the first row of the file must contain _____ with succeed-
    ing rows containing only _____.

Part V

♦

Extending
the Power of 1-2-3
through Macros

♦

15

The Macro Environment: Automating and Customizing Your Work in 1-2-3

In This Chapter...

Macro Basics

A *macro* is a set of written commands and keystroke instructions designed to perform specific tasks in 1-2-3. When you execute a macro, 1-2-3 automatically performs all the commands and keystrokes that the macro contains in the order in which they are entered.

Macros allow you to customize the way you work in 1-2-3 by automating repetitive or complex procedures. Macros are entered as labels in the worksheet and are assigned range names. As you are well aware, 1-2-3 commands are invoked by pressing the forward slash key (/) followed by the first letter of the names of each menu option used. Therefore, you can store any command sequence in a macro by entering the option letters preceded by a / symbol as a label. For example, you can store the command to save a worksheet, /File Save, by entering the keystrokes '/FS (the apostrophe is added to enter keystrokes as a label).

Representing Keys in Macros

Almost any key on the keyboard can be stored in a macro and replayed when the macro is executed. This includes all letter, number, and punctuation keys that you enter into a worksheet cell. Most other special keys on the IBM keyboard, including the function keys, editing keys, and pointer-movement keys, can also be stored in macros, although these cannot be entered directly, as can the alphanumeric and punctuation characters.

Lotus 1-2-3 macros use a special representation for keys, called *keystroke instructions*. By entering the keystroke instruction in the macro, you store its keystrokes so that it can be played back when the macro is executed just as if you had pressed it manually from the keyboard.

Table 15.1 shows the macro keystroke instructions for all the keys that can be represented in macros. You will notice that all keystroke instructions—with the exception of the tilde (˜), which represents the Enter key—are contained

♦ **Table 15.1:** *Macro Keystroke Instructions*

1-2-3 Key	Macro Keystroke Instruction
↵ *or* Enter	˜
←	{LEFT} (*or* {L} *in Release 2.2*)
→	{RIGHT} (*or* {R} *in Release 2.2*)
↑	{UP} (*or* {U} *in Release 2.2*)
↓	{DOWN} (*or* {D} *in Release 2.2*)

◆ **Table 15.1:** *Macro Keystroke Instructions (continued)*

1-2-3 Key	Macro Keystroke Instruction
{ (*open brace*)	{{}
} (*close brace*)	{}}
~ (*tilde*)	{~}
Abs (F4)	{ABS}
App1 (Alt-F7)	{APP1}
App2 (Alt-F8)	{APP2}
App3 (Alt-F9)	{APP3}
App4 (Alt-F10)	{APP4}
Backspace	{BACKSPACE} *or* {BS}
Backtab	{BIGLEFT}
Calc (F9)	{CALC}
Ctrl-←	{BIGLEFT}
Ctrl-→	{BIGRIGHT}
Del	{DELETE} *or* {DEL}
Edit (F2)	{EDIT}
End	{END}
Esc	{ESCAPE} *or* {ESC}
Goto (F5)	{GOTO}
Graph (F10)	{GRAPH}
Help (F1)	{HELP} (*Release 2.2 only*)
Home	{HOME}
Ins	{INSERT} *or* {INS}
Name (F3)	{NAME}
PgDn	{PGDN}
PgUp	{PGUP}
Query (F7)	{QUERY}
Tab	{BIGRIGHT}
Table (F8)	{TABLE}
Window (F6)	{WINDOW}

in a pair of braces, as in {EDIT} or {UP}. If you are using Release 2.2, you can abbreviate the arrow keys {LEFT}, {RIGHT}, {UP}, or {DOWN} to {L}, {R}, {U}, or {D}, respectively. If you are still using Release 2.01, you must spell out the entire key name within the braces.

Although this book follows the convention of entering the names for the keystroke instructions in all uppercase letters, you can enter them in all lowercase or a mixture of uppercase and lowercase letters as well.

Keys That Cannot Be Represented in Macros

A few keys that you can use in 1-2-3 cannot be included in your macros. These include:

- Caps Lock key
- Num Lock key
- Scroll Lock key
- Shift key
- Compose key (Alt-F1)
- Step key (Alt-F2)
- Run key (Alt-F3—Release 2.2)
- Undo key (Alt-F4—Release 2.2)
- Learn key (Alt-F5—Release 2.2)

Note that although you can't use the Shift or Compose key (Alt-F1) in a macro, you can still enter uppercase letters and special LICS characters in a macro as long as you enter them directly from the keyboard (see Appendix E for a list of LICS codes and information on how to use the Compose key).

If you are still using Release 2.01, you must add the Help key (F1) to the list of keys that can't be used in macros. In Release 2.2, however, you can now use the Help key to add help messages of your own to your macros.

Repeating Keystroke Instructions

It is often necessary in macros to instruct the program to repeat a keystroke more than once—for example, to move the cell pointer a specified number of times in a certain direction. To specify repetition of a key, you can enter the number of times the keystroke is to be repeated as part of its keystroke instruction. For instance, to have the pointer moved three cells to the right in a macro, you can enter {*RIGHT 3*} instead of {*RIGHT*}{*RIGHT*}{*RIGHT*}.

Entering a repetition factor as part of the keystroke instruction is not limited to cursor movement. You can enter such a factor into any special keystroke instruction listed in Table 15.1. For instance, if you want to have a macro change a cell reference into a mixed reference, with the column relative and the row absolute, you could enter {*ABS 2*} before the cell reference in the macro. This is the same as pressing the Absolute function key (F4) twice, thus producing a mixed address with the column relative and row absolute.

When entering a repetition factor, you do not have to enter a literal value such as 2 or 3. You can also enter a cell reference or a range name that contains such a value. For example, if cell A2 contains the number 3, you could enter this repetition factor as {*LEFT A2*}. The macro would then move the pointer three cells to the left. If cell A2 has been given the range name *Number*, you could produce the same cursor movement by entering {LEFT Number} in the macro.

You can also include a formula in the keystroke instruction. For example, if cell A2 contains the number 3 and B2 contains the value 2, you could move the cell pointer up five cells by entering {*UP A2+B2*}. Note that if any of the cells or formulas used as a repetition factor in a keystroke instruction contain an NA or ERR value, a label, or an empty cell when the macro is executed, the macro counts the repetition as 0 (meaning that the keystroke is ignored).

Since the keystroke instruction for the Enter key is not enclosed in braces, you cannot use this technique to indicate pressing the Enter key more than once. Whenever a macro requires you to press the Enter key several times in succession, you must enter a tilde for each time the Enter key is pressed. For example, to have the current cell in the worksheet formatted to Percent with one decimal place, you would enter

    '/RFP1 ˜ ˜

as the macro instruction. The first tilde signifies pressing the Enter key to set the number of decimal places to 1, and the second tilde signifies pressing the Enter key to accept the current cell as the range to be formatted.

Guidelines for Creating Macros

You must enter macro instructions into the worksheet as labels. You can include all macro instructions in a single cell (provided that they do not exceed 240 characters), or you can break them up into separate instructions.

Unless the macro contains very few instructions, you should always divide its commands and keystrokes among a range of cells. This not only makes the macro easier to interpret, but also makes it easier to find and fix any errors it might contain.

When using more than one cell for your macro, you must enter all of its instructions in a single column of consecutive cells with no blank cells intervening. When you execute a macro that is arranged in several cells of a column, 1-2-3 reads each instruction from left to right in each cell, moving down the column until it reaches a blank cell or a cell that contains a value, or encounters the advanced macro command {QUIT}.

When dividing a series of macro instructions, you should group each set of instructions that performs a single function or closely related functions in a single cell. This makes it easier to document a macro's purpose as well as to follow its function. Note that you can't split any keystroke instruction—that is, one that is enclosed in braces such as {RIGHT}—across two cells. All such instructions must be entered as part of one label in a single cell. Otherwise, this will cause an error when you execute the macro.

Whenever possible, use range names instead of cell addresses when referring to worksheet data in a macro. That way, if you have to move data referred to in a macro, your macro will continue to work as planned. If you use a cell address instead of a range name in the macro, this address will *not* automatically be updated in the macro when you move its data to a new location in the worksheet.

Entering Keystrokes in Macros

Because you must enter all macro instructions in the worksheet as labels, when an instruction begins with the following characters, it must be prefaced with a label prefix, usually the apostrophe ('):

/ (slash), \ (backslash), <, 0–9, +, –, @, . (period), (, #, or $

If the first character of the macro instruction that you are entering into a cell causes the program to go into LABEL mode, you do not need to preface it with an apostrophe. For example, you don't have to use a label prefix when entering a keystroke instruction such as {DOWN} because the program automatically interprets the open brace, {, as a label character.

Naming Macros

Once you enter a macro in your worksheet, you must assign a range name to it before you can run it. When assigning range names to macros, you must observe the following guidelines:

- Assign a range name that consists of a backslash (\) followed by a single letter (A–Z) if you are using Release 2.01 or if you want to be able to execute the macro by pressing Alt plus the letter in Release 2.2.

- Assign the range name \0 (zero) to a macro if you want 1-2-3 to automatically execute the macro as soon as you retrieve the worksheet that contains it.

✳ *New in 2.2*

- Assign a range name using any combination of characters (15 maximum), using the same rules as apply to naming any other ranges in 1-2-3 (see Naming a Cell Range in Chapter 4). To differentiate macro range names from regular range names, I suggest that you begin each range with a backslash (\), as you must when naming an Alt-key macro. Note that you can only do this if you are using Release 2.2. If you are using Release 2.01, you must name the macro with the single-letter \A to \Z codes.

- No macro range name should ever duplicate any commands, key names, macro instructions, or advanced macro commands (covered in Chapter 16).

Lotus 1-2-3 does not differentiate between capital and lowercase letters in range names. All range names entered in lowercase are automatically converted to their uppercase equivalents. If you are using Release 2.01, this means that you can assign only one macro to each letter key in a single worksheet file, which effectively limits the number of individual macros per worksheet to 26 (unless you create an Alt-0 autoexec macro, making 27). You can, however, assign different macros to the same letter keys as long as these macros are entered into different worksheet files.

When you assign a range name to the set of instructions entered into a single cell or cell range in the worksheet, you can use the /Range Name Create command. When the macro instructions are entered in a range of cells, you need only indicate the address of the first cell as the range; 1-2-3 automatically reads and executes the contents of all cells down the column range.

You can also assign range names to your macros by entering the name of the macro in the cell immediately to the left of the first cell of macro instructions and using the /Range Name Labels Right command. This is a favored method, because it allows you to structure the macro in a three-column layout, with the first column containing the macro name, the second the macro instructions, and the third comments that document the function of each set of macro instructions. Figure 15.1 illustrates this three-column layout for macros.

```
Y61: [W8] 'Name                                                      READY

        Y           Z               AA        AB      AC      AD
  61  Name        Macro instructions  Description
  62  \S          /FS{ESC}            Save worksheet the first time
  63
  64  \R          /FS~R               Save worksheet under same name
  65
  66  \D          @DATE({?},{?},{?})~ Enter date
  67              {DOWN}              move pointer down one row
  68
  69  \L          {EDIT}{HOME}'       Convert value into label
  70              {DOWN}              move pointer down one row
  71
  72  \V          {EDIT}{CALC}        Convert formula to calculated value
  73              {DOWN}              move pointer down one row
  74
  75  \E          /RE~                Erase current cell
  76
  77  \W          /WCS                Widen a column
  78
  79  \P          /PPAGPQ~            Print currently defined report again
  80
  MACROLIB.BAK                  UNDO
```

♦ **Figure 15.1:** *Sample macros with the macro name, instructions, and documentation arranged in three adjacent columns*

Remember that when the name of your macro begins with a backslash, as in Alt-key macros such as \S, you must preface the macro name with an apostrophe when you enter it into its cell. This is required because the backslash is normally used in Lotus 1-2-3 to create a repeating label. Therefore, to avoid entering the macro name SSSSSSSS in the cell rather than \S, you must actually enter '\S in the cell.

Using the /Range Name Labels Right command to name your macros when they are laid out in this three-column arrangement is more efficient than using the /Range Name Create command. This is because the /Range Name Labels command enables you to assign range names to all the macros you've entered in a worksheet in one operation. You must remember, however, to separate the last instruction in one macro from the first instruction of the next macro below it by at least one blank row when using this type of arrangement.

Documenting Your Macros

As you can see in Figure 15.1, a three-column layout for macros makes it easier not only to assign range names but also to document the function of each set of instructions. It is important to document the working of even the simplest macros, so that you can easily revise them later.

Because macros are executed from the first cell of the named range down its column, you can safely enter your comments to document the function of each set of instructions in the column immediately to the right. If you wish, you can place your comments in a column farther over to the right, leaving a blank column or columns between the macro contents and their associated descriptions. You will, however, want to make sure the column containing the macro instruction is wide enough so that all keystrokes and commands are visible in their cells.

When documenting a simple macro, you may have to add only a simple comment line describing the overall function of the macro rather than the function of each command. For instance, a macro that consists of the instruction /WCS10 ‾ can simply be described as *widen column to 10*. In a more complex macro made up of several steps, you will want to document each step, by describing either its function or its relation to other steps.

Executing Macros

To execute an Alt-key macro—that is, a macro whose range name consists of a backslash and a single letter—you press the Alt key and hold it down while you type the letter key. For instance, if you have assigned the range name \J to a macro, you execute it by pressing Alt-J.

* *New in 2.2*   If you are using Release 2.2 and you assigned your macro a range name other than one consisting of a \ (backslash) and a single letter, you must press the Run key (Alt-F3) and select its range name from line listing in response to the *Select macro to run:* prompt to execute it. When you press the Run key (Alt-F3), 1-2-3 displays a line listing of *all* range names defined in the worksheet, not just those assigned to macros. Therefore, to segregate and differentiate macro range names from other range names, you should begin all macro range names with the backslash (\). This places all macro range names together at the end of the line listing. Note that after you press the Run key (Alt-F3), you can always press the Name key (F3) to obtain a full-screen listing of all range names in the worksheet.

Before testing a macro for the first time, you should always save the worksheet by using the /File Save command. If the macro contains errors that might adversely affect the data in the worksheet, you can then retrieve the worksheet file and make any necessary corrections to its contents. Of course, any time you edit the contents of a macro, you can't be sure that you have not introduced potentially destructive errors into the macro. You should therefore use /File Save each time you edit a macro before testing its revised form.

Before executing a macro, you must determine whether you need to reposition the pointer for the macro to work properly and not damage the contents of the worksheet. This depends on the function of the macro. If you are executing a macro that erases the contents of the current cell (/RE ~), you will want to make sure that the pointer is positioned in a cell you don't mind deleting or that the Undo feature is activated (if you are using Release 2.2). However, if you are executing a macro that prints a copy of the currently defined report (/PPAGPQ), it doesn't matter where the pointer is located when you invoke the macro. In such a case, there would be no adverse effect on the macro even if the pointer is still located in the cell containing these macro instructions when you execute it.

To terminate a macro before it executes its instruction, you press Ctrl-Break. If you find that your macro contains errors that cause the program to go into ERROR mode, you can terminate the macro in this way. However, you will then have to press the Esc or Enter key to return to READY mode.

Creating an Automatically Executed Macro

If you create a macro that you want automatically executed as soon as you retrieve the worksheet, you will need to give it the range name \0 (zero). Any macro that has this name will be executed as soon as the file is retrieved, as long as the Autoexec macros setting is Yes (the program default). If you wish to change this setting to No and prevent 1-2-3 from automatically executing \0 macros, you need to select the No option from the /Worksheet Global Default Autoexec menu (/WGDAN).

Because you can't execute a macro that has the range name \0 manually (1-2-3 will just beep if you press Alt-0), you need to give your autoexec macros a second range name (using \ and a letter between A and Z). That way, you can then use the second range name to test the macro after it has been edited as well as to invoke it later.

Pausing Macros for User Input

You can have your macros pause during execution to allow you to enter data, choose a particular menu option, or enter a new setting. To enter a pause in a macro, enter {?}. When the program encounters a question mark enclosed in braces, it pauses and waits until you have had a chance to input data or respond to on-screen command prompts. During this time, you will see the CMD status indicator at the bottom of the screen. This lets you know that 1-2-3 is executing a macro but that it is currently paused. To continue execution of the macro, you press the Enter key.

Putting pauses in macros often makes them much more versatile. Because the pauses allow you to select new parameters each time you use the macros, you will find that you can use the same macro in many different situations. For example, consider a macro to help you enter dates with the @DATE function. To create a macro named \D that enters the serial date number for *January 11, 1990*, you could enter the instruction

>   @DATE(90,1,11) ˜

in a cell. After you assign the range name \D to this cell, when you press Alt-D, this macro enters the date number *32884* in the cell containing the pointer.

Such a macro is of limited usefulness (you can use it only when you need to enter the date January 11, 1990, in the worksheet). You could easily make it more versatile, however, by substituting pauses for the @DATE function arguments:

>   @DATE({?},{?},{?}) ˜

Now when you execute this version of the Alt-D macro, it enters *@DATE(* where it then encounters the first {?} causing the macro to pause. During this first pause, you can input the first @DATE argument (last two digits of the year). After doing this, you have to press Enter to resume the macro. The macro then enters a comma (,) and pauses again when it encounters the second {?}. During this pause, you can input the second @DATE argument (the number of the month). When you press the Enter key to resume the macro this time, it enters another comma (,) and then pauses one last time. During this pause, you enter the third @DATE argument (the number of the day). When you press the Enter key to resume the macro, it enters) to complete the @DATE function, and then the tilde at the end of the macro instruction enters the @function in the current cell.

The only thing to remember when adding pauses to your macros is that you must physically press the Enter key to continue their execution. Because 1-2-3 doesn't display an explicit prompt telling you that the macro has paused and is waiting for your input, the only clue you will have is the display of the CMD status indicator at the bottom of the screen.

Planning Your Macros

The first steps in creating a macro are to outline its functions, transcribe these into a set of keystroke and command instructions that can be read by 1-2-3, and then decide where to locate the instructions in the worksheet. You will often begin this process by going through the command keystrokes manually, writing down each command and prompt you encounter (note that if you are using Release 2.2, you can set up a learn range and have 1-2-3 enter the instructions in the worksheet as you run through them—see Creating Macros in

LEARN Mode, later in this chapter). Remember to transcribe special pointer-movement and function keys into their 1-2-3 keystroke instructions. This includes using a tilde (˜) each time you press the Enter key to signal a response to a prompt or to complete a command.

When you first outline the functions of the macro, decide what type of command sequences you want the macro to automate for you. As part of this process, estimate how often you will use these commands in the worksheet and in what contexts. Remember that because macros are entered as a part of the worksheet file, you can make them as application-specific as you deem necessary. However, there is a trade-off: if your macros are too finely tuned to a particular spreadsheet application, you will find yourself spending a great deal of time editing the macro or even recreating it when you begin working on a slightly different application.

Locating Your Macros in the Worksheet

Deciding where to locate your macros in the worksheet is as important in planning as deciding what they are to contain. Because macros are not actually a part of the data and formulas of the worksheet, they need to be located out of the way. At the same time, they can easily be corrupted or damaged if you forget their whereabouts when creating and editing the worksheet. Using the /Worksheet Delete command to delete an entire column or row of the worksheet can damage macros if any of their instructions are located in the deleted column or row. The /Worksheet Insert Row command can also disable your macros if it happens to introduce a blank row between macro instructions (the macros will then shut down prematurely when they reach the new blank cell). You should use these /Worksheet commands only after ascertaining that their use will have no adverse effect on your macros.

One way to avoid the possibility of damaging or disabling your macros with the /Worksheet Delete or /Worksheet Insert command is to locate all your macros together in an area below and to the right of your worksheet data. Because the macros are located in a panel to the right of the worksheet data, you can't harm them when using the /Worksheet Delete Column command. Because the macros are located below the worksheet data, you can't harm them when using either the /Worksheet Delete Row or /Worksheet Insert Row command. As your worksheet grows and you need more room in which to enter new data, you can move the macros farther over and down, as required, by using the /Worksheet Insert Column command and the /Worksheet Insert Row command in the columns to the left and the rows above the area that contains your macros.

Debugging Your Macros

Not all macros that you create will perform as intended when you first test them. If a macro gives you unexpected results, or terminates before it performs all the steps you had planned, you will need to *debug* it—that is, locate all the errors in the macro instructions and fix them.

When 1-2-3 encounters an error in your macro, the program beeps at you, goes into ERROR mode, and displays an error message, just as it does when it encounters any other kind of error in 1-2-3. The macro error message not only gives you a general description of the type of error encountered, but also gives the address of the cell where the error was encountered, as in

Unrecognized key/range name {...} {U61}

In this example, the keystroke instruction or range name that 1-2-3 can't decipher was encountered in cell U61, and you would examine the contents of this cell for typographical errors, missing braces, and the like for any range names or keystroke instructions entered there.

If you don't understand the error message that 1-2-3 displays, press the Help key (F1) and then press Enter to select the Error Message Index option. Then move the pointer to the name of the error message displayed (you may have to select the Continued option to bring new error messages in view—they are in alphabetical order). Then, press Enter to have the program display a help screen giving you information on the error message and what to do about it. To exit from the Help screen and return to the worksheet, press the Esc key.

To exit from ERROR mode and return to READY mode, you can press Esc, Ctrl-Break, or the Enter key. To locate the error, move the pointer to the cell address listed in the error message. When you spot the problem, press the Edit key (F2), correct the error, and press Enter.

Common Types of Macro Errors

The most common macro errors are the result of misspelling the names of keys, ranges, or advanced macro commands, or forgetting to include responses to all the prompts that appear when selecting a menu command sequence. The following list includes the types of problems to look for when 1-2-3 encounters a bug in your macro and its cause isn't self-evident:

 ◆ Typographical errors in a keystroke instruction, range name, or advanced macro command, such as {DWN} when you meant to enter {DOWN}

 ◆ Missing steps in a command sequence or steps out of order, such as /RF0, ˜ ˜ instead of /RF,0 ˜ ˜ to format the current cell with the Comma (,) format with 0 decimal places

* Missing tildes (for carriage returns), such as /PPOP55Q instead of /PPOP55 ˜ Q to set the page length to 55 lines

* Spaces where there shouldn't be any, as in @ ROUND(Balance,2) instead of @ROUND(Balance,2) to round a range named *Balance* to two decimal places

* No spaces where they are required, as in /FS{ESC} instead of /FS {ESC} to select /File Save and then clear the file name or search pattern

* Incorrect range names, cell addresses, or range names that duplicate key names or macro advanced commands, such as a range named END or WINDOW

* Incorrect arguments in 1-2-3 @functions

Because you can edit the contents of macros like any other cells in the worksheet, you can easily make modifications to a basic macro at any time, adding instructions or deleting them as you see fit. Just remember to save the worksheet each time you make any changes to it before testing the macro on your data.

Debugging Macros in STEP Mode

As you create more complex macros, you may find it difficult to locate the instructions that are causing errors in your macro. If, upon examining the contents of the macro, you can't spot any obvious errors such as typographical mistakes or an omission in the instructions, you can run the macro in STEP mode. In STEP mode, 1-2-3 runs the macro one instruction at a time. That way, you can see the effect that each instruction has on the worksheet. When you locate a step that causes an error to occur, you can abort the macro with Ctrl-Break and Esc and then fix the error.

To put the program in STEP mode, you press the Step key (Alt-F2) before you retest your macro. As soon as you press the Step key, you see the STEP indicator at the bottom of the screen. The macro is then executed one instruction at a time (if the macro is typing data, this translates to one keystroke at a time). To advance the macro to the next instruction, you can press any key, although I highly recommend the spacebar.

When you execute your next macro, this STEP mode indicator changes to SST. By pressing the spacebar, you can easily step through the macro, examining what happens after each instruction is executed until you locate the problem (at least the first problem—your macro could easily contain many). Once you spot the place at which the macro hangs up or causes the program to go into ERROR mode, you can press Esc or Ctrl-Break to terminate it and return to

READY mode. Then, you can edit the cell or cells that contain your errors, resave the worksheet, and test the macro again.

To exit from STEP mode so that macros are no longer executed one instruction at a time, you press the Step key (Alt-F2) a second time. Note that you can do this while a macro is paused and is waiting for you to press the spacebar to execute the next instruction or after the macro has completely finished executing. As soon as you press the Step key a second time, 1-2-3 lets you know that it is no longer in STEP mode by removing the STEP indicator from the status line.

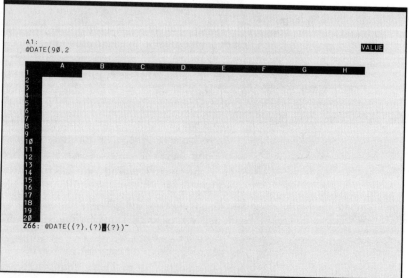

✻ *New in 2.2*

In Release 2.2, STEP mode has been improved. In place of the SST indicator on the status line, the program displays the address of the cell that contains instructions that are being executed, as well as the contents of that cell. In addition, the next instruction or keystroke to be executed (when you press the spacebar) is highlighted. This is shown in Figure 15.2, where a macro entered in cell Z66 is being executed in STEP mode. Here, the macro will enter the second comma separating the second and third argument of the @DATE function as soon as you press the spacebar (this is why this comma is highlighted on the status line).

If the macro is paused to allow you to enter data or respond to a prompt, the status line returns to normal: the macro instructions disappear and regular status indicators such as SST, NUM, or CAPS return to this line. As soon as you input your data or respond to the prompt and then press Enter to resume the

◆ **Figure 15.2:** *Executing a macro in STEP mode*

macro's execution, the current macro instructions return and all other status indicators disappear from the status line.

✳ New in 2.2

Creating Macros in LEARN Mode

Instead of typing all your macro instructions, you can use 1-2-3's learn feature to create simple macros. When you use this feature, you activate LEARN mode, wherein 1-2-3 records all of your keystrokes in a *learn range*—that is, a single column of cells that you have already defined. Creating macros with the new learn feature is essentially a five-step process:

1. Specify a single column of the worksheet as the learn range by selecting the /Worksheet Learn Range command (/WLR).

2. Turn on LEARN mode by pressing the Learn key (Alt-F5).

3. Select the 1-2-3 commands and/or type the data you want saved in your macro.

4. Turn off LEARN mode by pressing the Learn key (Alt-F5) again.

5. Move the pointer to the first cell of the learn range and assign a range name to it with the /Range Name Create command (/RNC).

When you select the /Worksheet Learn command (/WL), you are presented with the options

Range Cancel Erase

To define a new learn range, you select the Range option and then indicate the extent of the range in response to the *Enter learn range:* prompt. To cancel the currently defined learn range when you are about to create another macro with the learn feature, you select the Cancel option on the /Worksheet Learn menu. To actually erase the contents of the currently defined learn range when you want to redefine a macro in LEARN mode using the same learn range, you select the Erase option on this menu instead. When you select Erase, you are presented with the options

No Yes

To continue and have the contents of learn range erased, select Yes (Y). To abandon this operation and retain its contents, select No (N). Note that if you select the Yes option in error, you can restore the learn range by pressing the Undo key (Alt-F4).

When defining the learn range after selecting the /Worksheet Learn Range command, you need to make it large enough to contain all your keystrokes.

Remember that this range should consist of a single column (if you define a multiple-column range, 1-2-3 will reduce it to a single-column range automatically). If you enter more keystrokes than will fit in the learn range as you originally defined it, the program beeps at you, goes into ERROR mode, and displays the message

Learn range is full

At this point, you must exit from ERROR mode by pressing Esc or Enter, then enlarge the size of the learn range by selecting /Worksheet Learn Range and adding more rows to the learn range. If your macro is short, you can then select /Worksheet Learn Erase Yes to clear the learn range, turn on LEARN mode, and reenter all the keystrokes in your macro. If your macro is long, you can just turn on LEARN mode, and then begin entering keystrokes from the point you left off when the original range became full.

To avoid running into this error, you should always make the learn range bigger than you think might be required to contain your macro when you first define it. Note that the learn range doesn't take up any memory until you start recording keystrokes in it, so you needn't be concerned that creating a large learn range will use too much memory.

When recording your keystrokes in the learn range, the program uses abbreviations for all keystroke instructions, such as {R} for {RIGHT} or {D} for {DOWN}. Also, the program will record each press of a pointer- or cursor-movement key as a separate instruction, so if you press the Edit key and then press the ← key twice in LEARN mode, the program will record these keystrokes as

{EDIT}{L}{L}

If you wish, you can compact the transcription by manually editing this macro instruction and changing it to

{EDIT}{L 2}

which accomplishes the same thing.

Lotus 1-2-3 will not record any of the following keystrokes in the learn range:

- Shift

- Num Lock

- Scroll Lock

- Compose (Alt-F1)

- Run (Alt-F3)

- Undo (Alt-F4)

- Learn (Alt-F5)

You will notice that these are the same keys for which the program provides no keystroke instructions, so they can't be used in macros created manually either.

Lotus 1-2-3 won't actually place all the keystrokes that it is recording into the learn range until you turn off LEARN mode. Sometimes, you will see the CALC status indicator appear on the status line while you are recording a macro in LEARN mode. If this indicator remains displayed after you turn off LEARN mode, you need to press the Calc key (F9) to force 1-2-3 to place all the recorded keystrokes into the learn range.

Creating and Using Macro Libraries

There are certain utility macros, such as those used to save or reprint the worksheet, that you will want to use almost every time you start a new worksheet in 1-2-3 because they speed up the entry or editing of the worksheet. Rather than recreate such macros as you need them in each new worksheet that you begin, you can store them together in a separate worksheet file. This type of worksheet contains only macros that are retrieved and activated when you undertake a new worksheet. The worksheet shown in Figure 15.3 represents a typical macro library, containing a group of macros designed to make it easier to input, format, and edit worksheet data.

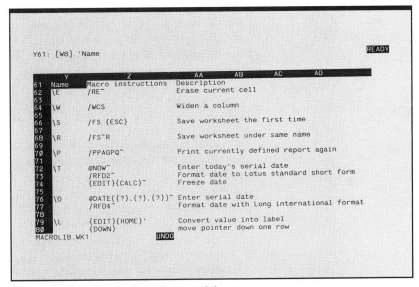

♦ **Figure 15.3:** *Typical macro library worksheet*

Once you have created it, you can use a macro library worksheet in two ways: you can retrieve the macro library worksheet with the /File Retrieve command and then build your worksheet in it, or you can start a new worksheet file and select the /File Combine Named/Specified-Range command to bring the cell range containing the macros into it.

If you choose the former method of creating your new worksheet in the macro library file, you *must* save the worksheet under a new file name to keep the macro library file from being overwritten with the worksheet data it contains. If you choose to use the second method of copying the macros from the library file into the current worksheet, you must use the /Range Name Labels Right command to rename all the copied macros before you can use them (remember that range names are not transferred when you use the /File Combine commands). You will get practice in using both methods in the macro exercises.

❊ *New in 2.2*

Release 2.2 introduces a new way to create and use macro libraries in 1-2-3 with the inclusion of its Macro Library Manager add-in program as part of the 1-2-3 software package. The Macro Library Manager, nicknamed *Hyperspace*, enables you to store collections of macros in a special library file that not only resides on the disk but also in RAM. Once you load the library file into memory, you can use the macros it contains with any worksheet that you begin or retrieve during the work session.

Because the Hyperspace macros remain in memory independent of any particular worksheet, a library file can even contain macros whose instructions erase the current worksheet from memory or retrieve a new one. You cannot use these types of file commands in a macro that is entered as part of a worksheet because such file commands would annihilate the macro from memory as soon as it erased the worksheet from RAM.

❊ *New in 2.2*

Attaching the Macro Library Manager Add-In

To create or use a Hyperspace macro library, you first need to attach the Macro Library Manager add-in program. Like the Allways add-in that you learned about in Chapter 10, this add-in program must be assigned to a particular Alt-function key combination between Alt-F7 and Alt-F10 when you load it into memory. Thereafter, you activate this add-in to create or use a Hyperspace macro library by pressing the Alt or Shift key plus the function key chosen.

The file name that 1-2-3 uses for the Macro Library Manager add-in program is *MACROMGR.ADN*. This file is located on the Install disk. If you are using 1-2-3 on a two-disk-drive system, you will want to replace the 1-2-3 System disk in drive A with a copy of the Install disk in drive A before you attempt to attach this program. If you are using 1-2-3 on a hard disk system, this file should already be copied in the same directory that holds the 1-2-3 program files (C:\123).

You need to take these steps to load the Macro Library manager into the memory of your computer:

1. **Select /Add-In Attach (/AA), then move the pointer to file MACROMGR.ADN, and press Enter.**

   You must now choose the key to assign to this add-in. This time, you should select 8 (for Alt-F8) because you already assigned 7 to Allways. That way, you can have both add-in programs attached at the same time.

2. **Type 8, then select the Quit option (Q) on the /Add-In menu.**

   Now, when you want to create a Hyperspace macro library or load one into memory, you can activate the Macro Library Manager simply by pressing Alt-F8 or Shift-F8.

Attaching the Macro Library Manager Add-In Automatically:
If you wish to have the Macro Library Manager add-in program attached automatically each time you start 1-2-3, you need to select the /Worksheet Global Default Other Add-In Set command (/WGDOAS). Select a number between 1 and 8 (if this is the only auto-attach add-in program, select *1*), then move the pointer to the *MACROMGR.ADN* file name, and press Enter. You will then be asked if you wish this add-in automatically invoked each time you start 1-2-3. Select the Yes option (Y). If the Macro Library Manager is already attached, 1-2-3 will assign it to the same Alt-key combination that you used when manually attaching the add-in. If not, you will have to choose between the No option and the numbers 7 through 10. After you select the key number, you will be returned to the /Worksheet Global Default Other Add-In menu. From here select the Quit option (Q), then select the Update option (U). Next, select the Quit option (Q) from the /Worksheet Global Default menu to return to READY mode. Thereafter, whenever you start 1-2-3, the program will automatically attach the Macro Library Manager add-in program after loading 1-2-3 into memory. This auto-invoke procedure ends by displaying the Macro Library Manager's menu, with which you can select the macro library file to be loaded.

✳ *New in 2.2* # Creating a Hyperspace Macro Library

Before you can create a Hyperspace macro library, you must create the macros it is to contain in a worksheet. You can prepare these macros by typing in the instructions or using the learn feature, whichever you find more convenient. When creating the macros in the worksheet for the Hyperspace library file, you must arrange them in a single column (remembering, of course, to skip a row between them) so that all the macros can be included in one range. You must also remember to assign range names to each of the macros *before* you copy them into a macro library.

After attaching the Macro Library Manager program, you need to activate its menu by pressing the Alt-function key that you assigned to this program (Alt-F8 in our case). When you do, you will see the following menu options:

Load Save Edit Remove Name-List Quit

To create a library containing the macros you have created in the current worksheet, you select the Save option (S) from this menu and enter a file name for the Hyperspace library file. All such files use the .MLB (for Macro Library) extension, and therefore the program will use the DOS search pattern *.MLB to display all existing library files in the current directory. When naming your macro library, you must follow the same rules as when naming worksheet files.

If the file name you select already exists on disk, the program will indicate this and prompt you for permission to overwrite the file. If you wish to replace the library file, select the Yes option (Y). If not, select No (N or Enter).

After indicating the macro library file name, you are prompted to enter the macro library range. Note that the range will already be anchored, so if the pointer is not already in the first cell of this range, you will have to press Esc to unanchor the range if you wish to define this range by pointing. If you used the three-column arrangement in laying out the macros, you can include all three columns in this range (although only the column containing the macro instructions must be included in the macro library range). Note that a macro library file can contain up to 16,376 cells.

After you define the range containing the macros, you will be asked if you wish to assign a password to the macro library file. If you select the No option (N or Enter), the macros in the designated range will be immediately copied into the library.

If you select the Yes option (Y), you will then be prompted to enter the password. Your password for a macro library file can be up to 80 characters long (with no spaces). When assigning a password, remember that it is case-sensitive, so uppercase and lowercase versions of the same letters are not considered matches. Note that unlike password-protecting a worksheet file, the

Macro Library Manager program doesn't require you to verify the password that you enter. This means that the program accepts whatever password you type as soon as you press the Enter key, and it immediately copies the macros in the designated range to this file.

You cannot edit or view password-protected libraries in STEP mode unless you correctly enter the password. You can, however, execute them without knowing or giving the password. This protects your macros from being tampered with while allowing them to be used.

When the Macro Library Manager copies the macros in the designated range to the library file, it actually removes them from the worksheet (that is, they are literally extracted from the worksheet—a process not followed elsewhere in 1-2-3, even when the process is called *extract*). As part of this process, the macros are not only saved in the macro library file but are *also* loaded into memory so that they are immediately available for use.

✳ *New in 2.2* Using Hyperspace Macros

To use a Hyperspace macro in a library that you have loaded into memory, you execute it just as you would if it were entered in the worksheet you are building.

If the macro you wish to use is an Alt-key macro, you press the Alt key plus the letter assigned as the second part of its range name. For example, if the macro's range name is \N, you would execute it by pressing Alt-N.

If the macro you wish to use is not an Alt-key macro, you press the Run key (Alt-F3). The program will then display a line listing of all named ranges in the current worksheet *as well as* those macro range names in the macro libraries loaded into RAM. Move the pointer to the range name of the macro you wish to execute and press Enter.

Selecting Macros with the Same Range Name

You may sometimes create a macro in the worksheet with the same range name as one in a Hyperspace macro whose library has been loaded into RAM. If it is an Alt-key macro and you press the Alt-letter key combination, 1-2-3 will execute the worksheet macro instead of the Hyperspace macro with the same name.

In such a situation, to execute the Hyperspace macro, you must use the Run key (Alt-F3). After that, you change the line listing to a full-screen listing by pressing the Name key (F3). In the full-screen listing, as you move the pointer to each range name, 1-2-3 lists its source under the prompt *Select the macro to run*. If the macro is in the current worksheet, the program lists its cell address. If the macro is a Hyperspace macro, the program lists the name of its macro library file. To execute the Hyperspace macro, you move the pointer to its range name in the full-screen listing rather than that of the worksheet macro and press Enter.

If you have loaded more than one Hyperspace macro library into RAM and duplicate Alt-key macro names are saved in different library files, 1-2-3 will run the macro in the library file that was first loaded into memory when you press the Alt-letter key combination. To execute a duplicate Alt-key macro from a different macro library file, you must also use the Run key (Alt-F3) with the Name key (F3) and select it from this screen according to its file name listing.

✳ *New in 2.2*   Managing Macro Library Files

The Macro Library Manager program enables you to create a table of all the macro range names in a macro library file that has been loaded into memory. This table consists of a single column that lists all the range names in alphabetical order. The table lists only the range names in the file, and not their location (as when using the /Range Name Table command), because Hyperspace macros occupy no cells and, therefore, have no cell addresses.

Obtaining a List of Macro Range Names in a Library File

To create a list of macro range names in a macro library file, you select the Name-List (N) option on the Macro Library Manager menu. You are then prompted to select the name of the macro library file. To do this, move the pointer to the name of the macro library file whose macro range names you wish listed, and press Enter. You are next prompted to enter the range for the list. In response to this prompt, move the pointer to the cell you wish to designate as the first cell of the table and press Enter. Be careful that no data exists in the column below this cell that can be overwritten by the table of macro range names.

As with range name tables created with the /Range Name Table command, the table of macro range names is static. If you edit the contents of a macro library file by either adding or deleting macros, this table is not automatically updated. To make it current, you need to recreate it with the Name-List option.

Loading More Than One Hyperspace Macro Library File into RAM

The Macro Library Manager program allows you to load multiple macro library files into RAM. To load another library file into memory, you select the Load (L) option on the Macro Manager Library menu, then move the pointer to the name of the file you wish to load, and press Enter.

The number of macro library files that you can load depends upon the amount of free memory, the size of the library file, and the size of the worksheet you are building. However, at no time can you have more than ten macro library files in memory, regardless of the amount of RAM available.

When you save a range of macros in a macro library file, 1-2-3 allocates a cell in *conventional* memory for every cell in the range whether it is empty or not (for a discussion of the types of memory and their usage, see Appendix A). Therefore, to conserve memory, you will want to make your macro range as compact as possible (individual macros must still be separated by blank cells, although you can omit the cells containing their range names and documentation).

Removing a Library File from Memory

To conserve memory, especially when you are building a large worksheet, you should retain in memory only those macro libraries that you are actively using. When you no longer need access to the Hyperspace macros in a particular macro library, you should unload the file to make more memory available. To do this, you select the Remove option (R) on the Macro Library Manager menu, then move the pointer to the name of the library file to be unloaded in response to the *Enter name of macro library to remove* prompt, and press Enter.

Editing a Macro Library File

To edit the contents of a macro library file, you must copy the macros into the worksheet using the Edit option on the Macro Library Manager menu. When you select Edit (E), the program lists all macro library files that are loaded into memory (you can't edit an MLB file directly from disk; it must first be loaded into RAM).

To select the library you want to edit, move the pointer to its name and press Enter. If you assigned a password to the macro library file when you saved it, you will then be prompted to enter it. If you cannot reproduce the password exactly as it was originally entered, 1-2-3 will beep, go into ERROR mode, and display the message

Incorrect password

When you press Esc or Enter to exit from ERROR mode, you will be returned immediately to READY mode in the worksheet, whereupon you will have to invoke the Macro Library Manager add-in program (using Alt-F8 or whatever key you assigned), select the Edit option, and choose the macro library file again.

After you select the file (and successfully enter the password, if one is assigned), the following options are displayed:

Ignore Overwrite

Choose the Ignore option (I) if you do not want 1-2-3 to replace duplicate range names in the worksheet. When you select Ignore, the program retains worksheet range names over identical library range names when the macro file is read into the worksheet for editing. This means that although the macro instructions for such ranges will be correctly read into the worksheet, their range names will no longer be assigned to the macro instructions, and they must be reassigned before you save these macros into a library file again. Choose the Overwrite option when you want 1-2-3 to retain the library range names that duplicate worksheet range names.

After you choose between Ignore and Overwrite, you are prompted to enter the range for the macro library. Here, you need only indicate the address of the first cell (in the upper left corner) of the range where you want the macros copied. As with other copied ranges, 1-2-3 will overwrite existing data when it copies the contents of the macro library into this range, so make sure you select an area that contains sufficient blank cells to contain this range.

Once the macros in the macro library have been copied into the worksheet, you can edit them as you would macros entered in a worksheet. After you have made all the desired editing changes, you can use the Save command to save changes in the same or a new macro library file. If you select the name of an existing macro library file, you select the Yes option (Y) when prompted by the program for permission to overwrite its contents.

Using Macro Libraries to Duplicate Data in Different Worksheets: Hyperspace macro libraries are primarily intended to hold collections of utility macros that you need when creating new worksheets. Because you can save data in them as well as macro instructions, however, you can also use Hyperspace macro libraries to copy the same data into different worksheets. After you input the data in a table that you wish to reuse, you save the range that contains this table in a macro library file using the Save option (S) on the Macro Library Manager menu. Then, when you start a new worksheet (during the same work session) that uses these data, you move the pointer to the location where you want the first cell of the table to be, select the Edit option (E) on the Macro Library Manager menu, choose the name of the library file that contains the table to be duplicated, and then press Enter twice (the first time to select Ignore, and the second to copy the contents of the macro library from the current cell on).

Erasing a Macro Library File

The Macro Library Manager menu doesn't include an option for deleting a macro library file from disk. If you wish to delete one of your files, you can use the /File Erase Other command, just as you would to erase any other 1-2-3 file from disk. To restrict the listing to just macro library files, you should select the /File Erase Other command (/FEO), press Esc to remove the *.* search pattern, then type *.*mlb* and press Enter.

After you locate the file you wish to erase, move the pointer to it, press Enter, and then select the Yes option (Y) when prompted by 1-2-3 for confirmation.

Practice Creating and Using Macros

In the exercises ahead, you will get a chance to create a variety of utility macros that will automate and simplify the building of new worksheets and the editing and printing of existing ones. All the macros that you create will then be saved in a macro library worksheet, which you will learn to copy in an existing worksheet or use in creating a new worksheet.

Creating Your First Macro in LEARN Mode

If you are using Release 2.2, you will use the learn feature to create your first macros. After some practice in using LEARN mode, however, you will then switch over to typing in your macros; you must use this method if you are using Release 2.01 or when creating macros that pause for user input.

1. **Begin a new worksheet; move the pointer to cell Y61 by pressing Tab three times and then PgDn three times.**
   You will create your first macros three screens to the right and three screen down from cell A1. This will place your macros to the right and below any worksheet data you might add, if you decide to create your worksheet using the macro library worksheet.

2. **Enter the heading *Name* in cell Y61, *Macro instructions* in cell Z61, and *Description* in cell AA61; then widen column Y to 8 characters and column Z to 20.**
   Your first macro will delete the current cell. This macro can be handy when you just need to erase the cell containing the pointer (and it's a lot faster than typing /RE and pressing Enter). You will name this macro \E, so that you can execute it by pressing Alt-E.

3. **Move the pointer to cell Y62, type '\E, and press the → key.**
    Remember that you have to type the apostrophe to prevent 1-2-3 from interpreting the \ (backslash) as the repeating-character label prefix. If you are using Release 2.01, you are ready to enter the keystrokes in cell Z62 as shown in step 4, and then complete steps 9–12. If you are using Release 2.2, you will have 1-2-3 enter these keystrokes for you in LEARN mode as you actually erase a cell; go ahead and define the learn range in step 5.

4. **With the pointer in cell Z62, type '/RE˜ and press Enter.**
    Remember that you must use the apostrophe to prevent 1-2-3 from accessing the menu, and that the tilde represents pressing the Enter key.

5. **With the pointer in cell Z62, select /Worksheet Learn Range (/WLR), type a period, move the pointer down to cell Z66, and press Enter.**
    You should always make the learn range bigger than you think you will need. Now that the learn range is set, you are ready to go through the keystrokes you want 1-2-3 to record in this macro.

6. **Move the pointer to cell AA62, type *Erase current cell*, and press Enter; then press the Learn key (Alt-F5) to turn on LEARN mode.**
    You should now see the LEARN status indicator on the status line. This indicates that all your keystrokes will be recorded until you press the Learn key a second time to turn off LEARN mode. Now you will erase the contents of cell AA62.

7. **Select /Range Erase (/RE) and press Enter; then press the Learn key (Alt-F5) to turn off LEARN mode.**
    As soon as you press the Learn key a second time, 1-2-3 stops recording keystrokes. You should notice that the LEARN indicator has disappeared from the status line and that the CALC indicator has appeared. To have 1-2-3 copy the recorded keystrokes into the learn range, you must press the Calc key.

8. **Press the Calc key (F9), and 1-2-3 copies the keystrokes '/re˜ in cell Z62.**
    Notice that 1-2-3 records the menu keystrokes in lowercase (the case makes no difference when the macro is executed). Next, you need to enter the macro description in AA62.

9. **Move the pointer to cell AA62, type *Erase current cell*, and press Enter.**

Now you are ready to assign the range name \E to this macro. Because this range name is already entered into cell Y62, you can use the /Range Name Labels Right command to assign it to cell Z62, which contains the macro instructions.

10. **Move the pointer to cell Y62, then select /Range Name Labels Right (/RNLR) and press Enter.**

    Before you test your macro, you will save your worksheet; that way, you can always retrieve it from disk if the macro goes awry and damages the worksheet.

11. **Save the worksheet under the file name MACROLIB.WK1; if you aren't sure that your PRACTICE directory is current, select /File Directory (/FD) before you save the worksheet with /File Save (/FS).**

    Now test your macro by entering a label in cell Y64 and using Alt-E to erase it.

12. **Move the pointer to cell Y64, type \W, and press Enter (this repeats Ws across the cell); then press Alt-E to erase it.**

    If you are using Release 2.01 and your macro doesn't work, check your macro keystrokes against those shown in Figure 15.4. If necessary, edit the keystrokes, save the worksheet again, and then test Alt-E in cell Y64.

Creating a Macro to Widen Columns

For your second macro exercise, you will create a macro that widens the current column. This task is one of the most frequently used when building a

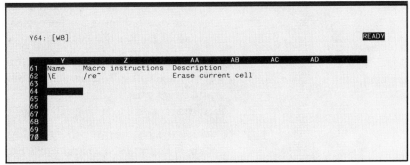

♦ **Figure 15.4:** *Macro library worksheet with the* \E *(Alt-E) macro*

worksheet (second only to the /Range Format command). You will name this macro \W, and it will type the keystrokes /WCS for you. If you are using Release 2.2, try creating this macro with the learn feature.

1. **With the pointer in cell Y64, type '\W and press the → key.**
   Note that you must place your second macro in row 64 to maintain at least one blank cell (Z63) between the macro instructions in cell Z62 and the ones you will enter in Z64. Without this blank cell, 1-2-3 would execute the keystrokes for the \E and \W macros whenever you pressed Alt-E. If you are using Release 2.01, you will now enter the keystrokes /WCS in cell Z64 in step 2, then complete steps 5–8. If you are using Release 2.2, go to step 3.

2. **With the pointer in Z64, type '/WCS and press the → key.**
   If you are using Release 2.2, you need to redefine the learn range before you turn on LEARN mode and have 1-2-3 record your keystrokes to widen a column.

3. **Select the /Worksheet Learn Cancel command (/WLC) to clear the current learn range; then select /Worksheet Learn Range (/WLR), move the pointer to cell Z64, type a period, move the pointer down to Z68, and press Enter.**
   Now all you have to do is turn on LEARN mode and go through the keystrokes to widen a single column.

4. **Press the Learn key (Alt-F5) to turn on LEARN mode, then select /Worksheet Column Set-Width (/WCS), press the Learn key a second time to turn off LEARN mode, and press Enter to set the column width (without changing it).**
   Notice that pressing Enter to set the column width also causes the worksheet to be recalculated so that the CALC indicator disappears and the recorded keystrokes are copied into Z64. Next, you need to document the function of this macro.

5. **Move the pointer to cell AA64 (it will already be in this cell, if you are using Release 2.01); then type *Widen current cell*, and press Enter.**
   All that remains is to assign the range name to this macro.

6. **Move the pointer to cell Y64, then select /Range Name Labels Right (/RNLR) and press Enter.**
   Before you test this macro, don't forget to save the worksheet.

7. **Save the worksheet under the same name.**
   To test the macro, use it to narrow column Y slightly.

8. **Press Alt-W, then press the ← key once to narrow the column width to 7, and press Enter to set it.**

Editing a Macro

If, after testing your macro, you find that you need to make some changes to it, you can do so. To see how this is done, you will now modify the functioning of the \W (Alt-W) macro slightly. Instead of having the macro terminate after selecting the /Worksheet Column Set-Width command as it does now, you will add a macro pause with {?}. During the time the macro is paused, you can change the width either by pressing the → or ← key or by typing in the number of characters. After the pause {?}, you will enter a tilde (˜) so that when you press the Enter key to resume the macro, the macro will enter a carriage return to set the new column width.

The only reason for making this revision to the macro is that adding a pause will cause 1-2-3 to display the CMD indicator. This indicator will help remind you to press the Enter key to resume the macro execution, thus setting the new column width (often, it is easy to forget to press the Enter key to set a new column width, especially when you use the → or ← key to change it).

1. **Move the pointer to cell Z64, then press the Edit key (F2).**
   Now you will type the transcription for pausing the macro, and pressing the Enter key.

2. **Type {?} ˜ at the end of the macro instructions '/WCS (be sure that you don't add a space between the pause {?} and the first part of the macro), and then press Enter.**
   Your macro should resemble the one shown in Figure 15.5. Before you test the working of this revised macro, you need to save the worksheet again.

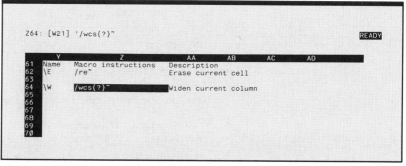

♦ **Figure 15.5:** *Macro library worksheet after revising the instructions for the \W (Alt-W) macro*

3. **Save the worksheet under the same name.**
   Now you are ready to test this revised macro. Note that it isn't necessary to redefine the range name when all you've done is revise the
   macro instructions.

4. **With the pointer in column Z, press Alt-W.**
   Notice that this time, the CMD status indicator is displayed on the
   status line, letting you know that the macro is paused, awaiting your
   input.

5. **Press the → key once to increase the width of column Z to
   22 characters, and then press Enter.**
   As soon as you press Enter to resume the macro, the CMD status
   indicator disappears, and the macro executes the tilde (˜) and presses
   the Enter key to set the new column width.

Creating Macros to Save Worksheets

The next two macros will save the worksheets that you create: the first one will
be used to save new worksheets that haven't yet been named, and the second
one will be used to save updates to a worksheet under the same file name. You
will most likely find that the second save macro actually persuades you to save
changes made to your worksheet more often, as it reduces the five-keystroke
command sequence of /FS←R to the simple two-keystroke sequence *Alt-R*.

The first save macro will be called \S. It will enter the save command keystrokes /FS. In addition, it will clear the DOS search pattern from the file name
prompt, leaving only the path name, by pressing the Esc key.

1. **Move the pointer to cell Y66, type '\S, then press the → key.**
   After entering the /FS keystrokes, you need to enter the keystroke
   instruction for pressing the Esc key—that is, {ESC}. To ensure that
   this key instruction is read properly when the macro is executed, you
   need to separate the save keystrokes and this keystroke instruction
   with a space.

2. **With the pointer in cell Z66, type '/FS   {ESC} and press the
   → key.**
   Next, document the function of this macro.

3. **With the pointer in cell AA66, enter *Save worksheet the
   first time*.**
   Before you assign a range name and test this macro, go on and create
   the second save macro. This save macro will enter the keystrokes

/FS ˜ R to save the worksheet using the Replace option. This macro can be used only with worksheets that have already been saved and named.

4. **Move the pointer to cell Y68, type '\R, and press the → key.**
   Enter the macro instructions in Z68.

5. **With the pointer in cell Z68, type '/FS ˜ R and press the → key.**
   Document the function of this macro in AA68.

6. **With the pointer in cell AA68, type** *Save worksheet under same name,* **and press Enter.**
   Because you have entered the macro range names for these two save macros, you can assign them to the macros in one operation using the /Range Name Labels Right command.

7. **Move the pointer to Y66, then select /Range Name Labels Right (/RNLR), then press the ↓ key until the pointer is in cell Y68 (the label range will be Y66..Y68), and press Enter.**
   Before you test these macros, you need to save the worksheet. Because the second save macro automates the save keystrokes you would now otherwise perform manually, you can use your \R (Alt-R) macro to do this. Do, however, check the macro instructions for this macro against those in Figure 15.6 before proceeding with the next step.

8. **Press Alt-R to save the changes to your worksheet under the same name.**

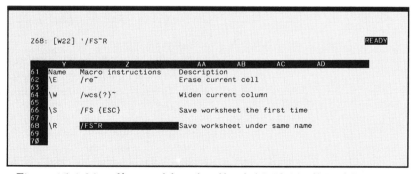

♦ **Figure 15.6:** *Macro library worksheet after adding the \S (Alt-S) and \R (Alt-R) macros*

Executing a Macro in STEP Mode

If you are using an 80286 or 80386 computer with a hard disk, you probably couldn't tell if the macro worked as planned because the WAIT mode indicator and disk light went on and off so quickly. If you are using a more vintage machine (especially with two disk drives), you most likely did witness these signs of the file being read to disk. In either case, to be sure that everything is as planned, you will now execute this save macro a second time in STEP mode.

1. **Press the Step key (Alt-F2).**
   You should see the STEP status indicator at the bottom of the screen.

2. **Press Alt-R to execute the macro in STEP mode.**
   If you are using Release 2.01, you will now see the 1-2-3 main menu at the top of the screen and the SST status indicator flashing at the bottom of the screen. If you are using Release 2.2, the 1-2-3 main menu will not yet be visible but you will see Z68: /FS ˜ R at the bottom of the screen, and you will also notice that the / (slash) is highlighted, indicating that this is the next keystroke to be played back.

3. **If you are using Release 2.2, press the spacebar once.**
   Now you can see the 1-2-3 main menu, with the F in /FS ˜ R highlighted at the bottom of the screen.

4. **Press the spacebar (both versions).**
   The /File menu now appears. If you are using Release 2.2, notice that the highlight is now on the S in /FS ˜ R.

5. **Press the spacebar again.**
   Now you see the file save prompt with the current file name, *MACROLIB.WK1*, displayed. If you are using Release 2.2, notice that the tilde (˜) in /FS ˜ R is highlighted.

6. **Press the spacebar again.**
   The tilde in the macro sends a carriage return (◄┘) so that the Cancel and Replace (and Backup, in Release 2.2) options are now displayed. If you are using Release 2.2, notice that the R in /FS ˜ R is highlighted.

7. **Press the spacebar one last time.**
   This time, 1-2-3 saves the file again and the macro terminates. If you are using Release 2.2, notice that the macro location and instructions have been replaced by the UNDO and STEP status indicators.

8. **Press the Step key (Alt-F2) to turn off STEP mode.**

Now test your \S (Alt-S) macro. It should start the /File Save procedure and then clear the file name *MACROLIB.WK1* before it terminates (when saving a new worksheet that hasn't yet been named, this
part of the macro will clear the **.wk1* search pattern, leaving you
room to enter a file name instead).

9. **Press Alt-S.**

You should see only the prompt *Enter name of file to save:* with the cursor
located after the colon. If you use this macro to save a new worksheet, it
will clear only the search pattern, not the entire path name.

Creating Date Macros

Entering dates in a 1-2-3 worksheet always seems like more work than it is
worth, what with having to use the @DATE function to enter the date numbers
and then use the /Range Format command to modify their display. To make
this job a lot easier, you will create two date macros: one that enters the current
date with the @NOW function, and another that allows you to enter the date
with the @DATE function.

You will split up macro instructions for the current date macro into several
cells. The first cell will contain the @NOW function, the second will contain
the instructions to use the Lotus standard short form date format, and the third
will contain the instructions to freeze the date (remember that the date number returned by the @NOW function is normally recalculated so that it will
remain current).

1. **Move the pointer to cell Y70, then type '\T and press the
→ key.**

Enter the instructions to enter the @NOW function.

2. **With the pointer in cell Z70, type '@NOW ˜ and press the
↓ key.**

Next, in the cell below, you will enter the instructions to format the
cell with the Lotus standard short form (D2).

3. **With the pointer in cell Z71, type '/RFD2 ˜ and press the
↓ key.**

To prevent this date from being recalculated each time you open the
worksheet, you will now enter the instructions to convert the serial
date returned by the @NOW function to its calculated value.

4. **With the pointer in cell Z72, type {EDIT}{CALC} ˜ and press Enter.**
    Now you need to document each step in this macro.

5. **Move the pointer to cell AA70, type *Enter today's serial date*, and press the ↓ key; then enter *Format date with Lotus standard short form* in cell AA71, press the ↓ key, enter *Freeze date* in cell AA72, and press Enter.**
    Next, you need to assign the range name \T to this macro.

6. **Move the pointer to cell Y70, then select /Range Name Labels Right (/RNLR) and press Enter.**
    Before you test this macro, you need to save the worksheet. You can use your \R (Alt-R) macro to do this.

7. **Press Alt-R to save the worksheet under the same name.**
    To test this macro, you will need to move to a blank cell.

8. **Move the pointer to cell Y74 and press Alt-T.**
    The day and month of today's date should now be displayed in cell Y74. Notice that the contents of the cell is a serial date number instead of the @NOW function itself. If your macro didn't work as planned, check your macro instructions against those shown in Figure 15.7 (note that your date in Y74 will differ from the one shown in

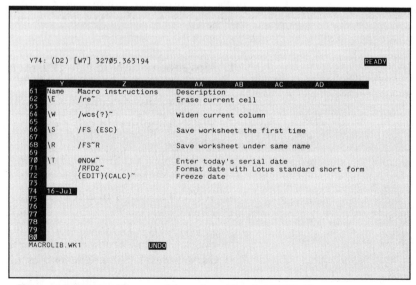

◆ **Figure 15.7:** *Macro library worksheet after adding the \T (Alt-T) macro*

this figure, unless you happen to be doing this exercise on July 16 as well). After you've gotten your macro to work properly, you will use your \E (Alt-E) macro to delete the current date.

9. **Press Alt-E to erase the date in cell Y74.**
   The second date macro that you will now create will use the @DATE function. It will contain three pauses: the first to allow you to enter the year argument, the second pause to enter the month argument, and the third pause to enter the day argument. It will then format the date using the long international format.

10. **Move the pointer to cell Y74, type '\D, and press the → key.**
    Now enter the @DATE function with the three strategic pauses.

11. **In cell Z74, type '@DATE({?},{?},{?})⁻ and then press the ↓ key.**
    Check the macro instruction in Z74 carefully, as it is easy to make a typographical error when having to alternate between so many shifted and unshifted characters. In cell Z75, you will enter the instructions to format the date number.

12. **In cell Z75, type '/RFD4⁻ and press Enter.**
    Document the function of these two macro instructions.

13. **Move the pointer to cell AA74, type *Enter date serial number*, and press the ↓ key; then type *Format date number with Long Intn'l format*, and press Enter.**
    Now assign the range name \D to this macro.

14. **Move the pointer to cell Y74, select /Range Name Labels Right (/RNLR), and press Enter.**
    Save the worksheet before testing this new macro.

15. **Press Alt-R to save the worksheet under the same name.**
    Next, test the macro in cell Y77.

16. **Move the pointer to cell Y77, then press Alt-D.**
    You should see *@DATE(* on the edit line at the top of the screen and the CMD status indicator at the bottom.

17. **Type 90, then press Enter.**
    When you press Enter to resume the macro, the macro types a comma before encountering the second pause.

18. **Type 2, then press Enter.**
    When you press Enter this time to resume the macro, the macro types a second comma before encountering the last pause.

19. **Type 19, then press Enter.**

    When you press Enter the third time, the macro inputs the @DATE function in cell Y77. Unfortunately, you can't see the result of the formatting because column Y is too narrow to display it. Use your \W (Alt-W) macro to widen it temporarily.

20. **Press Alt-W, then press the → key twice so that you can see the formatted date in Y77.**

    Your screen should now match the one shown in Figure 15.8.

21. **Press the ← key twice so that column Y is once again 7 characters wide; then press Enter to set the column width, and press Alt-E to delete the date in cell Z77.**

Creating Print Macros

For most users, print macros are as important as save macros. This is because 1-2-3 requires so many keystrokes just to obtain a second copy of the same report. You will create two variations of a basic print macro, analogous to the two versions of your save macro. The first print macro will print a copy of a report after pausing to enable you to define the print range. The second print macro will print another copy of the report using whatever print range has been previously defined.

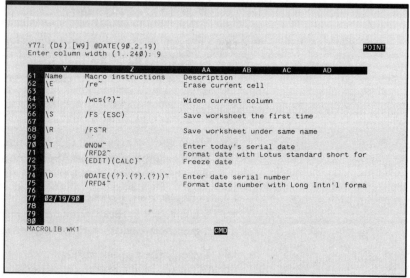

◆ **Figure 15.8:** *Macro library worksheet while testing the \D (Alt-D) macro*

1. **With the pointer still in cell Y77, type '\P, then press the → key.**
   This macro will select /Print Printer, then clear the previously defined range by selecting the Clear Range options. Then it will select the Range option and pause to allow you to define the print range. After you press Enter to resume the macro, it will select the Align Go Page and Quit options.

2. **With the pointer in cell Z77, type '/PPCRR{?}˜AGPQ, then press the → key.**
   Document this macro in cell AA77.

3. **With the pointer in cell AA77, type *Pause for print range, then print report* and press Enter.**
   Assign the range name \P to this macro.

4. **Move the pointer to cell Y77, then select /Range Name Labels Right (/RNLR), and press Enter.**
   Save this worksheet before testing it.

5. **Press Alt-R to save the worksheet under the same name.**
   Before you can test this macro, you must turn on your printer.

6. **Press Alt-P; when you are prompted to enter the print range, move the pointer to cell Y61, type a period to anchor, then move the pointer to cell AE77, and press Enter.**
   After you pressed Enter, the macro should have printed the print range (albeit on two pages, because you didn't change the left- and right-margin settings). If something went awry, check your macro instructions against those shown in Figure 15.9. Be sure that your macro has a tilde after the pause, as in {?} ˜ . Your second print macro is similar, except that it doesn't pause for you to define the print range.

7. **Move the pointer to cell Y79, type '\O (O as in *Otto*, not zero), then press the → key.**
   Enter the macro instructions in cell Z79.

8. **In cell Z79, enter '/PPAGPQ and press the → key.**
   Document the macro in cell AA79.

9. **In cell AA79, enter *Print report using same range and settings* and press Enter.**
   Now assign the range name \O to this macro.

10. **Move the pointer to cell Y79, then select /Range Name Labels Right (/RNLR), and press Enter.**
    Save the worksheet before testing this macro.

11. **Press Alt-R to save the worksheet under the same name.**
    Before you print the report with this macro, manually change the
    column widths and expand the print range to include the new print
    macro.

12. **Use your \W macro to narrow column Y to 5 characters
    and column Z to 20 characters; then select /Print Printer
    Range (/PPR), press the ↓ key to include row 79 in the print
    range, and press Enter.**
    Now test the macro by printing this report.

13. **Press Alt-O to print the report.**
    If all went as planned, you have a printout of all the macros you have
    created (all on one page). If you experienced any problem, check your
    \O macro against the one shown in Figure 15.10.

Using Your Macro Library Worksheet

By now, you have created quite a few useful macros that you will want to have
access to whenever you start a new worksheet. In the next two exercises, you
will practice methods for using the macros saved in your library when you build
a new worksheet or edit an existing one. If you are using Release 2.2, you will
want to perform these as well as the next two exercises, which give you practice in using a Hyperspace macro library created from these macros.

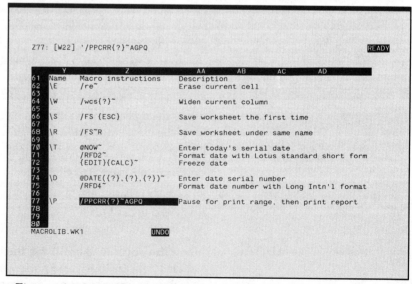

♦ **Figure 15.9:** *Macro library worksheet after adding the \P (Alt-P) macro*

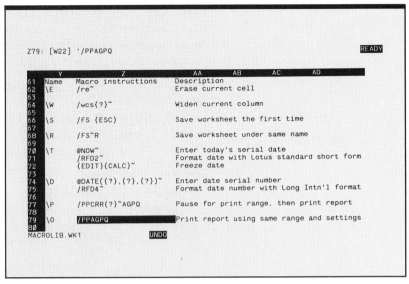

♦ **Figure 15.10:** *Macro library worksheet after adding the \O (Alt-O) macro*

Using Utility Macros in a New Worksheet

First, you will create a new worksheet using the *MACROLIB.WK1* file as its basis. When you do this, all your utility macros are immediately at your disposal; you need only be concerned about remembering to save your worksheet under a new name so that you don't save your data as part of the macro library worksheet.

Start this exercise by assigning a range name to all the macros in the library worksheet.

1. **Move the pointer to cell Y61, then select /Range Name Create (/RNC), type the range name MACROS, press Enter, move the pointer to cell AA79 (the range will be Y61..AA79), and press Enter.**

   Next, you need to save this worksheet under the same name.

2. **Press the Home key to move the pointer to A1, and then press Alt-R to save the newly defined range name as part of the worksheet.**

   Now assume that you have just started 1-2-3 and retrieved your *MACROLIB.WK1* file to start a new worksheet. Your new worksheet will be a sales database. Before you enter any data, you must save the file under a new name.

3. **Press Alt-S, type** *SALESDB* **for the file name, and press Enter.**
   By naming the worksheet right away, you avoid any possibility of saving data in your macro library worksheet (always make sure that you have a backup of this file on a different disk).

4. **Using Figure 15.11 as a guide, input the title** *SALES DATA-BASE 1990* **in cell A1, and then enter the field name** *FIRST.NAME* **in cell A3,** *LAST.NAME* **in cell B3,** *DATE.OF.SALE* **in cell C3, and** *"AMOUNT* **in cell D3.**
   Now you will use your \W macro to widen the columns of the database.

5. **Use your \W macro to widen column A to 12, column B to 17, and columns C and D to 13.**
   Notice from Figure 15.11 that all the dates in the DATE.OF.SALE field in column C are in the year 1990. Before you start entering these dates with the \D (Alt-D) macro, you should edit it so that the macro enters 90 for the first @DATE argument instead of a pause.

6. **Press the Goto key (F5), then the Name key (F3), and press Enter (the range name** *MACROS* **should be highlighted); move the pointer to cell Z73, press the Edit key (F2), press the ← key until the cursor is under the open brace { in the first pause {?}, then press Del three times, type 90, and press Enter.**
   Now you are ready to enter the few records shown in Figure 15.11. Begin with the one for John Thompson in row 4.

7. **Press the Home key to move the pointer to cell A1; move the pointer to cell A4 and enter** *John* **in this cell and** *Thompson* **in cell B4; then move the pointer to cell C4.**
   Use your \D (Alt-D) macro to enter the date of sale.

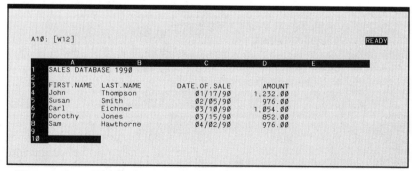

♦ **Figure 15.11:** *Sales database created from macro library worksheet file*

8. **With the pointer in cell C4, press Alt-D, type *1*, press Enter, type *17*, and press Enter; then move the pointer to cell D4 and enter *1232* in this cell.**
   Next, you need to finish entering the records for this database.

9. **Enter the four remaining records as they are shown in Figure 15.11. Remember to use your \D (Alt-D) macro to enter the date that each sale was made.**
   Now you are ready to save your work.

10. **Press Alt-R to save your updates to the database worksheet under the same file name, *SALESDB.WK1*.**

Copying Utility Macros into an Existing Worksheet

The second method for using a macro library worksheet is to bring it into the worksheet you are working on with the /File Combine Copy command. The major drawback to this method is that the /File Combine Copy command doesn't copy range names along with the data, and these macros won't function without range names. Therefore, this method requires two steps: first, copy the macros from the library worksheet into the current worksheet; second, assign range names to all of the macros.

To practice this method, you will use your new sales database. However, the first step you need to take is to delete the macros and their range names from this worksheet.

1. **Press the Goto key (F5), then the Name key (F3), and press Enter to move the pointer to the macros in your sales database worksheet.**
   Next, you will erase all the macros from the worksheet.

2. **Select /Range Erase (/RE), move the pointer to AA79, and press Enter.**
   Next, erase all the macro range names.

3. **Select /Range Name Reset (/RNR).**
   Now your sales database worksheet contains none of macros from your macro library worksheet. To have access to these macros as you continue building the database, you need to copy them from the *MACROLIB.WK1* file.

4. **With the pointer in cell Y61, select /File Combine Copy Named/Specified-Range (/FCCN), then type *macros*, press**

Enter, press the Name key (F3), move the pointer to the file name *MACROLIB.WK1*, and press Enter.

You should now see all of your macros copied from the macro library worksheet.

5. **Press Alt-W to widen column Y with the \W macro.**

The program beeps at you because the range names assigned to the macros in the *MACROLIB.WK1* file were not transferred to the current worksheet when you performed the /File Combine Copy operation.

6. **Select /Range Name Create (/RNC), type *macros*, press Enter, then move the pointer to cell AA79, and press Enter.**

Use the /Range Names Label command to assign the macro names in column Y to the appropriate macro instructions in column Z.

7. **Move the pointer to cell Y62, select /Range Name Labels Right (/RNLR), press the ↓ key until the pointer is on cell Y79, then press Enter.**

Save the worksheet now with the \R (Alt-R) macro.

8. **Press Alt-R to save the worksheet under the same name.**

Test out your \W (Alt-W) macro on the LAST.NAME field of your database.

9. **Press the Home key to move the pointer to cell A1, then move the pointer to B1, press Alt-W, press the ← key until the column is 13 characters wide, and press Enter.**

Save your changes to the database with your \R (Alt-R) macro.

10. **Press Alt-R to save the worksheet under the same name.**

Saving Your Macros in a Hyperspace Macro Library

✳ *New in 2.2*

If you are using Release 2.2, you will want to place your utility macros in a Hyperspace macro library so that they are available at any time during a work session independent of the worksheet you are building. To do this, you must first attach the Macro Library Manager add-in program. Then, you will use this program to copy your utility macros into a Hyperspace macro library file (with the extension .MLB). This library file will then remain in RAM until you either remove it with the Remove option on the Macro Library Manager menu or exit from 1-2-3.

If you are using Release 2.2 on a two-disk-drive system, you need to locate the Install disk that contains a copy of the *MACROMGR.ADN* file needed to attach the Macro Library Manager and replace the 1-2-3 System disk in drive A with the Install disk before you begin this exercise.

1. **Select /Add-In Attach (/AA), move the pointer to the file name *MACROMGR.ADN*, press Enter, then type 8, and select the Quit option (Q).**
   Now you will copy your utility macros in the sales database worksheet into a special library (MLB) file. Before you begin this operation, move the pointer to your macros.

2. **Press the Goto key (F5), then the Name key (F3), and press Enter to move the pointer to the first cell in the *MACROS* range.**
   Next, you will invoke the Macro Library Manager add-in program.

3. **Press Shift-F8 (or Alt-F8), select the Save option (S), type *utility* as the macro library file name, and press Enter; then move the pointer to cell AA79, press Enter again, and select the No option (N) when asked to use a password.**
   The macros in the range Y61..AA79 disappear from your screen. They are now saved in the file called *UTILITY.MLB*, which is not only saved on disk but also loaded into memory, meaning that you can use any of its macros.

4. **Press the Home key to move the pointer to cell A1, then press Alt-R to save the sales database worksheet under the same name.**
   Although the macros are no longer part of this worksheet, they are still available for use because they are now in RAM. The real advantage of Hyperspace macros, however, is that you can use them with any worksheet you retrieve or begin without having to use /File Combine Copy and the /Range Name commands.

5. **Retrieve your personnel database, *PERSNLDB.WK1*.**
   Use your \W (Alt-W) macro to narrow the supervisor field.

6. **Move the pointer to column G, press Alt-W, then press the ← key once to make the column 7 characters wide, and press Enter to set it.**

✳ *New in 2.2*   ## Editing Your Hyperspace Macro Library File

Now you will add your own record to the personnel database. When you do, you will input your start date with today's date using your \T (Alt-T) macro.

Notice, however, that the START.DATE field in the database uses the Lotus standard long form, whereas your \T macro formats the current date with the Lotus standard short form. Therefore, before you use this macro in entering your record, you will revise its contents slightly.

To edit a Hyperspace macro library file in memory (it must be in RAM before you can edit it), you need to copy it into a worksheet and then resave it.

1. **With the pointer in cell A1, press the Tab key three times to move the pointer to cell W1.**
   You need to be sure that the macros won't overwrite existing data.

2. **Press Shift-F8 (or Alt-F8), select the Edit option (E), press Enter to select *UTILITY.MLB* (which is highlighted), press Enter to select the Ignore option (there are no conflicting range names), and press Enter to indicate cell W1 as the first cell of the range for the macro library.**
   The contents of your utility macro library are now copied into columns W, X, and Y. Notice that you need to widen column X to see all the macro instructions.

3. **Move the pointer to column X, press Alt-W, then press the → key until you have widened the column to 20 characters.**
   Now you are ready to edit the formatting in your \T macro.

4. **Move the pointer to cell X11, press the Edit key (F2), press the ← key twice to move the cursor under the *2* in *'/RFD2 ˜*, then press the Del key, type *1*, and press Enter.**
   This is the only change that you need to make to the macros, so you are ready to save these macros under the same library file name.

5. **Move the pointer to cell W1, press Shift-F8 (or Alt-F8), select the Save option (S), press Enter to select *UTILITY.MLB* (which is highlighted), then select the Yes option (Y) to overwrite it, move the pointer to cell Y19, and press Enter; select the No option (N) when the program asks if you want to use a password to lock the library.**
   Before you add your record to the database, reset the width for column X.

6. **Move the pointer to column X and select /Worksheet Column Reset-Width (/WCR).**
   Position the pointer at the bottom of the database.

7. **Press the Home key to move the pointer to cell A1, press End ↓ to move to the last record in the database, and then press the ↓ key again to move it to the first blank row.**
Now add your record to the database.

8. **Enter 19 in the REC# field; enter '780–21–3456 in the SSN field; enter your first name in the FIRST.NAME field; enter your last name in the LAST.NAME field; enter ADMN in the DEPT field; enter President in the POSITION field; leave the SUPRVSR field blank; enter 225000 in the SALARY field and format it with the Comma (,) format with 0 decimal places; and then enter today's date in the START.DATE field by pressing Alt-T.**
Save the updated database worksheet.

9. **Press Home to move the pointer to cell A1, then press Alt-R to save the worksheet under the same name.**

Summary ◆

Troubleshooting

Question: I created a macro in my worksheet by placing \F in cell K44 and entering the macro instructions in cell L44. However, when I pressed Alt-F after saving the worksheet, nothing happened. What did I do wrong?

Answer: You forgot to assign the range name \F to the macro. You can do this either by placing the pointer in cell K44, typing /RNLR, and pressing Enter; or by placing the pointer in cell L44, typing /RNC, then typing \F, and pressing Enter twice.

Question: I created a macro and it was working properly. Then, after moving some of the data in the worksheet, I tried my macro and it no longer worked as planned. I checked the macro and verified that none of its instructions had been modified in any way. What could the problem be?

Answer: Most likely, the data you moved is referenced in your macro's instructions and, after moving this data to new cells in the worksheet, you didn't update the cell addresses in your macro. This is a common problem in macros that you can avoid by assigning a range name to all cells referenced in macros. That way, when you move data, the range names are updated and the macros remain current without requiring any editing.

Essential Techniques

To Create a Macro

1. Plan what keystrokes and commands the macro is to contain. Execute these keystrokes and commands manually, writing down the keystroke instruction for each key used.

2. Enter these keystrokes as labels in a single column of the worksheet, in an area where they can't be harmed by editing changes made to the worksheet. Enter discrete groups of macro instructions in separate cells in the column, making sure that you don't place any blank cells between them.

3. Assign a range name to the first cell of the macro. It must consist of a backslash (\) and a single letter between A and Z if you are using Release 2.01 or if you want to execute the macro by pressing Alt plus the letter key in Release 2.2.

4. Save your worksheet, then test your macro by executing it in a part of the worksheet where it can't damage your macro instructions.

To Debug a Macro in STEP Mode

1. Press the Step key (Alt-F2) to turn on STEP mode. The STEP indicator appears on the status line.

2. Execute your macro as you normally would.

3. Press the spacebar to step through each macro instruction, one at a time. When you locate an error you need to fix, press Ctrl-Break to abort the execution of the macro.

4. Press the Step key (Alt-F2) a second time to turn off STEP mode. The STEP indicator disappears from the status line.

Review

Important Terms You Should Know

Alt-key macro	learn range
debug	macro
Hyperspace	Run key (Alt-F3—Release 2.2)
keystroke instruction	Step key (Alt-F2—Release 2.2)
Learn key (Alt-F5—Release 2.2)	

Test Your Knowledge

1. When you want to indicate in a macro that 1-2-3 is to enter a carriage return, you enter a _____. When you want to indicate that 1-2-3 is to move the pointer directly to cell A1, you enter _____ in the macro.

2. If you want to have 1-2-3 move the pointer three cells to the right in a macro and you don't want to enter the keystroke instruction three times, you can enter _____ in the macro instead.

3. If you give the range \B to a macro, you execute it by pressing _____. If you give the range \BAK, you execute it by pressing _____ and then selecting \BAK from the line listing (Release 2.2 only).

4. To abort the execution of your macro prematurely, you press _____. Sometimes, you must also press _____ or _____ to return to READY mode.

5. To have a macro automatically executed as soon as you retrieve a worksheet, you must give it the range name _____.

6. To pause a macro for user input, you must enter _____ in the macro. To resume a macro's execution after pausing, you must press the _____ key.

7. To debug your macro in STEP mode, you press the _____ key before you execute the macro. To execute each new step, you press the _____.

8. To create a macro with the learn feature, you must first define a learn range with the _____ command. Then, you need to turn on LEARN mode by pressing _____ , enter your keystrokes and commands, and turn off LEARN mode by pressing _____.

9. To create a Hyperspace macro library in Release 2.2, you first need to create your macros in a worksheet, then attach the _____ add-in program, select its _____ option, and indicate the macro library name and the range that contains your macros.

Further Exercises

1. Retrieve your *MACROLIB.WK1* file and add the following macros:

   ♦ \U, a macro that enters repreating underscores (\–) in the current cell, then starts the /Copy command, selects the current cell as the FROM range, pauses the macro to allow you to indicate the TO range, and enters a carriage return when you press Enter to resume the macro's execution.

   ♦ \V, a macro that enters a centered vertical bar (|) in the current cell, then starts the /Copy command, selects the current cell as the FROM range, pauses the macro to allow you to indicate the TO range, and enters a carriage return when you press Enter to resume the macro's execution.

   ♦ \X, a macro that enters the abbreviated names of all 12 months (Jan, Feb, Mar, and so on) in the same row, starting with the current cell, and then centers them in their cells.

2. After you have created these macros, assigned their respective macro range names to them, and saved and tested each of them, enlarge the named range MACROS so that it includes your new macros before you save the *MACROLIB.WK1* file one last time.

16

Introduction to the Lotus Command Language

In This Chapter...

Command Language Basics

In Chapter 15, you learned how to create simple macros that automate procedures consisting solely of a series of keystrokes. In this chapter, you will be introduced to the Lotus Command Language, a language that enables you to create sophisticated macros that do a lot more than simply replay an unvarying series of keystrokes. For example, you can use this language to build an interactive macro that prompts the user for various inputs and then performs different procedures based on the user's response. You can also use this language to build menu macros that display your own custom menus (which look and work like standard 1-2-3 command menus). Such menu macros provide a familiar interface to users, with which they can comfortably select the procedures that they want the macro to perform.

The Lotus Command Language consists of 50 *advanced macro commands*, each of which initiates a specialized built-in command function. These advanced macro commands are divided into five groups: data manipulation, flow-of-control, screen control, interactive, and file manipulation. Each group of advanced macro commands performs different tasks:

- Data manipulation commands enable you to enter and erase data, change the contents of cells, or recalculate parts of a worksheet.

- Flow-of-control commands control the order in which macro instructions are executed; they allow your macros to incorporate conditional processing, branching, subroutine calls, and loops.

- Screen control commands enable you to control the appearance of the worksheet display and control panel, change the mode indicator, or sound the computer's bell.

- Interactive commands enable you to pause macros, obtain user input, determine the type of data that will be accepted, or display custom menus.

- File manipulation commands enable you to transfer data between a text file (that is, one saved in ASCII format) and a 1-2-3 worksheet.

Syntax of Advanced Macro Commands

Like 1-2-3 @functions, each advanced macro command has a specific structure or *syntax* that must be followed exactly. The first word in each advanced macro command is the *keyword*. Just as with the majority of @functions, most advanced macro commands also require one or more *arguments* that indicate what information the command is to process. The arguments required by the advanced macro command always follow the keyword. For example, in

{BEEP 3}

BEEP is the keyword and 3 is the argument that supplies the number of the tone that is to be sounded.

If the advanced macro command requires multiple arguments, you must separate each one with the global default argument separator in effect (initially, either the comma or semicolon will be accepted), as in

{LET Price,Cost∗1.5}

where *Price*, the first argument of the {LET} command, indicates the name of the range that is to receive the value calculated by the second argument, *Cost∗1.5*; and *Cost* is the range name of the cell that contains the cost of the item.

When you enter the keyword of an advanced macro command, it does not matter whether you use lowercase, uppercase, or mixed case. When you enter a range name as an advanced macro command argument, it also doesn't matter what case you use. Just be sure in both cases that you spell the keyword and range names correctly when inputting the advanced macro command. In this book, however, you will see the keywords for advanced macro commands entered in all uppercase letters.

Each advanced macro command, whether it consists of a single keyword, a keyword and a single argument, or a keyword and multiple arguments, must be enclosed in a pair of braces, just as you do when entering keystroke instructions. Furthermore, the entire advanced macro command, including its arguments and close brace, must be entered in a single cell. You cannot split an advanced macro command into different cells, as you can when entering 1-2-3 menu command keystrokes.

You must also use spaces correctly. Always enter a space between the keyword and the first argument of the advanced command, but do not include spaces between arguments after entering the argument separator. (You can enter spaces if they are part of the argument; enclose these arguments in quotation marks.) If the command keyword does not take any arguments, do not enter any spaces between the open brace, keyword, and close brace.

Types of Arguments

The advanced macro commands use various types of information as their arguments: numbers, strings (that is, labels), locations (cells or ranges), and conditions (logical formulas).

For *number* arguments, you can enter numbers, a numeric formula, or a range name or cell address that contains a number or numeric formula. For *string* arguments, you can enter a literal string (any sequence of characters enclosed in quotation marks), a string formula, or a range name or cell address that contains a string formula or a literal string. For *location* arguments, you can enter range names, cell addresses, or formulas that return a range name or cell address. For *condition* arguments, you usually enter logical formulas (which return logical 0 or 1). You can, however, use any other type of argument as a condition argument (such as a number, string, numeric or string formula, and so on).

✱ *New in 2.2*

Using a Link to Data in Another File as an Advanced Macro Command Argument: If you are using Release 2.2, you can use a formula that links to data in another worksheet file as an advanced macro command argument. When you do this, you enter the standard linking formula, with the appropriate file reference followed by the range name or cell address that contains the data you want used. For example, you could enter

{LET Newtotal, + < <INCSUM.WK1 > >Total}

to have the value that is saved in a cell named *Total*, which is located in your INCSUM worksheet file, stored in a cell named *Newtotal* in the current worksheet. For more information about linking formulas, see Chapter 7.

Using Range Names in Arguments   It is *always* preferable to use range names instead of cell addresses in the arguments of advanced macro commands. That way, if you have to move the data used in the argument to a new address in the worksheet, the range name will still refer to the appropriate data. This convention minimizes the possibility of introducing errors into your macros after you make layout changes to the data in the worksheet. When you assign range names to cells and cell ranges that are used as arguments in advanced macro commands, you use the same 1-2-3 commands (/Range Name Create or /Range Name Labels if you have entered the range name in a strategic position in the worksheet) and obey the same range naming conventions that you do when naming any range in 1-2-3.

Literal Strings within Arguments   Always enclose any literal string used as an advanced macro command argument in a pair of quotation marks to remove any ambiguity about its type, thus making it impossible for 1-2-3 to interpret it as anything other than a label (such as a range name, formula, or value of some sort). This is particularly important if you include a character such as a comma or an open or close brace in the argument that could easily be mistaken for part of the command statement.

For example, if you use the {LET} command to input data into a cell named *Total*, as in

> {LET Total,Year-to-Date}

1-2-3 will interpret Year-to-Date as a range name and input whatever value is stored in the cell that has this range name. If, however, you enter the {LET} command as

> {LET Total,"Year-to-Date"}

1-2-3 will enter *Year-to-Date* as a label in the cell named *Total*.

If you revise this {LET} command by using the value 1000, you enter it as

> {LET Total,1000}

and 1-2-3 will enter the value 1000 in the *Total* cell. If, however, you enclose this second argument in quotation marks, as in

> {LET Total,"1000"}

the program will enter 1000 as a left-aligned label (that is, a string) in the cell named *Total*.

Conventions Used to Represent the Syntax of Advanced Macro Commands

This book uses the same conventions in representing the syntax of advanced macro commands as does your 1-2-3 documentation. As you read through the information on specific commands and refer to the tables that describe the function of these commands in this chapter, keep in mind the following points:

- ◆ Advanced macro command keywords are always shown in all uppercase letters, as in {BEEP} or {INDICATE}, even though you can enter them in uppercase or lowercase letters.

- ◆ Advanced macro command arguments in syntax examples are shown in all lowercase letters, as in {LET *location,entry*}, where *location* and *entry* are the two arguments required by this command.

- Optional arguments in syntax examples are enclosed in square brackets [ ], as in {BEEP *[tone-number]*}, where you can add the *[tone-number]* argument to have the bell sound a different tone, but this argument isn't required to execute the command.

- When an argument in the syntax examples is italicized, this means that you must substitute something else for that argument when you use the command. For example, in the advanced macro command {BLANK *location*}, you substitute the actual range name or cell address of the cell you want the macro to erase for *location* when you enter this command in a macro.

- When an argument in the syntax examples is not italicized, this means that you must enter it exactly as it appears. For example, in the new Release 2.2 advanced macro command {GRAPHON *[named-graph]*,[nodisplay]}, if you want to make a new named graph current but you don't want to display it, you enter the nodisplay argument verbatim even though you substitute the actual graph name for the variable *named-graph* argument (it's italicized). For example, you use {GRAPHON COSTBAR,nodisplay} to make a bar graph named COST-BAR the current graph.

- Range names used in the arguments of sample advanced macro commands have the first letter capitalized, even though you can enter these in uppercase or lowercase letters.

- Strings used in the arguments of sample advanced macro commands are enclosed in quotation marks, even if they aren't required to make the macro run properly.

Entering and Manipulating Data in Macros

The first group of advanced macro commands that you are going to examine enables you to enter, edit, and recalculate data in the worksheet. Table 16.1 shows you the syntax for these commands and explains their function.

◆ **Table 16.1:** *Data Manipulation Macro Commands*

Keyword & Arguments	Function
{BLANK *location*}	Erases the cell or range specified by *location*.
{CONTENTS *target-location*, *source-location*, *[width,cell-format]*}	Stores the numeric value in the *target-location* as a label in the *source-location*. If you include an

♦ **Table 16.1:** *Data Manipulation Macro Commands (continued)*

Keyword & Arguments	Function
	optional *width* argument, the macro creates a label of that width. If you include an optional *cell-format* argument, the resulting label uses a value format specified by the argument's code number (see Table 16.2 for a list of codes and corresponding formats).
{LET *location,entry*}	Enters the value or label specified by *entry* into the cell or range specified by *location*. You can add a *:string* (abbreviated *:s*) or a *:value* (abbreviated *:v*) suffix to the entry argument to explicitly declare this argument to be a string or value.
{PUT *location,column-offset, row-offset,entry*}	Enters the value or label specified by *entry* at the *column-offset* and *row-offset* (both counted from 0) of the range specified by the *location* argument.
{RECALC *location, [condition],[iterations]*}	Recalculates the values in the range specified by *location*, starting with the cell in the upper left and proceeding row by row. With the optional *condition* argument, the macro recalculates the range until the condition is true. With the optional *iterations* argument, the macro recalculates the range the number of times specified by this argument.
{RECALCCOL *location, [condition],[iterations]*}	Same as the {RECALC} command, except that this command recalculates the values in the *location* range, starting with the cell in the upper left and proceeding column by column.

Entering Data in Your Macros

You can instruct a macro to input a particular entry into a cell of the worksheet either by having the macro move the pointer to the cell, then type the data, and press Enter, or by using the {LET} or {PUT} advanced macro command.

The major difference between using {LET} or {PUT} to enter data instead of keystroke instructions is that these advanced macro commands don't require moving the pointer to the cell that is to receive the entry. For example, if you want to use keystroke instructions to enter 4500 in a cell named *Expenses* when the pointer is in a cell named *Income*, you need to enter

{GOTO}Expenses ~ 4500 ~

to do it. If you use the {LET} advanced macro command to accomplish the same thing, you can omit the {GOTO} command:

{LET Expenses,4500} ~

In the first example with {GOTO}, the pointer is in the cell named *Expenses* after the command is executed. In the second example with {LET}, the pointer remains in the cell named *Income*.

You use the {LET} command to enter data in a particular cell of the worksheet, whose location is indicated most often by a range name or, on rare occasions, by a cell address. You can use this command to input labels, values, or the string or numeric formulas. Note that in the case of formulas, 1-2-3 enters the calculated result of the formula rather than the formula itself. For example, if the cell named *Income* contains 20,000 and the one named *Expenses* contains 10,000, when 1-2-3 executes the advanced macro command

{LET Profit,Income – Expenses} ~

the cell named *Profit* will contain 10,000.

Notice from Table 16.1 that you can add a :string or :value suffix to indicate the type of data you are inputting with the {LET} command. For instance, you can indicate that 1-2-3 is to enter the label *Income* rather than the value of 20,000 stored in a cell named *Income* as follows:

{LET Revenues,Income:s} ~

Of course, you can also accomplish the same thing by entering

{LET Revenues,"Income"} ~

where the quotation marks indicate that *Income* is to be entered verbatim (that is, as a string).

The {PUT} command differs from {LET} in that it is used to enter data in a particular cell of a data table. Because this command works with a table, it uses column- and row-offset arguments (which both start with 0) to indicate the location that is to get the data entry. In its use of offsets, this advanced macro command resembles the @INDEX function. Of course, its function is just the opposite: instead of returning the value of a cell at a particular column- and row-offset, it inputs a value there. For example, if you have a cell range A1..C3 named *Subtotal* and you want to put the value *1500* in cell B3, you would enter the following {PUT} command:

   {PUT Subtotal,1,2,1500} ˜

Note that the {PUT} command will return the macro error *Invalid offset in PUT* if you specify a column- or row-offset argument that is outside the range of the table as specified by the *location* argument.

Erasing Entries in the Worksheet

You can use the advanced macro command {BLANK} in a macro to erase a particular cell entry. This works the same way as entering the keystroke instructions for the /Range Erase command in a macro. For instance, to erase the entry in a cell named *Subtotal*, you can use {GOTO} with the /Range Erase keystrokes, as in

   {GOTO}Subtotal ˜ /RE ˜

or you can use the {BLANK} command, as in

   {BLANK Subtotal} ˜

Again, the major difference between these two statements is that {GOTO} moves the pointer to the cell called *Subtotal*, whereas the {BLANK} command does not require moving the pointer in order to erase the contents of this cell.

Recalculating the Worksheet

When you make new entries or deletions manually in a worksheet (assuming global recalculation is set to Automatic), 1-2-3 automatically updates the new values and recalculates all dependent formulas. This is not the case when you control input and erase data with advanced macro commands. Even when the worksheet recalculation method is set to Automatic, 1-2-3 doesn't recalculate all data in the worksheet when a macro is being executed.

Automatic recalculation of advanced macro commands occurs when the user presses Enter in response to a pause {?}, or if you have followed a command with a tilde (˜). For example, to have 1-2-3 recalculate the worksheet after using a {LET} command to store a new value in a range, you would terminate it with a tilde, as in

> {LET SalTotal,@SUM(Salaries)} ˜

Because this command statement is terminated with a tilde, 1-2-3 will actually total the numbers in the *Salaries* range and place this sum in the *SalTotal* cell when the macro executes this command.

To have your new values calculated in the worksheet, you can add the {CALC} keystroke instruction (or ˜ if global recalculation is set to Automatic). More effective than this method is the use of the {RECALC} and {RECALC-COL} commands. These advanced macro commands enable you to control the area of the worksheet that is to be recalculated at any given point in the macro's execution, and this significantly reduces the time it takes for the new values to be calculated and the macro execution to resume. The {RECALC} command recalculates the formulas row by row in the range specified as its argument. The {RECALCCOL} command recalculates them column by column within the specified range.

Converting Values to Labels in a Macro

When you need to convert a value to a label in your macro, as is the case when you want to concatenate strings or display messages using a variable, you can use the {CONTENTS} advanced macro command instead of the @STRING function, which performs essentially the same function. The {CONTENTS} command is superior because it gives you more control than @STRING over the display of the resulting label; you can add optional arguments that control the width of the display as well as the display format to be used.

The syntax of the {CONTENTS} command is

> {CONTENTS *target-location,source-location,[width,cell-format]*}

In this command, the *source-location* argument contains the value that you want the macro to convert to a left-aligned label, and the *target-location* argument contains the name or address of the cell where the macro is to enter this label. To specify the width of the converted label in the *target-location*, you add the optional *width* argument, which can be a number, numeric formula, or range name or cell reference that contains such a number or formula. To specify the format of the converted label in the *target-location*, you add the optional *cell-format* argument, which can be a format code number, a formula that returns such a number, or a range name or cell address that contains such a number or formula. Table 16.2 shows you the format code numbers and the corresponding display format that you can use in the *cell-format* argument of the {CONTENTS} command.

♦ **Table 16.2:** *Cell Format Codes for the {CONTENTS} Macro Command*

Code Number	Cell Format
0–15	Fixed, 0 to 15 decimal places
16–32	Scientific, 0 to 15 decimal places
33–47	Currency, 0 to 15 decimal places
48–63	Percent, 0 to 15 decimal places
64–79	Comma, 0 to 15 decimal places
112	+/−
113	General
114	D1 (DD-MMM-YY)
115	D2 (DD-MMM)
116	D3 (MMM-YY)
117	Text
118	Hidden
119	D6 (HH:MM:SS AM/PM)
120	D7 (HH:MM AM/PM)
121	D4 (Long Int'l)
122	D5 (Short Int'l)
123	D8 (Long Int'l)
124	D9 (Short Int'l)
127	Global cell format, as specified by /Worksheet Global Format

You can't specify a *cell-format* argument without using a *width* argument. If you omit the *width* argument, the macro will go into ERROR mode and display the error message

Invalid integer in CONTENTS

If you do not specify a width or display format, the program uses the same width and display format as the value in *source-location*.

To get an idea of how the {CONTENTS} command is used, consider the following example. The value 34566.778 has been entered into the *source-location* cell named *Balance*. The macro is to convert this value to a label formatted with the Currency format with 2 decimal places in a *target-location* cell named *BalString* by executing this statement:

{CONTENTS BalString,Balance,11,34}{CALC}

When the macro executes this command, the left-aligned label entered into BalString would appear as $34,556.78. The format code 34 specifies the use of the Currency format with 2 decimal places. Note that the width value of 11 does not actually change the width of the column that contains BalString to 11 characters (if its width is 9 characters, it will be displayed only if there is no entry in the cell on its right).

Nevertheless, you must specify a width of 11 to avoid a string of asterisks (the overflow indicator) in BalString across the Label cell. You have to use at least 11 for the *width* even though $34,556.78 uses only 10 characters, because you must include the new apostrophe label prefix (') that is added when this value is converted to a label.

Practice Creating Macros That Manipulate Worksheet Data

Now it's time to get some practice in using the advanced macro commands that enter and manipulate data. First, you will create an advanced macro that will look up related data when you enter the part number in a database lookup form. To do this, you will use the @VLOOKUP function as the *entry* argument of a series of {LET} commands. To see how this is done, you start a new worksheet where you will first enter a simple inventory database and lookup form.

1. **Clear the worksheet, then move the pointer to cell G1 and enter the sample inventory database shown in Figure 16.1; enter the part numbers *1000, 1001,* and *1002* in cells G4, G5, and G6 as labels by prefacing them with an apostrophe; when you have finished entering the data, widen column H to 16 and format the range J4..J6 to Comma (,) with 2 decimal places.**
    Now, before you create the lookup form in another part of the worksheet, assign a range name to this database.

2. **Move the pointer to cell G3, then select /Range Name Create (/RNC), type *db*, press Enter, move the pointer to cell J6, and press Enter again.**
    Now you are ready to create the lookup form where the macro will display data from this inventory database.

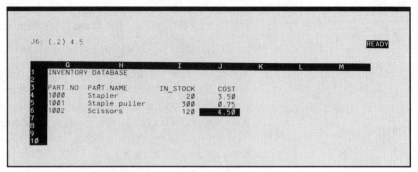

* **Figure 16.1:** *Inventory database to be used in lookup macro*

3. **Move the pointer to cell A1, then enter the lookup table shown in Figure 16.2. After you enter the labels and repeating hyphens, widen column A to 16 and column B to 13 characters.**
   You need to assign range names to the cells that will display information from the different fields of the inventory database.

4. **Assign the range name** PARTNO **to cell B3,** PARTNAME **to cell B5,** INSTOCK **to cell B7, and** COST **to cell B9; then assign the range name** INPUT **to the cell range B5..B9.**
   Before you begin your lookup macro, you should save your worksheet.

5. **Save this worksheet under the name** C16DBMAC.WK1.
   You will name your macro \L, and you will locate it in a new area of the worksheet.

6. **Move the pointer to cell Y61 and type '\L, press Enter, narrow this column to 4, then select the Range Name Labels Right command (/RNLR) and press Enter.**
   The first macro instruction will use the {BLANK} command to erase any entries in the PartNo and Input ranges that might be left from a previous execution of the \L macro.

7. **In cell Z61, type** {BLANK PartNo}{BLANK Input} ˜ **, then press the ↓ key.**
   Notice that you entered a tilde at the end of this statement. This forces the macro to carry out the two {BLANK} commands. The next instruction will move the pointer first to cell A1 and then to the cell named PartNo.

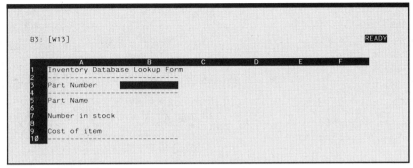

◆ **Figure 16.2:** *Lookup form to display information from the inventory database*

8. **In cell Z62, type {HOME}{GOTO}PartNo ˜ , then press the ↓ key.**

   The next instruction will enter the apostrophe label prefix for the user (all part numbers are entered as labels in the inventory database) and then suspend the macro by entering a pause. Note that to enter an apostrophe in the cell, you must enter two single apostrophes.

9. **In cell Z63, type ' '{?} ˜ , then press the ↓ key.**

   The next three statements in this macro use the {LET} command with an @VLOOKUP function as the *entry* argument and the appropriate range name for the *location* argument. In the @VLOOKUP function, you will use the range name PartNo for the *x* argument, the range name DB for the *table* argument, and the appropriate offset number (1, 2, or 3) for the *column-offset* argument. The first {LET} command will use 1 as the *column-offset* argument of the @VLOOKUP function and PartName as the *location* argument of the {LET} advanced macro command.

10. **In cell Z64, type {LET PartName, @VLOOKUP(PartNo, DB,1)}, then press the ↓ key.**

    The second {LET} command will use 2 as the *column-offset* argument of the @VLOOKUP function and InStock as the *location* argument of the {LET} advanced macro command.

11. **Copy the label in cell Z64 to cell Z65, then edit the label by changing PartName to InStock and 1 to 2.**

    The last {LET} command will use 3 as the *column-offset* argument of the @VLOOKUP function and Cost as the *location* argument of the {LET} advanced macro command.

12. **Copy the label in cell Z65 to cell Z66, then edit the label by changing *InStock* to *Cost* and 2 to 3, then add a tilde (˜) at the end of the {LET} statement right after the close brace }.**
    Now you need to document each step in this macro in column AA.

13. **Widen column Z to 37, then document the working of this macro by entering the descriptions shown in column AA in Figure 16.3. Put each description in its own cell immediately to the right of the macro instructions it describes.**
    Before you test this macro, you need to save the worksheet again.

14. **Save the worksheet under the same name.**
    The position of the pointer is not crucial when testing this macro, so go ahead and give it a try.

15. **Press Alt-L; when the macro pauses with the pointer in cell B3 after typing an apostrophe, you type *1000* and press Enter.**
    The macro should return the same results in the lookup form as shown in Figure 16.4. If you had a problem when you tested your macro, refer to the macro instructions shown in Figure 16.3 and try to find the problem. If you can't find the problem, execute the macro in STEP mode. If the macro works when you enter 1000 as the part number, go ahead and test it with a new part number.

16. **Press Alt-L again; then type *1002* and press Enter.**
    This time, you see *Staple puller* as the part name, with 300 in stock at a cost of 0.75. If you wish, you can test this macro a third time, this time entering *1001* as the part number.

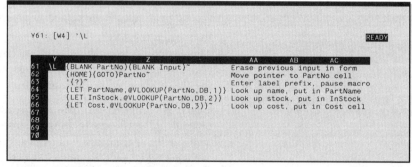

◆ **Figure 16.3:** *Completed lookup macro \L*

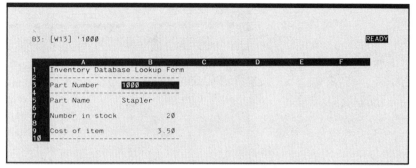

◆ **Figure 16.4:** *Completed input form*

Directing the Flow of Macro Execution

Macro instructions are normally executed in an unvarying order, starting with the first instruction in the macro range name and proceeding down the column until the macro encounters the {QUIT} command or a cell that contains a value or a formula, or is blank. Sometimes, however, you will want to redirect the flow of macro execution to different routines when certain conditions exist either in the macro or in the worksheet itself (a *routine* is simply a collection of macro instructions that performs a distinct procedure).

The Lotus Command Language contains two methods for redirecting the flow of a macro: with branches or with subroutine calls. When a macro *branches*, control goes to a new location in the macro instructions and execution continues from there. When the macro instructions at the new location are all executed, control of the macro does *not* automatically return to the original location.

A *subroutine call* also transfers control to a new location in the macro instructions. Unlike branching, however, a subroutine call *does* return control of the macro to the original location, and execution continues from there, once the macro instructions at the new location are all executed.

The advanced macro commands used to control the flow of macro execution are known as the *flow-of-control* macro commands. These commands are shown in Table 16.3. Notice that some commands in this table have alternate forms that begin with /X; for example, /XQ⁻ as an alternative for the {QUIT} advanced macro command, or /XR for {RETURN}. These /X (pronounced *slash X*) commands were first introduced in Release 1A of 1-2-3. Release 2.0 introduced the equivalent advanced macro commands that precede the /X (Lotus had originally developed these advanced macro commands for Symphony, its integrated software package). To assure full compatibility with macros created in Release 1A as users upgraded to new releases of 1-2-3, Releases 2.01, 2.2, and 3.0 all accept any of the /X commands.

◆ **Table 16.3:** *Flow-of-Control Macro Commands*

Keyword & Arguments	Function
{*subroutine* [*arg1*], [*arg2*],…,[*argn*]} *or* /XC*location* ~	Calls the subroutine that starts in the first cell of *subroutine* (or *location*, if using the /XC command). With the {*subroutine*} command, you can specify up to 31 optional arguments (*arg1*,*arg2*,…,*argn*) as long as you begin the subroutine with the {DEFINE} macro command (see {DEFINE} for more information on passing arguments to a subroutine).
{BRANCH *location*} *or* /XG*location* ~	Transfers macro control from the current column of macro instructions to *location*.
{DEFINE *location1*,*location2*, …,*locationn*}	Stores arguments passed to the subroutine in a {*subroutine*} command. Each *location* specifies the location for one argument. You can add a *:string* (abbreviated *:s*) or a *:value* (abbreviated *:v*) suffix to the location argument to explicitly declare this argument to be a string or a value.
{DISPATCH *location*}	Performs an indirect branch, transferring macro control to the first instruction in *location*.
{FOR *counter*,*start-number*, *stop-number*,*step-number*, *subroutine*}	Repeatedly calls *subroutine*, depending upon the *start-number*, *stop-number*, and *step-number* used. The number of the current repetition is stored in *counter*. As soon as the number in *counter* is greater than the *stop-number*, the macro continues execution at the instruction following the {FOR} command.

• **Table 16.3:** *Flow-of-Control Macro Commands (continued)*

Keyword & Arguments	Function
{FORBREAK}	Immediately terminates a FOR loop created with the {FOR} command and continues execution at the instruction following the {FOR} command.
{IF *condition*} *or* /XI*condition* ~	Evaluates *condition* as true or false, then executes the macro instruction immediately following the {IF} command in the same cell when the condition is true, or bypasses all further instructions in the same cell and executes the instruction in the cell immediately below if the condition is false.
{ONERROR *branch-location*, [*message-location*]}	Branches macro control to the first cell of *branch-location* when a 1-2-3 error occurs during the execution of the macro. If the optional *message-location* argument is included, it records the error message in this range.
{QUIT} *or* /XQ ~	Immediately terminates the execution of the macro and returns control of 1-2-3 to the user.
{RESTART}	Clears the subroutine stack, so that instead of returning to the original macro location when the macro instructions in the current sub-routine are executed, the macro ends.
{RETURN} *or* /XR	In a subroutine called by a {*subroutine*} or {MENUCALL} command, this command terminates the subroutine and resumes execution with the

♦ **Table 16.3:** *Flow-of-Control Macro Commands (continued)*

Keyword & Arguments	Function
	statement just below the subroutine call. In a subroutine called by a {FOR} command, it immediately terminates the current iteration of the subroutine and begins the next one.
{SYSTEM *command*}	Temporarily suspends 1-2-3 to execute the *command* in DOS. This *command* can be a DOS command, batch file, or command to run another program, and it must be enclosed in quotes. (Release 2.2 only)

Direct Branching in Macros

You can use the {BRANCH} (or /XG) advanced macro command to redirect the flow of a macro to a new location. As soon as the macro executes the {BRANCH} command, it stops executing the macro instructions in the current location and immediately begins executing the instructions in the first cell of the *location* argument. The type of branching accomplished with the {BRANCH} command is known as *direct branching*.

Direct branching is most often used with decision-making loops, where branches redirect the flow of a macro depending upon the outcome of the condition entered in an {IF} advanced macro command. You can also use direct branching to continuously loop through a series of macro instructions.

Practice with Macros That Loop Continuously

In the following exercise, you will create two simple keystroke macros. The first macro will convert a value in the current cell to a label and then move the pointer down one cell. The second macro will convert a label in the current cell to a value before it moves the pointer down. You can make both macros more useful by having them repeat their macro instructions continuously. That way, you can use them to convert a whole range of numbers to labels or vice versa without having to repeatedly execute the macro.

To cause the macros to repeat, you will add a {BRANCH} command in the last cell of the macro to redirect the macro to its first cell, in effect creating an *endless loop* that executes the same keystrokes over again. The only way you can stop such a macro is to manually press Ctrl-Break.

1. **Clear the worksheet, select /Data Fill (/DF), type a period to anchor the range, move the pointer to cell A20, and press Enter; then type *1* as the Start number, and press Enter three more times.**
   This fills the range with consecutive numbers. You will use these numbers to test your macros that convert numbers to labels and labels to numbers. You will call the first macro that converts values to labels \L.

2. **Move the pointer to cell Q41, type '\L, then press the → key.**
   This macro will use the Edit key to return the contents of the current cell to the edit line. Then it will use the Home key to move the cursor to the first character on the line, whereupon it will type the apostrophe label prefix, entering the edited contents as a label when it moves the pointer down to the next row.

3. **In cell R41, type {EDIT}{HOME}'{DOWN}, then press the ↓ key.**
   The keystrokes you just entered in cell R41 convert only a single cell. To have the macro process all cells in the column similarly, you will have the macro branch directly back to the macro instructions in \L (currently cell R41).

4. **In cell R42, type {BRANCH \L} and press Enter; then widen column R to 20 characters.**
   Now you need to document the function of the macro.

5. **In cell S41, enter the description *Add label prefix, move pointer down*; in cell S42, enter *Branch directly to \L*.**
   Assign the range name \L to this macro, and then you are ready to test it.

6. **Assign the range name \L to cell R41 by moving the pointer to cell Q41, selecting /Range Name Labels Right (/RNLR), and pressing Enter.**
   Save the worksheet before testing the macro.

7. **Save the worksheet under the file name *C16BRMAC.WK1*, then move the pointer to cell A1.**
   When you test this macro, you must be ready to press Ctrl-Break to stop it once it has finished converting the value *20* in cell A20 to the label '20.

8. **Press Alt-L; as soon as the macro converts the contents of A20 and the pointer moves into cell A21, press Ctrl-Break; then press the Esc key to exit from ERROR mode.**
   Notice that all the numeric entries in column A are now left-aligned in their cells. If you examine their contents, you will see that each one is now prefaced by the apostrophe label prefix.

9. **Move the pointer back to cell Q41; then copy the cell range Q41..S42 to cell Q44.**
   You will now edit this copy of the \L macro so that it converts labels to values. Start by changing the name of the macro to \V and assigning it as the range name.

10. **Move the pointer to cell Q44 and change \L to \V; then assign the range name \V to cell R44 by moving the pointer to cell Q44 and selecting /Range Name Labels Right (/RNLR), and press Enter.**
    Next, you need to edit the macro instructions in cell R44 so that this macro edits the cell, moves the cursor to the beginning of the line, deletes the apostrophe label prefix, and moves the pointer down to the next cell.

11. **Move the pointer to R44, press Edit (F2), move the cursor to the ' (apostrophe), and press the Del key; then type {DEL}, press the ↓ key, and widen column R to 24 characters.**
    Now edit the {BRANCH} command.

12. **Edit the {BRANCH} command in cell R45 by changing \L to \V.**
    Modify the documentation for this macro before you save the worksheet and test it.

13. **Change the description in cell S44 so that it reads *Delete label prefix, move pointer down*; then modify the description in S45 so that it says *Branch directly to* \V.**
    Your macros should now match the ones shown in Figure 16.5. If they do, save the worksheet now.

14. **Save the worksheet under the same name.**
    Test your macro on the labels in column A.

15. **Move the pointer to cell A1, then press Alt-V. When the macro has converted the label in cell A20 to a value and moved the pointer to cell A21, press Ctrl-Break and then Enter to return to READY mode.**

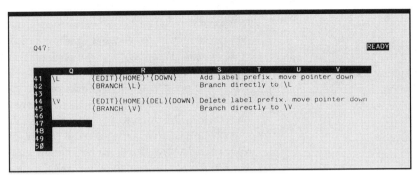

♦ **Figure 16.5:** *Worksheet showing the completed \L and \V macros*

Decision-Making in Macros

You perform conditional branching by using the {IF} (or /XI) advanced macro command. The syntax of this macro command is

{**IF** *condition*}

If the *condition* stated as its argument is met, the command executes the next instruction in the same cell; otherwise, it skips to the instruction in the next cell below.

For example, the {IF} command is often used with a counter to have a macro terminate after a certain number of iterations. This allows processing to continue as long as the count number entered in the {IF} condition has not yet been reached, as in

{IF Count = 10}{BRANCH Done}
{LET Count,Count + 1}
{BRANCH Main}

In this example, the macro branches to the cell range named Done only when the value in the cell range named Count is 10. Otherwise, it continues to process the instructions in the cells below the {IF} statement. In this example, the instructions are the {LET} statement, to increment the counter, and a {BRANCH} statement, to direct execution of the macro to instructions contained in the first cell of the range named Main.

Practice with Decision-Making in Macros

The best way to understand how the {IF} advanced macro command works is to put it to use. You can do just that in the \L and \V branching macros that you just created. There you can use the {IF} command to have the macros stop as soon as they have processed all the labels or all the values in the column.

To do this, you will add a counter loop that uses an IF condition to decide when the macro should shut down. The *condition* argument for the {IF} command will use the @COUNT function to return the number of cells in the column that must be processed; when the counter reaches this number, the macro will branch to a routine that terminates the macro.

Assuming that you still have the worksheet *C16BRMAC.WK1* that contains your \L and \V macros (if it's not current, begin by retrieving this worksheet), the first thing you need to do is name the range of numbers in column A.

1. **Move the pointer to cell A1 in your *C16BRMAC.WK1* worksheet, select /Range Name Create (/RNC), type *data*, press Enter, then move the pointer to cell A20, and press Enter again.**
    Now you are ready to add the counter loop with the {IF} command. You will start by modifying the \L macro that converts values to labels.

2. **Use the Goto key (F5) to move the pointer to cell Q41.**
    The macro that is currently called \L will need to be renamed, as it will now become the routine to which the \L macro branches after advancing the counter. You will now modify its name to *Label*.

3. **Change the name in Q41 from *\L* to *Label*.**
    The first step in this expanded version of the \L macro will be to set the counter back to zero. This has to be done to enable you to run this macro more than one time. This step, however, is not to be repeated each time the macro instructions in the Label routine are executed. Therefore, you will not want the {BRANCH} command in the Label routine to branch directly to \L. Instead, you will create a range named Loop containing the {IF} command that increments the counter. Before you create this part of the macro, you need to modify the {BRANCH} command and its description in the Label routine.

4. **Change the argument in the {BRANCH} command in R42 from *\L* to *Loop*, and change the comment in cell S42 to *Branch directly back to Loop*.**
    Now you are ready to add the first statement in the \L macro. You will do this in the area above the Label routine. The first statement will consist of a {LET} command that sets the *location* named *Counter* to 0.

5. **Enter ⁀\L in cell Q32, enter the command {*LET Counter,0*} in cell R32, then enter the comment *Reset Counter to 0* in cell S32.**
   Immediately below \L, you will enter the Counter routine that contains the {IF} command. Its *condition* will be *Counter=@COUNT-(Data)*. If this condition is true, the macro will branch to a range named Done.

6. **Enter *Loop* in Q33, enter the commands {*IF Counter = @COUNT(Data)*}{*BRANCH Done*} in cell R33, and then enter the comment *IF Counter = No. of cells in range, branch Done* in S33.**
   When the {IF} *condition* becomes true, the {BRANCH Done} command is executed (the Done routine will contain the command {QUIT} to immediately shut down the macro). Next, you will add the commands in cells R34 and R35 that are executed when the {IF} *condition* is false.

7. **Enter the command {*LET Counter,Counter + 1*} in cell R34 and the comment *Increment Counter* in cell S34.**
   This {LET} command adds 1 to whatever value the range named Counter currently contains each time the Loop routine is executed. Remember that when the macro begins, this value is set to 0 so that the Counter cell is incremented to 1 by the time the first value is converted to a label. Now you need to add the {BRANCH} statement that will make this happen.

8. **Enter the command {*BRANCH Label*} in cell R35 and the comment *Branch directly to Label* in S35.**
   Next, you must set up a cell named *Counter* to hold the current number of Loop iterations and another called *Done* that contains the advanced macro command {QUIT}.

9. **Enter the label *Counter* in cell Q37 and the comment *Store loop iteration No.* in cell S37 (be sure to leave cell R37 blank).**
   Next, add the Done routine in row 39.

10. **Enter the label *Done* in cell Q39, the command {*QUIT*} in R39, and the comment *Terminate macro* in S39.**
    Before you can test the macro, you need to name the macro ranges in column Q.

11. **Move the pointer to cell Q32, then select /Range Name Labels Right (/RNLR), move the pointer down to cell Q41, and press Enter.**

    Your macro ranges and instructions should match those shown in Figure 16.6. Check them carefully, then save the worksheet and move the pointer to cell A1.

12. **Widen column R to 39 characters, then save the worksheet under the same name, and press the Home key.**

    Test your macro. This time, you shouldn't need to press Ctrl-Break, as the macro should stop automatically as soon as it converts the last value in cell A20.

13. **Press Alt-L.**

    Now go ahead and expand your \V macro in the same way, so that it too shuts down automatically. Start by moving the \V macro instructions and comments down to make room for the {IF} command with its counter loop.

14. **Use the /Move command (/M) to move the range R44..S45 to cell R49.**

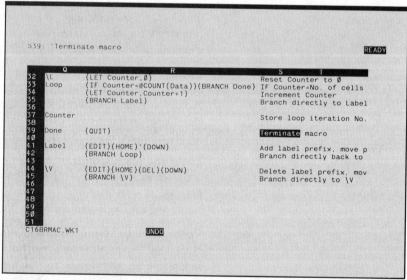

◆ **Figure 16.6:** *Expanded \L macro that shuts down automatically when all cells in the range are converted to labels*

You will call this routine *Value* and have it branch back to a routine called *V_Loop*. Now go ahead and add the *Value* label, and revise the {BRANCH} command in cell R49.

15. **Enter the label *Value* in cell Q49, change the argument of the {BRANCH} command in cell R50 from \V to *V_Loop*, and then change the reference in the comment from \V to *V_Loop* in cell S50.**

Because the instructions and comments for the \V macro are almost identical to those for the \L macro (they will both share the same Counter and Done ranges), you can save a lot of time by copying the range R32..S35.

16. **Use the /Copy command (/C) to copy the range R32..S35 to cell R44.**

Now add the name *V_Loop* to this copied routine in cell Q45.

17. **Enter the label *V_Loop* in cell Q45.**

You also need to modify the {BRANCH} *location* in cell R47 and the comment in S47.

18. **Change the argument in the {BRANCH} command from *Label* to *Value* in cell R47; then change *Label* to *Value* in the comment in cell S47.**

Assign the new range names.

19. **Move the pointer to cell Q44, then select /Range Name Labels Right (/RNLR), move the pointer down to cell Q49, and press Enter.**

Your \V macro should now match the one shown in Figure 16.7. When this is the case, save the worksheet in preparation to testing it.

20. **Save the worksheet under the same name, then press the Home key.**

Test your macro by converting the labels back to numbers in column A.

21. **Press Alt-V.**

This macro should shut down automatically when the last label in cell A20 is converted back into a value.

22. **Press Home, then Alt-L.**

Your values in this range are once again labels.

```
Q44: '\V                                                                  READY

       Q                              R                           S        T
 32  \L           {LET Counter,0}                        Reset Counter to 0
 33  Loop         {IF Counter=@COUNT(Data)}{BRANCH Done}  IF Counter=No. of cells
 34               {LET Counter,Counter+1}                 Increment Counter
 35               {BRANCH Label}                          Branch directly to Label
 36
 37  Counter                                         20  Store loop iteration No.
 38
 39  Done         {QUIT}                                  Terminate macro
 40
 41  Label        {EDIT}{HOME}'{DOWN}                     Add label prefix, move p
 42               {BRANCH Loop}                           Branch directly back to
 43
 44  \V           {LET Counter,0}                         Reset Counter to 0
 45  V_Loop       {IF Counter=@COUNT(Data)}{BRANCH Done}  IF Counter=No. of cells
 46               {LET Counter,Counter+1}                 Increment Counter
 47               {BRANCH Value}                          Branch directly to Value
 48
 49  Value        {EDIT}{HOME}{DEL}{DOWN}                 Delete label prefix, mov
 50               {BRANCH V_Loop}                         Branch directly to V_Loo
 51
C16BRMAC.WK1                          UNDO
```

+ **Figure 16.7:** *Expanded \V macro that shuts down automatically when all cells in the range are converted to values*

Indirect Branching in Macros

Both {IF} commands that you used in your \L and \V macros require only two branches: the *Done* branch, which is executed when the *condition* is true, and the *Label* or *Value* branch, which is executed when the *condition* is false. When the choices involve more than two possible branches (true or false), you have to resort to the use of multiple {IF} statements to perform direct branching.

For example, you could use multiple {IF} and {BRANCH} commands to evaluate the contents of a cell named Choice and then branch to the appropriately named routine, as in

        {IF Choice = "One"}{BRANCH One}
        {IF Choice = "Two"}{BRANCH Two}
        {IF Choice = "Three"}{BRANCH Three}
        {IF Choice = "Four"}{BRANCH Four}

The Lotus Command Language enables you to accomplish the same result in a macro by using the {DISPATCH} command. This command provides *indirect branching* and follows the syntax

        {DISPATCH *location*}

where *location* is the name of the routine whose instructions the macro branches to. Indirect branching gets its name from the fact that the macro doesn't branch (directly) to the name of the range used in the {DISPATCH} argument but (indirectly) to the routine named by this argument range.

Use of the {BRANCH} command can sometimes eliminate the need for multiple {IF} statements. For example, you could condense the four {IF} and {BRANCH} commands in the previous example to just

> **{DISPATCH Choice}**

if you use {DISPATCH}. Here, the macro evaluates the contents of the cell range named Choice and branches immediately to the name of the cell range that Choice contains. Following this example, if Choice contains the label One, the macro will branch to the routine named One; if Choice contains the label Two, it will branch to the routine named Two; and so on.

Practice with Indirect Branching in Macros

Try the next exercise to experience the difference between direct and indirect branching. In it, you will create a simple macro that prompts you to enter the name of your selection and then branches to the routine you name. When you first create this macro, you will use direct branching with multiple {IF} and {BRANCH} statements. Then, you will modify the macro and replace these with a single {DISPATCH} command.

Begin this exercise by clearing the worksheet.

1. **Clear the worksheet, then move the pointer to cell Q41.**
   You will call this macro \I.

2. **With the pointer in cell Q41, type '\I, then press the → key.**
   The first thing this macro will do is prompt you to enter a selection between One and Four. To do this, you will use the {GETLABEL} advanced macro command. This command uses two arguments: *message*, where you enter the prompt to be displayed, and *location*, where the response is stored.

3. **Enter {GETLABEL "Enter choice (One, Two, Three, or Four): ",Choice} in cell R41, then press the ↓ key.**
   Now you need to enter four {IF}/{BRANCH} statements in the cells below, one for each possible choice.

4. **Enter {IF Choice = "One"}{BRANCH One} in cell R42, then press the ↓ key.**
   Notice that you enclosed *One* in quotation marks when used as the argument of the {IF} command, but not when used as the argument of

the {BRANCH} command. The second {IF} statement will branch the macro to the routine named *Two*, if you type *Two* as your selection.

5. **Enter** *{IF Choice = "Two"}{BRANCH Two}* **in cell R43, then press the ↓ key.**
   Next, enter the third {IF} command.

6. **Enter** *{IF Choice = "Three"}{BRANCH Three}* **in cell R44, then press the ↓ key.**
   Now enter the fourth and last {IF} statement.

7. **Enter** *{IF Choice = "Four"}{BRANCH Four}* **in cell R45, then press Enter.**
   Next, you will enter the label *Choice*, which will be used to name cell R47 with the /Range Name Labels Right command. This cell will hold the reply that you enter when you respond to the {GETLABEL} prompt.

8. **Enter the label** *Choice* **in cell Q47.**
   All that remains is to enter the four routines named One, Two, Three, and Four. You will use {BEEP} as the command that is executed when each routine is selected. This command can take a *tone-number* argument that represents different pitches (1–4). When you use {BEEP} without a *tone-number* argument, it uses pitch 1.

9. **Enter the label** *One* **in cell Q49, then enter** *{BEEP}* **in cell R49.**
   To differentiate routine Two from routine One, you will sound two beeps using pitch 1 and pitch 2.

10. **Enter the label** *Two* **in cell Q51, then enter** *{BEEP}{BEEP 2}* **in cell R51.**
    Next, enter the label and commands for routine Three.

11. **Enter the label** *Three* **in cell Q53, then enter** *{BEEP}{BEEP 2}{BEEP 3}* **in cell R53.**
    Finally, enter the label and commands for routine Four.

12. **Enter the label** *Four* **in cell Q55, then enter** *{BEEP}{BEEP 2}{BEEP 3}{BEEP 4}* **in cell R55.**
    Name the macro and the routines using the /Range Name Labels Right command.

13. **Move the pointer to cell Q41, then select /Range Name Labels Right (/RNLR), move the pointer down to cell Q55, and press Enter.**
    Your macro should now match the one shown in Figure 16.8. If so, save the worksheet and then test the macro.

```
Q41: '\I                                                            READY

         Q        R       S       T       U       V       W       X
41  \I          {GETLABEL "Enter choice (One, Two, Three, or Four): ",Choice)
42              {IF Choice="One"}{BRANCH One}
43              {IF Choice="Two"}{BRANCH Two}
44              {IF Choice="Three"}{BRANCH Three}
45              {IF Choice="Four"}{BRANCH Four}
46
47  Choice
48
49  One         {BEEP}
50
51  Two         {BEEP}{BEEP 2}
52
53  Three       {BEEP}{BEEP 2}{BEEP 3}
54
55  Four        {BEEP}{BEEP 2}{BEEP 3}{BEEP 4}
56
57
58
59
60
C16IFMAC.WK1                    UNDO
```

♦ **Figure 16.8:** *Completed \I macro using multiple {IF}/{BRANCH} statements*

14. **Save this worksheet under the name C16IFMAC.WK1.**
    Test the macro in another part of the worksheet.

15. **Press Home, then press Alt-I, type *one* in response to the prompt in the control panel, and press Enter.**
    You should have heard one beep when you pressed Enter. Try it one more time, this time selecting routine Three.

16. **Press Alt-I, type *three*, and press Enter; then press Enter a second time to make the CALC indicator disappear (and to enter *three* in the cell named Choice).**
    This time, you should have heard three (slightly discordant) beeps. Now, before you test the other two routines, replace the multiple {IF}/{BRANCH} statements with a single {DISPATCH} statement. To do this, you will not erase these commands; rather, you will insert two blank rows below the one containing the {GETLABEL} command. This will introduce a blank cell between the {DISPATCH} command you are about to enter and the {IF} commands, in effect disengaging them from this macro.

17. **Move the pointer to cell R42, then select /Worksheet Insert Row (/WIR), press the ↓ key once to make the insert range R42..R43, then press Enter.**
    Now enter the {DISPATCH} command in cell R42.

18. **Enter {*DISPATCH Choice*} in cell R42.**
    Save the worksheet again, and then test the revised macro.

19. **Save the worksheet under the same name.**
    Test the Alt-I macro, this time selecting routine Two.

20. **Press the Home key, then type *two* in response to the prompt to enter your choice, and press Enter.**
    Before you leave this exercise, go ahead and try selecting routine Four.

21. **Press Alt-I, type *four*, and press Enter; then press Enter a second time to make the CALC indicator disappear (and to enter *four* into the cell named *Choice*).**

Subroutine Calls in Macros

The Release 2 version of the Lotus Command Language has no keyword for calling a subroutine (Release 1A uses /XC). To call a subroutine in a macro in Release 2.01 or 2.2, you simply enter the name of the routine in a pair of braces, as in {Print} or {Error_Trap}.

When your macro encounters such a subroutine call, it immediately begins executing the macro instructions in the cell that bears the same range name as the subroutine. When the macro reaches the end of the macro instructions in a subroutine (usually indicated by a blank cell), the program automatically returns to the place in the macro that contains the subroutine call, and the macro executes the instruction immediately following the subroutine.

Organizing related instructions into a subroutine and then entering a subroutine call is a perfect method for repeating discrete procedures in a macro. That way, instead of having to repeat the same macro instructions every time you need the procedure in a macro, you enter them once and then execute the procedure with a simple subroutine call whenever it's needed.

Using the {RETURN} Command to Interrupt Subroutines

You can use the {RETURN} command (or /XR) to have the macro terminate its execution of a subroutine and return immediately to the location of the subroutine call in the macro, where it will then execute the next instruction.

Most often, you use {RETURN} to terminate a subroutine prematurely when a particular condition exists in the macro or the worksheet. When you use it in this way, the {RETURN} command follows an {IF} command and is placed in the same cell where it represents the macro command to be executed when the condition is true. The remaining macro instructions in the subroutine are then placed in the cells below, where they represent the commands executed when the condition is false.

Note that you can also place {RETURN} as the last instruction in a subroutine, although this is unnecessary. Don't, however, confuse the functions of {RETURN} and {QUIT}. The {QUIT} advanced macro command terminates the macro completely, whereas the {RETURN} command returns control to the location in the macro that contains the subroutine call and the macro continues to run, executing whatever instructions follow.

Passing Values to Subroutines

When you define the subroutine call, you can include optional arguments that supply different variables for the subroutine procedure to process each time it is performed. This process is known as *passing values to a subroutine*. Values here are not restricted to numbers; they can be any type of data, including numbers, labels, formulas, or cell references.

To successfully pass values to a subroutine, be sure to do two things. First, you must enter the values you want passed as arguments of the subroutine call. Second, you must begin the subroutine's macro instructions with a {DEFINE} command. The arguments of the {DEFINE} command represent the locations of each value passed to the subroutine. When entering the arguments for the {DEFINE} command, you can use the optional suffixes of :value (abbreviate :v) or :string (abbreviated :s) to declare the type of data variable. If you do not use one of these suffixes to declare the type of argument, the program, by default, considers the data variable to be a string.

Figure 16.9 shows you an example macro that passes values to a subroutine to automatically widen the current column a particular width. By passing both the letter of the column and its width, this macro uses the same subroutine (Widen) to change three different columns (Q, R, and S) to different widths (15, 25, and then 30).

When the macro is executed, it begins by executing the first subroutine call, which passes the value Q to the cell called Col and the value to 15 to the cell called Width. These values are then used in the Widen subroutine to widen column Q to 15 characters. As soon as the last command in the Widen subroutine (/WCS{Width} ˜ in cell R47) is executed, the macro automatically returns to the {*subroutine*} statement that made the call, which is {Widen Q,15} in cell R41 in this case. Then, the macro continues by executing the statement below the calling subroutine, which is the subroutine call {Widen R,25} in cell R42. After executing the Widen subroutine a second time, this time using R as the Col value and 25 as the Width value, the macro returns to the calling subroutine ({Widen R,25} in cell R42) and executes the last subroutine call of {Widen S,30} in cell R43.

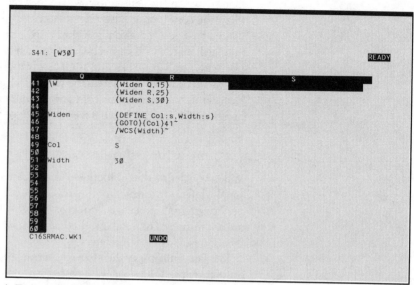

```
S41: [W30]                                                              READY

           Q                        R                        S
41  \W               {Widen Q,15}
42                   {Widen R,25}
43                   {Widen S,30}
44
45  Widen            {DEFINE Col:s,Width:s}
46                   {GOTO}{Col}41~
47                   /WCS{Width}~
48
49  Col              S
50
51  Width            30
52
53
54
55
56
57
58
59
60
C16SRMAC.WK1                   UNDO
```

* **Figure 16.9:** *Example macro that passes values to the Widen subroutine to widen three columns to three different widths*

Notice the {DEFINE} command in the Widen subroutine. This command indicates that the first value passed to the Widen subroutine is to be stored in a cell called Col and the second is to be stored in a cell called Width. The :s suffix declares that both these arguments are strings (this is why 30 in cell R51 in the figure is a left-aligned label).

The macro instructions in the Widen subroutine following the {DEFINE} command use the values stored in the Col and Width cells to determine which column is widened and how wide it will be. Notice that the second command in cell R46 is

   {GOTO}{Col}41 ˜

In Figure 16.9, you can see that the last time the macro processed this subroutine, the column letter S was passed and stored in the Col cell. When the macro executed this {GOTO} command, it therefore supplied S when it called the {Col} subroutine, making it the equivalent of {GOTO}S41 ˜ .

After positioning the pointer in cell S41, the macro executed the last statement in the Widen subroutine, which is

   /WCS{Width} ˜

During the last loop, when the macro passed the value S to Col, it also passed the value 30 to Width. Therefore, when the macro executed this /WCS command, the subroutine call to Width supplied 30, making the last command the equivalent of /WCS30˜.

Repeating Subroutines

When your macro requires repeated execution of a subroutine, either a specified number of times or until a particular condition is met, you can set up looping procedures in your subroutines by using the {FOR} advanced macro command. The {FOR} command requires several arguments:

{**FOR** *counter,start-number,stop-number,step-number,subroutine*}

The *counter* argument represents the name of the cell where the count numbers are stored. The *start-number* is the initial value entered into this cell. The *step-number* tells the macro how much to increment the value in the counter location each time the subroutine is executed. The *stop-value* tells the macro at what number to stop executing the subroutine. The *subroutine* argument is the name of the cell range that contains the procedure that is to be repeated.

For an example of how you can use the {FOR} command, consider the macro shown in Figure 16.10. This macro automatically widens each column in a table of data (given the range name *Data*) to 15 characters, and then moves the pointer to the first cell of the table and enters the names of all 12 months (using the three-letter abbreviation) across the top row.

To widen the current column to 15 characters, this macro uses a subroutine called Widen that contains the macro keystrokes

/WCS15˜{R}

These keystrokes select /Worksheet Column Set-Width, enter 15, press Enter, and then move the pointer to the next column to the right ({R} stands for

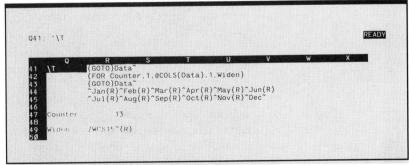

◆ **Figure 16.10:** *Sample macro with {FOR} loop to automatically widen each column in a table of data*

{RIGHT}, the keystroke instruction to move the pointer one cell to the right).

To repeat the Widen subroutine until all columns in the data table are widened to 15 characters, the macro moves the pointer to the first cell in the table with

{GOTO}Data ~

and then uses the following {FOR} command:

{FOR Counter,1,@COLS(Data),1,Widen}

In this case, the macro stores the starting number of 1 in the cell named Counter (cell R47 in Figure 16.9). Each time the Widen subroutine is executed, the number in this cell is incremented by 1 (the *step-number* argument). The *stop-number* argument in this macro is calculated by using the @COLS function to return the number of columns in the table named Data. When the number stored in the Counter cell exceeds this number, control passes to the next statement in the macro, which returns the pointer to the first cell of the table in preparation to entering the names of the months centered in the first 12 cells.

If you wish to add a condition under which the looping should be terminated before the counter reaches the *stop-number* value, you can add an {IF} statement followed by the {FORBREAK} advanced macro command. For example, in the macro shown in Figure 16.9, you could add the following {IF}/{FORBREAK} statement to the Widen subroutine of the \T macro to prevent the widening of any columns past column Z in the worksheet:

{IF @CELLPOINTER("col") = 27}{FORBREAK}
/WCS15 ~ {R}

In this case, if the pointer is located in cell AA (the 27th column of the worksheet) when the first loop of the {FOR} command is executed, the {FORBREAK} command aborts the subroutine and terminates looping by immediately transferring control of the macro to the statement following the {FOR} command.

Nesting Subroutines

You can nest many levels of subroutines in a macro—in other words, you can call one subroutine from within another. If your macro contains a series of nested subroutines, each of which calls another, you can use the {RESTART} command to clear the subroutine chain of command (clear the stack) and return control to the original calling macro.

Practice Using Subroutines

For your practice with subroutines, you will create a macro that prints your loan payment worksheet using different input values each time. If you remember, this worksheet enables you to input various principal amounts, interest rates, and terms, and then uses these values to calculate a table of monthly payments. Through the use of a print subroutine, you can have the print macro produce the same loan payment table using different input values.

1. **Retrieve the worksheet named *LOANPMT.WK1*.**
   Remember that this worksheet is globally protected. Only the three input cells C3, C4, and C5 are unprotected. To create a macro in this worksheet, you must first disable global protection.

2. **Select the /Worksheet Global Protection Disable (/WGPD) command.**
   Before you move to an unused area in the worksheet away from the loan payment table, where you can safely locate the print macro, you need to assign range names to the data here. You will assign range names to each of the three input cells as well as to the entire table.

3. **Assign the range name *PRIN* to cell C3, *RATE* to C4, and *TERM* to C5; then assign the range name *LOAN_TABLE* to the cell range A1..G17.**
   Now you're ready to begin creating the macro. You will name the macro \P.

4. **Move the pointer to cell Q41, then enter '\P in this cell, and press the → key.**
   This macro will first define the print range using *Loan_Table* as the print range.

5. **In cell R41, type '/PPRLoan_Table ˜ Q and press the ↓ key.**
   The next macro instruction will be a call to the subroutine that actually prints the defined range. This subroutine will be called *DO_Print*. As part of the subroutine call, you will enter arguments that pass values for the starting principal, interest rate, and term. In the first subroutine call, you will use *95000* as the initial principal, *.065* as the beginning interest rate, and *20* as the term.

6. **In cell R42, type {*DO_Print 95000,.065,20*}, then press the ↓ key.**
   After the macro prints the loan table using the values passed to the DO_Print subroutine, it will print the loan payment table a second time, using a new set of input values. This time, your subroutine call

will pass *175000* as the initial principal, *.11* as the starting interest rate, and *30* as the term.

7. **In cell R43, type {DO_Print 175000,.11,30} and press Enter.**

Now you are ready to create the DO_Print subroutine. Start by entering the subroutine name *DO_Print*.

8. **In cell Q46, enter *DO_Print*, then press the → key.**

The first command in this subroutine has to be the {DEFINE} command, which indicates where the values passed to this subroutine are to be stored. In this macro, you will store these values in the three input cells named Prin (C3), Rate (C4), and Term (C5), respectively. You will terminate each of these range names with the *:v* (abbreviation of :value) suffix to indicate the arguments they hold are values.

9. **In cell R46, type {DEFINE Prin:v, Rate:v, Term:v}, then press the ↓ key.**

Next, you need to enter the keystrokes to print the currently defined range, advance the page, and quit the /Print Printer menu.

10. **In cell R47, type '/PPAGPQ, then press Enter.**

Now you need to assign range names to the cell containing the first \P macro instruction and the first DO_Print subroutine instruction.

11. **Move the pointer to cell Q41, then select /Range Name Labels Right (/RNLR), move the pointer to cell Q46, and press Enter.**

Next, document the function of each macro step.

12. **Widen column R to 30 characters, then enter the comments for each step as they are shown in Figure 16.11.**

Now save the worksheet under a different file name.

13. **Save the worksheet under the new name *C16LNPMT.WK1*.**

Now test the macro. Be sure that your printer is turned on and has enough paper to print two pages.

14. **Turn on your printer, press the Home key, and then press Alt-P.**

If all went as planned, you should now have two printouts of the loan payment table with different values. Did you notice that the macro didn't update the table with the new input values and payments until after the table was printed? Let's improve the macro so that it shows you the new calculated values and then asks you if you want the table printed.

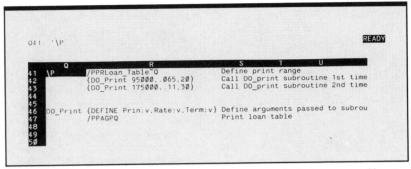

♦ **Figure 16.11:** *Print macro (\P) that uses subroutines to print loan payment table using different values*

15. **Move the pointer to cell R46, then use the /Move command to move the cell range R46..S47 to R47.**
    The first step in this revised DO_Print routine will be to move the pointer to the first cell of the loan table.

16. **In cell R46, enter {GOTO}Loan_Table˜, then press the ↓ key.**
    Next, you need to edit the instruction with the {DEFINE} command to have the table recalculated with these new values.

17. **With the pointer in cell R47, press the Edit key (F2), type {CALC}, and press the ↓ key.**
    Next, you need to insert two blank rows in the worksheet. In the first row, you will add the {GETLABEL} command to prompt the user for permission to print. In the second row, you will add the {IF} command that will evaluate the user's response.

18. **Select the /Worksheet Insert Row command (/WIR), press the ↓ key once, and press Enter.**
    Now you will use the {GETLABEL} command to have the macro prompt you to print this table.

19. **In cell R48, type {GETLABEL "Print this loan table? (Y/N): ",Response} and press Enter.**
    Next, you need to insert a step between the {DEFINE} command and the printing keystrokes. In this step, the macro will evaluate the response given by the user. If the response is N, the macro will return to the calling subroutine.

20. **Move the pointer to cell R49, type {IF Response = "N"} {RETURN} in this cell, and press Enter.**

Now you need to enter the range name *Response*, which will be used to name the cell where the {GETLABEL} command stores the user's response.

21. **Move the pointer to cell Q52, type *Response*, and press Enter.**
    Your \P macro should look like the one shown in Figure 16.12. Before you can try this revised macro, you need to reassign the *DO_Print* range name and assign *Response* to cell R52.

22. **Move the pointer to cell Q46, select /Range Name Labels Right (/RNLR), then move the pointer to cell Q52, and press Enter.**
    Now add the documentation for the new steps.

23. **Add the comments for the new steps, as shown in Figure 16.13.**
    Save the worksheet.

24. **Save the worksheet under the same name.**
    Now test the macro.

25. **Press Alt-P, type N, and press Enter when prompted to print the table the first time; then type Y when prompted the second time.**

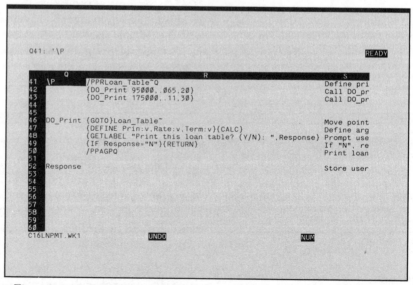

◆ **Figure 16.12:** *Revised print macro (\P) that prompts the user before printing the loan payment table*

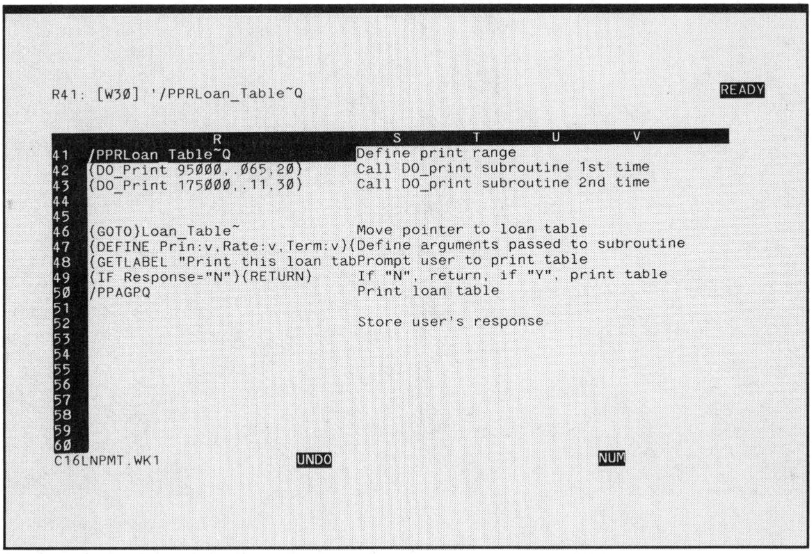

◆ **Figure 16.13:** *Comments for revised print macro (\P)*

Error Handling in Macros

If an error occurs during macro execution, the macro terminates execution and returns control to the user, displaying a 1-2-3 macro error message and going into ERROR mode. This can happen as a result of an input error or because the user has pressed Ctrl-Break.

To prevent a macro from being terminated by an error, you can use the {ONERROR} advanced macro command. When a macro error occurs, this command branches the macro to a new set of instructions designed to tell the user how to correct the error. You can also add an optional argument to have the macro record the 1-2-3 error message in a cell, which you can then display to the user.

The syntax of the {ONERROR} advanced macro command is

{**ONERROR** *branch-location,[message-location]*}

Figure 16.14 illustrates the use of this command. In the file retrieve macro \R shown there, the {ONERROR} command is used to run the ErrTrap routine. As part of this routine, the macro displays a 1-2-3 error message (*File does not exist* in this case) in a cell named ErrMsg. After suggesting what the problem might be, the {GETLABEL} command prompts the user to try again. If the user types N, the macro ends; otherwise, the macro branches back to \R and executes the file retrieve macro again.

```
Z61: '{ONERROR ErrTrap,ErrMsg}                                    READY

        Y        Z         AA        AB        AC        AD        AE        AF
61 \R           {ONERROR ErrTrap,ErrMsg}                                  Message
62              /FR {ESC}{?}~
63
64 ErrTrap      {GOTO}Message~
65              {BEEP}
66              The following 1-2-3 error has occurred: {DOWN}
67              /CErrMsg~~{DOWN}
68              You may have mistyped the name {DOWN}
69              or the file may be in another directory {DOWN}
70              {WAIT @NOW+@TIME(0,0,3)}~
71              {GOTO}Message~/RE{DOWN 4}~
72              {GETLABEL "Try again? (Y/N): ",Response}
73              {IF Response="N"}{CALC}{QUIT}
74              {BRANCH \R}
75
76 ErrMsg       File does not exist
77
78 Response n
79
80
ERRMAC.WK1                    UNDO
```

◆ **Figure 16.14:** *File retrieve macro with error-trapping routine*

Controlling the Screen Display

The Lotus Command Language contains several advanced macro commands that enable you to control the screen display during the execution of your macros. Table 16.4 shows you the screen-control advanced macro commands. As you can see from this list, all the commands in this group with the exception of {BEEP} are visual in nature, enabling you to control what the user sees (or doesn't see) as the macro is being executed.

Reducing Flicker When Macros Are Executed

Whenever your macros include instructions to select options from the 1-2-3 command menus, you will see a flicker as the program rapidly replays these macro instructions. In long macros containing many such command keystrokes, you can suppress this flickering by using the {WINDOWSOFF} and {PANELOFF} command keywords in the macro.

The {WINDOWSOFF} command freezes the worksheet display so that this area of the screen is not redrawn, even when the macro instructions affect a part of the worksheet. Using this advanced macro command helps to speed up a macro, because 1-2-3 does not have to take time to redraw the display screen.

The {PANELOFF} command clears the lines of the control panel and then suppresses further display of keystrokes in the control panel. This area of the display screen flickers the most as the macro rapidly executes the menu command sequences.

♦ **Table 16.4:** *Screen Control Macro Commands*

Keyword & Arguments	Function
{BEEP [*tone-number*]}	Sounds the computer's bell. *Tone-number* is an optional argument between 1 and 4 indicating the tone to be sounded when the computer beeps.
{BORDERSOFF}	Removes the display of the worksheet frame until the macro executes a {BORDERSON} or {FRAMEON} command. (Release 2.2 only)
{BORDERSON}	Redisplays the worksheet frame turned off with either a {BORDERSOFF} or {FRAMEOFF} command. (Release. 2.2 only)
{FRAMEOFF}	Identical to {BORDERSOFF} command. (Release 2.2 only)
{FRAMEON}	Identical to {BORDERSON} command. (Release 2.2 only)
{GRAPHOFF}	Removes the graph displayed with the {GRAPHON} command and redisplays the worksheet. (Release 2.2 only)
{GRAPHON [*named-graph*], [nodisplay]}	Displays a full-screen view of the current graph when no argument is specified. With the optional *named-graph* argument, the macro makes *named-graph* current and displays it. With the optional nodisplay argument, the macro makes the *named-graph* current but doesn't display it. (Release 2.2 only)
{INDICATE [*string*]}	Displays the *string* argument as the new mode indicator until the macro encounters {INDICATE} with no argument, or until you

◆ **Table 16.4:** *Screen Control Macro Commands (continued)*

Keyword & Arguments	Function
	retrieve a new worksheet, erase the worksheet in memory, or exit from 1-2-3.
{PANELOFF}	Freezes the control panel in its current state until the macro encounters a {PANELON} statement or the macro ends.
{PANELON}	Unfreezes the control panel initiated with {PANELOFF} so that it is once again redrawn and updated.
{WINDOWSOFF}	Freezes the worksheet display until the macro encounters a {WINDOWSON} statement or ends.
{WINDOWSON}	Unfreezes the worksheet display initiated with {WINDOWSON} so that it is once again redrawn and updated.

You can use both commands together in a macro to reduce the on-screen distractions caused by macro execution. You should not, however, add them to your macro until you have completed debugging it. Later in the macro, you can use the {WINDOWSON} and {PANELON} commands to unfreeze the display screen and control panel. If you do not add these commands, the {WINDOWS-OFF} and {PANELOFF} commands will automatically turn off when the macro terminates its execution.

✳ *New in 2.2*   ## Suppressing the Display of the Frame

Release 2.2 has added new advanced macro commands that enable you to turn off and on the display of the worksheet frame (that is, the borders area on the left and top of the worksheet display that contains the row numbers and column letters). To suppress the display of the frame while a macro is running, you can use either {BORDERSOFF} or {FRAMEOFF} (these commands are identical in usage and function).

Once the macro executes a {BORDERSOFF} or {FRAMEOFF} command, the display of the frame remains suppressed until either the macro encounters a {BORDERSON} or {FRAMEON} command, or the macro ends. Figure 16.15 shows you how the screen looks without the worksheet display. For this figure, a {FRAMEOFF} command has been added to the ErrTrap routine in the \R sample macro in Figure 16.14. This time, when a file name error occurs, the user message displayed in the range named Message appears on the screen without the usual cell references created with the worksheet frame.

Note that if a {WINDOWSOFF} command was executed earlier in the macro, you should be sure to add the {WINDOWSON} command before you use a {BORDERSOFF}, {BORDERSON}, {FRAMEOFF}, or {FRAMEON} command. This is because these frame display commands have no effect when the worksheet display isn't being redrawn.

Displaying Your Own Mode Indicator

You can have a macro display your own mode indicator in the upper right corner of the screen during the macro's execution. To do this, you add the {INDICATE} advanced macro command with an optional *string* argument containing the characters you want displayed in this area. For example, you could add the command

> {INDICATE "MACRO"}

to have MACRO displayed in the upper right corner of the screen as the new mode indicator.

When specifying the *string* argument for {INDICATE}, you can enter a literal string (as in the example), a reference to a cell that contains such an indicator string, or even a string formula that calculates the indicator string. In any

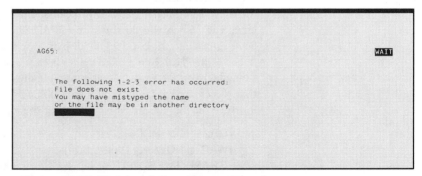

♦ **Figure 16.15:** *Worksheet display without worksheet frame*

case, the indicator string can contain as many characters as will fit within the first line of the control panel (up to 240 characters total).

Once your macro executes an {INDICATE} command that contains a *string* argument, the new mode indicator defined by this *string* remains on the screen until either the macro executes another {INDICATE} command, you retrieve a new worksheet with /File Retrieve, you clear the current worksheet with /Worksheet Erase, or you end your 1-2-3 work session.

To restore the regular display of mode indicators in 1-2-3 before you retrieve a new file, clear the worksheet display, or restart the program, you need to add

    {INDICATE}

—that is, the macro command without any optional *string* argument. To suppress the mode indicator display entirely, you enter

    {INDICATE ""}

in the macro.

✳ *New in 2.2*   Macro Commands for Displaying Graphs

Release 2.2 has added a {GRAPHON} command that makes it easy for you to display graphs during the execution of your macro. If you enter the {GRAPHON} command alone without the optional *named-graph* argument, 1-2-3 displays the current graph until either the macro ends, it reaches a {GRAPHOFF}, {INDICATE}, or {?} command, or it reaches an advanced macro command that displays a prompt or menu in the control panel.

To make a new graph current and display it, you add the optional *named-graph* argument, which specifies the name of the graph (the name you assigned to the graph with /Graph Name Create and saved as part of the worksheet, not the name you assigned with /Graph Save and saved as a PIC file). When you use the *named-graph* argument, you can add [nodisplay] as an optional second argument. When you do this, the {GRAPHON} macro command makes the *named-graph* current but does *not* display it on the screen.

The {GRAPHON} command makes it easy to create a graph slide show. For example, to create a macro that automatically displays each of the four graphs that you created in Chapter 9 in your *IS5YRCH9.WK1* worksheet in succession for three seconds apiece, you could enter the following commands:

```
{GRAPHON INCOMELN}
{WAIT @NOW + @TIME(0,0,3)}
{GRAPHON PRDCSTP}
{WAIT @NOW + @TIME(0,0,3)}
{GRAPHON COSTBAR}
```

{WAIT @NOW + @TIME(0,0,3)}
{GRAPHON TOTEXPSB}
{WAIT @NOW + @TIME(0,0,3)}

Each of these {GRAPHON} commands selects a particular named graph saved in your worksheet, and each {WAIT} command keeps the graph displayed for a total of three seconds (to learn more about {WAIT} and its arguments, see the discussion of this macro command in the Interactive Macro Commands section).

Sounding the Computer's Bell

In addition to the visual screen control commands, there is also an audio command, {BEEP}, which sounds the computer's bell (although it is called a bell, it is really more like an electronic buzz). You can use the {BEEP} advanced macro command whenever you want to alert the user to a change in processing, especially one that requires input, or to an error in processing.

The {BEEP} command can take an optional *tone-number* argument that specifies a number between 1 and 4 to sound one of the four tones used by the IBM computer. If you don't add this optional argument to your {BEEP} command, the macro will sound the same tone as when you specify 1 as its *tone-number* argument.

Interactive Macro Commands

The Lotus Command Language includes several interactive advanced macro commands that allow you to obtain and process new information supplied by the user of the macro. Table 16.5 lists the commands in this group.

The interactive advanced macro commands support several methods for suspending execution of the macro to accept user input for processing. You are already familiar with the macro pause command {?}, which simply suspends execution of the macro to allow you to access any 1-2-3 menu command or to type any keyboard character until you press Enter. In addition to this simple pause, the Lotus Command Language includes commands that enable you to prompt the user for specific information or even to create menu-driven applications.

Prompting the User for Input

The Lotus Command Language contains two commands that enable you to prompt the user for information: {GETLABEL} (or /XL) and {GETNUMBER} (or /XN). Both of these macro commands suspend the execution of the macro, display the message that you specify as the *prompt* argument on the control panel, and await the user's response in the cell named in the *location* argument

◆ **Table 16.5:** *Interactive Macro Commands*

Keyword & Arguments	Function
{?}	Suspends the macro execution until you press the Enter key, during which time you can enter data or move the pointer.
{BREAK}	Returns the program to READY mode (same effect as manually pressing Ctrl-Break in MENU mode).
{BREAKOFF}	Disables Ctrl-Break so that the macro can't be interrupted.
{BREAKON}	Enables Ctrl-Break after it has been disabled with {BREAKOFF}.
{GET *location*}	Suspends the macro until you press a key, and then it records the keystroke as a label in *location*.
{GETLABEL *prompt,location*} or /XL*prompt* ˜ [*location*] ˜	Displays *prompt* in the control panel and suspends the macro execution to allow you to enter a response. Your response is recorded as a label in *location*, and the macro resumes execution as soon as you press Enter.
{GETNUMBER *prompt,location*} or /XN*prompt* ˜ [*location*] ˜	Displays *prompt* in the control panel and suspends the macro execution to allow you to enter a response. Your response is recorded as a number in *location*, and the macro resumes execution as soon as you press Enter.
{LOOK *location*}	Checks the keyboard buffer for keystrokes, and records the first keystroke made as a label in *location*.

♦ **Table 16.5:** *Interactive Macro Commands (continued)*

Keyword & Arguments	Function
{MENUBRANCH *location*} or /XM*location* ~	Displays the macro menu that starts in the first cell of *location* in the control panel, pauses for you to select a menu item, and then branches to the macro instructions associated with the selected menu item.
{MENUCALL *location*}	Displays the macro menu that starts in the first cell of *location* in the control panel, pauses for you to select a menu item, and then performs a subroutine call to the macro instructions associated with the selected menu item.
{WAIT *time-number*}	Suspends the execution of the macro until the time specified by the *time-number* argument, then resumes execution. During this pause, WAIT is the mode indicator.

as soon as the user presses Enter. They differ, however, in the type of data that they accept from the user.

Use the {GETLABEL} command when you want the response given by the user to be accepted as a label (even when the response consists of numbers and is not prefaced by an apostrophe or some other label prefix).

You use the {GETNUMBER} command, on the other hand, when you want a numeric response from the user. If the user enters a label in response to a prompt displayed by a {GETNUMBER} command, 1-2-3 enters ERR in the cell specified as the *location* argument; this command accepts only numbers or numeric formulas (or references to a cell or range that contains such numbers or formulas).

You have already had some experience using the {GETLABEL} command in your macros. Figure 16.16 illustrates an application for the {GETNUMBER} command combined with the {FOR} command to print multiple copies of a report.

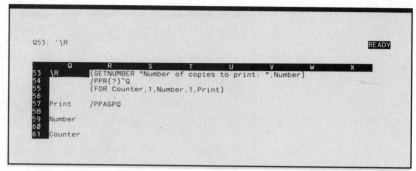

```
Q53: '\R                                                                    READY

        Q        R          S          T          U          V          W          X
53  \R           {GETNUMBER "Number of copies to print: ",Number}
54               /PPR(?)~Q
55               {FOR Counter,1,Number,1,Print}
56
57  Print        /PPAGPQ
58
59  Number
60
61  Counter
```

◆ **Figure 16.16:** *Macro with {GETNUMBER} used to print multiple copies of a report*

When you execute the \R macro in the figure, you will first see the message

Enter number of copies to be printed:

in the control panel. The number you enter on this line is stored in a cell named Number when you press the Enter key. This value is then used by the {FOR} command to control how many times the Print subroutine is executed. Notice that this macro also uses the {?} pause to allow you to specify the print range before the {FOR} repeats the Print subroutine the number of times you specified.

Evaluating a Single Keystroke

In addition to the {GETLABEL} and {GETNUMBER} commands, which accept a string of text or numeric input, the Lotus Command Language also includes the advanced macro command {GET}, which is useful whenever you require the user to press a single key to designate some kind of choice.

The {GET} statement suspends macro execution and waits until the user presses a single key, which it records in the cell named by the *location* argument, and then it immediately resumes execution. For example, you could have the user enter a single key to designate where the pointer should move next, as in

{GET Keystroke}
{IF Keystroke = "h"} {HOME}
{IF Keystroke = "e"} {END} {HOME}

This {GET} statement records the first key pressed in the cell named Keystroke. Then the {IF} commands evaluate the contents of this cell and move the pointer, depending upon its contents.

Along with {GET}, the Lotus Command Language includes the {LOOK} command, which checks the keyboard buffer for keystrokes and then records the first key pressed in the cell named as its *location* argument. The *keyboard buffer* (sometimes called the type-ahead buffer) stores all the keystrokes that you make during noninteractive parts of the macro. Each time you respond to an interactive command, this buffer is cleared.

Once a {LOOK} command has recorded the first keystroke made by the user in the *location* cell, you can then use an {IF} command to branch the macro according to its contents. Figure 16.17 illustrates this kind of usage. The \Z macro shown in this figure prompts you with the {GETLABEL} command to enter the name of the graph you want displayed. The Display routine contains a {WAIT} command (discussed next) that suspends the macro's execution for one second, then the {LOOK} command searches the keyboard buffer for the user's first keystroke. The {GET} command that immediately follows intercepts this keystroke and records it in the cell named Key_Press, which is used as the *location* argument for both commands.

The {IF} command then evaluates the contents of the Key_Press cell. If this cell is empty, the macro branches back to the Display routine and the graph continues to be displayed on the screen. If, however, the Key_Press cell contains any keystroke, the {GRAPHOFF} command is executed and the worksheet is displayed once again. In this way, you can continue to display the graph you have chosen until you press a key.

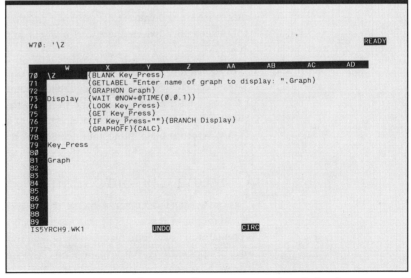

♦ **Figure 16.17:** *Macro with {GET} and {LOOK} commands to display the current graph until you press a key*

Suspending a Macro for a Period of Time

To suspend a macro's execution for a specified period of time, you use the {WAIT} advanced macro command. You can also use this command to delay the execution of a macro until a specific time. This is useful when you need a macro that will begin printing a lengthy report after office hours.

To suspend a macro's execution during a specified time, you must combine the {WAIT} statement with the @NO and @TIME functions, as in

    {WAIT @NOW + @TIME(0,1,0)}

This would suspend execution of the macro for one minute.

To delay processing until a specific hour, use the @INT(@NOW) or the @TODAY function with the @TIME function. For example, this command will delay execution until 8:00 PM on the current day:

    {WAIT @INT(@NOW) + @TIME(20,0,0)}

Disabling the Ctrl-Break Key

As you know, you can press the Ctrl-Break key to prematurely terminate the execution of a macro. You may sometimes want to prevent the user from using Ctrl-Break to interrupt the execution of your macro—for instance, when the macro is executing a procedure that imports data from a text file into a 1-2-3 worksheet. To disable Ctrl-Break, you enter the {BREAKOFF} command in the macro where you want it disabled. To enable the Ctrl-Break key again before the macro ends (whereupon Ctrl-Break is automatically enabled), you enter {BREAKON}.

✳ *New in 2.2* In addition to the {BREAKON} and {BREAKOFF} commands, Release 2.2 has introduced the {BREAK} advanced macro command. This command simulates pressing Ctrl-Break to return the program to READY mode. Note, however, that {BREAK} can't be used to interrupt the execution of a macro; its only function is to return 1-2-3 immediately to READY mode while the macro is running.

Creating Custom Menus

You can set up 1-2-3 macros so that they are entirely menu-driven. The command menus that you create in a macro appear and work like any other 1-2-3 command menu. Menu macros enable you to create highly specialized menu-driven applications that anyone who has minimal familiarity with 1-2-3 can use with confidence.

If you want to create a complex macro that *completely* customizes the workings of 1-2-3, you can name the menu macro \0 to have it executed automatically as soon as the worksheet file is retrieved. Then, you name the worksheet file that contains this menu macro under the file name *AUTO123.WK1* in the default directory. When you start 1-2-3, the program will automatically retrieve your *AUTO123.WK1* file; once this file is retrieved, the program will automatically execute the \0 macro. In this way, the user can perform all his or her work in the file only under the control of your custom menu macro.

Creating Menu Macros

To create a menu macro, you use either the {MENUBRANCH} (or /XM) or {MENUCALL} advanced macro command. The argument for both these commands is *location*, which is the name of the first cell of the range that contains the menu options. The {MENUCALL} command differs from {MENUBRANCH} in that it performs a subroutine call to the *location* argument rather than just branching to it. This means that the macro automatically returns to {MENUCALL} when you exit from the menu, whereupon it executes the command that follows.

When creating the menu at the *location* of the {MENUBRANCH} or the {MENUCALL} command, you start by entering the names of the menu options in a single row. These options appear on the first line of the control panel when you execute the menu macro. In the cell directly below the one containing each menu option, you enter a description of the option. These descriptions appear in the second line of the control panel when you execute the macro and then move the pointer to it.

In the cell below the description of each menu option, you place the macro instructions that are to be performed when that option is selected by the user. Many times, these instructions will consist solely of a {BRANCH} or {*subroutine*} command that directs the flow of the macro to a new area in the worksheet that contains the macro instructions.

When creating your menu for a menu macro, keep these guidelines in mind:

- A menu cannot contain more than eight options. However, you can have as many submenus attached to the menu options as you like.

- A menu option must be entered as a label; you can't use a string formula to create it.

- Begin each menu option with a different first letter. If possible, restrict the option name to a single word. If you must use more than one word, you should place a hyphen (no spaces) between the words so that it is clear to the user that it represents only a single menu choice.

♦ The menu option descriptions entered below each menu option can
be entered as strings or with string formulas. The total length of the
description cannot exceed the width of the screen, or an error will
occur.

Using Menu Macros

When you execute a menu macro, the program displays the menu options
listed in the first row of the *location* range on the first line of the control panel.
From that point on, the custom menu works just like all other 1-2-3 menus. To
select one of the menu options, you can either type the first letter of the option
name or use the cursor-movement keys to move the pointer to it and press
Enter. To leave a menu and return to 1-2-3 without selecting the Quit option
(assuming that you have provided one), you press Ctrl-Break.

If your menu macro uses several levels of menus, you can use the Esc key to
return to a previous level, or to READY mode if you are at the main menu level.

Practice Creating Custom Menus

For your last exercise with advanced macro commands, you will create a custom menu system for your personnel database stored in the PERSNLDB.WK1
worksheet. This menu will contain three options: the first option will enable
you to add a record to the database, the second option will allow you to sort the
data alphabetically either by name or department and starting date, and the
third option will let you quit the menu.

1. **Retrieve your database worksheet named** *PERSNLDB.WK1,*
   then move the pointer to cell W41.
   You will call the menu macro \M. It will use the {MENUBRANCH}
   command to branch to the menu location, which you will call *Main.*

2. **With the pointer in cell W41, enter** '\M, **then press the →**
   key and enter {*MENUBRANCH Main*} **in cell X41.**
   The main menu options will be Add, Sort, and Quit.

3. **Move the pointer to cell W43, type** *Main,* **then press the →**
   key, enter *Add* **in cell X43,** *Sort* **in cell Y43, and** *Quit* **in**
   cell Z43.
   Next, you need to enter the menu option descriptions in the cells
   below.

4. **Move the pointer to cell X44, type** *Add a new record to*
   database, **then press the → key, enter** *Sort database* **in cell**
   Y44, and enter *Return to 1-2-3* **in cell Z44.**

Although you don't have to widen columns X, Y, and Z to have your menu macro work properly, doing so will help you understand the working of this macro.

5. **Widen column X to 29 characters and Y to 19 characters.**
   Next, you need to add the macro instructions in the cells below the option descriptions. For the Add and Sort options, you will branch to routines that you will create below. For the Quit option, you will use the {QUIT} advanced macro command.

6. **Move the pointer to cell X45, type {BRANCH Add}, then press the → key; enter {BRANCH Sort} in cell Y45, and {QUIT} in cell Z45.**
   The Add routine will start by positioning the pointer in the first blank row beneath the last record of the database.

7. **Move the pointer to cell W47, type Add, then press the → key; type {HOME}{END}{DOWN 2} in cell X47 and then press the ↓ key.**
   The keystrokes {HOME}{END}{DOWN 2} will always locate the pointer in the correct cell for starting a new record. Pressing the Home key takes the pointer to cell A1, then End ↓ moves it to the first cell in the last record, and pressing the ↓ key a second time moves it to the first blank cell below. The first field is REC#. The macro will calculate this by adding 1 to the record number above it.

8. **With the pointer in cell X48, type ' + {UP} + 1{RIGHT}, then press the ↓ key.**
   The next field holds the social security number. This number is, however, entered as a label. Therefore, you will use the {GETLABEL} command to prompt the user to enter it.

9. **With the pointer in cell X49, type {GETLABEL "Enter social security number: ",Soc}, then press the ↓ key.**
   The social security number entered by the user will be saved in a cell named Soc. The macro must next copy the number stored in Soc to the field that holds the pointer.

10. **With the pointer in cell X50, type '/CSoc ˜ ˜ {RIGHT}, then press the ↓ key.**
    The next field holds the first name. You will use the same technique to prompt for this information as you did for the social security number.

11. **With the pointer in cell X51, type {GETLABEL "Enter first name: ",F_Name}, then press the ↓ key.**

Now use the same copy technique to copy the response stored in F_Name into the FIRST.NAME field.

12. With the pointer in cell X52, type '/CF_Name ~ ~ {RIGHT}, then press the ↓ key.

The next four fields in the database—LAST.NAME, DEPT, POSITION, and SUPRVSR—all use the same technique with similar commands to obtain the data and then copy them to the database. To cut down on the chance of errors in your macro, you should copy the {GETLABEL} and /C statements and then modify them.

13. Referring to Figure 16.18, use the /Copy command to copy the pair of {GETLABEL} and /C statements; then use the Edit key (F2) and modify them to create the contents of cells X53 through X60.

The field following SUPRVSR is SALARY. This field is numeric and requires a switch to the {GETNUMBER} command. In addition, the macro must also format the number before moving the pointer to the next cell to the right.

14. With the pointer in cell X61, type {GETNUMBER "Enter annual salary: ",Sal}, then press the ↓ key.

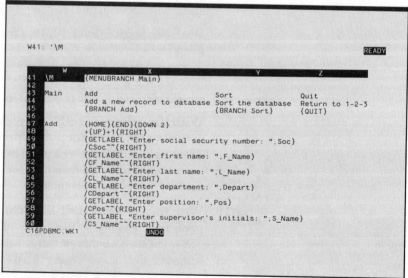

◆ **Figure 16.18:** *Menu macro with first part of the Add routine*

The next step will be to copy the number in the Sal field to the SAL-ARY field, format it using the Comma format with 0 decimal places, then move the pointer to the start date field.

15. **With the pointer in X62, type '/CSal ˜ ˜ /RF,0 ˜ ˜ {RIGHT}, then press the ↓ key.**
The last field in the database is the START.DATE field, which contains the date number of the date when each employee started working. To make the entry of this date easier, you will enter three {GETNUMBER} commands that will prompt the user for each part of the date (month, day, and year), and then plug this data into an @DATE function.

16. **With the pointer in cell X63, type {GETNUMBER "Enter the number of the start-date month: ",Month}, then press the ↓ key.**
Now, enter the {GETNUMBER} prompt for the day of the starting date.

17. **With the pointer in cell X64, type {GETNUMBER "Enter the day of the starting date: ",Day}, then press the ↓ key.**
Next, enter the {GETNUMBER} prompt for the year of the starting date.

18. **With the pointer in cell X65, type {GETNUMBER "Enter the last 2 digits of the start-date year: ",Year}, then press the ↓ key.**
Now you need to enter the @DATE function that will use the information stored in the Year, Month, and Day cells. After this @function enters the appropriate date number, the macro will have to format it using the Lotus standard long form date format.

19. **With the pointer in cell X66, type '@DATE(Year,Month,Day)/RFD1 ˜ ˜, then press the ↓ key.**
You need to add only one more command to your Add routine. This will be a {BRANCH} command that returns control to the \M menu macro. This command redisplays the menu, allowing the user to select the Add option again, or to select Sort or Quit.

20. **With the pointer in cell X67, type {BRANCH \M}, then press the Enter key.**
Before you enter the names of the ranges required by the Add routine, you should check the last part of this routine against the one shown in Figure 16.19, and then save your worksheet. When you save it, you will give the worksheet a new file name.

```
X68: [W29]                                                              READY
        W                    X                        Y           Z
49      {GETLABEL "Enter social security number: ",Soc}
50      /CSoc~~{RIGHT}
51      {GETLABEL "Enter first name: ",F_Name}
52      /CF_Name~~{RIGHT}
53      {GETLABEL "Enter last name: ",L_Name}
54      /CL_Name~~{RIGHT}
55      {GETLABEL "Enter department: ",Depart}
56      /CDepart~~{RIGHT}
57      {GETLABEL "Enter position: ",Pos}
58      /CPos~~{RIGHT}
59      {GETLABEL "Enter supervisor's initials: ",S_Name}
60      /CS_Name~~{RIGHT}
61      {GETNUMBER "Enter annual salary: ",Sal}
62      /CSal~~/RF,0~~{RIGHT}
63      {GETNUMBER "Enter the number of the start-date month: ",Month}
64      {GETNUMBER "Enter the day of the starting date: ",Day}
65      {GETNUMBER "Enter last 2 digits of the start-date year: ",Year}
66      @DATE(Year,Month,Day)~/RFD1~~
67      {BRANCH \M}
68
C16PDBMC.WK1                        UNDO
```

♦ **Figure 16.19:** *Menu macro with last part of the Add routine*

21. **Save the worksheet under the new file name,**
    C16PDBMC.WK1.
    The {GETLABEL} and {GETNUMBER} commands in the Add routine require several named cells in which to store the input made by the user before copying it to the database. Now you need to add these range names in the cells below.

22. **Referring to Figure 16.20, enter** *Soc* **in cell W69,** *F_Name* **in cell W70,** *L_Name* **in cell W71,** *Depart* **in cell W72,** *Pos* **in cell W73,** *S_Name* **in cell W74,** *Sal* **in cell W75,** *Month* **in cell W76,** *Day* **in cell W77, and** *Year* **in cell W78.**
    Save the worksheet again.

23. **Save the worksheet under the same name.**

Creating Submenus

You can arrange the menu macros that you create in a hierarchy containing multiple levels, just like the standard 1-2-3 command menus. To see how you go about creating submenus, you will now create one for your menu macro. This menu will give the user a chance to choose between sorting the data alphabetically by name, by department and starting date, or back to the original order by record number.

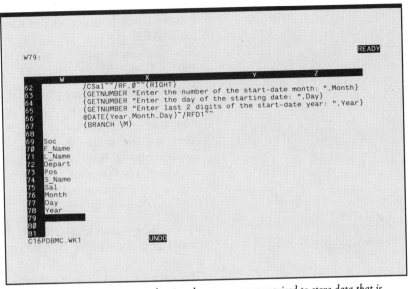

W79:

READY

```
        W           X              Y              Z
62          /CSa1~~/RF,Ø~~{RIGHT}
63          {GETNUMBER "Enter the number of the start-date month: ",Month}
64          {GETNUMBER "Enter the day of the starting date: ",Day}
65          {GETNUMBER "Enter last 2 digits of the start-date year: ",Year}
66          @DATE(Year,Month,Day)~/RFD1~~
67          {BRANCH \M}
68
69  Soc
70  F_Name
71  L_Name
72  Depart
73  Pos
74  S_Name
75  Sal
76  Month
77  Day
78  Year
79
80
81
C16PDBMC.WK1                    UNDO
```

◆ **Figure 16.20:** *Menu macro showing the range names required to store data that is input during the Add routine*

To create this second menu level, you need to add a {MENUBRANCH} command in the cell named Sort. That way, when you select the Sort option on the main menu, its {MENUBRANCH} command will transfer control to the Sort cell, which in turn will execute the second {MENUBRANCH} command, displaying the Sort menu options.

1. **Move the pointer to cell W80, type** *Sort,* **then press the → key and enter** {*MENUBRANCH Sort_Menu*} **in cell X80.**
   Now enter the options for the Sort menu.

2. **Enter** *Sort_Menu* **as the name for the sorting menu in cell W82, enter** *Name–Sort* **as the first option in cell X82, enter** *Department–Sort* **as the second option in cell Y82, enter** *Original–Sort* **as the third option in cell Z82, and then enter** *Return* **as the last option in cell AA82.**
   Next, enter the menu option descriptions.

3. **Enter** *Sort database alphabetically by last name and first name* **as the Name–Sort description in cell X83, enter** *Sort database by department and starting date* **as the Department–Sort option description in cell Y83, enter** *Sort database by record number to return it to original order* **as the Original–Sort option description in cell Z83, and enter**

Return to main menu as the Return option description in cell AA83.

Now you need to enter the macro instructions for each Sort menu option. These will all consist of {BRANCH} commands.

4. **Enter {BRANCH Name_Sort} in cell X84, enter {BRANCH Dept_Sort} in cell Y84, enter {BRANCH Rec_Sort} in cell Z84, and enter {BRANCH \M} in cell AA84.**

Next, you need to start the Name_Sort routine. Because sorting involves highlighting the data range and then rearranging data on the screen, the first commands in this routine will be {WINDOWS-OFF} to prevent redrawing the screen display and /Data Sort Reset (/DSR) to clear the data range.

5. **Move the pointer to cell W87, type *Name_Sort*, and press the → key; then enter {WINDOWSOFF}/DSR in cell X87, and press the ↓ key.**

The second group of commands will mark the data range by pointing. Remember that the sorting data range doesn't include the first row of field names.

6. **With the pointer in cell X88, type D{HOME}{DOWN}.{END}{RIGHT}{END}{DOWN} ˜ , then press the ↓ key.**

The *D* selects the Data-Range option, {HOME} moves the pointer to A1, {DOWN} moves it to A2 (the first cell of the data range), the period anchors the range, then {END}{RIGHT} highlights through the last field in the database, {END}{DOWN} highlights through the last record, and the tilde enters the new data range. Next, the macro will select the primary and secondary keys for sorting and then select the Go option to perform the sort.

7. **With the pointer in cell X89, type PLast.Name ˜ A ˜ SFirst.Name ˜ A ˜ G, then press the ↓ key.**

Because you assigned range names to the field entries in the first record of the database, you use them in the macro. The *P* selects the Primary-Key option, which enters the LAST.NAME field as the primary key, and then *A* selects ascending sort order. The *S* selects the Secondary-Key option, which enters the FIRST.NAME field as the secondary key, then *A* selects ascending sort order, and the *G* selects the Go option to perform the sort. Now enter the last macro instructions in this routine.

8. **With the pointer in cell X90, type {WINDOWSON}{BRANCH \M}, then press Enter.**

The Dept_Sort and Rec_Sort routines are identical to the Name-_Sort routine, except for the primary and secondary sorting keys that they use. The best way to complete this macro is to copy the Name-_Sort routine and then modify the third line of each set of macro instructions.

9. **Referring to Figure 16.21, enter the routine names Dept-_Sort in W92 and Rec_Sort in W97; copy the macro instructions from the Name_Sort routine; and modify the third line of each set of macro instructions in cells X94 and X99, as shown in the figure.**
Now you need to name the ranges used by this menu macro.

10. **Move the pointer to cell W41, select /Range Name Labels Right (/RNLR), move the pointer to cell W97, then press Enter.**
One more range must be named. In the Rec_Sort routine, you specified *Rec#* as the range name for the primary sorting key. This range name has not yet been assigned to the first record number in the database because you added the record numbers after you used the /Range Name Labels Down (/RNLD) command to name the others.

11. **Press the Home key to move the pointer to cell A1, then select /Range Name Labels Down (/RNLD), and press Enter.**
Save the worksheet now.

12. **Save the worksheet under the same file name.**

Testing and Using Your Menu Macro

Now you are ready to test your menu macro and see how it works. If you encounter any errors, note their location, and then check the macro instructions there against those in the preceding steps. If you still can't find the error, turn on STEP mode (Alt-F2), then execute the menu macro again, pressing the spacebar to advance the macro a step at a time until the error recurs.

1. **Press Alt-M.**
The main menu with the options Add, Sort, and Quit should now appear in the control panel.

2. **Press the → key to highlight the Sort option and then the Quit option; as you do, notice the descriptions beneath them in the control panel.**
As you move the pointer to each option, you see its description appear.

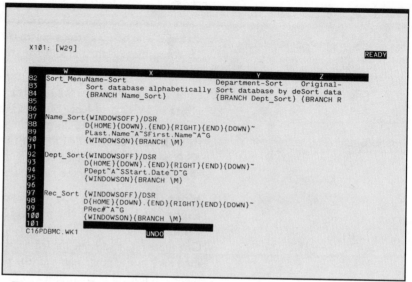

◆ **Figure 16.21:** *Sort_Menu routines for custom menu options*

3. **Type Q to select the Quit option.**
   The program should return you immediately to READY mode, and the custom menu should disappear.

4. **Press Alt-M, then type A to select the Add option.**
   The macro should automatically input the record number (20) in cell A21, and move the pointer to B21.

5. **Type 455–11–0344 in response to the prompt to enter the social security number, then press Enter.**
   Notice that it's no longer necessary to enter an apostrophe before you type this number, as {GETLABEL} does this for you.

6. **Type *Janet* as the first name, then press Enter.**
   Next, enter the last name.

7. **Type *Ball* as the last name, then press Enter.**
   Enter the department now.

8. **Type *ADMN* as the department, then press Enter.**
   Enter the position next.

9. **Type *Admn Asst* as the position, then press Enter.**
   Enter the initials of the supervisor.

10. **Type** *KN* **as the initials, then press Enter.**

    Next, enter the salary.

11. **Type 40000 as the annual salary, then press Enter.**

    Notice that the macro automatically formats this value with the Comma format and 0 decimal places.

12. **Type 4 as the number of the month for the starting date, then press Enter.**

    Next, you enter the day.

13. **Type** *11* **as the number of the day for the starting date, then press Enter.**

    Finally, you enter the year.

14. **Type 89 as the last two digits of the year for the starting date, then press Enter.**

    The macro should enter the date April 11, 1989, in cell I21 and format it to the Lotus standard long form, as shown in Figure 16.22.

15. **Type S to select the Sort option.**

    The Sort menu should now appear in the control panel, as shown in Figure 16.23.

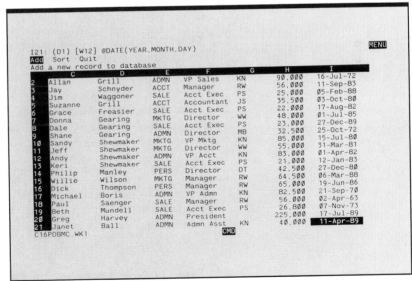

♦ **Figure 16.22:** *Adding a new record to the database using the Add menu option*

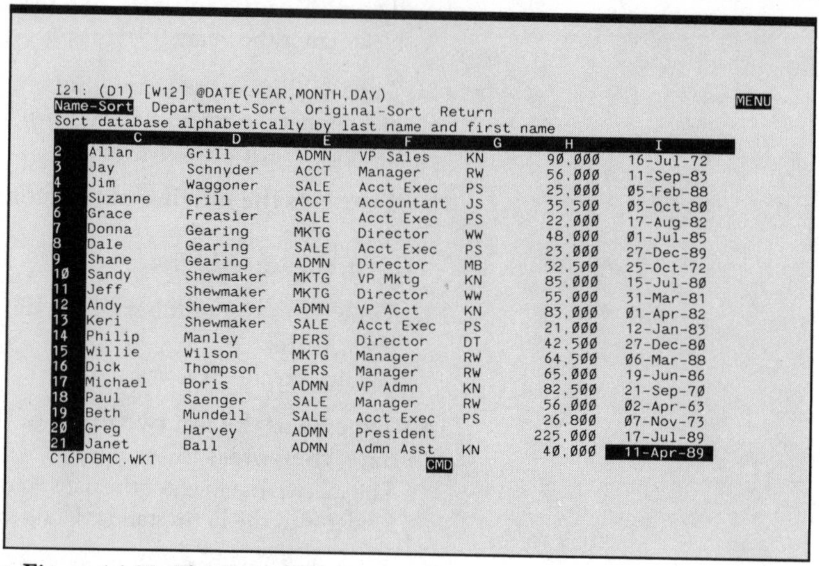

I21: (D1) [W12] @DATE(YEAR,MONTH,DAY) MENU
Name-Sort Department-Sort Original-Sort Return
Sort database alphabetically by last name and first name

	C	D	E	F	G	H	I
2	Allan	Grill	ADMN	VP Sales	KN	90,000	16-Jul-72
3	Jay	Schnyder	ACCT	Manager	RW	56,000	11-Sep-83
4	Jim	Waggoner	SALE	Acct Exec	PS	25,000	05-Feb-88
5	Suzanne	Grill	ACCT	Accountant	JS	35,500	03-Oct-80
6	Grace	Freasier	SALE	Acct Exec	PS	22,000	17-Aug-82
7	Donna	Gearing	MKTG	Director	WW	48,000	01-Jul-85
8	Dale	Gearing	SALE	Acct Exec	PS	23,000	27-Dec-89
9	Shane	Gearing	ADMN	Director	MB	32,500	25-Oct-72
10	Sandy	Shewmaker	MKTG	VP Mktg	KN	85,000	15-Jul-80
11	Jeff	Shewmaker	MKTG	Director	WW	55,000	31-Mar-81
12	Andy	Shewmaker	ADMN	VP Acct	KN	83,000	01-Apr-82
13	Keri	Shewmaker	SALE	Acct Exec	PS	21,000	12-Jan-83
14	Philip	Manley	PERS	Director	DT	42,500	27-Dec-80
15	Willie	Wilson	MKTG	Manager	RW	64,500	06-Mar-88
16	Dick	Thompson	PERS	Manager	RW	65,000	19-Jun-86
17	Michael	Boris	ADMN	VP Admn	KN	82,500	21-Sep-70
18	Paul	Saenger	SALE	Manager	RW	56,000	02-Apr-63
19	Beth	Mundell	SALE	Acct Exec	PS	26,800	07-Nov-73
20	Greg	Harvey	ADMN	President		225,000	17-Jul-89
21	Janet	Ball	ADMN	Admn Asst	KN	40,000	11-Apr-89

C16PDBMC.WK1 CMD

♦ **Figure 16.23:** *The custom Sort menu*

16. **Type *R* to select the Return option.**
    This should return you to the main menu of your custom menu.

17. **Type *SN* to sort the database by name.**
    The database should now be sorted alphabetically in last name and first name order.

18. **Type *SD* to sort the database by department and salary.**
    The database should now be sorted alphabetically by department and by salary in descending order (you won't be able to verify this, as the SALARY field isn't in view).

19. **Type *SO* to sort the database by record and return it to its original order.**
    The database should once again be numerically sorted by record number.

20. **Type *Q* to select the Quit option again.**

Transferring Data between Files

The file manipulation macro commands (shown in Figure 16.6) allow you to transfer data directly from a text file into a 1-2-3 worksheet or from a 1-2-3 worksheet without using the commands on the /File Import or /Print File menu. These commands can process two types of ASCII files: the standard text files, which store their data in a series of bytes divided by lines; or sequential files, which store their data as a continuous stream of bytes.

◆ **Table 16.6:** *File Manipulation Macro Commands*

Keyword & Arguments	Function
{CLOSE}	Closes the file previously opened with an {OPEN} statement.
{FILESIZE *location*}	Enters the size (in bytes) of the currently open file into the *location*.
{GETPOS *location*}	Determines the current position of the byte pointer in the open file and enters this value in the *location*.
{OPEN *file-name,access-type*}	Opens a text file for processing in read-only or read/write mode, depending upon the *access-type*, with *r* for read-only access, *m* for modify access, or *a* for append access for existing text files; and *w* for read/write access for new text files.
{READ *byte-count,location*}	Copies the number of bytes specified by the *byte-count* argument into *location*, starting at the current byte pointer position in the open text file.
{READLN *location*}	Copies the remainder of the current line into *location*, starting at the current byte pointer position in the open text file, and then advances the byte pointer to the beginning of the next line.

◆ **Table 16.6:** *File Manipulation Macro Commands (continued)*

Keyword & Arguments	Function
{SETPOS *offset-number*}	Positions the byte pointer in the open text file at *offset-number* bytes from the first byte in the file (which is counted as 0).
{WRITE *string*}	Copies *string* into the open text file, starting at the current postion of the byte pointer.
{WRITELN *string*}	Copies *string* into the open text file and adds a carriage return and linefeed to terminate the current line, starting at the current postion of the byte pointer.

The text file is the type created by most word processing software. Each line in this type of file is terminated by a carriage-return (ASCII code 13) and linefeed character (ASCII code 10). You can process this type of file by using the {READLN} command, which is set up to read text into a 1-2-3 worksheet file line by line rather than character by character. Each line of text in the file is read into and stored in a separate cell of the worksheet.

To transfer 1-2-3 data line by line to another file, you use the {WRITELN} command. This command transfers the contents of a worksheet cell to a new file as a single line of text.

To process a sequential ASCII file, you use the {READ} and {WRITE} commands. These commands read data into a worksheet file or write worksheet data to a new file character by character. The {READ} statement can copy up to 240 bytes from a sequential file into a 1-2-3 worksheet cell. The {WRITE} statement transfers one or more characters from a worksheet cell into the current position in the new file.

When you set up macros to process data between files using such commands, you begin by entering an {OPEN} statement, whose first argument specifies the complete *file-name* of the existing file to be used (if you are transferring data from it into a 1-2-3 worksheet) or the file name of a new file (if you are transferring data out of the worksheet).

After specifying the file name, you enter the *access-type* argument, which consists of a letter code (in uppercase or lowercase) that specifies the mode of transfer. The four possible letter codes are:

- R (read) opens an existing file with read-only access, which means that you can't write into the file but you can transfer data from the text file into the worksheet. The byte pointer is placed at the beginning of the file when you use this access type.

- W (write) opens a new file with read- and write-access, which you can use to transfer data from a worksheet to the ASCII file format.

- M (modify) opens an existing file with read- and write-access and places the byte pointer at the beginning of the file to allow transfer of data between the open file and the worksheet in either direction.

- A (append) opens an existing file with read- and write-access and places the byte pointer at the end of the file to allow transfer of data between the open file and the worksheet in either direction.

Note that if you use the W (write) code to open an *existing* file, 1-2-3 will erase its contents when it opens the file. For this reason, be sure that you open all existing files with the M (modify) or A (append) code when you want to add data to them.

Both text and sequential files number the position of each byte in the file, beginning with the first byte at position 0 and increasing by 1 for each subsequent byte until the last byte in the file is reached. The {FILESIZE} command obtains the total number of bytes in the file. The program maintains a byte pointer that indicates the current position. To obtain the current position of the pointer, you can use the {GETPOS} command. The {SETPOS} command resets the byte pointer to a new byte position in the file.

You can process data between only one worksheet and ASCII file at a time. When your macro has finished reading or writing data between the two, you must add a {CLOSE} statement before opening another file into which or out of which you will transfer data in the currently retrieved worksheet.

Summary

Troubleshooting

Question: When debugging my macros, I often receive the macro error message *Invalid range name in* followed by a reference to the cell containing the error. I know that this error is caused when a range name used in my macro doesn't yet exist. What can I do to prevent this kind of error?

Answer: When you are creating complex macros, it is easy to forget to name a range that is required by the macro. One of the best ways to prevent this type of problem is to use the /Range Name Table command (/RNT) after you complete your macro to obtain an up-to-date table of all range names. Next, print this range name table and print out the complete contents of your macro. You can then compare them to make sure that each range name you've referenced in the macro appears in the range name table.

Question: When I run my macro, some of the values critical to the worksheet aren't properly updated even though recalculation in the worksheet is set to Automatic. What is the problem, and how can I solve it?

Answer: The program seldom recalculates the worksheet when a macro is being executed. For this reason, you should add the {RECALC} or {RECALC-COL} command to your macro at any point where values in a particular range should be updated. As arguments for these commands, you enter the name of the range that contains the formulas to be recalculated. You can even set up logical formulas as the second argument for these commands to ensure that recalculation takes place until a certain condition is met.

Essential Techniques

To Create Menu Macros

1. Enter a {MENUBRANCH} or {MENUCALL} command that transfers control of the macro to the cell that contains the first menu option.

2. Enter single-word menu options (up to 8 total) in a single row of the worksheet. Make sure that each option is entered into its own cell, and that the cells are adjacent.

3. Enter descriptions for each menu option in the cells directly below the menu options. These descriptions cannot be longer than the width of the screen.

4. Enter the macro instructions for each menu option in the cells immediately below those that contain the menu option descriptions.

5. Assign a range name such as \M to the cell containing the {MENU-BRANCH} or {MENUCALL} command.

6. Assign the name you used as the *location* argument for the {MENU-BRANCH} or {MENUCALL} command as the range name for the cell that contains the first menu option.

To Have Your Custom Menu Automatically Displayed When You Start 1-2-3

1. Name the cell that contains the first {MENUBRANCH} or {MENU-CALL} command in your custom menu \0 (also give it another range name such as \M or \T so that you can execute it manually).

2. Save the final version of the worksheet that contains the custom menu *AUTO123.WK1*. Make sure that this worksheet is located in the designated default directory, that the cursor is located in the position where you want the user to see it when the file is retrieved, and that the menu is activated. Also, make sure the /Worksheet Global Default Autoexec setting is still set to Yes.

Review

Important Terms You Should Know

advanced macro command
branching
endless loop
indirect branching
keyword

passing values
routine
subroutine
subroutine call
/X commands

Test Your Knowledge

1. To have your macro enter *500* in a cell named *Income* in the worksheet, you enter the advanced macro command _____.

2. To have your macro enter *275* in the third column of the second row of a table named *Expenses*, you enter the advanced macro command

   _____.

3. To have your macro erase all the data in a data table named *Taxes*, you enter the advanced macro command _____.

4. To have 1-2-3 recalculate a range named *Orders* when a macro is running, you enter the advanced macro command _____.

5. To have your macro convert the value *5679* in a cell named *Total* to a label formatted with the Comma format with 2 decimal places in a cell called *NewTotal*, you enter the advanced macro command

   _____.

6. When using the {IF} command to branch a macro conditionally, you place the action you want performed if the condition is true

in _____ and the action you want performed if it isn't true in
_____.

7. If there are more than two possible outcomes and the name of the
   selection is the same as the name of the branch, you can use the
   _____ advanced macro command instead of the {IF} command.

8. To have a macro return to the place in the macro where a subroutine
   was called before all the instructions in the subroutine are executed,
   you use the _____ advanced macro command.

9. If you want to pass arguments to a subroutine, the subroutine must
   contain a _____ advanced macro command as its first command.

10. To have your macro repeat a subroutine named *Print* three times, you
    enter the advanced macro command _____.

11. To eliminate flicker in the control panel when a macro is running,
    you would enter the advanced macro command _____. To prevent
    flicker in the worksheet display during the execution of a macro, you
    enter the advanced macro command _____.

12. To have your macro display the mode indicator *IMPORT* during a
    macro's execution, you enter the advanced macro command
    _____. To return to the standard display of 1-2-3 mode indicators,
    you enter the advanced macro command _____ before the macro
    ends.

13. To have your macro prompt the user for his or her age and then store
    this information in a cell named *Ages*, you enter the advanced macro
    command _____.

14. To have your macro prompt the user to enter his or her address and
    then store this information in a cell named *Street*, you enter the
    advanced macro command _____.

15. To suspend the execution of your macro for 50 seconds, you enter the
    advanced macro command _____.

Further Exercises

1. Retrieve your worksheet *C16PDBMC.WK1* and add a Print menu
   option to your custom menu. Name the new option *Print*, and enter
   Print contents of the database as the menu option description. When
   the user selects this option, have the macro redefine the print range

(using the same technique the macro uses to redefine the data range to be sorted), and then print this range and return to READY mode.

2. After you have added your new Print option, save the worksheet under the same name. Test the Print option by sorting the worksheet by name before printing it, and then sorting it by department before printing it a second time.

a

Installation and Memory Usage

This appendix gives you detailed instructions on installing Release 2.2 on either a two-disk-drive or hard disk computer system. Following the installation instructions, you will find information on how 1-2-3 uses computer memory. If you need information on how to install the add-in program Allways, refer to Chapter 10, where you will find step-by-step instructions on how to install this print utility.

Disk Inventory

Release 2.2 of 1-2-3 is available in either 5¼-inch or 3½-inch format. If you have Release 2.2 in the 5¼-inch format, your package will contain the following 12 disks:

- System Disk
- Help Disk
- PrintGraph Disk
- Translate Disk
- Install Disk
- Install Library Disk
- Sample Files Disk
- Allways Setup Disk
- Allways Disk 2
- Allways Disk 3
- Allways Disk 4
- Allways Disk 5

If you have Release 2.2 in 3½-inch format, your package will contain these 6 disks:

- System, Help, and PrintGraph Disk
- Translate and Sample Files Disk
- Install and Install Library Disk
- Allways Setup Disk
- Allways Disk 2
- Allways Disk 3

Initializing the System Disk

Unlike Release 2.01 of 1-2-3, Release 2.2 is not copy-protected. Before you can use 1-2-3, however, you *must* initialize the original System disk by running the INIT program. When you run this simple program, 1-2-3 will prompt you to enter your name and the name of your company. After you verify this information, the INIT program will then copy this information onto the System disk. Thereafter, all backup copies that you make of the 1-2-3 System disk will contain this information, which is displayed when you start the program.

To run the INIT program, follow these steps:

1. **Power up your computer; if you are using a two-disk-drive system, you will need to put a copy of your DOS disk into drive A before you turn on the power; after the computer boots and the DOS prompt is displayed, remove the DOS disk.**
   Next, you need to find the original 1-2-3 System disk. The System disk must *not* be write-protected. If you use 5¼-inch disks, be sure that the notch on the System disk is not covered with a write-protect tab. If you use 3½-inch disks, be sure that the tab in the upper right corner covers the square hole. If you use 5¼-inch disks, be sure that you don't run the INIT program on a high-density drive (1.2Mb) if you plan to use 1-2-3 on a double-density drive (360K). If you run INIT on a high-density drive, you will no longer be able to use the System disk in a double-density drive!

2. **Place the System disk in drive A and close the door.**
   To run the INIT program, A: must be the default drive.

3. **Type A: and press Enter.**
   Now, enter the initialization program startup command.

4. **Type INIT and press Enter.**
   An opening screen will appear, explaining the purpose of the INIT program.

5. **Press Enter to continue.**
   A screen prompting you to enter your name will appear. You can enter up to 30 characters here. If you make a mistake in typing, press the Backspace key to delete your errors, and then retype the correct characters.

6. **Type your name and press Enter.**
   You will next be asked to confirm the spelling of your name. Be sure that you have spelled it correctly before you reply in the affirmative.

7. **Type Y to confirm the spelling of your name (if you spot an error, type N and then retype it).**
   Next, you need to enter the name of your company. If you don't use a company name, enter your name again.

8. **Type the name of your company (up to 30 characters) and press Enter.**
   Now you need to confirm the spelling of the company name.

9. **Type Y to confirm the spelling of the company name (if you spot an error, type N and then retype it).**
   A screen displaying your personal and company name will now appear.

10. **Check over the spelling of your name and company; if correct, press Enter to have the INIT program record this information on your System disk; if you see an error, press Ctrl-Break to end the initialization program without saving the changes.**
    As soon as the light in drive A goes out, you can safely remove the System disk.

Making Backup Copies of Your Disks

If you will be using 1-2-3 on a two-disk-drive system, you next need to make backup copies of all your program disks so that you can use them instead of the originals. To do this, you must have a formatted disk for each of the program disks included in your package. Follow these instructions to format disks and then copy the program files onto them:

1. **Place a copy of your DOS system disk in drive A and turn on the computer.**
   Next, you have to format new disks before you can copy the program disks.

2. **Place a new disk in drive B and close the door.**
   You must make sure that the disk you are about to format doesn't contain any data that you need to save, because formatting will erase all files.

3. **Format the new disk in drive B by typing the DOS FORMAT command *FORMAT B:* and pressing Enter; press Enter again when the program prompts you to start the formatting.**
   When the format is complete, you will be prompted to format another.

4. **Type Y when prompted to format another disk; then remove the formatted disk in drive B, replace it with a new disk, and press Enter again.**
   You will repeat this step until you have formatted a disk for each program disk.

5. **Repeat step 4 until you have formatted seven 5¹/₄-inch disks or three 3¹/₂-inch disks; then type *N* and press Enter when prompted to format another disk.**
   Before you copy the disks, you need to label them.

6. **Label your newly formatted disks, using the names as they appear on each original disk.**
   To copy each program disk, you will place the program disk in drive A in place of the DOS disk, and then issue the copy command. Before you put each original disk in drive A, it is a good idea to write-protect it. For 5¹/₄ inch disks, place a write-protect tab over the notch on the right. For 3¹/₂ inch disks, move the plastic tab up so that the square hole is open.

7. **Replace the DOS disk in drive A with one of the original 1-2-3 program disks; then place the blank formatted disk that is marked with the same name in drive B.**
   Now, you will use the DOS COPY command to copy all the files on the original disk in drive A to the blank disk in drive B.

8. **At the A:> prompt, type COPY A:*.* B: and press Enter.**
   DOS will then copy all program files to your backup disk.

9. **Repeat steps 7 and 8 until you have made copies of all your original program disks (except for the Allways disks, which you can't use without a hard disk).**
   Put your original program disks in a safe place.

Copying COMMAND.COM to the 1-2-3 System Disk

The Release 2.2 System disk has insufficient room for all the DOS boot files. This means that you will not be able to start your computer with the 1-2-3 System disk in drive A, as you may have become accustomed to doing if you used Release 1A. Instead, you will have to use a separate working copy of the DOS disk to load these operating-system files, and then replace it with your working copy of the 1-2-3 System disk each time you turn on your computer to do work with the program.

There is, however, still room to copy one of the DOS system files called COM-MAND.COM on the 1-2-3 System disk. By doing this, you will be able to return to the operating-system prompt when exiting from the program without getting the error message *Insert disk with COMMAND.COM in drive A and strike any key when ready.*

To copy this COMMAND.COM file onto the working copy of your 1-2-3 System disk, follow these steps:

1. **Place your DOS disk in drive A.**
   Next, find your working copy of the 1-2-3 System disk.

2. **Place the 1-2-3 System disk in drive B; make sure that this disk is not write-protected.**
   Now you are ready to copy the DOS file COMMAND.COM from the DOS disk in drive A to the 1-2-3 System disk in drive B.

3. **Type COPY and press the spacebar, type A:COMMAND.COM and press the spacebar, then type B: and press Enter.**

Copying on the Program onto Your Hard Disk

If you will be using 1-2-3 on a hard disk, you will want to copy all of the program files into their own directory on drive C. Most users find it convenient to name this directory \123 and place it directly beneath the root directory containing the DOS files (called C:). However, if you are upgrading to Release 2.2 and were previously using Release 2.01 or Release 1A on the hard disk, you may already have a \123 directory containing the 1-2-3 files for this version. In this case, you should delete all the Release 2.01 or 1A program files in this directory before copying the Release 2.2 files into it.

In the rare case that you wish to keep both versions of the program on the hard disk, you will have to create a new directory with a different name on drive C. Perhaps you could name this directory C:\123R2.2 to differentiate it from the Release 2.01 or 1A directory called C:\123.

To copy your 1-2-3 programs onto your hard disk, follow these steps:

1. **Turn on your computer (make sure that drive A is empty or that its door is not closed).**
   Next, you need to create a new directory where you will copy the 1-2-3 program files.

2. **At the C:> prompt, type *MD\123* and press Enter; if you already have a C:\123 directory that contains an earlier version of the program and you wish to maintain it, you need to type another name, such as *MD\123R2.2.***

Before you can copy the files into this new directory, you need to make it current.

3. **Type** *CD\123* **and press Enter.**
   Now locate your 1-2-3 program disks.

4. **Place the 1-2-3 System disk in drive A, close the door, then type COPY** A:*.* **and press Enter.**
   DOS will copy all the files from the System disk in drive A to the C:\123 directory.

5. **When DOS is finished copying files, replace the System disk with another program disk, press the function key F3 (which types COPY** A:*.* **for you), and press Enter; repeat this step until all the program disks are copied onto the hard disk.**
   Don't bother copying the Allways disks, as these are automatically copied when you install the program—see Chapter 10 for details. Also, you don't have to copy the sample worksheets on the Sample Files disk onto the hard disk, as you can use them in the A drive when you work through the 1-2-3 tutorials.

Installing 1-2-3

You can use 1-2-3 without using the Install program first. You will not, however, be able to print the worksheets that you create or display any graphs; to do this, you must run the Install program to configure 1-2-3 to the hardware you are using. Before running the Install program, you should take an inventory of your system. When you run the installation procedure, you will need to supply the program with information on the graphics capability of your system and type of monitor, the type of text printer(s), and the type of graphics printer(s).

When you install Release 2.2, you can designate more than the type of text printer and graphics printer to use in 1-2-3. Later, you can designate which text printer to use with the /Worksheet Global Default Printer Name command (see Appendix B). You can designate which of your graphics devices is to be used from the PrintGraph menu, which you access from the Lotus Access System menu (see Chapter 9).

All this information about your hardware system tells 1-2-3 which drivers to use. At the end of the process, these drivers are saved in a special file named 123.SET unless you give it another name. The file named 123.SET is always used as the default whenever you enter the program startup command *1-2-3* or choose this option from the Lotus Access System menu.

You can, however, store more than one hardware configuration (or driver set) on the System disk in separate files that carry the extension .SET. This enables you to use the same 1-2-3 System disk to run the program on different types of systems. To run 1-2-3 using drivers other than those saved in the default 123.SET file, you enter the startup command, press the spacebar, and then type the name of the SET file (you don't need to add the extension .SET), and press Enter. For example, if you have a driver set named TOSHIBA.SET and you want to use the 1-2-3 System disk on your laptop, you would enter

123 TOSHIBA

as the startup command.

Running the Install Program

To run the Install program, follow the steps outlined below. If you are using 1-2-3 on a hard disk, you must make the directory C:\123 (or whatever you named it) current before you run the program. If you are installing 1-2-3 on a two-disk-drive system, you must put the working copy of the Install disk in drive A.

1. **On a hard disk system, type *CD\123* at the C> prompt and press Enter to make C:\123 the current drive, then type *INSTALL* and press Enter; on a two-disk-drive system, type *INSTALL* and press Enter at the A> prompt.**
   When the Install program is loaded, you will see an opening screen giving you information about the Install program.

2. **Press Enter to begin the Install program.**
   You should now see the Install main menu screen, which looks like the one shown in Figure A.1. You will select the First-Time Installation option from this menu.

3. **Press Enter to select the First-Time Installation option, which is already highlighted.**
   This takes you to another information screen.

4. **Press Enter to continue.**
   Now you are asked if your computer can display graphs. If your system is equipped with some type of graphics adapter, such as a Hercules monochrome card or an EGA or VGA color card, you will answer yes.

5. **If your computer can display graphs, press Enter; if not, press the ↓ key to highlight No, then press Enter.**
   If you answered yes to the graphics question, you are next asked to

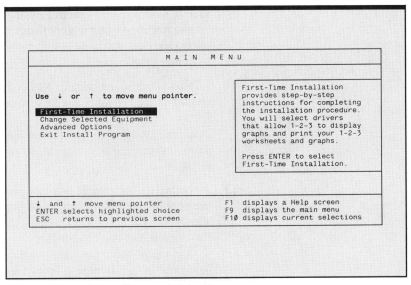

```
                    M A I N   M E N U

┌──────────────────────────────┬──────────────────────────┐
│                              │ First-Time Installation  │
│ Use ↓ or ↑ to move menu pointer. │ provides step-by-step    │
│                              │ instructions for completing│
│ ███████████████████████████  │ the installation procedure.│
│ First-Time Installation      │ You will select drivers  │
│ Change Selected Equipment    │ that allow 1-2-3 to display│
│ Advanced Options             │ graphs and print your 1-2-3│
│ Exit Install Program         │ worksheets and graphs.   │
│                              │                          │
│                              │ Press ENTER to select    │
│                              │ First-Time Installation. │
│                              │                          │
└──────────────────────────────┴──────────────────────────┘

  ↓ and ↑  move menu pointer      F1  displays a Help screen
  ENTER selects highlighted choice  F9  displays the main menu
  ESC   returns to previous screen  F1Ø displays current selections
```

◆ **Figure A.1:** *The Install program's main menu*

indicate how many monitors you have. If you have two monitors connected to your system, you can display text on one and graphics on the other.

6. **If you have only one monitor, press Enter; if you have two monitors, press the ↓ key to highlight No, then press Enter.**
   If you chose the One Monitor option, you are presented with a long list of graphics display options. If you chose the Two Monitors option, you will see a much shorter list. From here, you need to select the high-resolution graphics display that your system supports. Note that some of the options are the same, except that they enable you to display more rows and columns (80 by 25 is standard). If you choose to see more of the worksheet on the screen, the text in each cell will be smaller.

7. **Use the cursor-movement keys to move the pointer to the type of graphics display used by your computer, and press Enter.**
   After you select your graphics display (or if you chose not to display graphs), you will be asked if you have a text printer.

8. **Press Enter to answer yes, or press the ↓ key to highlight No if you don't have a printer connected to your computer.**
   When selecting the type of printer, you first select the brand name.

9. **Use the cursor-movement keys to move the pointer to the brand name of your text printer, and press Enter.**
After you select the brand name, a new screen displaying printer models appears.

10. **Use the cursor-movement keys to move the pointer to the model of text printer used by your computer, and press Enter.**
Next, you are asked if you have another text printer. If you have more than one printer connected to your computer, you can now install it.

11. **To install another text printer, press the ↓ key to move the pointer to the Yes option, then press Enter and repeat steps 9 and 10; when you finish installing all text printers, press Enter to select the No option.**
Now you are asked if you want to print graphs. Not all text printers have graphics capabilities. If yours does, you will now install the same printer(s) as a graphics printer. If you use a different printer or plotter for printing graphs, you must install it as the graphics device.

12. **Press Enter to select the Yes option, or press the ↓ key to move the pointer to No and press Enter if you don't have a printer that can print graphs.**
If you answered Yes, you again select the brand name from one screen of options and the model name from another.

13. **Select the brand and model of all graphics printers connected to your system. When you finish selecting them, select the No option.**
After you install your last graphics printer, you are asked if you want to name your driver set.

14. **Press Enter to answer No and have the Install program name your driver set *123.SET*; move the pointer to Yes and press Enter to give the driver set your own name, then type in your own file name (eight characters or less with no spaces), replacing *123*, and press Enter.**
If you answered No, you will see a new screen indicating that Install will save your selections as soon as you press Enter.

15. **Press Enter to save your changes in the default *123.SET* file; if you are using a two-disk-drive system, you will be prompted to change disks; before you switch disks, be sure that the disk you replace in drive A is not write-protected.**

After the driver set is saved, another screen of information appears. If you want to see the contents of the driver set, you press F10.

16. **Press Enter to leave the Install program; this takes you to the Exit screen, where you press the ↓ key to move the pointer to the Yes option and press Enter.**
This returns you to the DOS prompt, where you can start 1-2-3 (see Chapter 1 for details).

Changing Your Hardware

If, later, you make changes to your hardware—such as replacing your monochrome monitor with a VGA color monitor and graphics adapter—you will need to run the Install program to make the appropriate changes to your driver file by selecting the Change Selected Equipment option.

To do this, run the Install program from the operating-system prompt, or start this program by choosing the Install option from the Lotus Access System (you see this menu system whenever you enter *LOTUS* as the startup command). When the Install main menu appears, use the ↓ key to move the pointer to the Change Selected Equipment option, and press Enter. Then select either the Screen Display, Text Printer(s), or Graphics Printer(s) option, depending upon which type of equipment you wish to install.

Changing the Collating Sequence

You can also use the Install program to change the default sorting sequence. To do this, select Advanced Options from the Install main menu. For further details, refer to the section on Modifying the Collating Sequence in Chapter 11.

Lotus 1-2-3 and Computer Memory

Lotus 1-2-3 maintains the 1-2-3 program as well as all the data that you add to your worksheet in the computer's memory. If the amount of free memory available is 4,096 bytes or less, 1-2-3 displays a MEM indicator on the status line to warn you that the amount of memory is low. If you then continue to add data to your worksheet, you will eventually run out of memory and 1-2-3 will beep, go into ERROR mode, and display the error message *Memory full*.

IBM personal computers can utilize three different types of memory: conventional, expanded, and extended. Of these three types, Releases 2.01 and 2.2 support only the conventional and expanded types (extended memory is found only in computers using the Intel 80286 or 80386 microprocessor).

Conventional memory, which is also known as RAM, or random access memory, represents the basic memory of the computer of which only 640K (or kilobytes) is recognized by DOS.

Expanded memory is memory above 640K up to 8 megabytes. It is found primarily in IBM personal computers that use the Intel 8088 microprocessor, and it is used to overcome the 640K RAM barrier set up by DOS. Releases 2.01 and 2.2 of 1-2-3 support only expanded memory that meets the Lotus/Intel/Microsoft (or LIM) Expanded Memory Specification (version 4.0). As this is not the only type of expanded memory specification, you should always make sure that any expanded memory board that you purchase for use with 1-2-3 meets the LIM specification.

The Release 2.2 program requires a minimum of 320K RAM (conventional memory) to run. The memory not used to hold DOS and any other memory-resident utilities that you use is available for your worksheet data. Note, however, that when the Undo feature is enabled (the default when you install 1-2-3), you have only about half of this remaining conventional memory available. This is because the program stores a backup copy of the worksheet as it exists before you make a change in an undo buffer.

If you equip your computer with expanded memory, you can greatly increase the size of the worksheets that you can build. When Undo is disabled, the program can utilize up to 2 megabytes. When the Undo feature is active, 1-2-3 can handle between 4 and 5 megabytes of expanded memory, but half of this is used to create a copy of the previous version of all your files.

The program can store only labels, formulas, and real (decimal) numbers in expanded memory. All other parts of the worksheet, data, and program are stored in conventional memory at all times. This includes named ranges, graph settings, the results of string formulas, and all add-in programs that you attach. Moreover, for each entry in expanded memory, 1-2-3 must maintain a cell pointer in conventional memory (each cell pointer uses four bytes).

Because of this pointer system and the fact that many worksheet components remain in conventional memory, you will find that you can run out of conventional memory long before you have used up all of your expanded memory. Keep in mind that although adding expanded memory will enable you to create larger worksheets, it does not mean that there is a one-to-one correspondence between the size of the expanded memory and the maximum size of the worksheet (it is usually much less). To see how much conventional and expanded memory is available at any given time when using 1-2-3, use the /Worksheet Status command. On the status screen, the first number after the Conventional memory and Expanded memory headings represents the amount of memory (in bytes) that is still available.

b

Modifying the Program Defaults

Whenever you start up 1-2-3, the program looks for the default configuration in a file named 123.CNF located on the System disk. This file contains settings that control the following:

- The printer you are using and its interface.

- The margin settings, page length, and whether you use single sheets or continuous-feed paper (Wait) in printing.

- The directory where your 1-2-3 worksheets and graphs are to be saved and retrieved.

- Default settings for the display of currency and the punctuation in numbers, dates, and time. In Release 2.2, you can also control default settings for the display of negative values in the worksheet and whether the clock or worksheet file name is displayed on the status line.

- The configuration for accessing the online help.

※ *New in 2.2*   - Default settings that determine whether autoexec macros are automatically executed when their worksheets are retrieved, whether add-in programs are automatically attached when the program is started, and whether the Undo and Beep features are enabled.

You can customize all of these settings from the /Worksheet Global Default menu (/WGD). This menu, along with the Release 2.2 Default Settings sheet, is shown in Figure B.1. Remember that after you change any global default settings with these options, you need to select the Update option to have them saved in the 123.CNF file.

You have already learned how to change many of these defaults in earlier chapters, where you studied particular aspects of the program. This appendix covers the default settings that you haven't yet examined.

Changing the Help Default

The Help option allows you to choose between two methods for accessing the program's online help: Instant and Removable (the default). With the Removable method, the help file is closed when you leave help screens and return to the spreadsheet. This means that you can remove the disk with help files during your session. It also means that help access is slower than with the Instant method. If you use 1-2-3 on a two-disk-drive system, leave this default set to Removable.

With the Instant help method, the help file stays open after you use the help facility the first time. This gives you faster access to the various help screens

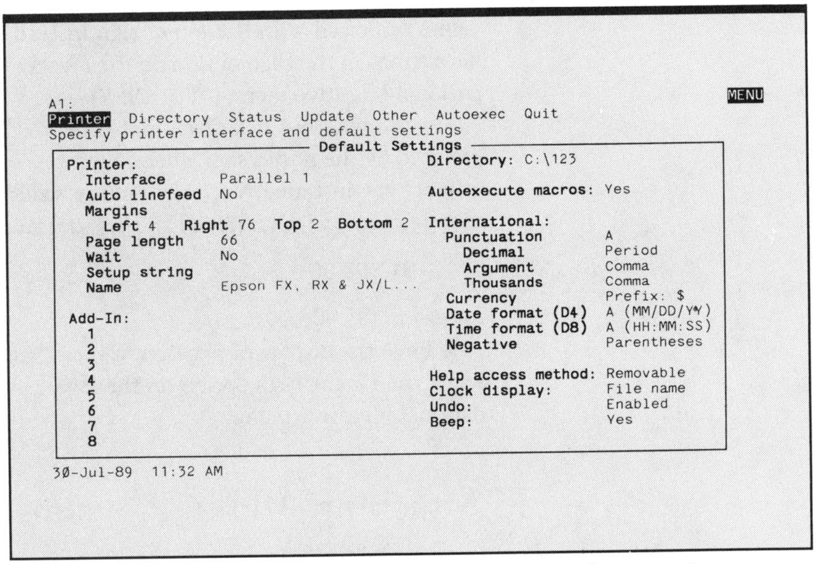

◆

```
A1:                                                          MENU
Printer  Directory  Status  Update  Other  Autoexec  Quit
Specify printer interface and default settings
                          ── Default Settings ──
  Printer:                              Directory: C:\123
    Interface      Parallel 1
    Auto linefeed  No              Autoexecute macros: Yes
    Margins
      Left 4  Right 76  Top 2  Bottom 2  International:
    Page length    66                  Punctuation    A
    Wait           No                    Decimal      Period
    Setup string                        Argument      Comma
    Name           Epson FX, RX & JX/L...  Thousands    Comma
                                        Currency      Prefix: $
  Add-In:                              Date format (D4)  A (MM/DD/YY)
    1                                  Time format (D8)  A (HH:MM:SS)
    2                                    Negative      Parentheses
    3
    4                               Help access method: Removable
    5                               Clock display:      File name
    6                               Undo:               Enabled
    7                               Beep:               Yes
    8

30-Jul-89  11:32 AM
```

◆ **Figure B.1:** *The /Worksheet Global Default menu with Default Settings sheet*

during your session in 1-2-3. Choose the Instant option if you use the program on a hard disk system.

✳ *New in 2.2* Turning Off the Beep

Whenever you make an error in moving the pointer, selecting a menu option, or entering or editing data, 1-2-3 then goes into ERROR mode and the program beeps at you. If you wish, you can permanently silence this beeping by selecting the No option on the /Worksheet Global Default Other Beep menu (/WGDOBN), and then selecting the Update option to save this change.

Note that doing this not only turns off the beep when you make an error or the program goes into ERROR mode, but also when you use the {BEEP} advanced macro command. This means that {BEEP} commands in all your macros will be ignored when you next execute them.

To turn the beep back on, select the Yes option on the /Worksheet Global Default Other Beep menu (/WGDOBY).

✳ *New in 2.2* Changing the Display of Negative Numbers

By default, 1-2-3 displays negative values in parentheses when you format them with the Comma (,) or Currency format using either the /Worksheet Global Format or /Range Format command. If you wish to have negative values displayed with the minus sign instead of enclosed in parentheses, you need to select the Sign option on the /Worksheet Global Default Other International Negative menu (/WGDOINS).

After you do this, negative numbers in cells of the worksheet will always be prefaced by the minus sign when formatted with the Comma (,) or Currency format. For instance, if you enter the value −1908 in the worksheet and then format it with Currency and two decimal places, it will appear as

   −$1,908.00

instead of ($1,908.00).

To have the display of negative values once again enclosed in parentheses, select the Parentheses option on the /Worksheet Global Default Other International Negative menu.

Attaching Add-In Programs Automatically upon Startup

✳ *New in 2.2*

As you know from studying the use of Allways in Chapter 10 and the Macro Library Manager in Chapter 15 (Appendix G lists other add-in programs available for Release 2.2), in Release 2.2 you attach such add-in programs after starting 1-2-3, using the Attach option on the /Add-In menu.

If you wish, you can have up to eight different add-in programs automatically attached when you start 1-2-3. Moreover, you can even have one of these eight automatically invoked. To designate that an add-in program be attached each time you start 1-2-3, you select the Add-In option on the /Worksheet Global Default Other menu (/WGDOA). This brings up the menu options

   Set Cancel Quit

Select the Set option (S), and you are presented with a menu of numbers 1–8. Select the number of the add-in program to be auto-attached, and 1-2-3 will display a list of the file names of all add-in programs (with the extension .ADN) installed in the directory from which you started 1-2-3. Move the pointer to the name of the add-in program and press Enter. You will then be presented with the options

   No-Key 7 8 9 10

Select the number of the function key (F7–F10) that you want to assign to the add-in, or select the No-Key option (N). After you assign the key, the program will display

   No Yes

If you select the Yes option (Y), 1-2-3 automatically invokes that program's menu or starts the add-in as soon as it has been loaded into memory (attached). Remember that you can designate only *one* add-in program as an auto-invoke program. Select the No option (N) to just have the program attached at startup.

If you later decide that you no longer want a particular add-in program automatically attached each time you start 1-2-3, you need to select the Cancel option on the /Worksheet Global Default Other Add-In menu (/WGDOAC). Then select the number (1–8) that you assigned to the add-in program, and choose the Quit option. Don't forget to select the Update option on the /Worksheet Global Default menu to have these saved in the 123.CNF file.

C

Lotus 1-2-3
Menu Trees

New in 2.2

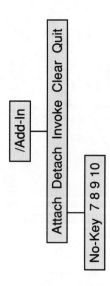

/Add-In

Attach   Detach   Invoke   Clear   Quit

No-Key   7   8   9   10

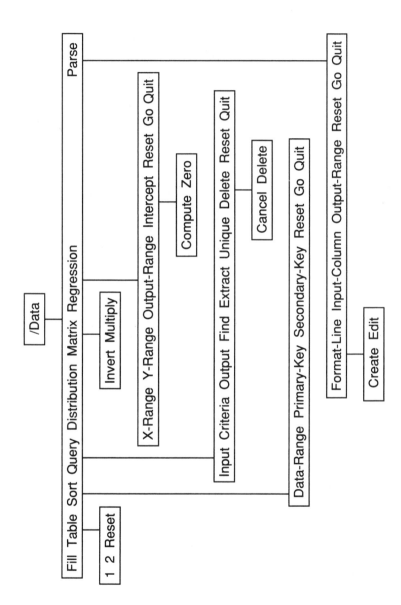

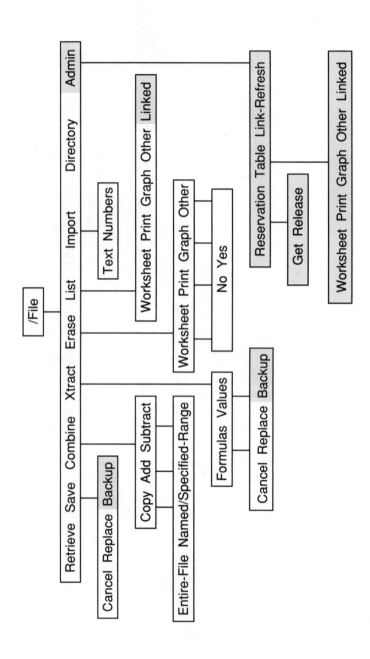

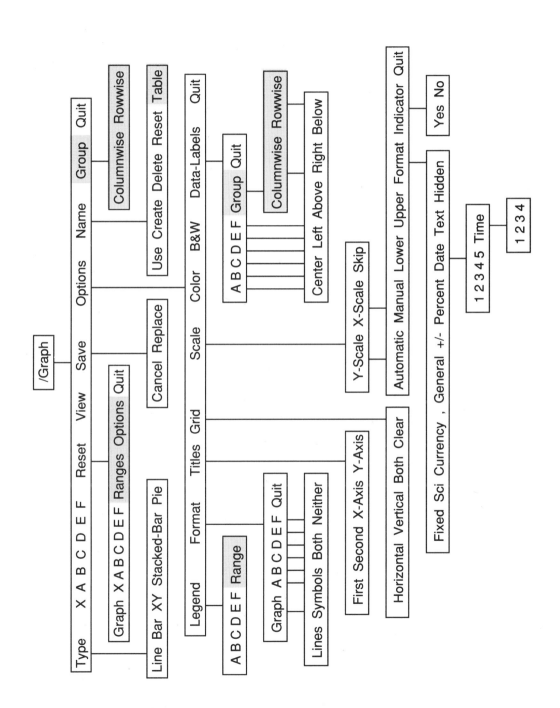

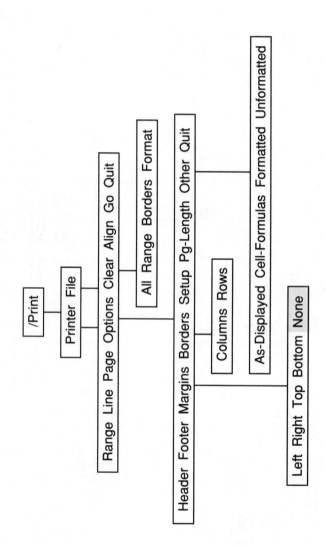

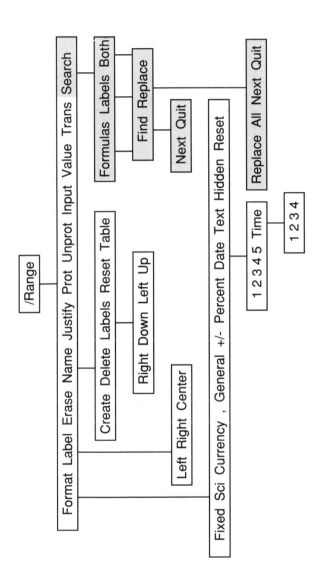

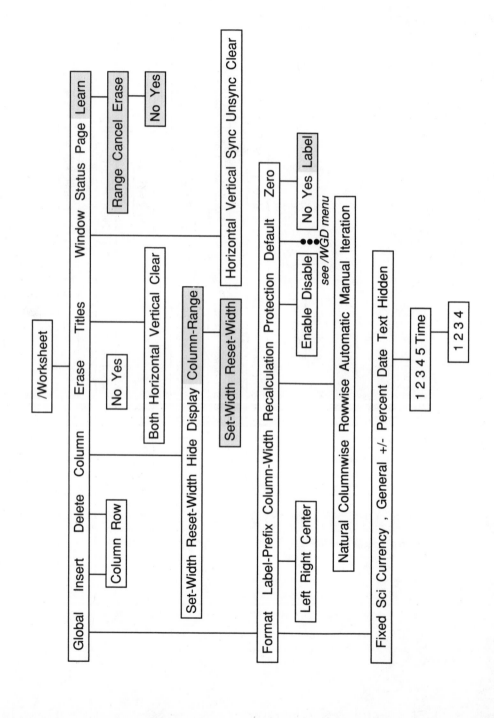

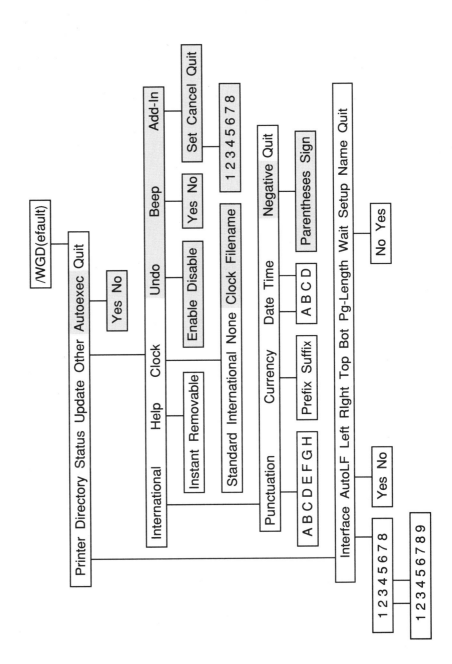

d

Networking
1-2-3

A networked version of Release 2.2 is available for all major PC networks, including those from IBM, Novell, 3Com Corporation, and Banyan Systems. Three editions of Release 2.2 are available for networks:

◆ Standard edition, which contains a complete set of 1-2-3 software and documentation, plus the license for one user on the network or on a standalone personal computer.

◆ Server edition, which contains a complete set of 1-2-3 software, network documentation, and administration software, a complete set of documentation on using 1-2-3, and the license for one user on the network.

◆ Node edition, which contains the license for one user on the network and a complete set of documentation on using 1-2-3 (no software is included).

Although the Standard edition can be installed on the network server, the Server edition (which costs $100 more) includes utilities designed to make it easier for the network administrator to install and manage all networked Lotus programs.

Sharing Worksheet Files on the Network

One of the most important benefits of using 1-2-3 on a network is that it is easy to share data generated with the program. To limit access to particular worksheets stored on the server, Release 2.2 relies upon the controls provided by the network's operating system (you can, of course, prevent a user from retrieving a worksheet file by password-protecting it—see Chapter 13 for information on how to do this).

Release 2.2 does, however, automatically limit concurrent access to worksheet files. Concurrency controls in 1-2-3 are referred to as reservations. A *reservation* is a file-locking device that prevents different users on the network from making changes to the same file at the same time.

Each file on the network has a reservation, and only one person can have that reservation at a time. The person who has the file's reservation is the only one who can save changes to the worksheet under the same file name.

The reservation status of a 1-2-3 file on the network is either *available* or *unavailable*. If you retrieve a worksheet that is available, 1-2-3 reads it into memory with its reservation so that you can save your changes under the same file name. If you attempt to retrieve a worksheet whose reservation is unavailable, the program will ask you if you want to retrieve the file without its reservation. If you say yes, 1-2-3 retrieves and displays the RO (read-only) indicator on the status line to let you know that you can't save changes to this file under its current file name.

When you use the /File Save command and try to save your changes under a file name that has already been used, the program will automatically get that file's reservation for you if it is then available.

Getting and Releasing Reservations

Release 2.2 includes a Reservation option on its new /File Admin menu that allows you to either get or release the current file's reservation. Although you will automatically get the file's reservation when you use /File Save, you can also use the /File Admin Reservation Get command (/FARG) to obtain it before you use /File Save, if the reservation was not available when you first retrieved the file.

When you are ready to give up a file's reservation, you can use the /File Admin Reservation Release command (/FARR) to do so before you exit from 1-2-3 or clear the worksheet from memory. Note, however, that you automatically lose the file's reservation when you select the /Worksheet Erase Yes command, use /File Retrieve to retrieve a new file, use /File Save and save the file under a new file name, or use the /Quit command to exit from 1-2-3.

You need to remember that once you release a file's reservation, its contents may be changed by another user. If this is the case, when you then try to get the file reservation later on during the work session (with the /File Admin Reservation Get command), 1-2-3 will display an error message letting you know that the current file has changed on disk and that this is why you can't get the reservation. When this happens, you need to use the /File Retrieve command to load the most current version of the worksheet file into memory.

e

LICS
(Lotus International Character Set)
Table

The Lotus International Character Set, or LICS for short, is shown in Table E.1. This special character set is made up of a series of decimal codes from 0 to 255. The first 128 codes, from 0 to 127, correspond to the ASCII codes. Codes above 127 are unique to the Lotus products, including Release 2 of 1-2-3 (Release 3.0 uses a superset of the LICS codes), Symphony, and Manuscript. As you can see from the table, most of these higher codes represent foreign-language symbols.

To enter one of the LICS characters in a worksheet, you press the Compose key (Alt-F1), then type the two characters shown in the last column of the table (known as the *compose sequence*). As soon as you type the second character of the compose sequence, 1-2-3 will display the LICS character (shown in the second column of this table) in the control panel. To then enter the LICS character in the current cell, you press the Enter key.

You will notice in the table that some LICS characters have more than one compose sequence listed. For example, you can create the cent sign (¢) by pressing the Compose key (Alt-F1) and then typing the compose sequence *c |* or *c/* (or *C |* or *C/*). Also, unless the compose sequence shown in the table is preceded by an asterisk (*), you can enter the characters listed in the compose sequence in any order to produce the LICS code. For example, you can create the cent sign (¢) just as well by typing the compose sequence *| c* instead of *c |* after pressing the Compose key. To create Pi (π), however, you must always enter the compose sequence *PI* or *pi* (never *IP* or *ip*) after pressing the Compose key.

In addition to using the Compose key and the compose sequence to produce an LICS character, you can also use the @CHAR function. When you enter @CHAR in a cell of the worksheet, you type in the LICS code (shown in the first column of the table). For example, to enter the symbol for PI (π) in a cell with the @CHAR function, you would enter *@CHAR(173)* and then press Enter.

Not all the characters in the LICS table can be displayed properly on the screen. When 1-2-3 can't exactly represent an LICS character on the screen, it uses an approximation known as a *fallback character*. Also, many printers can't interpret the LICS code correctly; when you print a worksheet that contains LICS characters produced with the higher codes (those above 127), you may find that the printed characters don't match the ones displayed in the worksheet on the screen.

◆ **Table E.1:** *The Lotus International Character Set*

LICS Code	Character	Description	Compose Sequence
32	(Space)		
33	!		
34	"		
35	#		++
36	$		
37	%		
38	&		
39	'	Apostrophe	
40	(		
41	)		
42	*		
43	+		
44	,		
45	—		
46	.		
47	/		
48	0		
49	1		
50	2		
51	3		
52	4		
53	5		
54	6		
55	7		
56	8		
57	9		
58	:		
59	;		
60	<		

◆ **Table E.1:** *The Lotus International Character Set (continued)*

LICS Code	Character	Description	Compose Sequence
61	=		
62	>		
63	?		
64	@		
65	A		aa *or* AA
66	B		
67	C		
68	D		
69	E		
70	F		
71	G		
72	H		
73	I		
74	J		
75	K		
76	L		
77	M		
78	N		
79	O		
80	P		
81	Q		
82	R		
83	S		
84	T		
85	U		
86	V		
87	W		
88	X		
89	Y		

◆ **Table E.1:** *The Lotus International Character Set (continued)*

LICS Code	Character	Description	Compose Sequence
90	Z		
91	[		((
92	\		//
93	]		))
94	^		vv
95	—		
96	`		
97	a		
98	b		
99	c		
100	d		
101	e		
102	f		
103	g		
104	h		
105	i		
106	j		
107	k		
108	l		
109	m		
110	n		
111	o		
112	p		
113	q		
114	r		
115	s		
116	t		
117	u		
118	v		

♦ **Table E.1:** *The Lotus International Character Set (continued)*

LICS Code	Character	Description	Compose Sequence
119	w		
120	x		
121	y		
122	z		
123	{		(—
124	¦		^ /
125	}		)—
126	~	Tilde	— —
127		Delete	
128	`	Uppercase grave	* ` spacebar
129	´	Uppercase acute	* ´ spacebar
130	^	Uppercase circumflex	* ^ spacebar
131	¨	Uppercase umlaut	* " spacebar
132	~	Uppercase tilde	* ~ spacebar
133	■	Unknown character (display only)	
134	■	Unknown character (display only)	
135	■	Unknown character (display only)	
136	■	Unknown character (display only)	
137	■	Unknown character (display only)	
138	■	Unknown character (display only)	
139	■	Unknown character (display only)	
140	■	Unknown character (display only)	
141	■	Unknown character (display only)	
142	■	Unknown character (display only)	
143	■	Unknown character (display only)	
144	`	Lowercase grave	* spacebar `
145	´	Lowercase acute	* spacebar ´
146	^	Lowercase circumflex	* spacebar ^
147	¨	Lowercase umlaut	* spacebar "

♦ **Table E.1:** *The Lotus International Character Set (continued)*

LICS Code	Character	Description	Compose Sequence
148	~	Lowercase tilde	spacebar ~
149	ı	Lowercase i without dot	i spacebar
150	_	Ordinal indicator	_ spacebar
151	▲	Begin attribute (display only)	ba
152	▼	End attribute (display only)	ea
153	■	Unknown character (display only)	
154	•	Hard space (display only)	spacebar spacebar
155	←	Merge character (display only)	mg
156	■	Unknown character (display only)	
157	■	Unknown character (display only)	
158	■	Unknown character (display only)	
159	■	Unknown character (display only)	
160	ƒ	Dutch Guilder	ff
161	©	Inverted exclamation mark	! !
162	¢	Cent sign	c| or C| or c/ or C/
163	£	Pound sign	L= or l= or L− or l−
164	"	Low opening double quotes	" ^
165	¥	Yen sign	Y= or y= or Y− or y−
166	P$_{ts}$	Pesetas sign	* PT or pt or Pt
167	§	Section sign	SO or so or So or s0
168	¤	General currency sign	XO or xo or Xo or x0
169	©	Copyright sign	CO or co or Co or c0
170	ª	Feminine ordinal	a _ or A _
171	«	Angle quotation mark left	< <
172	Δ	Delta	dd or DD
173	π	Pi	* PI or pi or Pi
174	≥	Greater than or equals	* >=
175	÷	Divide sign	:−
176	°	Degree sign	^0

◆ **Table E.1:** *The Lotus International Character Set (continued)*

LICS Code	Character	Description	Compose Sequence
177	±	Plus/minus sign	+ −
178	²	Superscript 2	^ 2
179	³	Superscript 3	^ 3
180	„	Low closing double quotes	" v
181	μ	Micro sign	* / u
182	¶	Paragraph sign	! p *or* ! P
183	•	Middle dot	^ .
184	TM	Trademark sign	TM *or* Tm *or* tm
185	¹	Superscript 1	^ 1
186	º	Masculine ordinal	o_ *or* O_
187	»	Angle quotation mark right	> >
188	¼	One quarter	* 1 4
189	½	One half	* 1 2
190	≤	Less than or equals	* = <
191	¿	Inverted question mark	? ?
192	À	Uppercase A with grave	A `
193	Á	Uppercase A with acute	A ´
194	Â	Uppercase A with circumflex	A ^
195	Ã	Uppercase A with tilde	A ~
196	Ä	Uppercase A with umlaut	A "
197	Å	Uppercase A with ring	A *
198	Æ	Uppercase AE with ligature	* A E
199	Ç	Uppercase C with cedilla	C ,
200	È	Uppercase E with grave	E `
201	É	Uppercase E with acute	E ´
202	Ê	Uppercase E with circumflex	E ^
203	Ë	Uppercase E with umlaut	E "
204	Ì	Uppercase I with grave	I `
205	Í	Uppercase I with acute	I ´

• **Table E.1:** *The Lotus International Character Set (continued)*

LICS Code	Character	Description	Compose Sequence
206	Î	Uppercase I with circumflex	I ^
207	Ï	Uppercase I with umlaut	I "
208	Đ	Uppercase eth (Icelandic)	D –
209	Ñ	Uppercase N with tilde	N ~
210	Ò	Uppercase O with grave	O `
211	Ó	Uppercase O with acute	O ´
212	Ô	Uppercase O with circumflex	O ^
213	Õ	Uppercase O with tilde	I ~
214	Ö	Uppercase O with umlaut	O "
215	Œ	Uppercase OE diphthong	* OE
216	Ø	Uppercase O with slash	O /
217	Ù	Uppercase U with grave	U `
218	Ú	Uppercase U with acute	U ´
219	Û	Uppercase U with circumflex	U ^
220	Ü	Uppercase U with umlaut	U "
221	Ÿ	Uppercase Y with umlaut	Y "
222	þ	Uppercase thorn (Icelandic)	P –
223	ß	Lowercase German sharp s	ss
224	à	Lowercase a with grave	a `
225	á	Lowercase a with acute	a ´
226	â	Lowercase a with circumflex	a ^
227	ã	Lowercase a with tilde	a ~
228	ä	Lowercase u with umlaut	a "
229	å	Lowercase a with ring	a *
230	æ	Lowercase ae with ligature	ae
231	ç	Lowercase c with cedilla	c ,
232	è	Lowercase e with grave	e `
233	é	Lowercase e with acute	e ´
234	ê	Lowercase e with circumflex	e ^

◆ **Table E.1:** *The Lotus International Character Set (continued)*

LICS Code	Character	Description	Compose Sequence
235	ë	Lowercase e with umlaut	e "
236	ì	Lowercase i with grave	i `
237	í	Lowercase i with acute	i ´
238	î	Lowercase i with circumflex	i ^
239	ï	Lowercase i with umlaut	i "
240	ð	Lowercase eth (Icelandic)	d —
241	ñ	Lowercase n with tilde	n ~
242	ò	Lowercase o with grave	o `
243	ó	Lowercase o with acute	o ´
244	ô	Lowercase o with circumflex	o ^
245	õ	Lowercase o with tilde	o ~
246	ö	Lowercase o with umlaut	o "
247	œ	Lowercase oe diphthong	* oe
248	ø	Lowercase o with slash	o /
249	ù	Lowercase u with grave	u `
250	ú	Lowercase u with acute	u ´
251	û	Lowercase u with circumflex	u ^
252	ü	Lowercase u with umlaut	u "
253	ÿ	Lowercase y with umlaut	y "
254	þ	Lowercase thorn (Icelandic)	p —
255	■	Unknown character (display only)	

* Indicates that you must enter the compose sequence in the order shown. Do not type the asterisk (*).

f

Answer
Key to Review
Questions

Part I:
Mastering
the 1-2-3
Spreadsheet

Chapter 1: The Worksheet Environment

1. column
   row
2. label
   value
3. long label
4. ' (apostrophe)
   left-
5. ^ (circumflex)

6. READY
7. / (slash)
8. type
9. Esc
   Break
10. Num Lock
    NUM

Chapter 2: Techniques for Adding and Editing Data

1. C:\123
   Lotus System disk
2. Lotus Access System
   Enter
   1
3. Home
4. →
   ↓
   F5
   D3
5. PgDn *or* Page Down
   PgUp *or* Page Up
6. Tab
   Ctrl-→
   Shift-Tab
   Ctrl-←
7. IV
   8192
   IV8192

8. →
   ↓
   F5
   B4
9. 'Net Sales
10. 1500
11. EDIT
12. '1990
13. @DATE(92,12,31)
    /Range Format Date
14. Esc
15. F2
16. /Range Erase
17. the Undo key (Alt-F4) in
    Release 2.2 only—no
    Undo in Release 2.01

Chapter 3: Building the Worksheet Step by Step

1. /Worksheet Erase
   Yes
   /File Save
2. Undo
   Alt-F4 (Release 2.2 only)
3. the Help key (F1)
4. Task Index
5. \#
6. @SUM

7. A3
   B3
   C3
8. /Range Label
   Right
9. /Worksheet Global Zero
   Yes
   No

Chapter 4: Cell Ranges: The Key to Managing Worksheet Data

1. first
   . (period)
   last
2. file reference
   << >> (angle brackets)
3. . (period)
   Esc
4. F5
   F3
5. Create
   Labels
   Up
6. , (Comma)—the Fixed
   format doesn't use
   parentheses for negative
   values
7. Enable
   /Worksheet Global
     Protect
   Disable
8. Esc
   Enter
9. /Move
   /Copy
10. down
    column

Chapter 5: Formulas and Functions: Performing Calculations

1. + (plus)
   & (ampersand)
2. conditional
   1
   0
3. +B2 > 25 #AND# B2 < 50
4. 1
5. copy
6. $C10
7. $EXPENSES
8. F9
   manual
9. /Worksheet Status
10. , (comma)
    ; (semicolon)

Chapter 6: Managing the Worksheet Environment

1. 10
   Horizontal
2. Window
   F6
3. 1 and 2
   beeping
4. A and B
5. Scroll Lock
6. SCROLL
   Scroll Lock
7. 4
   3

Chapter 7: Linking and Transferring Data between Worksheet Files

1. Entire-File
   /File Combine Copy
2. Named/Specified-Range
   /File Combine Add
   NAME (F3)

3. Subtract
   /File Combine
   the name of the current
   worksheet file
4. Formulas
   /File Xtract
5. file reference (Release 2.2
   only—Release 2.01
   doesn't support file
   linking)

6. path name
7. /File Admin Link-Refresh
   (Release 2.2 only)
8. last file
   Ctrl-End End
9. /File List Linked
   /File Admin Table Linked

Part II:
Generating
Reports and
Graphs

Chapter 8: Mastering Printing

1. Name
   /Worksheet Global
   Default Printer
2. interface
3. print range
   /Printer
   /Print
   Align
   Go
4. Page
5. Options Margins
   None
6. Header
   | | @
7. Footer
   | #
8. Setup
   the setup string
   right margin
   132

9. Setup
   the setup string
   page length
   88
10. the leftmost column of the
    print range in the row to
    appear on the new page
    /Worksheet Page
11. Yes
    /Worksheet Global
    Default Printer Wait
12. Cell-Formulas
    /Print Printer Options
    Other

Chapter 9: Representing Data Graphically

1. /Graph Group
   Columnwise
2. /Graph Options
   Format Symbols

3. /Graph Type
   Bar
4. X
   A

5. codes 1–7
   B
6. /Graph Options Legend
   Range
7. /Graph Options Scale
   Lower
   Upper
   Manual
8. /Graph Options Scale
   Format Percent
   0
9. /Graph Options
   Data-Labels
   Above

10. /Graph Name Create
    /Graph Name Use
11. /File Save
12. /Graph Save
13. quit
    PrintGraph
14. Settings Image Size Full
15. Ctrl-Break
    Esc

Chapter 10: Using Allways to Produce Perfect Reports

1. hard disk
2. F7
   F8
   F9
   F10
3. Detach
4. /Format Bold Set
   Alt-B
5. indicate the range
   pointing
   three
6. Alt-S
   /Worksheet Column
   Set-Width
7. /Layout Titles Header
   | | @
8. Font
   2
9. Font
   7
   Replace
   4 and press Enter
   20
   Use

10. Save
    /Format Font Library
    BUDGFNT
    Retrieve
    .AFS
    BUDGFNT.AFS
11. Add
    range
12. Set
    Go
    File
    .PRN
13. dashed
    first row
    Row
14. Tiny
    /Display Zoom
    F4
    4

Part III: Data Management and Analysis in 1-2-3

Chapter 11: The Database Environment

1. database
   field
   record
2. field names
   records
3. type
4. data range
   key
5. ascending
   descending
   ascending
6. duplicates
7. top
8. end
9. Find
10. Extract

11. Input
    Criteria
    Output
12. match exactly
13. row of copied field names
14. N2
    N3
    N1..N3
15. ˜CA
    N1..N2
16. +E3>500#AND#E3<=1000
    P2
    P1..P2
17. Query
    F7
18. output

Chapter 12: Data Analysis: What-If and Predictive

1. /Data Table 1
   one-variable data table
2. /Data Table 2
   two-variable data table
3. Table
   F8
4. intervals
   bin
5. columns
   rows

6. rows
   columns
7. square
8. dependent or y
   independent or x
9. 9
   2
10. Constant
    X Coefficient

Part IV: File Management and Organization

Chapter 13: Organizing and Maintaining Your Files

1. MD or MKDIR
2. CD or CHDIR
   /File Directory
3. files
   CD..
   RD or RMDIR

4. Directory
   /Worksheet Global Default
   Update
5. spacebar
   P
   the password (*NEPO*)

6. Esc or Backspace
   [Password Protected]
   Replace
7. Graph
   /File List
8. Graph
   /File Admin Table
   press Enter
   A100

9. /System
   EXIT
10. Worksheet
    /File Erase
    /System
    DEL (or DELETE)
    ERASE

Chapter 14: Translating Files: Exchanging Data between 1-2-3 and Other Programs

1. text or ASCII
   Numbers
   /File Import
2. Text
   /File Import
3. TYPE
4. comma
   quotation marks
5. /Data Parse
6. /Data Parse Format-Line
   Edit
   S (Skip block)

7. /File Retrieve (Release 3
   can read all Release 2
   files without translation)
8. Translate
9. dBASE III option in the
   Translate program
10. field names
    records

Part V: Extending the Power of 1-2-3 through Macros

Chapter 15: The Macro Environment: Automating and Customizing Your Work in 1-2-3

1. tilde (˜)
   {HOME}
2. {RIGHT 3} or {R 3} (if you
   are using Release 2.2)
3. Alt-B
   the Run key (Alt-F3)
4. Ctrl-Break
   Esc
   Enter

5. \0
6. {?}
   Enter
7. the Step key (Alt-F2)
   spacebar
8. /Worksheet Learn Range
   the Learn key (Alt-F5)
9. MACROMGR.ADN
   Save

Chapter 16: Introduction to the Lotus Command Language

1. {LET Income,500}
2. {PUT Expenses,2,1,275}
3. {BLANK Taxes}
4. {CALC}, {RECALC}, or {RECALCCOL}
5. {CONTENTS NewTotal, Total,9,66}
6. the same cell following the {IF} command the cell directly below
7. {DISPATCH}
8. {RETURN}
9. {DEFINE}
10. {FOR Counter,1,3,1,Print}
11. {PANELOFF} {WINDOWSOFF}
12. {INDICATE "IMPORT"} {INDICATE}
13. {GETNUMBER "Enter your age: ",Ages}
14. {GETLABEL "Enter your street address: ",Street}
15. {WAIT @NOW+@TIME(0,0,50)}

g

Using
Add-In Programs

Release 2.01 introduced the use of add-in programs to extend the power of 1-2-3. Add-in programs are auxiliary programs that are loaded into memory (attached) from within 1-2-3 itself. This means that you never have to leave the 1-2-3 worksheet to use them. Once an add-in program is attached to 1-2-3, you then use its own menu to select its various options.

Add-In versus Add-On Programs

Add-in programs aren't the only type of auxiliary programs available for use with 1-2-3. In addition to add-in programs, there are add-on programs as well. An add-on program differs from an add-in program primarily in that it is never started from *within* 1-2-3. This means that you don't have the option of loading the program in 1-2-3 and then removing the program when you no longer need it without having to exit from 1-2-3.

Some add-on programs, such as Freelance Plus (a complete business graphics package by Lotus Development), are run completely independently of 1-2-3. For example, although Freelance Plus uses the worksheets or PIC files that you have created in 1-2-3, it doesn't require the 1-2-3 program itself to run.

Other add-on programs such as HAL (Human Access Language, also by Lotus Development) are RAM-resident programs that fit between DOS and 1-2-3. Because HAL resides in the computer's memory along with 1-2-3, it resembles add-in programs such as Allways more than it does an add-on program such as Freelance Plus. Unlike Allways, however, HAL is always loaded into memory before 1-2-3—it can't be loaded from within 1-2-3. As a result, you can't remove HAL from memory until you quit 1-2-3.

HAL and Release 2.2:   If you routinely use HAL in doing your work in Release 2.01 of 1-2-3, you will probably be disappointed to learn that HAL is incompatible with Release 2.2. On the plus side, however, you will find that Release 2.2 now incorporates many of the extra features offered by HAL, including undo, search and replace, and linking worksheets. The most significant thing that you lose is the ability to phrase your requests in HAL's English-like language: you must use the standard 1-2-3 commands to accomplish all your tasks in Release 2.2.

Installing Add-In Programs

Before you can use any add-in program with 1-2-3, you must first install it. Most add-in programs include an install program that automates the installation procedure (check the documentation that accompanies the software for details). During this procedure, this program installs a copy of the Add-In Manager in your 1-2-3 driver set (by default, named *123.SET*).

Using the Add-In Manager

The /Add-In menu is used to attach, detach, or invoke add-in programs once they have been installed. In Release 2.01, this menu is not integrated into the 1-2-3 command menus, as it is now in Release 2.2. Instead of selecting /Add-In (/A) to bring up this menu as you do now in Release 2.2, you press Alt-F10 in Release 2.01.

The /Add-In menu for Release 2.2 contains the following options:

Attach Detach Invoke Clear Quit

You will find the Add-In menu for Release 2.01 identical, except that this earlier version contains a Setup option located between Clear and Quit. The Setup option is used to set auto-attach and auto-invoke add-ins. In Release 2.2, you do this by selecting the Add-In option on the /Worksheet Global Default Other menu (see Attaching Add-In Programs Automatically Upon Startup, in Appendix B, for details on how to set auto-attach and auto-invoke add-ins).

Attaching Add-In Programs

To attach an add-in program, you select the Attach option on the Add-In menu. The program will then display a line listing of all add-in program files (using the extension .ADN) that have been installed in the same directory as the one used in starting 1-2-3. This directory will be A:\ if you are using the program on a two-disk-drive system or C:\123 if you are using the program on a hard disk. You select the add-in program by moving the highlight to the appropriate ADN file name and pressing Enter.

After you select the file, you will be prompted to select the key to assign to the program. If you are using Release 2.2, choose between

No-Key 7 8 9 10

(If you are using Release 2.01, this menu will not include the last option, 10.) The options 7, 8, 9, and 10 represent the function keys F7, F8, F9, and F10, respectively. When you assign one of these keys to the add-in program you are attaching, you can start the program by pressing either Alt and the function key or Shift and the function key. For example, if you choose option 7, you can start the program by pressing Alt-F7 *or* Shift-F7.

Remember that in macros, the function key Alt-F7 is represented by {APP1}, Alt-F8 by {APP2}, Alt-F9 by {APP3}, and Alt-F10 by {APP4}. If you use any of these keystroke instructions in your macros, they will start the add-in program currently assigned to that particular key. In Release 2.01, {APP4} will display the Add-In menu. In Release 2.2, pressing Alt-F10 will also display the Add-In menu, provided that you haven't already assigned an add-in program to this key.

If you wish to use the Add-In menu to start the add-in program or you have already assigned the keys F7–F10 to add-in programs, you select the No-Key option. When you attach an add-in program with the No-key option, you must use the Invoke option on the Add-In menu and select the add-in program name when you wish to start it.

Removing an Add-In Program from Memory

As stated earlier, one of the primary advantages offered by add-in programs is that you can not only start them from within 1-2-3, but you can also remove them. To conserve RAM, you should always remove an add-in program from memory as soon as you have finished with it. To do this, you select the Detach option on the Add-In menu. The program then displays a line listing of all add-in programs that you have attached. To detach the one you no longer need, you move the pointer to its name (same as the program file name without the .ADN extension) and press Enter.

If you have more than one add-in program attached and you wish to remove all of them from memory at the same time, select the Clear option instead of Detach on the Add-In menu.

Source and Types of Add-In Programs

The types of add-in programs currently available for Release 2 of 1-2-3 are diverse. You will find a wide range of utility add-ins; for example, Note-It by Symantec enables you to document your worksheet by adding comments to any of its cells. You will find graphics add-ins, such as 3D-Graphics by Intex Solutions, that enable you to create three-dimensional graphs with your worksheet data.

Several database add-in programs are also available. Some programs, such as @BASE by Personics or Oracle for 1-2-3 by Oracle, actually enable you to create disk-based databases within 1-2-3 worksheets whose size is limited solely by available disk space. With Oracle for 1-2-3, you can create a true relational database that relates data from several different tables.

Besides those add-ins that enhance the graphics and database aspects of 1-2-3, you will find several add-in programs that specialize in the creation of certain types of worksheet applications. Chief among these is the new Budget Express add-in, which facilitates the creation of any type of budget, plan, or forecast.

Other add-ins enhance the printing of worksheets. For example, DataType by SWFTE makes available a wide range of fonts for printing worksheets with the HP LaserJet printer. If you are using Release 2.01 and don't plan to upgrade to 2.2 in the near future, you might want to consider Impress by PC Publishing. This add-in program offers the same presentation-quality printing of worksheet reports as does Allways. Unlike Allways, however, Impress enables you to edit your worksheet while using the program in display mode.

The *LOTUS Selects* catalog provides an excellent source of information on what add-ins (and add-ons as well) are available for use with 1-2-3. Not only does this catalog provide you with a general description of each add-in program that it offers, but it also gives a detailed list of its system requirements. You can order any add-in listed in the catalog directly from LOTUS Selects.

To obtain this catalog, you should send in the special LOTUS Selects request card that comes in your Release 2.2 package. If you no longer have this card, you can get on the mailing list by writing directly to:

> LOTUS Selects
> P.O. Box 9172
> Cambridge, MA 02139–9946

Compatibility of Add-In Programs in Release 2.2

Most add-in programs developed for use with Release 2.01 are compatible with Release 2.2. Some, however, weren't developed in strict accordance with the Lotus Developer Tools, which don't work properly with Release 2.2. Note that none of the add-in programs that work with Release 2.01 or 2.2 will work in Release 3.0. If you use both Release 2 and 3 in your office, you will have to obtain separate Release 3 versions of each add-in program you use with Release 2 as these become available.

If you experience problems with existing add-in programs when using them in Release 2.2, contact the add-in publishers directly for information on obtaining upgraded versions that are compatible with Release 2.2. When shopping for new add-in programs, always make sure to ask the vendor if they are compatible with Release 2.2 before you purchase them.

Also, if you purchased version 1.0 of Allways for use with Release 2.01, you can't use it with Release 2.2. You must install and use the version of Allways that comes as part of your Release 2.2 package.

✳ *New in 2.2*   ## Removing the Add-In Manager from a Driver Set

Most third-party add-in programs install a copy of the Add-In Manager program in your driver set file (123.SET by default) automatically as part of their installation procedure (this is not true of the Macro Manager or Allways add-ins supplied as part of Release 2.2). If you wish, you can remove the Add-In Manager from the driver set. Such a step is not necessary to run the add-in program, but it does free about 21K of RAM. To remove this program from your driver set, you follow these steps:

1. **On a hard disk system, use the CD command at the DOS prompt to make the directory that contains the 1-2-3 program current, as in** *CD\123;* **on a two-disk-drive system, put your working copy of the Install disk in drive A and the disk that contains your 1-2-3 driver set (usually, the 1-2-3 System disk) in drive B.**
   Next, you enter the command to delete the Add-In Manager from the driver set.

2. **Type** *DEL_MGR,* **press the spacebar, then type the file name of your driver set (including the** *.SET* **extension), and press Enter; for example, if you are deleting the Add-In Manager from your** *123.SET* **file, you type** *DEL_MGR* **and press the spacebar, then type** *123.SET* **and press Enter.**

Using Add-In @Functions

Some add-in programs include their own @functions. As soon as you attach such an add-in program with the /Add-In Attach (/AA) command, these @functions will be available when you create formulas in the worksheet. As with standard 1-2-3 @functions, add-in @functions have their own particular syntax that you must follow (check the documentation that accompanies the add-in program for the specific arguments).

Unlike the @functions built into 1-2-3, however, add-in @functions will work only when the add-in program that contains them is attached to 1-2-3. For that reason, you may want to designate such add-in programs as auto-attach add-ins if you use their add-in @functions extensively in your worksheets (see Attaching Add-In Programs Automatically Upon Startup, in Appendix B, for details on how to set auto-attach and auto-invoke add-ins).

Index

Lotus 1-2-3 Release 2 Handbook Sample Worksheets and Macros Available on Disk

If you would like to use the sample worksheets and macros described in the book but don't have the time or inclination to type them all in, you can order the disk that accompanies the text. This disk contains all the worksheet and macro files created in the handbook exercises *as well as* all the sample worksheet and macro files described in text and illustrated in the figures.

To order this disk, please fill out a copy or facsimile of the following order form and send it along with a check or money order in the amount of $18.00 for a 5¼-inch disk or $20.00 for a 3½-inch disk (California residents, please add 6% sales tax) to:

Greg Harvey

P.O. Box 1175

Point Reyes Station, CA 94956–1175

Name _____

Company _____

Address _____

City/State/Zip _____

Please specify the version of Lotus 1-2-3 that you use:

Release 2.0 or 2.01 _____

Release 2.2 _____

Please specify the disk format you need:

5¼ inch disk ($18.00) _____

3½ inch disk ($20.00) _____

Enclosed is my check or money order in U.S. currency. California residents add 6% sales tax ($19.08 total for a 5¼-inch disk or $21.20 for a 3½-inch disk). Please make the check payable to Greg Harvey.

SYBEX is not affiliated with Greg Harvey and assumes no responsibility for any defects in the disk or in the programs it contains.

SYBEX®

TO JOIN THE SYBEX MAILING LIST OR ORDER BOOKS
PLEASE COMPLETE THIS FORM

NAME _____ COMPANY _____

STREET _____ CITY _____

STATE _____ ZIP _____

☐ PLEASE MAIL ME MORE INFORMATION ABOUT **SYBEX** TITLES

ORDER FORM (There is no obligation to order)

PLEASE SEND ME THE FOLLOWING:

TITLE	QTY	PRICE
_____	____	____
_____	____	____
_____	____	____
_____	____	____

TOTAL BOOK ORDER   ____ $____

CUSTOMER SIGNATURE _____

SHIPPING AND HANDLING PLEASE ADD $2.00 PER BOOK VIA UPS   _____

FOR OVERSEAS SURFACE ADD $5.25 PER BOOK PLUS $4.40 REGISTRATION FEE   _____

FOR OVERSEAS AIRMAIL ADD $18.25 PER BOOK PLUS $4.40 REGISTRATION FEE   _____

CALIFORNIA RESIDENTS PLEASE ADD APPLICABLE SALES TAX   _____

TOTAL AMOUNT PAYABLE   _____

☐ CHECK ENCLOSED   ☐ VISA
☐ MASTERCARD   ☐ AMERICAN EXPRESS

ACCOUNT NUMBER _____

EXPIR. DATE _____ DAYTIME PHONE _____

CHECK AREA OF COMPUTER INTEREST:

☐ BUSINESS SOFTWARE

☐ TECHNICAL PROGRAMMING

☐ OTHER: _____

THE FACTOR THAT WAS MOST IMPORTANT IN YOUR SELECTION:

☐ THE SYBEX NAME

☐ QUALITY

☐ PRICE

☐ EXTRA FEATURES

☐ COMPREHENSIVENESS

☐ CLEAR WRITING

☐ OTHER _____

OTHER COMPUTER TITLES YOU WOULD LIKE TO SEE IN PRINT:

_____

_____

OCCUPATION

☐ PROGRAMMER   ☐ TEACHER

☐ SENIOR EXECUTIVE   ☐ HOMEMAKER

☐ COMPUTER CONSULTANT   ☐ RETIRED

☐ SUPERVISOR   ☐ STUDENT

☐ MIDDLE MANAGEMENT   ☐ OTHER:

☐ ENGINEER/TECHNICAL   _____

☐ CLERICAL/SERVICE

☐ BUSINESS OWNER/SELF EMPLOYED

CHECK YOUR LEVEL OF COMPUTER USE

☐ NEW TO COMPUTERS

☐ INFREQUENT COMPUTER USER

☐ FREQUENT USER OF ONE SOFTWARE

   PACKAGE:

   NAME _____

☐ FREQUENT USER OF MANY SOFTWARE

   PACKAGES

☐ PROFESSIONAL PROGRAMMER

OTHER COMMENTS:

_____

_____

_____

_____

_____

_____

_____

_____

PLEASE FOLD, SEAL, AND MAIL TO SYBEX

SYBEX, INC.

2021 CHALLENGER DR. #100

ALAMEDA, CALIFORNIA USA

       94501

SEAL

SYBEX Computer Books are different.

Here is why . . .

At SYBEX, each book is designed with you in mind. Every manuscript is carefully selected and supervised by our editors, who are themselves computer experts. We publish the best authors, whose technical expertise is matched by an ability to write clearly and to communicate effectively. Programs are thoroughly tested for accuracy by our technical staff. Our computerized production department goes to great lengths to make sure that each book is well-designed.

In the pursuit of timeliness, SYBEX has achieved many publishing firsts. SYBEX was among the first to integrate personal computers used by authors and staff into the publishing process. SYBEX was the first to publish books on the CP/M operating system, microprocessor interfacing techniques, word processing, and many more topics.

Expertise in computers and dedication to the highest quality product have made SYBEX a world leader in computer book publishing. Translated into fourteen languages, SYBEX books have helped millions of people around the world to get the most from their computers. We hope we have helped you, too.

For a complete catalog of our publications:

SYBEX, Inc. 2021 Challenger Drive, #100, Alameda, CA 94501
Tel: (415) 523-8233/(800) 227-2346   Telex: 336311
Fax: (415) 523-2373

Commonly Used Setup Strings

	Compressed	Expanded
C. Itoh 8510A	\027Q	\014
Epson FX, MX, or RX	\015	\027W1
Epson LQ1500	\027x0\015	\027W1
HP LaserJet	\027&k2S	—
HP ThinkJet	\027&k2S	\027&k1S
IBM 5182 Color Printer	\015	\027\087\001
IBM Color Jetprinter	\015	\027\087\001
IBM Graphics	\015	\027\087\001
IBM Proprinter	\015	\027\087\001\014
IBM Quietwriter, Models 1 & 2	—	\027\087\049
Okidata Microline	\029	\030\031
Okidata Pacemark	\027\066	\027\054\027\067
Star Micronics Gemini	\015	\027\087\001
TI 850, 850XL, 855, 856	\027P	\014
Toshiba P351, Pl350, Pl351, 321SL, 351SX, 321LC, 351C	\027*0\027[	\027!

	3 Lines per Inch (Double Spacing)	6 Lines per Inch	8 Lines per Inch
C. Itoh 8510A	\027T48	\027A	\027B
Epson FX, MX, or RX	\027\065\024	\0272	\0270
Epson LQ1500	\027\065\024	\0272	\0270
HP LaserJet	\027&l3D	\027&l6D	\027&l8D
HP ThinkJet	—	\027&l6D	\027&l8D
IBM 5182 Color Printer	—	\027\050	\027\048
IBM Color Jetprinter	\027\087\001	\027\050	\027\048
IBM Graphics	—	\027\050	\027\048
IBM Proprinter	\027\051\0272	\027\050	\027\048
IBM Quietwriter, Models 1 & 2	\027\065\024\027\050	\027\050	\027\048
Okidata Microline	\027\037\057\048	\027\054	\027\056
Okidata Pacemark	\027\037\057\048	\027\052	\027\053
Star Micronics Gemini	\027\065\024	\050	\0270\048
TI 850, 850XL, 855, 856	\027\065\024	\0272	\0270
Toshiba P351, Pl350, Pl351, 321SL, 351SX, 321LC, 351C	\027L16	\027L08	\027L06